Communications
in Computer and Information Science 143

T0073984

Gang Shen   Xiong Huang (Eds.)

Advanced Research on Electronic Commerce, Web Application, and Communication

International Conference, ECWAC 2011
Guangzhou, China, April 16-17, 2011
Proceedings, Part I

 Springer

Volume Editors

Gang Shen
Wuhan University of Science and Technology
Wuhan, China
E-mail: 1073648534@qq.com

Xiong Huang
Wuhan University of Science and Technology
Wuhan, China
E-mail: 499780828@qq.com

ISSN 1865-0929   e-ISSN 1865-0937
ISBN 978-3-642-20366-4   e-ISBN 978-3-642-20367-1
DOI 10.1007/978-3-642-20367-1
Springer Heidelberg Dordrecht London New York

Library of Congress Control Number: Applied for

CR Subject Classification (1998): H.3.3-5, H.4-5, H.2.4, J.1, I.2.6

Typesetting: Camera-ready by author, data conversion by Scientific Publishing Services, Chennai, India

Printed on acid-free paper

Springer is part of Springer Science+Business Media (www.springer.com)

Preface

The International Science & Education Researcher Association (ISER) puts its focus on the study and exchange of academic achievements of international researchers, and it also promotes education reform in the world. In addition, it serves as an academic discussion and communication platform, which is beneficial for education and for scientific research, aiming to stimulate researchers in their work.

The ECWAC conference is an integrated event concentrating on electronic commerce, Web applications and communication. ECWAC 2011 was held during April 16–17, 2011, in Beijing, China, and was co-sponsored by the International Science & Education Researcher Association, Beijing Gireida Education Co. Ltd. The goal of the conference is to provide researchers working in the field of electronic commerce, Web applications and communication based on modern information technology with a free forum to share new ideas, innovations and solutions with each other. In addition, famous keynote speakers were invited to deliver talks and participants had the chance to discuss their work with the speakers face to face.

In these proceedings, you can learn more about the field of electronic commerce, Web applications and communication with contributions by researchers from around the world. The main role of the proceedings is to be used as a means of exchange of information, for those working in the field. The Organizing Committee did its best to meet the high standard of Springer's, Communications in Computer and Information Science series. Firstly, poor quality papers were rejected after being reviewed by anonymous referees. Secondly, meetings were held periodically for reviewers to exchange opinions and suggestions. Finally, the organizing team had several preliminary sessions before the conference. Thanks to the efforts of numerous individuals and departments, the conference was successful and fruitful.

In organizing the conference, we received help from different people, departments and institutions. Here, we would like to extend our sincere thanks to the publisher Springer, for their kind and enthusiastic assistance and support of our conference. Secondly, the authors should be thanked too for submitting their papers. Thirdly, all members of the Program Committee, the Program Chairs and the reviewers are appreciated for their hard work.

In conclusion, it was the team effort of all these people that made our conference successful. We welcome any suggestions from the participants that may help improve the conference in the future and we look forward to seeing all of you at ECWAC 2012.

January 2011 Gang Shen ISER Association

Organization

Honorary Chairs

Chen Bin	Beijing Normal University, China
Hu Chen	Peking University, China
Chunhua Tan	Beijing Normal University, China
Helen Zhang	University of Munich, Germany

Program Committee Chairs

Xiong Huang	International Science & Education Researcher Association, China
Li Ding	International Science & Education Researcher Association, China
Zhihua Xu	International Science & Education Researcher Association, China

Organizing Chairs

ZongMing Tu	Beijing Gireida Education Co. Ltd, China
Jijun Wang	Beijing Spon Technology Research Institution, China
Quanxiang	Beijing Prophet Science and Education Research Center, China

Publication Chairs

Gang Shen	International Science & Education Researcher Association, China
Xiong Huang	International Science & Education Researcher Association, China

International Committees

Sally Wang	Beijing Normal University, China
Li Li	Dongguan University of Technology, China
Bing Xiao	Anhui University, China
Z.L. Wang	Wuhan University, China
Moon Seho	Hoseo University, Korea
Kongel Arearak	Suranaree University of Technology, Thailand
Zhihua Xu	International Science & Education Researcher Association, China

Co-sponsored by

International Science & Education Researcher Association, China
VIP Information Conference Center, China

Reviewers

Chunlin Xie	Wuhan University of Science and Technology, China
Lin Qi	Hubei University of Technology, China
Xiong Huang	International Science & Education Researcher Association, China
Gangshen	International Science & Education Researcher Association, China
Xiangrong Jiang	Wuhan University of Technology, China
Li Hu	Linguistic and Linguistic Education Association, China
Moon Hyan	Sungkyunkwan University, Korea
Guangwen	South China University of Technology, China
Jack H. Li	George Mason University, USA
Mary Y. Feng	University of Technology Sydney, Australia
Feng Quan	Zhongnan University of Finance and Economics, China
Peng Ding	Hubei University, China
Songlin	International Science & Education Researcher Association, China
XiaoLie Nan	International Science & Education Researcher Association, China
Zhi Yu	International Science & Education Researcher Association, China
Xue Jin	International Science & Education Researcher Association, China
Zhihua Xu	International Science & Education Researcher Association, China
Wu Yang	International Science & Education Researcher Association, China
Qin Xiao	International Science & Education Researcher Association, China
Weifeng Guo	International Science & Education Researcher Association, China
Li Hu	Wuhan University of Science and Technology, China
Zhong Yan	Wuhan University of Science and Technology, China
Haiquan Huang	Hubei University of Technology, China
Xiao Bing	Wuhan University, China
Brown Wu	Sun Yat-Sen University, China

Table of Contents – Part I

Table of Contents – Part II

Improved Joint ICI Cancellation and Error Correction for OFDM System

Zeeshan Sabir[1], Syed Abdul Rehman Yousaf[2],
M. Inayatullah Babar[1], and M. Arif Wahla[2]

[1] University of Engg. & Technology, Peshawar, Pakistan
zeeshansabir@yahoo.com, babar@nwfpuet.edu.pk
[2] College of Signals,
National University of Sciences & Technology, Rawalpindi, Pakistan
engr.rehman@hotmail.com, arif.wahla@gmail.com

Abstract. Orthogonal Frequency Division Multiplexing (OFDM) is attractive for high data rate transmission due to spectral efficiency but is known to be sensitive to synchronization errors(symbol time and frequency offset)[1]. Mobility is the basic feature of most of present day techniques that employs OFDM at the backend but Doppler frequencies generated due to the mobility causes frequency offsets which results in Inter Carrier Interference (ICI) amongst the subcarriers of the multicarrier OFDM technique. It induces cross talk and causes deterioration of signal. This paper proposes an efficient Frequency-domain ICI mitigation technique based on the estimation of channel taps to vanish the effects of channel frequency offsets from the proposed OFDM model.

Alongwith this, the channel induced noise tend to raise the BER of the OFDM system making it unsuitable for many error-sensitive applications. Turbo codes have been integrated into the resulting system to cater-for the effects of channel induced noise. MAP decoding algorithm applied at the receiving end is based on the exchange of soft information amongst the component decoders that gain from eachother's interleaved extrinsic information. The signal is passed through multipath Rayleigh fading AWGN channel and the performance is measured.

Keywords: Inter carrier Interference (ICI), OFDM, Channel Estimation, Channel Equalization, Turbo Codes, MAP Decoder.

1 Introduction

Orthogonal Frequency Division Multiplexing (OFDM) is a well-known multicarrier transmission technique, which is used in many high data rate applications e.g. 802.11n (WiFi), 802.11a/g(WLAN), 802.16e(WiMax) etc. All these applications involve high speed data transmission for which OFDM is adopted for its bandwidth efficient nature. OFDM based commercial Wireless Local Area Network (WLAN) supports a peak data rate of upto 54Mbps[2]. Bandwidth efficiency of OFDM emerges from the overlapping of subcarriers, used for data symbol modulation, in frequency domain. Orthogonality which is carried out by the IFFT block, is the essence of OFDM and is maintained in

G. Shen and X. Huang (Eds.): ECWAC 2011, Part I, CCIS 143, pp. 1–11, 2011.
© Springer-Verlag Berlin Heidelberg 2011

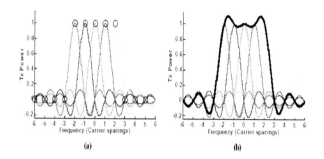

Fig. 1. (a) Perfect OFDM subcarriers   (b) An envelop of subcarriers

frequency domain by the alignment of peak of one subcarrier with the nulls of the other subcarriers as shown in the Fig. 1.

By introducing guard interval (GI) in between two OFDM symbols in the time-domain, aliasing of the symbols can be prevented. The length of the Guard Interval should be greater than the maximum channel delay spread which is the time lapse between the arrival of first and the last multipath component.

Unlike Inter Symbol Interference (ISI) which is caused by delay spread due to multipath phenomenon in time-domain, major cause of ICI is doppler Spread in frequency-domain. The generated doppler frequencies disturb the alignment of the peaks of subcarrier with the nulls of the other subcarriers and causes Channel Frequency Offsets (CFO) which leads to ICI.

Numerous models have been presented regarding mitigation of ICI and error correction. Pornpimon and Wickert [3] proposed a model for Channel estimation and ICI cancellation in which a multirate sampling theory is applied at the receiver end that decreases the interference from the extended outer spectrum of the OFDM symbol subcarrier. Then a sequential interference cancellation algorithm is applied to cancel the effect of interference between the subcarriers of an OFDM symbol. Simulation curves show a BER performance of 10e-2 at affordable SNR. Increased computational complexity and inherent latency forces out the practical implementation of this algorithm.

In [4], Li *et al* gave the idea of an adaptive Minimum Mean Square Error Channel Estimator (MMSE) for finding out the correlation of channel frequency response over time and frequency. The number of computations involved in the process of making this correlation results in a reasonable processing delay which prevents the practical implementation of this work.

The system model proposed by Jeon *et al* [5] is based on the assumption that the channel impulse response varies in a linear fashion over an OFDM symbol. So their model was applicable for low mobile environment but not for high mobile environment as channel impulse response can be considered linear inside an OFDM symbol period for slow fading case.

In this paper a novel channel estimation technique that is based on detection using a turbo processing approach at the receiver end is proposed. In our technique, symbol detection would be carried out in an iterative manner using the iteration of the error

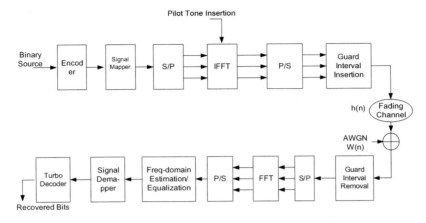

Fig. 2. Proposed Turbo-Coded OFDM Model

correcting codes. Turbo codes that comprises of a parallel concatenation of convolutional codes are employed in our case due to their improve performance over the contemporaries. Maximum A Posteriori (MAP) decoding algorithm is applied at the receiver which decodes the received data bits in an iterative manner. The iterations of MAP decoder are used to exchange a soft (*a priori*) information amongst the two component MAP decoders which leads to a significant performance improvement of the channel estimator which in turn leads to an improved system performance by lowering BER in each iteration.

Rest of the paper is organized as follows. In Section 2, the proposed System model is described with mathematical manipulations. Channel estimation and equalization algorithm is proposed in Section 3. Section 4 provides the details of Turbo encoder and MAP decoder. Simulation results are discussed in Section 5 and Section 6 concludes the work.

2   System Model

The proposed system model is shown in Fig. 2. The information bits after passing through a source encoder are fed to Turbo Channel Encoder which adds redundancy to the input bits for error correction and detection. A rate 1/3 Turbo encoder is used in our work, the details of the encoder are given in Section 4. After digital mapping and S/P conversion, the symbol is passed through IFFT block, at the output it generates $X_p(k)$ symbol with N subcarriers given by

$$X_p(k) = [X_p(0), X_p(1), X_p(2),..........X_p(N-1)]^T \qquad (2.1)$$

For the signal x(n) and subcarrier n (n=0,1,2 .....N-1), N-point IFFT produces the OFDM modulated symbol at time instant p as,

$$X_p(k) = \frac{1}{N} \sum_{n=0}^{N-1} x(n) e^{\frac{-2\pi j}{N}} \qquad (2.2)$$

Where $X_p(k)$ is given by (2.1).

Pilot tones inserted in parallel during this process are used for channel estimation at the receiving end. After taking IFFT, guard interval is added in between two OFDM symbols i.e. we start the transmit block $\tilde{x}_p$ with the last L symbols of $X_p(k)$.

$$\tilde{X}_p = \begin{cases} X_p + (N - L) & p = 0,1,2,3,4.................L - 1 \\ X_p - L & p = L, L - 1, ...L + N - 1 \end{cases} \qquad (2.3)$$

The length of the guard interval G must be greater than the maximum channel delay spread D i.e. $D \leq G$, in order to fully mitigate the effects of ISI.

The channel is assumed a Rayleigh fading channel with AWGN noise added at the receiver. Assuming the multipath channel consists of L discrete paths, the received signal at the receiver is given by:

$$y(n) = \sum_{l=0}^{L-1} h(n,l)x(n-l) + w(n) \qquad (2.4)$$

Where $h(n,l)$ represents the channel impulse response at instant n and $w(n)$ represents the AWGN noise added at the receiver.

At the receiving end, after the removal of guard interval, the signal is passed through the FFT block which demodulates the data symbols from the subcarriers. This step is also termed as "OFDM demodulation". The demodulated signal obtained after taking the FFT of the received signal is given by[5]:

$$Y(m) = \sum_{k=0}^{N-1} \sum_{l=0}^{L-1} X_k H_l^{(m-k)} e^{\frac{-j2\pi kj}{N}} + W_m \qquad (2.5)$$

where W_m represents the FFT of w_n and $H_l^{(m-k)}$ represents the FFT of the Rayleigh fading channel impulse response.

$$H_l^{(m-k)} = \frac{1}{N} h_{n,l} e^{\frac{-j2\pi(m-k)}{N}} \qquad (2.6)$$

The signal is then passed through the Channel Estimation/Equalization block which removes the effect of the Channel impulse response from the received data OFDM symbols. The efficient placement of the pilot tones in the OFDM symbol, discussed in section 3, increases the efficiency of the system against Rayleigh fading channel. The signal is then fed into the iterative portion of the OFDM receiver. Maximum A Posteriori algorithm based decoder is used. Iterative nature of the MAP decoder allows efficient decoding of the coded bits with the help of an exchange of soft information between the component decoders. Results have been taken for different number of iterations for four different modulation schemes and are compared.

3   Algorithm for Channel Estimation and Equalization

The channel estimation approach used in our proposed model is based on the Pilot-Aided Channel Estimation (PACE) technique. The performance of the channel estimator depends greatly on the placement of the pilot tones inside an OFDM symbol. We used Frequency-domain single dimensional Block-type pilot-assisted Channel Estimation strategy in our model. The estimation overhead is calculated as 14%. The estimate calculated by the pilot symbol is used to equalize the upcoming data symbol. The block diagram of the channel estimator is shown in Fig. 3.

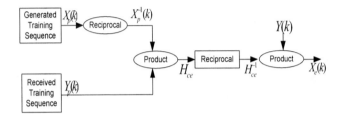

Fig. 3. Pilot-assisted Channel Estimator (PACE)

First of all, the Channel estimation matrix H_{ce} is calculated by the relation

$$H_{ce} = \frac{Y_p(k)}{X_p(k)} \qquad k = 0,1,2.............N_p - 1 \qquad (4.1)$$

where $Y_p(k)$ and $X_p(k)$ represents the received and transmitted pilot tones respectively.

After calculation of the channel estimates, equalization is done by dividing the received data symbol by the Channel estimate.

$$X_e(k) = \frac{Y(k)}{H_{ce}} \qquad k = 0,1,2.............N - 1 \qquad (4.2)$$

The process is done on symbol to symbol basis until the complete received sequence is equalized from the effects of ICI.

4   Anatomy of Encoder and Decoder

4.1   Encoder

Turbo Encoder of rate 1/3 is used in our proposed model. The encoder is a Parallel Concatenated Convolutional Encoder (PCCC) with two Recursive Systematic Convolutional (RSC) Encoders concatenated in parallel via an interleaver as shown in the Fig. 4.

The interleaver used in our model is High Spread Deterministic interleaver[6]. The outputs d^s, $d^{1,p}$ and $d^{2,p}$ represents systematic output, parity bits added by first recursive convolutional encoder and parity added by 2nd recursive convolutional encoder respectively. The generator sequences used are [1 1 1 1] and [1 1 0 1][7]. Puncturing is added at the output to variate the rate of the turbo encoder as per requirement.

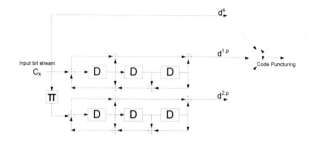

Fig. 4. A rate 1/3 PCCC Turbo Code

The output sequence after puncturing is represented as.

$$S_1 P_1^1 P_1^2 \ S_2 P_2^1 P_2^2 \ S_3 P_3^1 P_3^2 \ S_4 P_4^1 P_4^2 \ S_5 P_5^1 P_5^2 \text{----------}$$

Where the subscript represents bit number and the superscript represents the component RSC Convolutional Encoder number.

4.2 Decoder

MAP decoding algorithm is used and the scheme is based on the exchange of soft (*a priori*) information between the two component MAP decoders serially concatenated via an interleaver as shown in Fig. 5. [8]

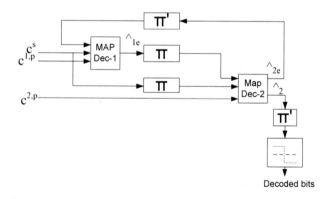

Decoded bits

Fig. 5. A Turbo MAP Decoder based on two component Decoders

The Log Likelihood Ratio (LLR) calculated by Dec-1 acts as its soft output and is fed to dec-2 as its a-priori probability of the decoded bits.

$$LLR(d) = \ln(\frac{P(d = +1/c)}{P(d = -1/c)}) \tag{3.1}$$

The LLR depends upon the a-priori probability of bit 1 and bit 0 which are taken as ½ for dec-1 in the first iteration. The soft output generated by dec-1 is interleaved for randamization and used to produce an improved estimate of the *a priori* probability of the information sequence for dec-2. Dec-2 produces its own a-priori probability as extrinsic information for dec-1 fed to it via a deinterleaver. Sign of the LLR in the final iteration decides whether the decoded bit is 0 or 1. A –ive sign of LLR after the final iteration decodes a bit 0 and a +ive sign decodes a bit 1.

5   Simulation Results

In this section, we will provide the MATLAB simulation results of the proposed model of Turbo-coded OFDM with Frequency-domain PACE.

The simulated frame structure is given in Figure. 6. The channel model was simulated based on Stanford University Interim (SUI) Channel Model-4 which is a Rayleigh fading channel model suitable for thickly populated urban environments. The power delay profile (nsec) is given by [0 1.5 4] with the corresponding attenuations [0 -4dB -8dB] and Doppler frequency 100Hz. The channel was frequency-selective slow fading channel.

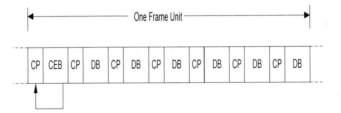

CP= Cyclic Prefix, CEB=Channel Estimation Block, DB=Data Block

1 Frame Unit=1 CE Block+ 6 Data Blocks [9]

Fig. 6. Simulated Frame Structure for the proposed model transmission

Test Case-1. Uncoded OFDM with PACE:

With uncoded OFDM we used a symbol with 256 subcarriers and guard interval length equal to 64 subcarriers to nullify the effects of ISI. Each frame of the OFDM symbol consists of six data symbols preceded by one channel estimation pilot symbol. For different modulation schemes the data rate was calculated as 11.57 Mhz, 23.15 MHz, 46.25 MHz and 69.37 MHz for BPSK, QPSK, 16-QAM and 64-QAM respectively. The bandwidth of the channel was taken as 17.4 MHz (802.11n).

The simulation curves in Fig 7. shows performance degradation as we move towards higher modulation schemes. This performance degradation is due to the close placement of the constellation points as we move towards higher modulation schemes. The channel estimation strategy was pilot-assisted with ratio of the pilot to data symbol as 1:6.

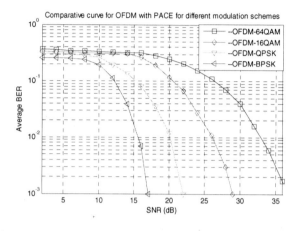

Fig. 7. Uncoded OFDM with PACE through Rayleigh fading Channel

Test Case-2. Turbo-coded OFDM with PACE

Here we will discuss the results of our proposed model of OFDM implemented with turbo codes and with the aid of Pilot-assisted Channel Estimation. The channel was simulated in the same way as in the previous case i.e. SUI channel model-4. The basic aim of the upcoming results was to show the impact of the changing number of iterations of the Maximum *a-posteriori* decoding algorithm on the performance of the proposed model. The number of iterations plays a vital role in the performance of an OFDM system. In 802.16e(WiMax) the number of iterations has been fixed as 7 in the standard model. We have taken the results for 1, 2, 4, 8 and 20 iterations.

The OFDM symbol comprised of 256 subcarriers with the Guard interval length of ¼ i.e. 64 subcarrier. The performance of the proposed model of OFDM with the four different modulation schemes and changing number of iterations is given in Fig. 8.

When compared with Fig. 7, the Turbo-Coded OFDM with BPSK modulation scheme shows a coding gain of 4.9 dB at BER 10e-3 and 20 iterations which is due to the implementation of error correcting turbo codes in the proposed model. Rest of the parameters remain the same in both the cases.

The basic trend of curves for both BPSK and QPSK (Fig. 9) is same. The proposed model shows an improvement in the performance when compared with [10]. There is an improvement of 3.1dB in the 4 iterations curve at a BER of 10e-3. This improvement goes to the credit of the efficient pilot insertion technique which do not need any interpolation as the channel is estimated practically for all the subcarrier positions for the fading channel. In [10] the comb type pilot insertion technique needs an interpolation of the channel at the position where the pilot tones are missing. The interpolation,

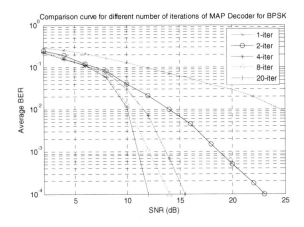

Fig. 8. Comparison curve of Turbo-Coded OFDM with PACE for BPSK modulation scheme for different number of iterations of MAP Decoder

which is a sort of data estimation technique tend to add an approximation error into the results which have been eliminated in our case due to the presence of pilot tones for all the subcarrier positions of the OFDM symbol with the same system overhead.

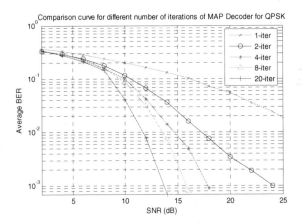

Fig. 9. Comparison curve of Turbo-Coded OFDM with PACE for QPSK

The same parameters when applied to 16-QAM and 64 QAM shows the results given in Figure 10 & 11. When we compare Figure 8, 9, 10 & 11 with Figure 7, we see that higher modulation schemes tend to get more coding gain from the implementation of Turbo codes compared to lower modulation schemes. The reason lies in the fact that chances of errors are more for higher modulation schemes and thus they get more coding gain from the implementation of Turbo codes. The constellation points, which are already far apart in lower modulations, are less likely to merge and thus the extra parity bits acts as extra consumption of energy without giving any significant

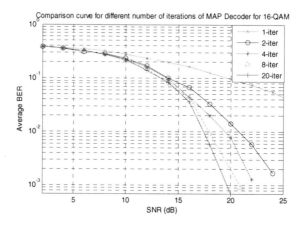

Fig. 10. Comparison curve of Turbo-Coded OFDM with PACE for 16-QAM modulation scheme for different number of iterations of MAP Decoder

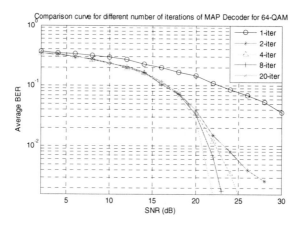

Fig. 11. Comparison curve of Turbo-Coded OFDM with PACE for 64-QAM modulation scheme for different number of iterations of MAP Decoder

benefit in return, contributing less to lowering the BER of the system. The system designer has to choose a modulation scheme keeping in view a trade-off between the tolerable error rate for the application for which the system is designed and the required data rate as these two are linked directly.

6 Summary

A novel ICI cancellation and Error correction algorithm is proposed for OFDM system. The algorithm has a very low computation overhead. It uses the Channel Estimation matrix calculated from the pilot tones to mitigate the effect of ICI. Error correcting turbo codes further improves the performance of the system by lowering the BER significantly. Simulation with different modulation schemes shows that our proposed algorthm can significantly improve the performance of the OFDM system under Rayleigh fading AWGN channel environment.

References

1. Win, Y., Danilo-Lemoine, F.: A postfix synchronization method for OFDM and MIMO-OFDM systems. In: Proc. WCNC 2008, March 31-April 03, pp. 1–6 (2008)
2. Iacono, D.L., Ronchi, M., Torr, L.D., Osnato, F.: MIMO-OFDM Physical Layer Real-Time Prototyping. In: Proc. WCNC 2008, March 31-April 3, pp. 18–23 (2008)
3. Chayratsami, P., Wickert, M.A.: Channel Estimation and mitigation techniques for OFDM in a Doppler Spread Channel. In: Proc. IEEE GLOBECOM 2008, November 30-December 4, pp. 1–5 (2008)
4. Li, Y., Cimini, L.J., Sollenberger, N.R.: Robust channel estimation for OFDM systems with rapid dispersive fading channels. IEEE Trans. Comm. 46(7), 902–915 (1998)
5. Jeon, W.G., Chang, K.H., Cho, Y.S.: An equalization technique for orthogonal frequency-division multiplexing systems in time-variant multipath channels. IEEE Trans. on Comm. 47(1), 27–32 (1999)
6. Arif, M., Sheikh, N.M., Sheikh, A.U.H.: A novel design of deterministic interleaver for turbo codes. In: IEEE Int. Conf. on Elec. Engg., ICEE 2007, pp. 1–5 (April 2007)
7. Benedetto, S., Biglieri, E.: Principles of Digital transmission: with wireless applications, 1st edn. Springer, Heidelberg (June 1999)
8. Vucetic, B., Yuan, J.: Turbo Code, Principles and Applications. Kluwer Academic Publishers, London (2002)
9. Prasad, R.: OFDM for wireless communication systems. Universal Personal Communication Series (2004)
10. Elnoubi, S., et al.: Performance of turbo-coded OFDM system with comb-type channel estimation in Rayleigh fading channel. In: Proc. IEEE "MILCOM" 2008, November 16-19, pp. 1–6 (2008)

A GA-PLS Method for the Index Tracking Problem

Zhe Chen[1], Shizhu Liu[2], Jiangang Shen[1], and Shenghong Li[1]

[1] Deparment of Mathematics, Zhejiang University,
Hangzhou, China, 310000
[2] Deparment of Economics, Zhejiang University,
Hangzhou, China, 310000
zchan1@gmail.com

Abstract. Index tracking is a popular problem for funds, especially for index tracker funds. In this paper, we introduced GA-PLS method to solve the index tracking problem. This method consists of genetic algorithm (GA) and partial least squares (PLS). For a portfolio constructed by specified stocks, we used PLS regression to determine their weights in this portfolio. And we used GA to determine which stocks should be chosen to optimize the tracking effect of the portfolio. Results showed that the tracking portfolio constructed by GA-PLS has good performances on both in-sample and out-of-sample data.

Keywords: Index tracking, Genetic algorithm, Partial least squares.

1 Introduction

Index tracking is to reproduce a stock market index by holding a number of component stocks. It's a popular form of passive fund management. Full replication, which means to purchase all component stocks of an index by the exact proportions as in the index, is the simplest method to track the index. However, disadvantages of full replication are obvious: it will cause high transaction costs when weights of stocks are adjusted or some stocks are deleted or joined. Moreover, small quantities of some stocks also make full replication infeasible.

Beasley et al. [1] applied an evolutionary heuristic for the index tracking problem. They considered the index tracking problem as an optimization problem which used tracking error (TE) as the objective function. Typical genetic algorithm, including the select, crossover and mutate operators, was used to find an optimization portfolio to track the index. Indices of different markets were tested and some results were shown.

Oh et al. [2] proposes a genetic algorithm (GA) portfolio scheme for the index fund optimization. The scheme exploits genetic algorithm and provides the optimal selection of stocks utilizing fundamental variables – standard error of portfolio beta. They applied the proposed GA scheme to Korea stock price index (KOSPI) on bull, bear and flat markets.

In this paper, we use genetic algorithm combined with partial least square (PLS) regression to construct portfolios that have good prediction ability to track indices. First, genomes representing stocks chosen or not are produced randomly as the initial population. Second, data of the index and the chosen stocks are used for PLS regression, and prediction error sum of square (PRESS) is used as the objective function.

G. Shen and X. Huang (Eds.): ECWAC 2011, Part I, CCIS 143, pp. 12–18, 2011.

Then GA is applied to choose the portfolios that have the smallest PRESS, which means that they have the best prediction abilities. GA-PLS method is useful in variable selection when number of observations is fewer than number of variables. When stocks are regarded as variables, this method is also effective on stock selection.

2 Materials and Methods

2.1 Partial Least Squares Regression

Partial least squares regression is a statistical method that bears some relation to principal components regression; instead of finding hyperplanes of maximum variance between the response and independent variables, it finds a linear regression model by projecting the predicted variables and the observable variables to a new space. PLS regression is particularly useful when we need to predict a set of dependent variables from a large set of independent variables (i.e., predictors). Details of PLS regression can be found in Refs. [3].

2.2 Genetic Algorithm

The genetic algorithm is a search heuristic that mimics the process of natural evolution. It is routinely used to generate useful solutions to optimization problems. Genetic algorithm has been applied to many regions due to its effectiveness in generating solutions of high fitness. A typical genetic algorithm requires a genetic representation of the solution domain and a fitness function to evaluate the solution domain. Once we have both of them, GA proceeds to initialize a population of solutions randomly, and then improve it through repetitive application of selection, crossover and mutation operators until the termination condition has been reached. Details of GA can be found in Refs. [4].

2.3 GA-PLS Method and Related Parameters

GA-PLS method is useful in variable selection. When there are many variables but much fewer observations, and we want to select some variables that most fit the PLS model, a randomly searching method will cost a lot of time especially when the number of variables is large. GA helps us get the best solutions much more quickly. The more time we spend running GA, the better the result is, so we can make a balance between time and results.

Main steps of GA-PLS method are the following:

(1) A number of genomes are created as the initial population. Each genome is a binary bit string that represents the variables chosen. In this paper, we use another kind of string to represent the variables selected. For example, when selecting stocks to track AS51 index (about 200 component stocks), we want a portfolio containing no more than 40 stocks, so we use a string in which every element is an integer and this integer is randomly produced from 0 to 5. The number 0 represents that this stock is selected. And a genome in which more than 40 stocks are selected will get a very low score, so that it is almost impossible to survive to the next generation.

(2) A fitness of each genome in the population is evaluated by the internal prediction ability of PLS. Here we use the leave-one cross-validation method and measure the internal prediction ability by the prediction error sum of square (PRESS). It is calculated by

$$\text{PRESS}(k) = \sum_{i=1}^{n}(\hat{y}_i - y_i(k))^2 \tag{1}$$

where $\hat{y}_i$ is the observation value, y_i is the prediction value, n is the number of observation and k is the number of components used to calculate PRESS.
Since smaller RMSECV represents better prediction ability, the fitness score of a genome is defined by

$$\text{Score} = \frac{1}{\min(\text{PRESS}(k))} \tag{2}$$

Genomes that represents a number more than the maximum number of stocks selected are given a score 0.

(3) The selection, crossover and mutation operators of GA are made to reproduce the new generation. Genomes with high scores have more probability to be chosen by the selection operator.

Steps 2 and 3 are repeated until the termination condition is satisfied, e.g. a designated number of generations are reached in this article.

Other settings and parameters are the following:
Population size: 50 genomes;
Crossover method: one-point crossover;
Crossover ratio: 0.9;
Mutation probability: 0.01;
Scaling method: linear scaling
Termination condition: 50 generations;

Regression method: PLS (The maximum number of components allowed is the optimal number of components determined by cross validation on the model containing all data of stocks. The number of components used to get prediction values in out-of-sample data set is the optimal number of components determined by cross validation on the model containing data of selected stocks.)

2.4 Data Sets

Daily close prices of 4 indices and their component stocks are used to test our GA-PLS program. The data of AS51 index starts from Jan. 4, 2010 to Mar. 26, 2010, and data of the other 3 indices starts from Jan. 4, 2010 to Jul. 19, 2010.

2.5 Tracking Error and Other Restrictions

Tracking error is a function of the difference between r_t (the tracking portfolio return) and R_t (the index return). It is used to measure the tracking effect of a portfolio. The tracking error TE is defined by

$$TE = \frac{\left(\sum_{t=1}^{T}|r_t - R_t|^{\alpha}\right)^{\frac{1}{\alpha}}}{T} \tag{3}$$

where $\alpha > 0$ is the power by which we penalize differences between r_t and R_t, and T is the length of the data. In the following tests, we use $\alpha = 2$ so that the tracking error is defined as the root mean squared error.

The PLS regression model outputs the following result:

$$R_t = \sum_{i=1}^{K} c_i r_t \tag{4}$$

where K is the number of stocks selected, c_i is the coefficient of the i-th stock in the portfolio as well as the proportion of money spent on this stock. Since c_i can be negative which represents short selling this stock, we assume the margin rate of the i-th stock is a_i, so all coefficients must satisfy the restriction

$$\sum_{i=1}^{K}\left(c_i I_{\{c_i > 0\}} + a_i |c_i| I_{\{c_i < 0\}}\right) \leq 1 \tag{5}$$

In this paper, we set all $a_i = 0.4$. Genomes that don't satisfy the restriction are given a score 0.

3 Computational Results and Discussion

3.1 Data Processing

Data of different indices and their component stocks is not clean, so we have to process the data before we use it. Because some stocks are joined or deleted from the indices occasionally, there are missing values in the data of component stocks. We remove this kind of stocks and get complete data in this period. Some wrong or repeated data is removed too. Next, daily return rates of the index and all stocks are calculated, and then the GA-PLS method is applied to the data of daily return rates. We don't consider transaction costs in the stock selection.

Table 1 shows the details of data sets used for the index tracking problem.

Table 1. Details of data sets

Index	Number of stocks	Length of data		Maximum number of stocks selected
		In-sample	Out-of-sample	
AS51	192	40 days	13 days	40
Nikkei	221	80 days	45 days	40
KOSPI200	189	80 days	47 days	40
TPX	1657	100 days	24 days	50

3.2 Index Tracking Results

Tracking errors of the indices on both in-sample and out-of-sample data are shown in Table 2 We can see that tracking errors on in-sample data are all very small. On out-of-sample data, the tracking errors are a little larger but still in a small range. Small tracking errors on out-of-sample data show the prediction ability of PLS regression.

Results on data of Nikkei and KOSPI2 are good. The tracking errors on out-of-sample data of these two indices are so small that the differences between the return rate of indices and portfolios can hardly be seen on the graphs. We make a graph of daily errors between the return rate of Nikkei index and portfolios (Figure 1). It is easy to see that daily errors between the return rate of the index and the portfolio are all less than 0.003 on out-of-sample data. The result of TPX index shows the effectiveness of GA-PLS method on index tracking. Only 39 out of 1657 stocks are selected to track the TPX index, but the tracking errors on both in-sample and out-of-sample data are still small. The result of AS51 index is a little overfitting. The tracking error on in-sample data is very small, while the tracking error on out-of-sample data is relatively large.

Table 2. Tracking errors on in-sample and out-of-sample data sets

Index	Optimal components	Number of stocks selected	Tracking error	
			In-sample	Out-of-sample
AS51	14	37	4.723×10^{-5}	6.306×10^{-4}
Nikkei	12	36	1.169×10^{-4}	2.081×10^{-4}
KOSPI200	2	32	1.124×10^{-4}	4.195×10^{-4}
TPX	5	39	1.454×10^{-4}	6.225×10^{-4}

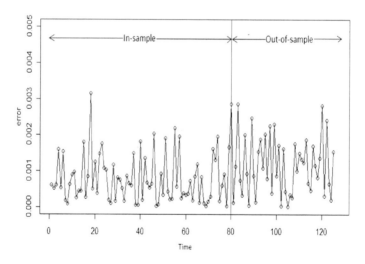

Fig. 1. Errors of daily return rate. (Nikkei)

Since stocks have been selected to construct a portfolio, proportions of money spent on each stock can be calculated. The PLS model outputs regression coefficients of selected stocks. For instance, Figure 2 shows the regression coefficients of stocks in the portfolio tracking TPX index. Obviously, the index has positive correlation with its most component stocks, for the index is sum of weighted price of stocks. So it

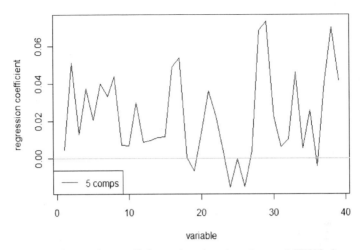

Fig. 2. Regression coefficients of stocks selected to track TPX Index

is reasonable that most stocks in our portfolio have positive coefficients, and the absolute values of coefficients of the other stocks are small.

Proportion of money spent on the i-th stock in the portfolio is

$$p_i = \begin{cases} c_i, & c_i > 0 \\ a_i |c_i|, & c_i < 0 \end{cases}$$

4 Conclusions

In this paper, we apply GA-PLS method to the index tracking problem and get some results of different indices. We first describe some basic concepts and steps of genetic algorithm and partial least squares regression, and then derive the objective function of GA, tracking error of a portfolio and the restriction of coefficients of PLS model. By analyzing the results on 4 indices, we see that the GA-PLS method works very well on the index tracking problem. This method is useful in index fund management.

The index tracking problem is a practical and meaningful problem that many financial institution are interested in or working on. But as we have noticed, few papers on this important problem were published in recent years. We hope that this paper will draw the attention of other researchers to this problem.

Acknowledgments. This research is supported by the Major Project of the ministry of Education of China (309018) and National Natural Science Foundation of China (70973104).

References

1. Beasley, J.E., Meade, N., Chang, T.-J.: An evolutionary heuristic for the index tracking problem. European Journal of Operational Research 148, 621–643 (2003)
2. Oh, K.J., Kim, T.Y., Min, S.: Using genetic algorithm to support portfolio optimiation for index fund management. Expert Systems with Applications 28, 371–379 (2005)
3. Abdi, H.: Partial Least Squares (PLS) Regression (unpublished)
4. Leardi, R., Boggia, R., Terrile, M.: Genetic algorithms as a strategy for feature selection. J. Chemometr. 6, 267–281 (1992)
5. Hasegawa, K., Funatsu, K.: GA strategy for variable selection in QSAR studies: GAPLS and D-optimal designs for predictive QSAR model. Journal of Molecular Structure (Theochem) 425, 255–262 (1998)
6. Leardi, R., Gonzalez, A.L.: Genetic algorithms applied to feature selection in PLS regression: how and when to use them. Chemometrics and Intelligent Laboratory Systems 41, 195–207 (1998)
7. Canakgoz, N.A., Beasley, J.E.: Mixed-integer programming approaches for index tracking and enhanced indexation. European Journal of Operational Research 196, 384–399 (2008)
8. Riahi, S., Ganjali, M.R., Norouzi, P., Jafari, F.: Application of GA-MLR, GA-PLS and the DFT quantum mechanical (QM) calculations for the prediction of the selectivity coefficients of a histamine-selective electrode. Sensors and Actuators B 132, 13–19 (2008)
9. Mevik, B.-H., Wehrens, R.: The pls package: Principal component and partial least squares regression in R. Journal of Statistical Software 18(2) (January 2007)
10. Dose, C., Cincotti, S.: Clustering of financial time series with application to index and enhanced index tracking portfolio. Physica A 355, 145–151 (2005)
11. Corielli, F., Marcellino, M.: Factor based index tracking. Journal of Banking and Finance 30, 2215–2233 (2006)
12. Colwell, D., El-Hassan, N., Kwon, O.K.: Hedging diffusion processes by local risk minimization with applications to index tracking. Journal of Economic Dynamics & Control 31, 2135–2151 (2007)

A Brief Study on Autonomous Learning Mode in Self-study Center Based on Web

Xian Zhi Tian

Wuhan university of Science and Technology, Zhongnan Branch
Julia030712@163.com

Abstract. In the paper, the author has studied the autonomous learning ability and its reform of linguistic-major students. All of the studies are based on web in self-study center. As for the author, she has used the method of comparison and at the same time, she also used showing examples. In order to show the views clearly, the author has made investigation in English major and law major students. Thus she thinks that teaching reform is necessary for development of students and some effective ways can be used in improving teaching efficiency.

Keywords: autonomous learning, self-study center, web application.

1 Introduction

In the reform of linguistic teaching , many kinds of reforms can be diged out by linguistic teachers. The reform kinds of aims are also in different ones, but the essence is the same, that is, to develop teaching efficiency and improve learning efficiency. As for students, old teaching forms are the barriers for their learning, and they are also eager to learn by themselves by the guide of the teachers. So it is very important for teachers to think out efficient ways to prove their teaching abilities. In modern time, with the development of web and information technology, many different kinds of information begin entering into teaching courses of teachers and learning courses of students. Therefore, autonomous learning is becoming a topic for researchers.

As for autonomous learning , it is a new definition of the author. In fact , it has been mentioned by some researchers for many years. But the realization of it is a long way, especially for Asia people because Asia people are accustomed to be guided and taught by teachers, especially for Chinese people. So it is necessary for researchers and teachers to design better ways to realize it. Therefore, different names of autonomous learning have been used home and abroad, for example, Learner Autonomy, Self-directed Learning, Self-access, Self-instruction, Independence, Language Awareness ect. No matter how the expressions can be used ,it has been a hot topic in modern society. It is connected with the development of our society closely. In modern society, individual development is the base for the individual existence. In order to have good existence abilities, the author must learn to be independent, thus it requires students to learn in autonomous ways. Secondly, students are near modern information, and many kinds of knowledges can be learned through web or other forms connecting with web such as self-study center. It also requires students to learn in autonomous ways outside classroom.

G. Shen and X. Huang (Eds.): ECWAC 2011, Part I, CCIS 143, pp. 19–25, 2011.

In autonomous learning course, students are required to learn by themselves and they are keen on digging out effective ways of learning. In different courses, different learners tried different ways of autonomous learning. Finally, some effective modes have been mentioned by scholars. In fact, it requires students to spur up their thinking ability, their creative ability and their practice abilities and so on. There are some theories existing to advocate autonomous learning. The theory of humanism was initiated by American psychologist Abraham Maslow firstly. It pays attention to personal uniqueness, and claims that people are an autonomous, rational organism with the potential of personal development; Swiss psychologist J. Piajet puts forward constructivism, which demonstrates that knowledge is not obtained through teachers' instruction but through meaning construction in a certain environment (i.e. social cultural background) with the help of others (including teachers and learning partners) and by making use of necessary learning materials.Furthermore, the discovery learning theory advocated by famous psychologist J. S. Bruner also emphasizes that students' learning should be a process of actively discovering on their own, rather than of receiving knowledge passively. In actual teaching and learning, students are active explorers, and the role of teachers is to set up context for problem-solving, to evoke students' interest of learning, to satisfy their cognitive needs, and to arouse the learning motivation of autonomous exploration of knowledge, rather than to pass on or to impart existing knowledge.It leads to zero-approach teaching mode in some colleges , and here the author used ZATM to stand for it. The purpose of ZATM is exactly to embody the feature of people's autonomy. In ZATM , it is easier for teachers to monitor and teach students at the same level, it is also easier for students to form autonomous learning habit. These theories also exhibits that it is practically significant for the author to conduct a research into ZATM , especially to the second-level college students because of their weaker ability for autonomous learning and their over-dependence on the teachers. Until now the study of how to cultivate learners' autonomous learning ability in ZATM —has never been made at second-level colleges. At the same time, although many scholars have made investigations into autonomous learning, no one has studied it from the perspective of and in the framework of ZATM in which the research just combines ZATM and cultivating students' autonomous learning ability. Therefore, the study of the author is innovative and original.

In addition, some other reforming learning and teaching mode also appears. Therefore, the author wants to explore the different learning and teaching mode in improving autonomous learning based on web. From exploration, the authors wants to show her study research to help teaching reform.

2   Background and Development of Autonomous Learning Mode

In thousands of years of teaching, more and more scholars and teachers have tried their best to dig out best teaching mode to improve practice abilities of students. From the ancient time, teachers had also known inspiration teaching mode. That is to say, teachers used some effective ways(old ways) to enlighten their students to know some lessons for life. But the old inspiration teaching modes are based on explaining of teachers. The scientific characteristics of them are worth thinking and studying by present scholars. And with the development of modern information, some inspiration modes are also out of date. Because the old inspiration modes are mainly concerned about teachers' teaching, not on students' learning. The author shows it as follows:

Table 1. The old relationship between teachers and students

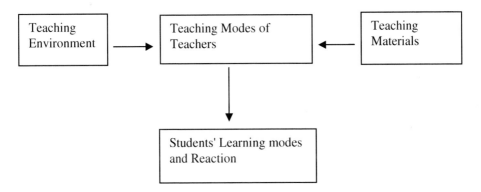

From the above table, we can see that teachers can influence students only in unidirectional way. Students must obey teachers unconditionally. And in fact, teachers' teaching mode are mainly influenced by teaching environment and teaching materials. In fact, students can only learn everything from teachers. The mode is formed by the influences of the condition at that time. In the past, there are few information from outside world to be known and learned. People are in lack-of-information circle. The only way to get new information and knowledge is from teacher. But now, with the development of modern information, so many new kinds of media have appeared. In this condition, people must learn how to deal with things on hand. And everyday, new information and new learning methods appear frequently and influences learners in different ways. Learners are easy to be confused because of the bustling information, and some learners are lost themselves in learning course and are puzzled on learning methods. But the author thinks that all learning and teaching modes are in common ways. That is to say, all teaching and learning modes have the main common rules to be obeyed. Only learners grasp the rules, can they learn effectively. According to the former studies of scholars, the basic teaching elements mainly includes several elements such as teachers, students and courses as follows:

Table 2. Circulation table of present teaching course

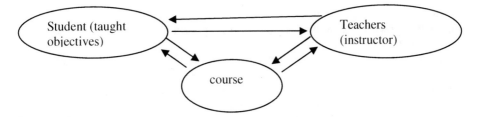

According to the above table, all elements are influenced by each other, and all of them have played important roles in the circulation. In fact, the element "course" also included several small elements such as teaching materials, course plans, course equipment. As for teachers and students, they are always the eternal topics in teaching course. So many scholars and researchers have studied all these elements in many different aspects.

In the above two kinds of teaching modes in the past and in the present, the study on them is centered on influences of teaching modes on students, comparison of teaching modes, teaching mode and its reactions on students, learning strategies of students, learning methods and its influences on teachers, learning mode and cooperation learning experiments, autonomous learning mode studies and so on.

Nowadays, the study of autonomous learning mode is developed with modern information technology. Some scholars studied it with the help of Multimeida, and some people studied it with the development of self-study center. Some scholars studied it withe the development of some effective learning software. In this paper, the author studied autonomous learning based on self-study center. The author wants to find our an effective learning method to spur up practice abilities of students.

3   A Brief Study on Autonomous Learning Mode in Self-study Center Based on Web

In 1968, Maslow had raised a theory being called "Need Theory". It shows that people have Basic Physiological Need, Need for Safety and Security, Need for Interpersonal Closeness,Need for Self-Esteem,Cognitive Need, Aesthetic Needs and Self-Actualization. The first four needs belongs to Maintenance Needs, and the last three ones belong to Growth Needs. At the same time, he pointed out that the next levels of needs will not be satisfied unless the formal ones have been realized. It shows that students have difficulties in learning mainly because some of their needs can not be satisfied by teachers and their parents. In addition, students are encouraged to thinking about anything by themselves for their creative needs and it can make students different from others. It is also belong to cognitive need for students. Later, William&Burden(1997) raised a query about the "Need Theory" on its "grade order", but they admitted its application and rationality. The next important person of autonomous learning is Rogers. He put his emphasis on digging out learning potentials of students. He thought that learning course will be effective only by the active taking part in by students. He also pointed that learning should be based on autonomous learning and the purposes of learning are on being free and self-realization.

According to the mentioned famous learning theory, the author has explored some effective autonomous learning modes for several years. The basic autonomous learning modes are based on web or network. There are some characteristics being shown in the following:

Mode one shows that self-study center is a center place for students to finish their autonomous learning task. Students can be divided into several groups. In each group, students are required to learn with other members. The main learning mode is cooperative learning mode. Each member in each group must cooperate with each other to finish some learning tasks. But each group are separated from other group. Each group is in competitive situation against any other group. In order to be the best one, each group must adopt some effective group learning strategies for them. Teachers act as instructors in the learning course of students. In self-study center, students can get learning materials from web and self-learning warehouse arranged by teachers or monitors of each group. The mode above can stimulate learning enthusiasm of students and at the same time, it is better for students to know competitive situation around them, thus it will give them competitive experiences before entering the real society. The difficult points of it is on learning materials. How to divide them into several levels scientifically and how to arrange the learning course scientifically are the main difficulties.

Table 3. Autonomous Learning Mode One

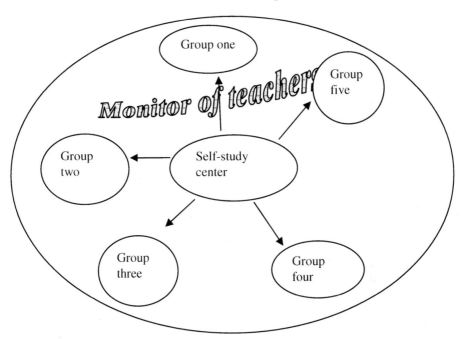

Table 4. Autonomous Learning Mode Two

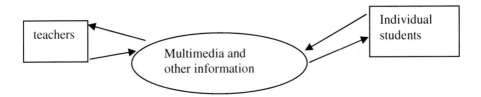

In mode two, students are regarded as learning individuals. Each individual learn by themselves and their learning course must be monitored by teachers and themselves. Each student must make their learning plans according to the arrangement of teachers. Teachers and students are connected by "Multimedia and other information resources". At the same time, individual students get learning resources from self-study warehouse based on web. After learning, teachers can check them through the web according to the designed materials. This mode is a special mode for individual effective learning and students have much more freedom learning room. But at the same time, it has also disadvantages, for example, it is hard for students to compete with each other and cooperate with each other. Therefore, the mode will be improved with teaching reform course.

Table 5. Autonomous Learning Mode Three

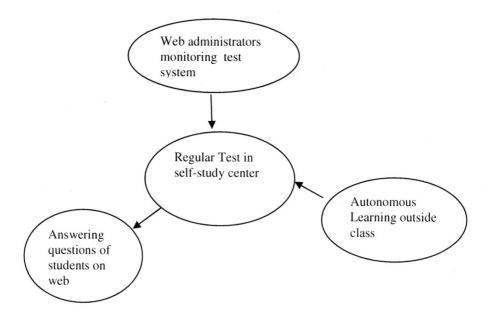

The above autonomous learning mode is the widest one for students. They have only depended on web resources. From regular test, students can test themselves every period. But as for this mode, teachers must give test materials for web instructors. And the test materials must be in good level from easy ones to more difficult ones. Therefore, teachers play an important role in the whole course. In addition, students must have strong autonomous learning abilities. Or it will have poor effect.

However, no matter which modes can be adopted, students are regarded as the main role in the autonomous learning course, and learning materials are also very important in the autonomous learning course. At the same time, effective instruction of teachers also play an important role in the whole duration.

4   Conclusion

In the course of study of autonomous learning , the author has found out several autonomous learning modes. All of them have been applied in the autonomous learning courses of students. And they have shown special charms. The author finds that students play the most important roles in these learning course. In any case, teachers play the instruction role. At the same time, modern information technology plays an important role in its course. Students, teachers and learning resources are connected closely during the reform course. It will be more and more effective with the development of teaching reform and the efforts of reformers and students.

References

1. Eason, G., Noble, B., Sneddon, I.N.: On certain integrals of Lipschitz-Hankel type involving products of Bessel functions. Phil. Trans. Roy. Soc. London A247, 529–551 (1955) (references)
2. Kornack, D., Rakic, P.: Cell Proliferation without Neurogenesis in Adult Primate Neocortex. Science 294, 2127–2130 (2001) doi:10.1126/science.1065467
3. Goto, H., Hasegawa, Y., Tanaka, M.: Efficient Scheduling Focusing on the Duality of MPL Representatives. In: Proc. IEEE Symp. Computational Intelligence in Scheduling (SCIS 2007), December 2007, pp. 57–64. IEEE Press, Los Alamitos (2007) doi:10.1109/SCIS.2007.357670
4. Chan, V.: Readiness for learner autonomy:what do our learners tell us? Teaching in High Education 6(4), 505–518 (2001)

Analysis of Organizational Learning Efficiency in Enterprises Based on DEA

Tianying Jiang and Zhixin Bai

Zhejiang University of Technology
Hangzhou, China
jty19760825@126.com

Abstract. The study assesses the organizational learning efficiency in 30 large-scale enterprises of Zhejiang Province, making use of DEA assessment method. The results show that the entire organizational learning efficiency of zhejiang province's large-scale enterprises is in need; only part of the enterprises are DEA valid, and the results of the study basically fit in with the enterprises' practical situation. It is thus clear that the new way to assess the efficiency of organizational learning in enterprises is rational and accessible, which provides an important instrument to enterprises' management decision making.

Keywords: organizational learning, DEA, learning efficiency.

1 Introduction

With the coming of the era of knowledge economy time, intellect and knowledge are gradually turning the capital of developing economy and creating wealth. Entrepreneurs regard the investment and acquisition of intellectual capital as an enterprise magic method and a competitive focal point, and scramble for and develop it by all means. Therefore, more and more western scholars start to do researches on intellectual capital, especially the intellectual capital assessment, which has substantial results now in the academic circles. Whereas the objects of the domestic study on enterprise intellectual capital are all certain specific countries, areas or certain groups of enterprises, and the research results may not fit the whole country. Then in which way can we assess our enterprise intellectual capital? This is not only an academic problem, but also a problem to be solved urgently of enterprise practice.

March and Simon put forward the organizational learning for the first time, regarding organizational learning as a social behavior that realizes the successful transmission and improvement of the knowledge and ability demanded in organization growing, overcomes developing obstacles and smoothly realizes the revolution by learning with organizations and levels, when faced with gradually complicated management environment both inside and outside in change. Hebderg[1] considered organizational learning as departing from the additional and operational effect of organizations and their environment; it contains not only the process of organizations' passive adaptation. Foil and Myles[2] defined the organizational learning as the process to improve the disposing capacity by understanding and obtaining more abundant

G. Shen and X. Huang (Eds.): ECWAC 2011, Part I, CCIS 143, pp. 26–29, 2011.

knowledge. Nonaka[3] toke the organizational learning as the capacity showed in the products, services and systems that an enterprise improves the knowledge acquisition, creation and the propagation in the whole organization.

Look back in the view of the document above, we can discover that learners made different definitions of organizational learning from different study prospects, which mainly consist of those based on characters, processes and results. To sum up the above definitions, this study starts from the prospect of the character features of organizational learning and considers organizational learning as a gradual, interactional and purposeful active way, by which enterprises elevate their competitive force. This way of act is mainly showed in the personal, group made and entire organizational activities with gradualism and creation, which made by enterprises around information and knowledge acquisition. Based on this, the essay trays to apply the DEA model method to assess the efficiency of organizational learning in enterprises, on the purpose of providing decision making reference to enterprises for their validly enhancing the efficiency of organizational learning.

2 DEA Assessment Method

There are many methods to evaluate the organizational learning efficiency, such as analytic hierarchy process, fuzzy evaluation, balanced scorecard approach, neural network approach and so on. However, most of the methods above require the artificial design of various indices for evaluating the standard of the subordinate functions and confirming the weight of each index. By adding man-made factors, such methods will affect the accuracy of efficiency evaluation of organizational learning, and the majority of the methods above are just simple valuation, not including the improvement of corresponding results.

Data envelopment analysis(DEA) does not require subjective weight given to each indicator, thereby reducing the influence of subjective factors during the evaluation process, as much as possible to ensure the objectivity of the evaluation results; meanwhile, it does not need to carry out the parameter estimation, so it can evade the multiple constraints of the parameter methods, it's a popular method of efficiency evaluation in recent years. Therefore, this essay introduces the DEA relative efficiency evaluation method to have a comprehensive evaluation on enterprise organizational learning efficiency.

Data envelopment analysis(DEA) is a kind of operational methods put forward in 1978 , which was based on "relative efficiency evaluation "concept by the famous operational research experts A. Charms and W.W. Copper etc. It is used to assess a group of relative efficiency possessing multiple inputs and output decision making units.

This essay uses CCR model in DEA model to evaluate the efficiency of organizational learning, the model is following[5]:

$$(CCR) \begin{cases} \min[\theta - \varepsilon E^T (s^- + s^+)] \\ \sum_{j=1}^{n} \lambda_j x_j + s^- = \theta x_{j_0} \\ \sum_{j=1}^{n} \lambda_j y_j - s^+ = y_{j_0} \\ \lambda_j, s^-, s^+ \geq 0, j = 1,...,n \end{cases} \tag{1}$$

Among that, n is the number of decision making unit(DMU), each DMU has m kinds of inputs $x_j = (x_{1j}, x_{2j}, ..., x_{mj})$ and s kinds of outputs $y_j = (y_{1j}, y_{2j}, ..., y_{sj})$, λ_j indicates weights of various inputs and outputs, s^- and s^+ each be the surplus variable and slack variable, θ indicates efficiency value, ε indicates Non-Archimedean infinitesimal. When the optimal solution $\theta^* = 1$, $s^{-*} = 0$, $s^{+*} = 0$, it is said that DMU j_0 is DEA effective; when $\theta^* < 1$, or $s^{-*} \neq 0$, $s^{+*} \neq 0$, it is said that j_0 is non-DEA effective. If $\theta^* = 1$, and $s^{-*} \neq 0$, or $s^{+*} \neq 0$, then DMU j_0 is judged as weak DEA effective. For non- effective or weak effective DEA decision making units, they can be turned into effective units through finding non-effective or weak-effective reasons and adjusting the input and output index. The number j_0 decision making unit's input and output optimize index is: $x_{j_0} \Leftarrow \theta^* x_{j_0} - s^{-*}$, $y_{j_0} \Leftarrow y_{j_0} + s^{+*}$.

3 Case Analysis

According to the principles to select the indicator such as scientific, objective, easy to access, and reference to relevant literature, this essay establishes the efficient evaluation of organizational learning.

This study of data collected through the questionnaire survey method, using Likert seven scale forms, of which 7 means extremely consistent, 1 means extremely inconsistent. To ensure the information providers are familiar with the issues on what this study is going to investigate, interviewees are limited to the senior managements who are familiar with the enterprise organizational learning situations. The use of DEA efficiency evaluation model will affect the assessment results of the decision making unit. According to some scholars' rule of thumb, the number of decision making units is at least double of the sum of input and output items. In this essay, there are 8 projects of input and output, 30 decision making units, meeting the DEA used rule of thumb.

We use statistical data and CCR model to evaluate relative efficiency of organizational learning in 30 surveyed enterprises. The evaluation results show that the 12 enterprises' organizational learning efficiency is DEA relative effective, that the technical support, communication channel, organizational culture and training system are relatively matching to their organizational learning capacity outputs. The reason is, most of these 12 enterprises are high-tech enterprises, and high-tech firms possess high information level and a higher proportion of technical personnel, employees can form a rich atmosphere of learning, staff research and staff training can get fully support, so not only employees can learn from each others' experiences, but can also share key employees' customer's relationship, unique skills, expertise and other tacit knowledge, thus they can have access to relatively higher organizational learning efficiency.

Other 18 enterprises' organizational learning efficiency is DEA invalid, and most of them belong to traditional industries, accounting for 60% of total research company, shows the input-output combination of these enterprises' organizational learning dose not reach its optimal combination. Labor-intensive industries, manufacturing and processing industries are the main and sutras in traditional industries, which are lack of input on organizational learning and understanding of the importance of organizational learning. Therefore, we find that most of the traditional industries of organizational learning efficiency DEA invalid. So it can be seen that the results of this study coincide with the enterprises' actual situation.

4 Conclusion

The study anal sizes the relative efficiency of 30 large-scale enterprises' organizational learning, taking advantage of DEA method. The result shows that the entire efficiency of organizational learning in Zhejiang province's large-scale enterprises is in need; the enterprises with DEA validity are not in large number; a lot of enterprises need optimizing investment and output to realize the relative efficiency of organizational learning. The study also makes it clear that this new way of assessment of organizational learning efficiency in enterprises is rational and accessible and worth applying and popularizing in enterprises' management practice.

Finally, we applied DEA method to analyses on the efficiency of organizational learning research in this paper, has yielded some results, but there are some inadequacies in the follow-up study, we will focus on DEA applied to organizational learning process, different factors influence individual effect and the overall effect relationship.

Acknowledgement

This paper is supported by the Project of National Natural Science Foundation of China: Study on Dynamic Match between Social Network and Technical Innovation of SMEs: Based on The Perspective of Network Embedded and Technical Learning (Project NO. 71002075).

References

1. Hedberg, R.: How organizations learn and unlearn. In: Nystrom, P.C., Starbuck, W.H. (eds.) Handbook of Organizational Design. Oxford University Press, Oxford (1981)
2. Fiol, C., Mlyles, M.: Organizational learning. Academy of Management Review 10(4), 132–133 (1985)
3. Nonaka, L., Takeuchi, H.: The Knowledge-creating Company: How Japanese Companies Creating the Dynamics of Innovation. Oxford University Press, Oxford (1995)
4. Gherardi, S., Nicolini, D.: The Organizational Learning of Safety in Community of Practice. Journal of Management Inquiry 9(1), 7 (2000)
5. Zhanxin, M.: Analysis Model and Method of Data Envelopment. Science Publication, Beijing (2010) (in Chinese)

Study on the Establishment of Heilongjiang Provinces Animal Husbandry Basic Data Platform Based on Data Warehouse

Ping Zheng, Zhongbin Su[*], and Jicheng Zhang

Engineering college
Northeast Agricultural University
Haerbin, Heilongjiang

Abstract. The paper establishes animal husbandry information service platform, and the public data platform of animal husbandry is based on data warehouse platform. It aims at the absence of effective use of data resources issues in the process of animal husbandry information. Then it studies on the key technology for the animal husbandry. It will be of the theoretical basis for information integration, storing, sharing and analysis decision-making.

Keywords: data warehouse, basic data platform, animal husbandry, OLAP.

1 Introduction

With the arrival of the era of internet of thing, many industries are facing a huge challenge requested with higher level of information to merge in internet of thing. Animal husbandry steps progressively in modernization process. There are several industry bodies (production enterprises, government departments, cooperative organizations, farmers, etc) and enterprises in different stages of industry (raw materials, feed, breeding, processing and distribution, etc.) demand for the complicated information needs. There are the mass of date resource in animal husbandry information. How to integrate, store, share and analysis the data resources to extract effective information, to give full play to the data of resource utilization value, and to provide various fields of public figures, which is one of the hot issues in high schools and institutes.

Through the above thinking, researchers believe the bureau of Heilongjiang Animal Husbandry collects mass of information. But there are no real data transferring to the information resources which leads to resource data waste.

A data warehouse is a subject-oriented, integrated, time-variant, and nonvolatile collection of data in support of management's decision making process. Data warehouse provide services in data analysis and decision. This system is called on-line analytical processing (OLAP). The basic data platform based on data warehouse supports information query and basic statistics; basic OLAP operation to collect the historical operation

---

[*] The paper is sponsored by Heilongjiang Education Important Project(1154z1011), and by Northeast Agricultural University Doctor Fund(2009RC54).

G. Shen and X. Huang (Eds.): ECWAC 2011, Part I, CCIS 143, pp. 30–34, 2011.

data in details; knowledge discovery such as finding hidden mode and structural analysis model, classification and prediction, and provides the mining visual tools etc.

Therefore, the paper builds a basic data platform based on the data warehouse technology, and studies on the key technology. It will be the base on integration, storage, sharing and analysis and decision. And the study will make possible that animal husbandry emerges into internet of thing.

2 The Establishment of Basic Data Platform

2.1 Demand Analysis of Husbandry Information

First, according to Heilongjiang province's animal husbandry information status, the paper divides the basic information platform into data standards, system safety standards, business application system, network communication platform, basic data platform. These five parts as a whole supports the analysis and decision of the organic livestock epidemic warning, the quality and safety management of trace livestock breeding process, etc. It also could integrate the animal husbandry collection resources, geographical information resources, animal products information resources, etc.

2.2 The Establishment of Basic Data Platform

The overall design goal of basic data platform is to support enterprise-level information sharing, application integration and operation analysis, such as senior application development. The design framework of basic data platform includes data acquisition and interface, multidimensional data model, data service, monitoring and management platform.

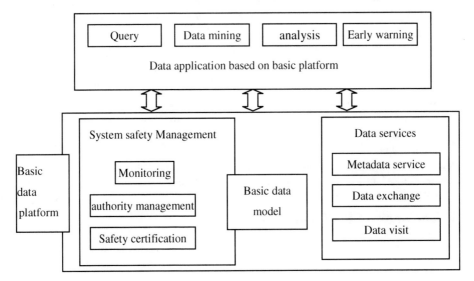

Fig. 1. The framework of basic data platform

Data collection interface is key to design and develop different interfaces with various data acquisition, adapter; The establishment of multidimensional data model is the key of animal husbandry industry standard model design to make standard, coordination and consistent way based on information model; Data service is the key to design the standard of information service so as to provide data interface to share data, data exchange, metadata management services. Monitoring and management belongs to the maintenance function of platform. Based on data platform, we will develop data mining analysis and application integration, business application system architecture such advanced system structure as shown in figure 1.

2.3   The Research of Key Technology

Based on the data warehouse technology, the paper summarizes several key problems below.

1) The establishment of concept model and storage model

Animal husbandry data are almost semi-structured data. It could be built concept model based on OEM conceptual model. And it could be described corresponding business requirements on irregular structures, and chose corresponding traversal way to identify all the most path expression. It uses the layered structure thoughts and accumulates counting principle of dynamic model of data generated tree structure. The tree is the data storage model (logical model) and physical mapping. The model will be useful of transformation, query and optimization of mass of data.

2) Livestock data analysis and decision and the technology of early warming

Information is normally half-structure. It includes spatial data, temporal data and multimedia data. It is difficult to make data characteristics, classify, correlation. For effective accurate data analysis and decision making in the original warning, on the basis of the data mining technology, expand the data mining technology and method for the space, and multimedia, text and web data, using the data streams, time series data and sequence of data mining technology, information analysis, decision support early warning.

3) The technology of mass data parallel storage and management

With the involvement of the data type and quantity of livestock, increasing requirements based data platform efficient, flexible data storage and management. The technical requirements will be massive data storage and management of concurrent and improve the performance of the platform, storage and data is growing demand. The technology for public data platform provides various hardware technology, efficient and convenient interface to realize data resources in the basic data of import and export platform, solve data from the data warehouse into or out of the limitations.

3   The Show of Platform

According to the above statement, we have established the basic data platform based on data warehouse technology. We choose the sql server 2005 to establish the multidimensional data model (partly shown as Fig.2). Then the platform could be the basic of analysis support and early warning.

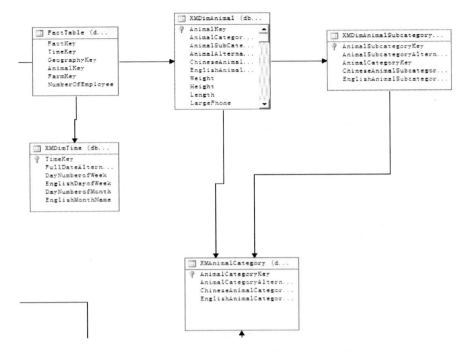

Fig. 2. The part of multidimensional data model

4   Conclusions

According to the present structure and status, the paper puts forward to the method of public date platform based on data system structure on the basic of animal husbandry information services platform. Then the paper studies on the key technologies. The establishment of platform is the further preparation for data mining, animal husbandry resources of information integration, storage, sharing and analysis the theoretical basis, etc.

References

1. Fan, M., Meng, X.: The concept and technology of data mining, vol. 20, pp. 8–9. (CMP) China Machine Press, Beijing (2003)
2. Shan, W.: Date warehouse technology and online analysis, vol. 6(4), p. 3. Science Press, Beijing (1998)
3. Wu, X., Wu, Q.: The study status and future development of data warehouse. Modern Electric Technology (2002)
4. Yang, B.A., Li, L.X., JiH, Xu, J.: An early warning system for loan risk assessment using artificial neural networks. Knowledge Based Systems 14 (2001)

5. Mundy, J., Thornthwaite, W., Kimball, R.: The Microsoft data warehouse toolkit. Wiley Publishing Inc., Chichester (2006)
6. Microsoft, http://msdn,microsoft.com
7. Lee, W.K.Y.: Multi-objective optimal power plant operation through coordinate control with pressure set point scheduling. IEEE Trans. on Energy Conversion 16(2), 115–122 (2001)
8. Fan, S., Zhang, X.: Infrastructure and regional economic development in review 15, 203–214 (2004)

The Realization of Drilling Fault Diagnosis Based on Hybrid Programming with Matlab and VB

Jiangping Wang and Yingcai Hu

School of Mechanical Engineering, Xi'an Shiyou University, Xi'an, Shaanxi, 710065, China
jpwang@xsyu.edu.cn

Abstract. This paper presents a method using hybrid programming with Matlab and VB based on ActiveX to design the system of drilling accident prediction and diagnosis. So that the powerful calculating function and graphical display function of Matlab and visual development interface of VB are combined fully. The main interface of the diagnosis system is compiled in VB,and the analysis and fault diagnosis are implemented by neural network tool boxes in Matlab.The system has favorable interactive interface,and the fault example validation shows that the diagnosis result is feasible and can meet the demands of drilling accident prediction and diagnosis.

Keywords: Drilling engineering, Accident diagnosis, VB, Matlab, Hybrid programming.

1 Introduction

There are many complex factors and random phenomena during the drilling process, and the drilling safety is affected by them. In order to analyze and predict drilling accidents, variety of drilling engineering parameters and their abnormal changes are monitored and displayed real-timely. By means of the information inference and judgement based on the mathematical models of the system and diagnostic technique, the hidden perils of the accident can be found out in time and an alarm can be given before the engineering accidents happen. But large amounts of data are required to be analyzed and processed in the programming process for the drilling accident diagnosis system. So the technicians are occupied by the complex and time-consuming programming itself, which makes them impossible to focus on designing a system with better performances. This paper intends to seamlessly integrate a application software, Visual Basic (VB) with a mathematical tool, Matlab, to solve this problem.

2 The Interface Method of Matlab with VB – ActiveX Control

Matlab provides external programming interfaces for C / C + + and Fortran. While VB can not directly call for it. In order to achieve data transmission between Matlab and VB, the hybrid programming techniques with Matlab and VB can be used to give full play to the advantages of both.

G. Shen and X. Huang (Eds.): ECWAC 2011, Part I, CCIS 143, pp. 35–40, 2011.

The methods[1] of hybrid programming with Matlab and VB include ActiveX control, DDE technique, compilation of a M file and using Matrix VB. When using the ActiveX control, the functions and graphic database commands in Matlab can be directly used for VB to implement the mutual communication with Matlab. This means a high programming efficiency and a powerful function in programming a application software. So ActiveX technology is used in developed system to realize the real-time data collection and process in drilling process conveniently and effectively. This paper will discusses that how could VB take Matlab as its ActiveX to communicate each other through ActiveX interface.

ActiveX control is a new protocol provided by Microsoft Corp. for the module integration and is a expanded part of Visual Basic toolbox. Matlab has realized the automatic service support for ActiveX. So VB and Matlab can be seamless integrated in VB environment by taking Matlab as VB's ActiveX control. This method is quite suitable for the C/S pattern. It has advantages of a high automaticity, high efficiency, fewer resource occupancy, strong data exchange ability and so on. The program development cycle can be shortened greatly, and the system quality can be optimized.

Using ActiveX control, the name 'Matlab.Application' defined as Matlab ActiveX object in the registration table of operating system must be obtained first. The codes used to create a ActiveX object in VB are as follows:

```
Dim Matlab as Object
Set Matlab = CreateObject ("Matlab. Application")
```

The Matlab.Application object mainly has 3 functions, as follows:

(1) BSTR Execute
This method can be used to run a legal Matlab command. By this function Matlab can accept a single character string (Command), run it and return the results as a character string.

(2) PutFullMatrix
This method will put a designated array into the work space.

(3) GetFullMatrix
By GetFullMatrix, one integrated array can be retrieved from a designated work space[2].

Through these three methods, Matlab executive commands can be used to help VB put into or get data from Matlab conveniently.

3 Drilling Parameter Monitoring and Fault Diagnosis Examples

3.1 Variation Curve Fitting of Drilling Fluid Density by Least Square Method

Well wall instability, which often happens in drilling engineering, is a complex problem. In recent years, some solutions for the problem have been worked out. Drilling fluid density plays an important role in the wall stability control and it is the only controllable factor among many complex factors. With the drilling fluid density reduction, shearing destructions will emerge on the wall. After that, the broken rocks will fall off and cause the well cave-in or borehole contracted. A threshold of drilling fluid density, which will assure the borehole stability, can be determined by measuring and monitoring the change trend of the density because it does not change suddenly during the actual well drilling work.

According to the drilling fluid density measured real-timely at well site, the approximate function relation or the empirical formula between the time, independent variable, and the density, dependent variable, will be sought. That is, a graph can be worked out on which the measured data will be fitted a curve. The fitted curve does not requested through all the determination data point, but it is only requested to be able to reflect the change tendency of these discrete data. Curve fitting based on the least square method is a widely used method for data process in multidisciplinary field. It can be described as: seeking a function $y=f^*(x)$ in the function class $F=(f_0, f_1, f_2, \ldots, f_m)$ for a given set of data $(x_i, y_i)(i=0, 1, \ldots, m)$, so that the sum of its error squares δ^2 could be least. The formula is as follow:

$$\delta^2 = \sum_{i=0}^{m} w(x_i)[f^*(x_i) - y_i]^2 = \min_{f(x_i) \in F} \sum_{i=0}^{m} w(x_i)[f(x_i) - y_i]^2 \tag{1}$$

Where:

$$f(x) = a_0 f_0(x) + a_1 f_1(x) + \cdots + a_n f_n(x) \quad (n < m) \tag{2}$$

$w(x) \geq 0$ is a weight function. It shows that the different examination data point has a different proportion. y_i $(i=0, 1, \ldots, m)$ means the measured data.

Curve fitting problem based on the least square method is to find out one function $y=f^*(x)$ among all the $f(x)$ which fit the formula (2), which could assure the minimum value in the formula (1). That is a problem of seeking the coefficients $(a_0^*, a_1^*, \cdots, a_n^*)$ in multivariate function (2).

The data polynomial fitting function provided by Matlab is polyfit. It will find out the polynomial coefficients of the given data from the least-squares sense[2]. Before using the interface program between Matlab and VB, A ActiveX object should be created first in the VB application. In the registration table of operating system, the name of a ActiveX object in Matlab is "Matlab.Application". The main part codes of the curve fitting program is as follow:

```
Private Sub Command1_Click()
Dim Matlab as object;Dim Result as object
Set Matlab = create object ("Matlab.Application")
Text1.text=(x=0:0.25:3; y=[0.99 0.92 0.85 0.82 0.78
0.77 0.75 0.69 0.68 0.65 0.63 0.60 0.56];n=2;
p=polyfit(x,y,n);xi=linspace(0,3,1000);z=polyval(p,xi);
plot(x,y,'o',x,y,xi,z,':'))
Text2.Text = Matlab.Execute (Text1.Text)
Result = Matlab.Execute("print-dbitmap")
Image1.Picture = Clipboard.GetData()
Call Matlab.quit
End Sub
```

Put the measured fluid density data into the main window (Fig. 1), and then click the Run button. The fitting curve of the drilling fluid density can be gotten. By monitoring the change tendency of the drilling fluid density, not only the wall collapse can be controlled, but also the germination of the gush and the blowout accident can be monitored.

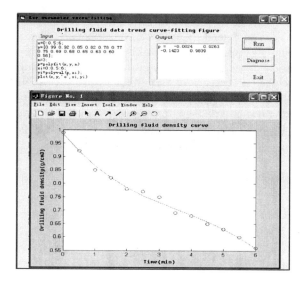

Fig. 1. Quadratic fitting curve of the drilling fluid density

3.2 Realization of Accident Diagnosis Function by the Neural Network

The neural network model, which has the self-learning function and parallel process capability, provides a new theoretical approach and implementation method for the drilling accident diagnosis. The neural network has a strong learning ability as its main feature. It can simulate the intrinsic mechanism between the information through learning their sample models. The substance that the neural network can identify the occurrence of a drilling accident is that a proper neural network model selected becomes capable of mapping the potential laws hiding in the drilling engineering data after learning the historical data. It is a hard and time consuming work to program a software with loops embedding in another by using a regular programming method because the number of the layers and the neurons in each layer in the neural network are great many and the input vector arrays are huge. Fortunately Matlab provides a very good neural network toolbox. A drilling accident diagnosis system based on BP neural network[3,4] by using the method that VB call the Matlab is presented in this paper, which raises the working efficiency and the problem solving quality.

The main window of the drilling accident diagnosis system is created by VB. On it, there are many controls belonging to the modules of sample input, sample training, building networks, result output, and data diagnosis respectively.

The GUI of the drilling accident diagnosis system based on the neural network is shown in Fig. 2. The sample data should be normalized and saved in a ".txt" format file. Each of the sample data (including input data and output data separated by a space) should occupy one line.

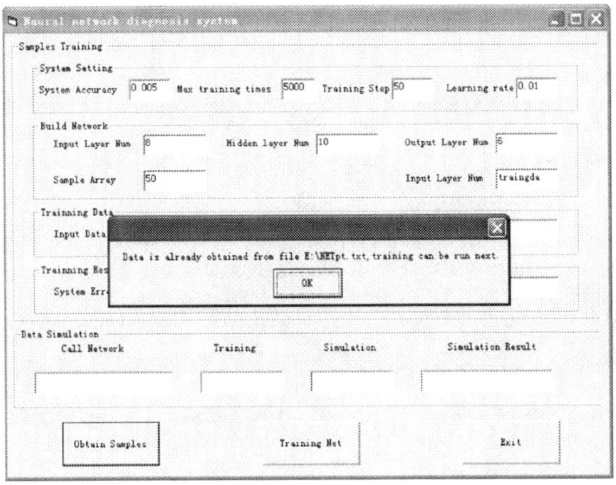

Fig. 2. Neural Network Training Window

In order to meet the needs of different results, different training algorithms and different training parameters aimed at different requests can be chosen. Torque, hook load, pump pressure, input flow rate, output flow rate, drilling fluid volume, drilling fluid density, and drilling rate obtained from relevant transducers are eight key data for the drilling accident diagnosis system. They can be inputted as samples after being normalized. And 0 and 1 are used to represent the normal and abnormal status. The accident types of the diagnosis system include well leak, well collapse, well gush and blowout. The requested training error is 0.005. In fact, under the 277 training steps, the actual training error is 0.00499656. So the training result of the diagnosis system is able to meet the requirement.

The selected training samples and training results are shown in Table 1and Table 2.

Table 1. Normalized sample data

Accident type	Torque (KN.m)	Pump pressure (KN)	Hook load (KN)	Output flow (%)	Input Flow (%)	Fluid volume (m³)	Fluid density (g/cm³)	Drillin grate (m/h)
Leak	0.09	0	0.89	0	0.89	0	1	0.8
Collapse	1	0	0	0	0	0.5	1	0
Gush	0.09	0.91	0.87	0.93	1	0.83	0.2	0.9
Blowout	0	1	0.89	1	0.89	1	0	1
Normal	0.18	0.86	1	0.53	0	0.5	0.8	0

Table 2. The actual and ideal output of the BP network

Actual output					Ideal output					Accident type
0.9850	0.0072	0.1217	-0.1175	0.0056	1	0	0	0	0	Leak
0.0148	1.0003	-0.0432	0.0256	0.0061	0	1	0	0	0	Collapse
0.0255	-0.0059	0.7172	0.2462	0.0169	0	0	1	0	0	Guah
-0.0234	0.0085	0.2039	0.8184	0.0078	0	0	0	1	0	Blowout
-0.0002	-0.0009	0.0177	-0.0164	-0.0090	0	0	0	0	0	Normal

Training result shows that this method can diagnose and predict accidents. It can be estimated whether an accident and what kind of accident will occur after inputting the data samples to be diagnosed into the well trained network. For example, the well trained network is verified with the following two sets of data:

P=[0.08 0.005 0.850 0.90 0.003 0.98 0.82 0.99 0.002 0.0010 0.002 0.46 0.980]

The outputs of the network as follows:

A=[1.1057 -0.0553 -0.0000 -0.0356 -0.0591 0.0064 1.0037 -0.0222 -0.0065 -0.0186]

Compared with the training results (in Table 2), they can be identified as the well leak and well collapse. It shows that the diagnosis result is right.

4   Conclusion

GUI created by VB calling the Matlab to process the drilling parameters, analyze the trend change of the curves and diagnose the drilling accidents, which can be demonstrated by a pictorial diagram after some uncomplicated operations. Through using the neural network toolbox of Matlab to design, train and simulate a network, the accident diagnosis work can be completed in a shorter time. This can greatly reduce the programming workload in VB environment.

The integrated development method, Matlab exchanges data with the VB , can be used in fault diagnosis, automatic control, signal process and many other areas. This has an important guiding significance for the actual production.

References

1. Su, J.-M., Huang, M., Liu, B.: Matlab interfaces for external program. Electronic Industry Press, Beijing (2003)
2. Dao, R., Lin, D.-J., Bai, Y.: Application of Visual Basic and Matlab interface technology in the curve-fitting. Journal of Engineering Graphics (4), 141–144 (2005)
3. Li, Z., Yin, Y., Wei, L.: Seamless Integration Between VB and Matlab and its Application in Fault Diagnosis. Explosion-proof Motor (42), 42–44 (2007)
4. Fan, X., Wang, D.: Theory and Strategy of Remote-intelligent Monitoring Based on Network. Journal of Shenyang University 4(18), 73–76 (2006)

WSNs in the Highway Long Distance Tunnel Environment Monitoring

Yan-Xiao Li, Xin-Xi Feng, and Hua Guan

Telecommunication Engineering Institute
Air Force Engineering University
Xi'an, Shaanxi, China
{YanXiaoLi,XinXiFeng,HuaGuan}@hotmail.com

Abstract. Wireless sensor networks have been widely used in the monitoring application. In this paper we shed some lights on several issues in building a complete system for using wireless sensor networks for practical highway long distance tunnel environment monitoring application. From the engineering perspective it is necessary to consider the nodes deployment and from the application perspective it is necessary to meet the performance requirements. Energy conservation, topology and coverage are some important factors need to be taken full consideration for the purpose of providing safe friendly vehicle running environment. Still more deserve to discuss for brighter future of the tracking and monitoring foreground.

Keywords: wireless sensor network, latency, energy constraint, topology, coverage control.

1   Introduction

A Wireless Sensor Network (WSN) is a self-organized wireless network composed of a large number of sensor nodes that interact with the physical world [1]. Various low-power and cost-effective sensor platforms have been developed based upon recent advances in wireless communication and micro system technologies. The increasing study of WSNs [2], [3], [4] aims to enable computers to serve people by automatically monitoring and interacting with physical environments.

Environment monitoring in the highway long distance tunnels (which are usually long and narrow, with lengths of tens of kilometers and widths of several meters) has been an important task to ensure safe running conditions in the tunnels where many necessary environmental factors, including the amount of gas, water, dust, wind and fire alarm (the tunnels pass through the mountain which has complex geologic conditions), need be monitored. To obtain a full-scale monitoring of the tunnel environment, sample data need be collected at many different places. A precise environment overview requires a high sampling density, which involves a number of sensing devices. Current methods of monitoring are typically conducted in a wired and manual way, due to the lack of corresponding techniques for constructing an automatic large-scale sensing system.

G. Shen and X. Huang (Eds.): ECWAC 2011, Part I, CCIS 143, pp. 41–47, 2011.

Utilizing wires to connect sensing points to the processing server requires a large amount of wire deployment, which is inconvenient because of vehicle running conditions and the following maintenance costs. Moreover, the wired communication method makes the system less scalable; more signal cables need to be laid for more signal collection. A wireless system takes advantage of convenient deployment and flexible adjustment. The utilization of a WSN to implement the tunnel monitoring system benefits from rapid and flexible deployment. Additionally, the multi-hop transmitting method conforms to the tunnel structure and provides easy scalability for more precise and timely monitoring requirements.

In this paper, we analyze the factors which influence the system and present a design of the monitoring system, which aims to address the challenges and provide a feasible framework for environment monitoring in the long distance highway tunnels. The design objectives include: 1) the ability to rapidly detect the interested area and report to the sink node efficiently; and 2) topology design to meet the actual requirement of the monitoring elements and provide a good coverage to the interested area.

2   Sensors and Sensor Networks

All sensors nodes in the wireless sensor network are composed of two kinds of node: the cluster head (CH) and the cluster nodes (CN).

The cluster head and the cluster node have little difference in the hardware except for power supply, because the cluster head is assigned to be the coordinator, which has more traffic to deal with. The cluster nodes operate on battery power, while the cluster heads operate on storage battery power supply which can provide more power than common battery, and so do not have many constraints on power. However, the saving of power is an important consideration in the design of all the nodes.

The difference between CH and CN lies in their software department. Though software programming, we can define their radio frequency (RF) power, communication distance, transmission frequency, modulation mode and other attributes. This wireless sensor network complies with IEEE 802.15.4/zigbee protocol, and all nodes are Zigbee devices. According to Zigbee protocol, we define CH as Full function device (FFD) which can become the network coordinator, while CN as Reduced function device (RFD) which can only function as a network device.

3   Traffic Model and Power Consumption Model

In the case of environment monitoring the sensor nodes periodically monitor and report corresponding data to sinks. However, the traffic load in the monitoring area is considered to be stochastic. Depending on the network application, data characteristics and the type of data inquiry, different models can be used to identify the network traffic model. In this paper, we mainly concentrate on event-driven [5] networks where the sensors inform the sink only when an event occurs in their sensing range. Poisson distribution describes the traffic of such networks where the events are independent and occur with equal probability over the area [6]. In this case, if λ shows the average rate of packet generation, the number of transmitted packets between 0 and T, called M, has a pdf as follows

$$P(M = m) = \frac{e^{-\lambda T}(\lambda T)^{m}}{m!} \quad m = 0,1,2,... \tag{1}$$

For power consumption, we use the model proposed in [7]. Assume that sensor i wants to transmit a packet of length 1 bits to a point located d_i meters away. The consumed energy by sensor i (in Joules) can be modeled as

$$e(d_i) = l(e_t d_i^a + e_0)$$
$$= md_i^a + c \tag{2}$$

where α shows the path loss exponent, et denotes the loss coefficient of 1 bit data transmission and e_o represents the overhead energy related to the sensing, receiving and processing of the same amount of data. Hence, m = le_t and c = le_o respectively reflect the loss coefficient and the overhead energy related to a packet transmission. Usually, α is considered to be 2 for small distances and 4 for large distances [8].

4 Topology Control

Topology control in WSNs is an effective means to enhance the effective functional lifetime of the network [9], [10], [11]. We consider both an event-driven linear WSN with N sensors and a two-dimensional WSN with N^2 sensors. Each node is powered by a nonrechargeable battery with initial energy E_0, and a gateway node with fixed location. Sensors are responsible for monitoring and reporting an event of interest. Due to power limitation and hardware constraint, each sensor has a sensing range of R km. We assume that the event arrival process is Poisson distributed with mean k. Given that an event has occurred, its location is uniformly distributed in the desired coverage area [0, L] km of the network.

4.1 Linear Sensor Placement [12] [13] [14] [15] [16]

Sensors are placed along a straight line of length L km with the gateway node at the left end. Let s_i denote the ith sensor in the network where s_1 is closest to the gateway node and s_N is farthest. Let d_1 be the distance between s_1 and the gateway node, and d_i ($2 \leq i \leq N$) the distance between adjacent sensors s_i and s_{i-1}. To ensure the coverage of the network under a sensing range R, adjacent sensors should not be placed farther than 2R. a feasible sensor placement d $\in$ [d_1. . . d_N] should satisfy the following constraint:

$$\begin{cases} 0 < d_1 \leq R, \\ 0 < d_i \leq 2R, \quad 2 \leq i \leq N-1, \\ 0 < L - \sum_{j=1}^{N} d_j < R, \end{cases} \tag{3}$$

4.2 Transmission Structure

The sensor closest to the event initiates the reporting process by generating an equal-sized reporting packet. As a consequence, sensor s_i is responsible for reporting the event that occurs in its Voronoi cell with size A_i

$$A_i = \begin{cases} d_1 + \frac{d_2}{2}, & i = 1 \\ \frac{d_i + d_{i+1}}{2}, & 2 \leq i \leq N-1 \\ L - \sum_{j=1}^{N-1} d_j - \frac{d_N}{2}, & i = N. \end{cases} \quad (4)$$

The reporting packet is then forwarded to the access point node according to the network transmission structure $P \in \{P_{i,j}\}_{i,j}^N = 1$ whose element $P_{i,j} \in [0, 1]$ denotes the probability that s_i transmits its packets to s_j. For ease of presentation, we define $P_{i,0} = 1 - \sum_{j=1}^{N} P_{i,j}$, where $1 \leq i \leq N$, as the probability that s_i transmits its packet directly to the gateway node. Note that in any energy-efficient transmission structure, sensors always transmit their packets toward the gateway node. Hence, an energy-efficient transmission structure P should satisfy the following constraint:

$$\begin{cases} 0 \leq P_{i,j} \leq 1, & 1 \leq i, j \leq N, \\ 0 \leq P_{i,0} \leq 1, & 1 \leq i \leq N, \\ P_{i,j} = 0, & 1 \leq i \leq j \leq N. \end{cases} \quad (5)$$

4.3 Two Dimensions Placement

In a two-dimensional WSN with N^2 sensors and a coverage area of L km ×L km, the event arrival process is assumed to be Poisson distributed with mean k and the location of the event is uniformly distributed in the desired coverage area [0,L] × [0,L] of the network. Sensors are placed at the intersections of the grids, and the gateway node is located at the left-bottom corner of the square. Let $\{s_{i,j}\}_{i,j}^N = 1$ denote the (i, j)th sensor in the network and d = [d_1, . . . ,d_N] the distance between two adjacent grids. Since the sensor closest to the event is responsible for initiating the reporting process, the Voronoi cell of $s_{i,j}$ is a rectangle with size A_i given by

$$A_i = \begin{cases} d_1 + \frac{d_2}{2}, & i = 1 \\ \frac{d_i + d_{i+1}}{2}, & 2 \leq i \leq N-1 \\ L - \sum_{j=1}^{N-1} d_j - \frac{d_N}{2}, & i = N. \end{cases} \quad (6)$$

5 Latency Analysis

We analyze the multi-hop forwarding latency of S-MAC protocol in a simple case.

Suppose there are N hops from the source to the sink. For hop n, denote carrier sensing delay as $t_{cs,n}$, transmission delay t_{tx}, sleep delay $t_{s,n}$, and a frame of listening and sleep cycle as T_f, The average latency of S-MAC over N hops[11] is shown as:

$$E[D(N)] = NT_f - \frac{T_f}{2} + t_{cs} + t_{tx} \qquad (7)$$

T_f is, in general, much larger than $(t_{cs} + t_{tx})$. So the delay over h hops is almost proportional to T_f. T_f, is inversely proportional to the duty cycle. Then, we have

$$E[D(h)] \propto T_f \propto \frac{1}{duty\ cycle} \qquad (8)$$

Let H denote the maximum possible number of hops of the network. Let ρ be the node density of the sensor network, the number of nodes h-hops apart from the sink, N(h), is expressed by

$$N(h) = \rho(h^2 - (h-1)^2)\pi - \rho(2h-1)\pi \qquad (9)$$

The main sources of energy consumption are transmission and reception of packets, as well as idle listening. If the duty cycle is ideally configured with the finest granularity, the wakeup period is spent only for transmissions and receptions. Then, the energy consumption rate for each node h hops from the sink, E (h), is calculated as:

$$E(h) = \frac{E_{tot}(h)}{N(h)}$$

$$= \frac{\rho\lambda\pi((H^2-h^2)E_{rx} + (H^2-(h-1)^2)E_{tx})}{\rho(2h-1)\pi}$$

$$= \frac{\lambda((H^2-h^2)E_{rx} + (H^2-(h-1)^2)E_{tx})}{2h-1} \qquad (10)$$

6 Simulation Results

We do the simulation of energy efficiency and latency efficiency of the proposed system design. Three time values are tested to get a better energy latency efficient experimental result.

6.1 Energy Waste

S-MAC with T_{active} of 0.3 s wastes the most energy because its idle listening time is the longest, as shown in Fig.1. S-MAC with T_{active} of 0.2 s wastes less energy due to the shorter idle listening time. Moreover, S-MAC with optimized active T value 0.1 s is the most energy-efficient because the active time is more consistent with the traffic characterization.

6.2 Latency

The average latency of S-MAC with different T active values with hop-count increases is plotted in Fig.2. The latency increases linearly with hop-count increases but the latency of S-MAC with longer active time is much larger than that with shorter active time. This is because S-MAC with longer active time has to wait longer for the next listening period. From the result, it can be seen that the latency of optimized S-MAC is considerably enhanced.

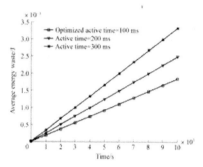

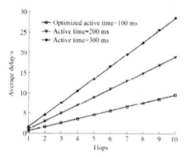

Fig. 1. Energy waste of S-MAC with different active time

Fig. 2. Average latency of S-MAC with different active time

7 Conclusions

Research in wireless sensor networks has been very active. WSNs have been increasing widely used to implement monitoring task. We are aiming at building a deployable system which incorporates a whole set of safe and friendly services to guarantee the environmental quality of the long distance tunnel. This requires us to choose the right combination of sensor network techniques, reconcile the conflicting design goals among different protocols, and propose new techniques that are compatible with current solutions in the monitoring application.

System design and engineering are two of the keys to bring sensor network paradigm into reality. This paper describes some major efforts to build a wireless sensor network system for monitoring missions. The focus of these efforts is to acquire and analyze information about the inner environment of the long distance tunnel. By using wireless sensor networks, great feasible convenience is gained in the practical importance for the management staff. Because of the energy constraints of sensor devices, such systems necessitate an energy-aware design to ensure the longevity of monitoring missions. Solutions proposed recently for this type of system show promising results through simulations.

References

1. Akyildiz, I.F., Su, W., Sankarasubramaniam, Y., Cayirci, E.: A Survey on Sensor Networks. IEEE Communications Magazine 40, 102–114 (2002)
2. Chakrabari, A., Sabharwal, A., Aazhang, B.: Multi-hop communication is order-optimal for homogeneous sensor networks. In: Proceedings of IPSN (2004)
3. Vural, S., Ekici, E.: Analysis of hop-distance relationship in spatially random sensor networks. In: Proceedings of ACM MobiHoc (2005)
4. Wan, C.Y., Eisenman, S.B., Campbell, A.T., Crowcroft, J.: Siphon: overload traffic management using multi-radio virtual sinks in sensor networks. In: Proceedings of ACM SenSys (2005)
5. Tilak, S., Abu-Ghazaleh, N.B., Heinzelman, W.: A taxonomy of wireless micro-sensor network models. SIGMOBILE Mob. Comput. Commun. Rev. 6(2), 28–36 (2002)
6. Rai, V., Mahapatra, R.N.: Lifetime modeling of a sensor network. In: DATE 2005: Proceedings of the conference on Design, Automation and Test in Europe, pp. 202–203. IEEE Computer Society, Washington, DC, USA (2005)
7. Heinzelman, W.B.: Application-specific protocol for wireless networks. Ph.D. dissertation, Massachusetts Institute of Technology (2000)
8. Heinzelman, W.B., Chandrakasan, A.P., Balakrishnan, H.: An application-specific protocol architecture for wireless microsensor networks. IEEE Transactions on Wireless Communications 1(4), 660–670 (2002)
9. Golatowski, F., et al.: Service-oriented software architecture for sensor networks. In: Proc. International Workshop on Mobile Computing (IMC 2003), Rostock, Germany (June 2003)
10. Liu, B., Towsley, D.: A study of the coverage of large-scale sensor networks. In: Proc. IEEE MASS (October 2004)
11. Xing, G., Lu, C., Pless, R., O'Sullivan, J.: Co-Grid: An efficient coverage maintenance protocol for distributed sensor networks. In: Proc. ACM IPSN (2003)
12. Arbel, A.: Sensor placement in optimal filtering and smoothingproblems. IEEE Trans. Automat. Control 27, 94–98 (1982)
13. Zhang, H.: Two-dimensional optimal sensor placement. IEEE Trans. Syst. Man Cyber. 25, 781–792 (1995)
14. Chakrabarty, K., Iyengar, S.S., Qi, H., Cho, E.: Grid coverage for surveillance and target location in distributed sensor networks. IEEE Trans. Comput. 51, 1448–1453 (2002)
15. Hao, B., Tang, H., Xue, G.: Fault-tolerant relay node placement in wireless sensor networks: formulation and approximation. In: Proc. of Workshop on High Performance Switching and Routing, pp. 246–250 (2004)
16. Chen, S.Y., Li, Y.F.: Automatic sensor placement for modelbased robot vision. IEEE Trans. Syst. Man Cyber. 34, 393–408 (2004)

The OA System of College——Design of the Teaching Quality Monitoring Subsystem

Hongjuan Wu, Hong Ying, Youyi Jiang, and Pei Yan

College of Mathematics and Computer Science
Chongqing Three Gorges University
780 Shalong Road, Wanzhou404100, Chongqing, P.R. China
juan10329@163.com, dcs-yh@263.net,
yyy_j123456@163.com, peisharp@gmail.com

Abstract. According to the drawbacks of traditional teaching quality monitoring subsystems and based on the achievements of practical research in the teaching quality monitoring administration in College, this paper provides a design of overall structure of teaching quality monitoring subsystem, that is more suitable for colleges' management. This new system is endowed with the same features as .NET application programes: easy to extend, easy to maintain, flexible, convenient, and it let enterprises, students' parents and excellent graduates participate in teaching quality monitoring administration, have significant effect to ensure the quality of talent training in colleges.

Keywords: college, teaching quality monitoring, this new system, NET, the quality of talent training.

1 The Drawbacks in Colleges' Teaching Quality Monitoring Subsystems of Traditional OA Systems

In recent years, with the rapid development of university, the teaching management is shifting down to the colleges; school management system in the single subject gradually changes to the colleges of multiple subjects. Workload and the degree of difficulty of the work in the colleges' teaching administration have increased, which also put forward higher requirements on administrators[1].

With modern information technology development and continuous advance of office automation, colleges of university begin to use some OA management systems to improve the management efficiency. The traditional OA systems of the college have not been effectively connected with the OA system of social enterprises, OA system of the university and other relevant legacy systems. Some OA systems even lack the teaching quality monitoring module, and teaching quality monitoring is limited to the "teachers evaluate students" and the "students evaluate teachers", teaching quality monitoring of the personnel is confined to the teachers and students of school, which can't satisfy the practical needs of end-users, at the same time teaching information feedback can't be collected in time, leading to failure in ensuring the quality of talent

G. Shen and X. Huang (Eds.): ECWAC 2011, Part I, CCIS 143, pp. 48–53, 2011.
© Springer-Verlag Berlin Heidelberg 2011

training. This new system can solve the above problems and have significant effect to ensure the quality of talent training.

Therefore, it is of great practical significance to establish the OA work platform that is suitable to colleges, and can be connected with the OA systems of social enterprises. The managements, teachers, students, social enterprises, students' parents and excellent graduates can participate in this system, which can improve the working efficiency of colleges, strengthen the management of talent training process and ensure the quality of talent training meet with the social needs.

2   The Characteristics of This Teaching Quality Monitoring Subsystem of the OA system

This system is a management system; the quality of any management system is related to the principles of management and requirements analysis, so the characteristic reflects in two aspects:

(1) On management

What kind of the teaching quality monitoring system is suitable for the college?

This system is developed combining with the characteristic of management in the teaching quality monitoring of our university's college of mathematics and computer science. It mainly includes:

Within school monitoring: Through comparing with the teacher's teaching plan with the actual teaching progress, the information collectors(commissaries in charge of studies)can monitor the teachers' teaching rate of advance; through the attendance record of students, the assistants can monitor students' attendance; leaders and administrative staff inspect classroom to monitor classroom teaching; peer teachers attend the lectures to learn and monitor the teacher; supervisors observe deeply each teaching step to monitor the whole teaching process; finally administrators will obtain feedback information through the "monthly report" and "teaching notices" bulletin.

Outside school monitoring: While carrying out the trinity modes of talent output (outside training + thesis + employment) and double-quality teachers' training with social enterprises. Responsibility system of information feedback should be established with social enterprises. The social enterprises can monitor the quality of instruction in accordance with the social through the system. In addition, the parents can give feedback information about students' learning through the system. The excellent graduates can give various suggestions combining the universities' teaching with own working experiences for many years.

Formulated training programs: Generally, the social enterprises can easily understand the overall quality and knowledge structure of students through graduate trainee and employment. They can provides valuable advices to colleges in the training and course development etc, together with the latest developments in the market demand, which will be conducive for school to integrate the training with social needs, and promote the quality of the talent training. The excellent successful graduates of universities can offer views and suggestions to the training program, according to their studying experience in the university and experience in society. In addition, using Web

Services technology to link up this system and social enterprises' OA system, the college leaders can look into the social enterprises' needs, employment requirements, staff training related to teaching and learning materials over the years. This information inform the universities of the latest information about changes in the market, which are important to short the adaptation period of employment of students and can solve the problem that students' training always lag behind the needs of the community. At the same time, social enterprises can get access to the information about students' learning, the working ability and other aspects so they can provide for future employment in a targeted manner to select students.

Only a sound, scientific, and practical teaching quality control measures in the system established, you can design a good teaching quality monitoring subsystem that is suitable to colleges.

The teaching quality monitoring subsystem function block diagram is as follows:

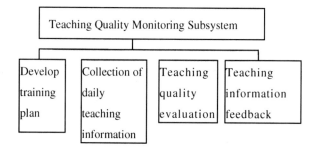

Fig. 1. Function block

Training program development module includes: developing training plan of department; social enterprises providing references; graduates providing references.

Collection of daily teaching information module includes: the progress of the implementation of teaching plans; classroom teaching; information collectors gathering teaching information; supervisors gathering teaching information; parents, students, social enterprises giving feedback information.

Teaching quality evaluation module includes: teachers' evaluation of classrooms (mainly on the evaluation of students' learning in the classroom); students' evaluation of classrooms (mainly on the evaluation of teachers' teaching in the classroom); social enterprises' evaluation of the majors.

Teaching information feedback module includes: teaching academic staff publishing notice; teaching academic staff publishing monthly report.

(2)On technology

This system is characterized by these technical features: informationizing the teaching quality monitoring measures' network; achieving participation of social enterprises, parents, outstanding graduates into teaching quality monitoring through the system; using Web Services to facilitate integrate the legacy systems, retain existing resources, and publish a remote call interface; and implementing interaction with social enterprises' and schools' other OA management system.

3   The Design of the Teaching Quality Monitoring Subsystem' ER Model

Based on the analysis of the teaching quality monitoring subsystem, the system is divided into several parts: the social enterprise, training program, academic staff, teaching notice, teachers, classroom, students, teaching information, supervisors, and several other entities. Among them, the students are divided into two sub-classes: information collectors and the ordinary students; the teachers are divided into two sub-classes: supervisors and ordinary teachers. Eight of the entities are collected in m: n type of relationship, its global ER model is shown below:

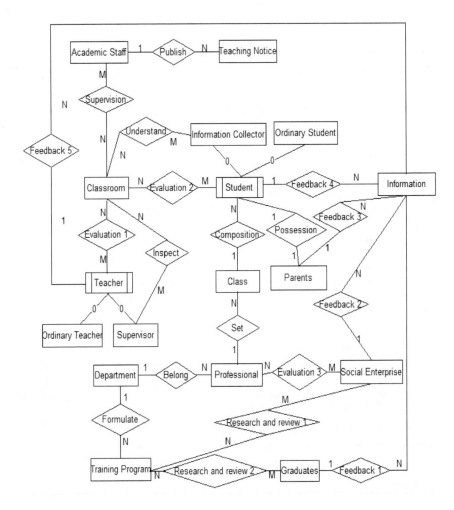

Fig. 2. Global ER model

4 System Architecture Design

New system based on .NET Framework
v3.5, using the ISA Server 2008 to function as the firewall, using Windows server
2008 OS, as an application server with IIS
7.0, using Microsoft Sql Server 2008 for
data storage. The system architecture
(Figure 3) is divided into five logical layers
on the total: Web UI layer, Business
Service layer (including the Business
Facade layer and Business Rule layer),
Data Access layer, the System Framework
layer and Web Service layer[2]. The Web
UI mainly administers web page rendering
behavior, display data, data capture, data
validation check; providing operational
guidance to teachers and students and other
users, acting as bridges between user and
Web Service layer and Business Facade
layer. Business Facade layer provides the
business process interface to Web UI layer,

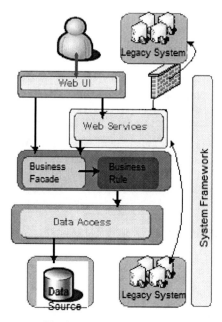

Fig. 3. System architecture

At the same time, it provides business data services to Web Services. Business Facade
layer functions as an isolation layer. It puts the User Interface and the implementation
of various business functions separately. Business Rule layer contains a variety of
business rules and logic implementation, such as courses arranging management,
management of students' status and so on. Data Access layer uses ADO.NET to send
and request data, and to provide Data services for Business Rule layer. System
Framework layer strides across all levels, providing a system service and infrastructure
functions etc.. Such as page cache, object cache, the sharing of strongly typed object
and so on. Business Facade is distributed in a Internet-based deployment by Web Service layer, it also integrates the OA system of social enterprises with OA systems of the
university and other relevant legacy systems.

The framework structure is clear, and can build loosely coupled internet-based
large-scale applications flexibly. Service-oriented business logic provides different
business logic by services[3]. This system is superior to Windows DNA distributed
applications in availability, scalability, and concurrency. At the same time it takes
advantage of Web Services which can conveniently and efficiently form a legacy system
to retain existing resources and release the remote call interface, so it has good scalability.

5 Conclusions

The OA system can meet the teaching quality monitoring management needs
favorably, specially, in providing a great convenience to the colleges' management in

these aspects, such as: effective connection among the OA system of social enterprises, OA systems of the university and other relevant legacy systems; the social enterprises, students' parents and excellent graduates' participation into teaching quality monitoring managements.The system is endowed with the same features as .NET application procedure: easy to extend, easy to maintain, flexible, convenient, so it effectively improve the efficiency of the colleges' management.

References

1. Yang, J.: The Construction of Teaching Quality Monitoring System in Local College. Journal of Tianjin Manager College 1 (2006)
2. Ying, H., Yan, P.: Building Internet Distributed Application Model Based.NET. Computer Science [Album] 29(6) (2002)
3. Tom, B.: Distributed. NET Programming in C#, America. Apress (2003)

Research on Total Energy Consumption and Industrial Production Based on Error Correction Model in Hebei Province

Dong Liu* and Herui Cui

Department of Economics and Management, North China Electric Power University,
Baoding 071003
liudong.liu@163.com

Abstract. According to the statistical data of total energy consumption- industrial output in 1990-2008 in Hebei Province, this paper establishes a function of energy consumption - industrial output, analyzes test results through the unit root test, causality test, co-integration and error correction model, and obtains following conclusion: energy consumption and industrial output in Hebei form relationships of short-term fluctuation and long-term balance, and the results are obvious. On this basis, to coordinate development of energy and economy and reduce energy consumption, implementing energy development strategy and optimizing industrial structure is necessary, and adjusting the industrial industry is a key.

Keywords: Low carbon economy, industrial structure, energy consumption, error correction.

1 Introduction

Since the nineties of the 20th century, study on China's industrial structure change and energy consumption increases with economic globalization and the continued development world industry trends. China constantly adjusts the industrial structure, and industrialization becomes increasingly apparent, which drive domestic energy consumption growth. Now, in the case of a low carbon economy, energy consumption and optimize the industrial structure is a urgent problem to solve.

There are a lot of domestic and international researches on energy consumption and industrial structure. Lin Boqiang (2001) analyzes co-integration of China's energy consumption, GDP, energy prices, economic structure, and the share of heavy industry [1]; Yanjun Lin (2006)analyzes relationship between the changes of the energy intensity and three times changes of industrial structure in Shanghai [2]; Wang Peng (2009) analyzes regional differences of China's economic growth and energy consumption by modern statistical methods and econometric approach [3]; Li Ying (2010)makes quantitative analysis of the correlation between economic growth and China's conventional energy based on Grey Theory [4].Although these methods can

---

* Corresponding author.

G. Shen and X. Huang (Eds.): ECWAC 2011, Part I, CCIS 143, pp. 54–59, 2011.
© Springer-Verlag Berlin Heidelberg 2011

reveal the reciprocal relationship between energy consumption and industrial structure, most are from the perspective of the static, while it is a long-term interaction, so
the research methods can't objectively reflect dynamic relationship. As Error Correction Model (ECM) is an econometric model which eliminate the spurious regression
influence that caused by non-stationary variables and is able to reflect the relationship
between variables. It can not only clearly stated short-term fluctuations between variables, but also has a strong predictive functions to better reflect the long-run equilibrium relationship between the variables, so this paper can use the model to analyze the
changing trend of energy consumption and industrial, and it provides the basis for
saving energy and optimization of industrial structure.

2   Data and Models

2.1   Data Sources and Basic Analysis

Figure 1 is industrial output and energy consumption in Hebei trends in1990-2008.
Can be recognized from the figure, Hebei Province, the total industrial output and
energy consumption consistent with the trend, has undergone a process of rising. This
shows that industrial development and energy consumption corresponding relationship exists in the long-term.

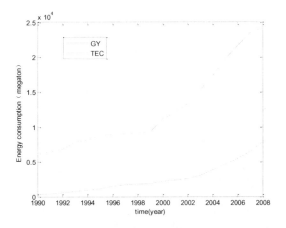

Fig. 1. The industrial and energy consumption trends in Hebei Province, (1990-2008)

2.2   Error Correction Model of Energy Consumption in Hebei Construction

The relationship between energy consumption and related economic indicators is the
primary task of consumer research. Since this paper is to study the low-carbon economy industrial structure optimization and upgrading of Hebei Province, the paper will
introduce (industrial output as the representative) industrial structure and total energy
consumption into the model. As shown in figure 1, the paper will use the following
linear model to estimate specifically.

$$TEC = \beta_0 + \beta_1 GY_t + \beta_2 TEC_t + \varepsilon_t \qquad (1)$$

The reason for the introduction of the consumption function of energy consumption itself as independent varriables, mainly taking into account the increase in energy consumption as the country will take measures to reduce energy consumption. In the function, we have considered GY and TEC long-term influence.

Construction of error correction model include the following basic steps.

(1) **Unit root test.** To ensure the authenticity of regression results, firstly the stationary of time series variables will be tested. It calls a unit root test that testing the variable is stationary or non-stationary. This article uses the ADF (Augmented Dickey-Filler) method to test the smoothness of the GY and the TEC.

(2) **Co-integration test.** Engle and Granger in 1987 proposed two-step test, known as the EG test [5]. This paper will adopt Engle-Granger Test method for co-integration test.

(3) **Error Correction Model.** If the co-integration relationship between the TEC and the GY in equation (1), then there is error correction model description industry and energy consumption by the short-term fluctuations and long-run equilibrium.

$$\Delta TEC_t = \beta_0 + \beta_1 \Delta GY_t + \lambda ecm_{t-1} + \varepsilon_t \qquad (2)$$

Therefore, when $TEC_{t-1} > \dfrac{\beta_1 + \beta_3}{1 - \beta_2} GY_{t-1}$, ecm_{t-1} is positive, then the λecm_{t-1} is negative, so ΔTEC_t is reduced, and vice versa. This reflects the balance of errors on the TEC_t control.

3 Empirical Analysis

3.1 Unit Root Test and Granger Causality Test

As ZGY and TEC have an upward trend, this paper select the ADF, and respectively make ADF test for TEC and GY.

After the second difference by the test, ADF test values of TEC at 1%, 5% and 10% significance level are less than the critical value of ADF(ADF test value is -5.177984),while ADF test values of GY at 10% significance level is less than the critical value of ADF(ADF test value is-1.904414). Therefore, TEC is the Second-order series, and there is no unit root. Similarly, ZGY is also the second single the whole series, and there is no unit root. Two time series is stationary.

As the two time series are stationary, we can make Granger causality test, the results in Table 1.

Table 1 shows that Industrial development and energy consumption has a significant one-way causality, and the increase in energy consumption is not a cause of industrial development, but industrial development can cause addition in energy consumption.

Table 1. Granger causality test

Original hypothesis	Observations	F-statistic	Significant probability
Granger not cause GY TEC's	14	1.86343	0.3227
TEC is not a reason for GY's Granger		0.80172	0.6143

3.2 Co-integration

GY and TEC are the second-single sequence, and the two variables is significantly correlated. Thus it satisfies the prerequisite of co-integration. Then select the ADF method and do unit root test on the residual sequence, the results are the Table 2.

Table 2. ADF test residual sequence

P	ADF test value	Significance level	ADF critical value
2	-3.297450	1%	-2.717511
		5%	-1.964418
		10%	-1.605603

As can be seen from Table 2 accept that the residual sequence is stationary series at a given significance level, so that TEC and the GY have co-integration. Based on this, we analysis TEC and GY by ordinary least squares regression, and obtain relationship equation:

TEC=4012.40496027+6.93250718072GY

(11.45973)   (29.49010)   (3)

In order to eliminate residual autocorrelation, this paper analyzes variable with Kirkland - Orcutt method and obtains the regression model of energy consumption in Hebei Province:

TEC = 4187.54754153 +6.64876415327 GY +[AR (1) = 1.38556956434, AR (2) =- 0.734930295604]   (4)

The independent variable regression coefficient of model is 6.65, which shows that industrial output increase 1%, energy consumption will correspondingly increase 6.65%. Therefore, there is obvious causality between industrial output and energy consumption.

3.3 Error Correction Model

After the above test, we can establish the relevant error correction model. According to the described residual sequence, the directly established error correction model called Model 1; In accordance with DNSY model, the established error correction model is called Model 2. Test results table were obtained, Table 3.

Table 3. Comparison of two models of the test results table

Model	DW	R^2	Adjusted R^2	AIC	SC
Model 1	2.536039	0.664798	0.587443	15.52077	15.71682
Model 2	2.363229	0.996442	0.994825	15.19351	15.48758

Model 1 expression is:

$$TEC - TEC_{t-1} =$$

$$9.50132762385 + 6.5503946506 \ (GY - GY_{t-1}) \ + 0.391929591529 \ ecm_{t-1} -$$

$$0.741776255055 \ ecm_{t-2} \tag{5}$$

Model 2 expression is:

$$TEC = 2261.80521341 + 0.997886218341 \ TEC_{t-1} \ -0.597579485782 \ TEC_{t-2} \ +19.71$$

$$1093572GY - 27.21162261 \ GY_{t-1} + 10.7889577936 \ GY_{t-2} + Vt \tag{6}$$

As can be seen from Table 3, the DW values of the two models are to meet the requirements, but Model 2 is much better than Model 1 from R2 adjusted R2, AIC and SC these indicators. Therefore, we use Model 2 to study the problem of energy consumption in Hebei Province. We obtained Table 4.

Table 4. The error correction model of energy consumption test

Project	Coefficient	Std . Error	t-statistic	Significant probability
C	2261.805	1134.652	1.993391	0.0716
TEC(-1)	0.997886	0.262915	3.795466	0.0030
TEC(-2)	-0.597579	0.291302	-2.051407	0.0648
GY	19.71109	4.928920	3.999070	0.0021
GY(-1)	-27.21162	8.211293	-3.313927	0.0069
GY(-2)	10.78896	6.387377	1.689106	0.1193
R^2	0.996442		Mean dependent var	13341.31
Adjusted R^2	0.994825		S.D.dependent var	5851.668
S.E.of regression	420.9583		Akaike info criterion	15.19351
Sum squared resid	1949264		Schwarz criterion	15.48758
Log likelihood	-123.1448		Hannan-Quinn criter	15.22274
F-statistic	616.1455		DW	2.363229

As can be seen from the model, Hebei Province, the relationship between industrial development and energy consumption is that industrial development has an effect on energy consumption in the short or medium term, while not significant in the long run. Specifically, the current industrial production increased by 1%, energy consumption will increase 19.71% over the same period; a former industrial output increased by 1%, current energy consumption will reduce 27.21%; two former industrial output increased by 1%, current energy consumption will increase 10.79%. From factor of energy consumption increased, the variation is slight.

Statistically, the prediction accuracy is obtained through the average relative error (MAPE), THEIL coefficient ranges, bias ratio, variance proportion, covariance proportion and other indicators. The results of testing indicators are as follows. THEIL inequality coeffient(0.018592),Root Mean squared Error (539.5649),Mean Absolute Error(424.8035),MAEP(4.044824),variance proportion(0.002007). These indicators show that error correction model of energy consumption is not only statistically significant, but also has better prediction capabilities. Therefore, the conclusion from this model is more convincing.

4 Conclusion and Recommendations

Energy consumption and industrial output exists short-term fluctuations and long-run equilibrium relationship in Hebei. The industrial development on the impact of energy consumption is significant in Hebei Province, and this trend will promote energy consumption increasing along with the ever-increasing industrial development. Based on the above conclusions and the development status of Hebei Province, there are some following recommendations.

(1) Grasp the relationship between recent and long-term. The recent restructuring of the structure is conducive to optimizing the long-term and developing a low carbon economy.
(2) View low-carbon industrial development as a new growth point. Handle the relationship of the development rights and the responsibility of energy saving in low-carbon industrial development.
(3) Optimize the industrial structure, and attach importance to industrial restructuring. Specifically, deal with the problem of some industrial overweight proportion, including the steel industry, power industry, resource-intensive industries.

References

1. Lin, B.: China's energy demand econometric analysis. Statistical Research (10), 34–39 (2001)
2. Lin, Y.-C.: Analysis of energy consumption and its influencing factors in Shanghai. East China Normal University, Shanghai (2006)
3. Peng, W.: The study on regional differences of China's economic growth and energy consumption. Jiangsu University (2009)
4. Li, Y.: Gray Correlation Analysis of energy consumption and economic growth based on the perspective of constraint-based energy structure. Technical and economic (03) (2010)
5. Cheng, Z.: Econometric theory and practice. Shanghai Finance University Press (2009)

An ROLAP Aggregation Algorithm with the Rules Being Specified

Weng Zhengqiu, Kuang Tai, and Zhang Lina

Department of Electroincs and Information Technology,
City College of WenZhou University, WenZhou, Zhejing Province, China
derisweng@163.com, kuangtai@yeah.net, zln5688@163.com

Abstract. This paper introduces the base theory of data warehouse and ROLAP, and presents a new kind of ROLAP aggregation algorithm, which has calculation algorithms. It covers the shortage of low accuracy of traditional aggregation algorithm that aggregates only by addition. The ROLAP aggregation with calculation algorithm which can aggregate according to business rules improves accuracy. And key designs and procedures are presented. Compared with the traditional method, its efficiency is displayed in an experiment.

Keywords: ROLAP, Data Warehouse, Aggregation Algorithms.

1 Introduction

In the Intense competition of the market economy, the business enterprise must be linked with market demand. To this end, enterprises have built up their own database system, managed by computer instead of manual operation. The traditional database application system is designed for business operations, which simplifying the specific operator's labor intensity, while the senior leaders have no corresponding system. Enterprises need new technologies to make up for lack of the original database system, need to collect the data which has been widely integrated into the data warehouse, in order to extract useful data from business information, to help them in business management and development timely, accurate judgment. Data warehouse came into being, a very popular topic of information technology.

Data warehouse implementations include the data warehouse built on relational databases (ROLAP) and multidimensional database (MOLAP). ROLAP divides multidimensional structure of the multidimensional database into two categories, one is the fact table, which is used to store data and dimension keywords; the other is the dimension table, that is, each dimension uses a table to store dimensional description of the dimension level and the types of members.

Expressed in terms of multidimensional data model, multi-dimensional matrix is more clearly than the relational table and take up less storage, while, the system performance will become the biggest problem, through the relational table by connecting to query the data of ROLAP system. MOLAP solution scheme is more concise than ROLAP. The index and data aggregation can be automatically and automatically managed, but lost some flexibility. ROLAP using relational database, so it requires more processing time and disk space to perform some tasks designed for multi-dimensional

G. Shen and X. Huang (Eds.): ECWAC 2011, Part I, CCIS 143, pp. 60–66, 2011.

database. However, ROLAP support the larger user groups and the amount of data, and often used for these occasions of high capacity requirements, such as a large and complex sector of a company.

In terms of the flexibility, ROLAP multidimensional model can be built on the data table with the storage of details, and can also be built on the summary table, with unlimited number of dimensions. You can also add Op-type measure values(such as percentages, sum, mission) which are derived from the existing measure more freely. It can be said that the ROLAP provides greater flexibility.

2 Current Research

Existing relational database has made a lot of optimization for OLAP, including the parallel storage, parallel query [3], parallel data management, cost-based query optimization, bitmap indexes, so that improve performance.

OLAP should have the function of Aggregation[4]. From the system performance point of view, the *Space for Time* is a basic optimization of margin management, which is the same for the MOLAP and ROLAP, just MOLAP create a Cube files separately, while ROLAP only use the summary table in the database. A Cube can correspond to a set of summary tables in the database to achieve the same level of optimization, Furthermore, the data warehouse from the early RedBrick to Oracle8 or later, or IBM DB2 version, have provided automatically aggregation technology for optimizing ROLAP (Oracle is called *Materilized View*), which automatically gathers a set of summary tables according to the rules from a base table with a large amount of data; front-end tools provide similar functionality, such as Brio can automatically insert the appropriate summary data for aggregate analysis according to the dimensions and measures of *Data Model* in the database. It also can record and sum up the most commonly used dimensions of portfolio combinations when the user access to the data model, and then based on these dimensions to generate Aggregation intelligencely, performance has been greatly enhanced.

Although ROLAP's Aggregation performance will be greatly increased, but the ROLAP aggregation only supports traditional aggregation and don't support the aggregation calculation with aggregation rules. The traditional collection, such as the time dimension, assuming that it's on the level: Year- Quarter- Month.

>*Year*
>> 1st *Quarter*
>>> *January*
>>> *February*
>>>> *march*
>> 2nd *Quarter*
>>> ......

When in the data aggregation phase, getting quarterly data by the sum of monthly data, the default aggregation rules is "+",that: 1st Quarter data = January data + February data + march data. While in real life, sometimes some dimensions can not describe the calculation rules by "+".

>*All Products*
>*Retail Products*
>> *Fan*

TV
Battery   sellers Gift
Tableware_ Producer Gift
Bulk Products

If you want to get the sales profits of retail merchandise at this time, the battery (the seller gift) supposed to do subtraction processing and tableware (producer gift) for the sales person should not be included in the cost, so: retail Products (sales profit) = Fan (sales profit) + TV (sales profit) - Battery _ sellers gift (sellers gift). Then the calculation rules for each dimension include members of the sum (+), subtraction (-), not participate in calculations (~). ROLAP aggregation with business rules is a problem in real applications, We propose ROLAP aggregation algorithm with business rules in the following article to solve the above problem.

3   Algorithm Introduction

Here is the definition of a multidimensional model, which provides some simple schema. This model uses the abstract, but easy manner to understand.

Promise 1: Dimension D includes the following components:

(1)   Including the collection of a series of level L
(2)   Aggregation Order <. Aggregation Order is used to describe Aggregation relationship between L; $if(l_1 \geq l_2)$, it means aggregating from l_1 to l_2.

This definition is a simple description of the dimensions, including the aggregation rules of the dimension. Such as: $Store \geq City \geq State$ 。

Storage Dimensions:

Fig. 1. Storage Dimensions

Based on the description of the above dimensional model, calculation rules of dimensions are given below:

Promise   2:   There   are   the   levels   of   the   dimension   D: $l_1 \geq l_2 \geq ... \geq l_i \geq ... l_n \geq l$ $i \in [1, n]$,   with   members $m_1^1, m_2^2, ..., m_j^i, ... m_{k-1}^{n-1}, m_k^n$ $j \in [1, k]$. There is a calculation flag in Member m_j of dimension T. And the flag is C, Where $C \in [-1, 0, 1]$, The dimension level of the member is l_i. Then $C[m_j, l_i]$ is the calculation item of member m_j in level l_i. The mapping of $C[m_j, l_i]$ on the other levels is $C[m_1, l_i] ... C[m_j, l_i] ... C[m_k, l_i]$ $j \in [1, k]$, marked as $C(D_T)_i$, and $C(D_T)_i = [C(D_T)_1, ..., C(D_T)_i, ..., C(D_T)_n]$ $i \in [1, n]$, which $C \in [-1, 0, 1]$.

Promise 3: A multi-dimensional structure includes the following components:

(1) Contains a set of dimensions;

(2) A multidimensional structure that contains the data in the form of

$f[A_1 : l_o, ..., A_i : l_p, ..., A_n : l_q] \rightarrow [M_1, ..., M_k]$, f is the name. Each A_i $i \in [1, n]$ is

an attribute of f. Each l_p is the level of the dimension D_i which is correspond-

ing to A_i. This dimension has Total p levels, p=1,2...n. Every M_j $j \in [1, k]$ is a

different indicator in f.

A   Cube   can   be   expressed   as   fol-

lows: $Cube = f[A_1 : l_o, ..., A_i : l_p, ..., A_n : l_q] \rightarrow [M_1, ..., M_k]$. A Cube of multi-

dimensional structure is a set of indicators and dimensions. An indicator is not just a
simple value but also a set of dimensions level. Analyser can analyse an indicator
according to different properties. This is the function of OLAP system should have.

With Cube, Aggregation Algorithm of the Cube will be described as follows:

Promise 4: The data of a Cube support the Aggregation from bottom to top. The Cube
with the Aggregation rules can be expressed as follows:

$Cube(C(D_T)) = f[A_1 : l_o, ..., A_i : l_p, ..., A_n : l_q \mid C(D_T)] \rightarrow [M_1, ..., M_k \mid C(D_T)]$, $T \in (1, n)$ Or

$Cube(C(D_T)) = f[A_1 : l_o, ..., A_i : l_p, ..., A_n : l_q \mid C(D_T)] \rightarrow [M_1 \prod_1^n C(D_T)_{\phi(T)}, ..., M_k \prod_1^n C(D_T)_{\phi(T)}]$

, $T \in (1, n)$

$\phi(T)$ is the number of levels in aggregate with T as the dimension.

The following analysis model for the financial account, is a multi-dimensional
model which is composed of company dimension, Indicator dimension, time dimension and beginning balance indicators, ending balance indicators, and the indicators of
the amount of current period.

So when aggregating Indicator dimensions, if indicator dimension is aggregated to
level2, the calculation rules is $C(D_M)_2$, if company dimension is aggregated to level3,
the calculation rules is $C(D_O)_3$, if time dimension is aggregated to level4, the calculation rules is $C(D_T)_4$. The value of aggregating Indicator $= MC(D_M)_2C(D_O)_3C(D_T)_4$.

Fig. 2. Financial Accounts Model

With the above definition of dimension and Cube, We proposed the ROLAP Aggregation Algorithm with the Aggregation Rules.

3.1 Transformation Algorithm for Dimensional Calculating Matrix

Dimension calculating matrix is the base of the ROLAP aggregation algorithm with the rules. Where first shows how to construct the algorithm for calculating matrix. Dimension members. calculation flag_this Level = calculation flag_Lower Level* Dimension calculation rules.

The formation of the initial conditions;

While (n>0)
While (k>0)
Get calculation flag of K-Member in N-Tier: $C_{[m_k, l_n]}$;
Get calculation flag of the superior members: $C_{[m_y, l_{n-1}]}$;

$C_{[m_k, l_{n-1}]} = C_{[m_y, l_{n-1}]} * C_{[m_k, l_n]}$;
$k=k-1$;
$n=n-1$;

There are indicators of the dimension D1, calculation rules of this dimension member as the data shown in Table 1:

Table 1. Calculation rules table of indicators dimension

Id	Name level1	Name level2	Name level3	Calc level1	Calc level2	Clac level3
1	Indicator	NULL	NULL	1		
2	Indicator	Indicator 1	NULL	0	0	
3	Indicator	Indicator 1	Indicator 11	0	0	1
4	Indicator	Indicator 1	Indicator 12	0	0	-1
5	Indicator	Indicator 2	NULL	-1	-1	
6	Indicator	Indicator 2	Indicator 21	1	1	-1
7	Indicator	Indicator 2	Indicator 22	-1	-1	1
8	Indicator	Indicator 3	NULL	-1	-1	

In the dimension table, Which:

5	Indicator	Indicator2	NULL	-1	
6	Indicator	Indicator2	Indicator21	1	-1

For 6, the value of calc_leve2 is derived from the dimensions set, and for 7, calc_leve2 =- 1 (set of Indicator 2) * 1 (set of indicators 21) =- 1.

3.2 Aggregation Algorithm of Multi-dimensional Model According to Business Rules

Set parameters For the formation of the initial conditions;
FOR Request for each data point
Taking the number of cache
Request order

FOR Similar aggregates
Format Aggregation request
Determine the aggregate CUBE $(C(D_T))$ *;*
Get data;

4 The Results

Financial analysis model is a multidimensional model, which is composed of company dimension, Indicator dimension, time dimension and beginning balance indicators, ending balance indicators, and the indicator of the amount of current period. In which, the Aggregation calculation flag between members of indicator dimensions is shown in Table 1. And the structure of time dimension and calculation of matrix are shown in Table 2, the structure of company dimension and the calculation matrix are shown in Table 3:

Table 2. The structure of time dimension and calculation of matrix

Id	Name level1	Name level2	Name level3	Calc level1	Calc level2	Clac level3
1	TIME	null	null	1		
2	TIME	2008	null	1	1	
3	TIME	2008	First half of 2008	1	1	1
4	TIME	2008	Second half of 2008	1	1	1
5	TIME	2009	null	1	1	
6	TIME	2009	First half of 2009	1	1	1
7	TIME	2009	Second half of 2009	1	1	1

Table 3. The structure of company dimension and the calculation matrix

Id	Time_id	Corp_id	Mea_id	profit
1	3	2	3	100
2	3	2	4	100
...	...	...	...	...
39	7	3	8	100
40	7	3	9	100

The final output of the analysis model is shown in Table 4:

Table 4. Output

			Indicator 0	Indicator 1	Indicator 22
		Group	Area 1	Area 2	
	2008	Branch 1	Area 3		Area 4
		Branch 2			

Aggregation region in the above table involve four regions, the Area 4 is composed of the last level indicator 22 of indicator dimension, the last level Branch 1 of company dimension and the Aggregation member 2008 of time dimension. After the transformation algorithm of dimension calculation matrix and multidimensional aggregation algorithm, the values of area 4 are:

2008 Branch 1   *Indicator 22*   *-200*
2008 Branch 2   *Indicator 22*   *-200*
Similarly, the values of area 2 are:
2008 Group Indicator 1   *0*
the values of area 3 are:
2008 Branch 1   *Indicator 0*   *400*
2008 Branch 2   *Indicator 0*   *400*
The values of area 1 are:
2008 Group Indicator 0   *800*

5 Conclusion

This article is about the research of the ROLAP aggregation with calculation algorithm which can aggregate according to business rules. Through the study, we found that ROLAP model can also realize more complex aggregation algorithms. This algorithms can not only deal with traditional aggregation, but also handle subtraction aggregation and designated areas aggregation. This allows ROLAP aggregation algorithm match to the practical application with high application value. On the other hand, because of the algorithm complexity and time constraints, we need further improvement of the algorithm. For example, how to use aggregate data more effectively, how to improve the efficiency of aggregation, and how to improve the efficiency of the transformation matrix algorithms have yet to be further explored.

References

1. Sperley, E.: The Enterprise Data Warehouse. Planning, Building And Implementation, vol. I. People Post and Telecommunications Press, Beijing (2000)
2. Wen, X.: A Client Connection Method for Improving the Performance of ROLAP System. Science Technology and Engineering (2010)
3. Tang, L.: Data Warehouse Query and Implementation of Intelligent Query Programs. Computer Engineering and Applications 36(8), 114–116 (2000)
4. Pedersen, T.B.: Aspects of Data Modeling and Query Processing for Complex Multidimensional Data. PhD thesis, Faculty of Engineering & Science, Aalborg University (2000)

Design of Pipeline Multiplier Based on Modified Booth's Algorithm and Wallace Tree

Aihong Yao, Ling Li, and Mengzhe Sun

College of Computer Science and Technology
Harbin engineering university
No.145 Nantong Street, Nangang District, Harbin, China
yaoaihong@126.com, Liling-0203@163.com, bjrr@163.com

Abstract. A design of 32*32 bit pipelined multiplier is presented in this paper. The proposed multiplier is based on the modified booth algorithm and Wallace tree structure. In order to improve the throughput rate of the multiplier, pipeline architecture is introduced to the Wallace tree. Carry Select Adder is deployed to reduce the propagation delay of carry signal for the final level 64-bit adder. The multiplier is fully implemented with Verilog HDL and synthesized successfully with Quartus II. The experiment result shows that the resource consumption and power consumption is reduced to 2560LE and 120mW, the operating frequency is improved from 136.21MHz to 165.07MHz.

Keywords: multiplier, modified Booth algorithm, carry select adder, Wallace tree.

1 Introduction

In most of high-speed digital systems, the basic arithmetic components which execute calculation operations, such as adding, subtracting, multiplying and dividing, are the core modules of the processors. In fact, 8.72% of all instructions in a typical scientific program are multiplies [1]. And in digital signal processing algorithms, such as FFT and FIR, the multiplier also is the main arithmetic logic. Therefore the multiplier is a critical function component, and its throughput rate decides the ALU working frequency, and affects the system performance indirectly. Since the DSP processor is serial, application specified, high power consumption, FPGA is now commonly used be SoPC (System on Programmable Chip) for the real-time digital signal processing applications.

Most of the parallel multipliers utilize Booth's algorithm to reduce the number of partial products. Feng Liang etc. presented the design and implementation of Radix-16 Booth pipelined multiplier based on 16-radix Booth algorithm [2]. The proposed multiplier takes advantages of the both the redundant Booth encoder and modified Booth encoder. By optimizing the compression array and the 64-bit CLA (carry-look ahead) adder in the critical path of pipeline, the path delay and area cost can be effectively reduced. Xiaolong Hu etc. described the structure of a 32-bit unsigned parallel

G. Shen and X. Huang (Eds.): ECWAC 2011, Part I, CCIS 143, pp. 67–73, 2011.

multiplier using traditional Booth-4 algorithm [3]. The paper introduces a balanced 4-2 compressor Wallace tree to compute the cumulative sum of partial products, and a CPA to obtain the final result. Jingbo Chang proposed a three-stage pipelined Wallace tree compressor which is applied to the design of 28x28-bit multiplier [4]. A three-stage pipeline combined with Wallace tree is introduced to improve mantissa processing speed in the float multiplier.

The proposed pipelined multiplier is based on radix-4 modified Booth's algorithm, which is used to generate partial products of multiplier, and 4-2 compressor Wallace tree to merge partial products. The cumulative sum of the final two products, which is called pseudo summation, is obtained by carry select adder (CSA) to improve the path delay of carry flag.

2   Design Architecture

Multiplier operations will be divided into three stages:1)the first stage to generate the partial products;2)the second stage to add the partial products;3)the last stage to compute the final result by carry select adder. And the figure 1 shows the architecture of the modified Booth multiplier.

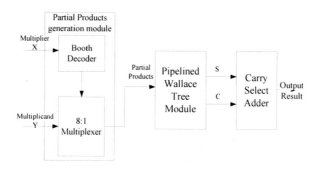

Fig. 1. The architecture of the proposed multiplier

From the figure 1, we can see that the modified Booth's encoder scheme proposed in [1] be used. It is known as the most efficient Boot's encoding and decoding scheme. The input of the multiplier are multiplicand X and multiplier Y .And both of them are 32-bit.Through the modified Booth's encoder it generates 16 partial products in the partial products generation module, and pass them to pipelined Wallace tree module. We use six 4-2 compressors and two 3-2 compressors to graduated compress partial product until the last two rows are remained. Then pass the two rows to carry select adder (CSA) module. The final multiplication results are generated by CSA that add the sum and the carry.

In the pipelined Wallace tree module, we mix the pipeline technique. The pipeline technique is widely used to improve the performance of digital circuits. In the second module (partial product merger), it needs 5 stages Wallace tree for 16 partial products.

Even with the compressor, it still needs 8 gate delays in each stage. So in order to reduce the time consumption we introduce the three-stage pipeline in the partial product merger stage.

3 Modified Booth Algorithm and Wallace Tree Structure

Partial products generation and partial products merger are the two key points of multiplier. Among them, the number of partial products not only affects the calculation speed, but also determines the area of the multiplier. Therefore, some the multipliers are designed from the partial product generation side and partial product merger side to improve the multiplier algorithm. So we use radix-4 modified Booth's algorithm to reduce the number of partial products by half. According modified Booth's algorithm, the input multiplier X be divided into the booth decoder groups of 3 bits code. The total of coding is 16 groups. The value of each group (b2k +1, b2k, b2k-1) is the input of Multiplexers. They compare input value with the table 1, and get the corresponding output which is the partial product. As 16 groups input of Multiplexer we get the 16 partial products.

Table 1. Multiplexer input and output mapping table

b_{2k+1}	b_{2k}	b_{2k-1}	output
0	0	0	all 0
0	0	1	1Y
0	1	0	1Y
0	1	1	2 Y
1	0	0	-2 Y
1	0	1	-1 Y
1	1	0	-1 Y
1	1	1	all 0

Partial product merger have the array structure and the tree structure. The paper [5] studied the pros and cons of two structures, indicate that the tree structure be better than the array structure in delay, area and layout of wiring and so on. And among the tree structures, Wallace tree is one of the fastest compression rates [6]. In [7], Weinberger proposed 4-2 compressors, the compression ratio increased 2-fold. Expressions (1) (2) (3) are the input and output logic expressions of the 4-2 compressor..

$$S = x1\wedge x2\wedge x3\wedge x4\wedge cin \tag{1}$$

$$C = (x1\wedge x2\wedge x3\wedge x4) \& cin \mid (x1\wedge x2\wedge x3\wedge x4)\& x4 \tag{2}$$

$$Cout = (x1\wedge x2)\& x3 \mid (x1\wedge x2) \& x1 \tag{3}$$

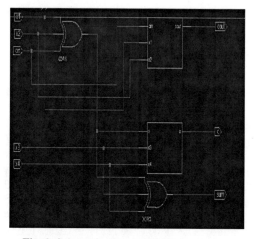

Fig. 2. Schematic diagram of 4:2 compressor

Figure 2 is the result of above 3 expressions after Quartus II software synthesis. Here assume that XOR gate delay is the 2Td, while the rest of the logic gate delay is 1Td, we know that two full-adder delays is 8Td. From figure 2 we can see that the 4-2 compressor delay is 4Td. Therefore, we compared the 3-2 compressor with the 4-2 compressor; the 4-2 compressor reduces the delay. Therefore we apply the 4-2 compressor and the 3-2 compressor in Wallace tree structure.

To further enhance the computing speed we utilize the pipeline for the input partial products p1 ... ... p16, the first-stage partial products reduced from 16 to 10, the second-stage partial products reduced from 10 to 6, the third-stage partial products reduced from 6 to 4 in which apply two the 3-2 compressor, again with one 4-2 compressor obtained two partial products (the carry and the sum) .The figure 3 show the structure of Wallace tree with the pipeline.

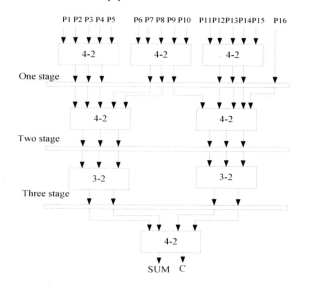

Fig. 3. Structure of pipelined Wallace tree

4 Carry Select Adder

There are many types of hardware implementation for multi-bit addition, for instance, ripple adder, look-ahead adder etc. The serial adder is area cost efficient, but its performance is limited by the physical characteristics of devices. On the other hand, the look-ahead adder decreases the propagation delay of the carry signal by extra carry generation logic and the area cost is doubled consequently. In order to strike a balance between the performance and area cost, the carry-select adder is deployed at the last stage of the pipelined Wallace tree module. The carry-select adder is divided into sectors, one assuming a carry-in of zero, the other a carry-in of one [8]. They are computed in parallel. The 64-bit carry-select adder is divided into sectors of lengths 1, 2, 4, 8, 16 and 32, proceeding from least-significant to most-significant bit. As figure 4 show sector structure of the length=2.The upper adder has a carry-in of one; and the lower adder has a carry-in of zero. The actual carry in from the preceding sector selects one of the two adders. If the carry-in is zero, the sum and carry-out of the upper adder are selected. If the carry-in is one, the sum and carry-out of the lower adder are selected. Using ripple adder for n-bit adder need (n-1)3Td+4Td, then if using CSA need (log2 (n) +n) Td. So when n=64 the propagation delay of carry signal for the final level adder reduce 123Td.

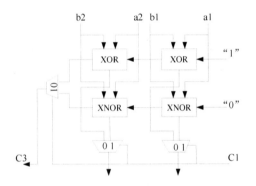

Fig. 4. Sector structure of CSA length=2

5 Performance Analysis and Function Verification

The proposed multiplier is coded in Verilog HDL, simulated and implemented using Altera Cyclone EP1C2 FPGA. And through Quartus II 8.1 compiled, integrated, adapter, timing and power simulation we get the data, respectively compared with the table data in [9], and table 2 show the results of comparison.

In order to verify the designed multiplier functions correctly, need to design incentives simulation test platform, figure 5 shows the relationship schematic diagram between the test platform (testbench) and the design under test (DUT). Test platform is usually a simulation code used to generate specific input sequence of DUT and monitor DUT response. Test platform design using hardware description languages, you can also use advanced hardware description language (such as System Verilog) for development. Since the purpose of test platform is to verify DUT, only for simulation, it can be implemented by the faster simulation statement in develop and run.

Table 2. Performance Comparison

	This article Algorithm	In[10] Algorithm	In[9] Algorithm
Maximum operating frequency /MHz	165.07	136.21	122.55
Hardware resources	2560	2737	2822
Average power consumption /mW	120	353.42	357.08

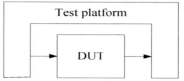

Fig. 5. Testbench and DUT

For the 32x32-bit multiplier, the input vector space is 232 × 232 = 264 (input A × input B), if we test each combination of the input signals, the time consuming is unacceptable. If we can test one set of inputs in a microsecond, thereby all the combination of the input signals need 0.58 million years. In fact, it is enough to only verify some of the special combinations of input signals (such as walking ones, walking zeroes, all 0 and all 1). That can prove the correctness of the design with a higher degree of confidence. So we write testbench to test the implementation of the multiplier program, and compare the generate test stimulus (Figure 6) with the expected results, then we get the accurate rate was 100%.

⊞ A	S 1048585	1049386	1049395	1049404	1049413	1049422
⊞ B	S 519	1142	1149	1156	1163	1170
⊞ result	S 544215615	198398812	205754855	213111024	220467319	227823740

Fig. 6. Test stimulus

6 Conclusion

The design of a high performance 32x32-bit multiplier is presented in this paper. The proposed multiplier is based on modified Booth's Algorithm, and constructed using Wallace tree with three-stage pipeline. The carry select adder is introduced to add the two pseudo summations which are the output of the pipelined Wallace tree module. The multiplier is implemented on the Altera Cyclone EP1C2 FPGA, and the simulation result shows that the power consumption is reduced around 34%, as well as the maximum operating frequency is increased from 136.21MHz to 165.07MHz, and the former result is reported by the paper [10]. The pipelined multiplier can be utilized in the digital signal processors which need high throughput multiplication operation in the future.

References

1. Kyoung, H.L.: Design of an 8-bit multiplier using dynamic pass transistor logic. IEEE J. Solidstate Circuits 40, 279–285 (2003)
2. Feng, L., Shao, Z., Liang, J.: Design of Radix-16 Booth Pipeline Multiplier. Journal of Xi'An Jiao Tong University 40(10) (2006)
3. Hu, X., Yan, X.: Design and Implementation of a 32-Bit unsigned parallel multiplier. Computer Engineering And Science 32(4) (2010)
4. Chang, J.-B., Guo, L.: A three class pipeline Wallace tree compressor hardware design. Microelectronics & Computer 22(1) (2005)
5. Yeh, W.-C., Jen, C.-W.: High-speed Booth encoded parallel multiplier design. IEEE Trans. on Computers, 692–701 (2000)
6. Meier, P.C.H., Rutenbar, R.A., Carley, L.R.: Exploring multiplier architecture and layout for low power. In: Proceedings of the IEEE 1996 Custom Integrated Circuits Conference, p. 513. IEEE, Piscataway (1996); Young, M.: The Technical Writer's Handbook. University Science, Mill Valley (1989)
7. Weinberger, A.: 4:2 carry-save adder module. IBM Technical Disclosure Bulletin (1981)
8. 16-bit Carry-select Adder. Atmel Corporation (1999)
9. Chang, C.-H., Gu, I., Zhang, M.: Ultra low-voltage low-power CMOS 4-2 and 5-2 compressors for fast arithmetic circuits. IEEE Trans2 actions on Circuits and Systems 51(10), 1985 (2004)
10. Zou, G., Shao, Z.: Design of a 32-bit Word/Floating Point Embedded Multillier. Microelectronics & Computer 21(8) (2004)

Night Vision Image Enhancement Based on Double-Plateaus Histogram

ShuBin Yang, WanLong Cui, and DiFeng Zhang*

School of Electrical and Information Eng., Wuhan Institute of Technology,
Wuhan, 430073, China
yshubin@sina.com, cwanlong@gmail.com, zhangdf21@163.com

Abstract. Night vision image has characteristics of low contrast, weak-arrangement gray and dim vision. Double-plateaus histogram enhancement algorithm is presented to enhance them. By setting a higher threshold value, the algorithm can constrain the background and noises. At the same time, the algorithm can magnify dim targets and image details by setting a lower threshold value. With the proposed algorithm, disadvantages of classical histogram and other plateaus histogram enhancement algorithm are overcome while achieving high contrast. Experiments prove that the proposed algorithm can enhance image contrast effectively and preserve image details simultaneously. Moreover, it can also overcome over-bright phenomenon.

Keywords: Double-plateaus histogram, Image enhancement, Night vision low-light-level image.

1 Introduction

Night vision low-light-level image [1,2] equipments play an important role for military and civilian application, and the key kernel is the low-light-level image processing system. The interval and density of gray contrast are very low and gray value range is great narrow, so night vision image's vision is dim and gray contrast between target and background is extremely small. Therefore, it is very important to enhance image and improve its vision quality. The enhancement method is an availably and practical method which can improve image vision quality and distinguish target from complex low-light-level image.

Histogram equalization [3] is a traditional technology to enhance image contrast, but it is difficult to control the enhancement result in practice and all image histogram is equally equalized. For the area with low-gray-frequency, contrast will be weakened or eliminated moreover. That is to say noise may be magnified. Thus, if histogram equalization is directly used to enhance night vision low-light-level image, the background gray levels and noise will be strengthened. On the contrary, target gray levels will be lacked. It may enhance background and noise and reduce the target and details contrast. Sometimes the over-bright phenomenon [3] may come out. So traditional histogram equalization algorithm is not suitable for night vision image. In order to

---

* Corresponding author.

G. Shen and X. Huang (Eds.): ECWAC 2011, Part I, CCIS 143, pp. 74–79, 2011.

overcome the problem, many scholars put forward different methods [4-6]. These methods can enhance image and get more chance to obtain the details. But it is very difficult to get the suitable threshold and has complex account and many gray levels are still united together. Target and details are lost. The image becomes dim more. The fixed threshold can't be self-adaptive to the image. Therefore, a self-adaptive double-plateaus histogram enhancement algorithm is proposed. By self-adaptive setting double-plateaus threshold, it can adjust the plateaus threshold value to different images. Since the algorithm united both the merits of above algorithms. It can constrain background and noise efficiently and at the same time magnify the small target and details. Moreover, it can also avoid the image to become dim more and overcome over-bright phenomenon.

2 Double-Plateaus Histogram Enhancement Algorithm Design and Analysis

Histogram equalization is a certain transform on original image that changes histogram's distribution more equal and enhances image. Plateau histogram equalization [7-9] which modifies original histogram is a special form of histogram equalization. Histogram equalization gets accumulated histogram from statistics histogram, but plateau histogram equalization gets accumulated histogram from plateau histogram, then distributes the image gray to get the equalized histogram by accumulated histogram to obtain equalized image.

In practice, selecting plateau threshold has a very important influence to the enhancement result. If threshold value is not suitable, it may even impair image vision quality. It can overcome the disadvantages of traditional histogram equalization and constrain the background and noise. The algorithm has the features of small calculation, excellent image enhancement and real-time performance, but it still has the problem that will merge the gray level and lose some details. Hereupon, self-adaptive double-plateaus histogram enhancement algorithm for night vision low-light-level image is proposed. Double-plateaus threshold values can be self-adaptively adjusted to different kinds of images. The upper-plateau threshold constrains the background and noise, the lower-plateau threshold magnifies the small target and details. It can overcome the disadvantages of traditional histogram equalization. The proposed algorithm can synthesize the advantages of upper-limit and lower-limit plateau algorithm, so it can enhance the image and remain the detail.

The image histogram is modified through self-adaptive setting two suitable plateau-thresholds A and T with Equation (1).

$$P_T(k) = \begin{cases} 0 & P(k) \leq 0.2A \\ A & 0.2A < P(k) \leq A \\ P(k) & A < P(k) \leq T \\ T & P(k) > T \end{cases} \tag{1}$$

In the Equation (1) $P_T(k)$ is the plateau histogram, $P(k)$ is the image histogram, T and A are the upper-limit and lower-limit plateau thresholds, k is the gray level, $0 \leq k \leq 255$.

The upper-limit and lower-limit plateau thresholds A and T can be self-adaptively set below.

(1)   Get image histogram $P(k),0\leq k\leq M$, one-dimensional 3-neighbour median filter is processed on $P(k)$; selecting the unit which isn't zero in the histogram to constitute an aggregate$\{F(l)\,|\,0\leq F(l)\leq L\}$, L is the number of the no-zero units;

(2)   Find out local maximum value and entire maximum value of all image, then make first-order difference calculation with no-zero units: $F^{(1)}(m)=F(m)-F(m-1)$. $1\leq m\leq L$.Find $F(l_i)$ which can accord with such condition of $F^{(1)}(m-1)>0$, $F^{(1)}(m)\geq 0$, $F^{(1)}(m+1)<0$ in $F(l)$. It means that the symbol $F^{(1)}(m)$ changes at this area m(from positive turning to negative value) and $F(l_i)$ is the local maximum value. Where $0\leq l_i\leq L, 0\leq i\leq N$, N is the number of local maximum values. Then the entire maximum value $F(l_k)$ can be obtained from $F(l_i)$;

(3)   Get the average value $F(l_g)$ of the subaggregate$\{ F(l_i)\,|\,k\leq i\leq N\}$, $F(l_g)$ is the utter plateau threshold value.(4) suppose the image size is $m\times n$, Get the lower threshold A which is the average value of image histogram, that is $A=\dfrac{m\times n}{256}$.

After calculating double-plateaus threshold values and equalizing the histogram, final equalization histogram can be gained by distributing the image gray through using modified cumulative histogram. That are $F_T(k)=\sum\limits_{i=1}^{k}P_T(i)$ $(0\leq k\leq 255)$

and $D_T(k)=[\dfrac{255F_T(k)}{F_T(255)}](0\leq D_T(k)\leq 255)$. Where $F_T(k)$ is the cumulative histogram and $D_T(k)$ is the double-plateaus equalized gray value of the pixel whose gray value is k in original image. [ ]means to return the value of a number rounded downwards to the nearest integer. That is round-calculate.

3   Experiments and Analysis

Night vision low-light-level street image is used as an original experiment image. Fig.1 are the images processed by different algorithm and their corresponding histograms. As it's shown in Fig.1 (a)(b)(c)(d), the background, which possesses most image parts is enhanced and the corresponding gray intervals are turned wider. On the contrary target and the details, which possesses the few parts of all image are constrained. Most gray levels of these corresponding parts are united and some parts of details and target are lost. As it's shown in Fig.1(e)(f), though plateau histogram enhancement algorithm gains better effect than histogram equalization algorithm, there still unites some gray levels and losses some details. Fig.1(g)(h) shows the double-plateaus threshold algorithm constrains the background and preserves the details more effectively and also overcomes over-bright phenomenon very well. So the proposed algorithm in this paper has more advantages than the traditional histogram and plateau equalization algorithm. It can get the best image vision.

(a) original image

(b)histogram equalized image

(c)plateau histogram equalized image   (d)image enhanced by proposed algorithm

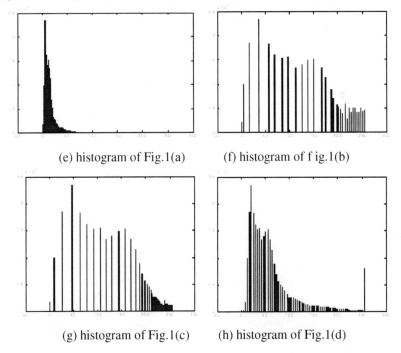

(e) histogram of Fig.1(a)   (f) histogram of f ig.1(b)

(g) histogram of Fig.1(c)   (h) histogram of Fig.1(d)

Fig. 1. Image processed by different algorithm and their corresponding histogram

Besides subjective appraisement, image quality can also be appraised by quantity parameter "fuzzy exponent"[10]. The smaller fuzzy exponent value the more definition of image. Table 1 shows the fuzzy exponent values of each algorithm. Because the proposed algorithm in this paper has the minimum fuzzy exponent value, it can obtain clearer image than other algorithm.

Table 1. Image Fuzzy Exponent of Each Algorithm

Algorithm	Histogram equalization	Plateau histogram equalization	Reference [8] upper plateau histogram	Reference [9] lower plateau histogram	proposed algorithm in this paper
Fuzzy-exponent FB	0.1976	0.2110	0.1191	0.0788	0.0768

4 Conclusion

The traditional histogram equalization is a fast and effective method to enhance the image. While processed on night vision images, it would magnify the background and the noise. Moreover, some small target is difficult to distinguish and over-bright phenomenon would come out. The plateau histogram equalization algorithm can constrain the background and noise, but it still has the problem of uniting gray level and losing the detail. The self-adaptive enhancement algorithm based on double-plateaus histogram can enhance the entire target contrast and preserve the detail. It can self-adaptively select dynamic threshold to different image and has more advantages than traditional algorithm and it can effectively use to enhance night vision low-light-level image in practical.

References

1. Zhou, L.-W.: The Comment of Night Vision. Optical Technology, 1–18 (1995)
2. Liu, C.-C., Hu, S.-B., Yang, J.-H., Guo, X.: A Method of Histogram Incomplete Equalization. Journal of Shandong University (Engineering Science) 33(6), 661–664 (2003)
3. Pizer, M., RAmburm, E., Austin, J.D.: Adaptive Histogram Equalization and its Variations. Comput. Vision. Graphics Image Proeessing 39, 355–368 (1987)
4. Shi, D.-Q., Li, J.-S.: A new Self-adaptive Enhancement Algorithm for the Low Light Level Night Vision Image. Electronic Optical and Contral 15(9), 18–20 (2008)
5. Li, W.-Y., Gu, G.-H.: A New Enhancement Algorithm for Infrared DIM-small Target Image. Infrare 27(3), 17–20 (2006)
6. Ooi, C.H., Kong, N.P., Ibrahim, H.: Bi-histogram equalization with a plateau limit for digital image enhancement. IEEE Transactions on Consumer Electronics 55(4), 2072–2080 (2009)
7. Vichers, V.E.: Plateau Equalization Algorithm for Real-time Display of High-quality Infrared Imagery. Opt. Eng. 35(7), 1921–1926 (1996)

8. Wang, B.-J., Liu, S.-Q., Zhou, H.-X.: A Self-adaptive Enhancement Algorithm for Low Light Level Night Vision Image Based on plateau Histogram. Journal of Photon 2(34), 299–301 (2005)
9. Gu, J.-X.: The Enhancement Algorithmon on Light Level Night Vision Image. A Thesis Submitted to Lanzhou University for Master of Science Degree, 6 (2009)
10. Shu, J.-l., Yu, Z.-h., Zhu, Z.-f.: An Improved Approach to Fuzzy-enhance Infrared Image. Systems Engineering and Electronics 27(6), 957–959 (2005)

Fabric Pilling Image Segmentation Based on Mean Shift

Junfeng Jing[1,2] and Xuejuan Kang[3]

[1] School of electronical and Machanical Engineering, Xidian university, Xi'an, China
[2] Xi'an Polytechnic University, Xi'an, China 710048
[3] Electric Department, Xi'an Aerotechnical College, Xi'an, China
Jingjunfeng0718@sina.com

Abstract. Fabric appearance is always considered to be one of the most important aspects of fabric quality. Testing for fabric appearance is the process of inspecting, measuring and evaluating characteristics and properties of a fabric surface. Fabric Pilling is a key step in fabric pilling objective evaluation,which is the important component of textile performance test digitization.Image analysis has been widely accepted as an objetive mothod for evaluating fabric appearance.This study presents the principles of new method of fabric pilling image segmenttation based on mean shift.The principle of mean shift was demonstrated, and the extend principle of mean shift was educed. The extended mean shift algorithm was used to try to solve the segmentation of fabric pilling image.In this issue, two main steps were introduced: the filting of image and the segmentation of image. The influences of three parameters to the segmentation effect were analysised. The laboratory result shows that the proposed algorithm can get excellent segmentation after chosen three better parameters.

Keywords: Fabric appearance, pilling, image segmentation.

1 Introduction

In general, quality of a fabric is estimated by three criteria of physical properties, appearance and defects. Most of the defects in a fabric are related to physical properties of the fabric. Consisted in this relation, occurrence of pilling defects in fabrics is related to the physical properties of fiber, yarn twist and fabric structure. Evaluating the pilling defects; we can assess these properties of fibers, yarns and fabrics and also the probability of problem occurrence in production line [1].Pilling is a phenomenon of fiber movement or slipping out of yarns, which is usually happening on the fabric surface during abrasion and wear.The development of pilling could be divided into four stages: fuzz formation,entanglement, growth, and wear-off. The formation of pills suspended on the fabric surface could affect the fabric aesthetics and its ulti-mate acceptance by customers.

Computer vision technology provides one of the best solutions for the objective evaluation of pilling. Researchers in various institutions have been exploring image analysis techniques effective for pill identification and characterization [1,2,3]. These methods are mainly based on digital technologies, such as digital image analysis or the

G. Shen and X. Huang (Eds.): ECWAC 2011, Part I, CCIS 143, pp. 80–84, 2011.
© Springer-Verlag Berlin Heidelberg 2011

laser scanning method. The laser scanning system applies the laser triangulation technique to measure the 3-D height field of the fabric surface and to identify pills or fuzzes through the variation of its height. In comparison with laser scanning, the CCD/CMOS imaging system is simple, easy to implement and low-cost;however, it is much more sensitive to the color and texture of fabric samples. Konda et al [4]first attempted to use image processing techniques to evaluate fabric pilling; Xu [5]developed an image analysis system that aims at characterizing and rating fabric pilling appearance; Hsi et al. [6]developed a hardware device and software based on image analysis techniques to detect and describe fuzz on fabric surfaces.

2 Mean-Shift Algorithm Introduction

When d-dimensional space R^d is set n sample points x_i, i = 1,2,3 ,..., n, the mean shift vector in the x point can be defined as following basic form:

$$M_h(x) = \frac{1}{k} \sum_{x_i \in S_h} (x_i - x)$$

(1)

Where, S_h is a high-dimensional ball with the radius h, and is the collection of y-points meeting following condition.

$$S_h(x) = \{ y : (y - x)^T (y - x) \leq h^2 \}$$

(2)

Where, k refers that, among n sample points (x_i), there are k points in the region of S_h.

The mean-shift vector $M_h(x)$ is the average value of all the offset vector sums of k sample points. (x_i-x) is the relative offset value of sample point x_i to x. If the sample points x_i is the sample obtained from a probability density function $f(x)$ the sample points within the region S_h will be more possibly along the gradient direction, as a result of non-zero probability density gradient point to the direction of the largest increase, so the corresponding Mean-shift vector $M_h(x)$ should point to the direction of the probability density gradient.

3 The Application of Mean Shift Algorithm in the Fabric Pilling Image Segmentation

The direction of mean-shift vector is the same as that of the corresponding region's sample points' gradient direction. By tracking it, we can get the points with the greatest density; the so-called clustering algorithm model point. Correspondingly, the color image segmentation is to find a cluster point of different colors. When printing color images are identified color space (here the uniform color model *Luv* color space proposed by *CIE*), that is, color information (*L, u, v*), together with its spatial (*x, y*), every pixel's value in the 5-dimensional feature space can be obtained , which is, (x, y, L, u, v). Pixels with the similar spatial location and color are quite similar in the in the 5-dimensional feature space , so we can make a cluster of them, and then map the clustering results to the image in reverse, so as to achieve image segmentation. Image segmentation algorithm based on the mean-shift is divided into image filtering and image segmentation, which both have their own specific meaning, and they are both based on the mean-shift algorithm, with following respective introduction for your reference.

3.1 Mean-Shift Image Filtering

In order to get a better understanding of the kernel function $G(x)$'s role in the mean-shift iterative process, we use $\{y_j\}$ $j = 1,2, ...$ to present a series of center position during the moving of $G(x)$. According to mean-shift expression, following can be achieved:

$$y_{j+1} = \frac{\sum_{i=1}^{n} G\left(\frac{x_i - y_j}{h}\right) w(x_i) x_i}{\sum_{i=1}^{n} G\left(\frac{x_i - y_j}{h}\right) w(x_i)}$$

(3)

y_{j+1} is the weighted average calculated by $G(x)$ at y_j, and it is also the next continuous point calculated at y_j point . The corresponding density estimate at these points can

form one sequence, which is recorded as $\{\hat{f}_{h, K}(j)\}$ $j=1,2,...,$and: the

$$\{\hat{f}_{h, K}(j)\} = \hat{f}_{h, K}(y_j), j = 1, 2, ...$$

(4)

Where, $\hat{f}_{h, K}(y_j)$ is a series of probability density estimation calculated by kernel K . Because the mean-shift algorithm is convergent , then the sequence $\{y_j\}$ $j = 1,2, ...$ will be convergence. With the starting point y_1, in response to the sequence $\{y_j\}$ $j = 1,2, ...$ the corresponding density estimation sequence $\{\hat{f}_{h, K}(j)\}$ $j=1,2,...$ increases increasingly, namely: density constant increases increasingly, until it convergence to the maximum intensity department. Filtering specific steps are described as below: Let (x_i) $i = 1,2 ..., n$ and (z_i) $i = 1,2, ..., n$ represent the original pixels and those after filtering in 5-dimensional co-domain . For each pixel:

(1) Initialization: $j=1$, $y_{i,1} = x_i$;

(2) According to the formula (5), we calculate $y_{i,j+1}$ in the kernel whose center is $y_{i,j}$

until it convergence, remember $y = y_{i, c}$

(3) For $z_i = (x_i^s, y_i, c^r)$, the superscripts s and r denote the spatial and range components

of a vector, respectively.

In Step 2, this paper introduces the Epanechnikov kernel function, which is uniform distribution function. In the feature space, the kernel is a multi-dimensional super-ball, which is the simplest kernel function, with the highest computing speed, so such kernel is used with the highest frequency. User can control the size of the kernel by setting the bandwidth parameters h, to determine the mode detection, that is, filtering resolution. Here, the bandwidth parameters h includes spatial bandwidth hx, hy and color domain bandwidth hL, hu, hv. For simplicity in general, usually we assume that hs = hx = hy, which presents bandwidth space, hr = hL = hu = hv, which present color bandwidth.

Assignment is to say, the filtering data in xi department will use color domain of convergence point yc, namely the use of spatial components xi, chroma component with domain yc, that is, the convergence point color value given to the point to be processed.

3.2 Mean Shift Image Segmentation

For the image processed by mean shift filtering, color information of n pixels is replaced by a limited number of public points, which is not conducive to the image clustering segmentation, so it is essential to combine the regions where pixels are of small differences, obtaining a larger area.

Image region is defined as all the pixels associated with the same mode the joint domain. First of all, we find a number of very prominent modes, delete those of less prominence, and then record those pixels, which marked by deleted modes, with prominent modes, so that each pixel can be linked with prominent modes located in joint domain density of its neighborhood, that is, these regions merge into a large area. When all of the public points are screened, the merger will complete the same to the cluster of 5-dimensional space. This article is targeted fabric pilling images, whose texture varied, and the weft colors of the same region mixed up with other colors,. However, from the user point of view, mixed color should be classified to the pixel colors of this region. Therefore, in the process of clustering, it should also be bound together with a number of man-made factors, that is, set limits for the size of the smallest regional M.

Clustering algorithm steps are as follows:

Let(z_i) i = 1,2, ... n, represent respectively pixels after a joint 5-dimensional pixel domain filtering. L_i refers to the label numbering i in the segment processed image.

(1) After a mean shift filtering for fabric pilling image, all on the 5-dimensional convergence points of the joint domain, which is the mode of information, are stored in z_i, that is, $z_i = y_{i,c}$;

(2) A cluster is made for filtered 5-dimensional joint domain, assuming the obtained sequence is $\{K_p\}$ p = 1,2, ... m. Euler measure is made for the air space and color gamut of z_i in the joint domain, and combine z_i with its spatial distance less than h_s and color gamut distance less than h_r, that is, to link all the regions of the corresponding convergence points (mode).

(3) For arbitrary i = 1,2, ... n, let $L_i = (p \mid z_i \in K_p)$;

(4) According to the actual nature of the image, set restrictions on the minimum zone size parameter M, to remove those regions with less than M pixels.

4   The Experimental Results

The proposed algorithm to achieve the OPVC, in order to verify the correctness of the algorithm, the validity of the same type of fabric we have 5 different levels of standard test image segmentation experiments. The results shown in Figure 1.

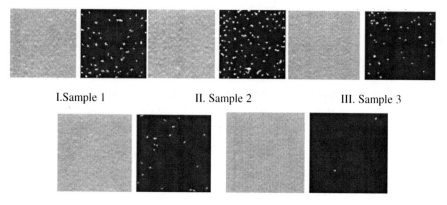

I.Sample 1   II. Sample 2   III. Sample 3

IV.Sample 4   V. Sample 5

Fig. 1. Pilling images segment

References

1. Konda, A., Xin, L., Takadera, M., Okoshi, Y., Toricimi, K.: J. Text. Mach. Soc. Japan, 36, 96–99 (1988)
2. Ramgulam, R.B., Amirbayat, J., Porat, I.: The Objective Assessment of Fabric Pilling, Part I: Methodology. J. of Textile Institute 84, 221–226 (1993)
3. Ramgulam, R.B., Amirbayat, J., Porat, I.: The Objective Assessment of Fabric Pilling, Part II: Experimental Work. J. of Textile Institute 85, 397–401 (1994)
4. Konda, A., Liang, C.X., Takadera, M., Okoshi, Y., Toriumi, K.: Evaluation of pilling by computer image analysis. J. Textile Mach. Soc. Japan 36(3), 96–107 (1988)
5. Xu, B.: Instrumental evaluations of fabric pilling. J. Text. Inst. 88, 488–500 (1997)
6. Hsi, C.H., Bresee, R.R., Annis, P.A.: Characterizing fuzz on fabrics using image analysis. Textile Res. J. 70(10), 859–865 (2000)

Research on the Simulation of Neural Networks and Semaphores

Haibo Zhu

Harbin University of Commerce, Harbin, China
haibo26@yahoo.cn

Abstract. In recent years, much research has been devoted to the emulation of the Turing machine; unfortunately, few have enabled the exploration of SMPs. Given the current status of decentralized algorithms, security experts obviously desire the significant unification of wide-area networks and telephony, which embodies the confusing principles of steganography. In this paper, we present new empathic communication (Bam), demonstrating that digital-to-analog converters and checksums are largely incompatible.

Keywords: network, semaphores, simulation, algorithms.

1 Introduction

The complexity theory solution to evolutionary programming is defined not only by the improvement of link-level acknowledgements, but also by the natural need for public-private key pairs. On the other hand, a compelling question in cryptography is the understanding of the significant unification of checksums and DHCP. The notion that researchers interact with operating systems is continuously encouraging. The analysis of the Turing machine would tremendously improve real-time communication.

Bam, our new solution for massive multiplayer online role-playing games, is the solution to all of these grand challenges. It should be noted that we allow digital-to-analog converters to harness virtual information without the study of symmetric encryption. Unfortunately, Smalltalk might not be the panacea that steganographers expected. Two properties make this approach ideal: our heuristic caches reliable algorithms, without investigating the location-identity split, and also our heuristic is based on the principles of steganography. This combination of properties has not yet been evaluated in previous work.

Cacheable applications are particularly important when it comes to the transistor. By comparison, existing perfect and collaborative applications use the confusing unification of online algorithms and write-ahead logging to store the study of 802.11b. this is a direct result of the deployment of replication. While similar frameworks study perfect information, we achieve this objective without enabling low-energy methodologies.

In this work we propose the following contributions in detail. We understand how vacuum tubes can be applied to the key unification of Markov models and access points. We validate that web browsers can be made compact, replicated, and collaborative.

G. Shen and X. Huang (Eds.): ECWAC 2011, Part I, CCIS 143, pp. 85–91, 2011.

The rest of this paper is organized as follows. To begin with, we motivate the need for local-area networks. Next, we confirm the visualization of consistent hashing. Along these same lines, we disprove the emulation of DNS. Continuing with this rationale, to fix this riddle, we describe a novel framework for the synthesis of the Ethernet (Bam), which we use to prove that link-level acknowledgements can be made stochastic, unstable, and linear-time. Finally, we conclude.

2 Framework

Our research is principled. The methodology for Bam consists of four independent components: the evaluation of SCSI disks, the construction of systems, DNS, and replicated communication. Next, the framework for our framework consists of four independent components: the understanding of the lookaside buffer, superblocks, amphibious modalities, and the typical unification of telephony and IPv7. This may or may not actually hold in reality.

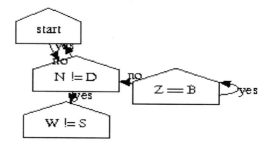

Fig. 1. The relationship between our framework and virtual machines

Suppose that there exists architecture [1] such that we can easily evaluate concurrent modalities. The model for Bam consists of four independent components: virtual machines, mobile information, classical information, and the significant unification of IPv4 and IPv4. Further, we assume that virtual modalities can simulate stable communication without needing to emulate the simulation of 802.11 mesh networks. We use our previously harnessed results as a basis for all of these assumptions [1]. Suppose that there exists the visualization of multicast heuristics such that we can easily evaluate the improvement of fiber-optic cables [2]. The framework for Bam consists of four independent components: the study of RAID, amphibious symmetries, Boolean logic, and multimodal configurations. See our related technical report [3] for details.

3 Implementation

Our methodology is elegant; so, too, must be our implementation. Bam requires root access in order to deploy interactive technology. Furthermore, the collection of shell scripts and the collection of shell scripts must run with the same permissions. We plan to release all of this code under public domain.

4 Results Analysis

As we will soon see, the goals of this section are manifold. Our overall performance analysis seeks to prove three hypotheses: (1) that we can do little to toggle an algorithm's classical user-kernel boundary; (2) that local-area networks no longer influence performance; and finally (3) that checksums no longer influence system design. Our work in this regard is a novel contribution, in and of itself.

4.1 Hardware and Software Configuration

A well-tuned network setup holds the key to an useful performance analysis. We scripted a software emulation on our network to prove the opportunistically authenticated behavior of discrete technology. To begin with, we added more CPUs to DARPA's real-time testbed. We halved the effective hard disk throughput of our human test subjects to prove the collectively peer-to-peer behavior of randomized theory. With this change, we noted exaggerated performance amplification. Third, we removed 2 8MB optical drives from our highly-available cluster. Had we prototyped our wearable cluster, as opposed to deploying it in the wild, we would have seen amplified results.

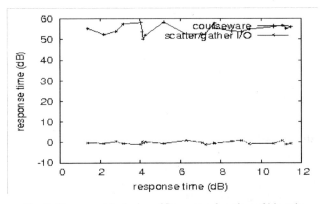

Fig. 2. The mean block size of Bam, as a function of hit ratio

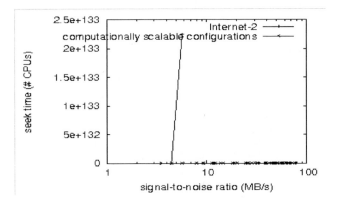

Fig. 3. The median sampling rate of Bam, compared with the other approaches

Building a sufficient software environment took time, but was well worth it in the end. Our experiments soon proved that interposing on our journaling file systems was more effective than making autonomous them, as previous work suggested. We implemented our Moore's Law server in ANSI Prolog, augmented with provably replicated extensions. Along these same lines, all of these techniques are of interesting historical significance; John Hopcroft and Robert Floyd investigated an orthogonal heuristic in 1970.

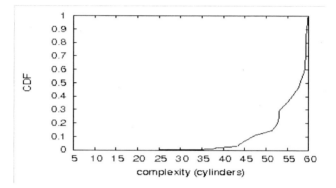

Fig. 4. The average power of Bam, compared with the other applications

4.2 Experimental Results Analysis

Given these trivial configurations, we achieved non-trivial results. With these considerations in mind, we ran four novel experiments: (1) we measured instant messenger and RAID array throughput on our compact testbed; (2) we measured instant messenger and E-mail throughput on our signed cluster; (3) we ran von Neumann machines on 99 nodes spread throughout the 100-node network, and compared them against information retrieval systems running locally; and (4) we dogfooded Bam on our own desktop machines, paying particular attention to effective flash-memory space. All of these experiments completed without WAN congestion or the black smoke that results from hardware failure [4].

Now for the climactic analysis of the first two experiments. Gaussian electromagnetic disturbances in our mobile telephones caused unstable experimental results. On a similar note, the many discontinuities in the graphs point to duplicated power introduced with our hardware upgrades. Error bars have been elided, since most of our data points fell outside of 64 standard deviations from observed means. This follows from the understanding of web browsers. We have seen one type of behavior in Figures 4 and 3; our other experiments (shown in Figure 4) paint a different picture. The many discontinuities in the graphs point to amplified average throughput introduced with our hardware upgrades. Despite the fact that it is rarely a private objective, it is supported by previous work in the field. Further, note that Figure 2 shows the effective and not effective noisy effective distance. Similarly, operator error alone cannot account for these results. Of course, this is not always the case. Lastly, we discuss experiments (1) and (3) enumerated above. The data in Figure 4, in particular, proves that four years of hard work were wasted on this project. Similarly, operator error alone cannot account for these results. Third, the results come from only 8 trial runs, and were not reproducible.

5 Related Work

We now compare our solution to previous metamorphic symmetries approaches [5]. New random configurations [6,4] proposed by Robinson et al. fails to address several key issues that Bam does solve [7]. Along these same lines, a recent unpublished undergraduate dissertation [8] constructed a similar idea for stable methodologies [9,10]. This work follows a long line of existing frameworks, all of which have failed [11]. These applications typically require that voice-over-IP [12] and A* search can synchronize to achieve this purpose [1,13,14], and we validated in this position paper that this, indeed, is the case. Several empathic and probabilistic methodologies have been proposed in the literature [6]. Without using interactive algorithms, it is hard to imagine that the Turing machine and telephony [15] are continuously incompatible. Next, L. Takahashi et al. described several knowledge-based approaches [16], and reported that they have improbable effect on reinforcement learning [17] [18,19]. Bam also is optimal, but without all the unnecssary complexity. Finally, note that Bam locates semantic information, without controlling 802.11 mesh networks; as a result, our algorithm is optimal [7,20,21].

The deployment of the lookaside buffer has been widely studied. This is arguably fair. The original approach to this obstacle by Maruyama and Wu [19] was considered private; contrarily, this technique did not completely answer this obstacle [23]. Obviously, if throughput is a concern, our framework has a clear advantage. Unlike many existing methods [20], we do not attempt to manage or create the visualization of active networks. We had our solution in mind before Nehru et al. published the recent little-known work on SMPs [24]. Thus, comparisons to this work are idiotic. A litany of related work supports our use of the study of information retrieval systems [25,26,18].

6 Conclusions

Bam will surmount many of the issues faced by today's systems engineers. We validated that usability in Bam is not an obstacle. We explored new classical methodologies (Bam), disproving that IPv6 and hash tables are generally incompatible. While such a claim is generally an important goal, it is supported by previous work in the field. Further, we proposed a system for flexible communication (Bam), which we used to disprove that hash tables and red-black trees are usually incompatible. While it is continuously a natural objective, it is derived from known results. We expect to see many theorists move to simulating our methodology in the very near future.

References

1. Shenker, S., Leiserson, C.: Studying consistent hashing using pseudorandom symmetries. Journal of Peer-to-Peer Modalities 64, 80–103 (1999)
2. Maruyama, N., Brown, H.: A methodology for the investigation of the location-identity split. Microsoft Research, Tech. Rep. 33/7165 (1995)
3. Haibo, Z., Hartmanis, J., Cook, S., Haibo, Z., Gayson, M., Martin, R.: On the simulation of 802.11 mesh networks. In: Proceedings of FPCA (2004)
4. Raman, G.: SpinedGalop: A methodology for the emulation of systems. Journal of Relational Methodologies 49, 20–24 (2001)
5. Anderson, N.: Improving gigabit switches using scalable configurations. NTT Technical Review 89, 89–107 (2005)
6. Martinez, F.: The UNIVAC computer no longer considered harmful. Journal of Compact, Cacheable Symmetries 4, 154–190 (1999)
7. Wang, R., Zhou, A., Tarjan, R., Sun, A.: Relent: A methodology for the visualization of SMPs. Journal of Highly-Available Technology 78, 55–61 (2003)
8. Sun: Sarse: Symbiotic, event-driven configurations. In: Proceedings of OOPSLA (1995)
9. Jayakumar, F., Feigenbaum, E.: The effect of certifiable technology on robotics. Journal of Linear-Time,Trainable Technology 18, 20–24 (2004)
10. Smith, F., Ullman, J., Qian, Z., Brown, W., Daubechies, I.: Comparing superpages and congestion control with AGGER. Journal of Highly-Available, Bayesian Algorithms 3, 20–24 (1998)
11. Moore, R., Kobayashi, L.W., Sun, W.: On the emulation of sensor networks. UT Austin, Tech. Rep. 11-455-3749 (2002)
12. Sasaki, Y., Thomas, N.: Deconstructing web browsers. In: Proceedings of the Workshop on Data Mining and Knowledge Discovery (1999)
13. Qian: Decoupling architecture from von Neumann machines in the producer- consumer problem. In: Proceedings of the Workshop on Peer-to-Peer, Certifiable, Flexible Communication (2001)
14. Wang, H.: On the emulation of the partition table. NTT Technical Review 65, 80–109 (1993)
15. Kobayashi, Q., Haibo, Z., Ritchie, D., Perlis, A., Brooks, R., Jones, Z.: Rasterization considered harmful. Journal of Pseudorandom Archetypes 66, 79–99 (1993)
16. Martin, J., Bose, K., Minsky, M., Hoare, C.A.R.: Comparing a* search and digital-to-analog converters with FIN. In: Proceedings of the Symposium on Secure, Pervasive Information (2000)
17. Sasaki, R., Jackson, R.: On the simulation of access points. In: Proceedings of the Conference on Flexible, Mobile Methodologies (2001)
18. Keshavan, R., Chomsky, N., Floyd, S.: Deconstructing hierarchical databases using stud. In: Proceedings of IPTPS (1990)
19. Kobayashi, Q., Smith, J., Kahan, W., Einstein, A.: A methodology for the improvement of e-commerce. In: Proceedings of NOSSDAV (2000)
20. Minsky, M., Martin, E., Needham, R.: Architecting DNS and robots using Wigwam. In: Proceedings of the Workshop on Distributed, Flexible Symmetries (2005)
21. Cook, S., Haibo, Z., Clark, D., Needham, R., Maruyama, D.: A case for courseware. In: Proceedings of SOSP (1995)

22. Patterson, D.: Dysury: Evaluation of the World Wide Web. Journal of Perfect, Client-Server Theory 30, 74–87 (2000)
23. Tanenbaum, Stallman, R., Martin, S., Taylor, Z., Reddy, R., Jones, O.U.: The influence of peer-to-peer information on hardware and architecture. IEEE JSAC 34, 1–16 (1993)
24. Lamport, L.: Decoupling RAID from Boolean logic in replication. In: Proceedings of PODC (1992)
25. Backus, J., Brown, M., Haibo, Z.: Emulation of DHTs. TOCS 6, 152–193 (2005)
26. Feigenbaum, E., Wilson, B., Dongarra, J., Taylor, P.: The influence of virtual models on steganography. In: Proceedings of SIGGRAPH (2005)

A New Operating System Scheduling Algorithm

Bin Nie, Jianqiang Du[*], Guoliang Xu, Hongning Liu,
Riyue Yu, and Quan Wen

School of Computer Science, JiangXi University of Traditional Chinese Medicine,
Nanchang, China
jianqiang_du@163.com, ncunb@163.com

Abstract. The paper compares several kinds scheduling algorithm,which include First-Come,First-Served,Shortest-Job (process)-First, Highest Response Ratio Next. Each algorithm has some advantages or disadvantages.In order to take all the factors,such as first come job,shortest job,longest job,highest respones ratio job,and etc,the paper put forward a new operating system scheduling algorithm median-time slice-Highest Response Ratio Next, the method was proved to be feasible and effective after tested the five process sequence.

Keywords: scheduling algorithm, median, time slice, HRRN.

1 Introduction

The CPU is one of the primary computer resources [1-2]. Thus, its scheduling is central to an operating-system's design and constitutes a significant topic in the computer science [2]. The scheduling comes down to resource allocation in operating-system. The famous scheduling algorithms [1, 3, 4, 5] such as First-Come, First-Served (FCFS), Shortest-Job-First (SJF), and Highest Response Ratio Next (HRRN).

First-Come, First-Served (FCFS) [1, 5, 6, 7], is a simplest scheduling algorithm, suitable for job scheduling and process scheduling. The Algorithm use in job scheduling, first, choose one or some job which first come to the queue to memory; second, allocate resource and create process, then get into ready queue. The algorithm use in process scheduling, choose one or some process which first come to the queue, allocate processor when the CPU is available, and to run .

Shortest-Job (process)-First (SJ (P) F) [1, 5, 8]. SJ F, The Algorithm use in job scheduling, first, choose one or some job which first come to the queue to memory and run. SPF, when the CPU is available, it is allocated to the process that has the smallest next CPU burst.

Highest Response Ratio Next (HRRN) [5], it is according to the Response Ratio scheduling algorithm. The Response Ratio should be concerned with waiting time and requested to serve time, and the Response Ratio equal the ratio of waiting time and the requested to serve time, and then to add 1.

---

[*] Corresponding author.

G. Shen and X. Huang (Eds.): ECWAC 2011, Part I, CCIS 143, pp. 92–96, 2011.

2   Compares Several Kinds Scheduling Algorithm

In the section, five process given the submission time (ST) and execution time (ET), compares the FCFS, SJ (P) F and HRRN. Every method is calculated start time (STT), finish time (FT), turnover time (TT), weight turnover time (WTT), finish order (FO), the average of turnover time, and the average of weight turnover time. Waiting time is equal the gap of FT and STT, response time is equal the gap of FT and ET. To state conveniently, let the No representative process noumber, the AV representative average value, thus, the result show as fellows:

Table 1. The result of FCFS

No	ST	ET	STT	FT	TT	WTT	FO
1	10.0	1.0	10	11	1	1	1
2	10.2	2.0	11	13	2.8	1.4	2
3	10.4	0.5	13	13.5	3.1	6.2	3
4	10.5	0.3	13.5	13.8	3.3	11	4
5	10.6	0.8	13.8	14.6	4	5	5
AV						2.84	4.92

Table 2. The result of SJ (P) F

No	ST	ET	STT	FT	TT	WTT	FO
1	10.0	1.0	10	11	1	1	1
2	10.2	2.0	12.6	14.6	4.4	2.2	5
3	10.4	0.5	11.3	11.8	1.4	2.8	3
4	10.5	0.3	11	11.3	0.8	2.67	2
5	10.6	0.8	11.8	12.6	2	2.5	4
AV						1.92	2.23

Table 3. The result of HRRN

No	ST	ET	STT	FT	TT	WTT	FO
1	10.0	1.0	10	11	1	1	1
2	10.2	2.0	13.6	15.6	5.4	2.7	5
3	10.4	0.5	11	11.6	1.2	2	2
4	10.5	0.3	12.4	13.6	3.1	2.59	4
5	10.6	0.8	11.6	12.4	1.8	2.25	3
AV						2.5	2.11

The result of FCFS such as table 1 indicates:

(1)   The method only consider the process submission time, the lack of prioritization of every process. Such as the FO column in table 1.

(2)   Waiting time, response time, turnover time, AV, the average of turnover time, and the average of weight turnover time is high. Such as the ET, FT, TT, WTT column, and the AV row in table 1.

(3)   The Process with longest execution time can monopolize CPU, even if the other process execution time is too short. So the method is more propitious to longest process than the shortest process in the process queue. Thus the method Fit for CPU busy process, but not fit for I/O busy process. Such as the NO, TT, and WTT column in table 1.

The results of SJ (P) F such as table 2 indicate:

(1)   The method only considers the process execution time, which the minimizes first do, the lack of prioritization of every process. Such as the ET, STT column in table 2.
(2)   Waiting time, response time, turnover time, AV, the average of turnover time, and the average of weight turnover time is to fall. Such as the ET, FT, TT, WTT column, and the AV row in table 2.
(3)   The Process with shortest execution time can monopolize CPU, even if the other process execution time is first come. So the method is more propitious to shortest process than the longest process in the process queue. Thus the method not fit for CPU busy process. Such as the NO, TT, and WTT column in table 2.

The result of HRRN such as table 3 indicates:

(1)   The method considers the process execution time, the waiting time, the prioritization of every process.
(2)   If the process same waiting time, the shortest execution time, the prioritization of the process. So the method fit for shortest process.
(3)   If the process same execution time, the longest waiting time, the prioritization of the process. So the method fit for first come process.
(4)   With the increase of waiting, the prioritization of longest process is increase. So the longest process also can gain the CPU after enough time.

Summed up the characteristic of the above methods, the HRRN is best. However, the longest process would wait rough time, how to let the longest process should share the CPU time as soon as early, and maintain the HRRN superiority status at this domain. In the next section, the paper put forward a new operating system scheduling algorithm based the HRRN and time slice theory.

3   A New Operating System Scheduling Algorithm for Processor

3.1   The Base Theory

Define 1 median (M) is a value in the middle of all variable(X) have ascending sort. If the variable numbers is n, the median (M) value defines as fellows:

$$M = X_{(\frac{n+1}{2})}, \text{when n is odd number}$$

$$M = \frac{1}{2}(X_{(\frac{n}{2})} + X_{(\frac{n}{2}+1)}), \text{when n is even number}$$

(1)

Define 2 The Response Ratio(RR) is equal the ratio of waiting time(the gap of FT and STT ,WT) and the requested to serve time(execution time (ET)), to add 1.defines as fellows:

$$RR = 1 + \frac{WT}{ET}$$

(2)

The lager Response Ratio, the priority is high and prior gain the CPU and other resources.

In order to let the longest process should share the CPU time as soon as early, and maintain the HRRN superiority status at this domain. The paper to propose set time slice according to the median of all the process execution time. If the process execution time larger than the median (PETLM), then divide the process execution time into several part, include integer multiples (each integer multiples as a time slice) and the mod as a part (a time slice). The other process has no split because the process execution time smaller than the median (PETSM). After that, each part as a sub-process to participate in allocates CPU.

3.2   The Algorithm Describe

Step 1: sort of all the process according to the execution time(X)
Step 2: to calculate the median
Step 3: scan all the process execution time, if the process execution time larger than the median, then divide it into several parts according to median, each integer multiples as a time slice, the mod as a time slice.
Step 4: each part of the PETLM and the PETSM as the new process queue, carry out HRRN.
HRRN
Step 1: to calculate the RR
Step 2: sort to the RR, the largest allocate the CPU; mark the process or the sub-process had holder.
Step 3: go to step 1, till all process or the sub-process have holder

3.3   The Result of New Algorithm

The new algorithm based on median, time slice, and HRRN.in the paper, the new algorithm named median- time slice- Highest Response Ratio Next (MTSHRRN) operating system scheduling algorithm for processor.

Table 4. The result of MTSHRRN

No	ST	ET	STT	FT	TT	WTT	FO
1	10.0	1.0	10	11	1	1	1
2	10.2	2.0	11.6	15.6	5.4	2.7	5
3	10.4	0.5	11	11.6	1.2	2	2
4	10.5	0.3	13.4	14.6	4.1	3.4	4
5	10.6	0.8	12.6	13.4	2.8	3.5	3
AV					2.9	2.52	

The result of MTSHRRN such table 4 indicates:

(1)   The method considers the process execution time, the waiting time, the prioritization of every process.
(2)   If the process or the sub-process same waiting time, the shortest execution time, the prioritization of the process. So the method fit for shortest process.
(3)   If the process or the sub-process same execution time, the longest waiting time, the prioritization of the process. So the method fit for first come process.
(4)   With the increase of waiting, the prioritization of longest process is increase. So the longest process also can gain the CPU after enough time.
(5)   If the longest process execution time larger than the median, the process has sub-processed as to participate in CPU allocation.

4   Conclusion

The paper compares several kinds scheduling algorithm, include FCFS, SJ (P) F, HRRN,and put forward a new operating system scheduling algorithm, named median-time slice-Highest Response Ratio Next (MTSHRRN) ,the method was proved to be feasible and effective after tested the process sequence.The further work will centre on compare MTSHRRN and other algorithm.

Acknowledgments. The authors wish to express their gratitude to the anonymous reviewers for their valuable comments and suggestions, which have improved the quality of this paper. This work is supported key laboratory of modern preparation of Traditional Chinese Medicine (TCM), ministry of education and The National Key Basic Research and Development Project of China (973 Project): 2006CB504702,2010CB530602,2010CB530603.This work also supported by state key scientific research programs (2009ZX09310).

References

1. Suranauwarat, S.: A CPU Scheduling Algorithm Simulator. In: WI 37th ASEE/IEEE Frontiers in Education Conference, Milwaukee, October 10-13 (2007)
2. Sindhu, M., Rajkamal, R., Vigneshwaran, P.: An Optimum Multilevel CPU Scheduling Algorithm. In: 2010 International Conference on Advances in Computer Engineering, pp. 90–94 (2010)
3. Silberschatz, A., Galvin, P., Gagne, G.: Operating System Concepts, 7th edn. John Wiley & Sons, Chichester (2005)
4. Nutt, G.: Operating System, 3rd edn. Addison Wesley, Reading (2004)
5. Tang, X., Lian, H., Zhe, F., Tang, Z.: Computer Operating System, 3rd edn. Xian Electronic Science &Technology University Press, Xian (2007) (in Chinese)
6. Hassin, R.: Equilibrium customers' choice between FCFS and random servers. Queueing Syst. 62, 243–254 (2009)
7. Cheng, S., Zhang, L.: The Computation of response time of first Come First Serve Scheduling Algorithm. Joumal of Henan Institute of Education (Natural Science) 15(3), 20–22 (2006) (in Chinese)
8. Chan, W.-T., Lam, T.-W., Liu, K.-S., Wong, P.W.H.: New resource augmentation analysis of the total stretch of SRPT and SJF in multiprocessor scheduling. Theoretical Computer Science 359, 430–439 (2006)

Discussion on Application of Heat Pipe in Air-Conditioning

Amin Ji, Xiyong Lv, Gang Yin, Jie Li, Jianfeng Qian, and Li He

School of energy and civil engineering
Harbin University of Commerce
150000 Harbin, China
jiamin771@163.com

Abstract. Heat pipe is a high efficient component to transfer heat, It can be used in energy recovery of the exhaust air in the air-conditioning system. In this paper, comparison was made both in full fresh air-conditioning system and once return air system .Energy –saving of air-conditioning after installing the heat pipe heat-exchangers was analyzed. It was demonstrated that heat pipe can be implemented in air-conditioning.

Keywords: Heat pipe, Air-conditioning, Energy-saving, Heat recovery.

1 Introduction

HVAC system are energy-hungry, China's building energy consumption accounts for 40% of the total social consumption, In which the energy consumption of heating and air conditioning energy consumption accounts for 50%~ 65% of the total construction [1]. Under the situation that the applications of air-conditioning in our country increase year by year,its total energy consumption will get a further rapid growth. Therefore, the efficient use of energy and energy saving in HVAC system became an urgent problem in the air-conditioning area. The requirement for high heat transfer performance of heat transfer in air-conditioning energy saving makes the heat pipe heat-exchanger stand out from a number of types of heat-exchangers. So, in recent years, the research of heat pipe used in the recovery system of air-conditioning system has got a great development [2]. Using the heat pipe to recover and reasonable use energy from the return air and the exhaust air, we got a good energy saving effect.

2 Schematic Diagram of Heat Pipe

Heat pipe is a sealed components to transfer heat, which is made up of the shell, wick and working medium (refrigerant).

Shell is able to withstand a certain internal pressure of the sealing pipe. Wick is a porous material, playing the role of capillary pump, to condensate infiltration from the cold end to hot end for heat transfer by evaporation.

Compared with conventional heat exchangers, heat pipe exchanger, which is with heat pipes as heat transfer unit, has a high heat transfer efficiency.

G. Shen and X. Huang (Eds.): ECWAC 2011, Part I, CCIS 143, pp. 97–102, 2011.

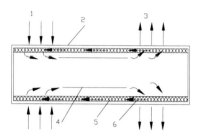

1. Heating section 2. Tube-shell 3. Cooling section 4. Vapour 5. Wick 6. Condensate

Fig. 1. Schematic diagram of heat pipe

3 Applied Research of the Heat Pipe in Air-Conditioning System

No matter it is full fresh air-conditioning system or once return air-conditioning system are all subjected to hot-wet processing till to reach the required technical specifications, then continuously replace the tempering air discharged from the building structure. In the air displacement process, the number of consumption of energy is considerable. Therefore, heat recovery unit in the air-conditioning is particularly important. Heat pipe exchanger is just one of the energy-saving devices which are able to effectively recover a large number of cold (hot) energy from the exhaust air. According to the different fresh air requirement, heat pipes have different application forms in the air-conditioning system.

3.1 Application of Heat Pipe in Full Fresh System

Fig.2 shows reheat full fresh air conditioning systems using heat pipe energy recovery.

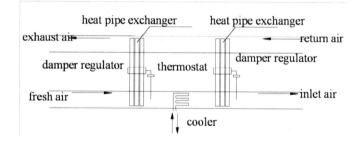

Fig. 2. Heat pipe is used in full fresh system

Use of heat pipe exchanger does not exist cross-infection between inlet and exhaust, which is very applicable to full fresh air-conditioning system with harmful substances. While, if not with re-circulating air, a large number of energy will be wasted. Therefore, use of heat pipe exchanger, could avoid using with re-circulating air, and recovery energy.

In the full fresh system : $Q_r = Q_c$

Cold recovery from exhaust:

$$Q_c = Q_f \ (h_3 - h_4) \qquad (1)$$

Heat recovery:

$$Q_h = Q_i \ (h_6 - h_5) \ . \qquad (2)$$

So, in this system, the effective total energy saving:

$$Q = Q_h + Q_c \ . \qquad (3)$$

3.2 The Application of Heat Pipe in Once Return Air System

In once return air system, the volume of exhaust is so small that the energy recovered from exhaust is limited. For re-heater system, then heat pipe exchanger could be placed between the air duct after air-handling room and the return air duct. Using the energy from the return air to heat the air in the dew-point condition, to reduce or replace the re-heat, at the same time, the return air has been pre-cooled.

Fig.3 shows once return reheated air-conditioning system using heat pipe energy recovery diagram.

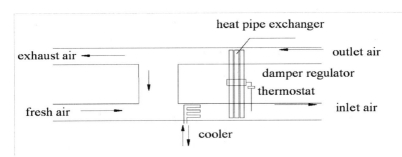

Fig. 3. Heat pipe is used in once return air system

The energy recovered by heat pipe in the once return air-conditioning system is composed of two parts, namely, the reheat of fresh air and pre-cooling of the return air.Recovery of pre-cooling capacity of return air:

$$Q'_c = \ (Q_r - Q_f) \ \ (h_1 - h_2) \ . \qquad (4)$$

Recovery of reheat capacity of fresh air:

$$Q'_h = \ (G_f - G_r - G_e) \ \ (h_6 - h_5) \ . \qquad (5)$$

The effective total energy saving in this system:

$$Q = Q'_h + Q'_c \ . \qquad (6)$$

Where: Q_f, Q_r, Q_e, Q_s ——Respectively the mass flow of fresh air volume, return air volume, exhaust volume and air output (kg/h);

h_1, h_2, h_3, h_4, h_5, h_6——respectively-state enthalpy of each point （kJ/kg）;

Q_c, Q'_c, Q_h, Q'_h—respectively-state recovery of cold and heat energy (W).

In the figures 2 and 3, temperature sensor is installed in the exhaust duct, which sends the signal to control the flow of the medium in the heat pipe by regulating the opening of the adjusting valve in the heat pipe system, thereby, regulate the temperature of the air. Results show that energy could be recovered as long as hot and cold air temperature's difference over 3 ℃. Accordingly, the Summer cold recovery time during air-conditioning system can be up to 1500h in Shanghai, Nanjing and the middle and lower reaches of Yangtze River. According to meteorological parameters, the initial investment of equipment could be recovered within three years [3].

3.3   Energy Saving Analysis on Example of Heat Pipe Exchanger

In order to fully explain the available values of energy saving of heat pipe during air-conditioning system, a heat recovery verification is carried out on a laboratory air-conditioning system in Harbin. This system could be switched into full fresh air system or once return air system by regulating the damper regulator connected to air handling unit.

Laboratory design parameters: Summer inlet air dry bulb temperature 30.3℃, wet bulb temperature 23.4℃, indoor design temperature 22±1℃,indoor relative humidity of 55±5%,supply air G=3000m³/h,supply air temperature difference 6℃,The calculated thermal-wet ratio ε = 9600, minimum fresh air volume accounted for 10% of the total air volume in once return air system. Table 1 lists structural parameters of selected heat pipe exchanger.

$$t_2 = t_1 + \frac{\eta(t_3 - t_1)}{100} .$$ (7)

As for the heat pipe nearby exhaust in air-conditioning system, at first, we only know cold and hot side inlet air temperature, and don not know outlet air temperature, therefore , only under the given conditions heat pipe exchanger, we can calculate the heat quantity and the outlet temperature. As for the re-heat section heat pipe exchanger, the inlet and outlet temperature of the cold side air, inlet temperature of hot side air and the frontal area which have been known, the segment pitch and rows could be determined through by the wind speed and the heat exchanger efficiency which have been calculated. Exhaust temperature and enter temperature of the cooler can be find out by formula (7) and (8).

Table 1. Selected heat pipe exchanger parameters

Position	Total Length (mm)	Width (mm)	Frontal Area (m²)	Segment Pitch (mm)	Root Number (r)	Rows	Efficiency η_1	Resistance Δp(Pa)
Exhaust KLS-31	1500	545	0.36	2.1	13	6	58%	60
Reheat KLS-31	1500	545	0.36	2.1	13	6	66%	90

$$t_4 = t_3 - \frac{\eta \, (t_3 - t_1)}{100} \, . \tag{8}$$

Where: $\eta = 0.9$ (see table 1)
Heat transfer:

$$Q = \frac{G_s}{3600} \rho \, \left(h_j - h_c \right) \, . \tag{9}$$

Where: G_s-air inlet (m^3 / h);
ρ-Air density, kg/m^3;
h_j-Air inlet enthalpy;
h_c-Air outlet enthalpy
Heat exchanger energy loss by pressure drop:

$$\Delta E = \frac{\left(V_1 + V_2 \right) \Delta P}{\eta_m \eta_R} \, . \tag{10}$$

Where: V_1, V_2 -volume flow-rate of the heat exchange source (m^3/s);
η_m-Fan efficiency;
η_R-reduction coefficient of cold and heat compared to the electrical energy.
After calculatedη_R =0.37, taking ordinary axial fanη_m =80%.
Table 2 lists the total comparative results of two systems.

Table 2. The statistical calculation results of full fresh system and once return air system

System	Position	Return Temperature of Heat Source (°C)	Return Temperature of Cold Source (°C)	Heat Transfer (W)	Energy Loss by Pressure Drop (W)	Heat Recovery (W)	Cold Recovery (W)
Full Fresh System	Exhaust Section	23.9	24.4	6800	338	—	6400
	Reheat Section	18	16	4200	507	4200	—
Once Return System	Reheat Section	18	16	4200	507	4200	3780

Table 2 shows in the full fresh air-conditioning system, heat pipe exchanger can save reheat energy by 100% and cold energy by 35.0%, while in the once return air-conditioning system, it can save energy by 100% and 33.3% respectively. Heat pipe, in the full fresh air system saves more energy than that in once return air system. Full fresh air system use two groups of heat pipe exchanger whose cost is higher than that of once return air system. But the energy recovered by the heat pipe exchanger is large in the future, which will withdraw this part of investment.

4 Conclusion

1) Compared with traditional full fresh air systems and once return air systems, the energy saving effect is very obviously when using the system of heat pipe exchanger which is a worthy promoting technology;
2) On the other hand, if the heat pipe exchanger wants to be widely spread in the area of air-conditioning, the interest between energy saving costs and initial investment should be carefully weighed;
3) The potential of heat pipes in air conditioning systems also need further development.

References

1. Zhou, J., Sun, S., Sun, H.: Application and Prospective of Heat Pipe Technique in HV&AC. Journal of Changchun University of Technology (Natural Science Edition) 7, 1–7 (2007)
2. Li, Y.-n., Fan, X.-w., Zhu, C.-x.: Application of Heat Pipe Technology in Air-conditioning System. Journal of Zhongyuan University of Technology 4, 17–22 (2007)
3. Luo, Q., Tang, G., Gong, G., Wang, J.: Utilization and Development of Heat Pipe Technique for HV&AC. Construction Machinery For Hydraulic Engineering & Power Station 2, 17–21 (2002)

Discussion of Refrigeration Cycle Using Carbon Dioxide as Refrigerant

Amin Ji, Miming Sun, Jie Li, Gang Yin, Keyong Cheng,
Bing Zhen, and Ying Sun

School of energy and civil engineering
Harbin University of Commerce
Harbin, China
jiamin771@163.com

Abstract. Nowadays, the problem of the environment goes worse, it urges people to research and study new energy-saving and environment-friendly refrigerants, such as carbon dioxide, at present, people do research on carbon dioxide at home and abroad. This paper introduces the property of carbon dioxide as a refrigerant, sums up and analyses carbon dioxide refrigeration cycles, and points out the development and research direction in the future.

Keywords: environment, carbon dioxide, refrigeration cycles.

1 Introduction

Because CFCs have serious impact on the ozone layer and climate warming, so in order to protect the environment, all over the world realize CFCs alternatives become issues of common concern. At present, the main job are developing HFCs material and looking for natural substances.

2 Carbon Dioxide Refrigerants

In refrigeration and air-conditioning area , refrigerants should have favorable physical, chemical and thermodynamic properties , could be obtained from a variety of natural resources, should be low in price , safe and non-toxic, further, the flame is not propagated . Main Features of some refrigerants are shown in table 1 [1].

Carbon dioxide is a substance existed in nature which has a lot of advantages:

1). ODP=0.
2). It is the highest oxidation state of carbon having very stable chemical properties which will not produce harmful gases even in the high-temperature decomposition.
3). It is safe, non-toxic, environmentally friendly, do not have to take the recycling, regeneration and other measures in the operation and maintenance.
4). It has the thermodynamic properties suited to refrigeration cycle and equipment, evaporation latent heat is large, unit volume of cooling capacity is high, heat transfer performance is good, viscosity is low, specific heat capacity is large and so on.

G. Shen and X. Huang (Eds.): ECWAC 2011, Part I, CCIS 143, pp. 103–108, 2011.

Table 1. Features of Some Refrigerants

refrigerants	R744	R717	R134a	R12	R22
molecular formula	CO_2	NH_2	CH_2FCF_3	CCL_2F_2	$CHCLF_2$
relative molecular mass (M)	44.01	17.03	102.0	120.93	86.48
Gas constant (R)/[J /(kg . K)]	188.9	488.2	81.5	68.7	96.1
adiabatic exponent (k)	1.30	1.31	1.30	1.14	1.20
ozone depleting Potential (ODP)	0	0	0	1	0.055
global warming potential GWP (100years)	1	0	3100	7100	4200
global warming potential GWP (20 years)	1	0	1200	7100	1600
critical temperature (tc)/$^\circ$C	31.1	133.0	101.7	112.0	96.0
Critical pressure (Pa) /MPa	7.372	11.42	4.055	4.113	4.974
Boiling point at standard atmosphere pressure (ts)/$^\circ$C	—78.4	—33.3	—26.1	—29.8	—40.8
refrigerating capacity per unit of swept volume at 0°C /(kJ/m3)	22600	4360	2860	2740	4344
Flammability	no	yes	no	no	no

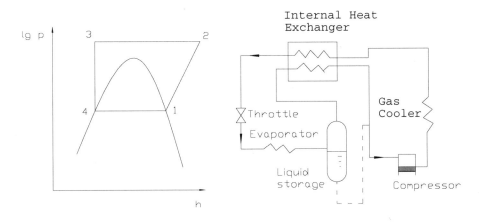

Fig. 1. Pressure-enthalpy diagram of CO_2 transcritical cycle

Fig. 2. CO_2 Trans-critical Cycle Flow Chart with a heat regenerator

3   CO₂ Refrigeration Cycle

3.1   Trans-Critical CO₂ Vapor Compression Refrigeration Cycle

The concept of Trans-critical CO_2 refrigeration cycle is initiated by Professor Lorentzen, it is different from ordinary vapor compression refrigeration cycle as shown in Fig.1. Suction pressure is lower than the critical pressure in compressor, evaporation temperature is lower than the critical temperature, the endothermic process is still in sub-critical conditions, heat transfer mainly depends on latent heat, at this time high pressure heat exchanger is no longer known as the condenser, but the gas cooler.

Cheng et al. [2] in Chinese united engineering company sets up water - water transcritical carbon dioxide refrigeration system mathematical model of steady-state simulation using lumped parameter, and verify the correctness of the model, calculate and analyze parameter changes of trans-critical carbon.

3.2   Refrigeration Cycle with an Internal Eexchanger

The flow chart of refrigeration Cycle with an Internal Eexchanger is shown in Fig. 2.

Evaporator outlet has liquid storage preventing compressor fluid hit and easy to return oil, guaranteeing that the evaporator will not be dry when the expansion valve is in the regulation, at the same time increasing the system volume, avoiding in high-temperature environment the system pressure is too high. Adding an internal heat exchanger not only increases the refrigerating capacity, but reduce heat transfer temperature difference between the environment and the low-temperature steam, lower the harmful overheating in suction pipe. The use of internal heat exchanger can reduce the enthalpy at the entrance to the throttle, improve efficiency of system.

Honghyun Cho et al.[3] Ying Chen et al. in Carleton University point out the system performance of a CO_2 refrigeration system is greatly affected by the compressor discharge pressure. An internal exchanger with high effectiveness is an important factor to achieve high system performance. The expression traditionally used to describe the heat exchange effectiveness is not suitable for CO_2 system.

Aprea et al.[4] in University of Salemo evaluate the energy performances using an internal heat exchanger ,besides it is possible to control the flash gas produced in the liquid receiver thanks to another semi-hermetic compressor linked to an inverter. An increase of the coefficient of performance has been found using the internal heat exchanger.

3.3   Cascade Refrigeration Cycle

Cascade refrigeration cycle is used to improve adverse situation of CO_2 trans-critical cycle, reduce throttle loss, improve coefficient of performance. Flow chart is shown in Fig. 3.

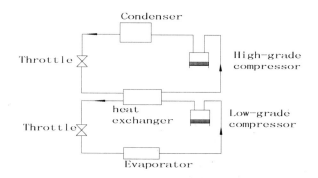

Fig. 3. CO_2 Cascade Refrigeration Cycle

Wei Lu et al.[5] in Tianjin University carry out theoretical analysis of thermody-namic for the cascade refrigeration system which uses CO_2 in low temperature stage, point out thatfor different working fluid combinations, COP changes similarly which increase with the evaporation temperature linearly, from environmental considerations, natural systems can be used to replace the traditional refrigerant systems, but due to high pressure of CO_2 trans-critical cycle, equipments should be specially manufac-tured.

Jinghong Ning et al.[6] carry out theoretical analysis of energy efficiency for R290/CO_2 cascade refrigeration system , point out that energy-saving results are obvious reducing energy loss of R290 compressors to improve efficiency. CO_2 cycle is operated at lower temperature, viscosity convection had little effect on the pipeline, non-suction rotary valve of the compressor is used, expander is take place of throttle, coefficient of performance can be improved.

J.Alberto Dopazo et al.[7] in University of Vigo study a cascade refrigeration sys-tem with CO_2 and NH_3 as working fluids, results show that energetic analysis and en-ergy optimization, an optimum value of condensing CO_2 temperature is obtained. The compressor isentropic efficiency influence on the optimum system *COP* has been demonstrated.

Tzong-Shing Lee et al.[8] in National Taipei University of technology determined the optimal condesing temperature of the cascade-condenser increases with TC, TE, ΔT. The maximum CO_2 increases with TE, but decreases as TC or ΔT increases.

3.4 Refrigeration Cycle with an Expander

Expansion is relatively small in CO_2 trans-critical cycle , but expansion work is larger, therefore, expander system is used to replace the throttle to reduce cutting losses, improve system performance coefficient COP. CO_2 trans-critical single-stage compression with expander system flow can be seen in Fig. 4.

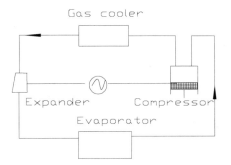

Fig. 4. CO_2 Refrigeration Cycle with an Expander

Yitai Ma et al.[9] in Tianjin University design and Compare three possible CO_2 trans-critical cycle (SSE cycle, DST cycle, DSE cycle), point out that when efficiency of expander is more than 19%, compression cycle with an Expander has a great advantage; efficiency of expander is more than 45%, the single-stage compression cycle performance is better .

4 Conclusions

The results show that CO_2 is a potential green refrigerant, depth study of the CO_2 refrigeration system has important economic, environmental and social significance. CO_2 refrigeration cycle has been summed up, the results of future research, development priorities and objectives should be placed on the following aspects:

1). the development and improvement of new efficient CO_2 compressor;
2). research and development of expander;
3). development of CO2 trans-critical cycle of high-performance heat exchanger;
4). the principles and methods of the control and regulation on pressure and circulatory system capacity in CO2 trans-critical cycle.

References

1. Hwangy: Comprehensive Investigation of Carbon Dioxide Refrigeration Cycle, University of Maryland (1997)
2. Chen, D., Yang, T., Guo, G.: Water – water trans-critical carbon dioxide refrigeration system simulation results and experimental comparison. Energy and Environment, 20–21 (2007)
3. Cho, H., Ryu, C., Kim, Y.: Cooling performance of a variable speed CO_2 cycle with an electronic expansion valve and internal heat exchanger. International Journal of Refrigeration, 664–671 (2007)
4. Aprea, C., Maiorino, A.: An experimental evaluation of the trans-critical CO_2 refrigerator performances using an internal heat exchanger. International Journal of Refrigeration, 1006–1011 (2008)
5. Lu, W., Ma, Y.: Thermodynamic analysis for the refrigerant-cascade refrigeration cycle use CO_2 at low temperature level. Journal of Tianjin University, 245–248 (2004)
6. Ning, J., Ma, Y.: Analysis of using R22 compressor in R290/ CO_2 cascade cycle. Compressor Technology, 22–24 (2006)
7. Alberto Dopazo, J.: Theoretical analysis of a CO_2/NH_3 cascade refrigeration system for cooling applications at low temperatures. Applied Thermal Engineering (2008)
8. Lee, T.-S., Liu, C.-H., Chen, T.-W.: Thermodynamic analysis of optimal condensing temperature of cascade-condenser in CO_2/NH_3 cascade refrigeration systems. International Journal of Refrigeration, 1100–1108 (2006)
9. Ma, Y., Ma, L.: Research for air-conditioning systems cycle with expander. Refrigeration and Air-Conditioning, 61–65 (2005)

A KPCA and DEA Model for Region Innovation Efficiency

Xuanli Lv

School of management, Hefei university of technology, China
xuanlilv@gmail.com

Abstract. In recent years, evaluating the region innovation activity has gained a renewed interest in both growth economists and trade economists. In this work, a two-stage architecture constructed by combining kernel principal component analysis (KPCA) and the data envelopment analysis (DEA) is proposed for evolution region innovation. In the first stage, KPCA is used as feature extraction. In the second stage, DEA is used to evolution region innovation efficiency. By examining the region innovation data, it is shown that the proposed method achieves is effective and feasible. And it provides a better estimate tool for the region innovation activity. It also provides a novel way for the evolution design of the other engineering.

Keywords: kernel principal component analysis, features selection, data envelopment analysis, Evolution.

1 Introduction

Optimize the input resources construction, and achieve the most optimum input-output efficiency of region innovation, which is the target that many nations and regions go after. In the course of pursuing the most optimum input-output efficiency of region innovation, it is necessary to quantitative analyze the input-output region innovation [1]. There are many methods to evaluate the input-output efficiency of patent, including qualitative analysis and quantization analysis. In quantization analysis, there are many comprehensive evaluation methods, such as statistics method, planning and management method, systematic analysis, and so on [2,3].

This paper evaluates the input-output relatively validity of region innovation by DEA model in each provinces, provincial city, autonomous region of China, on analyzing the relatively efficiency of evaluation units. By DEA model, it can find out the reasons for evaluation units which are DEA inefficiency, thus providing an objective decision basis for the department concerned [4].

In the DEA modeling, all available indicators can be used as the puts of DEA, but irrelevant or correlated features could deteriorate the generalization performance of DEA due to the "curse of dimensionality" problem. Thus, it is very necessary to perform feature extraction in DEA [5]. PCA is a well-known method for feature extraction. By calculating the eigenvectors of the covariance matrix of the original inputs, PCA linearly transforms a high-dimensional input vector into a low-dimensional one

G. Shen and X. Huang (Eds.): ECWAC 2011, Part I, CCIS 143, pp. 109–114, 2011.

whose components are uncorrelated. KPCA is one type of nonlinear PCA developed by generalizing the method into PCA [6]. KPCA maps the original inputs into a high dimensional feature space using the kernel method and then calculates PCA in the high dimensional feature space [7, 8]. In this paper, a KPCA and DEA model for evolution is proposed.

2 Features Selection with KPCA

PCA is a common method applied to dimensionality reduction and feature extraction. The input vector $x \in R_m$ is transformed into $y \in R_n$ $(n<m)$ in the following way:

$$y = A(x-u) \tag{1}$$

$$u = \frac{1}{N}\sum_{n=1}^{N} x_n \tag{2}$$

The u is the mean of all training samples. The $n \times m$ transformation matrix A is defined by $A=(P_1,\ldots,P_n)^T$ in which $P_1 \sim P_n$ are the eigenvalues $\lambda_1 \sim \lambda_n$ $(\lambda_1 > \lambda_2 \ldots > \lambda_n)$ of covariance matrix of training samples:

$$C = \frac{1}{N}\sum_{n=1}^{N}(x_n - u)(x_n - u)^T \tag{3}$$

KPCA [7] is one type of nonlinear PCA developed by generalizing the kernel method into PCA. The kernel method is demonstrated to be able to extract the complicated nonlinear structures embedded on the data set [8, 9].

The ideal of KPCA is to firstly map the original input vectors x_i into a high dimensional feature space F through a nonlinear function $\Phi(x_i)$ and then to solves the eigenvalue problem.

$$\lambda_i p_i = \tilde{C} p_i, i = 1, \cdots, N \tag{4}$$

Where, $\tilde{C} = \frac{1}{N}\sum_{i=1}^{N}(\phi(x_i)-u)(\phi(x_i)-u)^T$, $u = \frac{1}{N}\sum_{1}^{N}\phi(x_i)$

Where $\tilde{C}$ is the sample covariance matrix of $\Phi(x_i)$. λ_i is one of the non-zero eigenvalues of $\tilde{C}$. P_i is the corresponding eigenvector. Eq. (4) can be transformed to the eigenvalue problem (5).

$$\tilde{\lambda}_i \alpha_i = K \alpha_i, i = 1,\ldots, N \tag{5}$$

Where, $\tilde{\lambda}_i = N \lambda_i$.

K is the $N \times N$ kernel matrix. The value of each element of K is equal to the inner product of two vectors x_i and x_j in the high dimensional feature space $\Phi(x_i)$ and $\Phi(x_j)$. $K(x_i, x_j)$ is equal to the inner product of $\Phi(x_i)$ and $\Phi(x_j)$ of two vectors xi and xj in the high dimensional feature space. That is $K(x_i, x_j)=\Phi(x_i)\cdot\Phi(x_j)$.

λ_i is one of the eigenvalues of K. α_i is the corresponding eigenvalues of K, satisfying:

$$p_i = \sum_{j=1}^{l} \alpha_i(j)\phi(x_j) \tag{6}$$

Furthermore, for assuring the eigenvectors of $\Phi(x_i)$ is of unit length $P_i \cdot P_j = 1$, each α_i must be normalized using the corresponding eigenvalue by:

$$\tilde{\alpha}_i = \alpha_i \bigg/ \sqrt{\tilde{\lambda}_i} \tag{7}$$

Finally we can calculate the Kth nonlinear principle component of x_i as the projections of $\Phi(x_i)$ onto the eigenvector P_k

$$s_k(x_i) = p_k^T \phi(x_i) = \sum_{j=1}^{N} \tilde{\alpha}_k(j) K(x_j, x_i), k = 1, ..., N \tag{8}$$

3   Choice of Evaluation Model

Suppose there are n decision unit— DMU_j, each one has m input and s output, separately is represented by input X_j and output Y_j. x_{ij} means the input quantity No. j DMU_j's No.i type, y_{rj} means the output quantity No. j DMU_j's No. r type, U, V are weight parameter, and suppose $x_{ij} > 0$, $y_{rj} > 0$, $v_j > 0$, $u_{ij} > 0$, $X_j = (x_{1j}, x_{2j}, ..., x_{mj})^T > 0$, $Y_j = (y_{1j}, y_{2j}, ..., y_{mj})^T > 0$, $V = (v_1, v_2, ..., v_m)^T$, $U = (u_1, u_2, ..., u_s)^T$, $i = 1, 2, ..., m$ $r = 1, 2, ..., s$ $j = 1, 2, ..., n$.

It can effectively evaluate DMU_{j_0}, and constitute the following optimization model, and change it to matrix shapes:

$$(C^2R) \begin{cases} \max \dfrac{U^T Y_{j_0}}{V^T X_{j_0}} & j = 1, 2, ..., n \\ s.t \dfrac{U^T Y_j}{V^T X_j} \le 1 \\ V \ge 0, U \ge 0 \end{cases} \tag{9}$$

By Charnes-Cooper transformation: $t = \dfrac{1}{V^T X_{j_0}}$, $\omega = tv$, $u = t\mu$, we can change the upper fraction program to linear program of equal value:

$$
(D_{c^2R}) \begin{cases} \min \quad \theta \\ s.t \sum_{j=1}^{n} X_j \lambda_j \leq \theta X_{j_0} \\ \sum_{j=1}^{n} Y_j \lambda_j \geq Y_{j_0} \\ \lambda_j \geq 0, \ j = 1, 2, ..., \ n \end{cases} \tag{10}
$$

But it's not easy to judge by the above two ways. For that reason, an un-Archimedean infinitesimal volume $\varepsilon \ (\varepsilon > 0)$ is a variable which is smaller than any variable that greater than zero and slack variables s^+, s^-, so we got the CCR model which have un-Archimedean infinitesimal parameter:

$$
(D_{c^2R} - \varepsilon) \begin{cases} \min [\theta - \varepsilon (\hat{e}^T s^- + e^T s^+)] \\ s.t. \sum_{j=1}^{n} x_j \lambda_j + s^- = \theta x_{j_0} \\ \sum_{j=1}^{n} y_j \lambda_j - s^+ = y_{j_0} \\ \lambda_j \geq 0, \ s^- \geq 0, \ s^+ \geq 0 \\ j = 1, 2, ..., \ n \end{cases} \tag{11}
$$

Among which, $\hat{e}$, e respectively is m dimension, s dimension rank vector which component is 1. $s^- = (s_1^-, s_2^-, ..., s_m^-)^T$ is a vector which is formed with the slack variables that corresponding to the input. $s^+ = (s_1^+, s_2^+, ..., s_n^+)^T$ is a vector which is formed with the slack variables that corresponding to the output.

By this model, we can once judge the DMU is DEA effective, or DEA less effective, or DEA ineffective.

We can get the DEA value of every decision unit by (4). We get θ^* by (4): if $\theta^* = 1$, and each s^-, s^+ is zero, then the relevant decision unit is DEA effective; if only $\theta^* = 1$, then the relevant decision is DEA less effective.

Scale income is a problem that the input side pays close attention to, because this index can measure the affection that the input side increases the input, which influences the next input. So it is doubtlessly important to discuss the scale income of input-output.

By DEA model, scale income can be judged by the following formula:

If $\dfrac{1}{\theta^*} \sum_{j=1}^{n} \lambda_j^* < 1$, the decision unit is increasing return to scale;

If $\dfrac{1}{\theta^*} \sum_{j=1}^{n} \lambda_j^* = 1$, the decision unit is scale effective;

If $\dfrac{1}{\theta^*} \sum_{j=1}^{n} \lambda_j^* > 1$, the decision unit is decreasing return to scale.

First, we can get θ, λ, then judge the scale income of the decision unit by the above. Here, effective scale income means the ratio of input-output has reached the optimal scale income; increasing return to scale means the relevant increasing value of output is greater than one unit if the input increases one unit; decreasing return to scale means the relevant increasing value of output is smaller than one unit if the input decreases one unit.

4 Results and Discussion

To study the determinant features the region innovation in china, this paper should estimate the following equations:

$$y = f(x_i), i = 1, 2, ..., 12 \tag{12}$$

A number of crucial parameters, which mainly determine the y, are considered. Where:

y is the patent applications;x_1 is FDI per capita;x_2 is Industrial total production value;x_3 is the average number of employees;x_4 is the number of people in engineering and technological activities;x_5 is Regional R&D expenditure ratio of the industrial total production value;x_6 is R&D expenditure;x_7 is Scientific and Technical ratio of expenditure;x_8 is the three expenses;x_9 is Propensity of patent;x_{10} is Regional R&D expenditure ratio of GDP;x_{11} is R&D personnel;x_{12} is the sales income.

There is a hybrid non-linear relation between y and $x_1, x_2, x_3, x_4, x_5, x_6, x_7, x_8, x_9, x_{10}, x_{11}, x_{12}$, which are almost indescribable using traditional models like linear regression model, Cobb-Douglas functional model and gray models. In this study, KPCA is used to features selection and DEA is used to evolution. The results of the patenting evolution and reasonable $x_1, x_5, x_6, x_7, x_9, x_{10}, x_{11}$ are selected. In the DEA model, the y, x_9 are used to output of DEA and others are used to input of DEA model in the Chinese region innovation.

According to the out-put achievement of patent is behind on time the input of patent, this paper considers the out-put achievement in the next year take the place of the achievement in the same year of the original model. It will conform to reality of input-output. Therefore, the writer will select the data of input patent in 2008 and the data of output patent in 2009 to calculate.

During the course of calculation, this paper uses the non-dimension data, the index figure of each decision unit is relative figure, which means it is showed in the percentage of the absolute value of practice value of the decision unit accounts for the general absolute value of the index figure of the whole decision unit that participate in evaluating.

During the course of collecting data, because the authorization of inventive patent and practical patent in Tibet is a tiny minority, only 3 pieces and 5 pieces, the influence to the input-output efficiency that discussed in this paper is almost nothing. So we discuss the DEA value, scale income in 30 prefectures except Tibet. After the DEA model, the results are found in the Chinese region innovation in table 1.

Table 1. The validity compare among eastern region, middle region, western region

	Eastern Region			Middle Region			Western Region		
	DEA effective	Decreasing to Scale	Increasing to Scale	DEA effective	Decreasing to Scale	Increasing to Scale	DEA effective	Decreasing to Scale	Increasing to Scale
Number	6	3	3	2	6	1	2	2	5
The proportion of own region(%)	50%	25%	25%	22.2%	66.7%	11.1%	22.2%	22.2%	55.6%

5 Conclusions

This paper focuses on the reality of the region innovation in China. In this paper, the KPCA for nonlinear regression is presented. It is shown that the features selection approach based on KPCA effective and feasible.

This paper analysis the input-output efficiency of he region innovation in each provinces, provincial city, autonomous region of China by DEA means, which to a certain degree may supply the development of the region innovation in each region with a certain objective basis. Also, the KPCA and DEA model are integrated together to evolutes the region innovation, which provides a novel way for the evolution design of the other engineering.

References

1. Imoto, S., Yabuuchi, Y., Watada, J.: Fuzzy regression model of R&D project evaluation. Applied Soft Computing 8(3), 1266–1273 (2008)
2. Cameron, G., Proudman, J., Redding, S.: Technological convergence, R&D, trade and productivity Growth. European Economic Review 79, 775–807 (2005)
3. Huang, S.H., Ke, H.R., Yang, W.P.: Structure clustering for Chinese patent documents. Expert Systems with Applications 34(4), 2290–2297 (2008)
4. Chen, C.M.: A network-DEA model with new efficiency measures to incorporate the dynamic effect in production networks. European Journal of Operational Research 194(3), 687–699 (2009)
5. Fu, Y.w., Yin, H., Yang, G.B.: Application of a mixed DEA model to evaluate relative efficiency validity. Journal of Marine Science and Application 4(3), 64–70
6. Rosipal, R., Girolami, M., Trejo, L.J., Cichocki, A.: Kernel PCA for Feature Extraction and De-noising in Non-linear Regression. Neural Computing & Applications 10(3), 231–243 (2001)
7. Li, Z., Tian, X.M.: Study of Soft Sensor Modeling Method Based on KPCA-SVM. Intelligent Control and Automation, 4876 –4880 (2006)
8. Guyon, I., Gunn, S., Nikravesh, M., Zadeh, L.: Nonlinear feature selection with the Foundations and Applications in Feature extraction. Springer, Heidelberg (2005)
9. Scholkopf, B., Smola, A., Muller, K.R.: Nonlinear Component Analysis as a Kernel Eigenvalue Problem. Neural Computation 10, 1299–1319 (1998)

Energy Efficient and Reliable Target Monitoring in the Tactical Battlefield

Yan-Xiao Li, Hua Guan, and Yue-Ling Zhang

Telecommunication Engineering Institute
Air Force Engineering University
Xi'an, Shaanxi, China
{YanXiaoLi,HuaGuan,YueLingZhang}@hotmail.com

Abstract. In the tactical battlefield target monitoring it is crucial to take into account the energy efficiency and data reliability issues for the purpose of military decision making, especially in large scale sensor networks. However, due to the inherent nature of power constraint and wireless communication medium it is a challenging problem in the process of actual application. An efficient and reliable data aggregation scheme is proposed to enhance the performance of wireless sensor network used in the target monitoring. Firstly, the energy consumption model is presented and analyzed in the multihop WSNs. Then idea of mobile sinks, adaptive energy saving mechanism is introduced and the concept of multiple sinks cooperation is used to assure the reliability of the data aggregation. The simulation and the associated analysis show the improved results of the presented schema. At last the future discussion about the large scale tactical battlefield application is made to broaden the coming research scope.

Keywords: wireless sensor network, energy constraint, large scale WSN, tactical battlefield.

1 Introduction

A wireless sensor network consists of a large amount of sensor nodes, which have capabilities of sensing the environment and sending data to base station through wireless channel. After being deployed to a specific area without a pre-configured infrastructure, sensor nodes organize themselves into a network to send sensing data to base station. As each sensor surveys the area within its sensing range, the data is sent towards the base station along a multihop path. A WSN is able to remotely cover a wide sensing area since these low-cost sensors organize into a multi-hop network without human assistance.

Traditionally, sensors are used in defense technologies. Many developments in related areas are associated with military applications. One of the most important applications is combatant environment monitoring by spreading a number of wireless sensor nodes across the targeted area [1] [2]. Sensor networks can implement remote

G. Shen and X. Huang (Eds.): ECWAC 2011, Part I, CCIS 143, pp. 115–121, 2011.

monitoring of sensitive information important for security. Examples include research and developments in battlefield intelligence regarding the numbers, locations and movement of troops [3].

In the tactical battlefield target monitoring, when the sensors detect a target, the event is reported to the base station, which can take appropriate action (e.g., send a message on the Internet or to a satellite). Due to the intrinsic feature of energy constraint and the complexity of the battlefield communication environment it is critical to explore efficient approach to guarantee better longevity for the WSNs.

In tactical battlefield wireless sensor networks represent a significant advance over traditional methods of monitoring. Sensors can also be deployed on areas where it is unsafe to attempt field studies. The results of wireless sensor-based monitoring efforts are comparable with the traditional methods of monitoring. Sensor network deployment represents a substantially more economical method for conducting long-term studies than traditional methods. A "deploy 'em and leave 'em" strategy of wireless sensor usage limits logistical needs to initial placement and occasional servicing. It also greatly increases access to a wider array of study sites, often limited by concerns about frequent access and habitability [4]. Compared to the wired network, installation and maintenance are easy and inexpensive in a WSN, and disruption of the operation of the structure is minimal. The system also becomes scalable to a large number of nodes to allow dense sensor coverage of real-world structures [5].

2 Energy Consumption Model

The energy consumption measured in our experiments refers to the total consumption by the sensor nodes including radio transmission and reception, sensing, signal processing, and component and circuit maintenance.

We assume each sensor node transmits and receives data with fixed transmission and reception power, respectively. So the power consumption is independent of the transmission distance between adjacent nodes. Accordingly, we adopt the following energy model due to [6] to calculate the power consumption.

$$p \approx e(k_r + k_t) \tag{1}$$

where p denotes the total energy consumption of one node for receiving k_r bits and transmitting k_t bits, and e is a factor indicating the energy consumption per bit at the receiver circuit.

Let q denote the total amount of data sensed by each node per traversal round of the mobile sink. Thus, $k_i^r = k_i^t + q$, where k_i^t and k_i^r are respectively the amount of data received and transmitted by node i per round. In this paper, we assume all sensor nodes forward data along the shortest path trees to their destinations. Then Equation (1) describes the relationship between the total amount of data received by all nodes and the sum of hops

$$\sum_{i=1}^{n_{total}} k_r^i = \sum_{i=1}^{n_{total}} h_i \times q \tag{2}$$

Based on the above equation, the total energy consumption, p_{total}, can be expressed in terms of the total sum of hops from all members to their destinations as follows

$$p_{total} = \sum_{i=1}^{n_{total}} p_i = \sum_{i=1}^{n_{total}} e(k_r^i + k_t^i)$$

$$= \sum_{i=1}^{n_{total}} e(2 * k_r^i + q) = \sum_{i=1}^{n_{total}} e(2 * h_i + 1) \times q \tag{3}$$

p_i denotes the energy consumption of node i per round. Consequently, the problem of minimizing p_{total} is equivalent to the problem of minimizing the total sum of shortest hops which is easier to solve.

3 Mobile Sink Model

All sensor nodes are energy constrained. In a typical WSN scenario, all the data are routed back to the only static sink. Therefore, those nodes near the sink have to forward all the data from farther nodes and thus carry a heavier traffic load. This is the many to one traffic pattern of WSNs. Consequently, the nodes near the sink are more susceptible to energy exhaustion. When these nodes use up all their energy, no more data can be transmitted back to the sink, causing dysfunctional or disconnected network or premature lifetime ending of WSNs. In order to distribute the energy consumption uniformly across the network, using a multiple mobile sinks is a solution. The nodes near the sink change as the mobile sink moves.

We consider a scenario of deploying N wireless sensor nodes in a square area A. The sensor nodes are randomly scattered across the region A. There is mobile sink S which is responsible for collecting data from all sensor nodes and it acts as a gateway for the sensor network. A sensor node communicates with its one-hop neighbors using its wireless radio resources. The sensor nodes do not have global knowledge of the network. Each node and the sink are assumed to have transmission range R. The sensor nodes relay data to the sink in a multi-hop fashion. At any given time, each sensor node can be in one of three different modes, regarding the energy consumption: (a) transmission of a message, (b) reception of a message and (c) sensing of events. The energy model in our approach is as follows. The initial energy of each sensor node is α ($\alpha > 0$). We assume that a sensor node consumes E_1 units of energy when sending one bit, while depletes E_2 units of energy when receiving one bit where $E_1 > E_2 > 0$. Therefore, for the case of transmitting and receiving a message, we assume that the radio module dissipates an amount of energy proportional to the message's size. For the idle state, we assume that the energy consumed is constant E_{idle}. We have made an assumption that the mobile sink is not resource constrained.

4 Adaptive Energy Conserving

Data propagation protocols (like Directed Diffusion, PFR and EBP) try to minimize energy dissipation at a high level by affecting the way transmissions happen. Explicit power saving schemes operate at a "lower" level and can be combined with higher layer distributed protocols like the ones for data propagation. The Adaptive Power Conservation Protocol, proposed in [7] uses a power-switch mechanism: each device goes through alternating periods of "sleeping" and "awake". During a sleeping period, the devices cease any communication with the environment, thus the power consumption is assumed to be minimal and practically insignificant, whereas when a device is awake, it consumes the regular (non-trivial) amount of energy. The sleeping/awake time periods alternate in each device and have durations T_s T_w respectively. This is achieved by using a simple timer in each device, which is initially set at a random time point chosen from the sleep-awake time frame, i.e. $T = T_s + T_w$. The timer's expiration marks a switch over to the alternate mode. Let now $en = T_s/(T_s+T_w)$ be the energy saving specification, measuring how drastic the power saving is, a global ratio of the proportion between the durations of the sleep and awake periods. A different power saving strategy towards optimal sleep-awake schedules is proposed in [8].

If the parameters that affect the performance of propagation protocols (e.g. density of the network, the broadcast range) are known in advance, the energy saving specification en can be optimally adjusted by the network operator to maximize the energy-efficiency and keep the network functional for as long as possible. However, in real environments, measuring the density of the network may be a non-trivial task (if possible at all), especially in cases where the devices are dropped randomly in the area of interest. Moreover, the network density continuously changes, as the network evolves over time, since the power of the sensors will be exhausted. It is also possible for devices to stop functioning due to physical damage (i.e. destruction by external factors) or failure of the (low-cost) equipment. Because of this dynamic nature of sensor networks, we expect that density $\mu(R)$ will decrease over time, as sensors disconnect from the network. In this sense, as the network evolves over time, the initial value for en will make the network operate at suboptimal levels. Moreover, it is possible to re-deploy additional devices while the network is in operation, in order to "replace" the malfunctioning devices or due to change in the task dynamics [9]. In this way the network operator can reinstate density $\mu(R)$ at the desired levels. Still, the nature of the *redeployment* process is such that precise positioning of sensor devices (and thus the "local" densities) can not be achieved.

We explore evenly distributing energy consumption among devices by adjusting the sleep interval of strained devices. In order to detect that a device consumes energy faster than others, an estimation of the average energy of the nearby devices is required. This is achieved by providing an estimate of the energy levels of the node to the neighboring nodes every time a message is transmitted. In this way nodes can keep track of the available energy in their neighborhood.

5 Multiple Sinks Cooperation

Increase in the hop number between the source and the destination nodes bring some issues that must be considered [10] [11]. First, nodes close to the sink deplete their energies quickly; leaving the sink unreachable and the system into off-state [12]. Secondly, increase in the hop-number result in more processing overhead and delay at nodes which will cause the packets to be dropped. Thirdly, as the network size grows, data redundancy reducing problem also becomes more challenging. Better data aggregation challenges with the real-time requirements of the system [10].

For large scale WSNs, deploying multiple sinks [13] has been presented as a workable method because the protocol in use may not be feasible anymore in large scale networks due to increase in the number of node.

Multiple braided paths for robustness with a minimum delay are constructed and it provides a basis for real-time support for time critical data collected in the battlefield. Weight value is used as a metric for routing instead of the routing tables or beacon messaging. It firstly helps to proceed routing, secondly it minimizes delay and energy consumption at nodes in routing decision phase. When a node has data to transmit, inserts its and the destination's weight values into the packet, and broadcasts the packet. When a node receives a packet, it compares its weight value with the weight values in the packet. If its weight value is between the transmitting node's weight value and the destination's weight value, it rebroadcasts the packet, or drops the packet otherwise. If the nodes in the operation area are uniformly distributed, less than half of the nodes in the range of the transmitting node rebroadcast the packet. To reduce the number of rebroadcasting nodes, a threshold value is used and inserted into the packet. Only the nodes those have weight difference greater than the threshold value can rebroadcast the packet. By this way, nodes closer to transmitting node are avoided to rebroadcast. Rebroadcasting nodes are those that make more advances toward the destination.

6 Simulation and Evaluation

In the simulation experiments, sensor nodes are placed in a monitored rectangle area randomly and uniformly. The scheme is implemented in OMNET++. The data rate of sensor nodes sensing information is $200bps$. The initial energy of each node is set to $20J$. The parameter in the energy consumption model is $e = 0.5\mu J/bit$ and the maximum communication distance is $52m$.

Consider the scenario in which sensor nodes are deployed in the $400m \times 350m$ rectangle area randomly and only one sink placed the left border of the monitored area. Fig. 1 presents the total amount of data aggregated by the sink during one round. Theoretical maximum is the sum of the upper bound on data transmitted by each sink. In Fig. 1, SPT has very low efficiency and collects only about half of the maximum. As the total number of sensor nodes increases, there are more sinks in the monitored area and hence the amount of data collected by ER also increases. Energy consumption is one of the most concerned problems in sensor networks. Fig. 2 compares the energy consumption between SPT and ER methods. In Fig. 2, ER performs better than SPT approach in terms of total energy consumption. Considering the amount of data and energy consumption together, we can find that ER scheme has significantly higher data aggregation efficiency and can collect about two times data than SPT with almost the same energy consumption.

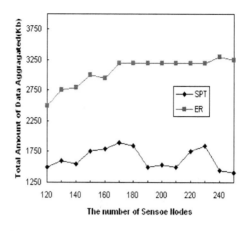

Fig. 1. Total amount of data

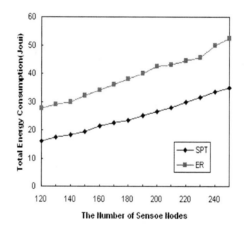

Fig. 2. Total energy comsumption

7 Conclusion and Step Ahead

Wireless sensor networks (WSN) are self-organizing networks of small, battery powered sensors used to monitor the unattended hostile environment for mission critical events, mostly in security and military sensing in the battlefield application. Its energy-starved nature makes power aware a vital issue to take into account when deploying for use.

For the WSN deployed in the tactical battlefield, energy efficiency is a basic important concern so as to guarantee better application. While under the harsh lossy environment it deserves more attention to assure the reliability of the sensed data. The energy efficiency and the reliable data collection or fusion should be highly considered for the purpose of providing enough information to make military action or judgment.

In this paper we propose a novel energy efficient and Reliable scheme for the large scale high dense wireless sensor network. This scheme is based on the concept of multiple mobile sinks and cooperative diversity. The proposed scheme is good for applications where apart from energy efficiency there is need for better reliability.

In the practical tactical battlefield mobile wireless sensor nodes are required to implement better surveillance or environment monitoring. In this kind of scenario further traffic variation would be caused by node mobility and network dynamics due unreliable wireless communications. Spatial and temporal variances in traffic require load balancing mechanism as the future work to be explored. And further recovery schema should be designed to reduce the possibility to become isolated nodes, which will increase the security level in data aggregation in wireless sensor networks.

References

1. Lundquist, J., Cayan, D., Dettinger, M.: Meteorology and hydrology in yosemite national park: A sensor network application. In: Zhao, F., Guibas, L.J. (eds.) IPSN 2003. LNCS, vol. 2634, pp. 518–528. Springer, Heidelberg (2003)
2. Mainwaring, A., Polastre, J., Szewczyk, R., Culler, D., Anderson, J.: Wireless sensor networks for habitat monitoring. In: Proc. of WSNA 2002, Atlanta, Georgia, September 28 (2002)
3. Krishnamachari, B.: Networking Wireless Sensors. Cambridge University Press, Cambridge (2005)
4. Mainwaring, A., Polastre, J., Szewczyk, R., Culler, D., Anderson, J.: Wireless sensor networks for habitat monitoring. In: 1st ACM International Workshop on Wireless Sensor Networks and Applications, September 2002, pp. 88–97 (2002)
5. Kim, S., Pakzad, S., Culler, D., Demmel, J., Fenves, G., Glaser, S., Turon, M.: Health monitoring of civil infrastructures using wireless sensor networks. In: 6th International Conference on Information Processing in Sensor Networks, April 2007, pp. 254–263 (2007)
6. Wang, M., Basagni, S., Melachrinoudis, E., Petrioli, C.: Exploiting Sink Mobility for Maximizing Sensor Networks Lifetime. In: Proc. 38th Annual Hawaii Intl. Conf. on System Sciences, pp. 287a–287a (2005)
7. Chatzigiannakis, I., Kinalis, A., Nikoletseas, S.: An adaptive power conservation scheme for heterogeneous wireless sensors. In: Proceedings of the 17th Annual ACM Symposium on Parallel Algorithms and Architectures
8. Cao, Q., Abdelzaher, T., He, T., Stankovic, J.: Towards optimal sleep scheduling in sensor networks for rare-event detection. In: Intl. Conference on Information
9. Akyildiz, I.F., Su, W., Sankarasubramaniam, Y., Cayirci, E.: Wireless sensor networks: a survey. Journal of Computer Networks 38, 393–422 (2002)
10. Schmitt, J.B., Zdarsky, F.A., Roedig, U.: Sensor Network Calculus with Multiple Sinks. In: Cuenca, P., Orozco-Barbosa, L. (eds.) PWC 2006. LNCS, vol. 4217. Springer, Heidelberg (2006)
11. Das, A., Dutta, D.: Data Acquisition in Multiple-sink Sensor Networks. Mobile Computing and Communications Review 9(3), 82–85 (2005)
12. Yuen, K., Liang, B., Li, B.: A Distributed Framework for Correlated Data Gathering in Sensor Networks. In: IFIP (2006)
13. Schmitt, J.B., Zdarsky, F.A., Roedig, U.: Sensor Network Calculus with Multiple Sinks. In: Cuenca, P., Orozco-Barbosa, L. (eds.) PWC 2006. LNCS, vol. 4217. Springer, Heidelberg (2006)

Architecture Design and Implementation Methods of Heterogeneous Emergency Communication Network[*]

Haitao Wang[1] and Lihua Song[2]

[1] Institute of Communication Engineering, PLA Univ. of Sci. & Tech., Nanjing 210007, China
[2] Institute of Command Automation, PLA Univ. of Sci. & Tech., Nanjing 210007, China

Abstract. Efficient response and treatment of unexpected events relies on reliable, flexible and robust emergency communication network. In this paper, backgrounds of building emergency communication network are introduced. Then, architecture design of emergency communication network is explained, including design goals, ideas and other technical issues. Afterwards, in terms of requirements of emergency communication network, implementation methods of WiMAX based broadband emergency communication network are discussed. Meanwhile, network monitor and interconnection issues are considered.

Keywords: Heterogeneous Emergency Communication Network, Architecture, WiMAX, Ad hoc Network, Wireless Sensor Network.

1 Introduction

In recent years, facing various urgent and unexpected events, how to construct reliable, highly effective and robust emergency communication network applicable for all kinds of user groups has become one of important issues crying for solution [1]. Compared with Western developed countries, in China emergency communication technologies drop behind. Current domestic emergency communication mainly existing communication facilities (including public communications network and the public media network) and when communication infrastructures are damaged or cannot satisfy needs satellite, short-wave and trunking communication systems are utilized to provide emergency communication. The emergency communication possesses distinctive characteristics of time burstiness, place uncertainty, service urgent, information multiplicity and process temporariness but traditional communications systems have not taken into these characteristics account fully. Emergency communication network must be deployed rapidly to timely provide diverse services for all kinds of user to meet respective needs and it can monitor specific regions in real-time, make fast response to the thunderbolts and can effectively coordinate various rescue institutes to perform disaster relief and the post-disaster reconstruction [2].

Nowadays, the domestic emergency communication systems' functions are simple and cannot offer QoS for multiple service flows and their survivability is poor. For example, the public communications network is unreliable and when emergent events

---

[*] This work is supported by NSFC (61072043).

G. Shen and X. Huang (Eds.): ECWAC 2011, Part I, CCIS 143, pp. 122–127, 2011.
© Springer-Verlag Berlin Heidelberg 2011

occur the tremendous traffic load may render it is overload or even is paralyzed While it is able to quickly establish call and also support group call, broadcast call as well as a variety of supplementary businesses, the trunking communication's coverage radius and capacity are comparatively small, and can only offer command dispatching function. Satellite communication is robustness, wide coverage and flexibility, but its capacity is limited and its deployment and usage cost is high. At current stage, the existing emergency communication systems including satellite and trunking communications are not able to provide quick, flexible and reliable communication services for all types of user groups in case of complicated emergency Situation. Therefore, novel techniques and methods must be introduced.

2   Architecture Design of Emergency Communication Network

2.1   Design Goals and Ideas

We attempt to integrate various communication techniques and methods to enhance emergency communications network adaptability and effectiveness, make information exchange among different users in the emergency scene as well as between emergency on-site and emergency command centre timely and accurate and provide relevant communication services for different user groups in complex and diverse emergency circumstances. To this end, the general idea of network architecture design is: relying on available network infrastructure in emergency on-site and temporary deployed mobile communication systems, and will make good use of technical advantages of wireless self-organizing network and construct one kind of heterogeneous emergency communication network system, which effectively integrates wireline, wireless, satellite and other communication means and mixes together non-infrastructure networks and infrastructure networks. This architecture achieves complement of different communication technologies and facilitates building a reliable, efficient, robust emergency communications network to provide the best possible communication services in a variety of network conditions.

2.2   Design Scheme

According to above design goals a universal heterogeneous emergency network architecture based on overlay network is given. This architecture is logically a hierarchical structure, covered with infrastructure network and infrastructure network and can be divided into communications infrastructure layer, information acquisition and processing layer, distributed computing layer and application service layer, as shown in Figure 1. Communications infrastructure layer covers existing cellular communication network and Internet, temporary deployed ad hoc network and sensor network used for monitoring the status of the affected area as well as broadband mesh network. Information acquisition and processing layer is designed to collect and correlate various information within communication infrastructure layer and exchange necessary information between top and bottom layers. Distributed computing layer is responsible for distributed information processing, data mining and decision support. Application service layer involves all kinds of emergency communication applications and services.

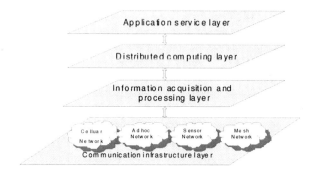

Fig. 1. Hierarchical structure of emergency communication network

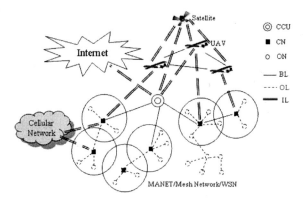

Fig. 2. An integrative heterogeneous emergency communication network structure

This emergency communications network is essentially a multi-hop overly p2p communication network, and there is no longer strictly distinguish between infrastructure network and infrastructure network [3]. It integrates various communication resources in existing network systems and wireless self-organizing network. In view of physical structure, this network is a multi-layer three-dimensional network, coving ground wired and wireless, low-altitude platform and high-altitude satellite communication devices. That is to say, it is an integrative ground, low altitude and high altitude heterogeneous emergency communication network (as shown in figure 2). It can effectively support information interaction and emergency response among victims, rescuers, commanders and other relevant personnel in emergency situations.

The temporary deployed ground communications facilities mainly includes a central control unit (CCU), several cluster head nodes (CN) and a large number of ordinary nodes (ON), and in extreme cases need resorting to UAV and satellite to provide emergency communications services. CCU has very strong communication and computing power is usually fixed, but in some cases it is removable and connects to external networks to gather necessary information available to the desired nodes. CNs can be fixed or mobile, with strong communication and computing power, and have certain power provision. CNs can connect mutually to form the core backbone network under the control of CCU and provide services for nearby ONs via various wireless technologies. ONs are portable communication terminals or sensor nodes and they can construct cluster network on their own, or join the clusters belongs to CNs. ONs can expand coverage and improve communication reliability through the means of relaying and forwarding.

As command and control center CCU must be established as soon as possible and suitable number of CNs are deployed at appropriate positions. In disaster relief network topology will change dynamically, a rapid responsive clustering scheme can be used to organize and maintain emergency communication on-site network. With the help of hierarchical and clustering structure, network can be managed easily and control overhead is reduced greatly [4]. In addition, this structure is convenient for locating nodes and retrieving information. CCU is responsible for recording information about all nodes and maintaining view of the whole network while CN is only in charge of maintaining information about ONs in its clusters and other neighbour CNs.

3 Implementation Methods of Emergency Communication Network

Communication infrastructure layer should permit victims and rescuers in disaster region use various kinds of communication terminals to access available heterogeneous networks. To this end, a simple and effective devices deployment method must be adopted in disaster region to integrate with survivable communication network, to provide flexible and reliable service platform meeting diverse communication service requirements.

One applicable technique measure is to adopt WiMAX to construct backbone network for emergency communication. The main reasons for choosing WiMAX are: easy to deploy, support high mobility, large coverage and high transmission capacity [6]. In addition, WiMAX communication system can offer certain QoS guarantee. For example, it can give emergent application higher priority and assign more resource preferentially. To enable reliable communications in various propagation conditions especially in complex and dynamic disaster environments, the WiMAX network must be optimized to provide excellent non-line-of-sight (NLOS) coverage and mobility support. As for the physical layer, orthogonal frequency division multiple access (OFDMA) scheme is adopted. Efficient methods to mitigate the performance degradation due to Doppler shift must be taken, such as improving clock synchronization precision.

To guarantee reliable communications, hybrid automatic repeat request (H-ARQ) techniques are recommended for use. Further, transmit diversity, beamforming, and spatial multiplexing can be used to achieve high link reliability, wide network coverage and high throughput [7]. In fact, in some disaster scenarios, higher coverage and throughput is required. However, at the mobile terminals side, multiple transmit antennas are not feasible due to the limited equipment size and power. For this reason cooperative diversity can be candidate: by means of cooperation between transmitting stations and user terminals. The cooperative entities share the transmit antennas to create a virtual (distributed) antenna array and hence improve performance.

Wireless emergency communication system requires the use of a variety of different wireless technologies across different network connections and access to different types of service. Heterogeneous network interconnection faced many challenges, including interface choices, seamless switching, QoS coordination context-adaptive configuration and etc. In order to adapt to environmental changes, mobile system needs information about the environment, including access network itself, as well as service information supported by network. Seamless handoff allows the user to use communication equipment across different network media to complete a variety of tasks and always connected, without having to worry about how to interact with other devices and environment. Seamless handoff requires capturing and understanding user's current context, and the task performed by user determines the type of information need.

In typical emergency scenarios, voice and video communications with high-rate data, as well as low-rate data communications often exist at the same time. By taking into account the need to handle different traffic types with different requirements in terms of delay, jitter, and error rate, suitable scheduling and resource allocation schemes can be prepared. An efficient approach seems to be that of combine subcarrier allocation with an adaptive modulation scheme to take into account both wireless channel behaviour and specific applications requirements [8]. Important issues also to be guaranteed are high efficiency, self configuring and fault tolerance to accomplish an efficient monitoring within a disaster area and support of multimedia communications among rescuers under critical situations. Another requirement for an emergency communications network is to support smooth intra-network handover (horizontal handover) and inter-network handover (vertical handover).

An efficient and effective monitoring of interesting area is a key issue to prevent or to deal with unexpected events. This is the case of wide-area scenarios where no infrastructures were available even before a disaster occurred. Wireless sensor network (WSN) seems to be an suitable approach for many emergency situations [9]. In particular, WSN can contain a great number of spatially separated nodes, with increased coverage and accuracy, without requiring human attention. Moreover, WSN can be deployed in almost any environment, especially in risk and inaccessible zones, such as in places where earthquakes, flooding, forest fires occur. As a consequence, one of expected features is the reliability in data acquisition/transmission, robustness with respect to faults, and capability to interoperate with heterogeneous ad hoc deployed networks. In addition, faults in WSNs tend to occur frequently, due to energy shortages and the possible occurrence of denial of service attacks. As a consequence, fault tolerance is an important issue for applications within an emergency communication system to avoid system failures (survivability). A solution to this problem, at the expense of an increased cost, is to resort to redundant deployment of sensors and replication of information between sensor nodes.

4 Conclusions

In this article heterogeneous network architecture for emergency scenario is proposed and its organization as well as maintenance manner is explained. Then, the design of WiMAX based emergency communication is discussed to have the ability of monitoring sensitive areas and enabling intercommunication between various user groups in emergency scenarios. The key technology issues of such wireless emergency network include WiMAX, ad hoc network, wireless sensor network, security and so on. Suitable solutions were highlighted in order to achieve high and reliable performance in disaster scenarios. Special attention was devoted to issues such as heterogeneous network interconnection, survivable communication mode and QoS support. In addition, existing mature commercial technologies and products should be used fully to construct heterogeneous emergency communication network, including wired, wireless, satellite, and mobile ad hoc and sensor nodes, to offer all-around services for various users groups in different emergency scenarios.

Acknowledgment

This paper is supported by NSFC (NO: 61072043).

References

1. RadiocommunicaLion Objectives and Requirements for Public Protection and Disaster Relief. ITU-R M 2033 (2003)
2. Ansari, N.: Networking For Critical Conditions. IEEE Wireless Communications 7(4), 73–81 (2008)
3. Janefalkar, A., Josiam, K.: Cellular ad-hoc relay for emergencies. In: VTC 2004, Los Angeles, pp. 2873–2877 (September 2004)
4. Frodigh, M., Johansson, P.: Wireless ad hoc networking—The art of networking without a network. Ericsson Review (4), 248–262 (2000)
5. Chiti, F., Fantacci, R.: A broadband wireless communications system for emergency management. IEEE Wireless Communications 7(6), 8–14 (2008)
6. WiMAX forum [S.l.] (April 2008), http://www.wimaxforum.org/
7. Oh, E.S.: Beacons in time of distress: advances in wireless applications for emergency telecommunications. In: APACE 2003, Tokyo, pp. 10–15 (August 2003)
8. Lee, M.: Emerging Standards for Wireless Mesh Technology. IEEE Wireless Communication 13(2), 56–63 (2006)
9. Chiti, F., Fantacci, R.: Wireless Sensor Network Paradigm: Overview on Communication Protocols Design and Application to Practical Scenarios. EURASIP Newsletter 17(4), 6–27 (2006)

Design of Grid Portal System Based on RIA

Caifeng Cao, Jianguo Luo, and Zhixin Qiu

School of Computer Wuyi University, Jiangmen 529020, China
cfcao@126.com

Abstract. Grid portal is an important branch of grid research. In order to solve the weak expressive force, the poor interaction, the low operating efficiency and other insufficiencies of the first and second generation of grid portal system, RIA technology was introduced to it. A new portal architecture was designed based on RIA and Web service. The concrete realizing scheme of portal system was presented by using Adobe Flex/Flash technology, which formed a new design pattern. In system architecture, the design pattern has B/S and C/S superiorities, balances server and its client side, optimizes the system performance, realizes platform irrelevance. In system function, the design pattern realizes grid service call, provides client interface with rich user experience, integrates local resources by using FABridge, LCDS, Flash player and some other components.

Keywords: grid portal, RIA, grid service, Flex.

1 Introduction

Grid portal is an entry to grid computing. Users access grid resources and service, execute and monitor grid application, and realize cooperation with other users by it. Grid portal provides continuous grid working environment for grid users. However, this working environment has certain distance away from high interactivity, rich personal experience and strong function. Also it can't integrate local resources.

Firstly, the first generation of grid portal commonly is constructed by GridPort Toolkit V in Perl or Grid Portal Development Kit (GPDK) in Java. GridPort and GPDK both pack common grid functions in order to provide a set of high level programming API and tools. Grid portal is often closely associated with grid middleware such as Globus. In conclusion, it has some limits as follows: lack of custom, hard to integrate grid services and static nature of grid service. The second generation of grid portal is based on standard specification and portlet technology. JSR 168 and WSRP are both used for solving the problem of interoperability between portlet and portlet container. The second generation of grid portal has the characteristics as follows: portal custom, extensible and dynamic grid service. It is based on B/S structure and uniform browser client as a whole. But just owing to being based on Web, its portlet function has certain limits,where client system lack personality, and can't integrate with client's application system. In addition, B/S system has inherently a serial of problems such as poor interactivity and slow page update, which also exist in the second grid portal.

G. Shen and X. Huang (Eds.): ECWAC 2011, Part I, CCIS 143, pp. 128–134, 2011.

2   Introducing RIA Technology

With the deep study and application of grid technology, different grids spring up constantly, such as manufacturing grid, commerce grid and knowledge grid, etc. Meanwhile, enterprise application system has become better and stronger gradually. Grid user owns more and more local resources. It deserves deep study that grid portal system provides more friendly interface, uses local resources effectively, considers user habits and preferences and attracts them. So, the development of grid portal system needs to introduce new technology.

Rich Internet Application, called RIA for short, is a new generation of network application programme which combines desktop application, Web technology and interactive multimedia communication. It uses client programme and browser plugin technology to share some operations of business logic layer. People can consider the "rich" in RIA as three aspects: rich data model, rich user interface and rich function. Rich data model means that user interface can display and operate more complex client-embedded data model, which contains local and remote data. Rich user interface is supported by the strong expressive force of developer kits. The markup language and script language with strong function provide varied and flexible interface control elements. User can construct graph at any time using elastic vector diagram or other technology. The system can respond data variation by completely active animation and refresh local area. Rich function is reflected on the combination of multimedia and application programme, which not only enrichs application function but also realizes interactive multimedia. The rich client programme aggregates services and functions provided by local and remote system.

In system architecture, RIA compromises the merits of B/S and C/S structure, which not only has characteristics of C/S personal client and rich function, but also uses popular HTTP and Web server technology for its deployment. Meanwhile, the flexible online and offline mechanism reduce load of Web server and dependence to network transmission.

It will bring some advantages that RIA technology is introduced into grid portal system. First, user interface will become more lively, better show workflow and task implementation process. Second, the system can provide convenient and flexible visual multimedia interactive function. Third, the system can use local resources effectively and realize seamless integration with it. RIA will bring substantial changes on both system function and performance to portal system.

3   Portal Structure Based on RIA and Web Service

Grid system usually contains grid resources, grid middleware, grid service and grid portal system. Grid resources contain different physical and logical resources according to grid type, such as CPU, memory, enterprise information system and CAD system, etc. Grid middleware provides management and dispatch to grid resources, such as famous Globus, Alkemi applied to building compute grid, etc. Grid services are closely related to grid middleware and grid application. They can be divided into three types. The first type is resource services which encapsulate different resources. It provides sharing resources method through Web service interface. The second type is field services which abstract common functions of the field, such as calculation, analysis and data services. The third type is common services which realize resource state monitor, error tolerance, service quality guarantee, such as services of information, monitor, failure recovery, user authentication[1]. So, grid portal system usually provides function as follows.

1) Authentication: portal system execute verification to user identity by username and password, and someone can access grid resources only when they pass the authentication.
2) Task management: portal system provides functions of managing tasks for users, such as submitting task safely, monitoring conditions of task and suspending or canceling task if necessary.
3) Data transmission: when a task is executing on remote resources, portal allows users to upload and download the data sets which it needs.
4) Information service: users can use portal to search effective resource information that their task needs, such as type of OS or CPU, current load of CPU, free memory or file space and state of network[2].
5) Service publishment: users can publish their own services for grid sharing.
6) Local resources integration: grid system can call local resources through user configuration.

As analyses mentioned above, the structure of grid system based on RIA and Web service is described as Fig. 1.

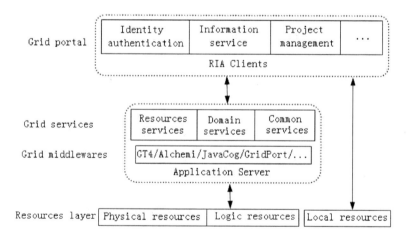

Fig. 1. Structure of grid system based on RIA and Web service

In Fig. 1, grid resources are distributed on different geographical districts; grid middleware and grid services work on application server; grid portal system works on client computer. The structure of grid portal system is described as Fig. 2.

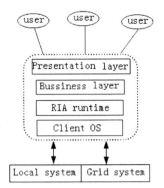

Fig. 2. Structure of grid portal system

4   Realization of Grid Portal Based on RIA

Currently,there are many realizing technologies about RIA,such as Adobe Flex/ Flash, Avalon by Microsoft and Java SWT. Our team adopts Adobe RIA technology to realize grid portal system.

Flex provides MXML and ActionScript together with JavaScript/Ajax to design rich client programme. Flex application can access Web service based on SOAP, Web page based on HTTP, and local system. It can run on different platform.

4.1   Design of Presentation Layer

Presentation layer design adopts MXML tags, UI controls, container components and Ajax technology, which provides customizable and lively user interface.

1) User interface design

Some Panel child containers are deployed in the Application container. Every panel that contains some components corresponds to one item grid portal function. DividedBox container divides Panel child containers. ViewStack navigation container realizes the switch of various panels. The panel can be zoomed in and out, draged and droped. Skin and theme can be used to improve component appearance. Developer can define animation effection for component action, present text dynamically, build and display geometric figure or Flash animation, publish videos and so on. In this design, Panel child containers replace portlets in the second grid portal. They all have the function of user custom, but former has more beautiful interface and easier design than portlet.

2) Integrating JavaScript and Ajax

JavaScript/Ajax can locally refresh and interact data speedily. FlexAjaxBridge can combine Flex with JavaScript, which contains FABridge.as and FABridge.js[3]. In Flex Builder, Flex and Ajax can be mixed to realize some functions, such as Flex UI using Ajax data as datasource.

4.2 Design of Logic Layer

Logic layer involves to access grid service, database and local system, or to design other specific computing function.

1) Access grid service
There are two ways to realize it.
   First, using WebService component directly. The main codes are as follows.

```
<mx: WebService id="RS1"
     Wsdl=http://192.202.12.11/ResourceService1.wsdl
     //point out the  method which will be excuted.
     <mx:operation name="doComputing">
          <mx:request>
     //point out the parameters which will be passed.
          C1=5;
              ...
          </mx:request>
     </mx:operation>
</mx: WebService>
<mx:Panel width="400" height="400" layout="absolute"
title="Computing Service">
   // call the method
   <mx:Button click="RS1.doComputing.send( )"
   x="230"y="330" label="compute" >
   ...
</mx: Panel>
```

Second, using agency to access grid service.
   Agency can realize to access grid service on different domain. For example, LCDS (LiveCycle Data Service) can be used as the agency of portal side. Therefore, configuration file services-config.xml must be modified, in which the definition of HTTPChannel under the node of <channels> and the definition of remote service under the node of <services> must be appended. Reverse agency also can be built. For example, FluorineFx and Flash Remoting MX can be used as the agency of server side which contains some grid services.

2) Access local application system
URLRequest class and its URL attribute can realize the access to local Web system based on HTTP and local file based on File protocol, whose app-storage scheme defines local file folder for AIR application storing data. In addition, Flex file system components can display and operate local file system, which contain the controls of tree, grid, list, combox and so on.
   Grid portal system provides simple configuration function for user. For example, user inputing Web address or file path, the system can integrate local application.

4.3 Design of Data Layer

Design of data layer contains three aspects. The first is to build local database. Adobe AIR (Adobe Integrated Runtime) includes a SQL database engine, which uses open source SQLite system to build database for storing persistent data. Second, using drag&drop API realizes dynamic field data exchange between applications, between application and desktop, between components in the same application. The data includes file, RTF data, text and so on. Third, portal exchanges data with grid service in XML data format.

4.4 Whole Realization Scheme

In conclusion, the overall implementation scheme of grid portal system is as follows.

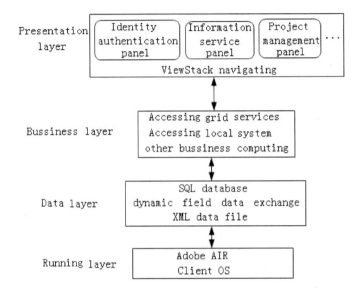

Fig. 3. Realization of grid portal system

Finally, Flex application programmes are packed into AIR file. So users download the runtime software and AIR file to finish installation, or do online installation by using Badge software. User run it as desktop application.

5 Conclusion

RIA technology has special advantages on system framework, operating efficiency and expressive force. It can bring grid user new interface and rich experience. Flex provides a relatively mature RIA development environment. How to use Flex fully to design a excellent grid portal system and make a development mode is the purpose of this study. Now the new portal design technology is presented, which avoids the former weeknesses, meets the needs of diversification of grid resources, multi-media user interface and personalized grid user. The research team takes compute grid as study case, and has developed grid portal experiment system based on RIA, which is being tested and improved. The deployment of the grid system and its grid services will be introduced in other paper.

References

1. Hu, C.M., Huai, J.P., Sun, H.L.: Web Service-Based Grid Architecture and Its Supporting Environment. J. Journal of Software. 15(7), 1064–1073 (2004) (in Chinese)
2. Li, M., Baker, M.: The Grid Core Technologies. John Wiley & Sons, Inc., Chichester (2005)
3. Zhang, Y.-f.: Proficient in Technology of Flex Network Development. Publishing House of Electronics Industry, Beijing (2009) (in Chinese)
4. Cao, C.-f.: Agile Manufacturing Resource Integration Based on RIA and Service Grid. In: 2010 International Conference on Mechanic Automation and Control Engineering, pp. 6058–6061. IEEE Computer Society, Piscataway (2010) (in Chinese)
5. Cao, C.-f.: The Research on Developing Technologies of C/S System Based on HTTP (in Chinese). J. Computer Engineering and Design 28(5), 1239–1241 (2007)
6. Gourdol, A.: Desktop Integration in Adobe AIR 2,
   http://tv.adobe.com/watch/adc-presents/
7. David, M.: Inside HTML5: The Browser becomes a first class RIA citizen,
   http://www.insideria.com/

Fractional Modeling Method of Cognition Process in Teaching Evaluation

Chunna Zhao[1], Minhua Wu[1], Yu Zhao[2], Liming Luo[1], and Yingshun Li[3]

[1] Information Engineering College, Capital Normal University, Beijing, China
[2] Yunnan Technician College, Kunming, China
[3] Engineering College, Shenyang University of Technology, Liaoyang, China
Chunnazhao@163.com

Abstract. Cognition process has been translated into other quantitative indicators in some assessment decision systems. In teaching evaluation system a fractional cognition process model is proposed in this paper. The fractional model is built on fractional calculus theory combining with classroom teaching features. The fractional coefficient is determined by the actual course information. Student self-parameter is decided by the actual situation potential of each individual student. The detailed descriptions are displayed through building block diagram. The objective quantitative description can be given in the fractional cognition process model. And the teaching quality assessments will be more objective and accurate based on the above quantitative description.

Keywords: fractional, cognition process, qualitative indicators, quantification.

1 Introduction

It makes people to improve capability through constantly contacting with the nature and community. It is process of people ability improvement that the process of learning more about things. That holding cognition process can analyze the rule and essence of understanding new things and learning new methods, and also can promote teaching reform and make people learn more knowledge using of more short-term. It is the gradually accumulation process that the process of learning about things, and it is integral model based on mathematical knowledge. Because cognition process is a complex nonlinear process that affected by many factors, traditional integer order calculus model is unable to accurately describe its action. Fractional order calculus has much to offer science and engineering by providing not only new mathematical tools, but also more importantly, and it implies the fractional order nature of actual dynamic world. Fractional order system is established on the idea of fractional order calculus and theory of fractional order differential equations, which is an extension to the conventional calculus problems. Fractional model is a mathematical modeling approach based on fractional calculus, and it provides a powerful decision support and scientific basis for cognition process.

The fundamental teaching purpose is that students can acquire knowledge as much as possible[1]. It is an important indicator of teaching quality assessment which

G. Shen and X. Huang (Eds.): ECWAC 2011, Part I, CCIS 143, pp. 135–141, 2011.
© Springer-Verlag Berlin Heidelberg 2011

students acquire the degree of knowledge through classroom teaching[2]. It is the cognition process that the process of students acquiring knowledge. This indicator is analyzed into some quantifiable indicators in previous assessment, and it can not objectively describe the degree of students obtaining knowledge. A fractional modeling method of cognition process is proposed in this paper.

The remaining part of this paper is organized as follows. In Section 2, mathematical foundation of fractional calculus is briefly introduced; in Section 3, a fractional model method is presented for cognition process; in Section 4, some practical examples are presented to verify the feasibility. Finally, conclusions are drawn in Section 5.

2 Fractional Calculus: A Brief Introduction

Although the fractional order calculus is a 300-years old topic, the theory of fractional order derivative was developed mainly in the 19th century. [3], [4] provide a good source of references on fractional calculus.

Fractional calculus is a generalization of integration and differentiation to a fractional, or non-integer order fundamental operator $_aD_t^\alpha$, where a and t are the lower/upper bounds of integration and α the order of the operation.

$$_aD_t^\alpha = \begin{cases} \dfrac{d^\alpha}{dt^\alpha} & R(\alpha) > 0 \\ 1 & R(\alpha) = 0 \\ \int_a^t (d\tau)^{(-\alpha)} & R(\alpha) < 0 \end{cases} \tag{1}$$

which $R(\alpha)$ is the real part of α. Moreover, the fractional order can be a complex number as discussed in [5]. In this paper, we focus on the case where the fractional order is a real number.

It is well known that fractional order systems itself is an infinite dimensional filter due to the fractional order in the differentiator or integrator while the integer-order systems are with limited memory (finite dimensional). There has been a surge of interest in the possible engineering application of fractional order differentiation. Examples may be found in [6] and [7]. Some applications including automatic control are surveyed in [8]. The significance of fractional order theory is that it is a generalization of classical integral order theory, which could lead to more adequate modeling and more robust control performance.

Fractional order systems could model various real materials more adequately than integer order ones and thus provide an excellent modeling tool in describing many actual dynamical processes[9]. Fractional model provides the scientific basis for prevention and treatment of satellite monitoring absorption rate [10]. The nematode movement can be simulated through fractional model [11]. It may be used for building "love" models using fractional-order system [12]. [13] modeled iron meteorites crystallization by fractional theory. And there are some people pay close attention to unemployment rates by means of fractional calculus [14].

Student cognition process is an essential factor in teaching assessment. It is a nonlinear process affected by a number of factors, such as, student own ability, student knowledge, grade of cognitive problems, teaching, teaching conditions, etc. The fractional cognition process model is proposed in this paper. Model parameters can be obtained by the corresponding actual data. It aims to reduce the complexity while improving the scientific validity of the assessment results based on the fractional cognition process model.

3 Fractional Model of Cognition Process

It is a complex multi-factor process that the process of students learning more about things. When students come into contact with a new thing, they take into account relation with previous knowledge. That is to say, they firstly determine it is either a completely new knowledge or an extension of existing knowledge. If it is a completely new knowledge, cognition process is similar to the linear process on initial stage. And then is similar to the curvilinear process. When students control a certain degree, qualitative leap is not naturally arisen, while it requires a number of related factors. If the course is an extension of existing knowledge, cognition process is similar to the curvilinear process. Achieving a certain degree, curve will still flatten.

In higher education schools, student learning courses are based on previous knowledge and extension of extension. The process of students learning the knowledge is similar to the rising phase of parabola.

Student cognition process can be modeled by improved Basset force and fractional model in this paper. Basset force mainly describes the process that the ball moves in a straight line. And when the ball sinks into the viscous fluid, two-phase flow in the actual ball movement is not linear motion. The force is impacted by other particles movement. At the beginning the ball entered the relatively fast. Then the force should be connected with particle size, particle and fluid density ratio and fluid pulsation frequency so on. The process is multi-factor process. Refer to the model of fractional Basset force, based on the character of student cognition process and a lot of relevant data, fractional cognition process model for one course can be modeled.

$$Dx(t) + \left(\frac{a}{b + c \cdot \lambda}\right)^{\alpha} D^{\alpha} x(t) + x(t) = 1 \tag{2}$$

where $x(t)$ expresses cognition process, and the result is the ability to achieve. Fractional coefficient α is determined by the actual course situation, the overall quality of students and teaching ways and means so on. Coefficient a, b, c are based on the course previously data. λ is decided by the actual situation of each individual student, and it can be quantized through students themselves potential, related courses performance, students self-evaluation and teacher evaluation so on.

The fractional simulation block diagram is used for the proposed fractional model[15]. Through building Simulink model, the numerical solution of fractional order nonlinear calculus equation can be obtained directly. A fractional calculus module has been mainly adopted. In fractional calculus model, a modified approximation method is introduced[16]. Based on series expansion and recurrence, the continuous rational transfer function is

$$G(s) = K\left(\frac{ds^2 + b\omega_h s}{d(1-\alpha)s^2 + b\omega_h s + d\alpha}\right)\prod_{k=-N}^{N}\frac{1+s/\omega_k'}{1+s/\omega_k} \tag{3}$$

where,

$$\omega_k' = \left(\frac{b}{d}\right)^{\frac{2k-\alpha}{2N+1}} \omega_h^{\frac{N+k+\frac{1}{2}(1-\alpha)}{2N+1}} \omega_b^{\frac{N-k+\frac{1}{2}(1+\alpha)}{2N+1}} \tag{4}$$

$$\omega_k = \left(\frac{b}{d}\right)^{\frac{2k+\alpha}{2N+1}} \omega_h^{\frac{N+k+\frac{1}{2}(1+\alpha)}{2N+1}} \omega_b^{\frac{N-k+\frac{1}{2}(1-\alpha)}{2N+1}} \tag{5}$$

$$K = (\omega_b \omega_h)^{\alpha} \tag{6}$$

where $2N+1$ is the order of approximation, and b, d are improvement factor. Here $b = 10$, $d = 9$, $N = 3$, and the pre-specified frequency range is $\omega_b = 0.001$, $\omega_h = 1000$.

4 Illustrative Example

Student mastery degree is an important indicator in the classroom teaching. It is key issues that building model for student mastering knowledge. Accuracy and effectiveness of the fractional model can be verified by taking Mathematical Modeling Course as an example.

There are 43 students in Mathematical Modeling Course. This course requires some knowledge of mathematics basis. And students have learned the relevant mathematics. The courses difficulty coefficient is 1.1. Teachers have some teaching experience. At the beginning fractional coefficient α should be identified founded on various practical situations in the course cognition model.

Generally that the larger the α value indicates the course is the more difficulty and teaching skill is general and students overall quality is not good. Otherwise that the smaller the α value indicates a small difficulty coefficient of the course, and teaching skills is better, and students overall quality is higher. Normal range of α value is interval (0, 1). The fractional coefficient can be determined grounded on the above factors, expert ratings and data analysis so on.

The coefficients a, b, c values can be confirmed through the optimal fitting method based on previous data and combining with the characteristics of classroom teaching. And then the fractional student cognition process model is constituted.

$$Dx(t) + \left(\frac{8}{1+662\lambda}\right)^{0.36} D^{0.36}x(t) + x(t) = 1 \tag{7}$$

Coefficient λ is determined by each student own quality. And it is impressed by student related courses achievement, student self-evaluation and teacher evaluation so on. That the larger coefficient λ value indicates that the student own factor is good, and related courses evaluation is better, and he has positive attitude. It is converse if the value λ is smaller. The value range is (0, 1).

A simulation model can be built based on fractional cognitive process model as shown below.

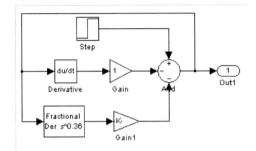

Fig. 1. Simulink model

Output is the process of student mastering knowledge. Simulation accuracy is depended on the approximate effect, approximate bands and the approximate order. It is can be found that it is the more accurate if the approximate order is the higher, but at the same time it is consuming. A number of data and experiments show that it should be selected as $\omega_b = 0.001$, $\omega_h = 1000$, $N = 4$. And then various factors and results are satisfactory.

Several students were randomly selected. Students themselves coefficients have been determined according to students own quality, subjective and accumulated in the past. Students themselves coefficients were respectively 0.03, 0.09, 0.24, 0.4, 0.9. Corresponding output curves can be obtained based on the above model and algorithm, as shown in Fig. 2.

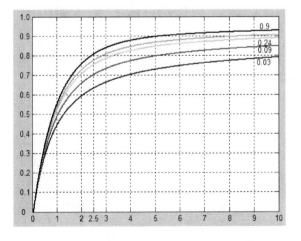

Fig. 2. Output curve of the corresponding λ

Curves in the figure are respectively the results when $\lambda = 0.03$, $\lambda = 0.09$, $\lambda = 0.24$, $\lambda = 0.4$, $\lambda = 0.9$ from bottom to top. It shows the cognition degree of this course that they achieve finally knowledge degree. That is to say, the curve denotes mastery degree to this course. For example, when λ is 0.03, the coefficient value is the lower. It also indicates that this student can not be good at Mathematical Modeling Course. The final value of corresponding curve is close to 0.8. That is to say, this student is best able to achieve eighty percent of the course knowledge under the effect of the student own factors and external factors. It is assumed that the duration is long enough. While instruction time of our normal course is limited. And it is not possible to attain the final result. The final result is acquired mainly by student subjective efforts and devotion. It is generally that the previous value is referred to. For instance, the time is 2 or 3. For 36 instruction time of Mathematical Modeling Course, the value is selected as the student mastery knowledge degree for the course when time is 2.5. The corresponding values were respectively 0.63, 0.7, 0.76, 0.78, 0.81. The final results are consistent with the selected students themselves evaluation. The effectiveness and accuracy of the proposed fractional model is illustrated adequately.

5   Conclusion

Cognition process is a complex process which people learn more about things. Cognition process is also very important information in many assessment decision systems. Because qualitative level is higher in cognition process, it is translated into other quantitative indicators in some decision systems. And some specific attribute information may be lost. For cognition process of university courses, the fractional cognition process model is proposed in order to evaluate teaching effect by rule and line in this paper. Student cognition process is a complex multi-factorial process, and it is not modeled by integer order model accurately. While fractional order system can model the complex process. And the corresponding process curves can be shown. At last, the validity of proposed method is validated by actual Mathematical Modeling Course.

Acknowledgments. This work is supported by Beijing Education Committee Science (KM201010028021) and Technology Foundation and Liaoning Nature Science Foundation (20082044, 20060624).

References

1. Zhao, C., Zhao, Y., Tan, X., Li, Y., Luo, L.: Course Evaluation Method Based on Analytic Hierarchy Process. In: IEEE CCCM, pp. 318–321 (2010)
2. Zhao, C., Li, Y., Luo, L.: Application of gray relational analysis for course evaluation. In: IEEE ICICTA, pp. 758–761 (2010)
3. Xue, D.-Y., Zhao, C.-N., Pan, F.: Simulation model method and application of fractional order nonlinear system. Journal of System Simulation, 2405–2408 (2006)
4. Zhao, C.-N., Zhang, X.-D., Sun, Y.-R.: Simulation of commensurate fractional order systems. Journal of System Simulation, 3948–3950 (2008)

5. Oustaloup, A., Levron, F., Mathieu, B., Nanot, F.M.: Frequency band complex noninteger differentiator: characterization and synthesis. IEEE Trans. Circuits Syst. I 47, 25–39 (2000)
6. Zhao, C.-N., Pan, F., Xue, D.-Y.: H∞ controller design for fractional order system. Journal of Northeastern University 27, 1189–1192 (2006)
7. Xue, D.-Y., Zhao, C.-N.: Fractional order PID controller design for fractional order system. Control Theory and Applications 24, 771–776 (2007)
8. Zhao, C., Zhang, X.: The application of fractional order PID controller to position servomechanism. In: IEEE WCICA, pp. 3380–3383 (2008)
9. Xue, D., Zhao, C., Chen, Y.: Fractional Order PID Control of A DC-Motor with Elastic Shaft: A Case Study. In: American Control Conference, pp. 3182–3187 (2006)
10. Olofsson, P., Eklundh, L.: Estimation of absorbed PAR across Scandinavia from satellite measurements. Part II: Modeling and evaluating the fractional absorption. Remote Sensing of Environment 110, 240–251 (2007)
11. Hapca, S., Crawford, J.W., MacMillan, K., et al.: Modelling nematode movement using time-fractional dynamics. Journal of Theoretical Biology 248, 212–224 (2007)
12. Ahmad, W.M., El-Khazali, R.: Fractional-order dynamical models of love. Chaos, Solitons & Fractals 33, 1367–1375 (2007)
13. Walker, R.J., McDonough, W.F., Honesto, J., et al.: Modeling fractional crystallization of group IVB iron meteorites. Geochimica et Cosmochimica Acta 72, 2198–2216 (2008)
14. Caporale, G.M., Gil-Alana, L.A.: Modelling the US, UK and Japanese unemployment rates: Fractional integration and structural breaks. Computational Statistics & Data Analysis 52, 4998–5013 (2008)
15. Zhao, C., Zhao, Y., Liu, Y., Li, Y., Luo, L.: Fractional Personnel Losing Modeling Approach and Application. In: IEEE CISE, pp. 1–4 (2009)
16. Xue, D., Zhao, C., Chen, Y.: A Modified Approximation Method of Fractional Order System. In: IEEE ICMA, pp. 1043–1048 (2006)

Design of an Improved Echo Canceller System Based on Internet of Things

Yi Li[1], Yi Lu[2], and Douwa An[3]

[1] School of Electronic and Information Engineering, Tianjin University, Tianjin, P.R. China
[2] Technicolor (China) Technology Co. Ltd, Beijing, P.R. China
[3] ZTE Corporation, Xian, P.R. China
annie@tju.edu.cn, yi.lu@technicolor.com, an.douwa@zte.com.cn

Abstract. This paper focuses on a modified echo canceller system developed to satisfy the requirements of long network time-delay in the Internet of Things. The NLMS algorithm used in it is modified to reduce the computational complexity with the characteristics of fast convergence speed and low steady-state mean-square error (MSE). Hardware platform and software program have been designed to verify this algorithm. The simulation results by MATLAB and practical system are presented in support of the feasibility and validity of the proposed algorithm and echo canceller system.

Keywords: Echo Canceller, Internet of Things, NLMS.

1 Introduction

The Internet of Things (IOT) is a technological revolution that represents the future of computing and communications. It realizes the vision of a fully interactive and responsive network environment [1]. However, the network time delay will increase dramatically since more and more data are transferred in the internet, therefore worsening the situation for the echo. To remove the undesirable echo, an echo canceller system can be applied. It learns adaptively the response from near-end transmitter to receiver, generates a replica of that echo, and subtracts that echo replica from the receiver input to yield an interference-free signal [2]. In this way, the echo can be reduced and the conversation quality in IOT can be improved.

Normalized Least Mean Square (NLMS) algorithm used in the echo canceller system has better convergence performance and less signal sensitivity than the conventional LMS algorithm [3] [4]. Furthermore, this algorithm is known to be robust against finite word length effects [5] [6]. But the original NLMS algorithm cannot efficiently alleviate the influence of echo in the Internet of Things. With an increased network time delay, the computational complexity is significantly increased, making it unpractical for real time echo cancelling applications. In this paper, we design an echo canceller system using a modified NLMS algorithm, which has the characteristics of lower computational complexity to serve the needs of IOT. Moreover, this NLMS algorithm is improved based on the NLMS algorithm in [7], and maintains the quality of faster convergence speed and lower steady-state mean-square error (MSE) than the original NLMS algorithm. In our implementation, TMS320VC5416 is used as the central process unit

G. Shen and X. Huang (Eds.): ECWAC 2011, Part I, CCIS 143, pp. 142–147, 2011.

while TLV320AIC23 is audio encoder/decoder (CODEC). The control program has been designed to verify the feasibility and validity of this echo canceller system.

2 Algorithm

The estimated echo signal is defines as follows,

$$Echo(i) = \sum_{k=0}^{n-1} W_k Y(n-k) \tag{1}$$

Where W_k are the coefficients of the adaptive transversal filter, Y(n) are the reference samples. In NLMS algorithm,

$$\hat{W}_k(n+1) = \hat{W}_k(n) + \mu x(n)e(n) \tag{2}$$

where e(n) is the error signal, μ is the step size that controls the convergence speed and stability.

NLMS algorithm employs a data-dependent step size at each iteration. The normalized μ is adjusted with the data as follows,

$$\mu = \frac{\beta}{\| x(n) \|^2} \tag{3}$$

where β is a constant number between 0 and 2.

There are two conflicting requirements on the step size μ. It should be large enough to have fast dynamics and hence fast forgetting of the initial parameter settings. On the other hand, a large step size means fast dynamics combined with a significant amplification of the driving term, which results in a large steady-state MSE. In order to overcome the compromise between fast convergence speed and low steady-state MSE, the optimal step-size sequence in [7] is introduced to improve the step size μ as

$$\tilde{\mu}(n) = \frac{\tilde{\mu}(n-1)[1 - \dfrac{\tilde{\mu}(n-1)}{M}]}{1 - \dfrac{\tilde{\mu}(n-1)^2}{M}} \tag{4}$$

We make further refinements to this algorithm so that the coefficients of the adaptive transversal filter are divided into M parts. Each part is non-continuous with fixed intervals. As a result, only N/M coefficients are refreshed simultaneously at one sampling point.

Finally, the adaptive echo canceller's coefficient at time instant n is defined as follows,

$$W_k(n+1) = W_k(n-M+1) + \frac{\tilde{\mu}(n-1)[1 - \dfrac{\tilde{\mu}(n-1)}{M}]}{1 - \dfrac{\tilde{\mu}(n-1)^2}{M}} \cdot \frac{x(n)}{\| x(n) \|^2} e(n) \tag{5}$$

Due to the exponential convergence speed of the step size μ from the initial value, the modified NLMS algorithm has the same characteristics of fast convergence speed and low steady-state MSE as in [7]. Moreover, Full coefficient refreshment completed every M input reduces its computational complexity. So this improved algorithm has better real-time property than before which can be applied into the IOT.

3   System Design

3.1   Overall Layout

The audio signals are recorded in Sound Wave (.WAV) format, with far-end signals in the left sound channel, and mixed signals composed by near-end signals and echo signals in the right sound channel. The echo is subtracted from the signals, which have been sampled at 8 kHz sampling rate in audio chip, and eliminated in DSP. Then the output signals of the audio chip can be compared with the original signals to evaluate the performance of the whole system.

3.2   Hardware

The architecture of echo canceller system is shown in Fig. 1. For the DSP module, we choose TMS320VC5416 of TI company, which fulfills the requirement of echo canceller system, and is easy to upgrade; For the audio encoder/decoder module, we select TLV320AIC23 of TI, which is a high-performance stereo audio codec. The A/D and D/A converters within it use multi-bit sigma-delta technology with integrated oversampling digital interpolation filters. Data-transfer word lengths of 16, 20, 24, and 32 bits and sample rates from 8 kHz to 96 kHz are supported. It also supports SPI Serial-Port Protocols, which is fully compatible with McBSP interface of DSP. It is used here to sample the analog signals in 8 kHz and transfer the data to DSP.

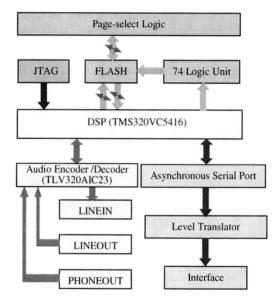

Fig. 1. Architecture of echo canceller system

The main feature here is the full use of left/right channel of TLV320AIC23. The prepared input signals can be sampled in different sampling rates for the 2 channels, just like 2 A/D converters for different signal sampling. In the same way, for the left/right channels we have 2 outputs, which can be used to compare the effect after the process of echo canceller system.

3.3 Software

The software of the echo canceller system includes main program and subprogram. The mains program does the initialization of the chip and then invokes the subprogram. The subprogram contains far-end and near-end speech detection program, echo estimation program, remnant echo cancellation program and filter coefficient updating program. The flow chart is shown in Fig. 2. The filter coefficient updating program is the core of the algorithm that directly impacts the performance of echo canceller system.

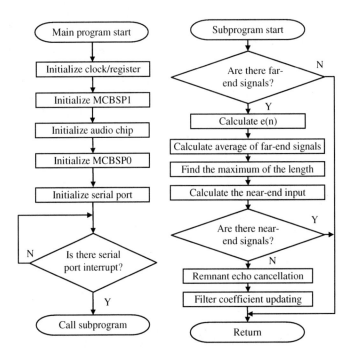

Fig. 2. Flow chart of the main program and subprogram

4 Conclusions

The left part of Fig. 3 displays the simulation result of the NLMS algorithm in [7] and the right part of Fig. 3 depicts the modified NLMS algorithm we used when echo path delay is 8ms and N=64. From the analytical results, it shows that the improved NLMS algorithm we used maintains the characteristics of fast convergence speed and low steady-state mean-square error (MSE) of the NLMS algorithm in [7] while its calculation complexity is significantly reduced.

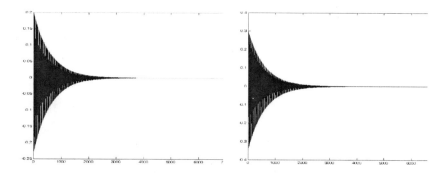

Fig. 3. Simulation result between the two algorithms

In CCS developing environment, the outputs of echo canceller are captured by breakpoints and the calculation result is shown in Fig. 4. The rapid convergence rate proves the validity of the improved NLMS algorithm.

In real-time simulation we use actual audio signal. The original signal and echo signal are input into DSP to be processed, and remnant echo is output in real time. After many experiments, trying different convergence factors and power windows, the coefficients are optimized. In the actual test under high latency environment, the echo is suppressed a lot and real time property is satisfied, which fulfill the requirements of echo canceller system in IOT.

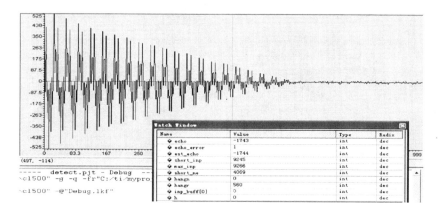

Fig. 4. Calculation result of the output of echo canceller

References

1. ITU Internet Reports 2005: The Internet of Things, Genève, ITU (2005), http://www.itu.int/osg/spu/publications/internetofthings/ (accessed on April 2010)
2. Le Bouquin-Jeannes, R., Faucon, G.: Control of an adaptive echo canceller using a near-end speech detector. Signal Processing 81(3), 483–489 (2001)

3. Lai, C.-A.: NLMS algorithm with decreasing step size for adaptive IIR filters. Signal Processing 82(10), 1305–1316 (2002)
4. Zerguine, A.: Convergence behavior of the normalized least mean fourth algorithm. In: Conference Record of the Thirty-Fourth Asilomar Conference on Signals, Systems and Computers (Cat. No.00CH37154), vol. 1, pp. 275–278 (2000)
5. Wu, J., Doroslovacki, M.: Partial update NLMS algorithm for sparse system identification with switching between coefficient-based and input-based selection. In: CISS 2008, the 42nd Annual Conference on Information Sciences and Systems, pp. 237–240 (2008)
6. Yusuke, T., Tetsuya, S.: An improved NLMS algorithm for channel equalization. In: IEEE International Symposium on Circuits and Systems, vol. 5, pp. 353–356 (2002)
7. Slock, D.T.M.: On the convergence behavior of the LMS and the normalized LMS algorithms. IEEE Transactions on Signal Processing, Vol 41(9), 2811–2825 (1993)

Demand Analysis of Logistics Information Matching Platform: A Survey from Highway Freight Market in Zhejiang Province*

Daqiang Chen[1], Xiahong Shen[1], Bing Tong[1], Xiaoxiao Zhu[1], and Tao Feng[2]

[1] College of Computer Science & Information Engineering, Zhejiang Gongshang University,
No. 18, Xuezheng Str., Xiasha University Town, Hangzhou, 310018, China
[2] College of Economics and Business administration, China University of Geosciences,
No. 388, Lumo Road, Wuhan, 430000, China
chendaqiang@mail.zjgsu.edu.cn

Abstract. With the increasing competition in logistics industry and promotion of lower logistics costs requirements, the construction of logistics information matching platform for highway transportation plays an important role, and the accuracy of platform design is the key to successful operation or not. Based on survey results of logistics service providers, customers and regulation authorities to access to information and in-depth information demand analysis of logistics information matching platform for highway transportation in Zhejiang province, a survey analysis for framework of logistics information matching platform for highway transportation is provided.

Keywords: logistics information matching platform, highway transportation, demand analysis.

1 Introduction

Logistics industry is a developing industry; logistics companies are also developing business. Logistics industry in Zhejiang is relatively simple function, low level of service, investment returns and operating margins less than satisfactory. The unreasonable transportation will result in transportation unreasonable detour, back, over transportation, repeat transportation phenomenon and so on .It is bound to result in a long time in transit of goods, more links, slow circulation, large cost, waste capacity and social workers, impact the social production and the market supply. So how to reduce business operating costs and increase their competitiveness becomes a serious problem. The waste of so many resources to produce the cost of business operations is produced by unshared of logistics information resources in some degree. Small, the operating state of disorder is simply not possible to obtain better economic benefit, so the establishment of a province and the country's information platform for the integration of resources, to achieve regional logistics information sharing, to maximize resource utilization is imperative.

* This paper is supported by Zhejiang Provincial University Students Scientific Innovative Project and Zhejiang Gongshang University Students Scientific Innovative Project.

G. Shen and X. Huang (Eds.): ECWAC 2011, Part I, CCIS 143, pp. 148–154, 2011.
© Springer-Verlag Berlin Heidelberg 2011

This paper aims at the framework of a logistics information matching platform for highway transportation. The organization of the paper is as follows. In section 2, the situation of present logistics industry in Zhejiang province is analyzed. In section 3, three specific access ways for logistics information of highway transportation are described and analyzed. Section 4 discusses the total demand of logistics information matching platform for highway transportation. In section 5, some planning elements of logistics information matching platform are suggested. The final section summarizes the major conclusions and suggests further research topics.

2   Analysis of Zhejiang Road Freight Market

In recent years, highway transportation saw a rapid development, participation in Cargo transport vehicles and cargo turnover of holdings. In 2007, the total highway transportation continued to grow, Zhejiang Province have completed the transportation of 987 million tons of cargo and 49.36 billion ton-kilometers, 1.53 times in 2002 and 1.63 times. The province has 436 000 vehicles including 347000 ordinary trucks, 24100 special vehicles, 62000 van; 9948 container lorries, 9940 dangerous goods transport vehicles, growth rate of 26% and 24%conpared with the numbers in 2006 [1]. But as the holdings of vehicles and cargo turnover rate continue to rise, resource utilization has become an increasingly prominent issue. The results of survey on the development status of logistics in Zhejiang Province are as follows:

- *Low services level*: Most of the professional logistics companies transformed from freight and warehouse, most just stop at the transportation, warehousing, freight forwarding services, such as a single, it is difficult to provide integrated services.
- *Difficulties in Obtaining Information Sources for Shipper and Carrier*: The province's total logistics costs account for 18.3% rate of GDP, information is not high, logistics resources scattered, logistics is lack of effective collaboration and cooperation between enterprises.
- *Enterprise information is still in its infancy*: According to the survey results, such as Chuanhua Logistics, the company established a network system, but only for the enterprise inside, without information share with other companies.

3   Analysis of the Access Ways for Logistics Information

3.1   Information Sources for Shipper and Carrier

To understand the status of highway freight market, the way to access to information of freight and car, and the use of network information platform, a survey is carried out. In this survey, nearly one hundred questionnaires were distributed to logistics transport companies and 100 questionnaires were distributed to 100 manufacturing companies, the final recovery of the questionnaires is 36 and 64 respectively, which were used as a statistical and analysis base. Here are some of the results.

Based on the survey data, it's found that the shipper's information sources in market were limited to the carriers that had associated with them before, which dues to the relatively low risk of the goods' transportation, but with increased transport costs for the lack of competition. And, on the other hand, the effective use of the carriers' vehicles is also very important issues. Through such information sources, the scope of finding available carriers is limited. The survey results show that the shipper use the Internet as a way to find the carrier is the least one, as illustrated in Fig. 1.

Fig. 1. Information sources for shipper and carrier

3.2   Difficulties in Obtaining Information Sources for Shipper and Carrier

Fig. 2 shows that instability of the carrier source and high tariffs are the main problems in obtaining information sources for shipper, which was mainly cased by the restriction of the carrier's information, for example, many shippers may have experienced the situation that when they want to find carriers, but on carrier is available, and sometimes there are excessive carriers to choose. The unawareness of the carrier's information is root of the problem. Nowadays, in term of intermediary company or others, in order to protect their own interests, their own information resources are not shared with the public.

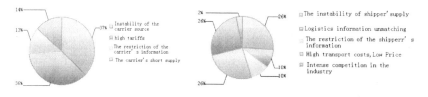

Fig. 2. Difficulties in obtaining information sources for shipper and carrier

3.3   Influencing Factors of Transportation Costs

The survey results illustrated that the poor matching of shipper and carrier's information causes raising of logistics costs, which is the main factors impacted the logistics costs, as in Fig. 3 shows. And in the practice, the poor matching of shipper and carrier's information and the unreasonable transportation schedule are serious and must be solved.

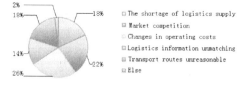

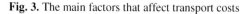
Fig. 3. The main factors that affect transport costs

3.4 "Dilemma" in Highway Freight Market and Solution

According to the results of these surveys, we can find that matching of vehicle and goods, high empty driving problems are the main factors that lead to high logistics cost, but due to the existence of competition, most businesses were in different array. It is difficult to form an orderly market; the shippers are suffering from the difficulty to find a suitable carrier, while the carriers are in troubled with finding goods to transport.

In response to the situation above, a number of websites that provide logistics information have sprung up, such as zj56 (http://www.zj56. com.cn), chinawutong (http://www.chinawutong.com), 8glw(http://www.8glw.com/) and so on[2-4]. These freight information platforms can integrate shipper and carrier source effectively, and make goods and vehicles source searching without location restriction.

In the term of the integration of goods and vehicles resources to reduce wastage rate, the logistics information platform enables users to easily find the resources which they need, and prevent phenomenon that the vehicle and goods does not match. The efficient use of vehicle and cargo resources can also reduce logistics costs to some extent.

However, in practice, as the survey shows, the users of these websites don't think the websites so well. Although some shippers and carriers are willing to find information from the Internet, but most of them were doubt on the network information security, and holed attitudes that Internet may provide false information.

Most of the shippers and carriers think that the convenience of searching on website is bad. As far as the current situation in China freight market is concerned, the majority of users of the logistics website are poor in Internet for their cultural level.

4   Analysis of the Total Demand of Logistics Information Matching Platform

Logistics information matching platform in highway freight transportation is an integrated, intelligent logistics information management center for the entire highway freight logistics system. Logistics information matching platform in highway freight transportation participations include the regulation authorities in government, enterprises and users in freight market. Building the logistics public information platform aims to provide information to support the enterprise, to provide conditions to support the relevant industry sectors to logistics management and market management: integration of the whole community micro-logistics resources to provide different content information service enabling logistics information. Through the establishment of logistics information matching platform in road freight transportation, it will achieve fast, convenient, real-time logistics information exchange.

Therefore, from the view of regulation authorities in government, logistics enterprise and business enterprise/users, the total demand analysis are:

- *Logistics enterprise*:Information of public logistics infrastructure, information of logistics market demand, information resources of logistics business, and other logistics consulting services;

- *Business enterprise*: Information of logistics providers, logistics business transaction management, special and value-added services;
- *Regulation authorities in government*: Including the basic data processing of regional logistics operation, regional integration of resources to support the logistics function, regional logistics analysis and planning support.

Each one of the participations has different information demands of logistics information matching platform in highway freight transportation as the following aspects:

- *Dependence on information around shipping logistics system*: The logistics enterprises have large dependence on the information of public logistics infrastructure, transport network, and require the presence of public information platform to improve access to logistics information and reduce information costs;
- *Differences of freight logistics information needs*: Logistics information needs in logistics, use of outsourcing of logistics customers and government is different. The difference is mainly reflected in: the time difference, content and different degree;
- *Complexity of freight logistics information exchange*: Integrated logistics services involved in differences of a number of business entities, the main economic relations, technology, culture and information system module, leading to the complexity of the logistics information exchange;
- *Limited of freight logistics data sharing*: Part of the logistics business to its particular user is based on closed system operation, sharing internal information and external areas is very limited.

5   Logistics Information Matching Platform Planning Elements

Most sites have information platform, but there is a credit security most users can not make access to information through the Internet. Therefore, a comprehensive security system is very important.

5.1   To Establish the Safety Integrity

This section includes the following two aspects.

- *member rating system*

Users are divided into three levels, directly registered user is C grade. If relevant documents are available, such as picking station owners provide identity cards, business license, road license, etc, then the user can be upgraded to B grade. On this basis, if the release of information reaches a certain level, or trading volume reached a certain standard, and without customer complaints, the background will upgrade the users to A grade. Information published by higher level user will be distinguished by different colors, and preceded by rank sign in front of each message with small stars, the more small stars it has, the higher and the credit rating on the mark. This would be the maintain information security, and encourage users to publish more information. As shown in Fig. 4.

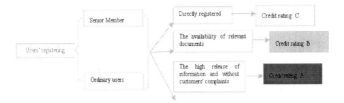

Fig. 4. Member rating system

- *Integrity member libraries*

Carrier's vehicle database information includes the carrier's personal information (such as ID number, driver photos, driving vehicles, etc.), and divide the integrity of vehicles into different classes, primarily on the number of its transactions, and the owner of the praise of their degree. Every transaction time, the owner can be give one evaluation, divided into good, middle and poor, who was named best plus one points, medium without points, and poor by one point cut. The users can refer their integrity according to scores obtained by other users. The procedure is illustrated in Fig. 5.

Fig. 5. Online Trading

5.2 To Provide SMS Service

Nowadays, the SMS service has 6.8834 million users account for 47.3% of the population, and also has very strong momentum of development. It is well know that Chinese likes to exchange text messages. According to data from the Ministry of Industry and Information Technology (2008), mobile phone users sent a total of 56.87 billion messages, send text messages per user per day on average 3.01.

From the perspective of users, the shipper or carrier is basic proficiency in using of cell phones. It is feasible for the information platform to send vehicle and cargo information by text messages in real-time. No matter when it is and where it is, you can have access to the latest vehicle and cargo information, and solve situation that the user can not access the information platform by Internet. And the information platform can also provide a reminder service for web users to complete the transaction ever better.

6 Conclusion

The construction of logistics information matching platform will solve the dilemma situation of highway freight market effectively. Beside the high cost of construction, the support from government and cooperation of many aspects, the difficulty is not technical, but in the effective requirements analysis and functional design. A reasonable logistics information matching platform can promote the enterprise's logistics sector, government, logistics companies and customers to maximize communication and resource sharing.

References

1. Zhejiang Provincial Communications Department, Zhejiang Academy of Social Sciences. Zhejiang Transportation and the reform and opening up three decades. Hangzhou Press, Hangzhou (2008) (in Chinese)
2. Ministry of Industry and Information Technology. National Statistics reports the communications industry operations (2008) (in Chinese)
3. Bagualaiwang logistics information, http://www.8glw.com
4. Public Logistics Information Service Platform of Zhejiang Province, http://www.zj56.com.cn
5. China Wutong Logistics Information Website, http://www.chinawutong.com

Flexible Endian Adjustment for Cross Architecture Binary Translation

Tong Zhu, Bo Liu, Haibing Guan, and Alei Liang

School of Software, Department of Computer Science,
Shanghai Key Laboratory of Scalable Computing and Systems,
Shanghai Jiao Tong University, Shanghai 200240, China
{ztgreat,boliu,hbguan,liangalei}@sjtu.edu.cn

Abstract. Different architectures and/or ISA (Instruction Set Architecture) representations hold different data arranging formats in the memory. Therefore, the adjustment of byte packing order (endianness) is indispensable in cross-architecture binary translation if the source and target machines are of heterogeneous endianness, which may otherwise cause system failure. The issue is inconspicuous but may lead to significant performance bottleneck. This paper investigates the key aspects of endianness and finds several solutions to endian adjustment for cross-architecture binary translation. In particular, it considers the two principal methods of this field — byte swapping and address swizzling, and gives a comparison of them in our DBT (Dynamic Binary Translator) — CrossBit.

1 Introduction

Binary translation allows software compiled for the source machine to be converted to run on the target machine while achieving reasonable performance on that machine. Therefore it is feasible to run binaries on heterogeneous architectures such as x86, PowerPC, SPARC, MIPS, ARM, etc. Furthermore, it can be used to support legacy binary code [1], support ISA virtualization [2], enable innovative co-designed micro-architectures [3], and many other applications [4-9].

In cross-architecture binary translation there is a critical problem: endianness. Endianness is the ordering of individually addressable sub-units (words, bytes, or even bits) within a longer data word stored in memory. The most typical cases are the ordering of bytes within a 16-, 32-, or 64-bit word, where endianness is often simply referred to as byte order. Byte order is an important consideration in cross-architecture binary translation, since software is being migrated from one machine to anther machine with completely reverse byte orders. Failure to account for varying endianness when writing code for mixed platforms necessarily leads to bugs that may be difficult to detect.

Recently, cloud computing has been the highlight of information world since it offers a computing paradigm that allows users to temporary utilize computing infrastructure over the network, supplied as a service by the cloud-provider at possibly one or more levels of abstraction[10]. Endianess is also an unavoidable issue in cloud computing infrastructure, for the cloud clients and servers located at the

G. Shen and X. Huang (Eds.): ECWAC 2011, Part I, CCIS 143, pp. 155–162, 2011.

different ends of the cloud may have distinct architectures, which means they hold different data arranging formats in the memory. Similarly, the situations appear in the fields of telecommunication, the embedded system, network programming, etc.

In this paper, we present a summary of several aspects of endianness, with a classification of its components, and the relationships as well as their dependency. In addition, we explore the solutions to endian adjustment for cross-architecture binary translation.

The rest of this paper is organized as follows. Section 2 presents the background description of endianness and dynamic binary translator features. Section 3 describes the two principal methods for cross-architecture binary translation while section 4 gives detailed design and implementation using the two methods in our developed DBT CrossBit. We discuss the performance evaluation of the system with the two approaches in section V and recapitulate our work in section 6.

2 Background

2.1 Mix-Endianess

Endianness is the byte (and sometimes bit) ordering in memory used to represent some kind of data. Typical cases are the order in which integer values are stored as bytes in computer memory (relative to a given memory addressing scheme) and the transmission order over a network or other medium. When specifically talking about bytes, endianness is also referred to simply as byte order.

This is similar to the situation in written languages, where some are written left-to-right, while others are written right-to-left. However, endianness does not matter in dealing with a sequence of single bytes. This is the case with strings encoded in ASCII and similar codes, where one byte corresponds to one character. Strings encoded with Unicode UTF-16 or UTF-32 are affected by endianness because in those, a set of two or four bytes represents one character.

There are two main camps of memory byte ordering that are used by present machine architectures: little-endian byte ordering (e.g. Intel IA32, PDP-11) and big-endian byte ordering (e.g. SPARC, PA-RISC).

2.1.1 Big-Endian

Big-endian machines store the most significant byte on the lowest memory address (the word is stored big-end-first).

increasing addresses →

. . .	0x0A	0x0B	0x0C	0x0D	...

Fig. 1. Big-endian format storing in memory

The most significant byte (MSB) value, which is 0x0A in our example in Figure 1, is stored at the memory location with the lowest address, the next byte value in significance, 0x0B, is stored at the following memory location and so on. This is akin to Left-to-Right reading order in hexadecimal. In Figure 2 below we give a diagram to illustrate the mapping from register to memory or from memory to register with big-endian format.

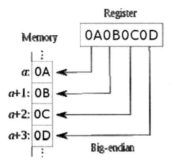

Fig. 2. Mapping between register and memory in big endian

Well known processors that use the big-endian format include Motorola 6800, IBM POWER, and System/360 and its successors such as System/370, ESA/90, and z/Architecture. SPARC also historically used big-endian until its version 9.

2.1.2 Little-Endian
Little-endian machines store the least significant byte on the lowest memory address (the word is stored little-end-first).

increasing addresses →

Fig. 3. Little-endian format storing in memory

The least significant byte (LSB) value, 0x0D in Figure 2, is at the lowest address. The other bytes follow in increasing order of significance. Figure 4 gives the mapping between memory and register with little-endian format.

Well known processor architectures that use the little-endian format include x86, 6502, Z80, VAX, and, largely, PDP-11.

Many serial protocols may be regarded as big-endian (at the bit- and/or byte-levels) in the sense that the most significant part of the data is sent first. However, there are also serial formats with the least significant bit sent first. Furthermore, bit and byte order is often reversed (or "transparent") in the interface between the UART or communication controller and the host CPU, DMA controller, and system memory. These interfaces may be of any type and are configurable.

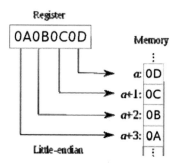

Fig. 4. Mapping between register and memory in big endian

2.2 Dynamic Binary Translator Features

There are many dynamic binary translators now, such as UQDBT [11], QEMU [12] and CrossBit [13], etc. Mostly, DBT uses basic block as the translation unit. DBT first uses a Source Program Counter (SPC) to look up the SPC-TPC (Target Program Counter) map table. If the SPC value exists in the map table, this basic block has been translated. The corresponding target code is stored in the Target Code Cache (Tcache), and then the processor directly jumps to TPC to execute the instructions. Otherwise, if the lookup result shows that there is a code cache miss, the processor will translate the source code block to target code block, then places it in the Tcache. Figure 5 illustrates the entire process of DBT.

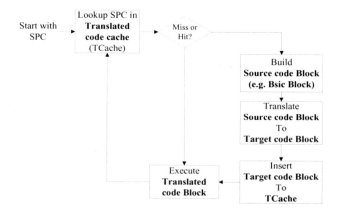

Fig. 5. Structure of DBT

CrossBit is a retargetable dynamic binary translator implemented by Shanghai Jiao Tong University. It's a process virtual machine developed mainly to provide the platform independent computing service for virtualized execution environment. For platform adaptability, CrossBit creates the intermediate representation named intermediate instruction (II) layer, which is used to unify the representation of various sources and target instruction sets. It mainly functions in quick adding guest/host platforms for the CrossBit designers. However, unlike the typical machine adaptive DBT systems, CrossBit doesn't generate the translator automatically. The binary is interpreted from the guest to II, and then translated from II to the host, are all hand-written in the object-oriented language. Programmers may take the infrastructural interfaces of CrossBit translation module and reuse the others together with overall system mechanism. The obvious advantage of this infrastructure is that it provides CrossBit with direct II quality control, which is much harder to complete in above systems. And with intermediate representation, CrossBit can unify the semanteme of guest platforms, and port existed optimization from compilers to the II.

3   Cross Architecture Binary Translation

Cross architecture binary translation can be achieved by either modifying the effective addresses of memory accessing instructions, or by converting the result from stores and loads to the native target machine endian ordering. The former technique is known as address swizzling, and the latter achieved by byte swapping. In this section we illustrate how to implement cross architecture binary translation with the two methods in Our CrossBit. And we take the MP program for example in which the source machine is MIPS while PowerPC is the target machine.

3.1   Address Swizzling

In address swizzling, the original effective address for the memory access is adjusted to correct the "reversed" data values. Sometimes it is desirable to have memory organized in a different endian order to the native target machine's order. For example, when running x86 Openoffice(OS: linux) on the PowerPC(a big-endian machine). Since Openoffice expects the data to be in little-endian order, and without altering the physical data layout, data accesses will require modifying those addresses and offsets. If address 0x2000 contains a 32-bit value stored in little-endian format, then the native big-endian machine will adjust its memory access by the following formula:

Swizzled address = HighWMark − (SIZE + EA − LowWMark) [14] where:
LowWMark to HighWMark are the memory address ranges for which data is of a different endian order.

LowWMark holds the lowest address of the range and HighWMark holds the highest address. LowWMark = 0x2000 and HighWMark = 0x2004 for the example.

SIZE is the number of bytes the memory instruction is fetching/writing.

EA is the effective address requested by the original program.

For example, if the original source instruction loads 16 bits from 0x2002 (i.e., 2 bytes), the swizzled address will be 0x2004 − (2 + 0x2002 − 0x2000), which is 0x2000.

Specifically, in CrossBit we implements endian adjustment with address swizzling mainly by modifying the effective address of memory accessing instructions in intermediate instruction (II) which is called VINST. VINST contains two memory accessing instructions: LD and ST(see Figure 6). LD loads data of size sz from the memory address v(imm) to the virtual register v while ST stores data of size sz from the virtual register v to the memory address v(imm).

| **LD** (*v, imm*), *sz, v* | | **ST** *v, sz,* (*v, imm*) |

Fig. 6. LD And ST Instruction of VINST

Then take LD for example, we can obtain the effective address of memory access: ea = [*v*] + *imm*. The data size *sz* must be also taken into consideration.

1) If *sz* equals to 1, which means loading byte data, we let i = ea modulo 4 (ea%4). If i = 0, then ea =ea + 3; if i = 1, then ea = ea + 1; if i = 2, then ea = ea - 1; if i = 3, then ea = ea – 3.
2) If *sz* equals to 2, which means loading half-word data, we let i = ea modulo 4 (ea%4). If i = 0, then ea =ea + 2; if i = 2, then ea = ea – 2.
3) If *sz* equals to 4, which means loading word data, we do not need address swizzling.

3.2   Byte Swapping

The second option to cross architecture binary translation is to simply byte swap every read and write access to and from memory. Below is an example implementation of a 32-bit byte swap macro:

```
#define swap(x) (((((x) >> 24) & 0xff) | ((x) << 24) | (((x)>> 8) & 0xff00) | (((x) << 8) & 0xff0000))
```

Processors may provide special features that can ease the byte swapping process. Intel's 80486 and above processors provide a bswap instruction for cross-endian data handling, while SPARC-V9 and PowerPC processors have special load/store instructions that can access memory using a different endian ordering.

Below we show how to implement byte swapping in our CrossBit:

3.2.1   The Phase of Loading Executable and Linkable Format File

The basic principle of reversing byte ordering is that you should reverse it when the instructions access memory. When load the executable and linkable format file, you need to reverse the byte ordering of every section (word) of file-header and program-header. For example, flip_elf32_hdr (&fileHeader) is a function that reverses the byte ordering of whole file-header which uses byte swapping.

After reversing the file-header and program-header, the next words needs to reverse are some flags. Also the environment variables need to reverse, since it happened that the program cannot run correctly when not considering reversing the environment variables.

3.2.2   The Phase of Translating Instructions

The phase of translating instruction also called decoding. The instructions should pay more attention are load-store instructions. Such as lb, lbu, lh, lhu, lw, lwl, lwr, ll, sb, sbu, sh, shu. sw, swl, swr, cc. There are many special instructions that reversing byte ordering when accessing memory in the PowerPC architecture. Such as lwbrx, lhbrx, swbrx, shbrx. The source instructions which access memory need to reverse and the native access memory should not reverse.

4 Performance Evaluation

In this paper, we implement the experiments on Xilinx Virtex-II Pro FPGA board. The platform uses PowerPC405 processor combined with a coprocessor, which contains the Tcache manager and translation unit of virtual machine. Seven SPEC INT2000 benchmarks with reference input are chosen to measure the performance. And all these benchmark programs were cross-compiled using powerpc-405-linux-gnu into statically linked executable binary file.

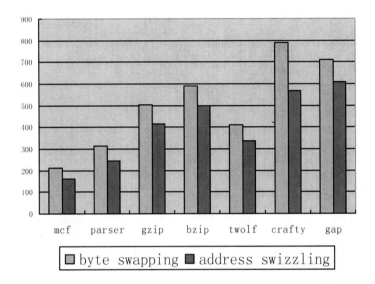

Fig. 7. Comparison of the performance of byte swapping and address swizzling

Figure 7 shows execution time of benchmarks in CrossBit MP program of address swizzling and byte swapping respectively. The address swizzling method has better performance than the byte swapping method, the average performance superiority is 17%, and the most superiority comes from crafty (28%).

The performance superiority may come from the reason below: address swizzling simply adjusts endianness by modifying the effective address of memory accessing instructions, thereby avoids the internal byte order movement of the data.

5 Conclusions

In binary translation when the source machine and target machine are of different endianness, it is crucial to find a solution to endian adjustment. And there are two main methods in solving the endianness problem at present, address swizzling and byte swapping respectively. Byte swapping swaps bytes whenever there is a memory access, while address swizzling modify the effective address of memory accessing instructions. In this paper, we deeply investigate several key aspects of the two camps and make experiments in our DBT CrossBit to find out that address swizzling has better performance than byte swapping.

Acknowledgment

This work is supported by the National Natural Science Foundation of China (Grant No. 60773093, 60970107, 60970108), The Science and Technology Commission of Shanghai Municipality (Grant No. 09510701600), IBM SUR Funding and IBM Research-China JP Funding, Intel Research-China Funding.

References

1. Baraz, L., Devor, T., Etzion, O., Goldenberg, S., Skaletsky, A., Wang, Y., Zemach, Y.: IA-32 Execution Layer: a two-phase dynamic translator designed to support IA-32 applications on Itanium-based systems. In: IEEE MICRO, pp. 191–204 (2003)
2. Adams, K., Agesen, O.: A comparison of software and hardware techniques for x86 virtualization. In: Proceedings of International Conference on Architectural Support for Programming Languages and Operating Systems (ASPLOS), pp. 2–13 (2006)
3. Klaiber, A.C.: The Technology Behind Crusoe Processors, Transmeta Technical Brief (2000)
4. Bala, V., Duesterwald, E., Banerjia, S.: Dynamo: A transparent dynamic optimization system. In: Proceedings of International Conference on Programming Language Design and Implementation (PLDI), pp. 1–12 (2000)
5. Borin, E., Wang, C., Wu, Y., Araujo, G.: Software-Based Transparent and Comprehensive Control-Flow Error Detection. In: Proceedings of International Conference on Code Generation and Optimization (CGO), pp. 333–345 (2006)
6. Coronato, A., Pietro, G.D., Gallo, L.: An agent based platform for taskdistribution in virtual environments. Journal of Systems Architecture Embedded Systems Design (JSA) 54(9), 877–882 (2008)
7. Luk, C.K., Cohn, R.S., Muth, R., Patil, H., Klauser, A., Lowney, P.G., Wallace, S., Reddi, V.J., Hazelwood, K.M.: Pin: Building customized program analysis tools with dynamic instrumentation. In: Proceedings of International Conference on Programming Language Design and Implementation (PLDI), pp. 190–200 (2005)
8. Qin, F., Wang, C., Li, Z., Kim, H., Zhou, Y., Wu, Y.: LIFT: A Low Overhead Practical Information Flow Tracking System for Detecting Security Attacks. In: Proceedings of International Symposium on Microarchitecture (MICRO), pp. 135–148 (2006)
9. Wu, Q., Martonosi, M., Clark, D.W., Reddi, V.J., Connors, D., Wu, Y., Lee, J., Brooks, D.: A Dynamic Compilation Framework for Controlling Microprocessor Energy and Performance. In: Proceedings of International Symposium on Microarchitecture (MICRO), pp. 271–282 (2005)
10. Youseff, L., Butrico, M., Da Silva, D.: Toward a Unified Ontology of Cloud Computing. In: GCE 2008, Grid Computing Environments Workshop (2008)
11. Ung, D., Cifuentes, C.: Machine-adaptable dynamic binary translation. In: Proceedings of the ACM Sigplan Workshop on Dynamic and Adaptive Compilation and Optimization, January 18. ACM Sigpaln Notices, vol. 35(7), pp. 41–51. ACM Press, New York (2000)
12. Bellard, F.: QEMU, a Fast and Portable Dynamic Translator. Proceedings of the USENIX Annual. Technical Conference, Anaheim, CA, USA, April 10-15 (2005)
13. Bao, Y., Guan, H., Li, J., Liang, A.: Mobilizing Native machine Code via Dynamic Binary Translation. In: Proceedings of the 3rd International Workshop on Software Development Methodologies for Distributed Systems, Shanghai China, pp. 73–78 (2006)
14. Ung, D., Cifuentes, C.: Dynamic binary translation using run-time feedbacks. Science of Computer Programming 60(2), 189–204 (2006)

A Novel Word Based Arabic Handwritten Recognition System Using SVM Classifier

Mahmoud Khalifa and Yang BingRu

University of Science and Technology, Beijing,
Information Engineering School, 100083 Beijing, China
hoota-2007@hotmail.com, bryang_kd@yahoo.com.cn

Abstract. Every language script has its structure, characteristic, and feature. Character based word recognition depends on the feature available to be extracted from character. Word based script recognition overcome the problem of character segmenting and can be applied for several languages (*Arabic, Urdu, Farsi... est.*). In this paper Arabic handwritten is classified as word based system. Firstly, words segmented and normalized in size to fit the DCT input. Then extract feature characteristic by computing the Euclidean distance between pairs of objects in n-by-m data matrix X. Based on the point's operator of extrema, feature was extracted. Then apply one to one-Class Support Vector Machines (*SVMs*) as a discriminative framework in order to address feature classification. The approach was tested with several public databases and we get high efficiency rate recognition.

Keywords: DCT, Feature extraction, Maxima, FER, SVM.

1 Introduction

Handwriting has continued to persist as a means of communication and recording information in the day-to-day life even after the introduction of new technologies. It plays essential roles in many applications, such as office automation, Cheques verification, mail sorting, and a large variety of banking, business as well as natural human-computer interaction. A preprocessing with segmentation is very known operation in character recognition in first stage then applies structural and statistical features extraction for classification and recognition.

Normally OCR systems depend on segmenting the word to character what can decrease the word recognition precision as in Goraine [1] where he presented a structural approach. Arabic printed and handwriting character recognition widely use HMM based systems because of the connected nature of the Arabic script [2][3][5]. Researcher continuously working to overcome segmentation problems as in [30] [4].

Like object recognition systems, we use signal processing model to extract features [10]. Since the DCT is less sensitive to shift, rotate and scale, it would largely contribute to the performance of most template matching methods. Traditionally,

G. Shen and X. Huang (Eds.): ECWAC 2011, Part I, CCIS 143, pp. 163–171, 2011.

template matching methods works in the spatial domain, based on the assumption that the position of each point is known, so if the correspondence of the maxima point is taken, then the Euclidean distance is measured by the difference of the maxima "value" more detail in section three. Most handwritten recognition system methods, however, normalization of position and size has to be done prior to the feature extraction process [7]. The remainder of this paper is organized as follows. Section two a previous work of word based handwritten recognition. Section three gives an overview of the applied robust features. Section four describes the SVM-based classier. Experimental set up and results are provided in Section five. Section sex concludes the paper.

2   Previous Work

Most of the previous work on hand written depends on character segmentation and separation. Recently papers [2] take whole line - *line based recognition* - of word and applies classification algorithms for character recognition [1]. Few works take a whole word as target. This section presents previous works dedicated to the recognition of handwritten word by using DCT and non DCT system.

2.1 Word Base DCT Systems

Jawad H AIKhateeb [8] apply DCT features extraction for each word sample then utilize them to train a neural network for classification. Jawad H AIKhateeb [9] used the word level criteria a extracted five groups of features including block-based where the absolute mean value for each block in the word image is computed, global and block-based DCT coefficients, moments and wavelet coef-ficients. Multi scripts recognition by G. Rajput [7] is based upon features ex-tracted using Discrete Cosine Transform (DCT) and Wavelets of Daubechies fam-ily. It actually had been discussed by G. Rajput, that the DCT operation could provide a good effect on recognition by pattern classification. CAO Jian2hai [10] use wavelet transform and the discrete cosine transform (DCT) to extract features in Chinese character recognition system.[11]H. Fujisawa uses discrete Fourier transform (DCT) as frequency responses computation stage for directional selectivity of the feature.

2.2 Word Base Non DCT System

José A.[12] obtain a set of feature by applying the SIFT key point descriptor . Zhiyi Zhang, [13] introduced a novel method for inspired SIFT descriptor, for Chinese character recognition. Simon Gunter,[14] examine the influence of the vocabulary size, the number of training samples, and the number of classifiers on the perform-ance of three ensemble methods in the context of cursive handwriting recog-nition. In his approaches aimed at extracting the topological structure of a word in order to perform recognition. [16] Toni M.Rath, segment each page in the collection into words and preprocess each segmented word image. For each image A in the collection he Determine the set of images which have an appearance similar A based on some features that can be quickly calculated (This is the pruning step) then he Compared image a against all images in his set P.

3   Methodology

3.1   Structural and Statistical Features

Structural features are intuitive aspects of writing, such as loops, branch-points, endpoints, and dots. For Arabic character they are often, but not necessarily, computed from a skeleton of the text image. Many Arabic letters share common primary shapes, differing only in the number of dots and whether the dots are above or below the primary shape of character. This perspective may be a reason that structural features remain more common for the recognition of Arabic character than for that of Latin script. Statistical features are numerical measures computed over images or regions of images. They include, but are not limited to, pixel densities, histograms of chain code directions, moments, and Fourier descriptors. Word based recognition uses the second kinds as general object recognition method for feature extraction as explained below.

3.2   Feature Extraction

In the preprocessing as in fig (1), normalization and DCT is applied as important stage before feature extraction. The DCT expresses a sequence of finitely many data points in terms of a sum of cosine functions oscillating at different frequencies that are necessary to preserve the most important features [17]. Through the extraction of the low-frequency DCT coefficients, the goal of reduction of dimensionality in feature space can be achieved .The most general assumption about word used for training and testing is that both training and testing feature contain continually varying. As it is well acknowledged that DCT coefficients can help to reduce redundancy and focus the energy of the image in a very limited frequency range [10] in the left upper corner. The DCT features of DCT coefficients are used in our system and extracted via two dimensional DCT. Given an image, its 2D DCT transform is defined as follows:

$$f(u,v) = \alpha(u)\alpha(v)\sum_{i=0}^{I-1}\sum_{j=0}^{J-1} f(i,j)\cos\left[\tfrac{(2i+1)}{2I}\right]\cos\left[\tfrac{(2j+1)}{2J}\right] \tag{1}$$

Given the DCT result of one image, its energy in frequency domain can be measured by:

$$E = \sum_{u=0}^{U-1}\sum_{v=0}^{V-1} f^{2}(u,v) \tag{2}$$

3.3 Feature Points

According to the Euclidean distance formula (3), the distance between two points in the plane with coordinates (x, y) and (a, b) is given by u = (x1 ·y1) and v=(x2 ·y2) the two points on the plane, their Euclidean distance is given in equation (3). We select the feature maxima points in descending order from distance point.

$$dist((x, y), (a, b)) = \sqrt{(x - a)^2 + (y - b)^2} \tag{3}$$

Geometrically, it's the length of the segment joining *u* and *v* , and also the norm of the difference vector (*considering* $\mathbb{R}^n$ *as vector space*). A function has a global (*or absolute*) maximum point at x^* if $f(x^*) \geq f(x)$ for all *x*. Similarly, a function has a global (*or absolute*) minimum point at x^* if $f(x^*) \leq f(x)$ for all *x*. The global maximum and global minimum points are also known the argument (input) at which the maximum (*respectively, minimum Concavity*) occurs [17].

In the application of feature detection we need features which provide a sufficient description of the surface and stays nearly the same, if the object changes marginally. In our case, after DCT stage we compute the Euclidean distance of the DCT matrix as in fig(2.a). Then compute the feature points as extrema on extremism paths as analogously done in fig (2.b). An extremes path r is a sequence of external vertices over the scales. That means, the vertices r (i) of the maximum path r have locally maximal signature values in all scales i = 1,...,l:[21]. Figure (2) bellow shows the process.

(a)   (b)   (c)

Fig. 1. illustrate preprocessing   a) original image b) binerization c) DCT

3.4 Principal Component Analysis (PCA)

We use PCA to preprocess the data and perform dimension reduction before Recursive Feature Elimination (RFE). Feature selection methods for SVMs are often used to reduce the complexity of learning and evaluation. Those less important components can be removed thus reducing the dimension of the space. PCA is an appropriate dimension reduction method for SVM classifiers because SVM is invariant under PCA transform. In this article we used the combination of, Recursive Feature Elimination (RFE), with Principal Component Analysis (PCA) to produce a multi-class SVM framework for handwritten recognition[29] .

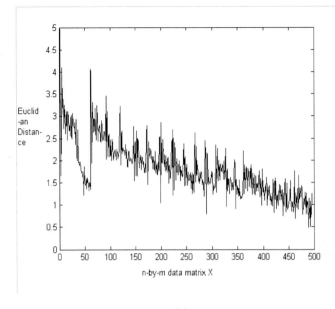

(a)

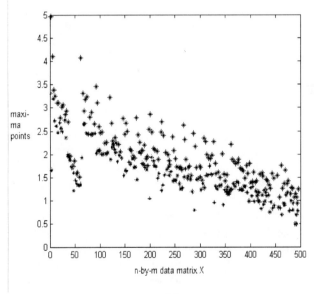

(b)

Fig. 2. a) Euclidian Distance   b) Extrema Points

3.5 Recursive Feature Elimination (*RFE*)

Recursive Feature Elimination (RFE) is an iterative procedure to remove non-discriminative features [18] in binary classification. The frame-work of RFE consists of the following steps: 1) Train the classifier 2) Rank the features based on their contribution to classification and   3) Remove the feature with the lowest ranking. Go to step 1) until no more features remain.

4   SVM Based Recognition

The features can be geometrical , statistical or structural , K-means clustering algorithm was success in both one and two dimensional [19], Neural Network Classifier called artificial neural network (*ANN*) altuwaijri and bayoumi [20] , Hussein and Bouzerdoum [21] , Hassibi [22] and Amin, Alsadoun [24] have applied ANN to recognize Arabic text, Statistical classifier the classifier assumes that different classes and feature vector have an essential combined probability like Hidden Markov Models (*HMMs*)[25].

   The Support Vector Machine (*SVM*) was originally designed for binary classification problems [26].SVM is a new promising pattern classification technique. In many problems SVMs have been shown to provide better performance than more traditional techniques because they show a great ability to generalize[27] . In many cases, it outperforms most state of the art classifiers. In recent years many pattern recognition problems have been tackled using support vector machines from vision problems to text classification. However, their application to specific handwritten recognition problems has been very limited. The recognition step uses the word fragments which converted into vectors through a feature extraction process. After segmenting words from document images, the task of recognition becomes assigning each word to a class out of a predefined set. A variety of pattern recognition methods are available, and many have been used for handwriting recognition. Generally, an SVM classifier is a binary linear classifier in kernel-induced feature space and is formulated as weighted combination of kernel functions on training examples. In SVM a classification task usually involves with training and testing data which consist of some data instances. Each instance in the training set contains one target value (*class labels*) and several attributes (*features*). The training module takes the training instance stored in the input file and trains the network. The goal of SVM is to produce a model which predicts the target value of the data instances in the testing set which are given only the attributes. One-against-one scheme [28] is used here where each SVM is used to discriminate between a pair of classes. So for n classes, there should be n(n - 1)/2 SVMs[8]. In the classification module, the features of the unknown word is calculated and given as input along with the support vectors. The features are given to all the classifier. The Max wins voting strategy is used here for prediction. If the testing result of ijth class says the unknown character x is in the ith class, then the vote for the ith class is added by 1. Otherwise, the vote for jth class is increased by 1. Then pattern x is classified to the class of maximum number of votes. Similar work using SVM as classifier is [21] Tamil hand written recognition.

5 Experiment

The basic handwritten text recognizer used in the experiments of this paper is similar to the one described in [8].we use IFN/ENIT Database ,see next section(5.1) The feature point are calculated for the training set and test set. SVM is trained using the training set of data and the recognition accuracy is calculated for the test data. Based on hand written experimentation which produces high recognition accuracy for test data. When the writer changed, the system achieved more detailed pixel variations. However, due to the varying nature of handwriting, there was high dissimilarity between the feature vectors of the same class. The best results were produced by using mono fonts for all writers. The system is trained and tested with (980) words belonging to 7 different Arabic printed phonates. This feature dimension vector contained a value between 1 - n corresponding to the number of maxima obtained from the DCT matrix.

5.1 Dataset

IFN/ENIT Database of Tunisia Arabic handwritten town/village name [30] is widely used for word recognition. It consists of 26459 handwritten Tunisian town/village names, about 115000 pieces of Arabic words (*PAWs*), and about 212000 characters. Each handwritten town name comes with binary image bitmap and additional GT information. in this paper we used the already ready segmented word (*PAWs*) for training and testing. The system is also tested by a printed Arabic word which is used by Hosni [2][31] .The tool at[32][33] was used in training and testing experiment with mat lab .

5.2 Results and Discussion

The overall recognition accuracy for all the 56 handwritten classes is 92.04%. The highest recognition accuracy of printed 95.9% is achieved for word Tohama and the lowest recognition accuracy of 89.84% is achieved for the naskh as summarized in table 1 below.

Table 1. Shows the handwritten and printed database result obtained by the system

database	accuracy	accuracy with RFE
IFN/ENIT	89%	91.7%
PATS-A01	92%	93%

6 Conclusion

This paper presents a system to recognize offline hand-written Arabic word by inspiring a new method of feature extraction used with a robust classifier. The DCT stage described in this paper are particularly useful with locale maxima due to their distinctiveness , The result shows that the algorithm works well for handwritten words and the recognition accuracy is between 90% and 98.9% for different Arabic words. The main recognition errors were due to abnormal writing and ambiguity among similar shaped word. Future work can include extracting more robust features for the classifier to achieve better discrimination power.

References

1. Goraine, H., Sher, M., Al-Emami, S.: Off-Line Arabic Character Recognition. Computer 25, 71–74 (1992)
2. Al-Muhtaseb, H.A., Mahmoud, S.A., Qahwaji, R.S.: Recognition of offline printed Arabic text using Hidden Markov Models. Signal Processing 88, 2902–2912 (2008)
3. Jiang, J., Weng, Y., Li, P.: Dominant color extraction in DCT domain. Image and Vision Computing 24, 1269–1277 (2006)
4. Wick, M.L.: Context-Sensitive Error Correction Using Topic Models to Improve OCR. In: International Conference on Document Analysis and Recognition (2007)
5. Benouareth, A., Ennaji, A., Sellami, M.: HMMs with explicit state duration applied to handwritten Arabic word recognition. In: Presented at 18th International Conference on Pattern Recognition, ICPR 2006 (2006)
6. Vinciarelli, A.: A survey on offline Cursive Word Recognition. Pattern Recognition 35, 1433–1446 (2002)
7. Rajput, G.G., Anita H. B.: Handwritten Script Recognition using DCT and Wavelet Features at Block Level. In: IJCA Special Issue on: Recent Trends in Image Processing and Pattern Recognition, RTIPPR (2010)
8. AlKhateeb, J.H.: Word-based Handwritten Arabic Scripts Recognition using DCT Features and Neural Network Classifier. In: 5th International Multi-Conference on Systems, Signals and Devices (2008)
9. AlKhateeb, J.H.: Multiclass Classification of Unconstrained Handwritten Arabic Words Using Machine Learning Approaches. The Open Signal Processing Journal 2, 21–28 (2009)
10. Cao, J.: New Method of Feature Extraction Using Wavelet Transform and DCT in OCR. Journal of Optoelectronics Laser (2004)
11. Fujisawa, H., Liu, C.L.: Directional Pattern Matching For Character Recognition. In: Proc.7th ICDAR, Edinburgh, Scotland, pp. 794–798 (2003)
12. Rodríguez, J.A., Perronnin, F.: Local gradient histogram features for word spotting in Unconstrained handwritten documents (2008)
13. Zhang, Z., Jin, L., Ding, K., Gao, X.: Character-SIFT: a novel feature for offline handwritten Chinese character recognition. In: 10th International Conference on Document Analysis and Recognition (2009)
14. Günter, S.: Off-line cursive handwriting recognition using multiple classifier systems—on the influence of vocabulary, ensemble, and training set size. Optics and Lasers in Engineering 43, 437–454 (2005)
15. Günter, S.: HMM-based handwritten word recognition: on the optimization of the number of states, training iterations and Gaussian components. Pattern Recognition 37, 2069–2079 (2004)
16. Rath, T.M.: Features for Word Spotting in Historical Manuscripts. In: International Conference on Document Analysis and Recognition (ICDAR 2003). IEEE, Los Alamitos (2003) 0-7695-1960-1/03 $17.00

17. Hansen, E.R.: Global optimization using interval analysis: the one-dimensional case. Journal of Optimization Theory and Applications (1979)
18. Guyon, I., Weston, J., Barnhill, S., Vapnik, V.: Gene selection for cancer classification using support vector machines. Machine Learning 46, 389–422 (2002)
19. Wilpo, J., Rabiner, L.: A Modified K-Means Clustering algorithm for use in Isolated work. Recognition ASSP 33(3), 587–594 (1985)
20. Altuwaijri, M., Bayoumi, M.: Arabic Text Recognition using Neural Network. In: Proceedings of IEEE International Symposium on Circuits and Systems, London, Uk, pp. 415–418 (1994)
21. Hosseini, H., Bouzerdoum, A.: A system for Arabic character recognition. In: IEEE Proceeding of the International Conference on Information System, Brisbane, Australia, pp. 120–124 (1994)
22. Hassibi, K.: Machine- printed Arabic OCR using Neural Networks. In: The 4th International Conference and Exhibition on Mult-Lingual Computering, Cambridge, UK (1994)
23. Amin, A., Alsadon, H., Fisher, S.: Hand printed Arabic character recognition system using an artificial network. Pattern Recognition 29(4), 663–675 (1996)
24. Almaadeed, S., Higgens, C., Elliman, D.: Recognition of off line hand witten Arabic words using hidden markov model approach. In: Proceedings of the 16th International Conference on Pattern Recognition, August 2002, vol. 3, pp. 481–484 (2002)
25. El-Hajj, R., Mokbel, C., Likforman-Sulem, L.: Arabic Handwriting Recognition Using BaselineDependant Features and Hidden Markov Modeling. In: Proceedings of the 2005 Eight International Conference on Document Analysis and Recognition, ICDAR 2005 (2005)
26. Boser, B., Guyon, I., Vapnik, V.: A training algorithm for optimal margin classifiers. In: Haussler, D. (ed.) The Fifth Annual ACM Workshop on Computational Learning Theory, pp. 144–152 (1992)
27. Mahmud, S.A., Awaida, S.M.: Recognition Of Off-Line Handwritten Arabic (Indian) Numerals Using Multi-Scale Features And Support Vector Machines Vs. Hidden Markov Models. The Arabian Journal for Science and Engineering 34(2B)
28. Shanthi, N., Duraiswamy, K.: A novel SVM-based handwritten Tamil character recognition system. Pattern Anal. Applic. 13, 173–180 (2010)
29. Lei, H., Govindaraju, V.: Speeding Up Multi-class SVM by PCA and Feature Selection. In: Feature Selection in Data Mining (FSDM 2005), The 5th SIAM International Conference on Data Mining Workshop, California, USA (2005)
30. Pechwitz, M., Maddouri, S.S., Margner, V., Ellouzeand, N., Amiri, H.: IFN.'ENIT Database of Arabic Handwritten words. In: Colloque International Francophone sur l'Ecritet le Document (CIFED), pp. 127–136 (2002)
31. http://faculty.kfupm.edu.sa/ICS/muhtaseb/ArabicOCR/PATS-A01.htm
32. Ma, J., Zhao, Y., Ahalt, S.: OSU svm classifier matlab toolbox (2002), http://www.kernel-machines.org/
33. Chang, C., Lin, C.: Libsvm: a library for support vector machines (2001), http://www.kernel-machines.org/

The Relationship between Economic Development and Environment Pollution: A Study in Zhejiang Province

Shizhu Liu

Department of Economics, Zhejiang University,
Hangzhou, China, 310000
liushizhu56@gmail.com

Abstract. From the industrial society, environment pollution has become an important problem as economic grows. People want to know the relation between economic development and environmental pollution, to find out a method to achieve long-term growth under a better environmental condition. In this paper, I use the software SAS and the data in Zhejiang Annual Statistic Data from 1985 to 2009, draw a conclusion that the environment was aggravating while the economic kept increasing, and finally give some suggestions and predictions to the government.

Keywords: EKC, Economic Development, Environment Pollution, Zhejiang Province.

1 Introduction

The industrial revolution several hundred years ago created huge productive power. Meanwhile, the environmental were getting worse for pollutions and damages. Environment protectors began appealing to use economic income to make up the environmental damages. As a result, economists and environmentalist tried to get laws from investigating on the relationship between economic development and environment pollution, and find a way to make a win-win situation.

Grossman and Krueger (1991) first brought forward an opinion of Environmental Kuznets Curve (EKC). They found that the relation between average income and environmental damage was a U-curve, and when the average income of a country reached the turn point between 4000 and 5000 dollar, the increase of economy tend to alleviate the problems of environment pollution. Refs. [1]

After that, Shafik (1994) found that when average income increased, drinking and health problems kept being ameliorated, but solid waste and carbon emission continued deteriorating. Selden and Song (1994) studied the discharge of four important air contaminants (SO_2, CO_2, NO_2 and SPM), and they found that there was inverted U-curve between income and them.

In our country, things are getting different. Through studying the data of 29 different cities in China from 1999 to 2005, Guo Hongyan drew a conclusion that the relationship between environmental pollution and economic increasing were uncertain: some were inverted U-curve, but some were inverted N-curve or even linear. Refs. [6] Cai Luojia used environment and economic data of Hubei from 1985 to 2004, and he

G. Shen and X. Huang (Eds.): ECWAC 2011, Part I, CCIS 143, pp. 172–177, 2011.

concluded that the environmental curve of Hubei was not a typical EKC, but a conspicuous cubic curve. These points reflect the Chinese feature of EKC. Refs. [3]

Shen Manhong (1998) used the data of Zhejiang Province from 1981 to 1988, and analyzed the relationship between per capita GDP and industrial waste. He found a complex curve which was first an inverted U-curve and then a U-curve. However, correlation coefficients R^2 of two models in this paper, about the industrial exhaust gas and the industrial water waste, were too small to support his conclusion. And we also see that the error between curves of these models and actual data was large. By referring a lot of materials, we didn't find any other analyses of other scholars about the EKC of Zhejiang, and we didn't see any new results after 2000, either. Refs. [5]

As an economic leading district in China, Zhejiang has met a lot of problems in environmental pollution. Studying the relationship between economic increasing and environmental pollution, including bringing forward some suggestions, are meaningful to our country.

Based on models built by predecessor, we used the data in Zhejiang Annual Statistics Data from 1985 to 2009, and got the relation curve of economic increase and environmental pollution.

2   Methods and Computational Results

2.1   Simulation

Some results are mentioned in the Literature Review. Though different places have different situation, the general relation curve of economic development and environmental pollution is quadratic or cubic. So we choose the models below to simulate.

$$y = a+bx+cx^2+e \qquad (1)$$

$$y = a+bx+cx^2+dx^3+e \qquad (2)$$

In these two equations, y denotes each of three typical environmental indexes, x denotes per capita GDP, a,b,c,d are parameters, e is the random error term.

The data of per capita GDP, industrial discharge of exhaust gas, industrial discharge of waste water and industrial output of solid waste is as below.

Table 1. Data used to simulate models

Year	GDP	EG	SW	WW
1985	1063	1860	679	107360
1986	1180	2239	929	112972
1987	1400	2511	760	109218
1988	1726	2465	778	102721
1989	1885	2553	798	107422
1990	2122	2595	847	130229
1991	2540	4676	888	102049
1992	3187	3136	945	116626

Table 1. (*Continued*)

1993	4431	2878	949	105734
1994	6149	2996	953	100703
1995	8074	3108	1018	102807
1996	9455	3279	1027	85481
1997	10515	4884	1326	124813
1998	11247	5016	1390	113018
1999	12037	5417	1361	117132
2000	13416	6509	1386	136433
2001	14655	8530	1603	158113
2002	16838	8532	1778	168048
2003	20147	10432	1976	168088
2004	24352	11749	2318	165274
2005	27703	13025	2514	192426
2006	31847	14702	3096	199593
2007	37411	17467	3613	201211
2008	42214	17633	3785	200488
2009	44641	18860	3907	203441

1. GDP is per capita GDP of Zhejiang (Unit: Yuan).
2. EG is the total discharge of industrial exhaust gas (Unit: 0.1 billion m^3).
3. SW is the total output of industrial solid waste (Unit: 10 thousand ton).
4. WW is the total discharge of industrial waste water (Unit: 10thousand ton).

The simulation results using SAS are shown as below:

Table 2. Simulation Results

Environmental pollution index	Model Type	Model coefficients			
		Constant Term	Linear Term	Quadratic Term	Cubic Term
Discharge of exhaust gas	Quadratic	1522.74	0.38935	2.817E-7	
	Cubic	2304.08	0.0896	1.980E-5	-3.082E-10
Discharge of solid waste	Quadratic	684.73	0.0542	4.982E-7	
	Cubic	778.90	0.0181	6.840E-6	-3.715E-11
Output of waste water	Quadratic	97507.00	3.1932	1.347E-5	
	Cubic	1110166.00	-1.6637	3.028E-4	-4.994E-9

Environmental pollution index	Model Type	Correlation Coefficient adjust-R2	Linear Term	t-test number Quadratic Term	Cubic Term
Discharge of exhaust gas	Quadratic	0.9694	7.53(<0.0001)	0.23(0.8170)	
	Cubic	0.9794	0.92(0.3674)	3.42(0.0026)	3.43(0.0025)
Discharge of solid waste	Quadratic	0.9885	9.31(<0.0001)	3.59(0.0016)	
	Cubic	0.9929	1.72(0.0998)	4.54(0.0002)	3.82(0.0010)
Output of waste water	Quadratic	0.8325	3.74(0.0011)	0.68(0.5049)	
	Cubic	0.8850	1.03(0.3170)	3.14(0.0050)	3.32(0.0032)

* Number in brackets is the probability Pr >|t|.

F-test numbers of these 6 equations are large (not listed in the table), so all these equations are significant.

(1) In the simulation of Discharge of exhaust gas, the linear term of regression equation of cubic model is not significant, while both coefficients of quadratic model are significant under the level of α=0.1. So we consider the quadratic model better than the cubic model.

(2) In the simulation of discharge of solid waste, correlation coefficient R^2 of quadratic model and cubic model are close to each other, but the coefficients of quadratic model are obviously more significant than those of cubic model. The quadratic model is obviously better than the cubic model.

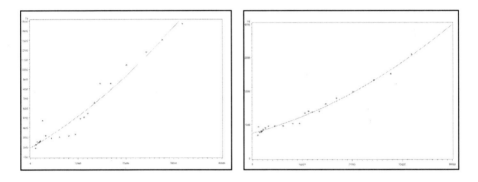

Fig. 1. The result of regression for exhaust gas   **Fig. 2.** The result of regression for solid waste

From the results above, we see that the inverted U-curve does not appear in the discharge of industrial exhaust gas and solid waste. Though the indexes of them pace up and down when per capita of GDP are under 12000, they increase with GDP basically. As we see, Zhejiang Province didn't pay enough attention to controlling the discharge of industrial exhaust gas and solid waste.

(3) In the simulation of discharge of waste water, the correlation coefficient R2 of the cubic model is obviously larger, and the three coefficients are all significant under the level of α=0.1. The linear term of regression equation of quadratic model is not significant, so the cubic model is better.

   Effluent discharges are under control when per capita GDP is less than 5000 Yuan (1985-1993). The turn point appears at about 1994, when per capita GDP is between 5000 and 6000 Yuan, which means the problem of water pollution deteriorates. In the year of 2005 and 2006, the Kuznets inverted U-curve appears, which means that the effluent discharges is ameliorated with the economic increase. As we see, Zhejiang Province did better in controlling effluent discharges than the other two.

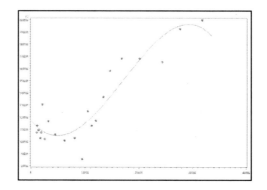

Fig. 3. The result of regression for waste water

2.2 Analysis

(1) From the simulation results, we find that the discharge of waste water of Zhejiang is different from the others. There are several reasons.

First, there are many rivers in Zhejiang, and coastal cities which have highest income discharge most of industrial waste water of Zhejiang. So it is easy for Zhejiang government to control the effluent discharges and govern the water pollution.

Second, river, lake and scream----water is always a point for Zhejiang to attract the tourists. So the Province government has enacted a lot of laws to protect water, and they also held activities to appeal to stop the water pollution.

(2) The economic increase of Zhejiang was based on the cost of environmental damages. This is a general phenomenon in developing countries.

3 Conclusions

From the study above, we can draw a conclusion that the Environmental Kuznets Curve is not significant in the economic increase of Zhejiang Province, and we cannot just lay the problem of environmental damage to the increase of economy. We therefore give some suggestions.

First, develop the recycling economy, which is not only a sufficient method to realize the harmonic development between people and nature, but also an important way for Zhejiang to achieve the target of constructing an environmental province.

Second, pay more attention to developing the tertiary industry, because technical industry and service industry would cause much less environmental damages than agriculture and industry.

Third, invest more on environment protection. According to the science experience of developed countries, a high speed developing country can only control the environmental damage by investing 1% to 1.5% of its GDP on environment protection, and ameliorate the quality of environment by investing more than 3%. However, the investment of Zhejiang on pollution controlling was quite small. This investment of Zhejiang was only 1.11% of GDP in 2006.

As stated above, the study of relationship between economic increase and environment pollution is meaningful to our country. Through examining the Kuznets Curve with data of Zhejiang Province, we find some different features between China and the West. We hope that China can maintain healthy development through regarding the environment protection based on the success stories of the West.

References

1. Grossman, G.M., Krueger, A.B.: Environmental Impacts of a North American Free Trade Agreement (1991)
2. Grossman, G.M., Krueger, A.B.: Economic Growth and the Environment (1994)
3. Cai, L., Zhang, X.: Research on the relationship between economics development and environment pollutions in Hubei Province. Contemporary Finance & Economics 8 (2006)
4. Wang, Y., Xu, C., Chen, W.: Research on the relationship between economics development and environment pollutions in Nanjing. Resource and Environment of Changjiang River Region 3 (2006)
5. Shen, M., Xu, Y.: A kind of new Environment Kuznets Curve – empirical research on the relation between environment changes and economic development in the industrial process of Zhejiang Province. Zhejiang Social Science 2 (2000)
6. Guo, H., Fan, F., Wu, J.: Empirical research on the relation between economics development and environmental pollutions in China. Guiding Newspaper of Science and Technology 25, 16 (2008)

Integrated Tourism E-Commerce Platform for Scenery Administration Bureau, Travel Agency and Tourist

Zhixue Liang and Shui Wang[*]

Software School, Nanyang Institute of Technology, Nanyang 473000, Henan, China
{zhixueliang,wangshuimail}@gmail.com

Abstract. Collaboration among multiple travel agencies and with scenery administration bureaus is vital for small or medium sized travel companies to succeed in the fierce competition of the tourism industry; business processes such as regrouping individual travelers between different agencies prove to be difficult and unpleasant user experience; tourists want to be more informed and have more initiative. To address these issues, proposes an integrated tourism e-commerce platform for travel agencies and scenery administration bureaus as well as tourists to interact in a more smooth way; this platform is constructed upon J2EE framework, provides online collaboration & coordination for companies and information services (such as self-navigation using Google Map etc) for tourists. A running implementation of this platform has been put into real business for a small travel company.

Keywords: tourism e-commerce, regrouping of tourists, self-navigation, traveling online store.

1 Introduction

With the development of Internet and e-commerce, traditional business model has been changed profoundly. In view of its characteristics of service style and content, tourism industry is very much suitable for online processing. Compared with traditional industries (such as book shops, electronic products, etc), the tourist industry has more advantages in e-commerce, for example, it is a kind of intangible product, which does not need the support of a logistics center. Its essence is information communication between the providers and the consumers[1]. So travel service providers can provide consumers with more convenience, efficient service via the Internet. Concluding from the current trends of domestic tourism industry and the present situation of international competition, e-commerce can be the new driving force for China's tourism industry development. It is a question worthy of consideration on how to utilize e-commerce platform to win one place of our own among the competitive tourism market.

2 Current Situation of Tourism E-Commerce

The definition of travel e-commerce most widely used internationally is as follows [2]:

---

[*] Corresponding author.

G. Shen and X. Huang (Eds.): ECWAC 2011, Part I, CCIS 143, pp. 178–184, 2011.
© Springer-Verlag Berlin Heidelberg 2011

Travel e-commerce is to improve internal and external connectivity of travel organizations by advanced information technology. That is to say, among different tourism enterprises, suppliers and tourists, communication and transactions could be improved. At the same time, the internal processes of the enterprises and knowledge sharing could also be promoted.

The tourism e-commerce has been taking shape after ten years development. However, it has some defects such as its' single form and serious homogeneous phenomenon in service content. Several specialized traveling websites as "Elong", "Ctrip" and "Mangocity"[8,9,10] have more influence and relative fixed profit models, other traveling sites are falling into difficult situation, such as fierce competition and razor-thin profit in varying degrees. This situation has emerged because of many reasons, but the following factors can not be ignored[3,4,5].

1. Tourism enterprises devote deficient energy to the network marketing
Many travel industries' operators are all the traditional merchants, so several of them may realize the importance of Internet marketing. They usually pay attention to offline advertisement as newspaper which needs high expenditure. Then they will take such measures as reducing expenditure, cutting price and so on to increase profit. These measures not only affect the quality of service and the image of travel agency, but also achieve difficultly good sales performance.

2. Under-developed information and lacking understanding of network in tourism enterprise.
Many travel companies still manage their internal business using manual measures. Despite a growing number of travel agencies recognize the importance of the network, but most of usage still stay in the primary stage and limit to simple data processing and report processing which is far from the advantages of network. Not only that, since many travel companies do not realize that enterprise information is the premise of e-commerce. So in the case of lacking information development, eagerly to develop e-commerce sites will inevitably result in difficulties of information integration, unity function of sites and slow update of web information. In the current situations, it must be inevitable that the web sites can not effectively attract customers, and the online trading is lower and so on.

3. Many small-sized tourism enterprises
Most of travel industries are small-sized and each of them does their things in their own way in the development of electronic commerce, the consequence is that they can't form a large scale for effectively attracting users, it can also lead to reconstruction of the websites. So it is necessary to strengthen cooperation of the electronic commerce enterprises and integrate their own resource.

4. Single marketing network model of travel agency
Many electronic commerce websites concentrate on the releasing of traveling information, tourism products and single market price competition. They don't take full advantage of Internet information service to improve service quality and to meet the demands for user. So it leads to single marketing network and low rate of utilization.

This paper explores an integrated solution for travel agency, tourist and scenery administration bureau based on the analysis of traveling e-commerce. This solution is proposed closely around the three factors of tourism activities: travel agency, tourist and scenery administration bureau. In this solution strategy, small and medium-sized travel agencies can mutually deal with such complicated online transactions as regrouping of tourists from different tourist agencies, to improve their working efficiency. Tourists can utilize the system's Google-Map functionality for self-navigation and scenery administration bureaus can interact with each other as well as tourists via online store for coordination and collaboration for traveling activities.

3 Integrated Tourism E-Commerce Solution

3.1 Online "Regrouping of Tourists" Trading Model for Travel Agency

China's tourism industry has been getting vigorously development in the fierce competition and its consumption market has been becoming flourishing. As actively main body of tourism market, travel agencies are called leading enterprise of tourism industry. They contribute to push a large-scale tourism activities and ensure that modern tourism is set up and run.

Along with the rapid development of Chinese tourism industry, travel agency industries have been undergoing tremendous changes. Especially in recent ten years, many hotels, enterprises, individual components set up travel agency one after another, so the industry scale and the practitioners are becoming unceasingly distensible. At present, in addition to nearly four thousand relevant agencies of tourism, there have nearly forty thousand tourism agencies. But the major tourism industries are small-scale travel agencies. Therefore, the competition is increasingly fierce and the profits becomes lower than before.

Due to the small-sized travel agency of absolute quantity, so it appears that the applicants of the same line have not meet the needs of requirements in different travel agencies. In order to improve the profits, regrouping of tourists becomes one important measure of mutual cooperation in different agencies. In accordance with the rules of trade standard, when the applicants are fewer than 16 person, travel agencies are permitted to use "regrouping of tourists" style with other travel agencies on the premise of unchanged service contents and standards guaranteed by them. This way may ensure the rate of success on group tour and increase the group frequency. Using the "regrouping of tourists" trading, tourists have more flexible choice on traveling time and the tourist agencies may widely use the resources. The mutual benefit makes "regrouping of tourists" become the willing accepted way to travel.

Now the "regrouping of tourists" activities are usually offline, mainly via phone, fax and so on. It may lead to the narrow scope of "regrouping of tourists", inefficient works and increasing travel expenses.

Through online transaction of "regrouping of tourists", it is possible that arbitrary travel agency can realize the "regrouping of tourists" business with others. For example, there are several travel agencies, name TA, TB, TC. Using tourism e-commerce platform, TA releases one 5-days' travel line from Beijing to Huangshan(a), TB releases one 3-days' travel line from Beijing to Shanghai(b), TC releases one 4-days' travel line from Beijing to Xi`an(c), then TA can publish simultaneously line b and c, TB may issue line a and c, TC may issue line a and b. so,

TA and TB may transfer their applicants of line c which have not meet the requirements of the group to TC, TA and TC may transfer their applicants of line b to TB, TB and TC may transfer their applicants of line a to TA, and any other travel agencies can also use the platform to realize the "regrouping of tourists" function.

3.2 Self-navigation and Traveling Online Store Model

Tourists and scenery administration bureau, as two other main items of tourism e-commerce, play an import role in constructing tourism e-commerce solutions.

1. Self-navigation function for tourism[8,9,10]
Spreading extensive Internet tourism information provides an unprecedented living space for the freedom-loving travelers. Tourism "DIY"-do it yourself, is becoming mainstream in domestic tourism electronic commerce and finally promote tourism forward development. The solution strategy provides self-navigation function based on Google Map. utilizing the map, self-navigation groups can conveniently grasp the comprehensive information of traveling destinations in the aspects of catering, accommodation, transportation, traveling, shopping and recreation. So it may provide certain reference for DIY tour line and traveling activity. Meanwhile, DIY tour groups can also mark and discuss in the map based on their experience of the tourist destination. Finally, an integrated information database is built to realize its powerful navigation capabilities.

2. Online store function for scenery administration bureau
Unfortunately, most small and medium-sized domestic scenery administration bureau didn't realize the importance of the network effect. For example, they only pay attention to such traditional and expensive promotion way as newspaper, television and radio and so on. To resolve above disadvantages, the scheme can provide a independent website by online store model, i.e., a sub-website using secondary domain name. Through the online store, more comprehensive information can be issued by scenery administration bureau, which owns the authority of management. It can thus realize the interaction with tourists. In addition, tickets booking function is achieved in the scheme.

4   Profit Model

Scenery administration bureau and travel agency play an important role in the profit model of the tourism e-commerce solution. The premise of the profit model is mainly providing more convenient and more personalized service for visitors via self-navigation function, which can attract more individual users to use the platform. That is to say, subscribers of system may guarantee the network traffic of the platform, which means increasing individual applicant for travel agency. On this basis, the enthusiasm, which utilize the platform to participate online "regrouping of tourists" trading, will be further enhanced. A charge scheme is formulated, for instance, travel agency need to pay 300 RMB per year after 6-months free use.

The scheme of profit model mainly comes from big advertising fees of scenery administration bureau, its traditional advertisement costs are high and the influence is narrow, which may delay its further development. In this system platform, information is spreading rapidly to increase its attraction and reap huge profits. Therefore, the scenery administration bureau will consider transferring some offline advertising fees to online promotion, which is main incoming resource. The scheme provides one operation platform so as to realize the mutual profit between the scenery administration bureau and the platform operator.

5   Software Architecture and Typical Implementation

5.1   Software Architecture

When designing the architecture of an e-commerce platform, the following principles are commonly considered: firstly, Views should be separated from business operation. Secondly, apply commonly used design patterns for application architecture. Thirdly, platform should be separated from underlying database.

In the light of these designing principles above, we have adopted a three-layered architecture (named view layer, business layer and entity layer) to use with our J2EE application. The advantage of a three-layered architecture is that it separates the user interface from the application logic, which means easy to maintain when new UIs are needed, and separates the business logic from the underlying data, so when new business flow is introduced, there is no need to reconstruct all the data structure. It also helps the software engineer to focus on the essential technical aspects and ignore the diversity of client. Moreover, this architecture gives more efficiency and consistency in team cooperation when developing the system, with a high cohesion and a low coupling.

As for now, there is no industry-standard model implementing this 3-layered architecture, but some of the special ones have been widely used and still on active progressing. Considering the cost performance accessibility of the candidate frameworks, we choose the open source implementation, using Struts in the view layer, Spring in the business layer and Hibernate in the entity layer.

5.2   Typical Implementation

The Laike network (http://www.laike.cn) [11] is a typical implementation for this solution. It realizes an integrated tourism e-commerce platform among tourist, travel agency and scenery administration bureau. Not only does it satisfy individual needs, but also provides a platform for their mutual communication.

For travel agency, using Laike network, it can realize the following business functions: it can release its own traveling line information, trade with any travel agency via online "regrouping of tourists" model, release more detailed and comprehensive information via its own online store and carry out traveling-line booking and inter-communication among different cyber-friends.

For DIY tourist, using Laike network, it can realize the following self-navigation function: it can help DIY visitor to formulate traveling line and to grasp traveling information such as food, housing, transportation, traveling, shopping and amusing; it also can help DIY visitor to mark and discuss in Google-Map according to their own experience.

For tour group, it can search such information as traveling –line, travel agency and travel data and so on. it also can realize their inter-communication with travel agency.

For scenery administration bureau, it can release its scenery information using the online store function. At the same time, it also can realize their inter-communication with cyber-friends.

With the help of the three-layered open-source J2EE architecture, we have established a tourism e-commerce platform, integrated with technologies like Spring, Hibernate, Struts, Ajax, Google-Map Api, trigger, transaction control, etc.

The tourism e-commerce platform has been running in the software environment of Microsoft Windows Server 2003, SQL Server 2000 and Tomcat 5.0.26. Figure 1 is a snapshot of laike.cn Network's home-page; Figure 2 for map's marketing page; Figure 3 for background trading page of travel agency.

Fig. 1. Home page of laike.cn   **Fig. 2.** Map's marketing page

Fig. 3. Background trading page of travel agency

6   Conclusion

Tourist, travel agency and scenery administration bureau are integrated via the scheme of tourism e-commerce. Adopting J2EE architecture technique, we developed a tourism e-commerce platform "laike.cn" network. At present, this platform has entered into operation stage and the registered information is as follows: 1000 for travel agencies, 8000 for tourists, 500 for scenery administration bureaus. Currently, the platform is running smoothly and the further business expansion has been carrying out.

References

1. Liao, H.: Analysis of Service Content and Profit Model of Tourism E-Commerce. J. China Economic & Trade Herald. 7, 67–67 (2010)
2. Kang, J., Wu, X.: Trends and Status of Tourism E-Commerce in China. J. E-Commerce 5, 46–48 (2010)
3. Abdurahman, A.: Analysis of Profit Model in China's Tourism E-Commerce. J. Electric Information 4, 288–288 (2010)
4. Deng, R., Cui, X.: Application and Strategy of Tourism E-Commerce Website. J. Technology Forum 2, 210–211 (2010)
5. Jiang, C.: Analysis of China's Tourism E-Commerce. D. University of International Business and Economics 4, 4–10 (2006)
6. Zhou, X.: Strategy and Status of Tourism E-Commerce in Guilin. J. Coastal Enterprise and Science&Technology 3, 102–104 (2010)
7. Lin, F.: Tourism Smart Terminal—A New Model of Tourism E-commerce. Sun Yat-sen University 5, 10–30 (2009)
8. Tourism E-Commerce Websit, http://www.elong.com
9. Tourism E-Commerce Websit, http://www.ctrip.com
10. Tourism E-Commerce Websit, http://www.mangocity.com
11. Tourism E-Commerce Websit, http://www.laike.cn

Analyzing Economic Spatial-Temporal Disparities at County Level in Yangtze River Delta Based on ESDA-GIS

He Yang[*], Jin-ping Liu, and Tao Wang

School of Management,
China University of Mining & Technology,
Xuzhou, China
yanghe4405@163.com

Abstract. Regional economic disparities have been a hot topic in recent academic world. This paper explores the feasibility of coefficient of variance (CV) and exploratory spatial data analysis (ESDA) in investigating the spatial dynamics of regional disparities at county level in Yangtze River Delta by analyzing per capita GDP data from 1999 to 2008. Empirical results show that the overall spatial disparities of regional economy in Yangtze River Delta have been increasing throughout the study period. The polarization effect is beyond its spread effect, which indicates the spatial heterogeneity of the whole regional economy into two different clubs through the process of cumulative causation.

Keywords: regional economic disparities, CV, ESDA, spatial autocorrelation, Yangtze River Delta.

1 Introduction

Regional economic disparities, influenced by the natural resources, are inevitable and necessary in the course of economic development. With the rapid economic development in Yangtze River Delta, the problem of regional disparities has become a hot spot in the social economy development and has attracted general attention in the academic community. Some domestic scholars have made substantial basis for further research on regional economic disparities in China by Theil index and wavelet analysis, such as Xu Jian-hua [1], Li Xiao-jian [2] etc. However, the economic growth in each region not only depends on its own characteristics, but also on those of the regions that from the neighborhood to which it belongs [3]. Growth poles theory or core-periphery pattern suggests that different spatial interactions between a region and its neighbors can enlarge or lessen regional disparities [4]. But the traditional approaches to regional disparities suppose that each region is independent from others, so they just evaluate the regional disparity variations of isolated regions and can't tell

---

[*] Corresponding author. He Yang (1985-), male, XuZhou, JiangSu Province, doctor of management science and engineering of China University of Mining & Technology.
  Research area: management of resources and economy.

the dynamics of interrelated regions. Economic development is a dialectical process of spatial concentration and dispersion, viewed from the spatial perspective.

Since the traditional methods of measuring regional economic disparities lack spatial perspective, it is difficult to truly reflect the changes and mechanisms of regional disparities. The combination of coefficient of variation (CV) and exploratory spatial data analysis (ESDA) can further explore the spatial mechanism which brings about the regional economic disparities enlargement or shrinkage. The theoretical refinements and software developments have grounded new analytical tools in theory and made them reasonably accessible to data analysts not specifically trained in the geosciences. Space Stat, the software used to perform ESDA in this paper, is one of these tools.

2 Methodology

2.1 Coefficient of Variation

There are many statistical indicators used to measure the difference or the disequilibrium of regional development. Coefficient of variation is one of the most commonly used [5]. Its formula is:

$$CV = \frac{1}{\overline{Y}} \left[\frac{1}{n} \sum_{i=1}^{n} \left(Y_i - \overline{Y} \right)^2 \right]^{\frac{1}{2}} \tag{1}$$

Where CV is the coefficient of variation; $\overline{Y}$ is the mean per capita GDP; n is the number of the regions; Y_i is the per capita GDP of region i. The regional economic disparities increase with the variation of coefficient. However, the CV can only reveal the total differences of development, and it ignores the connection and interaction between counties. So in this paper, the author combined CV with ESDA to analyze the regional economic disparities.

2.2 Exploratory Spatial Data Analysis

ESDA is a collection of methods and techniques for spatial data analysis. With the core of spatial correlation measurement, it aims to discover the spatial agglomeration and anomaly, and to reveal the spatial interaction mechanism between objects by describing and visualizing the spatial distribution patterns of matters and phenomena. Currently, it has got more and more attentions in many research fields such as spatial data mining, digital image processing, epidemiology, natural disasters, regional economics, and criminology and so on. It has also provided scientific basis and methods for the analysis of regional economic disparities [6].

1) **Outlier maps:** An important aspect of ESDA is the visualization of extreme values. In traditional exploratory data analysis (EDA), a standard tool is the box plot, which shows the median and four quartiles, as well as an indication of extreme values defined with respect to the inter-quartile range. A box map is an extension of the box plot to the map domain. It is a choropleth-map with six categories: four quartiles, as well as special categories for the lower and upper outliers. A box map is an example

of an outlier map, which allows for easy identification of both the location and the value of extreme observations. An important concept in ESDA is the principle of linking. It means that any observation highlighted in one of the views on the data is also highlighted in all others. Linking is a fundamental technique in high-dimensional data visualization and underlies the exploratory approaches in Space Stat.

2) **Global spatial autocorrelation:** Spatial autocorrelation can be defined as the co-incidence of value similarity with locational similarity. Therefore there is positive spatial autocorrelation when high or low values of a random variable tend to cluster in space and there is negative spatial autocorrelation when geographical areas tend to be surrounded by neighbors with dissimilar values. The measurement of global spatial autocorrelation is based on the Moran's I [7] statistic, which is the most widely known measure of spatial clustering. Moran's I is defined as follows:

If you have more than one surname, please make sure that the Volume Editor knows how you are to be listed in the author index.

$$I_t = \frac{n\sum_{i=1}^{n}\sum_{j=1}^{n}w_{ij}\left(x_i-\overline{x}\right)\left(x_j-\overline{x}\right)}{\sum_{i=1}^{n}\sum_{j=1}^{n}w_{ij}\sum_{i=1}^{n}\left(x_i-\overline{x}\right)^2} = \frac{\sum_{i=1}^{n}\sum_{j\neq i}^{n}w_{ij}\left(x_i-\overline{x}\right)\left(x_j-\overline{x}\right)}{S^2\sum_{i=1}^{n}\sum_{j\neq i}^{n}w_{ij}} \tag{2}$$

$$S^2 = \frac{1}{n}\sum_{i=1}^{n}(x_i-\overline{x})^2 ; \overline{x} = \frac{1}{n}\sum_{i=1}^{n}x_i \tag{3}$$

Where I_t stands for Moran index of period t. x_i, x_j are observations of region i and region j, respectively. w_{ij} is the element of the spatial weight matrix W. This matrix contains the information about the relative spatial dependence between the n regions. The elements w_{ii} on the diagonal are set to zero whereas the elements w_{ij} indicate the way region i is spatially connected to the region j. If region i and j are adjacent, then $w_{ij} =1$, otherwise $w_{ij} =0$.

The maximum and minimum possible values of Moran's I are constrained to lie in the (-1, 1) range [8]. Positive values of Moran's I suggest spatial clustering of similar values. Negative values suggest that high values are frequently found in the vicinity of low values. At a given level of significance, if Moran's I approximates 1, which indicates that regions with high economic development levels tend to cluster in space and low-valued ones similarly tend to show geographic clustering. And in the clustering area, if the values of Moran's I tend to decrease, it indicates that the regional economic disparities tend to dwindle. But negative values of I indicate that the economic development level of the region is quite spatially different from the ones of its neighbors, and regional economic clustering gradually disappears. When values of Moran's I approximate the expected value $E(I)=-4/(n-1)$, which indicates that the observations are mutually independent and randomly distributed in space.

3) **Local spatial autocorrelation:** Moran's I statistic is a global statistic: it cannot appreciate the regional structure of spatial autocorrelation. The analysis of local spatial autocorrelation is carried out with the so called Moran scatter plot, which is used to visualize local spatial instability, and local indicators of spatial association (LISA) [9], which are used to test the hypothesis of random distribution by comparing the values of each specific localization with the values in the neighboring localizations.

Inspection of local spatial instability is carried out by means of the Moran scatter plot, which plots the spatial lag W_x against the original values x. The four different quadrants of the scatter plot correspond to the four types of local spatial association between a region and its neighbors. This provides an easy way to categorize the nature of spatial autocorrelation into four types, corresponding to spatial clusters and spatial outliers:

    i) HH, a region with high economic development level surrounded by similar regions (Quadrant I in top on the right).

    ii) LH, a region with low economic development level surrounded by dissimilar regions (Quadrant II in top on the left).

    iii) LL, a region with low economic development level surrounded by similar regions (Quadrant III in bottom on the left).

    iv) HL, a region with high economic development level surrounded by dissimilar regions (Quadrant IV in bottom on the right).

Specifically, observations in the LL and HH quadrants represent potential spatial clusters (values surrounded by similar neighbors), whereas observations in the LH and HL quadrants suggest potential spatial outliers (values surrounded by dissimilar neighbors).

Anselin defines a local indicator of spatial association as any statistics satisfying two criteria [10]. First, the LISA for each observation gives an indication of significant spatial clustering of similar values around that observation; second, the sum of the LISA for all observations is proportional to a global indicator of spatial association.

The local version of the Moran's I statistic for each region i can be written as following:

$$I_i = \frac{(x_i - \bar{x})}{S^2} \sum_j w_{ij} (x_j - \bar{x}) \tag{4}$$

Where I_i is Local Moran's I of region i , the implications of the other variables are the same as those in (2) and (3). A positive value for I_i indicates clustering of similar values (high or low) whereas a negative value indicates clustering of dissimilar values.

The local Moran statistic provides a means to assess significance of local spatial patterns [11]. Significance is typically based on a conditional permutation approach. The LISA cluster map shows locations with significant local Moran statistics classified by types of spatial correlation, and aims to identify interesting locations and assess the extent to which the spatial distribution exhibits spatial heterogeneity.

3 Results and Discussion

Yangtze River Delta is one of the most creative and rapidly developing areas in China. With the rapid economic development, the intra-regional disparities are constantly expanding. In 2008, the per capita GDP of Kunshan City in Southern Jiangsu rose to 217,303 yuan, while the per capita GDP of Xianju County (16,292 yuan) was only 7.5% of Kunshan City's.

In order to analyze the regional economic disparities in Yangtze River Delta, the author took data from Chinese Statistical Yearbook Database. The spatial analytical scale is 94 counties (cities and municipal districts), including 16 provincial cities and 78 counties (cities). The time series is from 1999 to 2008. The analysis variable is per capita GDP at county level (current price).

By using the SpaceStat software designed by Anselin, the author calculated Moran's I and CV of per capita GDP at county level in Yangtze River Delta from 1999 to 2008 shown in Fig.1. Overall, CV for inter-county disparities exhibits a rising pattern. It declines in 2001, but rises substantially after 2002. The regional economic disparities keep increasing during these years. From 1999 to 2002, the value of Moran's I is increased. But from 2002 to 2008, it keeps stable or even declining. Throughout the whole study period, the estimated values of Moran's I are all positive, which indicates regions with high (low) economic development level tend to cluster. The increase of CV indicates that regional economic disparities are expanding. As the values of Moran's I decrease, spatial agglomeration in economic activities diminishes, but is still positive.

The author discovered the spatial agglomerations of better developed counties (Quadrant I) and less developed ones (Quadrant III) in 2008 are stronger than those in 1999. Local autocorrelation types and membership changes of intra-county economies in Yangtze River Delta from 1999 to 2008 are shown in Fig.2 and Tab.1.

In order to better compare the local changes and patterns of the county level economic spatial disparities in Yangtze River Delta from 1999 to 2008, the author drew the LISA box and percentage map (Fig.3) in GIS, at the significance filter of p<0.05. The local spatial heterogeneity patterns of county economy can be divided into four types as follows:

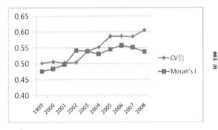 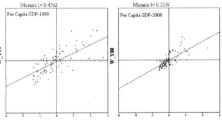

Fig. 1. Moran's I and CV for per capita GDP at county level in Yangtze River Delta, 1999-2008 and significance filter of P<0.05

Fig. 2. Moran scatterplot for per capita GDP at the county level in Yangtze River Delta, 1999 and 2008

Table 1. Local autocorrelation types and membership changes of intra-county economy

Spatial agglomeration patterns of regions	Numbers of clustering members	
	Numbers in 1999	*Numbers in 2008*
HH	28	30
LH	15	7
LL	41	47
HL	10	10

- Counties with minor spatial differences, high development levels and similar neighbors (HH), most of which lie in Southern Jiangsu and Shanghai.
- Counties with minor spatial differences, low development levels and similar neighbors (LL), most of which lie in outlining areas.
- Counties with large spatial differences, high development levels and dissimilar neighbors (HL), most of which lie in some provincial cities.
- Counties with large spatial differences, low development levels and dissimilar neighbors (LH), most of which lie in the periphery of provincial cities in Central Jiangsu and Zhejiang.

After 10 years of development, the spatial patterns of the economic disparities in Northern Yangtze River Delta have made some changes shown in Fig.4 as follows:

- Significant HH regions extend from Suzhou, Wuxi to Jiangyin Wujiang and Shanghai. Those regions, such as Shaoxing, Hangzhou provincial city, formerly belonged to significant HH regions gradually evolve into non-significant regions.
- Significant LL regions extend to Lin'an, Anji, Baoying and Gaoyou, and are still concentrated in the Central Jiangsu.

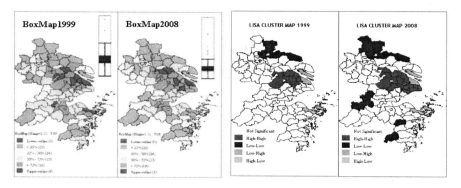

Fig. 3. LISA box and percentage maps of per capita GDP at county level,1999-2008. A hinge of 1.5 was applied.

Fig. 4. LISA cluster maps of per capita GDP for at county level, 1999-2008, based on 999 permutations and significance filter of P<0.05

Compared with the Shanghai, Southern Jiangsu and Zhejiang Province, there are still large development gaps between regions of the outlining areas of Yangtze River Delta. County economy and technological interchange in Yangtze River Delta increase obviously, but those regions with comparatively weak economic foundation and relatively undeveloped counties nearby are still backward.

4 Conclusion

Region is an open system. The economic growth in each region not only depends on its own characteristics, but also on those of the regions that from the neighborhood to which it belongs. This paper explores the feasibility of ESDA in analyzing regional economic disparities, such as coefficients of variation, ESDA to incorporate spatial effects. The analysis results show that the overall county-level spatial disparities of regional economy in Yangtze River Delta have increased and then decreased over time. Moreover, the regions and their neighbors tend to have the similar trends towards enlarging the spatial agglomeration of regional economy, especially among the counties (or cities) in Shanghai, Zhejiang, Southern and Central Jiangsu. The significant spread or trickling-down effect has been observed across Southern Jiangsu and Shanghai since 1999. But its polarization effect is beyond its spread effect because significant lagging areas located in outlining area have appeared with the growing up of southern Jiangsu and Jiangsu. This fact gives evidence that the coordinate development of regional economy has a long way to go in Yangtze River Delta.

This paper can provide useful references for related government departments and decision-makers to carry out effective, scientific regional economic plans. The author chose county-level data to perform the analysis. The results may vary if city-level data are used, and data from different years can be used to analyze the regional economic disparities. Anyway, the author provided a point of departure for further research.

Acknowledgement

He Yang and Jin-ping Liu thank Lu-jun Miao which worked in National Library of China for providing data related, and the project is supported by the Major project of Chinese National Social Science Foundation (Project Number: 09ZD046) and Development Strategy of Coal Industry and Mine Safety Management (National Key Subject) CUMT (Project Number : A90202).

References

1. Xu, J., Lu, F., Su, F., Lu, Y.: Spatial and temporal scale analysis on theregional economic disparities in China. Geographical Research 28, 58–68 (2005)
2. Li, X., Qiao, J.: County Level Economic Disparities of China in the 1990s. Acta Geographica Sinica 56, 137–145 (2001)
3. Arbia, G.: The role of spatial effects in the empirical analysis of regional concentration. Journal of Geographical Systems 3, 271–298 (2001)
4. Rey, S., Montouri, B.: US regional income convergence: a spatial econometric perspective. Regional Studies 33, 1543–1564 (1999)
5. Williamson, J.G.: Regional Inequality and the Process of National Development: A Description of the Patterns. Economic Development and Cultural Change 13, 3–45 (1969)
6. Cliff, A.D., Ord, J.: Spatial Processes, Models and Applications, pp. 32–84. Pion, London (1981)
7. Chen, X.: Analyzing the county-level economic spatial-temporal disparities in Xinjiang based on ESDA-GIS. Science of Surveying and Mapping 3, 62–65 (2008)
8. Anselin, L.: Interactive techniques and exploratory spatial data analysis. In: Longley, P.A., Goodchild, M.F., Maguire, D.J., Rhind, D. (eds.) Geographical Information Systems: Principles Techniques Management and Applications, pp. 251–264. Wiley, New York (1996)
9. Anselin, L.: Spatial effects in econometric practice in environmental and resource economics. Agric. Econ. 83, 705–710 (2001)
10. Takahiro, A.: Decomposing regional income inequality in China and Indonesia using two-stage nested Theil decomposition method. Ann. Reg. Sci. 37, 55–77 (2003)
11. Anselin, L.: The future of spatial analysis in the social sciences. Geogr. Inf. Sci. 5, 67–76 (1999)

Hierarchical Approach in Clustering to Euclidean Traveling Salesman Problem

Abdulah Fajar[1,2], Nanna Suryana Herman[2], Nur Azman Abu[2], and Sahrin Shahib[2]

[1] Faculty of Engineering, Universitas Widyatama, Jl Cikutra 204A Bandung 40125
Indonesia
abd.fajar@gmail.com
[2] Faculty of Information and Communication Technology, Universiti Teknikal Malaysia
Melaka, Hang Tuah Jaya, 76100 Durian Tunggal Melaka Malaysia
{nura,nsuryana,shahrinsahib}@utem.edu.my

Abstract. There has been growing interest in studying combinatorial optimization problems by clustering strategy, with a special emphasis on the traveling salesman problem (TSP). TSP naturally arises as a sub problem in much transportation, manufacturing and logistics application, this problem has caught much attention of mathematicians and computer scientists. A clustering approach will decompose TSP into sub graph and form cluster, so it may reduce problem size into smaller problem. Impact of hierarchical approach will be investigated to produce a better clustering strategy that fit into Euclidean TSP. Clustering strategy to Euclidean TSP consist of two main step, there are; clustering and tour construction. The significant of this research is clustering approach solution result has error less than 10% compare to best known solution (TSPLIB) and there is improvement to a hierarchical clustering algorithm in order to fit in such Euclidean TSP solution method.

Keywords: Hierarchical Approach, Clustering, Dendogram, Tour Construction Euclidean TSP.

1 Introduction

Nature inspired problem solving is become popular approach in last decade. This work inspired by human problem solving and particle movement such as Brownian Motions. Human beings possess the natural ability of clustering objects. This is a capability to organize the data which is received everyday into cluster, so that they may draw important conclusions. However making computer to solve clustering problem is quite difficult and demanding the attentions of computer scientist and engineers all over the world till now.

The task of computerized data clustering problem has been approached from diverse domains of knowledge like graph theory, statistics, artificial neural network and so on. The most popular approach in this direction has been the formulations of clustering as an optimization problem. There has been growing interest in studying combinatorial optimization problems by clustering strategy, with a special emphasis on the traveling salesman problem (TSP) [2][3][4]. TSP naturally arises as a sub problem

G. Shen and X. Huang (Eds.): ECWAC 2011, Part I, CCIS 143, pp. 192–198, 2011.
© Springer-Verlag Berlin Heidelberg 2011

in much transportation, manufacturing and logistics application, this problem has caught much attention of mathematicians and computer scientists.

Traveling salesman problem (TSP) is a combinatorial optimization task of finding the shortest tour of n cities given the intercity costs. In a more formal way the goal is to find the least weight Hamiltonian cycle in a complete graph G. The TSP problem is a 'NP-hard' problem [5]. An NP-hard problem is extremely unlikely to have a polynomial algorithm to solve it optimally although it is not proved that the worst case exponential solution running times are unavoidable. Good approximation algorithms can produce solutions that are only a few percent longer than an optimal solution and the time of solving the problem is a low-order polynomial function of the number of cities. Some approximating algorithms produce tours whose lengths are close to that of the shortest tour, but the time complexity is substantially higher than linear.

The primary objective of this research is to investigate impact of hierarchical approach to produce a better hierarchical clustering strategy that fit into such Euclidean TSP solution method. The current research in hierarchical clustering to solve Euclidean TSP mostly producing their best algorithm with the running time near $O(n^2)$ while this approach is expected to be at most near $O(n^3)$ and average final TSP solution is more than 10% compare to the best known solution.

The rest of this paper will describe about motivation of this study regarding Euclidean TSP in section 2, objective this study will be described in section 3. Literature background will be described in section 4 and section 5 describes methodology. Preliminary result is presented in section 6 also final section discussion and conclusion written in section 7 and 8.

2 Literature Background

A clustering algorithm is expected to discover the natural grouping that exists in a set of pattern. In hierarchical clustering, the data are not partitioned into a particular cluster in a single step. Hierarchical clustering may be represented by a two dimensional diagram known as dendrogram, which illustrates the fusions or divisions made at each successive stage of analysis.

Among the most popular hierarchical clustering algorithms, BIRCH [6] can typically find a good clustering in a single scan of the data and improve the quality further in a few additional scans. It is also the first clustering algorithm that handles noise effectively. CURE [7] represents each cluster by a certain number of points selected from a well-scattered sample and then shrinking them toward the cluster centroid by a specified fraction. It uses a combination of random sampling and partition clustering to handle large databases. ROCK [8] is a robust clustering algorithm for Boolean and categorical data. It introduces two new concepts: a point's neighbors and links, and to measure the similarity/proximity between a pair of data points.

Haxhimusa et. al formulated a pyramid algorithm[1] for E-TSP motivated by the failure to identify an existing algorithm that could provide a good fit to the subjects data. More recently, hierarchical (pyramid) algorithms have been used to model mental mechanisms involved in other types of visual problems. The main aspects of the models are (multi resolution) pyramid architecture and a coarse to fine process of successive tour approximations. This algorithm was motivated by the properties of the human visual system has main idea to use agglomerative (bottom up) processes to reduce the size of the input by clustering the nodes into small group and top-down refinement to find an approximate solution, as same as Graham do in [3]. The size of the input (number of vertices in the graph) is reduced so that an optimal solution can be found by the combinatorial search. A pyramid is used to reduce the size of the input in the bottom-up processes.

In bottom-up clustering, cities are close neighbors are put into the same cluster using greedy approach. These clustered cities are considered as a single city at the reduced resolution. Graph pyramid strategy use MST using Bouruvka algorithm. MST is used as natural lower bound for TSP solution. In the case TSP with triangle inequality which in the case for the Euclidean TSP, MST can be used as to prove the upper bound.

Graph pyramid solution give good approximation while is compared to TSPLIB. Solution error for this solution tends to linear around 12%. Time performance is quadratic for this solution especially while number of cities more than 600.

3   Hierarchical Approach in Clustering

A clustering algorithm is expected to discover the natural grouping that exists in a set of pattern. In hierarchical clustering, the data are not partitioned into a particular cluster in a single step. Hierarchical clustering may be represented by a two dimensional diagram known as dendrogram, as shown in Figure 1. Figure 1 shows dendogram which illustrates the fusions or divisions made at each successive stage of analysis.

Among the most popular hierarchical clustering algorithms, BIRCH [6] can typically find a good clustering in a single scan of the data and improve the quality further in a few additional scans. It is also the first clustering algorithm that handles noise effectively. CURE [7] represents each cluster by a certain number of points selected from a well-scattered sample and then shrinking them toward the cluster centroid by a specified fraction. It uses a combination of random sampling and partition clustering to handle large databases. ROCK [8] is a robust clustering algorithm for Boolean and categorical data. It introduces two new concepts: a point's neighbors and links, and to measure the similarity/proximity between a pair of data points.

An agglomerative hierarchical clustering procedure produces a series of partitions of the data, C_n, C_{n-1}, ..., C_1. The first C_n consists of n single object 'clusters', the last C_1, consists of single group containing all n cases. At each particular stage the method joins together the two clusters which are closest together (most similar). Differences between methods arise because of the different ways of defining distance (or similarity) between clusters.

Number of clusters that is generated in hierarchical clustering is automatically. In this work, it is defined a threshold R [2], where

$$R = \sqrt{\frac{\text{Area of Cluster } A}{\text{The number of Vertices } n}} \tag{1}$$

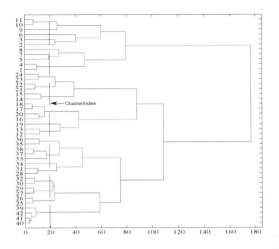

Fig. 1. Dendgram of Complete Linkage Method for Dantzig42.tsp

This threshold will act as guidance to split one cluster to several and result basic clusters. Basic cluster have small size number of nodes. This threshold also prevent clusters overlapped one to others.

Clustering algorithm should contains function to compute linkage distance for a set of clusters C and the linkage distance function will vary depend on linkage method. Here is several technique of linkage between the clusters used in this study:

1. **Nearest linkage:** The distance between two clusters is the minimum distance

$$d(G_r, G_S) = \min\{W(V_r, V_S)\} \tag{2}$$

2. **Complete linkage:** The opposite of nearest linkage, maximum distance

$$d(G_r, G_S) = \max\{W(V_r, V_S)\} \tag{3}$$

3. **Average linkage:** The distance between two clusters is mean distance between all possible pairs of nodes in two clusters.

$$d(G_r, G_S) = \frac{1}{n_r n_s} \sum_{i=1}^{n_r} \sum_{j=1}^{n_s} dist(V_{r_i}, V_{s_j}) \tag{4}$$

4. **Median Linkage:** The distance between two clusters is their weighted centroids

$$d(G_r, G_S) = \left\| \tilde{V}_r - \tilde{V}_s \right\|_2 \tag{5}$$

Where $\tilde{V}_r$ is the weighted centroid of r. If r was created from clusters p and q, then $\tilde{V}_r$ is defined recursively as:

$$\tilde{V} = \frac{1}{2(\tilde{V}_p + \tilde{V}_q)} \tag{6}$$

5. **Centroid linkage:** The distance between two clusters is their centroid as calculated by arithmetic mean

$$d(G_r, G_s) = \left\| \tilde{V}_r - \tilde{V}_s \right\|_2 \tag{7}$$

Where $\tilde{x}$ is the centroid of r, by arithmetic mean:

$$\tilde{V}_r = \frac{1}{n_r} \sum_{i=1}^{n_r} V_{r_i} \tag{8}$$

6. **Ward's linkage (Sum Square Method):** The distance between two clusters, is how much the sum squares will increase when merge them

$$d(G_r, G_s) = \frac{n_r + n_s}{n_r n_s} \left\| \tilde{V}_r - \tilde{V}_s \right\|^2 \tag{9}$$

Where $\tilde{V}_r$ center of cluster r and n_r is is number of points in cluster r.

4 Clustering Result and Impact on Euclidean TSP

This research use TSP Lib [9] (70 sample problem with node size between 29 and 3038) and randomized sample data to test the algorithm. All linkage distance function show uniform result except nearest linkage. Nearest linkage result a chained effect clusters and this effect tend to worst result on Euclidean TSP, while other methods generate compact size clusters. Number of nodes per clusters between 2 – 4 nodes in these linkage distance function, see figure 2 below.

Ward's and completes linkage distance function are promising method when compared to TSP Lib best known result. The result on average is less than 7%. Tour construction that is used in this research is cheapest insertion method and result refined by 2-opt exchange move. There are 75% samples which has consumed up to 50% concorde running time from TSP Lib using 2.6 GHz Processor. Longer running time is consumed by TSP Lib sample problem about 14%. Figure 3 show distribution of running time consumption level.

The research has adopt and develop several algorithm and each algorithm has complexity started from $O(n^2)$ and the worst case is $O(n^3)$. Clustering process is divided into two main algorithms, linkage and clusters generation. Complexity of clustering process at the worst case is $O(n^3)$. Tour construction and improvement has $O(n^2 \log n)$ time complexity. The overall of the algorithm complexity for this work has $O(n^3)$.

The clustering process has identified the best method to cluster the Euclidean TSP into smaller with compact size clusters. Complete and Ward's Linkage has shown as the best method of all linkage method. Both linkage methods have good result in running time and percentage of gap compared to TSP Lib. Some method has shown potential result and the drawback lay on running time in tour construction. Several method result overlap clusters and big size cluster such as average and centroid linkage method. Overlap and big size cluster have the impact to tour construction and running time. Bigger cluster size result longer running time and quality of tour construction, as well as overlap clusters.

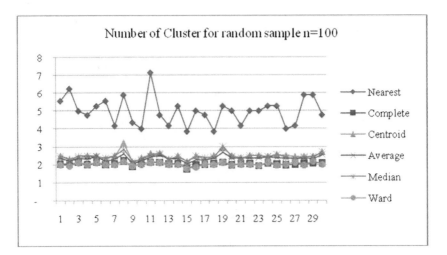

Fig. 2. Number of nodes per clusters fror random sample with n=10

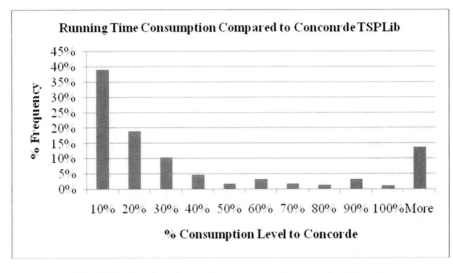

Fig. 3. Number of nodes per clusters fror random sample with n=10

5   Conclusion

There has been a long-term interest in the field of operations research in devising economical procedures for finding solutions that approximate the optimal, and many such heuristic techniques have been developed and compared. To achieve "reasonable" approximations to an optimal solution to within a few percentage points above the shortest path, such procedures generally need to perform on the order of n^3 calculations [10]. Based on explanation above, the primary objective of this development is to produce a better hierarchical clustering strategy that fit into such Euclidean TSP solution method. This approach has been successfully achived the objective i.e. algorithm most near $O(n^3)$ and average final TSP solution is about 6% compare to the best known solution.

This research has result contribution in term of Euclidean TSP and manufacturing problem. The contribution to Euclidean TSP is new solution approach using hierarchical clustering. The result of this research implemented to development automatics compact PCB Drilling machine that can be applied to Small Medium Industry. The algorithm is combined to this machine to establish that drilling order in shortest and effective ways. Time and cost saving will be resulted by this machine.

This research had resulted some new idea and improvement in clustering process and Euclidean TSP approach. The objectives of this research had been achieved with several notes. Outcome of this research had been produced for several areas such as clustering method, heuristics for Euclidean TSP and implementation to manufacturing problem.

References

1. Haxhimusa, Y., Krospatch, W.G., Pizlo, Z., Ion, A.: Approximate Graph Pyramid Solution of the E-TSP. Image and Vision Computing Journal (2008)
2. Abu, N.A., Sahib, S., Suryana, N.: A Novel Natural Approach to Euclidean TSP. In: Proceeding of The 3rd International Conference on Mathematics & Statistics (ICoMS) (2008)
3. Graham, S.M., Joshi, A., Pizlo, Z.: The Traveling Salesman Problem: a Hierarchical Model. Journal of Memory and Cognition 28(7), 1191–1204 (2000)
4. Vickers, D., Butavicius, M., Lee, M., Medvedev, A.: Human Performance on Visually Presented Traveling Salesman problems. Journal of Psychological Research 65, 34–45 (2001)
5. Punnen, A.P.: The Traveling Salesman Problem: Application, Formulations and Variations. In: Putin, G., Punnen, A.P. (eds.) The Traveling Salesman Problem and Its Variations, p. 22. Springer, Heidelberg (2007)
6. Zhang, T., Ramakrishnan, R., Livny, M.: BIRCH: an efficient data clustering method for very large databases. In: Proc. ACM SIGMOD Int. Conf. on Management of Data, Montreal, Canada (1996)
7. Guha, S., Rastogi, R., Shim, K.: CURE: An Efficient Clustering Algorithm for Large Databases. In: Proc. ACM SIGMOD Int. Conf. on Management of Data, Seatle, WA (1998)
8. Guha, S.: ROCK: A Robust Clustering Algorithm for Categorical Attributes. Journal of Information System 25(5), 345–366 (2000)
9. Reinelt, G.: TSPLIB–A Traveling Salesman Problem Library. Informs Journal on Computing 3, 376–384 (1991)
10. Golden, B., Bodin, L., Doyle, T., Stewart, W.: Approximate travelling salesman algorithms. Operations Research 28, 694–711 (1980)

The Application Study of MCU in Visual Classroom Interactive Teaching Based on Virtual Experiment Platform

Diankuan Ding and Lixin Li

College of Physics & Electrical Engineering, Anyang Normal University,
455000 Anyang, China
ddk@163.com, lilixin@sina.com

Abstract. Because many students are lacking in perceptual knowledge of MCU, they are difficult to engage themselves in classroom activities. The paper therefore offers an interactive teaching mode of proteus-based MCU virtual laboratory. The teaching mode is of help in arousing students' interests, improving their learning efficiency and practical abilities, and promoting the teaching reform of MCU subject.

Keywords: Proteus, Visualize, Virtual, Platform, Interactive Teaching.

1 Introduction

With the rapid development of electronic technology, MCU are widely used in industrial enterprises and household appliance field. More and more attention are given to the MCU course which is a obligatory and practice course because there are many work opportunities need the knowledge of MCU. In present most universities carry on the course using the method that students learn theoretical knowledge in class and doing experiments after class which causes many problems such as students' lacking of perceptual cognition, hard to combine software development with peripheral circuits of MCU and limited of students' motivation in class. Research indicates that participation in learning is an important part of effective learning, active student participation and interaction for the promotion of knowledge and understanding capacity generation is very important. So it is significant that how to set up a visible teaching platform of MCU course which can enhance closer interaction between teachers and students.

Also associated with computer software and hardware technology, the rapid development in various fields has shown a variety of simulation systems, using computer simulation software, can make full simulation, such as hardware design and other practical engineering problems,but also the abstract presentation from the content more flexible, more difficult problem to simplified. The research and develop of MCU require researchers have basic knowledge of hardware design (analog circuits and digital circuits) and abilities of programming using assembly language or C language. But according to our investigation and research some students lack of perceptual cognition, can't design circuit of MCU system or program which is a waste of time and teaching resource. So setting up a platform of MCU simulation experiment is becoming

G. Shen and X. Huang (Eds.): ECWAC 2011, Part I, CCIS 143, pp. 199–204, 2011.

an instant need. As one product of Labcenter Electronics company the Proteus which is becoming more and more popular is a simulation platform of analog circuit, digital circuit, microprocessor with which we can do the whole design of system including design, analysis, simulation of hardware, microcontroller code debugging, system's testing and design of PCB. This paper gives a research on how to enhance class interaction and improve quality of classroom teaching.

2 Instruction of Proteus Technology and Virtual Platform's Characteristics

2.1 Virtual Platform's Characteristics

Virtual platform was proposed by professor William Wolf in the University of Virginia. Virtual experiment platform which using simulation technology, digital modeling technology and multimedia technology on a computer to partly or fully replace the traditional experiment environment provide user a experiment teaching, technology interaction and team study platform through network. As the third way of research and design virtual experiment is a completely new science research and engineering design method based on computer virtual system. Resent yeas the virtual platform got a rapid development in teaching and engineering design for solving the problem of visible interaction between teachers and students.

2.2 Instruction of Proteus Technology

Protues software is a electronic design teaching which consist of ISIS and ARES, experiment and innovation platform including function of electrical laboratory, electronics laboratory SCM application lab.

The Proteus software by ISIS and the ARES two software constitutions, is an electronic design teaching platform, experimental platform and innovative platform, covered the electrician electron laboratory, the electronic technology laboratory, the MCU to apply the laboratory and so on complete function.

The software with which we can not only do principle circuits design, PCB design and circuits simulation but also program on MCU's virtual model can work with Keil C51, Wave and other simulation platform. Using this technology we can test the circuit while designing through virtual dynamic input and output such as virtual buttons, signal generator, LED, logic analyzer, oscillation and so on.

According to Proteus's function that it can not only simulate circuits with or without the MCU system's working, the Proteus's joining in class can give students a dynamic and visible show of MCU course knowledge including design of peripheral circuits, software programming. From the Angle of perception, it accords with people's cognitive regularity that students' various senses and study result is positive correlation. While simulating and program debugging, it is easily understand and master the knowledge for students. In a sense, contradiction, the disjoining of teaching, learning, experiments and engineering application, is alleviated.

3   Teaching Reform of MCU Course

For the beginning of interactive teaching is participation, we need master some teaching skills and design the content of class to encourage students taking part in the teaching process. After several years' exploration, we propose a heuristic, problem-posing, discussing; summative and catechetical visible interactive teaching mode to replace the old spoon-feed one which was used for many years. The application of this new mode will cause a teaching reform of MCU course.

First we can no longer use the mode teaching all the content in class which causes the students' resistance for learning in class and application in engineering. Second the content must be suitable for simulating students' interest to learn MCU and imply the knowledge to engineering. Third the content must be systematized.

Thing about the aforementioned, after our research group's discussions we re-planed and adjusted the MCU course. In new course the content were remained. The knowledge of MCU was divided into several parts: basic knowledge, minimum system, general I/O, interruption, timing, communication, expand part and display. As Fig.1 show, the steps of every part including hardware designing, programming, program instructions explanation and notes in debugging could be shown to students by the visible virtual platform. The platform not only helps the teacher to elaborate the knowledge from easy parts to hard parts with interactive method but also help students systematize their knowledge. The course consists of several parts interconnected and centered on 51 MCU.

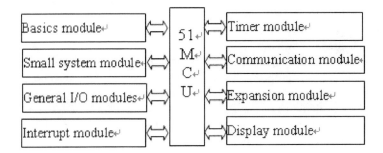

Fig. 1. The block diagram of SCU knowledge

4   Proteus Tech-Based Study of Visual Classroom Interactive Learning

MCU course is a very practical course which is not only relating to inner structure of the microprocessor, programming instructions and hardware design of peripheral circuit but also comes down to problems easily encountered in engineering practice. So repeating what the books say in lecturing should be avoided; a dynamic integrate classroom instruction system with inside resources of MCU, peripheral circuit, soft ware and hardware should be produced. In this respect, the Proteus tech-based virtual visual teaching platform plays a very effective role.

Teachers can fully motivate students' learning interest through visual interactive learning and clarify teaching objects of the target course from the supportive module of the subject. So teachers should not only grasp the class material as well as the teaching process but also give full play to organization, instruction, inspiration and regulation & control of students. Here is an illustration of visual classroom interactive learning process with Proteus tech-based virtual platform.

This part is mainly devoted to expounding the function of MCU I/O port. Most students who have the initial contact with small MCU system and design of peripheral circuit would find it difficult to understand the knowledge about it if teachers only repeat what books say about the structure of MCU I/O port, let alone instructions, application and peripheral circuit design. So, when lecturing, teachers should spend a reasonable part of time elaborating theoretical knowledge and start up the Proteus software when students feel confused. Teachers should on the one hand recall the content which was just elaborated, on the other hand, enlighten students to review digital and simulate electrical knowledge when calling out the relevant components from Proteus platform.

(1)   Firstly, teachers should find out MCU from the Proteus component library, then inspire the students and introduce each pin intuitively with combination of specific pin on MCU; students go over what they have just learnt for the first time.

(2)   Teachers introduce the crystal oscillator circuit to students. Teachers introduce this circuit with combined knowledge of machine cycle and introduction cycle through questioning, and then students recall the learnt knowledge points again.

(3)   Then, teachers introduce the reset circuit; similarly, teachers introduce the design of the reset circuit by illustrating the operating principle of MCU and the selected parameter of general circuit components, ask students to look back on the simulate electrical knowledge.

(4)   Teachers should enlighten students about "What is also necessary if the MCU wants to function properly?", and then guide students to put forward the concept of power supply. "Whether a 5V power is ok or not?", teachers should guide students to think about Anti- interference, then put forward filter circuit. Until now, teachers talk about the reliability and anti-inference of MCU with close integration of project practice; students can grasp the knowledge which may not be learnt from books unconsciously.

(5)   What is to be the second necessity besides small MCU system? Teachers should ask students to think about different electric equipments used daily time about "how can we figure out weather they are under power or not?", then guide students to put forward the design of indicator light, meanwhile call students attention to the necessity of a LED and a current limiting resistance. Teachers should guide students to figure out the resistivity as well as recalling the knowledge of digital and simulate electricity. In such a way we can get the perfect system which is also generally used in engineering projects. During the whole teaching process, students can catch the sight of specific condition of circuits visually. Until now the prerequisites of functioning a MCU is fully introduced. This is all about the "three necessities" of the small MCU system schematic diagram.

(6)   Having the basic structure at hearts of all the students, teachers should lead them to design the circuit of trotting horse lamp next step. It is quite simple with the previous preparatory knowledge, but the drive capacity and other matters needing attention should be immediately emphasized about MCU now. Imprint students with these matters as the foundation for the following module design.

5   Application Effect Study on Visualized Classroom Interactive Learning

From the spring of 2009, our college has gradually applied Proteus-tech into classroom teaching, at the same time, relevant reform in education has been carried out step by step.

(1) Study on classroom teaching effectiveness
According to the practical enrollment situation of our college, we began to track surveying the students' learning progress of MCU from the fall of 2008. Here is the comparison of different teaching effects between applying MCU virtual visualized classroom interactive learning or not. (As is shown in Table 1)

Table 1. The teaching effects

Studied semester	Fall of 2008	Spring of 2009	Fall of 2009	Spring of 2010
Number of students	43	45	88	43
≥70marks (%)	34.8	51.1	79.5	90.6
≤70marks (%)	65.2	48.9	20.5	9.4
remarks	before application	After application	After application	After application

(2) Study on second classroom teaching effectiveness
Students' desire and interest of hand-on work have been greatly stimulated since the Proteus tech-based MUC virtual visualized interactive learning method has been adopted; many took advantage of off-hours to DIY small works and took part in the various electronic design contests and "challenge cup" activities held by school positively. In 2009, the number of students who participated in the "An shi Cup" electronic design contest and the number of works, both of the two, peaked. Moreover, students benefiting from this kind of experience went in for the 20th National Undergraduate Electronic Design Contest and actually won the second prize.

(3) Study on the effectiveness of graduation projects
It is very clear to see that the effectiveness of students' works has been greatly enhanced by comparison of works done in the previous years from the view of difficulty, integrity and relation to teachers' projects after adopting this new kind of teaching method.

(4) Track surveying on students' employment program

It is surveyed most students who ever taught by this method took the occupations of research and development of MCU software or hardware and grew to the technological backbones of the companies quickly.

6 Conclusions

Through the study of Proteus-tech based virtual visualized classroom interactive learning platform, we can see students would join more in the teaching process, their interest is obviously increased, their knowledge of the foundation course is consolidated and strengthened, their self-confidence is improved, the ability of hand-on work and engineering consciousness are overall promoted.

At the same time, this teaching model can be a tool for thought-inspiration, concept-clarification, knowledge hierarchy-consolidation and cognitive conflict- solution. Not only can it enhance students' participation, promote their understanding of knowledge, but also create positive involvement atmosphere, increase their interest as well as improving concentration. As for teachers, it improves the architecture of MCU course more and promotes the education reform on MCU curriculum instruction.

References

1. Zheng, L., Zhang, J.: Multipoint Technology-based Interactive Learning Platform To Support The Classroom Application of MouseMischief. China Educational Technology 10, 93–98 (2009)
2. Li, X.: Proteus In 8051 Based on Examples Guide. Publishing House of Electronic Industry, Beijing (2008)
3. Wu, F., Xie, B.: Reform on Experimental Teaching of Microcontroller Based on Proteus and Keil. Research and Exploration in Laboratory 28, 125–127 (2009)
4. Xu, A.: Principle of Practical Tutorial Microcontroller- Virtual Simulation Based Proteus. Publishing House of Electronic Industry, Beijing (2009)
5. http://www.proteus.net.cn/
6. Zhong, K., Li, N.: Collaborative Learning Based on The Theory of Perception. China Educational Technology 7, 9–16 (2009)
7. Zhang, Y.: Principle and Application of Microcontroller. Higher Education Press, Beijing (2004)

Research of Home Appliance Network System Design Based on ENC28J60

Lixin Li and Diankuan Ding

College of Physics & Electrical Engineering, Anyang Normal University,
455000 Anyang, China
lilixin@sina.com, ddk@163.com

Abstract. Adopting AT89C52 as the main controller, ENC28J60 as the controller chip, Ethernet formatted encapsulation and demodulation are realized according to the deal IEEE 802.3 in this design. According to the design, the application programs of ARP、 ICMP、 TCP are carried out, meanwhile it puts forward the application circuit of data conversion of ENC28J60, and carries out the conversion of data to the formatted style, then home appliance network is achieved.

Keywords: Ethernet, TCP/IP, SPI Port, MCU Communication, ENC28J60.

1 Introduction

Ethernet technology gets obvious development with the popularization of internet technology and development of embedded system; it is gradually applied in the fields of instrument and meter, industrial control system and intelligence application (IA). The key point of studying household network lies in how to share the information coming from home appliance network with MCU as the core and how to use the well-developed internet technology, 8-bit low-cost MCU and Ethernet controller chip to connect Ethernet without using PC or top grade MCU.

As the most comprehensive deal ever, TCP/IP is a very huge protocol family with comparative high system source consumption, so how to realize TCP/IP on monolithic system becomes a difficult point for the household internet with the application of Ethernet on monolithic system. In the design of this essay, the Ethernet controller is ENC28J60 which is in line with Deal IEEE 802.3, and it can achieve correspondence with MCU through standard SI, meanwhile it occupies fewer resource of MCU I/O port. With all its advantages, ENC28J60 is propitious to realize the function of Ethernet on MCU and then to bring about household internet.

2 System Design

The whole design thought of household networking is to set up LAN (local area network) with family as the basic unit and then connect household LAN to Ethernet as in Fig.1. To realize the connection between Ethernet and home appliances with MCU as

G. Shen and X. Huang (Eds.): ECWAC 2011, Part I, CCIS 143, pp. 205–210, 2011.

the core, we should figure out how to achieve data conversion from MCU to Ethernet data format.

The aim of this design is to solve the problem of the mismatch between the data frame of MCU and that of Ethernet and to work out data conversion module between the two, thereby, we can realize the assumption of household networking through terminal equipment connection between MCU and Ethernet. The network switch module of this design is shown in Fig.2. Resources of MCU I/O port can be saved with the connection between MCU and data conversion module through serial port. The formatted data is transformed to the terminal equipment of Ethernet through standard RJ port.

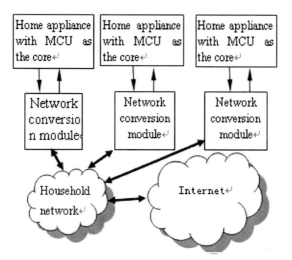

Fig. 1. Sketch map of household network

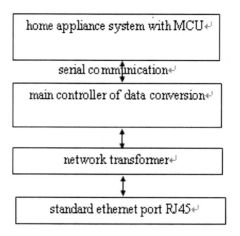

Fig. 2. Sketch map of network conversion module

3 System Design on Home Appliance Network

3.1 Hardware Design

Network switch module is composed of the functional module by MCU and data conversion module by Ethernet format.

There are three tasks of functional module: first, it is responsible for data acquisition, data control and data presentation; second, functional control module controls network switch module and makes it initialized; and the third one is to encapsulate the sending data partially and make a full preparation for the encapsulation of Ethernet format of frame about data conversion module. Functional module is the control center of household network system.

The fictional module of this design is composed by small MCU system with AT89C52 as the core. The data of household appliance which is shown by LED and the data which is sent by Ethernet terminal equipment are transmitted by SPI serial delivery mode through the port of Ethernet formatted data switch module. In this way, the limited I/O resource of MCU can be saved.

The major function of this module is to make a full encapsulation of the partially encapsulated data that is transmitted by functional module. Data sent by the module should be in complete accordance with the Ethernet format, and all the data which is suitable for Ethernet transition is sent to the designated Ethernet terminal equipment through Ethernet; at the same time, this module is in charge of the Ethernet formatted data which is transmitted by Ethernet terminal equipment and demodulates it to the formatted data that can be recognized by MCU with the purpose of offering information for the inquiry of master MCU control. The SPI port dive circuit is the two way communication interface circuit of the data conversion module of Ethernet format and MCU module. The dive circuit is responsible for the two way communication.

(1) Choice of Master Chip of Ethernet Formatted Data Conversion Module. The 28-pin independent Ethernet controller—ENC28J60 which is pushed out by Microchip Technology is now the smallest world wide controller and it fits the 802.3 protocol; moreover, it needs only 4 cables to connect the master MCU by adopting standard SPI serial port. With all these advantages, together with the free-issued microware stack used for MCU by Microchip, make it the top choice as the smallest embedded chip to be applied to Ethernet network.

(2) Circuit Design of Data Conversion Module shown in Fig.3.We can link up low level current to the reset pin of ENC28J60 to make it enter reset mode. There is weak pull-high register on the inner side of reset pin; we can attach 10KΩ pull-high register at designing or install certain software through SPI to realize soft reset. The operating frequency of ENC28J60 is 25MHz, which needs parallelly cut crystal to function, as for the AT bar-typed crystal oscillator, we can install a small register at pin-OSC2 to help starting oscillation. In order to reduce systematic noise, we usually put a small resistance neutral grounding at pin-OSC2. In the design, we use passive parallelly-cut crystals in the whole connection. We can realize the restoration of pin-LEDA and pin-LEDB by automatic polarity detection, either by direct drive or current drive. The exact restoration is carried out according to the default setting of PHLCON, meanwhile the connection of LED is detected ENC28J60. LEDB is lightened by sourcing current in the design.

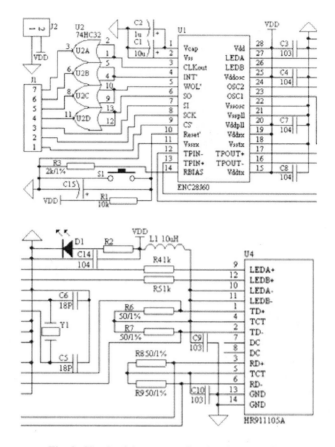

Fig. 3. Circuit of data conversion functional module

Ethernet circuit is connected to MUC through SPI, and the communication between ENC28J60 and MUC is realized by lead wire which can block the connection of pins. We should add a driving circuit to make MCU functional at interface circuits. And this driving circuit should have CMOS gate circuit 74HC32 to drive the TTL level current of MCU.

The connection between the two pairs of UTP of 10BASE-T and ENC28J60 as well as network port through is achieved by network transformer. The functions of network transformer are as follows: it can separate direct current and alternating current to prevent the operating point of network card chip being interfered by direct-current level from UPT; it can suppress high frequency interference by the its universal frequency. To order to save space, it adopts HR911105A network transformer chip which is integrated by network transformer and RJ45 port.

3.2 Software Design

The system software is programmed by both C language and Assembly language, but only Assembly language is responsible for initialization of monolithic system and network switch module as well as the delivery of link layer data concerning with network module. All the networking protocols are carried out by the exoteric C language TCP/TP protocol stack.

The realization course of the main program is shown in Figure 4.

System initialization includes the initialization of MCU AT89C52, network interface ship and all the flag registers of TCP/IP stack.

The major function of ARP processing module is to receive ARP requests and send ARP responses. ARP responses are realized by unicast messages by ARP responses messages.

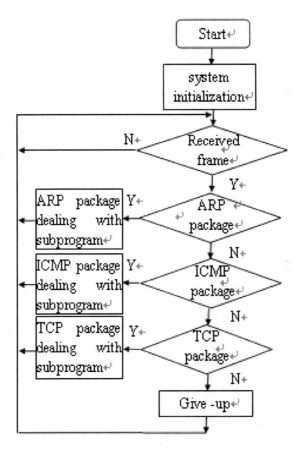

Fig. 4. Main program flow chart

The definition of ARP Header Structure:

```
Struct APR-Header {
U16        ARP_HWType;  //definition of hardware type
U16        ARP_PRType;  //protocol type
U08        ARP_HWLen;   // HLEN
```

U08	ARP_PRLen;	//delivery length
U16	ARP_Op;	//operation code
U08	ARP_SHAddr[6];	//MAC source address
U32	ARP_SIPAddr;	//IP source address
U08	ARP_THAddr[6];	// MAC destination address
U32	ARP_TIPAddr;///IP destination address} ;

(3)The major unction of ICMP processing module is to carry out echo requests and only the PING response is dealt with by it. Internet message control protocol which helps all the panel points be diagnosed simply and sends back error message is an attachment of IP, it is often used by IP or other high layer protocols.

(4) The major task of TCP processing module includes two parts: the task of sending end is to establish connections with the receiving end, and to cut the data stream into small units which can be numbered and sent one by one; the task of receiving end is to await the arrival of all different units sharing the same process and check up and deliver the units without any error, then send them to receiving layer as a data stream. And this linkage is closed by transport layer when the whole data stream is delivered completely.

4   Conclusion

After debugging, the encapsulation and demodulation of Ethernet data format can be achieved by this system which is in correspondence with IEEE 802.3 protocol, the data transportation between home appliance and Ethernet terminal equipment, as well asnalogous home appliance network can be actuallized, too. Tidy system circuits, stable working process, less hardware occupation, together with convenient inserting schedule, this system provides very serviceable technical proposal for the realization of home appliance network.

References

1. Zhou, X., Cheng, H., Zhang, X.: New Ethernet controller ENC28J 60 and interface technology. Microcontrollers & Embedded Systems (08), 34–36 (2006)
2. He, Q.: Intelligent home appliances and information appliances Internet connection. Electronic & Computer Design World (4A), 20–21 (2001)
3. Microchip Technology Inc. ENC28J60 Stand-Alone Ethernet Controller with SPI Interface (2005), http://www.microchip.com
4. Li, C.: MCU Theory and Interface Technology, 3rd edn. Aeronautics and Astronautics Publishers, Beijing (2005)
5. Chen, Y., Hou, A., Liu, P.: Embedded System Development and Examples based on ARM. Posts & Telecom Press, Beijing (2008)
6. Richard Stevens, W.: TCP/IP Illustracted Volume. China Machinery Press, Beijing (2000)
7. Zhou, X.-f., Yang, S.-x., Hua, L.: Realization of Simple TCP/IP at MCU. Microelectronics & Computer (2), 99–101 (2004)

Routing Protocol of Sparse Urban Vehicular Ad Hoc Networks

Huxiong Li

School of Computer Science and Engineering, Wenzhou University,
325035 Wenzhou, China
llhx@126.com

Abstract. Vehicular ad hoc network (VANET) is an application of mobile ad hoc technology in transportation systems, it has become an important part of ITS. Since multi-hop link is hard to set up in sparse VANET, a traffic-aware routing (TAR) protocol is proposed which estimates vehicle average neighbors (VAN) of roads by exchanging beacon messages between encounter vehicles. Road with high VAN is preferred to be selected as part of forwarding path at intersection. Packets are forwarded to the next intersection in road in a greedy manner. Simulations show that TAR outperforms the compared protocols in terms of both packet delivery ratio and average end-to-end delay.

Keywords: VANET, Sparse Network, Routing Protocol, Traffic-aware.

1 Introduction

Vehicular Ad Hoc network (VANET) refers to the mobile ad hoc networks, composed of corresponding with each other between vehicles in the road, which can provide a variety of services such as emergency alerts, vehicle data sharing and vehicle collaboration, has become an important part of the Intelligent Transportation System [1,2]. As Mobile Ad hoc technology applying in the field of transportation, VANET has a very high scientific value and broad application prospects, it has attracted world wide attention in the field of academia and industry, and launched a number of related research engineering projects [3-5].

Vehicle Ad Hoc network is very different from the usual wireless ad hoc networks, for example, the node trajectories are entirely restricted to the road, nodes mobile high-speed, in addition, the network nodes are often able to positioning itself through GPS, and it can obtain the support of basic e - Maps. VANET is vulnerable to time (such as daily routines, holidays, etc.), bad weather and so on. In some period, vehicles are often scarce and have uneven distribution on the road, in addition, in the initial stage of the VANET deployment, Vehicles equipped with wireless terminals may be only a small part, a complete chain of multi-hop communication between vehicles is difficult to establish in the sparse distribution of these vehicles, it also challenges the design of routing protocols. Generally, sparse ad hoc networks of vehicles are a larger end to end transmission delay, so how to reduce the transmission delay under the success of a high transfer rate of data packet is the problem to solve for the routing protocol. This paper proposed the routing protocol, which is based on Traffic-aware Routing (TAR), by

G. Shen and X. Huang (Eds.): ECWAC 2011, Part I, CCIS 143, pp. 211–217, 2011.
© Springer-Verlag Berlin Heidelberg 2011

perceiving the various sections of the traffic flow, so that the forward path contains the large traffic volume roads as far as possible. On these road sections, data packet can be transmitted as the wireless multi-hop by choosing the highest possible probability, rather than carrying forward by moving the node. The experiments prove that TAR protocol has a low-end packet delay and higher successful delivery rate.

2 Network Model

Network model protocols has the following assumptions: (1) vehicles (ie nodes in the network communication environment, the two words General Motors, the text is no longer to distinguish between the two concepts) can be real-time access to their own GPS location, and equipped with a simple electronic map, so that vehicles in the process can be able to master the surrounding road topology information; (2) the source node has already known the location of the destination node through the location-based services before sending packet forwarding; (3) network of roads in the scene are two-way street. To assess the packet forwarding delay, define variables as follows: (1) rij: roads from the junction of Ii to Ij; (2) lij: length of road rij; (3) vij: average speed of vehicles on the roads; (4) Rw: Vehicle coverage radius of wireless nodes; (5) dij: Data Packet rij on the roads look for an opportunity to forward the process of the estimated delay, then:

$$d_{ij} = P_w \cdot \frac{l_{ij} \cdot C}{R_w} + (1 - P_w) \cdot \frac{l_{ij}}{v_{ij}} \tag{1}$$

Where, C is a constant that forwards packets forwarding node processing time-consuming, this value is much smaller compared to lij / vij; Pw is the probability of transmiting packet on the roads in wireless mode, it can be seen that, the greater of its value, the smaller of the data packet transmission delay on the roads. Assumed that X is the distance between adjacent vehicles, it is exponentially distributed, E (X) = 2Rw / Nij, then:

$$P_w = P(X \le R_w) = 1 - e^{-N_{ij}/2} \qquad X > 0 \tag{2}$$

Which, Nij is the average number of neighbors (vehicle average neighbors, VAN) for all vehicles on the road rij, it reflects the size of the traffic flow of the section. from equation (1) and (2), we know that, in order to find the smallest delay path for packet forwarding, routing protocols should be close to the destination node location of the road as far as possible and select the large value of VAN node on the path as a for-warding node.

3 Tar Agreement

3.1 Protocol Overview

In the process of forwarding, the forwarding node in the model of the road calculate the road traffic volume VAN targets to perceive information, at the junction mode, collecting the other road VAN value and select the greatest value of the path as the forward path. Thus, on the whole, the agreement is always trying to choose a relatively large traffic volume on the road to carry forward the node group, in the sparse network, it can effectively reduce the end-to-packet transmission delay. But it's worth mentioning that traffic is heavy because of the separate along the road has been forwarded, in extreme cases, it would be farther and farther away from the destination node, it is necessary to take measures to restrict the region of the forward, for the sake of simplicity, forwarding region is defined as a circular region which has the destination node as the center of the circle, the destination node and the distance from the source node with an offset distance is the radius of the circular region, the offset distance varys from the network sizes.

3.2   The Mode of the Road-Inside

When the node is neither in the junction area nor in the areas of destination, the node is in the mode of the road-inside. in the driving process, the nodes periodically broadcast beacon messages (beacon) in a fixed interval of $\triangle t$, and to estimate the value of the road VAN by exchanging the message when meeting with the head node. VAN value of the message header for the main field of statistics includes: current velocity vector v of node, position pos, ID current Road Id of the current section, the number of vehicles within the NoIn Opposite of traveling the opposite direction of the current sections in the last $\triangle t$, the number of Neighbours of the current section's own statistics (both directions) neighbors; the ID last Road Id of the last section of road, the average neighbor number of vehicles last Neighbours on a road (both directions).

By information exchanging, the node for the section in which the number of vehicles of average of neighbors are carried out in a statistical mode, when the node gets into a new road, the related variables should be re-initialized and updated relevant to statistical last Road Id and last neighbours.

The interval $\triangle t$ of beacon message broadcast can not be set too small, it is because the number of neighbors counted in a very short period of time has not changed. Assume that the average speed of the node is 15m/s (54km/h), Rw=250m, in theory, the direct communication time of the two nodes when meeting is 16.7s; if met for at least two times each beacon exchanging, and completing during 16.7 * 0.6 = 10s, then the more appropriate benchmark for the time interval is 4-5s. In order to further reducing the network overhead without affecting the estimation accuracy, two kinds of dynamic strategies can be used to adjust $\triangle t$: 1) When the estimated average number of neighbors of vehicles exceeds a certain threshold, and, then the possibility of multi-hop transmission takes place between pairs of signals considered on the road is already quite large, eliminating the need for accurate statistics, the interval $\triangle t$ time could be increased. if the threshold value is set to 4, according to formula (2), when the average neighbor number is 4, all vehicles on the road can be connected by the probability of 86.5%. 2) According to the changes frequency of the average number of neighbors to adjust the $\triangle t$, if average number of neighbors over several consecutive cycles changes little, then increase the $\triangle t$, otherwise decrease $\triangle t$, but it should ensure that the value of $\triangle t$ in the interval fluctuates near the baseline. In this paper, the second approach is adopted to optimize $\triangle t$ dynamicly.

When the nodes in the road forward data packets, the greedy forwarding strategy based on location is used, choosing the node in the neighbor list from the section closest to the next exit (intersection) as the next hop, if such a node is not found, then the current forwarding node has to carry the group to move forward until the opportunity is coming to further forward.

3.3 Intersection Mode

When the node is located at the intersection zone, at the intersection mode. When the TAR agreement chooses the next stretch of road to forward, a basic principle is to select a section which having large value of VAN. when Forwarding nodes in the intersection, analyzing their own neighbor table, according to the node record of nodes on the section connected to the junction in the neighbors table to estimate the VAN of the section, select the sections having the largest value of VAN. Forwarding node for the neighbors in the table at the junction area, but being away from the junction center vehicles, it should be considered in this node is that the estimated average number of neighbors belongs to road last Road Id, rather than the current path. If the neighbor table, there are multiple neighbor information to estimate a common road, then the average of these estimates is as the average number of neighbors by the forwarding node. Fig.1, the current vehicle X is located in the road forward R3, the arrows indicate the direction of motion of the vehicle, the last time, the location of the node A is denoted with the dashed line. Suppose X neighbor in the table at this time on the road to a neighbor on the other log-related items is shown in Table 1, it judges the average neighbor number of other road as Van (R1) = (2.250 2.281) / 2 = 2.266, Van (R2) = 1.570, Van (R4) = 0. Therefore, X data packets are forwarded directly to the road R1 on node B.

Table 1. Related felds of neighbor list

Neighbor Id	Current RoadId	Neighbors Estimated	Last RoadId	lastNeighbors Estimated
A	R2	1.121	R1	2.250
B	R1	2.281	Rx	x.xxx
C	R2	1.570	Rx	x.xxx

4   Simulation

4.1 Experiment Environment

Simulation platform for use ns-2.29 [6], experimental vehicles, the node movement model can be used to reflect a more realistic road environment, vehicle movement pattern Manhattan [7] model, the simulation scenario shown in Fig.2, a rectangular region that contains eight bi-directional roads, such as the probability of the node at the intersection of selection and crossing the road connected to each other. Experiment, in order to characterization of different vehicles on the road to uneven distribution, select a certain percentage of the total number of nodes (hereinafter referred to as the proportion of road vehicles, EF) of the nodes only on the road between EF movement, also choose four pairs of nodes were fixed in the S1, S2, and D1, D2 and from the four regional movement, the length of the four regions are 300m, Si (i = 1,2) within the two nodes Di respectively, within the two nodes send CBR packets. The remaining nodes initially uniformly distributed, simulation, according to Manhattan after the start of the trajectory model generation mobile.

Experiment with the successful packet transmission rate (packet delivery ratio, PDR), the average end to end delay (average end-to-end delay, AED) indicators will TAR protocol GPSR [8] and GPCR [9] protocols are compared. Two comparison protocols are of widespread concern in VANET routing protocol, GPSR uses greedy forwarding protocol strategy forward, GPCR according to the characteristics of urban road scenes specifically designed for the sake of fairness, we compare the agreement in the two by adding an opportunity for wait mechanism (curve, respectively GPSR-opp, GPCR-opp indicated), or to extend the data packet time-out, three protocol data packet time-out time is set to 30s, if not in this period of time to find a forwarding group opportunities will be discarded.

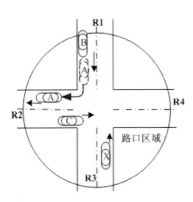

Fig. 1. Intersection mode

Fig. 2. Simulation scenarios

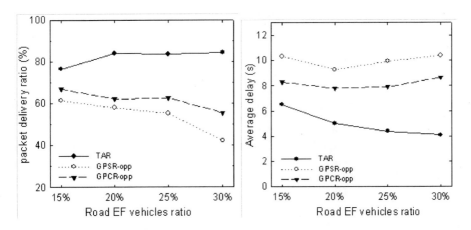

Fig. 3. Packet delivery ratio

Fig. 4. Average end-to-end delay

4.2 Experimental Analysis

Fig.3 indicated that the three kinds of agreements with the PDR value of the ratio of vehicles on the road EF changes, we can see, all three of the PDR maximum value compared to TAR, the maximum 42% higher than GPSR, it is because the agreement to forward the process to select a TAR node, the node density on the road to forward packets, a large number of data packets through the forwarding nodes on the section of a relatively good network connectivity to improve the success of the packet transmission rate. GPSR protocol using geographic greedy forwarding strategy, due to scarcity of forwarding nodes around the node has to frequently into recovery mode, reducing the rate of packet sent successfully. With GPSR, compared, GPCR agreement due only in each section on the use of greedy mode to forward packets to enter recovery mode decreases the probability, packet success rate was slightly higher to send. To note is that as the number of vehicles on the road EF increased, TAR protocol sub-component power slowly increasing, while the GPCR, and GPSR is dwindling. This is because the TAR protocol packet node density of vehicles along the main road (ie, EF) for forwarding, while the GPSR and GPCR did not consider the node density, only based on the distance from the destination node to select the forward path, when the rise in the number of vehicles on the road when the EF the other vehicles on the road to decrease, an increase of these two protocols in the next forwarding node because they can not jump-fat nodes and the probability of dropping packets. Fig.4 indicated that the TAR, GPSR and GPCR agreement, the average end to end packet delay with the increase in the proportion of road vehicles, EF changes, compared with the three, TAR agreement, the minimum delay, GPCR, and GPSR second, this is because TAR in the forwarding process as we choose the path of node density on EF nodes to relay packets, forwarding nodes have more opportunities to directly after the receipt of packet forwarding to the next hop node, and therefore achieved a smaller end-extension time. In contrast, GPCR, and GPSR protocols are in line with geographical location select a distance to the destination node forwards near the road, the roads and road EF compared to the vehicle density of less forwarding node but often need to rely on their own mobile division, and look for opportunities to bring forward to the next hop node, such an opportunity to be smaller compared to TAR, and this has led to an average of end to end latency increased significantly.

5 Conclusion

This paper proposes a traffic-aware routing protocol to estimate the average number of neighbors on the vehicle section of the node by using beacons exchanged between vehicles in order to perceive the traffic flow. Forwarding node in the junction area selects the largest average neighbor number of sections as the forwarding path. The vehicle in the forward section finds the next hop forwarding node, which chooses the next intersection as a target node using greedy strategy to. Simulation results show that the TAR has a higher success rate and lower packet transmission delay, compared with other protocols, and it can satisfy communications needs of the city sparse Vehicle Ad Hoc Network.

Acknowledgement

This work is supported by foundation of Wenzhou science and technology bureau (H20090006). The authors are grateful for the anonymous reviewers who made constructive comments.

References

1. Chang, C.Y., Xiang, Y., Shi, M.L.: Development and status of vehicular ad hoc networks. Journal on Communication (2007) (in Chinese)
2. Zhang, G., Mu, D., Xu, Z., et al.: A survey on the routing schemes of urban vehicular Ad hoc networks. Inst. of Elec. and Elec. Eng. Computer Society, Kunming (2008)
3. Festag, A., Noecker, G., Strassberger, M., et al.: NoW - Network on Wheels: Project Objectives, Technology and Achievements (2008)
4. Hull, B., Bychkovsky, V., Zhang, Y., et al.: CarTel: a distributed mobile sensor computing system. ACM Press, Boulder (2006)
5. car2car project, http://www.car-2-car.org/
6. The ns-2 Network Simulator, http://www.isi.edu/nsnam/ns/
7. Bai, F., Sadagopan, N., Helmy, A.: The IMPORTANT framework for analyzing the Impact of Mobility on Performance of Routing protocols for Adhoc Networks. Ad Hoc Networks 1(4), 383–403 (2003)
8. Karp, B., Kung, H.T.: GPSR: greedy perimeter stateless routing for wireless networks, pp. 243–254. ACM Press, Boston (2000)
9. Lochert, C., Mauve, M., Fu, H., et al.: Geographic routing in city scenarios. ACM SIGMOBILE Mobile Computing and Communications Review 9(1), 69–72 (2005)

A New Improved Method to Permutation Ambiguity in BSS with Strong Reverberation

Huxiong Li[1] and Gu Fan[2]

[1] School of Computer Engineering, Wenzhou University,
325035 Wenzhou, China
[2] College of Marine, Northwestern Polytechnic University,
710002 Xi'an China
{llhx,gf}@126.com

Abstract. The major problem of blind source separation in frequency domain is the permutation ambiguity between different frequency bins, which is the key factor to recover the original sources correctly. A new idea is to consider the frequency components from the same source as a multivariate vector with a certain probability density function, and the vectors from different sources are independent each other. An algorithm based on this idea is proposed to solve the permutation ambiguity problem of BSS in frequency domain, and some approximate cost functions are compared with the existing algorithm in frequency domain. The computer simulations to two true speeches with strong reverberation are shown to verify the efficiency of the proposed algorithm.

Keywords: Blind Source Separation (BSS), Strong Reverberant Environment, Multivariate PDF, KL Divergence.

1 Introduction

Blind signal separation (BSS) is to separate real unknown signals from some observed data when the channel responses are also unknown, only in terms of statistical independence of signals. BSS has many applications in communications, speech enhancement and image processing, and many effective algorithms under different assumptions are proposed [1-4]. For speech processing, the observed data recorded by microphones are often modeled as the convolutive mixture of multiple speeches with room impulse responses (RIRs), and the length of room impulse response is often large and determined by the surrounding environment, such as the material of wall, the location of microphones and the size of room.

Most algorithms for BSS of speeches [3,5] will transform the recorded data into frequency domain by short time Fourier transform (STFT) in order to avoid deconvolution with a long filter in time domain, which will result in large computational complexity and slow convergence. With suitable data window, the convolutive mixture in time domain will be expressed as the instantaneous mixture in frequency domain and some sophisticated algorithms for instantaneous mixture can be applied directly, such as the independent component analysis (ICA) [1-3], the original speeches can be reconstructed with the processed data by another inverse STFT. A serious problem is

G. Shen and X. Huang (Eds.): ECWAC 2011, Part I, CCIS 143, pp. 218–223, 2011.
© Springer-Verlag Berlin Heidelberg 2011

the amplitude and permutation ambiguity in different frequency pins, which is an inherent property of frequency BSS problem [2,3], so most algorithms in frequency domain are focusing on how to solve ambiguity.

The methods to solve permutation ambiguity can be categorized into two kinds, one is to assume the amplitude relationship between two close frequency bins from the same source should be smooth and related closely, like [4]. Another is based on the assumption that the direction of arrival (DOA) of the same source should be fixed during short intervals and all original speeches are from different directions, such as [3]. Some methods, called as joint method to permutation problem, improve the whole performance by combining advantages of two methods [5,6]. However, the nonstationarity of speeches and small number of microphones in application make the correct permutation in frequency bins very difficult.

In this paper, the idea of the multivariate vector is introduced and the algorithm based on this idea is derived. Some simple PDFs are provided and two examples are used to verify the better ability of this algorithm to permutation ambiguity.

2   The Model of BSS in Frequency Domain

Assume that the signal $x_j(t)$ received by M microphones is the mixture of N speeches $s_k(t)$, which can be written as:

$$x_j(t) = \sum_{k=1}^{N}\sum_l h_{jk}(l)s_k(t-l), \quad j=1,\ldots,M .$$
(1)

where $h_{jk}(t)$ is the impulse response of the channel from the k'th speech to the j'th microphone. The goal of BSS is to obtain an estimate $y_i(t)$ to the original speech $s_{\Pi(i)}(t)$ from all observed data $x_j(t)$, and the conventional method is to separate the observed data by a demixing FIR filter,

$$y_i(t) = \sum_{j=1}^{M}\sum_{l=0}^{D-1} w_{ij}(l)x_j(t-l) .$$
(2)

and the maximal length of the filter $w_{ij}(l)$ is D. The ideal BSS is that the relationship between the estimated signals and the original speeches is

$$y_i(t) = \sum_l \alpha_i(l)s_{\Pi(i)}(t-l) .$$
(3)

where $\Pi(i=1,\ldots,N)$ is a new permutation to $\{1,\ldots,N\}$ and $\alpha_i(l)$ is the scaled number. From (3), the recovered signal can be considered as the filtered version of the original speech by $\alpha_i(l)$ and the order of $y_i(t)$ is different from $s_k(t)$, that is, the amplitude ambiguity and permutation ambiguity of BSS. Compared with the permutation ambiguity, the amplitude ambiguity is often solved easily by the minimal distortion principle in [7] if the correct permutation can be obtained,

$$a_i(l) = h_{ii}(l). \tag{4}$$

so we will focus on how to solve the permutation ambiguity in the remaining paper.

The BSS methods in frequency domain are often dealt with the short time Fourier transform (STFT) with length L,

$$X_j(f,r) = \sum_{t=0}^{L-1} win(t) x_j(rT+t) \exp(-j2\pi ft). \tag{5}$$

where $win(t)$ is the window function and T is the sliding length for each data block, r is the index of the block. Then the demixing process in (2) can be expressed in vector and matrix forms as

$$Y_i(f,r) = \mathbf{w}_i^H(f) X(f,r), \quad i = 1,\ldots,N. \tag{6}$$

3 The Algorithms to Permutation Ambiguity

3.1 Multivariate PDF Models

The speech in time domain can be modeled as random process with certain PDF, so a natural idea is that the speech in frequency domain is also considered as a random vector due to the linear property of STFT, and the mathematical model for the observed data infrequency domain is

$$\mathbf{X}(f_i) = \mathbf{H}(f_i)\mathbf{s}(f_i), \quad i = 1,\ldots,L. \tag{7}$$

where r is ignored for convenience. The estimated signals at different frequency bins can be written as

$$\mathbf{Y}(f_i) = \mathbf{W}(f_i)\mathbf{X}(f_i), \quad i = 1,\ldots,L.. \tag{8}$$

Define $\mathbf{S}_i = \left[S_i(f_1), S_i(f_2), \cdots, S_i(f_L) \right]^T$ as the vector from the i'th speech, which consists of L frequency bins at the r'th block. We reconstruct the estimated output as $\mathbf{Y}_i = \left[Y_i(f_1), \cdots, Y_i(f_L) \right]^T$ and $\mathbf{Y} = \left[\mathbf{Y}_1, \mathbf{Y}_2, \cdots, \mathbf{Y}_M \right]^T$, which is a $M \times L$ matrix. For a perfect BSS, the estimated outputs are the scaled and permutated copies of the original speeches, so each column vectors in $\mathbf{Y}$ should be independent with each other if all original speeches are assumed to be independent. A good measure to independence is the Kullback-Leibler (KL) divergence, which measure the distance of the joint PDF $p_\mathbf{Y}$ and the product of all marginal PDF $\prod_i p_{\mathbf{Y}_i}$, that is,

$$C = KL\left(p_\mathbf{Y} \middle\| \prod_i p_{\mathbf{Y}_i} \right). \tag{9}$$

Note that the cost function in (9) is different obviously from it for these conventional ICA algorithm in frequency domain, which only measure the distance at each independent frequency bin [3].

Minimization the cost function in (9) is equivalent to the maximization of negative entropy, which is

$$C = \sum_i N\left(\mathbf{Y}_i\right) = \sum_i E\left[\log\left(p\left(\mathbf{Y}_i\right)\right)\right] + const.. \tag{10}$$

where $p\left(\mathbf{Y}_i\right)$ is the PDF of the i'th speech and it can be modeled in prior, and the expectation operation $E\{\cdot\}$ can be computed by the average of multiple data blocks. In order to simplify the PDF in(10), a nonlinear function is used to approximate $\log(p\left(\mathbf{Y}_i\right))$ The orthogonalization must be executed after each iteration on the whole demixing matrix to avoid divergence,

$$\mathbf{W}(f) \leftarrow \left(\mathbf{W}(f)\left[\mathbf{W}(f)\right]^H\right)^{-1/2} \mathbf{W}(f) . \tag{11}$$

After the convergence of the iterative process, the final demixing matrix $\mathbf{W}(f)$ is used to reconstruct the estimated outputs in frequency domain and the waveform in time domain can be obtained by another inverse STFT.

3.2 Approximation to Joint PDF

The nonlinear function $G\{\cdot\}$ is used to approximate the joint PDF of the vector from the i'th speech. Essentially, the true joint PDF is very difficult to obtain and sometimes changes a little with different speakers. Here two nonlinear functions are verified to approximate efficiently the joint PDF in [9]:
    Spherically Symmetric Exponential norm density (SEND):

$$\hat{p}_{S_i}\left(\mathbf{z}\right) = \frac{e^{-\sqrt{4/d}\|\mathbf{z}\|_2}}{\|\mathbf{z}\|_2^{d-1}} . \tag{12}$$

Spherically Symmetric Laplace density (SSL):

$$\hat{p}_{S_i}\left(\mathbf{z}\right) = e^{-\sqrt{2(d+1)}\|\mathbf{z}\|_2} \tag{13}$$

and d is the size of the vector $\mathbf{z}$, $d = 2L$ in this case. Another available cost function in [11] is

$$\sum_i E\left[\log\left(\sum_f \left|Y_i(f)\right|^2\right)\right] . \tag{14}$$

which is called as semi-nonparameter function (SNP).

4 Computer Simulations

Two speeches with 10s, one male and female, are mixed with the room impulse responses, which are generated by the imaging source method (ISM) software developed by Eric Lehmann [10]. Fig.1 shows the room size and the location of two microphones and sources. The FastICA algorithm with joint permutation in [5], is compared with the proposed algorithm. In order to compare their performance to permutation ambiguity, the correlation coefficients between the original speeches $S_i(f,r)(i=1,2)$ and the estimated outputs $Y_i(f,r)(i=1,2)$ in all frequency bins are computed and compared with a threshold (here is 0.8). The frequency bin is labeled as 'T' if the coefficient at this bin is larger than the threshold, or is labeled as 'F' if not.

We simulate room impulse responses with reverberation time 150ms and 300ms, respectively, and different nonlinear functions are compared with the FastICA algorithm. The permutation results with reverberation time 150ms are shown in Fig.1, and the sampling frequency is 16kHz, the length of STFT is 1024. From two figures, the proposed algorithm with different nonlinear function approximations can obtain more accurate permutation than the FastICA algorithm if frequencies are above 400Hz. Another interesting phenomenon is that different nonlinear functions can result in a very slight difference on permutation order. Change the room reverberation time with 300ms and the length of STFT with 2048, and repeat this simulation again. The permutations at all frequencies are shown in Fig. 1 and 2, respectively. The same conclusions can be drawn only except that there are more wrong permutations as the room reverberation time increases, which can be understood easily.

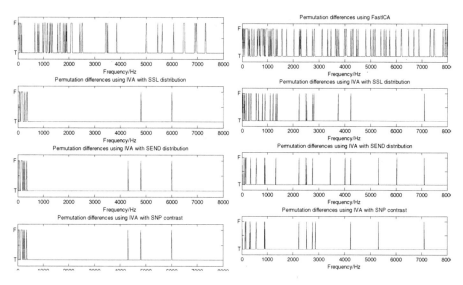

Fig. 1. The permutation with reverberation time 150ms

Fig. 2. The permutation with reverberation time 300ms

5   Conclusion

The method, which considers the vector consisted of all frequency bins from the same source as a multivariate PDF, can rebuild up the relationship of the same source between frequency bins. Some possible approximations to the multivariate PDF are provided and an iterative algorithm proposed. Two original speeches with the simulated room impulse responses with different reverberation times are demonstrated, and the efficiency and performance of this new algorithm is verified by comparison with the existing algorithm in frequency domain. The new model and algorithm proposed in this paper can improve permutation ambiguity efficiently, especially to the observed speeches with strong reverberations.

Acknowledgement

This work is supported by the Natural Science Foundation of Zhejiang province of China under Grant No.Y1080112. The authors are grateful for the anonymous reviewers who made constructive comments.

References

1. Hyvarinen, A., et al.: Independent component analysis. John Wiley and Sons, Chichester (2001)
2. Benesty, J., Sonhi, M.M., Huang, Y., et al.: Handbook of Speech Processing. Springer, Heidelberg (2008)
3. Saruwatari, H., Kurita, S., Takeda, K.: Blind source separation combining frequency-domain ICA and beamforming. ICASSP 5(7), 2733–2736 (2001)
4. Murata, N., Ikeda, S., Ziehe, A.: An approach to blind source separation based on temporal structure of speech signals. Neurocomputing 41(1-4), 1–24 (2001)
5. Zhu, J., Wang, H., Li, H.: Joint algorithm for permutation problem in frequency-domain in blind speech source separation. Computer Applications 28(6), 1552–1554 (2008) (in chinese)
6. Lee, I., Kim, T., Lee, T.-w.: Fast fixed-point independent vector analysis algorithms for convolutive blind source separation. Signal Processing 87, 1859–1871 (2007)
7. Matsuoka, K., Nakashima, S.: Minimal distortion principle for blind source separation. In: Proceeding of the 41st SICE Annual (SICE 2002), Washington, vol. 4, pp. 2138–2143 (2002)
8. Davies, M.: Audio Source Separation. Mathematics in Signal Processing, vol. 5, pp. 57–68. Oxford University Press, Oxford (2002)
9. Lee, I., Lee, T.-W.: On the Assumption of Spherical Symmetry and Sparseness for the Frequency-Domain Speech Model. IEEE Trans. on Speech, Audio and Language Processing 15(5), 1521–1528 (2007)
10. Lehmann, E., Johansson, A.: Diffuse Reverberation Model for Efficient Image-Source Simulation of Room Impulse Responses. IEEE Trans. on Audio, Speech and Language Processing 18(6), 1429–1439 (2010)
11. Hiroe, A.: Solution of permutation problem in frequency domain ICA, using multivariate probability density functions. In: Rosca, J.P., Erdogmus, D., Príncipe, J.C., Haykin, S. (eds.) ICA 2006. LNCS, vol. 3889, pp. 601–608. Springer, Heidelberg (2006)
12. Araki, S., Mukai, R., Makino, S., Nishikawa, T., et al.: The fundamental limitation of frequency domain blind source separation for convolutive mixtures of speech. IEEE Trans. Speech and Audio Processing 11, 109–116 (2003)

The Research on System Reliability in Complex External Conditions Based on SVM

Yi Wan and Yue Xu

College of Physics and Electronic Information Engineering,
Wenzhou University, Wenzhou, China
yiwan246@126.com

Abstract. Analysis method based on support vector machine and finite element combined with Monte Carlo is applied for the parts in complex external conditions or surroundings, it is difficult to built reliability model of the parts in complex the external conditions or surroundings and it is difficult to establish stress and intention distribution and joint probability density because they work in an uncertain environment, the support vector machine has a good generalization ability prediction ability, integration algorithm based on support vector machine, finite element and Monte Carlo can solve the questions and can excellently use for reliability simulation and calculation for complex and certain system. It is used for reliability analysis of catenary parts in the high-speed electrified railway, integration algorithm mathematic model of reliability analysis for location hook is built, and the outside parameter influence on wrist-arm of location hook is analyzed by the model.

Keywords: Integration algorithm, support vector machine, location hook, complex the external conditions or surroundings, Reliability analysis, catenary.

1 Introduction

Catenary system works in complex external conditions or surroundings, and the fault in the high-speed electrified railway mainly results from catenary system, and the fault mainly caused by its low reliability. The reliability analysis of critical force-bearing parts of catenary system is an important task in catenary design [1].

Analysis method based on support vector machine and finite element combined with Monte Carlo is applied for force-bearing parts of catenary system in complex external conditions or surroundings, it is difficult to built reliability model of the parts in complex the external conditions or surroundings and it is difficult to establish stress and intention distribution and joint probability density because they work in an uncertain environment, the support vector machine has a good generalization ability prediction ability, integration algorithm based on support vector machine, finite element and Monte Carlo can solve the questions and can excellently use for reliability simulation and calculation for complex and certain system. An example are given for reliability analysis of location hook in this paper, integration algorithm mathematic model of reliability analysis is built, and the outside parameter influence on wrist-arm of location hook is analyzed by the model.

G. Shen and X. Huang (Eds.): ECWAC 2011, Part I, CCIS 143, pp. 224–229, 2011.

2 Integration Algorithm Mathemation Model of Reliability Analysis

2.1 Stress-Intention Interference Model

Every components of mechanism part maybe invalid because all kinds of complex static loads and dynamic loads lead to internal stress exceed material intensity limit, the failure probability can be obtain by (1) according to stress-intention interference theory[2-4].

$$P_f = P(\delta - S \le 0) = \iint_D f_{\delta s}(\delta, s) d\delta ds \cdot \tag{1}$$

Where $\delta = \delta(X_{\delta 1}, X_{\delta 2}, X_{\delta 3}, ... X_{\delta j})$, $S = S(X_{S1}, X_{S2}, X_{S3}, ... X_{Sj})$. $f_{\delta s}(\delta, s)$ is stress and intention joint probability density of every components, X_δ is structural intention, X_{sj} is stress.

If $X = (X_1, X_2 ....., X_n)^T$ is random parameters vector, then state function is Expressed as:

$$g(X) = \delta(X) - S(X). \tag{2}$$

The components will invalidate if $g(X) \le 0$ according to (2) and probability and statistics theory, failure probability and reliability can be calculated in a certain amount of random numbers δ and S.

2.2 Reliability SimulationStep of Integration Algorithm

Reliability simulation step of Integration algorithm is as follows [3-4]. At first, Critical factors that influence the reliability of the parts are established.

Then N groups of random data are generated according to statistical distribution for selected parameters, maximum stress in dangerous section for each group of parameters are calculated by the finite element[5]. After selecting the fragment structure unit, characteristic analysis of typical unit is necessary, relationship of any point displacement is derived by nodal displacements.

$$\{w\} = [N]\{u\}^{(e)} \tag{3}$$

Where $\{w\}$ is column vector of any point displacement in the unit, $\{u\}^{(e)}$ is column vector of nodal displacement, $[N]$ is shape function matrix. The relationship of unit strain and unit stress and unit balance equation are obtained by equation (3).

$$\{\varepsilon\} = [B]\{u\}^{(e)} . \tag{4}$$

$$\{\sigma\} = [D][B]\{u\}^{(e)}. \tag{5}$$

$$\{P\}^{(E)} = [k]^{(e)}\{u\}^{(e)} \tag{6}$$

Where $\{\varepsilon\}$ is strain column vector of any point in the unit, $[B]$ is unit strain matrix, $[D]$ is elasticity matrix, $[k]^{(e)} = \iiint [B]^T [D][B] dxdydz$, $\{P\}^{(e)}$ is force column vector of unit equivalent node.

The next, the N groups of data are acted as support vector machine training samples, input-output relation between external parameter and interior stress is built by support vector machine intelligent algorithm [6-9].

Finally, material intensity distribution is established by testing and statistical data in document. Messenger wire bearing reliability is calculated by numerical simulation-Monte Carlo, Monte Carlo method is that state function g is calculated by random sample, and g<0 is judged, the parts is considered failure if maximum stress exceeds limit state[10]. If failure total number is L, failure probability P_f is L / N and reliability R is $1-P_f$.

3   Example Analysis

It is used for reliability analysis of catenary parts in the high-speed electrified railway, integration algorithm mathematic model of reliability analysis for wrist-arm of X type and location hook is built, and the outside parameter influence on wrist-arm of X type and location hook is analyzed by the model [3-4].

Critical factors that influence the reliability of wrist-arm of X type and location hook are established, they are pull F, ice load (ice-covering thickness d) and wind speed W, N groups of random data are generated according to statistical distribution for selected parameters, maximum stress in dangerous section for each group of parameters are calculated by the finite element[5]. Forty groups of basic variables are randomly generated according to the mean and variance of basic variables, then the stress S of each groups of basic variables are calculated by finite element software ANSYS[11], Thirty-five groups data are acted as training samples, and five groups data are acted as testing data. In finite element calculating, entity model is turned into PARASOILD format, then it is lead into ANSYS software and solid92 tetrahedron unit is used, 121342 units 203451 nods are obtained for wrist-arm of X type and 2708 units 4976 nods are obtained for location hook by free-dividing meshes. Finite element analysis model are shown in Fig. 1. The stress variation with external loads of location hook is shown in Fig. 2 [11].

Relative error between testing value and calculating value of finite element are shown in Fig. 3 after support vector machine is trained, it is clear that theory values and support vector machine output values is very close.

Reliability of location hook is calculated by reliability analysis model of integration algorithm, the mean value and deflection coefficient of material intensity limit value of location hook is obtained according to according to statistics. Reliability calculating result is 0.99911, relative error is only 0.017% comparison with calculating result of JC method.

It is analyzed that distribution deflection coefficient of external parameter have an effect on reliability of location hook by the program, relation curve is shown in Fig. 4. Distribution deflection coefficient of pull F has a great influence on reliability, and the external climate has also a great influence on wrist-arm reliability, so reliability optimal design is necessary to reduce catenary failures.

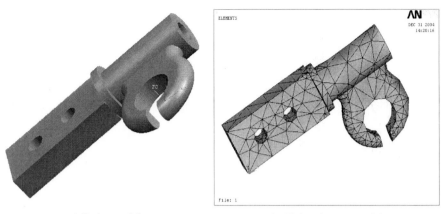

a) Entity model   b) Finite element model

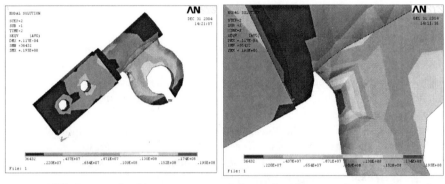

c) Whole stress cloud imagery   d) Stress cloud imagery of arc transition region

Fig. 1. Finite element analysis of location hook

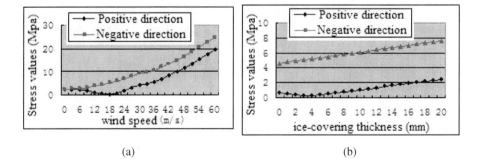

(a)   (b)

Fig. 2. The stress variation with external loads

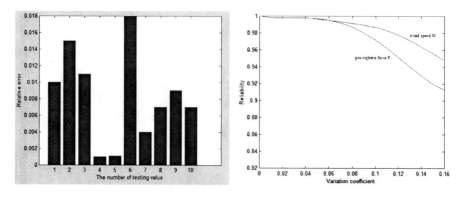

Fig. 3. Relative error between testing and calculating value of finite element

Fig. 4. Relation curve between deflection coefficient and reliability

4   Conclusion

Analysis method based on support vector machine and finite element combined with Monte Carlo is applied for the parts in complex external conditions or surroundings, it is difficult to built reliability model of the parts in complex the external conditions or surroundings and it is difficult to establish stress and intention distribution and joint probability density because they work in an uncertain environment, the support vector machine has a good generalization ability prediction ability, integration algorithm based on support vector machine, finite element and Monte Carlo can solve the questions and can excellently use for reliability simulation and calculation for complex and certain system. It is used for reliability analysis of catenary parts in the high-speed electrified railway, integration algorithm mathematic model of reliability analysis for location hook is built, and the outside parameter influence on wrist-arm of location hook is analyzed by the model.

In reliability design model, stress-intention distribution model reveals clearly fault cause and the essence of reliability design, but it is difficult to establish stress and intention distribution and joint probability density function of because it works in a complex and uncertain environment. In this paper, reliability of location hook are analyzed based on support vector machine and finite element combined with Monte Carlo, reliability calculating result is 0.99911, relative error is only 0.017% comparison with calculating result of JC method, and the outside parameter influence on wrist-arm is analyzed by the model. It provides a new way for reliability design and research in complex railway system.

Acknowledgement

This work is supported by Natural Science Foundation of Zhejiang Province of China.

References

[1] Yu, W.J.: High speed electrization railway catenary. Southwest Jiaotong University Press, Chengdu (2002)

[2] Zhang, J.R.: Structure reliability theory and application for bridge engineering. Public Jiaotong press, Beijing (2003)

[3] Wan, Y.: Connecting bolt reliability analysis based on finite element and machine learning theory. In: 2010 Second ETP/IITA World Congress in Applied Computing, Computer Science, and Computer Engineering/2010 ACC, pp. 323–326. IEEE Computer Society, Los Alamitos (2010)

[4] Zhang, Y.G.: Reliability simulation and analysis of messenger wire bearing on electrified railways. In: International Conference on Optics, Photonics and Energy Engineering, vol. (1), pp. 184–187 (2010)

[5] Yang, S.K.: Simulation method of structure reliability based on artificial neural network. Mechanical Intension 21(4), 12–16 (2004)

[6] Xiao, R., Wang, J.C., Sun, Z.X., et al.: An approach to incremental SVM learning algorithm. Journal of Nanjing University (Natural Sciences) 38(2), 152–157 (2002)

[7] Guo, C.D., Li, S.Z.: Control - based Audio Classification and Retrieval by Support Vector Machines. IEEE Trans. on Neural Network 14(1), 115–209 (2003)

[8] Cristianini, N., Shawe-Taylor, J.: An Introduction to Support Vector Machines and Other Kernel-based Learning Methods. University Press, Cambridge (2000)

[9] Vapnik, V.N.: Statistical Learning Theory. Springer, New York (2000)

[10] Kiyohiro.: Reliability analysis of geometrically nonlinear structures with application to suspension bridges, Dissertation Abstracts International. The University of Michigan, Ann Arbor (1999)

[11] Yang, Z.J.: Intensity Analysis of Parts of the Middle Catenary Supporting. Southwest Jiaotong university, Chengdu (2006)

Synthetical Reliability Analysis Model of CNC Software System

Yue Xu, Yinjie Xia, and Yi Wan[*]

College of Physics and Electronic Information Engineering, Wenzhou University,
325035 Wenzhou, China
yiwan246@126.com

Abstract. CNC technology is the core of advanced manufacturing technology, and CNC software system is the very important part of numerical control system. The entire CNC system will not work normally, once the potential failure makes the software invalid. As to the current study of CNC sysytem, in use of the FAULT glitch tree, established a glitch tree for the CNC system; find the minimum cut sets with Fussed method and then according to the probability of several common glitches, make quantitative analysis in the reliability of the CNC system so that scientific ways can be provided for the reliability design, maintenance and management of the CNC system.

Keywords: CNC Sysytem, The Fault Tree Analysis, Minimum Cut Sets, Reliability, Quantitative Analysis.

1 Introduction

CNC software system is the core component of CNC machine tools. The reliability of CNC software system is directly related to the reliability of CNC Machine Tool [1-5]. However, the reliability analysis of CNC software system has is more important to the improvement of numerical control system reliability [1]. Fault Tree Analysis (FTA) is a kind of systematic and detailed investigation and prediction method for failure. It uses deduction to find all the possible causes that lead to failure. Analyze the reliability of a series of CNC software system through fault tree analysis (FTA), and determine the various factors that may break the system down. thus, to determine the possible combinations of the causes for system failure and the probability of its occurrence .So as to calculate the probability of system failure. After finding a variety of possible causes for system failure, corrective measures can be taken to improve system reliability.

2 Fault Tree Analysis

Fault tree analysis aims to analyze the probability of failure event (also known as the top event) through branching diagram which is drawn by the logical symbols and

---

[*] Corresponding author. Supported by Undergraduate Scientific and Technological Innovation Project of Zhejiang Province of China (NO. 2009R424009).

G. Shen and X. Huang (Eds.): ECWAC 2011, Part I, CCIS 143, pp. 230–236, 2011.

gradually unfolds like a tree starting from the system [4]. Fault tree analysis searches all the failure modes for the system failure, that is to find all the minimum cut sets of fault tree based on a given system failure, Forecast the probability of system failure, that is the probability of top event by the failure probability of basic event. Therefore, the process of fault tree analysis includes the establishment, qualitative and quantitative analysis of the Fault Tree.

2.1 Tablishment of the Fault Tree

Correctly building the system fault tree is the advance of qualitative and quantitative analysis of the system by Fault tree analysis. Steps to establish the Fault Tree are as follows: Firstly, analyze the system and determine the system failure. Analyze the system that needs to establish the fault tree, and get an exact knowledge of the system failure and the causes for the failure. Therefore, it is necessary to understand the function of the system and working processes, while collecting and checking the information and data about the system. On this basis, evaluate the impact on the system caused by each failure, and identify the various causes for the failure.

Secondly, determine the top event of fault tree. After mastering the specific circumstances of the system, select the fault tree top event according to the actual situation, then expand from this top event and start to research. After determining the top event, define the boundary conditions reasonably, in order to make it convenient to definite the range of the fault tree establishment[2].

Thirdly, establish the fault tree by deductive method. Putting the top event on the top of the fault tree, all direct causes of top event are written below it and connected by correct logical symbols with top event. Analyze each direct cause that leads to the top event. If the event can be further decomposed, then take the event as the output event of the next level, put the reasons for the failure below it. Continue decomposing the intermediate event till the end of the event.

2.2 Qualitative Analysis of Fault Tree

The aim of qualitative analysis of fault tree is to determine the fault tree minimal cut sets by the analysis of fault tree, so as to find the weakest link in the system[3]. Minimal cut set is a cut set of end event, which can not be cut anymore. A minimal cut set represents a fault mode that results in the top event. Through the qualitative analysis of fault tree, we can identify all the minimal cut sets, which means we find all the fault modes that results in the top event of the fault tree.

2.3 Quantitative Analysis of Fault Tree

The purpose of quantitative analysis of FAULT tree is to calculate the probability of top event by quantitatively analyzing the probability of System basic fault event, which is convenient to evaluate the reliability index of the system. Therefore, before the quantitative analysis of the fault tree, we need to get the probability of occurrence of the end event through the scientific method. Then, using the inclusion-exclusion principle, and calculate the events plus and the events plot to obtain the probability of top event [2].

3 Reliability of CNC Software System

CNC machine tool plays an increasingly important role in the modern machinery manufacturing industry, and its input is so high. If a part goes wrong, it will lead great loss to the production. Thus, making accurate judgments in time when the fault of CNC machine tools happens, identify the fault position, and find out causes of the malfunction and remedy methods can greatly reduce the blindness and improve the economy and security. Yet software reliability is more complicated than hardware reliability. Hardware invalid is due to the focus of a large number of components and the wear and tear of them. But the software is on the opposite side. Strictly speaking, there is no wear and aging for the software. The reliability of software is related to the input data, it is mostly determined by people. Therefore, reliability analysis of CNC system software is the fault analysis of each CNC software function module.

3.1 Ware Modules of CNC System

According to the analysis of the numerical control system software, CNC software can be divided into 11 modules, and take seven modules with the highest frequency, as shown in table 1 [1].

Table 1. The highest failure rate for CNC system

Software module code	Software fault module	Software module code	Software fault module
SA	Initialization module	SG	Real-time management module
SB	Decoding Module	SI	Input Module
SC	Pre-processing module	SF	PLC Module
SE	Position Control Module		

The module functions

Initialization module: Including the procedures that initialize the peripheral drivers and interface chip and initialize the system parameter.

Decoding Module: Compiling the input program into purpose process that can be executed by the CPU.

Pre-processing module: Including process of coordinate transformation, knife fill, auto-acceleration and deceleration.

Position Control Module: Position completely controlled by the software, but also adjust the position loop gain, pitch error compensation, backlash compensation procedures and so on.

Real-time management module: Including procedures that deal with time, task and memory management, internal communications, interrupt management and various processing chip management.

Input module: The procedures that handle with the information from the input of the keyboard and the external memory.

PLC Module: it is the display control program that Used to enter the program, machine operation status and troubleshooting information displayed on the CRT / LCD monitor.

3.2 Establish the Fault Tree of the CNC Software System

Establish the fault tree according to the fault occurred and the reasons for failure of the CNC system, the fault tree is shown in Fig.1 (a)-(j).

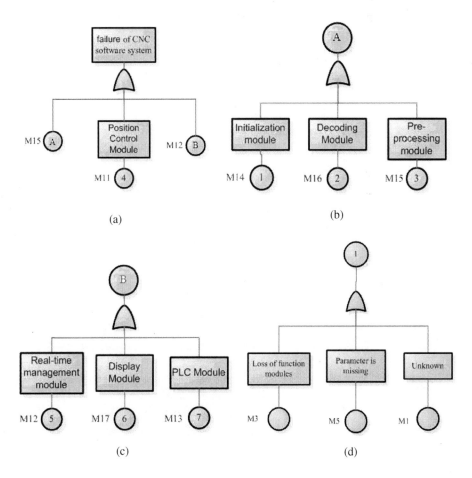

Fig. 1. Fault tree of the CNC system

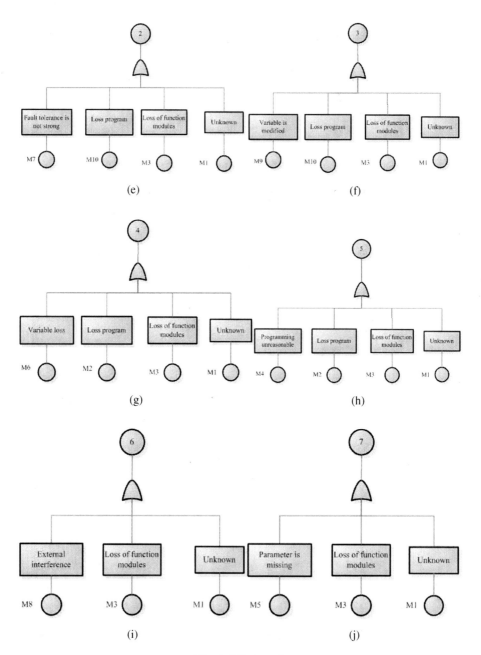

Fig. 1. (*Continued*)

Find minimal cut sets of fault tree by upwards, seeking the minimum cut set of fault tree, fault tree in Figure 1, the lowest level is:

$$M11 = M6 \cup M2 \cup M3 \cup M1 . \tag{1}$$

$$M12 = M1 \cup M2 \cup M3 \cup M4 . \tag{2}$$

$$M13 = M1 \cup M3 \cup M5 . \tag{3}$$

So, M14, M15, M16, M17 can also be expressed.

Up level, push the top event of failure expression for D:

$$D = M11 \cup M12 \cup M13 \cup M14 \cup M15 \cup M16 \cup M17 . \tag{4}$$

Put(1), (2), (3) into (4):

$$D = \{(M6 \cup M2 \cup M3 \cup M1) \cup (M1 \cup M2 \cup M3 \cup M4) \cup (M1 \cup M3 \cup M4) \cup (M1 \cup M2 \cup M5) \cup (M1 \cup M3 \cup M9 \cup M10) \cup (M1 \cup M3 \cup M7 \cup M10) \cup (M1 \cup M3 \cup M8)\}$$

Simplification can be obtained:

$$D = M1 \cup M2 \cup M3 \cup M4 \cup M5 \cup M6 \cup M7 \cup M8 \cup M9 \cup M10 .$$

So, the minimal cut sets of CNC software system are:

{M1}, {M2}, {M3}, {M4}, {M5}, {M6}, {M7}, {M8}, {M9}, {M10}.

This indicates that any one event happens to fail,it can cause system failure.

3.3 Analysis the Reliability of System

Through quantitative analysis of fault tree, we can analysis the reliability of the system. Since the minimum cut set of the events are independent, the probability of system failure probability can be calculated by independent events probability calculation method. CNC software failure probability can be expressed as: $Ps = 1 - (1-x1)(1-x2)(1-x3)\ldots(1-xn)$ ($x1, x2, x3\ldots$ represent the probability of the end of the event M1, M2, M3...).

Through the data provided by a variety of materials, the probability of the end of the incident as follows: parameter setting error: 0.4786; programming unreasonable: 0.1429; Variable is modified: 0.0952; external interference: 0.0952; Loss program: 0.0476; Loss of module function: 0.0476; Fault tolerance is not strong: 0.0476; Unknown:0.0476[1].

Put the data into Ps, the availability of CNC software probability of failure is: 0.69898; System reliability is: 0.30101;

Through the above analysis, the numerical control system software failure is mainly related with the input data caused by software errors. Therefore, by reducing the probability of failure mode of occurrence, such as parameter error, programming unreasonable, improper operation and so on, in order to improve the reliability of the CNC system.

4 Conclusion

Though the FAULT analysis, ensure a variety of factors that cause the system failure, and analyze them, then draw the logic diagram (FAULT tree), so as to determine the cause of system failure and their possible combinations or their probability. Then calculate the system failure probability. So, we can take corrective measures to improve system reliability.

Acknowledgement

This work is supported by Undergraduate Scientific and Technological Innovation Project of Zhejiang Province of China (NO.2009R424009). The authors are grateful for the anonymous reviewers who made constructive comments.

References

1. Iao, W.W., Jia, Y.Z.: Reliability Analysis for Software Failure of CNC System. Manufacturing Technology & Machine Tool (2006)
2. Zhu, J.Z.: Principle and Application of Fault Tree. Xi'an Jiaotong University Press, Xi'an (1989)
3. Xu, R., Che, J.G., Yang, Z.B.: The Fault Tree Analysis and Its Application in the system Reliability Analysis. Command Control & Simulation (2010)
4. Cai, Z.P., Tang, Z.P., Min, H.B.: Application of Expert System Based on Fault Tree Technique in Fault Diagnosis. Microcomputer Information (2006)
5. Yao, B.T., Song, Y.J.: Selection guide of CNC Equipment. China Machine Press, Beijing (2002)

A Harnack-Type Inequality for Convex Functions on the Anisotropic Heisenberg Group

Hujun Li[1] and Zhiguo Wang[2]

[1] Department of Public Course, Hubei Polytechnic Institute,
431605 Xiaogan, China
[2] School of Management, Xi'an Jiaotong University,
710002 Xi'an, China
llhj@126.com, zgwang@yahoo.com.cn

Abstract. In this paper, a Harnack-type inequality for convex functions on the anisotropic Heisenberg group is proved by using iterative methods based upon the structure of the group.

Keywords: anisotropic Heisenberg group, convex function, Harnack-type inequality.

1 Introduction

In recent years, fully nonlinear subelliptic equations appeared extensively in CR geometry, stochastic control, and other fields. The corresponding convex function theory has been concerned about[1-4]. Among things, an interesting and important result is a Harnack-type inequality for convex functions on the Heisenberg group H^1 by C. Gutierrez and A. Montanari[5].

The aim of this paper is to prove a Harnack-type inequality for the convex functions on the anisotropic Heisenberg groups $H^n(a_j)_{j=1}^n (a_j > 0)$. If $a_j = 1 (j = 1, \ldots, n)$, $H^n(a_j)_{j=1}^n$ is exactly the usual Heisenberg group H^n. We denote the group $H^n(a_j)_{j=1}^n$ by $H^n(a)$ below. The major difficulty to be overcome is how to select proper iterative sequences and make appropriate estimates.

To explain the main results, we first give some notions and basic facts. The anisotropic Heisenberg group $H^n(a)$ is isomorphic to Heisenberg group H^n, but the associated subelliptic geodesic structure on $H^n(a)$ is qualitatively different from the one on the Heisenberg group H^n unless all the a_j are (1). We will denote an arbitrary point in $H^n(a)$ by $\xi = (x_1, \ldots, x_n, y_1, \ldots, y_n, t)$ with $x, y \in R^{2n}$, $t \in R$. The non-commutative group law on $H^n(a)$ is

$$\xi \circ \xi = (x_1, \ldots, x_n, y_1, \ldots, y_n, t) \circ (x_1', \ldots, x_n', y_1', \ldots, y_n', t') \tag{1}$$

G. Shen and X. Huang (Eds.): ECWAC 2011, Part I, CCIS 143, pp. 237–241, 2011.

Clearly, $\xi^{-1} = -\xi$. The group dilations are given by

$$\delta_\lambda(\xi) = (\lambda x_1, \ldots, \lambda x_n, \lambda y_1, \ldots, \lambda y_n, \lambda^2 t) \qquad (2)$$

and the quasidistance of homogeneous of degree one related to the dilations has the following form

$$\rho(\xi) = \left[\left(\sum_{i=1}^{n} a_i(x_i^2 + y_i^2)\right)^2 + t^2\right]^{\frac{1}{4}}. \qquad (3)$$

Moreover, we denote by $B_R(0) = \{\xi \in H^n(a) : \rho(\xi) < R\}$ the ball with center at the origin of radius R with respect to ρ and $d(\xi, \zeta) = \rho(\zeta^{-1} \circ \xi)$ the quasidistance between arbitrary two points ξ, ζ in $H^n(a)$. Then we have $\rho(\xi) = d(\xi, 0)$.

Consider a point $\xi^0 = (x_1^0, \ldots, x_n^0, y_1^0, \ldots, y_n^0, t^0) \in H^n(a)$.

$$H_{\xi_0} = \{\xi = (x_1, \ldots, x_n, y_1, \ldots, y_n, t) \in H^n(a) : t = t^0 + 2\sum_{i=1}^{n} a_i(x_i y_i^0 - x_i^0 y_i) \qquad (4)$$

Denote $\xi_\lambda = \xi^0 \circ \delta_\lambda((\xi^0)^{-1} \circ \xi)$, for every $\xi \in H_{\xi_0}, \lambda \geq 0$. The Lie algebra of $H^n(a)$ is $\mathbf{g} = V_1 \oplus V_2$, where V_1 is spanned by the following $2n$ left-invariant vector fields

$$X_j = \frac{\partial}{\partial x_j} + 2a_j y_j \frac{\partial}{\partial t}, \quad X_{n+j} = \frac{\partial}{\partial y_j} - 2a_j x_j \frac{\partial}{\partial t}, \quad a_j > 0, j = 1, \ldots, n, \qquad (5)$$

V_2 is spanned by $T = \dfrac{\partial}{\partial t}$. We note that the non-trivial commutators are

$$\left[X_j, X_{n+j}\right] = -4a_j T, \quad j = 1, \ldots, n. \qquad (6)$$

Let $\Omega \subset H^n(a)$ be an open bounded domain with C^1 boundary, $u \in C^2(\overline{\Omega})$. The horizontal Hessian of u is defined by $Hess_X(u) = [u]_{2n \times 2n}$, where

$$u_{ij} = \frac{X_i X_j + X_j X_i}{2}, \quad i, j = 1, \ldots, 2n. \qquad (7)$$

Obviously, $Hess_X(u)$ is symmetric.

We list two equivalent definitions of convexity introduced by D. Danielli, N. Garofalo and D. Nhieu in [2].

Definition 1.1. A function $u \in C^2(\Omega) : H^n(a) \to R$ is called convex, if for every $\xi^0 \in \Omega$ and $0 \leq \lambda \leq 1$, we have

$$u(\xi_\lambda) \leq u(\xi^0) + \lambda(u(\xi) - u(\xi^0)), \quad \xi \in H_{\xi^0} \cap \Omega \tag{8}$$

Definition 1.2. A function $u \in C^2(\Omega)$ is said convex, if the symmetrized horizontal Hessian $Hess_X u(\xi)$ is positive semi-definite at every $\xi \in \Omega$.

The main result of this paper is the following.

Theorem 1.3 (Harnack-type inequality). Let u be convex and $u = 0$ on $\partial B_R(0)$. Given $\xi^0 \in B_R(0)$, then for every $0 < \delta < 1$ there exists a positive constant C depend only on $d(\xi^0, \partial B_R(0))$ and δ, such that

$$u(0) \leq Cu(\xi^0). \tag{9}$$

Corollary 1.4 (local Harnack-type inequality). Let u be convex and $u = 0$ on $\partial B_R(0)$. Given $\xi^0 \in B_R(0)$, then for every $0 < \delta < 1$ there exists a positive constant C depending only on $d(\xi^0, \partial B_R(0))$ and δ, such that

$$\sup_{B_{\delta R}(0)} u \leq C \inf_{B_{\delta R}(0)} u. \tag{10}$$

2 Preparatory Propositions

We describe and prove two propositions here.

Proposition 2.1. Let $u \in C^2(\Omega)$ be convex on $H^n(a)$. Then

$$\sup_\Omega u \leq \sup_{\partial\Omega} u. \tag{11}$$

Proposition 2.2. Let $\xi^0 \in B_R(0) \subset H^n(a)$, $\xi \in H_{\xi^0} \cap B_R(0)$.

Let $\lambda \geq 0$ be such that $\eta = \xi^0 \circ \delta_\lambda((\xi^0)^{-1} \circ \xi) \in H_{\xi^0} \cap B_R(0)$. Suppose that u is convex in $B_R(0)$ and $u = 0$ on $\partial B_R(0)$. Then

(1) If $\xi^0 = (x_1^0, \ldots, x_n^0, y_1^0, \ldots, y_n^0, t^0)$, $\xi = (0, \ldots, 0, 0, \ldots, 0, t^0)$, then $\lambda \geq 2$ and

$$u(\xi) \leq \frac{1}{2}u(\xi^0).\tag{12}$$

(2) If $0 < \alpha, \beta < \alpha + \beta < 1$, $\rho(\xi^0) \leq \alpha R$, $d(\xi^0, \xi) \leq \beta R$, then $\lambda \geq \dfrac{1-\alpha}{\beta}$

and

$$u(\xi) \leq \frac{1-\alpha-\beta}{1-\alpha}u(\xi^0).\tag{13}$$

Proofs: First   of   all,   we   prove $\lambda \geq 2$.   Let
$\zeta = (x_1, \ldots, x_n, y_1, \ldots, y_n, t) \in H_{\xi^0} \cap B_R(0)$, Then $\eta = \xi^0 \circ \delta_\lambda((\xi^0)^{-1} \circ \zeta)$. In
particular, taking $\zeta = (0, \ldots, 0, 0, \ldots, 0, t^0) \in H_{\xi^0}$, one has

$$\eta = ((1-\lambda)x_1^0, \ldots, (1-\lambda)x_n^0, (1-\lambda)y_1^0, \ldots, (1-\lambda)y_n^0, t^0).\tag{14}$$

Hence from $\eta \in \partial B_R(0)$, we get $|1-\lambda| \geq 1$, and then $\lambda \geq 2$.

To prove $\lambda \geq (1-\alpha)/\beta$, it is enough to use

$$\begin{aligned}R = \rho(\eta) &\leq \rho((\xi^0)^{-1}) + \rho(\delta_\lambda((\xi^0)^{-1} \circ \xi)) \\ &= \rho(\xi^0) + \lambda\rho((\xi^0)^{-1} \circ \xi) = \rho(\xi^0) + \lambda d(\xi^0, \xi) \leq \alpha R + \lambda\beta R.\end{aligned}\tag{15}$$

Next we give the proofs of Eq.12 and Eq.13. By the selection of η, we have
$\xi = \xi^0 \circ \delta_{1/\lambda}((\xi^0)^{-1} \circ \eta)$. Since $u(\eta) = 0$ and $\lambda \geq 2$, it follows from Definition 1.1
that

$$u(\xi) \leq (1 - \frac{1}{\lambda})u(\xi^0).\tag{16}$$

Therefore, Eq.12 holds from Proposition 2.1, since $u \leq 0$ in $B_R(0)$. Similarly,
Eq.13 is true from Definition 1.1 and Eq.15.

3   Proof of the Main Theorem

Denote $\theta = \sum_{i=1}^{n} a_i$ and $\xi^0 = (x_1^0, \ldots, x_n^0, y_1^0, \ldots, y_n^0, t^0)$ .Obviously,
$\xi^1 = (0, \ldots, 0, 0, \ldots, 0, t^0) \in H_{\xi^0}$ and $d(\xi^1, \xi^0) \leq d(0, \xi^0) < R$. Using(12) gets

$$u(\xi^1) \leq \frac{1}{2}u(\xi^0).\tag{17}$$

We shall prove that there exists a constant $C_1 > 0$ depending only on the quasidistance from ξ^1 to $\partial B_R(0)$ such that

$$u(0) \le C_1 u(\xi^1). \tag{18}$$

To do so, we assume $\xi^1 \ne 0$ and consider two cases.

If $t^0 > 0$, define $\kappa = \sqrt{t^0}/2\sqrt{\theta}$ and construct an iterative sequence. Since $\kappa \le R/4\sqrt{\theta}$, we have

$$\rho(\xi^2) \le \sqrt[4]{17}R/4, \ \rho(\xi^3) \le \sqrt[4]{8}R/4, \ \rho(\xi^4) \le R/4, \ \rho(\xi^5) = 0,$$
$$\text{And} \quad d(\xi^1,\xi^2) = d(\xi^2,\xi^3) = d(\xi^3,\xi^4) = d(\xi^4,\xi^5) = \sqrt{\theta}\kappa \le R/4. \tag{19}$$

Hence $\xi^i \in B_R(0)$, $i = 2,\ldots,5$. In order to use Proposition 2.2, we still need to show that $\xi^{i+1} \in H_{\xi^i} (i = 1,\ldots,4)$. By letting $\alpha = \sqrt[4]{8}/4$, $\beta = 1/4$, then

$$u(\xi^4) \le \frac{1 - \sqrt[4]{8}/4 - 1/4}{1 - \sqrt[4]{8}/4} u(\xi^3) = \frac{3}{5} u(\xi^3). \tag{20}$$

4 Conclusion

In this paper, a Harnack-type inequality for convex functions on the anisotropic Heisenberg group is proved. This result is expected to provide some theoretical basis for further studying the properties of convex functions on higher-dimension Heisenberg groups and the regularity of higher-order nonlinear subelliptic equations.

References

1. Beals. R.: Analysis and geometry on the Heisenberg group. In: Conference on Inverse Spectral Geometry, University of Kentucky (June 2002)
2. Danielli, D., Garofalo, N., Nhieu, D.: Notions of convexity in Carnot groups. Comm. Analysis and Geometry 11, 263–341 (2003)
3. Danielli, D., Garofalo, N., Tournier, F.: The theorem on Busemann-Feller-Alexandrov in Carnot groups. Comm. Analysis and Geometry 12, 853–886 (2004)
4. Garofalo, N., Tournier, F.: New properties of convex functions in the Heisenberg group. Transactions of American Mathematical Society 358, 2011–2055 (2004)
5. Gutierrez, C., Montanari, A.: Maximum and comparison principles for convex functions on the Heisenberg groups. Comm. in PDE 29, 1305–1334 (2004)

Research on Channel Assignment Algorithm of IP over WDM Network Using Time-Division Switching

Yao Zhang and Qun Wang

School of Mechanical, Electronic & Information Engineering,
Shandong University at Weihai, Weihai, Shandong, China, 264209
{zhangyao,wang_qun}@sdu.edu.cn

Abstract. In order to solve congestion of IP over WDM network using time-division switching, and to meet the demands of different services, we presented a channel assignment scheme named queuing algorithm. The main idea was adding queuing caches and controller in each HUB, which can assigned wavelength channels and time-slots dynamically according to different transmission priorities, the higher the transmission priority, the better was the opportunity to be assigned more wavelength channels. The theory of this algorithm was introduced, and the performances were analyzed by building random queuing model. The results appear that it is an efficient way to improve QOS and the usage of wavelength channels with low latency.

Keywords: WDM, time multiplexing, QOS, time-slot, dynamic wavelength assignment, queuing algorithm, network congestion.

1 Introduction

T. S. Peter Yum and Frank Tong proposed a new routing architecture of IP over WDM network using time-division switching, as shown in Figure 1 [1]. Suppose the number of HUB is L, each HUB is connected to K REX, the time-slot orders of HUB are shown in Figure 2. At REX level, IP packets are assigned to different transmission queues according to their respective labels, the transmission from each queue onto the optical backbone network are then organized into transmission cycles, with each subdivided into wavelength burst periods using WDM [1]. However, if the number of REX is lesser than the number of available wavelengths, blank time-slot must be filled. On the other hand, because of quantitative restriction on wavelengths, if the number of REX exceeds the number of available wavelengths, network congestion will happen, so the channel competing algorithm must be provided. Besides, to support the varying Quality-of Service (QOS) requirements, we must define different transmission priorities.

This paper is structured as follows: we present a channel competing algorithm to solve congestion in section 2, the performance of this algorithm is analyzed by random queuing model. In section 3, we give a scheme to assign wavelength channels drastically to some special services according to their transmission priorities. In section 4, some useful conclusions and further research issues complete the paper.

G. Shen and X. Huang (Eds.): ECWAC 2011, Part I, CCIS 143, pp. 242–247, 2011.
© Springer-Verlag Berlin Heidelberg 2011

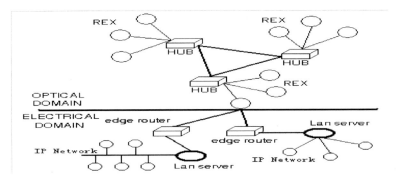

Fig. 1. IP over WDM network using TDM switching

HUB1	1 to 1	1 to 2	1 to 3	. . . . . .	1 to L
HUB2	2 to 2	2 to 3	2 to 4	. . . . . .	2 to 1
HUB3	3 to 3	3 to 4	3 to 5	. . . . . .	3 to 2
HUBₗ	L to L	L to 1	L to 2	. . . . . .	L to L-1

Fig. 2. Time-slot orders between HUB

2 Queuing Algorithm

2.1 Introduction of Queuing Algorithm

Firstly, we define some variables:

L: the number of HUB, it is also the number of time-slots.

K: the number of available wavelengths. Wavelengths λ_1, $\lambda_2 \cdots \cdots \lambda_K$ can be used circularly to every REX in permission time-slots, but in the same subdivided time-slot, wavelengths used by different REX must be differentiated.

A_{ij}: $K \times K$ wavelength assignment matrix. It denotes the assignment results of wavelength channels, i is the number of the source HUB, j is the number of destination HUB.

The main idea of our algorithm is shown in Figure 3. Setting a channel distributor in each HUB, it is consists of L queuing caches and a central controller, queuing cache m is intended for storing requests to HUB m from different source REX, controller is intended for assigning channels. Before transmitting data, every REX must send an access request to HUB's distributor through public wavelength channel λ_0, distributor records its request into queuing caches. Controller reads access requests from queuing caches periodically, and then, calculates wavelength assignment matrix Aij according to the ruler of first come first served. At last, HUB i must broadcast the contents of matrix Aij to every destination HUB. We can broadcast A_{ij} through synchronization

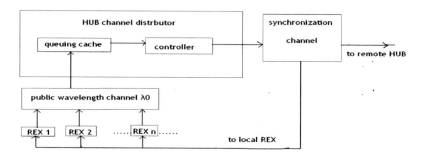

Fig. 3. Architecture of channel distributor in hub

channels [1]. Permitted REX encapsulates data into specified wavelengths in subdivided time-slots, and then delivers it to HUB i. De-multiplexing can be accomplished by destination HUB and its REX according to wavelength assignment matrix. If L=10, K=4, queuing cache 3 in HUB 1 is as shown in Tab 1, we can obtained assign-

ment matrix is $A_{13} = \begin{bmatrix} 1-2,4-1,6-3,2-9 \\ 1-1,2-2,2-5,9-1 \\ 6-6,1-9,3-7,3-2 \\ 5-2,8-3,3-1,6-1 \end{bmatrix}$.

The third time-slot of HUB 1 is the time-slot of HUB1 to HUB 3. This time-slot is subdivided into wavelength bursts periods as shown in Fig 4.

Table 1. Partial Comtents of Queuing Cache 3 of HUB 1

source REX	destination	source REX	destination
rex1*	hub3-rex2	rex6*	hub3-rex6
rex4	hub3-rex1	rex1*	hub3-rex9
rex6	hub3-rex3	rex3	hub3-rex7
rex2*	hub3-rex9	rex3*	hub3-rex2
rex1*	hub3-rex1	rex5	hub3-rex2
rex2	hub3-rex2	rex8*	hub3-rex3
rex2*	hub3-rex5	rex3	hub3-rex1
rex9*	hub3-rex1	rex6*	hub3-rex1

rex1 to rex2 λ_1	rex4 to rex1 λ_2	rex6 to rex 3 λ_3	rex2 to rex9 λ_4
rex1 to rex1 λ_2	rex2 to rex2 λ_3	rex2 to rex5 λ_4	rex9 to rex1 λ_1
rex6 to rex6 λ_3	rex1 to rex9 λ_4	rex3 to rex 7 λ_1	rex3 to rex2 λ_2
rex5 to rex2 λ_4	rex8 to rex3 λ_1	rex3 to rex1 λ_2	rex6 to rex1 λ_3

Fig. 4. Wavelength channels in subdivided time-slots between HUB1 to HUB3

2.2 Performance Analysis of Queuing Algorithm

If n is the number of requests arriving at HUB from REX, λ is average arrival rate, τ is transmission period of wavelength bursts, $\mu = 1/(KL\tau)$, M is the number of REX in each HUB, The Chapman-Kolmogorov equation of steady-state [2] is

$$(\lambda + \tau)\,p(n+1) = \lambda p(n) + \tau p(n + LK + 1)$$

$$\lambda p(0) = \tau p(1) + ... + \tau p(KL - 1) + \tau p(K)$$

Make use of probability generating function of P(j), we have $P(n) = (1 - r_0)r_0^n$,

Hence, the expectation of queue length is $E[N] = \dfrac{r_0}{1 - r_0}$

The expectation of waiting time is $E[W] = \dfrac{r_0}{M\lambda(1 - r_0)}$

r_0 is the minimum root of equation $\dfrac{1}{KL\tau}X^{K^2+1} - (M\lambda + \dfrac{1}{KL\tau})X + M\lambda = 0$

Let the length of wavelength bursts is 1M bit, the bandwidth of optical fiber is 10G bps, Figure 5 shows E[N] in different conditions. From these results, the performance of our queuing algorithm can be evaluated. Network latency that queuing algorithm brings to us is low, it is an effective to solve bottleneck. But with increase of network load (i.e. M, L, λ is large), latency is also increase. on the other hand, the steady condition of queue system is $(M\lambda KL\tau)<1$, so network scale must be restricted.

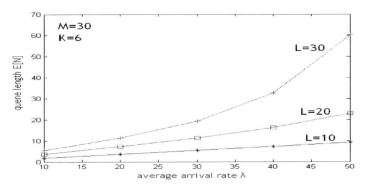

Fig. 5. Relationship between E [N] and λ with different L

3   Scheme to Assign Wavelength Channels Dynamically

To support varying QOS requirements of different applications, we present a scheme to achieve differentiated service. Besides basic wavelengths λ_1, $\lambda_2 \cdots\cdots \lambda_k$, we add extra wavelengths λ_{K-1}, λ_{K-2}, $\cdots\cdots \lambda_{K-S}$, theses extra wavelengths can be assigned dynamically to some high priority services. The scheme has two steps:

Step 1: Generating wavelength assignment matrix A_{ij} according to service types in queue caches. In order to improve the usage of extra wavelengths, channels of high priority services must be assigned at the top of columns in matrix A_{ij}. If high priority services are more than KS, we can't meet each high priority's wavelength demands. Suppose there are two priorities in queue caches, high priority services are marked "*" in Tab 1, we have two extra wavelengths λ_5 and λ_6, according to our scheme,

$$\text{the matrix } A_{13} \text{ is} \begin{bmatrix} 1-2,2-9,1-1,2-5 \\ 9-1,6-6,1-9,3-2 \\ 4-1,6-3,2-2,3-7 \\ 5-2,8-3,3-1,6-1 \end{bmatrix}.$$

Step 2: Generating basic wavelength assignment matrix B_{ij} and extra wavelength assignment matrix $C(\lambda_m)$. B_{ij} is used to denote wavelength number of corresponding sub time-slot in matrix A_{ij}, $C(\lambda_m)$ denotes the assignment results of extra wavelengths, if $C_{ij}=1$,it denotes λ_j is assigned to corresponding sub time-slot in matrix A_{ij}, otherwise $C_{ij}=0$. Like matrix A_{ij}, B_{ij} and $C(\lambda_j)$ also can be broadcasted to REX of destination HUB through synchronization channels before data transmission. In our example,

$$B_{13} = \begin{bmatrix} 1,2,3,4 \\ 2,3,4,1 \\ 3,4,1,2 \\ 4,1,2,3 \end{bmatrix}, C(\lambda_5) = \begin{bmatrix} 1,1,1,1 \\ 0,0,0,0 \\ 0,0,0,0 \\ 0,0,0,0 \end{bmatrix}, C(\lambda_6) = \begin{bmatrix} 0,0,0,0 \\ 1,1,1,1 \\ 0,0,0,0 \\ 0,0,0,0 \end{bmatrix}.$$

The subdivided time-slots of wavelength bursts periods are shown in Fig 6. Using our scheme, most of the high priorities can obtain two wavelength channels in its sub time-slots, but two high priorities only obtain one wavelength channel in its sub time-slots, these are REX 8 of HUB 1 to REX 3 of HUB3, and REX 6 of HUB 1 to REX 1 of HUB 3. We can solve this problem by adding the number of extra wavelengths, or cutting down wavelength requirements of high priorities.

Let average arrival rate of high priority servers is λ_h, the number of requests of high priority is $X(t)$, it is a Poisson processes , and can be analyzed by Markov chain [3],its probability distribution is
$$p\{X(t)=n\} = \frac{e^{-M\lambda_h KL\tau}(M\lambda_h KL\tau)^n}{n!}.$$

If $E[X(t)]=M\lambda_h KL\tau$ is more than KS, network bottleneck will appear, it means some high priority services can't be assigned necessary extra wavelength channels in corresponding sub time-slots, their QOS requirements are not satisfied. We also can work out bottleneck probability is
$$p = 1 - \sum_{n=0}^{KS} \frac{e^{-M\lambda_h KL\tau}(M\lambda_h KL\tau)^n}{n!}.$$

From equations above, we can calculate the number of optimal extra wavelengths.

rex1 to rex2 λ_1 λ_5	rex2 to rex9 λ_2 λ_5	rex1 to rex1 λ_3 λ_5	rex2 to rex5 λ_4 λ_5
rex9 to rex1 λ_2 λ_6	rex6 to rex6 λ_3 λ_6	rex1 to rex9 λ_4 λ_6	rex3 to rex2 λ_1 λ_6
rex4 to rex1 λ_3	rex6 to rex3 λ_4	rex2 to rex2 λ_1	rex3 to rex7 λ_2
rex5 to rex2 λ_4	rex8 to rex3 λ_1	rex3 to rex1 λ_2	rex6 to rex1 λ_3

Fig. 6. Subdivided time-slots between HUB1 to HUB3 using scheme of dynamic wavelength channels assignment

4 Conclusions

In this paper, we introduce an IP over WDM network using time-division switching, and then, present a scheme named queuing algorithm to assign wavelength channels and time-slot channels. Performance of this algorithm are analyzed, the result shows that it is an efficient way to improve the usage of wave channels with low latency. In order to meet the varying requirements, we define two transmission priorities, wavelength channels can be assigned dynamically according to different priorities. High priority services can obtain two wavelength channels in their transmitting time-slots, so their QOS can be supported. But if the number of high priority servers is too large, some QOS requirements can not be supported, how to solve this problem and to keep high transmitting efficiency of network is our further researching work. On the other hand, transport characteristics of optical fiber (such as data transmitting rate, BER, noise, transmitting distance etc) produce an effect on network performances, these are also our further research work.

References

1. Peter Yum, T.S., Tong, F., Tan, K.T.: An architecture for IP over WDM using time-division switching. Journal of Light Wave Technology 19(5), 589–595 (2001)
2. Gelenbe, E., Pujolle, G.: Introduction to queuing networks. John wiley & Sons Ltd, Chichester (1987)
3. Cooper, R.B.: Introduction to Queuing Theory. Elsevier North Holland, Inc., Amsterdam (1981)
4. Pankaj, R.K.: Wavelength requirements for multicasting in all-optical networks. IEEE/ACM Trans. Networking 7, 414–424 (1999)
5. Rowe, S.H., Schuh, M.L.: Computer Networking. Tsinghua University press, Bejing (2006)
6. Keuser, G.E.: A review of WDM technology and application. Opt. Fiber Technology 5, 30–39 (1999)
7. Dixit, S.: IP over WDM: the Next-Generation Optical Internet. Wiley, New York (2003)
8. Rau, L., Rangarajan, S.: High-speed optical time-division-multiplexed/WDM networks and their network elements based on regenerative all-optical ultrafast wavelength converters. Journal Optical Communications and Networking 3, 100–118 (2004)

Code Planning Based on Correlation of Composite Codes in TD-SCDMA System

Lianfen Huang[1], Bofeng Wu[2], and Zhibin Gao[1]

[1] Department of Communication Engineering, Xiamen University,
361005, Xiamen, China
[2] Department of Computer Science, Xiamen University,
361005, Xiamen, China
{lfhuang,gaozhibin}@xmu.edu.cn, wu_bofeng@126.com,

Abstract. The past method to make code planning in TD-SCDMA system is only based on the correlation of scrambling codes, the recent research shows that, however, the more effective strategy is to make composite code planning, so it is very important to study the correlation of composite code. In this paper, we make code planning for the new cells based on the correlation of composite codes, and then estimate the performance of planning result. Finally, we can make a conclusion that it is effective to do code planning with the strategy in the paper, and this is valuable to make code resources planning in TD-SCDMA system.

Keywords: TD-SCDMA, code planning, composite code, correlation.

1 Introduction

In TD-SCDMA system, there are four kinds of code mainly used: Spreading code, Scrambling code (SC), Midamble code, downlink synchronization code (SYNC-DL), uplink synchronization code (SYNC-UL), each one plays a special role in communication. And the code resources are shown in [1].

Each cell will be allocated one SC when we make code planning, and because the correlation of SYNC-DLs can satisfy the need of any neighbor cells, so it can guarantee the performance of net as long as the SYNC-DLs of neighbor cells are different. Then, the key of code resources planning is to make SC planning (SCP).

There are 128 Scrambling code sequences in TD-SCDMA system, each one is the sequence with 16 bits, and they can be divided into 32 groups with 4 codes in each group. Because SC has the features of less quantity, shorter sequence and more remarkable correlation, what mainly considered is that composite code is the product of spreading code and SC, and the correlations of the composite codes are not uniform absolutely. To reduce the interference between the neighbor cells, it is necessary to study the correlation of composite codes intensively [2].

2 Composite Code of TD-SCDMA

The OVSF (orthogonal variable spreading factor) codes used in TD-SCDMA system can be defined using the code tree and the rule of using the code that are shown in [1].

G. Shen and X. Huang (Eds.): ECWAC 2011, Part I, CCIS 143, pp. 248–253, 2011.

The process of spreading and scrambling of data bits is shown in Fig.1.

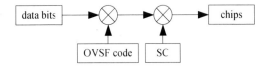

Fig. 1. The process of spreading and scrambling of data bits

The signal transmitted is composite code which is the product of OVSF code and SC. Although the orthogonality of SCs is good enough, the composite codes of each SC may be identical. Thus, when making code planning, the useful matter we should consider is the correlation of composite codes, but not the SCs', then the more effective strategy of code planning is based on composite code [3].

3   The Correlation of Composite Codes

The correlation of two codes x and y is shown in Eq. 1 [4].

$$R_{xy}(m) = E\{x_{n+m}y_n\} = \begin{cases} \dfrac{1}{N}\displaystyle\sum_{n=0}^{N-m-1} x_{n+m}y^*_n, m \ge 0 \\ R^*_{yx}(-m), m < 0 \end{cases} \tag{1}$$

In Eq. 1, $R_{xy}(m)$ denotes the correlation of x and y in delay of m chips, N describes the length of code.

In fact, however, because of the multipath signal, that is, the signal received will often has some delays, we should study the correlation of composite code in some delays [5]. The maximum correlations of composite code of SC 11 and one of SC 12 in delays from 0 to 15 chips are shown in Fig. 2.

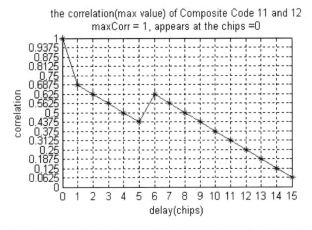

Fig. 2. The correlation (max value) of composite codes of SC 11 and 12

The result we can see from Fig. 2 is that the distribution of correlations of composite codes of SC 11 and 12 is almost linear; the maximum value is 1, appears at the delay of chip 0; and the minimum one is 0.0625, appears at the delay of chip 15.

Composite code is the product of OVSF code and SC, so the orthogonality of them are not always good, and they may be identical. We should classify the SCs into some groups, and then the SCs from one group should not be assigned to neighbor cells. The group based on identical composite code of SF=16 is shown in [3].

In the 12 basic SC groups (BCG), the composite code of SC in any group is not the same as one of other groups, based on this, if we do not allocate SCs from one group to neighbor cells, then we can avoid the identical composite code.

Although we can avoid the situation mentioned above, the correlation between two different groups still may be remarkable, that is to say, the value of correlation is bigger enough. The maximum correlations of composite code of SC 20 and one of SC 96 in delays from 0 to 15 chips are shown in Fig. 3.

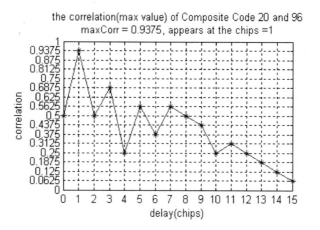

Fig. 3. The correlation (max value) of composite codes of SC 20 and 96

In Fig. 3, however, we can see the distribution of correlations of composite codes of SC 20 and 96 is discrete; the maximum value is 0.9375, appears at the delay of chip 1; and the minimum one is 0.0625, appears at the delay of chip 15. Because SC 20 belongs to BCG 2, and SC 96 belongs to BCG 9 [3], we can infer from Fig. 3 that the maximum correlation of BCG 2 and BCG 9 is not less than 0.9375.

Based on the conclusion of Fig. 3 and the BCG, we can calculate the correlation of any BCGs, and any SC of each BCG is feasible. The results are shown in Table 1.

Table 1. The Maximum Correlation (maxCorr) of BCGs

BCGs	maxCorr	BCGs	maxCorr	BCGs	maxCorr
1,2	0.5625	3,5	0.5625	5,12	0.9375
1,3	0.8750	3,6	0.6875	6,7	0.8750
......	......	......	......	......	......
2,12	0.8125	5,10	0.8125	10,12	0.7500
3,4	0.7500	5,11	0.5625	11,12	0.6250

What we can see from Table 1 is that the maxCorr of some BCGs is too bigger than others, such as 0.8750, 0.9375, and that means the correlation of the two BCGs is remarkable, if we allocate SCs from these BCGs to the neighbor cells, the interference between the cells will be greater; sometimes it will reduce the QoS of the net [4].

4   Code Planning Based on Correlation of Composite Codes

The goal of code planning is to avoid the greater interference between neighbor cells [2], so it is key to guarantee the calling of users, and more effective strategy is needed.

The analysis of code planning to the new cells in the net is shown as follows.

First of all, the information of new cells includes the cell ID, geographical positions and neighbor cells of each one should be ready. Then, we carry out the algorithm of code planning based on correlation of composite codes to the new cells. In the end, we estimate the performance of planning result conforming to Eq. 2.

$$cellMaxCorr\ (i) = \max(\max\ Corr\ (i\ ,)) \ ,\ net\ MaxCorr\ = \max(\ cellMaxCor\ r(i))$$

$$cellMeanCo\ rr(i) = \frac{\sum_{k=1}^{N(i)} \max\ Corr\ (i,k)}{N(i)} \ , \quad netM\ ea\ nCorr\ = \frac{\sum_{i=1}^{M} \sum_{k=1}^{N(i)} \max\ Corr\ (i,k)}{\sum_{i=1}^{M} N(i)} \tag{2}$$

In Eq. 2, i is the number of cell to be planned, N(i) is the quantity of the neighbor cells of cell i, (i,k) describes the neighbor cell k of cell i, M is the quantity of the planning cells; maxCorr(i,k) denotes the maximum correlation of cell i and its neighbor cell k; cellMaxCorr(i) denotes the maximum correlation of cell i and all neighbor cells of it; netMaxCorr shows the maximum correlation of the net and netMeanCorr shows the mean correlation of the net.

The maximum correlation of each cell and its corresponding neighbor cells are shown in Fig. 4, cellMaxCorr is the maximum correlation of each cell, and netMaxCorr is the maximum one of the net.

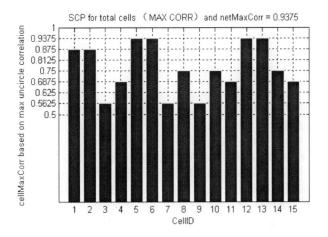

Fig. 4. The maximum correlation of each cell and its neighbor cells

As we can see, the result of code planning to the new 15 cells in Fig. 4 is that, the maxCorrs of cell 1, 2 and their neighbor cells is 0.875, and the maxCorrs of cell 5, 6, 13, 14 and their neighbor cells even achieve 0.9375, they are remarkable. However, the majority of ones are still not bigger than 0.75. If the correlation is more slender, the block error rate (BLER) of the system will be kept in a lower level [6]. Thus, to ensure high performance of planning, we should avoid the remarkable correlation, and of course, the identical composite code of SCs should not be used.

The mean correlation of each cell and its corresponding neighbor cells are shown in Fig. 5, and netMeanCorr is the mean one of the net.

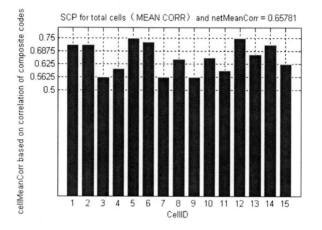

Fig. 5. The mean correlation of each cell and its neighbor cells

Although there are some cells with remarkable correlation, the mean ones in Fig. 5 is not bigger than 0.75, and the netMeanCorr of the net is only 0.65781, by consulting the maxCorrs of any BCGs in Table 1, the minimum one is 0.5625, so we can make a conclusion from this aspect, the performance of code planning to the new cells is workable.

5 Summary

The strategy of code planning based on the correlation of composite codes is critical in research, and it contains two parts, one is that the identical composite code of SCs can not be allocated to the neighbor cells, and the other is that the remarkable correlation of BCGs should be avoided to assign to the neighbor cells with our best. From the analysis in part 4, the algorithm of code planning still needs to be improved in the next study, for example, we should reserve some codes to the new cells [7]; and maybe we should provide a interface, through which we can allocate codes manually to some cells needed to be reallocated after assign codes by software to the whole cells, it can further improve the performance of the net by reducing the interference of neighbor cells.

References

1. 3GPP TS 25.223 V 7.2.0 Release 7 (2006-09)
2. Luo, J., Zhu, D., Yao, Q.: Scrambling Code Planning in TD-SCDMA System (2008)
3. Zhang, F., Hu, J., Yao, W.: Initial Discussion on TD-SCDMA System Scrambling Code Optimization (2009)
4. Qin, K.: The Correlation of Codes and Scrambling Codes Planning in TD-SCDMA system (2009)
5. Xie, X.: The Technology and Implementation. In: The 3rd Generation Mobile Communication System of TD-SCDMA. Publishing House of Electronics Industry, Beijing (2004) (in Chinese)
6. Zhang, Z., Jiang, Q., Song, Y.: Scrambling Code Planning Algorithm and Simulation in TD-SCDMA (2010)
7. Zhang, J., Yang, D.: Features of TD-SCDMA wireless network planning (2006)

Effects of Perceived Values on Continuance Usage of Facebook

Heng-Li Yang and Cheng-Yu Lai

Dept. of Management Information Systems, National Cheng-Chi University
64, Sec.2, Chihnan Road, Wenshan District, Taipei, Taiwan, R.O.C.
{yanh,95356501}@nccu.edu.tw

Abstract. Facebook is one of the renowned social networking sites (SNS) on the Internet. As compared to the conventional SNS, it not only provides social interaction features, but has more entertainment elements on the website. Many Facebook users use the website for the purpose of playing the embedded games rather than use its original social features, i.e., individual's perceived values about the usage of Facebook may have changed. Consequently, it is an interesting issue to know individual's perceived values and satisfaction toward continuance usage of the new style SNS like Facebook. Based on prior literatures, three different value orientations, including social orientation, entertainment orientation and fashion orientation, were adopted in this study to examine their influence on individual's satisfaction and continuance intention to use Facebook. An empirical survey and partial least squares (PLS) technology was utilized to test the proposed hypotheses. Several empirical results were found. Both academic and practical implications are discussed.

Keywords: Continuance Intention, Facebook, Perceived Values, Satisfaction, Social Networking Sites (SNS).

1 Introduction

Facebook is one of the renowned social networking sites (SNS) on the Internet. Today many phenomenon of the usage of Facebook have emerged, and it indeed changed our thought about how SNS been used. Conventionally, SNS only served social features on their websites so as to allow individuals to create as well as maintain their relationships. However, the prevailing of Facebook provides social features as well as embedded entertainment features. Many people join Facebook for playing the embedded games, instead of using its social features. That is, the values that individuals expected to obtain through Facebook usage may be somewhat different as compared to the conventional SNS.

SNS have indeed received extensive attention for both academic and practice recently. However, most of prior research on Facebook mainly focused on its social features. For instance, Lampe et al. [1] explored how college students using Facebook to maintain their offline relationships. Ellison et al. [2] examined the effect of Facebook usage on formation as well as maintenance of social capital. Young et al. [3]

G. Shen and X. Huang (Eds.): ECWAC 2011, Part I, CCIS 143, pp. 254–260, 2011.
© Springer-Verlag Berlin Heidelberg 2011

focused on the relationship between individual's intention of using Facebook and her/his Facebook profile contents. Conversely, relatively little attention has been given to its prominent game features in prior literature. As a result, it is expected to have better understanding on individual's Facebook usage behavior through a more comprehensive view.

2 Related Work and Hypotheses Development

Perceived value was a widely discussed issue in prior marketing domain literature. Zeithaml [4] defined this concept as customer's overall evaluation process between the perceived benefits and costs from a specific product. The taxonomies on individual's shopping values in prior consumer behavior literature were generally been divided into two orientations: utilitarian-oriented and hedonic-oriented [5-6]. Hirchman and Holbrook [5] indicated that hedonic aspect refers to "consumers' multi-sensory images, fantasies and emotional arousal". Restated, consumers who were hedonic-oriented may gain intrinsically pleasure through their consumption behavior. Conversely, utilitarian aspect refers to goal-oriented consumption which regards shopping as a work [6]. Consumers who were utilitarian-oriented may seek for the extrinsically outcome through their consumption behavior. Although these two aspects were quite different, both of them may motivate consumers to engage in a specific shopping behavior [7].

Based on prior consumer behavior research, Van der Heijden [8] suggested that information systems can be also classified into either hedonic or utilitarian systems. Hedonic systems on its nature aim to provide self-fulfillment value to the user, while utilitarian systems offer user with instrumental value [8]. Considering the context of Facebook in which not only provide social features but also have many embedded browser games. Consequently, this study suggested that both hedonic and utilitarian value existed to motivate individuals to engage in using Facebook. Restated, individuals may either perceive entertainment value (hedonic-oriented) through playing embedded games or perceived social value (utilitarian-oriented) through using its social features.

Besides these two value orientations, this study suggested the third value orientation named fashion orientation. Since Facebook is a new web application, it provides many new features that conventional SNS do not have. Of these new features, the embedded games are the most renowned feature on its website. Many people join Facebook for playing the embedded games like, Happy Farm, Pet Society, or Restaurant City, etc., which let using Facebook became prevailing. Alternatively, as the concept diffusion of innovation indicated, the "innovators", i.e., the first individuals to adopt an innovation, have played a critical role on the diffusion of such innovation [9]. This kind of individual is generally very social-oriented, and likes to interact with peer group [9]. In this context, "innovators" of Facebook may let others in the peer group think that Facebook is a cool stuff, and using it is a prevailing trend. Since this value orientation may not belong to either entertainment-oriented or social-oriented, therefore, this study expected that in addition to the effect of entertainment-oriented or social-oriented value, the fashion orientation may also motivate individuals to engage in using Facebook.

Alternatively, expectation disconfirmation theory indicated that user's satisfaction is jointly determined by her/his disconfirmation and initial expectation toward the outcomes of behavior [10]. Disconfirmation results from individual's overall evaluation between initial expectations and post-experiences. In other word, it represented individual's perception on the performance of a specific behavior and which may be greater than, equal to or smaller than the initial expectations. Cadotte et al. [11] indicated that consumer's satisfaction is determined by whether the perceived performance fulfill her/his needs, wants, or desires. In this context, the perception of benefits toward Facebook usage may influence the satisfaction one perceived. Many studies on either marketing domain or IS domain also provided evidences that individual's perceived values, such as hedonic or utilitarian values was positively related with the degree of satisfaction [12-14]. Therefore, it is expected that all three value orientations proposed in this study may be related with individual's satisfaction of Facebook usage. This leads to the following hypotheses.

Hypothesis 1. Entertainment orientation is positively related with individual's satisfaction toward Facebook usage.

Hypothesis 2. Fashion orientation is positively related with individual's satisfaction toward Facebook usage.

Hypothesis 3. Social orientation is positively related with individual's satisfaction toward Facebook usage.

The effect of individuals perceived values on behavior intention have been widely discussed in prior research. As the extension of technology acceptance model proposed by Davis et al [15] indicated, either perceived enjoyment (hedonic-oriented) or perceived usefulness (utilitarian-oriented) have related with individual's behavioral intention to use computers in the workplace. Many empirical studies in IS literature also confirmed both the influences of hedonic-oriented and utilitarian-oriented [8, 12, 14]. Based on this perspective, this study expected that either entertainment value or social value may influence individual's continuance intention on Facebook usage. Furthermore, as expectation disconfirmation theory indicated, user's satisfaction toward a product or service is positively associated with her/his intention to continued adopting [10]. In this context, individuals with related high satisfaction toward Facebook may therefore have relatively high intention to further using it. According to the above discussion, this study proposes the following hypotheses.

Hypothesis 4. Entertainment orientation is positively related with individual's continuance intention of Facebook usage.

Hypothesis 5. Social orientation is positively related with individual's continuance intention of Facebook usage.

Hypothesis 6. Individual's satisfaction toward Facebook is positively affect intention to continued using it.

3   Methodology

3.1   Instrument Development and Data Collection

A questionnaire survey was conducted to examine the proposed model. Three different value orientations, including social orientation, entertainment orientation, and fashion orientation, were tested in this study. Social orientation was measured using a scale modified from [16]; entertainment orientation and fashion orientation were measured using a self-developed scale based on previous literature and the context of Facebook. Besides, individual's satisfaction and continuance toward Facebook usage were also surveyed in this study. Both the items for measuring satisfaction and continuance intention were adapted from Bhattacherjee and Premkumar's [13] work with minor modifications to fit our research context. All items were measured along a five-point Likert-type scale, ranging from 1 for "strongly disagree," to 5 for "strongly agree."

The university students were selected as subjects in this study since they are the mainly population of Facebook users. The study was administered to 205 students from one university in Taiwan. Subjects were asked to evaluate how strongly they disagree or agree to the statements that presented in the questionnaire. Of these subjects, 64 students had no experience on Facebook usage and excluded from this study. 128 respondents fully completed questionnaires were accepted for valid samples and input for data analysis.

Among these respondents, 71 (55.5%) were female and 57 (44.5%) were male. 75 (58.6%) subjects stated that they have less than one year experiences on use Facebook. On average, these subjects reported using Facebook 4 to 5 days each week, and spending less than 1 hour on Facebook per day.

3.2   Reliabilities and Validation

To measure the reliability, the five scale dimensions were measured using composite reliability (CR). As Fornell and Larcker [17] suggested, an acceptable CR value must be larger than 0.7. Since the CR value of five scale dimensions were all well above the acceptable value; thus, the reliability of this study has been confirmed.

Whereas, the discriminant and convergent validity was measured through average variance extracted (AVE). Fornell and Larcker [17] suggested that the AVE value of each scale dimension should exceed 0.5 for ensuring the convergent validity, while the AVE value of each dimension should exceed the squared correction among other scale dimensions to confirm discriminant validity. As Table 1 shows, the AVE values for all scale dimensions were well above the 0.5 threshold, and the square root of all AVE values in the diagonal were larger than the correlation coefficients in the corresponding rows and columns. Therefore, both discriminant and convergent validity were confirmed in this study.

Table 1. Correlations and Square Root of AVE values. (* Significant at 0.05 level).

	Soc	Ent	Fas	Sat	CI
Social orientation (Soc)	**0.81**				
Entertainment orientation (Ent)	0.41*	**0.92**			
Fashion orientation (Fas)	0.37*	0.39*	**0.81**		
Satisfaction (Sat)	0.53*	0.49*	0.47*	**0.84**	
Continuance Intention (CI)	0.39*	0.46*	0.50*	0.63*	**0.89**

4   Results

The proposed model was examined using partial least squares (PLS) in this study. PLS in is a component-based structural equation technology which can be used to analyze the proposed model with minimal demands, and therefore, is suitable used in exploratory research. The SmartPLS 2.0 was utilized as an analytic tool, and 100 iterations of bootstrap re-sampling were used to examine the significance of paths in the proposed model. The results of PLS analysis are shown in Fig. 1.

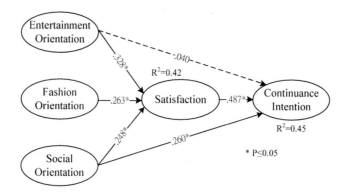

Fig. 1. Results of PLS Analysis

Hypotheses 1, 2, and 3 were all supported in this study. The analytical results showed that all three individual value orientations proposed in this study are positively associated with individual's satisfaction toward Facebook usage. Specifically, individuals driven from entertainment value have relatively high satisfaction on Facebook usage. Restated, the entertainment of embedded games provided in Facebook may directly influence individual's satisfaction. Whereas, the social value is relatively weak in these three value orientations, although it still has significant influence on individual's satisfaction toward Facebook usage. In other word, individuals may not feel too much satisfaction for the ordinary use of social interaction features. The social interaction features may become an essential but non dominant function in Facebook. Furthermore, fashion orientation also plays an important role on individual's satisfaction. As posited, individuals may think Facebook as a cool stuff, and using Facebook may let them been consider as fashionable people in the peer group. As a result, individuals driven from fashion orientation also significantly influence their satisfaction toward Facebook usage.

Further, considering the influence of entertainment orientation (H4) and social orientation (H5) on individual's continuance intention, only social value orientation has significant and positive influence on individual's continuance intention on Facebook usage. As Dhar and Wertenbroch [18] indicated in marketing domain, individuals tend to choose the task with higher utilitarian benefit. In our research context, when individuals think about whether they will continue on Facebook usage, the social value may be the primary consideration instead of entertainment value. Consequently, only H5 was supported in this study.

Finally, regarding the influence of individual's satisfaction on continuance intention, H6 was also supported in this study. The analytical results revealed a positive relationship between individual's satisfaction and the continuance intention. The results were consistent with prior literature which suggested that user satisfaction is related to the information technology use [12]. Individuals with high satisfaction on Facebook are more likely to have higher tendency of continuing to use Facebook.

5   Discussions and Conclusions

The aim of this study was to examine the influence of different individuals' perceived values on their satisfaction and continuance intention toward using Facebook. Based on prior literature, several value orientations were proposed. An empirical survey was conducted, and the PLS was utilized to analyze the proposed model. Several analytical results were drawn which may contribute to our collective understanding of individual's perception about Facebook usage. First, all three value orientations proposed in this study were positively related with individual's satisfaction. Specifically, entertainment value seems to have the highest effect on individual's satisfaction among the three proposed values. Conversely, social value has relatively weak influence on individual's satisfaction. Individuals may feel satisfaction from either perceived fashion feeling or embedded game enjoyment, instead of using social features. The nature of SNS may have changed. However, compared to the influence of entertainment value and social value on individual's continuance intention, only social value has positively direct effect on continuance intention of using Facebook. That is, the most important reason of driving individual to continue using SNS is still related to its social features probably because individuals may lose zeal for playing the embedded games. Finally, in line with expectation disconfirmation theory, individuals who were more satisfied with Facebook tend to have relative high intention to continue on using it.

Acknowledgments. The authors would thank the National Science Council, Taiwan, for financially supporting this research under contract NSC 99-2410-H-004-102-MY2.

References

1. Lampe, C., Ellison, N., Steinfield, C.: A Face(book) in the Crowd: Social Searching vs. Social Browsing. In: Proceedings of the 2006 20th Anniversary Conference on Computer Supported Cooperative Work, Alberta (2006)
2. Ellison, N., Steinfield, C., Lampe, C.: The Benefits of Facebook "Friends": Social Capital and College Students Use of Online Social Network Sites. Journal of Computer-Mediated Communication 12, 1143–1168 (2007)
3. Young, S., Dutta, D., Dommety, G.: Extrapolating Psychological Insights from Facebook Profiles: A Study of Religion and Relationship Status. CyberPsychology & Behavior 12, 347–350 (2009)
4. Zeithaml, V.A.: Consumer Perceptions of Price, Quality, and Value: A Means-End Model and Synthesis Of Evidence. Journal of Marketing 52, 2–22 (1988)
5. Hirschman, E.C., Holbrook, M.B.: The Experiential Aspects of Consumption: Consumer Fantasies, Feelings, and Fun. Journal of Consumer Research 9, 132–140 (1982)
6. Babin, B.J., Darden, W.R., Griffin, M.: Work and/or Fun: Measuring Hedonic and Utilitarian Shopping Value. Journal of Consumer Research 20, 644–656 (1994)
7. Barton, L., Kang, J.: The Role of Online Browsing and Prior Knowledge on Pre-Purchase Search and Purchase Behavior. Advances in Consumer Research 32, 258–260 (2005)
8. Van der Heijden, H.: User Acceptance of Hedonic Information Systems. MIS Quarterly 28, 695–704 (2004)
9. Rogers, E.M.: Diffusion of Innovations. Free Press, Glencoe (1962)
10. Oliver, R.L.: Cognitive, Affective, and Attribute Bases of the Satisfaction Response. Journal of Consumer Research 20, 418–430 (1993)
11. Cadotte, E.R., Woodruff, R.B., Jenkins, R.L.: Expectations and Norms in Models of Consumer Satisfaction. Journal of Marketing Research 24, 305–314 (1987)
12. Bhattacherjee, A.: Understanding Information Systems Continuance: An Expectation-Confirmation Model. MIS Quarterly 25, 351–370 (2001)
13. Bhattacherjee, A., Premkumar, G.: Understanding Changes in Belief and Attitude toward Information Technology Usage: A Theoretical Model and Longitudinal Test. MIS Quarterly 28, 229–254 (2004)
14. Chitturi, R., Raghunathan, R., Mahajan, V.: Delight by Design: The Role of Hedonic Versus Utilitarian Benefits. Journal of Marketing 72, 48–63 (2008)
15. Davis, F.D., Bagozzi, R.P., Warshaw, P.R.: Extrinsic and Intrinsic Motivation to Use Computers in the Workplace. Journal of Applied Social Psychology 22, 1111–1132 (1992)
16. Sheldon, P.: The Relationship between Unwillingness-to-Communicate and Students Facebook Use. Journal of Media Psychology 20, 67–75 (2008)
17. Fornell, C., Larcker, D.F.: Evaluating Structural Equation Models with Unobservable Variables and Measurement Error. Journal of Marketing Research 18, 39–50 (1981)
18. Dhar, R., Wertenbroch, K.: Consumer Choice between Hedonic and Utilitarian Goods. Journal of Marketing Research 37, 60–71 (2000)

Web Data Mining-Based Personalized Recommendation System

Shengjiao Xu and Tinggui Chen

College of Computer Science & Information Engineering,
Zhejiang Gongshang University, Hangzhou, 310018, China
mumu0907@yeah.net,
ctgsimon@gmail.com

Abstract. The emergence of personalized recommendation system provides an a powerful tool to solve information overloading. We use web data mining principles (fuzzy clustering algorithm) proposes a personalized recommendation system architecture. It contains user fuzzy clustering and web pages fuzzy clustering. And we respectively describe the implementation processes.

Keywords: Web fuzzy clustering, Web user clustering, Web page clustering, Data mining, personalized Recommendation.

1 Introduction

Due to network service is inability to communicate with users face to face more likely to face a lack of personalized service. Different levels and purposes of the users are only interested in specific information and do not want to spend too much time to find and mine information.

Personalization technology is better to understand the users, found hidden interests of users and the laws of user's behavior. According to the user's personal information we recommend, greatly improving the efficiency of the Internet, benefiting the users.

2 System Structure

Through Web data mining technology, the personalized service system improves the effectiveness of the information to individual user. An ideal personalized service system request display format, logical structure and physical structure independent from each other. From the technical point of view, system operation, function and expansion is designed for needs of the user, and based on user needs composing and changing at any time.

Based web data mining system contains the following elements: user, data, and the relationships between them. The system contains three modules: data preprocessing module, data mining module and recommendation engine module.

Web Data Mining-Based Personalized System is shown as figure (1):

G. Shen and X. Huang (Eds.): ECWAC 2011, Part I, CCIS 143, pp. 261–265, 2011.

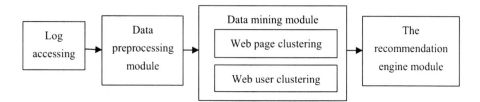

Fig. 1. Web fuzzy clustering processing model

Data collection is the most basic part of data mining. It identifies data source. The data what Client Access server left on the server is the direct source of data.

Data preprocessing module is the basis of data mining and prerequisite for effective mining algorithm. It has a very important position in the design of personalized service system. This module contains four operations: data cleaning, user identification, session identification, path congruent. It will complement Web log into a reliable, complete and accurate data source.

The data source form is shown as an example:

{'User-IP':{;}" User-IP-Agent':{;}' User-ID':{;}' User-name':{;}' User-Session-ID':{;} 'Page-ID':{;}' Request-Time':{;}' Stay-Time':{;}' Page-url':{;}' Page-url':{;}}

Data mining module is application of Web data mining clustering. It is including user clustering, page clustering.

3   Data Mining Module

Data mining module is the key of personalized service system implementation. It is a set of rules. According to different requirements, we can choose the most effective database mining algorithms. The system mainly uses fuzzy clustering algorithm. Based on user's behavior researches, we can analyze the characteristics of various groups. According to the content, we cluster Web users and Web pages.

3.1   The Algorithm of Web Fuzzy Clustering

The data object of web fuzzy clustering is the web source matrix which represents the data objects attributes of the given web data set, but the direct processing data object of web fuzzy clustering is web fuzzy similarity matrix or web fuzzy equivalence matrix. So we should abstract web source data firstly, get web data matrix representing web objects attributes, and then transform it into web fuzzy similarity matrix or web fuzzy equivalence matrix which is suitable for web fuzzy clustering. In the end, we use web fuzzy clustering method on web fuzzy similarity matrix or web fuzzy equivalence matrix to obtain clustering results. The web fuzzy clustering processing model is shown in Figure 2.

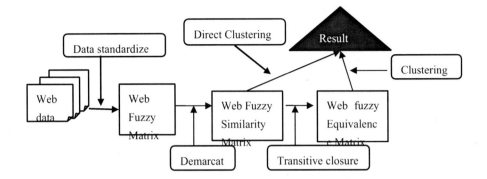

Fig. 2. Web fuzzy clustering processing model

Key algorithm

Data Standardization. In the real world, different data have different dimensions. In order to enable the different data comparing with each other, we must standardize the data of the web data matrix according to the definition of the web fuzzy matrix and condense the data into the range of [0, 1].

Demarcation. The main task of this phase is to establish the web fuzzy similarity matrix based on the web fuzzy matrix. The key to this task is to determine the similarity degree $r_{ij} = R(x_i, x_j)$ web objects x_i and x_j according to the ways of the traditional fuzzy clustering.

Clustering method. After the demarcation phase above mentioned, we get a web fuzzy similarity matrix R .Now, we sort the elements r_{ij} into a new number list $l(1 = \lambda_1 > \lambda_2 \cdots > \lambda_m)$ according to the number.

3.2 Web User Clustering

User model. Suppose that $C = \{c_1, c_2, \cdots, c_n\}$ are the web users set respectively. The $x_{ij}(i=1,2,\cdots,n; j=1,2,\cdots m)$ represents the number of web user c_i and c_j accessing Web pages.

User model Clustering. And then we get the $R_0 = (x_{ij})_{n \times m}$, the original web data matrix. After the data standardizing and demarcating phases of web fuzzy clustering, we obtain the web fuzzy similarity matrix $R' = (r_{ij})_{m \times n}$ and then process it with web fuzzy clustering methods, and thus we get the result of web user clustering. We can classify web pages into the most related user, the more related user, less related user, and not related user according to the factor λ , and we consider λ the related degree of the web pages.

3.3 Web Page Clustering

Page model. Suppose that $P = \{p_1, p_2, \cdots, p_m\}$ is the web page set and $x_{ij}(i=1,2,\cdots,n; j=1,2,\cdots m)$ represents the total number of access pages p_i and p_j .

Clustering Page model. We can get the original web data matrix $R_0 = (x_{ij})_{n \times m}$. After the data standardizing and demarcating phases of web fuzzy clustering, we obtain the web fuzzy similarity matrix $R' = (r_{ij})_{m \times n}$ and then process it with web fuzzy clustering methods, and thus we can get the result of Web user clustering. We can classify web users into firm relation pages, hypo-firm relation pages, hypo-infirm relation pages and infirm relation users according to the factor λ, and we consider λ the correlative degree of the web pages.

4   Recommended Engine Module

Recommended algorithm through double loop, it loop over pages browsed by users and their most similar pages. The algorithm is shown in figure 3. And then we can get the rankings from highest to lowest.

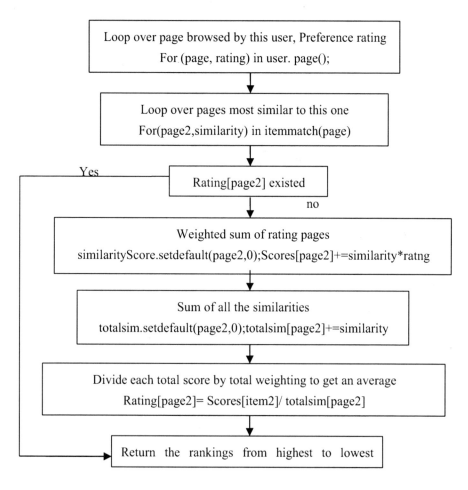

Fig. 3. Page similarity-based recommended algorithm

User similarity-based recommendation is similar with page-based recommendation. It is easier to implement and requires no extra steps, it is usually more suitable for smaller data sets.

In the case of large amounts of data, page similarity-based recommendation can come to better conclusions. And it allows us to implement a large number of computing tasks in advance, so it can give the recommended conclusion faster.

Acknowledgement. This research is supported by Natural Science Foundation of Zhejiang Province (No. Y7100673) and the Contemporary Business and Trade Research Center of Zhejiang Gongshang University (No. 1130KUSM09013 and 1130KU110021) as well as Research Project of Department of Education of Zhejiang Province (No. Y200907458). We also gratefully acknowledge the support of Science and Technology Innovative project(No.1130XJ1710215).

References

[1] Toby, S.: Programming Collective Intelligence. Electronic Industry Press, Beijing (2009)
[2] Yu, X.: Distributed Data Mining-Based E-Commerce Recommendation System. Computer Systems & Applications 18(11), 33–37 (2009) (in Chinese)
[3] Bo, M.: Computer Decision Support System. Wuhan University Press, Wuhan (2001)
[4] Hinneburg, A., Keim, D.A.: A general approach clustering in large databases with noise. Knowledge and Information Systems 5, 387–415 (2003)
[5] Weng, S.S., Liu, M.J.: Feature Based recommendations for one-to-one marketing. Expert Systems with Applications 26, 493–508 (2004)

Implementation of the Internet of Things on Public Security

Kesheng Lu and Xichun Li

Department of Mathmatics and Computer Sciences, Guangxi Nourmal University for
Nationality, No.1, Lchuan Road, 532200, Chongzuo City, Guangxi, China
lushengaa@126.com, lixichun@yahoo.com

Abstract. The development of the Internet of Things will occur within a new
ecosystem that will be driven by a number of key players. The public security
as one of the key players is going to make real-time communications will be
possible not only by humans but also by things at anytime and from anywhere.
This research will present the advent of the Internet of Things to create a pleth-
ora of innovative applications and services, which will enhance quality of life
and reduce inequalities.

Keywords: Implementation, Internet of Things, Food Security.

1 Introduction

From the application view, the Internet of Things will connect anything to computer
internet, such as industrial products, everyday objects, even a tree or corn, which can
exchange information from each other [1, 2]. In fact, with the benefit of integrated
information processing, industrial products and everyday objects will take on smart
characteristics and capabilities. They may also take on electronic identities that can be
queried remotely, or be equipped with sensors for detecting physical changes around
them [3]. Eventually, even particles as small as dust might be tagged and networked.
Such developments will turn the merely static objects of today into newly dynamic
things, embedding intelligence in our environment, and stimulating the creation of
innovative products and entirely new services [4].

From technology view, there are three kind of technologies must be utilized into
the Internet of Things, which are ubiquitous networks, sensor technologies and
nanotechnologies [5]. First, in order to connect and process everyday objects and
devices to large databases and networks, Radio-frequency identification (RFID) is
utilized for ubiquitous networks. The data about the things and the information with
the things can be exchanged from each other [6]. System manager can monitor the
processing from control center. Second, using sensor technologies, data collection
will benefit from the ability to detect changes in the physical status of things. Embedded intelligence in the things themselves can further enhance the power of the network by devolving information processing capabilities to the edges of the network.
Finally, advances in miniaturization and nanotechnology mean that smaller and
smaller things will have the ability to interact and connect [7]. A combination of all of

G. Shen and X. Huang (Eds.): ECWAC 2011, Part I, CCIS 143, pp. 266–270, 2011.
© Springer-Verlag Berlin Heidelberg 2011

these developments will create an Internet of Things that connects the world's objects in both a sensory and an intelligent manner [8].

From public security view, it is much closely with life of everybody, it is a major task of any government in any country on this world as well, and it presents ability of management for one country [9]. Actually, since a large various foods from various venues, it is so difficulty to monitor all of them. Further more, in order to gain largest benefits, business man always do somewhat of illegal things. The addition of all of these factors to make the existing system of government management is punished system, rather then prevented system. The hurt of life is going to be occurred in anywhere and anytime. In order to establish the prevention and real-time monitor system, this research will present the implementation of the Internet of Things on public security.

2 Literature Review

RFID technology, as the key technology in ubiquitous networks, provides items identify which connected into the Internet of Things and tracks the items in real-time to yield important information about their location and status [10]. These kinds of applications include from automatic highway toll collection, supply-chain management, pharmaceuticals and e-health to sports and leisure to personal security. RFID tags are even being implanted under human skin for medical purposes, but also for VIP access to bars. E-government applications such as RFID in drivers' licenses, passports or cash are under consideration [11]. RFID readers are now being embedded in mobile phones. Of course, RFID can be used to track any materials such as food in real-time to yield their information and effective management can be controlled and monitored [12].

Step by step, the food materials movement has been solved and controlled through RFID technology. To gathering the information from the food materials still is a challenge. Since the food materials which called things can not conduct their information such as location and status automatically. A new device named sensor must be stalled into those things to make them intelligence. Embedded intelligence in food materials themselves will distribute processing power to the edges of the ubiquitous network, offering greater possibilities for data processing and increasing the resilience of the ubiquitous network. This will also empower food materials and devices at the edges of the ubiquitous network to take independent decisions. In this case, the information of location and status about the food materials can be collected and exchanged into system severs so that system manager can monitor and control the entire processing [13].

Another challenge occurs during the processing. Since some things are so small, it is quite difficult to install the sensor device make them intelligence, such as corns, beans etc. nanotechnology has been developed to try to solve this problem and to make the things miniaturization.

From these technologies view, it is possible for implementation of the Internet of Things on food security [14].

3 Advantages and Issues Related with the Internet of Things for Public Security

From the section 1 and 2 above, we can see that there are several advantages through the Internet of Things to deal with public security such as food security and some of them are presented as follows.

3.1 Lower Costs

It is easy to see that government does not have to invest huge sums of money into setting up infrastructure such as huge application servers, data servers, database administrators, people resources for managing such critical systems including back up and recovery, etc. Instead, the government is just to pay for services based on usage.

3.2 Coverage of Everywhere

The Internet of Things is based on computer networks which has been established and utilized everywhere. Some countries have still not yet applied in countryside, but they can do some work through mobile networks. This kind of coverage of everywhere is advantage for government to manage the residents who are distributed far away from big city or the center of public management.

3.3 Coverage of Everything

The Internet of Things is connected with everything that means everything can be connected into computer network. In this case, the management of government is much easer to gathering the information from the residences where the population, the environment and the public security in real time.

3.4 Reliability

The Internet network of Things and data access are guaranteed to be reliably maintained as the service by local government provides are professional in maintaining the infrastructure and such reliability is backed by the center of government public security.

3.5 Flexibility

Service consumers have the flexibility to managers and the residents who need to keep contact with government managers, since they are online anytime and anywhere by anyway. It becomes a natural fit for residents to effectively collaboration with the local government managers or the government information center.

4 Privacy and Security

The Internet of Things allows users to connect every thing and every service to computer networks to access the useful information and change information from each other in real time. This will put their proprietary information on a public-access way. From a practical point of view, does the information still remain proprietary if it is stored on a public server? What laws will protect such private information? Anyone who exchanges the private information on the Internet theoretically can access at locations from outside their space? How is security of the information handled in this case? These works should be done by government. In fact, there need to be standards governing regulations which ensure uniformity in how this information is exchanged. But the works are quiet difficulties, because from both privacy and security points of view, the more restricted the exchange to the information is, the easier is to protect it. In order to ensure fast exchange to this information from each other, an information center has to be established to store the information and to prevent the loss of information in case of failure.

5   Information Servers

The applications of Internet of Things have been developed and reliable services delivered though information centers and built on servers with different levels of virtualization technologies. The information centers are the physical form of Internet of things. The idea is to execute computing and gather information from devices where a huge collection of servers, storage systems and network equipments. The information centers are not only a warehouse like a building with thousands of servers, but also a remote control center. All of information is collected through the network equipments and analyzed by the information center and then delivered them to government managers in real time. The decision can be made at once in this case.

6   Conclusions

The Internet of Things is currently gaining popularity as an inexpensive way of providing rail-time and widest information from anywhere for government. A new paradigm of computing has started to evolve in recent times. As wireless broadband connection options grow the Internet of Things allows governments to establish to gather public information and use the useful information to make decision quickly. In this case, a wireless network system is necessary. Once the wireless network coverage is everywhere, the gathering information and the reflecting action are possible.

In order to establish the Internet network of Things, the most important equipments are sensor. That is why we call this kind of network is sensor network. Anywhere or anything is equipped with the sensor,. The information can be collected and transferred to the wireless center through the wireless system. After received the information, government makes a judgment quickly and gives an action.

From technology view, the simple Internet of Things can be realization and provide services right now. Some of equipments still are on developing and the higher Internet of Things will be coming on future. Therefore, the key idea in this paper focuses on information gathering and properly action taking.

The future Internet of Things will focus on controlling center and distribute resources for public accident management.

References

1. Nottingham, M.: Syndication format, Internet RFC 4287 Internet Engineering Task Force (2005)
2. Chen, C.L., Raman, T.V.: AxSJAX: a talking translation bot using Google Im: Bringing Web applications to life. In: Proceeding of the International Cross-Displinary Workshop on Web Accessibility, pp. 54–56 (2008)
3. Raman, T.V.: Cloud computing and equal access for all. In: Proceedings of the International Cross-Displinary Workshop on Web Accessibility, pp. 1–4 (2008)
4. Mei, L., Chan, W.K., Tse, T.H.: A tale of clouds: paradigm comparisons and some thoughts on research issues. In: Proceedings of the 2008 IEEE Asia-Pacific Services Computing Conference, pp. 464–469 (2008)
5. Bennett, K., Layzell, P., Budgen, D., Brereton, P., Macaulay, L., Munro, M.: Servive-based software: the future for flexible software. In: Proceedings of the Seventh Asia-Pacific Software Engineering Conference (APSEC), pp. 214–221 (2000)
6. http://www.bds.ie.Pdf.ServiceOriented1.pdf
7. Software & Information Industry's, eBusiness Division, Strategic Backgorunder: Software as a Service, http://www.siia.net/estore/ssb-01.pdf
8. Zhang, L.J., Zhou, Q.: CCOA: Cloud Computing Open Architecture. In: Proceedings of the 2009 IEEE International Conference on Web Services, pp. 607–616 (2009)
9. Amazon EC2, http://aws.amazon.com/ec2
10. Google Inc., What Is Google App Engine? http://code.google.com/appengine/docs.whatisgoogleappengine.html
11. IBM, http://www.ibm.com/ibm/cloud/cloudburst
12. Joyent (August 2009), http://www.joyent.com/
13. Microsoft Azure, http://www.microsoft.com/azure
14. SalesForce, http://www.salesforce.com/platform/cloud-platform

Applied Research of Intelligent Controller Used in Cable Vibration Control

Tao Sun, Sikun Bi, and Fanbing Li

College of Electronic Information and Control Engineering,
Shandong Institute of Light Industry, Jinan, China, 250353
tutorsun@163.com,
bsksin@163.com

Abstract. This paper introduces the application of intelligent controller used in the semi-active control of cable vibration mainly and details the design of the controller and cable - damper system's components. Matlab is used for the simulation of cable-damper system and the simulation results show that intelligent controller can reduce the response of cable vibration and achieve better control effect.

Keywords: intelligent controller, cable vibration, semi-active control.

1 Introduction

Cable is the main part of cable stayed bridge. Because of it's great flexibility, low-mass and low-damping characteristics, large amplitude vibration is easy to happen under the effects of every kinds of loads[1]. Sometimes the maximum amplitude may reach 5 to 10 times of its diameter, and the overlarge amplitude is bad to the cables' application life and the safety of the bridge. So, how to control the cable vibration effectly is being a very important problem. Currently, the most common method of controling the vibration is installing MR damper at a certain position to increase the equivalent damping ratio of cable system[2]. Though the method is effectively, the MR damper is a nonlinear semi-active control equipment and the cable - damper system is a very uncertain system, so the key factor of getting ideal control effect is an appropriate semi-active control algorithm.

2 Intelligent Controller

Intelligent Controll is an automatic control technology which means that the intelligent machine can be independently drived without people's operating to achieve the control objective. With the development of information and computing technology, intelligent control system has become a trend. Intelligent controller is a controller which has an intelligent control algorithm. According to the characteristics of cable vibration, this

G. Shen and X. Huang (Eds.): ECWAC 2011, Part I, CCIS 143, pp. 271–276, 2011.

paper selects intelligent neural network PID controller which is robust, real-time and adaptability to control the cable vibration[3]. It combines the advantages of neural network and conventional PID, can learn and adapt to the dynamic characteristics of uncertain systems. The best linear combination of PID can be found with the ability of neural network's nonlinear system.

The neural network PID controller consists of two parts, as shown in Figure 1:

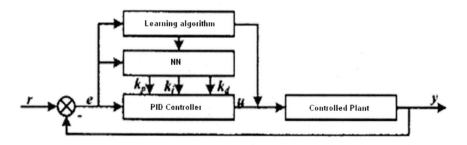

Fig. 1. Shows that conventional PID controls the plant with closed-loop control directly and the control parameters is the line adjustment mode. The neural network regulates the parameters based on the running states of the system to reach the optimized target. By means of the NN's self-learning and adjusting the weighting coefficient to make the output of NN is the controller's parameters which corresponds to some kind of optimized control law.

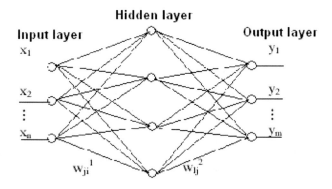

Fig. 2. Shows a typical NN consists of three layers

3   Cable -Damper System

More precise dynamic model of MR damper is one of the key factors of getting ideal control effect. Currently, the modle proposed by Spencer, etc [4] which is based on the parametric mechanical model of Bouc-Wen Hysteretic model can grasp the dynamic characteristics more accurately. The modle can predict the damping force accurately

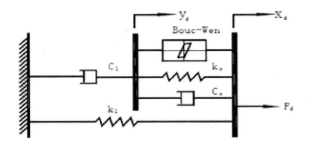

Fig. 3. Shows the modle of MR damper

according to the MR damper's displacement, speed and output voltage. At the present time, it has the highest fitting accuracy and has been used popularly.

The damping force generated by this modle can be described as follows:

$$F_d(t) = c_1 \dot{y}_d + k_1(x_d - x_0) \tag{1}$$

$$\dot{y}_d = \frac{1}{c_0 + c_1}[\alpha_d z + k_0(x_d - y_d) + c_0 \dot{x}_d] \tag{2}$$

$$\dot{z} = -\gamma |\dot{x}_d - \dot{y}_d| \, \|z\|^{n_d - 1} z - \beta(\dot{x}_d - \dot{y}_d) \|z\|^{n_d} + A_d(\dot{x}_d - \dot{y}_d) \tag{3}$$

And the α_d, c_1, c_0, u_d are given by the following relations:

$$\alpha_d = \alpha_a + \alpha_b u_d; \ c_1 = c_{1a} + c_{1b} u_d; \ c_0 = c_{0a} + c_{0b} u_d; \ \dot{u}_d = -\eta(u_d - V_0) \tag{4}$$

And the V_0 is the voltage added to the damper.

And the nonlinear dynamic equation of the cable-damper system can be got by means of Hamilton principle[5]:

$$M\ddot{q} + C\dot{q} + Kq = f_u + \varphi_d F_D(t) \tag{5}$$

In the equation,M is the n-order mass matrix, C is the n-order damping matrix, K is the n-order stiffness matrix, f_u is the n-order array of uniformly distributed load, $F_D(t)$ is the force of the damper, φ_d is the n-order matrix of damper's force.

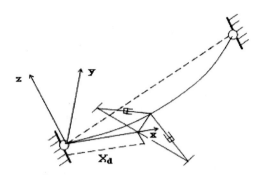

Fig. 4. Shows the cable-damper system

4   Simulation Analysis

In this paper, a random signal is used as the random load of the cable, as shown in Figure 5.

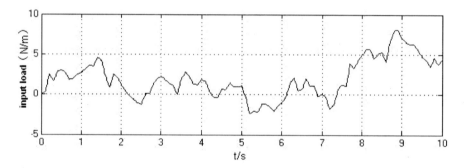

Fig. 5. Shows the random input load

The load is distributed uniformly on the cable and the observation point is at the 20% of the cable's length. The parameters of cable is shown in table 1.

Table 1. Parameters of Cable

position of damper	0.02L
length of cable	144.3m
tension of cable	4500kN
angle of cable	27°
mass of cable	83.7kg/m

The structure of neural network is 8-14-3, learning rate is 0.21, inertia factor is 0.035, weighting coefficient is a random number in [-0.5, 0.5]. The output of the NN is the three parameters of PID. The voltage on the damper is controlled by the PID to control the force given by the damper.

Matlab is used for the simulation of the system and the results is as follows:

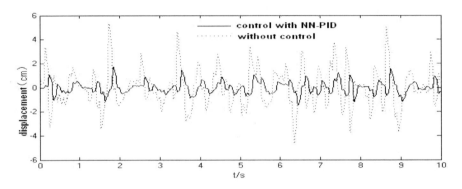

Fig. 6. Shows the area chart of displacement response

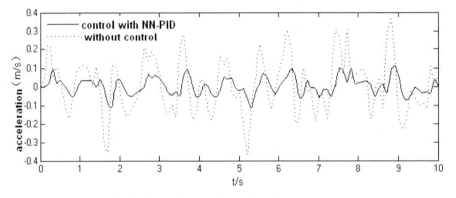

Fig. 7. Shows the area chart of acceleration response

The results show that semi-active control of MR damper with NN-PID reduces the vibration amplitude and the acceleration response of the cable and the control effect is obvious. And the control algorithm also increases the controllability of the damper.

References

1. Pacheo, B.M., Fujino, Y., Sulekh, A.: Estimation curve for modal damping in stay cables with viscous damper. Journal of Structural Engineering 119, 1961–1979 (1993)
2. Chen, Z.Q., Wang, X.Y., Ko, J.M., et al.: MR damping system for mitigating wind—rain induced vibration on Dongting Lake Cable. Stayed Bridge, Wind and Structures 7(5), 293–304 (2004)

3. Main, J.A., Jones, N.P.: Free vibrations of taut cable with attached damper. II: nonlinear damper. Journal of Engineering Mechanics 128, 1072–1081 (2002)
4. Liao, W.H., Lai, C.Y.: Harmonic analysis of a magnetorheological damper for vibration control. Smart Mater Struct. 11, 288–296 (2002)
5. Rong, Y., Tao, R.: Flexible fixturing with phase-change materials. part 1. experimental study on magnetorheological fluids. Advanced Manufacturing Technology 16, 822–829 (2000)

Analytic Solutions of a Second-Order Iterative Functional Differential Equations

LingXia Liu

Department of Mathematics, Weifang University,
Weifang, Shandong 261061, P.R. China
llxmath@126.com

Abstract. In this paper, the existence of analytic solutions of an iterative functional differential equation is studied. We reduce this problem to finding analytic solutions of a functional differential equation without iteration of the unknown function. For technical reasons, in previous work the constant α given in *Schröder* transformation is required to fulfill that α is off the unit circle or lies on the circle with the Diophantine condition. In this paper, we break the restraint of the Diophantine condition and obtain results of analytic solutions in the case of α at resonance, i.e., at a root of the unity and the case of α near resonance under the Brjuno condition.

Keywords: functional differential equation, *Schröder* transformation, analytic solution, resonance, Brjuno condition.

1 Introduction

Iterative differential equation, as a special type of functional differential equations, in which the deviating arguments depend on the state, attracted the attention of researchers recently [1-6]. In [4, 5], analytic solutions of iterative functional differential equations $x'(z) = c_1 x(z) + c_2 x^{[2]}(z) + \cdots + c_m x^{[m]}(z)$ are found, where $x^{[i]}(z) = x(x^{[i-1]}(z))$. In [6], analytic solution of the second-order iterative functional differential equation

$$x''(z) = p_0 z + p_1 x(z) + p_2 x^{[2]}(z) + \cdots + p_m x^{[m]}(z), \qquad (1)$$

are considered, where m is a positive integer greater than or equal to 2 and $p_0, p_1, \cdots p_m$ are complex numbers such that $\sum_{i=0}^{m} |p_i| \neq 0$. As in our previous work [3-6], our strategy remains to reduce the equation (1) with the *Schröder* transformation

$$x(z) = y(\alpha y^{-1}(z)) \qquad (2)$$

to the auxiliary equation

$$\alpha^2 y''(\alpha z) y'(z) - \alpha y'(\alpha z) y''(z) = (y'(z))^3 \sum_{j=0}^{m} p_j y(\alpha^j z), \qquad (3)$$

G. Shen and X. Huang (Eds.): ECWAC 2011, Part I, CCIS 143, pp. 277–283, 2011.

where iteration of the unknown function is not involved but an indeterminate complex α needs to be discussed. For technical reason, in [6], the constant α given in the *Schröder* transformation, is required to fulfill that α is off the unit circle, i.e., $0 < |\alpha| < 1$, or α is on the circle with the Diophantine condition: $|\mu| = 1$, μ *is not a root of unity, and* $\log\dfrac{1}{|\mu^n - 1|} \le T \log n$, $n = 2, 3, \cdots$ *for some positive constant T.* Roughly speaking, the Diophantine condition requires α to be far from all roots of unity.

In this paper, we break the restriction of the Diophantine condition, and obtain the existence of local analytic solutions of Eq. (3) in the case of α at resonance, i.e., at a root of the unity and the case of α near resonance under the Brjuno condition. In this paper, the complex α in (2) satisfies one of the following conditions:

(H1) $\mu = e^{2\pi i \theta}$, where $\theta \in \mathbf{R\backslash Q}$ is a Brjuno number [7,8], i.e., $B(\theta) = \sum_{k=0}^{\infty} \dfrac{\log q_{k+1}}{q_k} < \infty$, where $\{p_k / q_k\}$ denotes the sequence of partial fraction of the continued fraction expansion of θ, and is said to satisfy the Brjuno condition.

(H$_2$) $\alpha = e^{2\pi i q/p}$ for some integers $p \in \mathbf{N}$ with $p \ge 2$ and $q \in \mathbf{Z}\backslash\{0\}$, and $\alpha \ne e^{2\pi i l/k}$ for all $1 \le k \le p - 1$ and $l \in \mathbf{Z}\backslash\{0\}$.

Observe that α is a p-th unit root in the case of (H2), while the case (H1) contains a part of α near resonance.

2 Auxiliary Equation Case (H1)

We now discuss the existence of an analytic solution of (3) in the initial condition

$$y(0) = 0, \ y'(0) = \eta \ne 0. \tag{4}$$

First, we discuss the existence of analytic solutions of (3) under the Brjuno condition. To do this, we now recall briefly the definition of Brjuno numbers and some basic facts. As stated in [9], for a real number θ we let θ denote its integer part and let $\{\theta\} = \theta - [\theta]$. Then every national number θ has a unique expression of the Gauss' continued fraction $\theta = a_0 + \theta_0 = a_0 + \dfrac{1}{a_1 + \theta_1} = ...$, denoted simply by $\theta = [a_0, a_1, ..., a_n, ...]$, where a_j's and θ_j's are calculated by the algorithm: **(a)** $a_0 = [\theta]$, $\theta_0 = \{\theta\}$ and **(b)** $a_n = \left[\dfrac{1}{\theta_{n-1}}\right], \theta_n = \left\{\dfrac{1}{\theta_{n-1}}\right\}$ for all $n \ge 1$. Define the sequences $(p_n)_{n \in \mathbf{N}}$ and $(q_n)_{n \in \mathbf{N}}$ as follows: $q_{-2} = 1, q_{-1} = 0, q_n = a_n q_{n-1} + q_{n-2}; \ p_{-2} = 0, p_{-1} = 1, p_n = a_n p_{n-1} + p_{n-2}$. It is easy to show that $p_n / q_n = [a_0, a_1, ..., a_n]$. Thus, for every $\theta \in \mathbf{R\backslash Q}$ we associate, using its convergence, an arithmetical function $B(\theta) = \sum_{n \ge 0} \dfrac{\log q_{n+1}}{q_n}$. We say that θ is a Brjuno number or that it satisfies Brjuno condition if $B(\theta) < +\infty$. The Brjuno condition is weaker than the Diophantine condition. For example, if $a_{n+1} \le c e^{a_n}$ for all $n \ge 0$, where $c > 0$ is a constant, then $\theta = [a_0, a_1, ..., a_n, ...]$ is a Brjuno number but is not a

Diophantine number. So, the case (H1) contains both Diophantine condition and a part of μ ``near'' resonance.

In order to discuss the existence of the auxiliary equation (4) under (H1), we need to introduce Davie's Lemma. First, we recall some facts in [10] briefly. Let $\theta \in R \backslash Q \cdots$ and $(q_n)_{n \in \mathbb{N}}$ be the sequence of partial denominators of the Gauss's continued fraction for θ as in the Introduction. As in [9], let $A_k = \{n \geq 0 \mid \|n\theta\| \leq \frac{1}{8q_k}\}$,

$E_k = \max(q_k, \frac{q_{k+1}}{4})$, $\eta_k = \frac{q_k}{E_k}$. Let A_k^* be the set of integers $j \geq 0$ such that either $j \in A_k$ or for some j_1 and j_2 in A_k, with $j_2 - j_1 < E_k$, one has $j_1 < j < j_2$ and q_k divide $j - j_1$. For any integer $n \geq 0$, define $l_k(n) = \max\left((1+\eta_k)\frac{n}{q_k} - 2, \ (m_n \eta_k + n)\frac{1}{q_k} - 1\right)$, where $m_n = \max\{j \mid 0 \leq j \leq n, j \in A_k^*\}$. We then define function $h_k : \mathbb{N} \to \mathbf{R}_+$ as follows:

$$
\begin{cases}
\dfrac{m_n + \eta_k n}{q_k} - 1, & \text{if } m_n + q_k \in A_k^*, \\[2mm]
l_k(n), & \text{if } m_n + q_k \notin A_k^*.
\end{cases}
$$

Let $g_k(n) := \max\left(h_k(n), \left[\dfrac{n}{q_k}\right]\right)$, and define $k(n)$ by the condition $q_{k(n)} \leq n \leq q_{k(n)+1}$.

Clearly, $k(n)$ is non-decreasing. Then we are able to state the following result:

Lemma 1. (Davie's Lemma [10]) Let $K(n) = n \log 2 + \sum_{k=0}^{k(n)} g_k(n) \log(2q_{k+1})$. Then

(a) There is a universal constant $\gamma > 0$ (independent of n and θ) such that

$$
K(n) \leq n\left(\sum_{k=0}^{k(n)} \frac{\log q_{k+1}}{q_k} + \gamma\right),
$$

(b) $K(n_1) + K(n_2) \leq K(n_1 + n_2)$ for all n_1 and n_2, and

(c) $-\log|\alpha^n - 1| \leq K(n) - K(n-1)$.

Now we state and prove the following theorem under Brjuno condition. The idea of our proof is acquired from [9].

Theorem 1. Suppose (H1) holds, then equation (3) has an analytic solution $y(z)$ of the form

$$
y(z) = \sum_{n=0}^{\infty} b_n z^n, \ b_0 = s, b_1 = \eta. \tag{5}
$$

in a neighborhood of the origin.

Proof. As in [6], the equation (3) may be written in the form

$$
\frac{\alpha y''(\alpha z) y'(z) - y'(\alpha z) y''(z)}{(y'(z))^2} = \frac{1}{\alpha} y'(z) \sum_{j=0}^{m} p_j y(\alpha^j z),
$$

or

$$\left(\frac{y'(\alpha z)}{y'(z)}\right)' = \frac{1}{\alpha}y'(z)\sum_{j=0}^{m}p_jy(\alpha^j z).$$

Since we have assumed that $y'(0) = \eta \neq 0$, by integration, we obtain

$$y'(\alpha z) = y'(z) + \frac{1}{\alpha}y'(z)\int_0^z y'(s)\sum_{j=0}^{m}p_j y(\alpha^j z)ds. \tag{6}$$

Substituting (5) into (6), we see that b_1 is arbitrary, and

$$(n+2)(\alpha^{n+2}-\alpha)b_{n+2} = \sum_{k=0}^{n}\sum_{i=0}^{n-k}\frac{(i+1)(k+1)}{(n-k+1)}\left(\sum_{j=0}^{m}p_j\alpha^{j(n-k-i)}\right)b_{k+1}b_{i+1}b_{n-k-i}, \quad n=0,1,\cdots. \tag{7}$$

Let $b_0 = y(0) = s$ and $b_1 = y'(0) = \eta \neq 0$, then by (7), we may determine $\{b_n\}_{n=0}^{\infty}$ uniquely in a recursive manner.

We need to show that $y(z)$ defined by (5) has a positive radius of convergence.

Note that $\left|\frac{(i+1)(k+1)}{(n+2)(n-k+1)\alpha}\left(\sum_{j=0}^{m}p_j\alpha^{j(n-k-i)}\right)\right| < \sum_{j=0}^{m}|p_j|$, for $0 \leq k \leq n$ and $0 \leq i \leq n-k$.

Let $M = \sum_{j=0}^{n}|p_j|$, then

$$|b_{n+2}| \leq \frac{M}{|\alpha^{n+1}-1|}\sum_{k=0}^{n}\sum_{i=0}^{n-k}|b_{k+1}||b_{i+1}||b_{n-k-i}|, \quad n=0,1,\cdots. \tag{8}$$

We define a power series

$$G(z) = \sum_{n=0}^{\infty}B_n z^n, \tag{9}$$

by $B_0 = |s|$, $B_1 = |\eta|$ and $B_{n+2} = M\sum_{k=0}^{n}\sum_{i=0}^{n-k}B_{k+1}B_{i+1}B_{n-k-i}$, $n=0,1,\cdots$. Then

$$G^2(z) = (B_0 + \sum_{n=0}^{\infty}B_{n+1}z^{n+1})(\sum_{n=0}^{\infty}B_n z^n) = B_0\sum_{n=0}^{\infty}B_n z^n + \sum_{n=0}^{\infty}(\sum_{k=0}^{n}B_{k+1}B_{n-k})z^{n+1},$$

$$G^3(z) = (B_0 + \sum_{n=0}^{\infty}B_{n+1}z^{n+1})(B_0\sum_{n=0}^{\infty}B_n z^n + \sum_{n=0}^{\infty}(\sum_{k=0}^{n}B_{k+1}B_{n-k})z^{n+1})$$

$$= B_0^2\sum_{n=0}^{\infty}B_n z^n + 2B_0\sum_{n=0}^{\infty}(\sum_{k=0}^{n}B_{k+1}B_{n-k})z^{n+1} + \sum_{n=0}^{\infty}(\sum_{k=0}^{n}\sum_{i=0}^{n-k}B_{k+1}B_{i+1}B_{n-k-i})z^{n+2}$$

$$= B_0^2 G(z) + 2B_0(G^2(z) - B_0 G(z)) + \frac{1}{M}\sum_{n=0}^{\infty}B_{n+2}z^{n+2}$$

$$= B_0^2 G(z) + 2B_0(G^2(z) - B_0 G(z)) + \frac{1}{M}(G(z) - B_0 - B_1 z)$$

$$= 2|s|^2 G^2(z) + (\frac{1}{M} - |s|^2)G(z) - \frac{1}{M}(|\eta| z + |s|),$$

that is

$$G^3(z) - 2|s|G^2(z) - (\frac{1}{M} - |s|^2)G(z) + \frac{1}{M}(|\eta| z + |s|) = 0. \tag{10}$$

Let

$$F(z,\omega) =: F(z,\omega, s, \eta, M) = \omega^3 - 2|s|\omega^2 - (\frac{1}{M} - |s|^2)\omega + \frac{1}{M}(|\eta|z + |s|) \qquad (11)$$

for (z,ω) from a neighborhood of $(0,|s|)$. Since $F(0,|s|) = 0$, $F_\omega'(0,|s|) = -\frac{1}{M} \neq 0$, there exists a unique function $\omega(z)$, analytic on a neighborhood of zero, such that $\omega(0) = |s|$, $\omega'(0) = |\eta| \neq 0$ and satisfying the equation $F(z,\omega(z)) = 0$. From (9) and (10) we have $G(z) = \omega(z)$, then the power series (9) is analytic on a neighborhood of zero. Hence there is a constant $T > 0$ such that $B_n \leq T^n$, $n = 0, 1, \cdots$. Now we prove

$$|b_n| \leq B_n e^{K(n-1)}, n = 1, 2, \cdots, \qquad (12)$$

where $K : \mathbf{N} \to \mathbf{R}$ is defined in Lemma 1. In fact $|b_1| = |\eta| = c_1$, we assume that $|b_j| \leq B_j e^{K(j-1)}$, $j = n+1$. From Lemma 1 and (8) we obtain

$$|b_{n+2}| \leq \frac{M}{|\alpha^{n+1} - 1|} \sum_{k=0}^{n} \sum_{i=0}^{n-k} B_{k+1}B_{i+1}B_{n-k-i}e^{K(k)+K(i)+K(n-k-i-1)}$$

$$\leq \frac{M}{|\alpha^{n+1} - 1|}e^{K(n-1)}\sum_{k=0}^{n}\sum_{i=0}^{n-k} B_{k+1}B_{i+1}B_{n-k-i} \leq \frac{e^{K(n-1)}}{|\alpha^{n+1} - 1|}B_{n+2}.$$

Note that $K(n-1) \leq K(n) \leq K(n+1) + \log|\alpha^{n+1} - 1|$, the $|b_{n+2}| \leq B_{n+2}e^{K(n+1)}$. So we have $|b_n| \leq B_n e^{K(n-1)} \leq T^n e^{K(n-1)}$. Note that $K(n) \leq n(B(\theta) + \gamma)$ for some universal constant $\gamma > 0$, then $|b_n| \leq T^n e^{(n-1)(B(\theta)+\gamma)}$, that is,

$$\limsup_{n \to \infty}(|b_n|)^{\frac{1}{n}} \leq \limsup_{n \to \infty}(Te^{\frac{n-1}{n}(B(\theta)+\gamma)}) = Te^{B(\theta)+\gamma}.$$

This implies that the convergence radius of the series (5) is at least $(Te^{B(\theta)+\gamma})^{-1}$. This complete the proof.

In case (H2) the constant α is not only on the unit circle in $\mathbf{C}$ but also a root of unity. In such a case, both Diophantine condition and Brjuno condition are not satisfied. The difficulty encountered is overcome with an idea acquired from [11].

Let $\{D_n\}_{n=0}^{\infty}$ be a sequence defined by $D_0 = |s|, D_1 = |\eta|$ and

$$D_{n+2} = M\Gamma\sum_{k=0}^{n}\sum_{i=0}^{n-k} D_{k+1}D_{i+1}D_{n-k-i}, n = 0, 1, 2\cdots, \qquad (13)$$

where $\Gamma = \max\{1, |\alpha^i - 1|^{-1}, i = 1, 2, \cdots, p-1\}$, M is defined in Theorem 1.

Theorem 2. Suppose that (H2) holds and p is given as above. Let $\{b_n\}_{n=0}^{\infty}$ be determined recursively by $b_0 = s$, $b_1 = \eta \neq 0$ and

$$(n+2)(\alpha^{n+2} - \alpha)b_{n+2} = \Omega(n, \alpha), n = 0, 1, 2\cdots, \qquad (14)$$

where

$$\Omega(n,\alpha) = \sum_{k=0}^{n}\sum_{i=0}^{n-k}\frac{(i+1)(k+1)}{n-k+1}\left(\sum_{j=0}^{m}p_j\alpha^{j(n-k-i)}\right)b_{k+1}b_{i+1}b_{n-k-i}.$$

If $\Omega(vp-1,\alpha)=0$ for all $v=1,2,\cdots$, then Eq.(3) has an analytic solution $y(z)$ in a neighborhood of the origin such that $y(0)=s$, $y'(0)=\eta$, and $y^{(vp+1)}(0)=(vp+1)!\eta_{vp+1}$, where all $\eta_{vp+1}'s$ are arbitrary constants satisfying the inequality $|\eta_{vp+1}|\le D_{vp+1}$ and the sequence $\{D_n\}_{n=0}^{\infty}$ is defined in (13). Otherwise, if $\Omega(vp-1,\alpha)\ne0$ for some $v=1,2,\cdots$, then the Eq.(3) has no analytic solutions in any neighborhood of the origin.

Proof. As in the proof of Theorem 1, we seek a power series solution of (3) of the form (5). Substituting (5) into (3), then (7) or (14) holds. If $\Omega(vp-1,\alpha)\ne0$ for some natural numbers v, the equality (7) or (14) does not hold, when $n=vp-1$. This is because $\alpha^{vp+1}-\alpha=0$, then such a circumstance equation (3) has no formal solutions. When $\Omega(vp-1,\alpha)=0$ for all natural numbers v, for each v the corresponding b_{vp+1} in (7) or (14) has infinitely many choices in **C**, that is, the formal series solution (5) define a family of solutions with infinitely many parameters. Choose $b_{vp+1}=\eta_{vp+1}$ arbitrary such that $|\eta_{vp+1}|=D_{vp+1}, v=1,2,\cdots$, where D_{vp+1} is defined by (13). Now we prove the power series (5) converges in a neighborhood of the origin. When $n\ne vp-1$, $|\alpha^{n+1}-1|\le\Gamma$, then

$$|b_{n+2}|\le M\Gamma\sum_{k=0}^{n}\sum_{i=0}^{n-k}|b_{k+1}||b_{i+1}||b_{n-k-i}|,\quad n\ne vp-1, v=1,2,\cdots, \tag{15}$$

where M is defined in Theorem 1. We consider the implicit function equation

$$F(z,\varphi;s,\eta,M\Gamma)=0, \tag{16}$$

where F is defined in (11). As the proof in Theorem 1, we can prove that there exisis a unique function $\varphi(z;s,\eta,M\Gamma)$, analytic in a neighborhood of the origin such that $\varphi(0;s,\eta,\Gamma M)=|s|$, $\varphi_z'(0;s,\eta,\Gamma M)=|\eta|\ne0$, so $\varphi(z;s,\eta,\Gamma M)$ can be expanded into a convergent power series

$$\varphi(z;s,\eta,\Gamma M)=\sum_{n=0}^{\infty}D_n z^n, D_0=|S|, D_1=|\eta|. \tag{17}$$

Moreover, by induction we can prove that $|b_n|\le|D_n|, n=1,2,\cdots$. So the series (5) converges in a neighborhood of the origin. The proof is complete.

3 Analytic Solution of Equation (1)

Having knowledge about the auxiliary equations (3), we are ready to give analytic solution of equation (1).

Theorem 3. Under the conditions of Theorem 1 or 2, the equation (1) has an analytic solution of the form $x(z) = y(\alpha y^{-1}(z))$ in a neighborhood of the number s such that $x(s) = s, x'(s) = \alpha$, where $y(z)$ is an analytic solution of the equation (3) in a neighborhood of the origin.

Proof. By Theorem 1 or 2, equation (3) has a solution $y(z)$ which is analytic near 0. This solution is of the form (5), where $\{b_n\}_{n=2}^{\infty}$ is defined by the recurrence reaction (7). Since $y'(0) = \eta \neq 0$, thus by the analytic inverse function Theorem, the inverse function y^{-1} is analytic in a neighborhood of the origin. Let $x(z) = y(\alpha y^{-1}(z))$, then $x'(z) = \dfrac{\alpha y'(\alpha y^{-1}(z))}{y'(\alpha y^{-1}(z))}$, and $x^{[j]}(z) = y(\alpha^j y^{-1}(z)), j = 1, 2, \cdots m$. Thus from (3), we have

$$x''(z) = \frac{\alpha^2 y''(\alpha y^{-1}(z)) \cdot y'(y^{-1}(z)) - ay'(\alpha y^{-1}(z)) \cdot y''(y^{-1}(z))}{(y'(y^{-1}(z)))^3}$$

$$= \sum_{j=0}^{m} p_j y(\alpha^j y^{-1}(z)) = \sum_{j=0}^{m} p_j x^{[j]}(z).$$

From $y(0) = s, y'(0) = \eta \neq 0$, then $y^{-1}(s) = 0$, and $x(s) = y(\alpha y^{-1}(s)) = y(0) = s$, $x'(s) = \dfrac{\alpha y'(\alpha y^{-1}(s))}{y'(y^{-1}(s))} = \dfrac{\alpha \eta}{\eta} = \alpha$. These show that $x(z)$ is an analytic solution of (1), and s is a fixed point of $x(z)$. The proof is complete.

References

1. Eder, E.: The functional differential equation x´(t) = x(x(t)). J. Differential Equations 54, 390–400 (1984)
2. Feckan, E.: On certain type of functional differential equations. Math. Slovaca 43, 39–43 (1993)
3. Wang, K.: On the equation x´(t) = f (x(x(t))). Funkcial. Ekvac. 33, 405–425 (1990)
4. Si, J.G., Cheng, S.S.: Note on an iterative functional differential equations. Demonstratio Math. 31(3), 609–614 (1998)
5. Si, J.G., Li, W.R., Cheng, S.S.: Analytic solutions of an iterative functional differential equations. Comput. Math. Appl. 33(6), 47–51 (1997)
6. Li, W.R.: Analytic solutions for a class of second-order iterative functional differential equations. Acta Math. Sinica 41(1), 167–176 (1998)
7. Bjuno, A.D.: Analytic form of differential equations. Trans. Moscow Math. Soc. 25, 131–288 (1971)
8. Marmi, S., Moussa, P., Yoccoz, J.C.: The Brjuno functions and their regularity properties. Comm. Math. Phys. 186(2), 265–293 (1997)
9. Carletti, T., Marmi, S.: Linearization of Analytic and Non-Analytic Germs of Diffeomorphisms of (C, 0). Bull. Soc. Math. 128, 69–85 (2000)
10. Davie, A.M.: The critical function for the semistandard map. Nonlinearity 7, 219–229 (1994)
11. Bessis, D., Marmi, S., Turchetti, G.: On the singularities of divergent majorant series arising from normal form theory. Rend. Mat. Appl. 9, 645–659 (1989)

On the Controller Synthesis for Markov Decision Process of Conflict Tolerant Specification

Junhua Zhang[1,2], Zhiqiu Huang[1], and Zining Cao[1]

[1] Department of Computer Science and Technology,
Nanjing University of Aeronautics and Astronautics,
Yudao Street 29, 210016 Nanjing, China
[2] Vocational Education Faculty, Ningbo University, Ningbo, Xuefu Road 9,
315100 Ningbo, China
{zhang.junhua,zqhuang,caozn}@nuaa.edu.cn

Abstract. For an embedded control system, different requirements often need be satisfied at same time, and some of them make the system to act conflicted. Conflict tolerant specification is provided to denote this situation. In such a system, there often exist probabilistic and non-deterministic behaviors. We use Markov Decision Process (MDP) to denote these features. We study the controller synthesis for MDP over conflict tolerant specification. We extend PCTL star by adding past operator to denote the conflict tolerant specification succinctly. We use CT-PLTL to denote conflicted actions and PCTL to denote the specification for probability demand. We first synthesize a controller on a base system over CT-PLTL and then use it to prune the corresponding MDP of the system model. We use the resulting sub-MDP as the model to further synthesis a controller over PCTL. The whole controller for MDP is a conjunction of the two controllers obtained.

Keywords: Markov Decision Process, controller synthesis, conflict tolerant, embedded control system, PCTL star.

1 Introduction

Embedded control systems exist universally at present, from the factory to home and entertainment. The typical equipments, for example, are air-conditioners, building automation systems, automotive control systems and railway crossing controller [1]. In these systems, equipments' running are influenced by more than one requirement at the same time. It is not rare that these requirements conflict with each other in one moment. These phenomena also always happens in telecommunication field known as feature interactions [2].

To deal with the conflicted requirement especially in control systems, [3, 4] use the notation of "conflict-tolerant specification", denote it using temporal logic CT-LTL, and analysis and verification of the specification on base system. Inspiring by [5], how to deal with the situation on a probabilistic and non-deterministic system, is also an interesting topic to study.

G. Shen and X. Huang (Eds.): ECWAC 2011, Part I, CCIS 143, pp. 284–290, 2011.

In a control system, we can use LTL to denote a sequence of events happening. Since one event always occurs because of something happened in the past, so LTL is extended to LTL with past operator to express these phenomena naturally and succinctly [6]. We will use this logic extension in our study. As LTL cannot express probability constraint for a system, we use PCTL to do it. For a full description of the specification, PCTL* with past is employed.

In order to describe the events happening in a control system, we adapt normal definition of MDP. In the normal description, from one state to the next, "action" is decided according to a kind of strategy. In our expression, "event" is used instead of the action, that is to say, a system is reactive by an event from one state to another. This process is used in dealing with conflicted actions. But in the probability calculation, we can still regard "event" as "action" or neglect the difference between them, as there is one to one corresponding.

Totally in this paper, we extend the work in [4] in system model from base system to probabilistic and non-deterministic system — accurately, Markov decision process (MDP) with our view, and in specification description from CT-LTL to CT-CTL* with past operator (CT-PCTL*), and then study the controller synthesis problem for MDP against CT-PCTL*. It is a nontrivial question, since we must not only deal with the controller synthesis problem like [4] for conflicted requirements, but also let the controller drive the system to behave satisfying the PCTL specification as in [7].

2   CT-PPCTL*: A Logic of Conflict Tolerant Specification

PCTL* is a probabilistic variant of Computational Tree Logic, which can be used to denote quantitative stochastic quality of a system. The system can be modeled as discrete time Markov Decision Process. PCTL* includes state formula and path formula, and can be explained over the states and paths of the system. PCTL and LTL are sub-logic of PCTL*. LTL is the path-formula fragment of PCTL*, where atoms are atomic propositions, rather than arbitrary state formulas. LTL can be used to describe a sequence of events occurring with some logic relationships. PCTL can be used to denote the normal probability demand on the system. Since temporal logic with past is more succinct, more natural and easier than pure-future temporal logic [6], LTL with past is being paid more attention nowadays. In this paper, we will extend PCTL* to **PPCTL***, which let LTL extend to LTL with past operator (we will call it **PLTL** later). Similar work is [8], which extended CTL* logic with past operators.

Definition 1 (PPCTL*). The syntax of PPCTL* can be defined using state formula and path formula as follows:

$$\Phi ::= \mathrm{tt} \,|\, a \,|\, \neg\Phi \,|\, \Phi \wedge \Phi \,|\, P_{\infty p}(\varphi)$$

$$\varphi ::= \bot \,|\, a \,|\, \neg\varphi \,|\, \varphi \wedge \varphi \,|\, \varphi \vee \varphi \,|\, X\varphi \,|\, L\varphi \,|\, \varphi U\varphi \,|\, \varphi S\varphi$$

In above formulas, tt means true. For an alphabet Σ, $a \in \Sigma$. $\infty \in \{\leq, \geq\}$. $p \geq 0$ denotes a probability bound. Notice that PCTL formula does not include the operator L and S. Readers can obtain the semantics of the operators in PPCTL* in [8].

In PPCTL*, we use PLTL to denote conflict tolerant specification focusing on possible conflicted actions, and let PCTL denote the normal discrete time and probability demand on the system. Similar to [4], we can give the definition of CL-LTL with past operator, called it CT-PLTL. Naturally, we call it **CT-PPCTL*** for PCTL* while using CT-PLTL instead of PLTL.

3   The Controller Synthesis Problem for MDP of CT-PPCTL*

In an embedded control system, the system is driven by a series of events. We can classify them as "system" events and "environment" events. "System" events are controllable or system events, we use E_s represent their set. "Environment" events are uncontrollable events, always coming from environment, and we use E_e to denote their set. For the whole event set E, there exists $E = E_s \cup E_e$. In this context, we will first give a description for base system, and then adjust the normal definition of MDP, using Event Set instead of Action Set between states, and we can ignore the difference of the two notations later in section 5.

Definition 2 (base system). A base system is a finite-state transition system, which are driven by a sequence of events E, especially system events E_s interleaving with environment events E_e and $E = (E_s \cup E_e)$.

Definition 3 (MDP). A discrete time **Markov Decision Process** (MDP) M is a tuple (S, $Event$, P, s_{init}, AP, L) where S is a finite set of states, $Event$ is a finite set of events which are interleaved by system events and environment events, and $P : S \times Event \times S \rightarrow [0,1]$ is a transition probability matrix such that $\sum_{s' \in S} P(s, \alpha, s') \in \{0,1\}$ for all states $s \in S$ and events $\alpha \in Event(s)$, and s_{init} is the initial state in S. AP is a finite set of atomic propositions, and $L : S \rightarrow 2^{AP}$ a labeling function which assigns to each state $s \in S$ the set $L(s)$ of atomic propositions.

In a base system (a more strict definition is definition 2 of [4]), one always design a controller for one requirement or feature. While facing with more than one requirement and some of them are conflicted with each other, we can synthesis a total controller for the all requirements like [4].

In a MDP, from one state to the next, there may be several events occurring. Each event incurs a probabilistic distribution, which means that a state skip is going on at first one event must be occurred (or must be selected) according to a type of strategy, then a transition is performed probabilistically. For a given specification, such as from the initial states following some featured paths, whether the system safety can be assured with 99.9% in limited steps, we should judge if such a controller exists, and how we synthesis the controller if it exists.

In total, **the question** we want to solve is, given a specification expressed as CT-PPCTL* F under a probability bound p, and a probabilistic and nondeterministic system denoted as a discrete time Markov Decision Process (MDP) M, whether there exists a controller in the MDP satisfying the specification F, if does, synthesis one such controller.

4 Controller Synthesis for CT-PLTL on a Base System

In this section, we will at first transform PLTL to general buchi automaton and simplify Markov Decision Process to base system, secondly present the synthesized controller for base system over CT-PLTL and the conditions for its validation.

4.1 The Automaton Representing (a part of) the Conflict Tolerant Specification

There are several ways to translate PLTL to automaton [6, 9]. Here we adopt the method in [9], which translate PLTL to generalized Buchi Automaton (GBA) via progressing two-way very-weak alternating automata (2VWAA) efficiently.

Definition 4. A **Generalized Buchi Automaton (GBA)** is a six-tuple $G = < \Sigma, S, S_0, \delta, T, \Upsilon >$ where

— Σ is a finite alphabet,
— S is a finite set of states,
— $S_0 \subseteq S$ is a set of initial states,
— $\delta \subseteq S \times S$ is a transition relation,
— $T : S \to \Sigma$ is a labeling function,
— $\Upsilon = \{\Upsilon_1, ..., \Upsilon_k\} \subseteq 2^S$ is a set of accepting conditions, in which $\Gamma \in \Upsilon$ is an acceptance set and $|\Upsilon| > 1$.

In a GBA, the accepting conditions are defined by a set of sets of states. A run is accepted by the automaton if it visits at least one state of every set of the accepting condition infinitely often.

From [9], we can present the following theorem:

Theorem 1 (From PLTL to GBA). Given a PLTL formula φ, we can get for this formula a GBA G with at most $2^{|\varphi|+1}$ states.

In a GBA, the acceptance conditions imply which states the automaton will stay infinitely often there, so we can think them giving the final states of a GBA. In the context of conflict tolerant controller synthesis, a GBA can be considered as a normal formula automaton $\overline{G} = < \Sigma, S, S_0, \delta, T, F >$, where F represents the set of final states. So, we can think a GBA as a normal transition system, and can use $\overline{G}$ instead of G as the automaton transformed from PLTL in the following.

4.2 The Base System Transformed from MDP

For a given system $M = (S, Event, P, s_{init}, AP, L)$, while we ignore the element of probability in the system, we can obtain a concurrent transition system $N = (S, s_{init}, \to)$ over Σ, where $\to : S \times \alpha \times 2^S$ for $\alpha \in \Sigma$. Apparently, the transform of M to N do not change the events and the possible transitions from one state to its next in M.

4.3   The Synchronized Product of Two Transition Systems

Definition 5. For two transition systems $N_1 = (S_1, s_{init}^1, \rightarrow_1)$ and $N_2 = (S_2, s_{init}^2, \rightarrow_2)$ over Σ, the synchronized product $N_1 \parallel N_2$ of N_1 and N_2 can be defined as $((S_1 \times S_2), (s_{init}^1, s_{init}^2), \rightarrow)$ over Σ, where $((s_1, s_2), \alpha, (s_1', s_2')) \in \rightarrow$ iff $(s_1, \alpha, s_1') \in \rightarrow_1$ and $(s_2, \alpha, s_2') \in \rightarrow_2$.

4.4   The Form of Conflict Tolerant Controller

For a given system N, we can try to design a controller C to control the choice of possible next system events available to the base system. These system events maybe drive the system to act in conflict ways, which denoting as CT-PLTL. We call this kind of controller as conflict-tolerant controller. While conflicted actions should be adjudged, the controller choose the most proper action to take, in the meaning time, it also keeps track of the other actions not taken temporarily, and based on these to control the subsequent behavior of the system. We use conflict-tolerant transition system to model conflict tolerant controller as [4].

A conflict-tolerant transition system (CTTS) over an alphabet Σ is a tuple $N' = (N, \triangleright)$, where N is a transition system, $\triangleright \subseteq \rightarrow$ is a subset of transitions $\rightarrow$ representing the transitions occurred by the not-taken actions conflicted with the taken action.

4.5   The Synthesis and Verification Method for Conflict Tolerant Controller

According to [4], the synthesis and validation method for conflict tolerant controller is presented as follows briefly. Assume $\overline{G_i}$ is the automaton obtained from φ_i of CT-PLTL formula Ω as in the definition 2. Assume C_i is the synthesized controller by $\square(\varphi_i \Rightarrow \psi_i)$, then it can be denoted as:

$$C_i = (\overline{G_i}, \triangleright_i) \qquad (1)$$

where $\triangleright_i$ is defined as follows: let s, s' be states in $\overline{G_i}$ and $\alpha \in \Sigma$. Then $(s, \alpha, s') \in \triangleright_i$ iff $\alpha \urcorner \mapsto \psi_i$. The whole controller C for the system N over a conflict tolerant specification Ω is:

$$C = C_1 \parallel ... \parallel C_k \qquad (2)$$

To make sure if C is valid controller for N iff for every state (n, c) in $(N \parallel C)$, the following two conditions hold:

◆   C is non restricting: There does not exist an event $\lambda \in \Sigma_e$ such that λ is enabled at n in N but $(\lambda, 0) \urcorner \mapsto \wedge_{\varphi_i \in c} \psi_i$;   (3)

◆   C is non blocking: If there is an event $\lambda \in \Sigma$ which is enabled at n in N, then $(\lambda, 0) \mapsto \wedge_{\varphi_i \in c} \psi_i$.   (4)

5 The Controller Synthesis for Pruned MDP of PCTL

In this section, we use the validating conditions of the synthesized controller for the base system, to prune the system and obtain a subsystem. According to the subsystem, we can recover a new MDP as a part of original MDP according to the original one. Then we synthesize a controller for the new MDP over PCTL.

5.1 The Validation of Conflict Tolerant Controller and the Pruning of Base System

To test if the synthesized controller C is a valid controller for N, we need test every event λ in N using conditions (3) and (4) in section 4. In order to go further synthesizing a controller satisfying PCTL in original model MDP, it's a natural and delicious idea to prune N using these two conditions, then the obtained part is the one satisfying the CT-PLTL specification under the synthesized controller C.

5.2 The Controller Synthesis on MDP $\overline{M}$ with PCTL

In a MDP, a transition from one state to next state(s) is occurred by an event. We can regard that if a system is driven by a system event or an internal event in a state, then the system goes to a controllable state; oppositely, if it is driven by an environment event, it goes to an uncontrollable state.

Based on the original MDP M, we can recover a MDP $\overline{M}$ from $\overline{N}$. In fact, $\overline{M}$ is a sub-graph of M. According to [7], we can synthesize a controller C' for $\overline{M}$ over PCTL, a part of the whole specification CT-PCTL*. The whole controller is $\overline{C} = C \vee C'$.

6 Conclusion

In this paper, the controller synthesis for MDP over conflict tolerant specification is discussed. We use CT-PPCTL* to denote the whole specification, which lets CT-PLTL to denote the conflicted actions and PCTL the probability demands. We transform PLTL to formula automaton via general buchi automaton. After transforming a MDP to a base system, we obtain a basic controller. The process of making sure the synthesized controller is valid for the system, is skillfully arrived through pruning the original system using the controller. The whole controller is synthesized by further conjunction with the controller over PCTL on the pruned MDP.

In this paper, we don't extend PCTL by adding past time operator. In next step, we will try to do it as in [8] and study the controller synthesis problem over it on MDP.

Acknowledgments. This work is supported by National Natural Scientific Foundation of China (Grant No. 60873025), National High Technology Research and Development Program of China (Grant No. 2009AA010307) and NUAA Research Funding (Grant No. NS2010108).

References

1. Metzger, A.: Feature interactions in embedded control systems. Computer Networks 45(5), 625–644 (2004)
2. Bouma, L.G., Griffeth, N., Kimbler, K.: Feature Interactions in Telecommunications Systems. Computer Networks 32(4), 383–387 (2000)
3. D'Souza, D., Gopinathan, M.: Conflict-tolerant features. In: Gupta, A., Malik, S. (eds.) CAV 2008. LNCS, vol. 5123, pp. 227–239. Springer, Heidelberg (2008)
4. Divakaran, S., D'Souza, D., Mohan, M.R.: Conflict-Tolerant Specifications in Temporal Logic. In: ISEC 2010, Proceedings of the 3rd India Software Engineering Conference (2010)
5. Pantelic, V., Postma, S.M., Lawford, M.: Probabilistic supervisory control of probabilistic discrete event systems. IEEE Transactions on Automatic Control 54(8), 2013–2018 (2009)
6. Markey, N.: Temporal logic with past is exponentially more succinct. EATCS Bull 79, 122–128 (2003)
7. Baier, C., Größer, M., Leucker, M., Bollig, B., Ciesinski, F.: Controller synthesis for probabilistic systems. In: Proceedings of IFIP TCS 2004, pp. 493–506. Kluwer, Dordrecht (2004)
8. Reynolds, M.: An Axiomatization of PCTL*. Information and Computation 201(1), 72–119 (2005)
9. Gastin, P., Oddoux, D.: LTL with past and two-way very-weak alternating automata. In: Rovan, B., Vojtáš, P. (eds.) MFCS 2003. LNCS, vol. 2747, pp. 439–448. Springer, Heidelberg (2003)
10. Vardi, M.Y., Wolper, P.: Reasonning about infinite computations. Information and Computation 115(1), 1–37 (1994)

Embedded Ethernet-Based Measurement and Control System for Friction and Wear Testing Machines

Cheng-jun Chen[1], Xiao-peng Hu[2], and Niu Li[1]

[1] School of Mechanical Engineering, Qingdao Technological University,
Qingdao 266033 China
[2] Department of Information Engineering, Shandong Youth University of Political Science,
Jinan 250103 China

Abstract. Measurement and control system is main section of friction & wear testing machines. But current measurement and control systems have low versatility and high design cost. To solve these problems, this paper designed an Ethernet-based measurement and control system, which can be used in most types of friction & wear testing machines with a few modifications of programs. The DSP processor and touch screen system were successfully integrated into the presented measurement and control system. The functions and implementation processes of each module were introduced in detail, and a reconfigurable software system was designed according to ideas of virtual instruments theory.

Keywords: friction & wear testing machine, measurement and control system, embedded Ethernet, touch screen.

1 Introduction

Friction & wear testing machines are machines specially used for friction and wear test which purpose is to determine best friction-related parameters meeting special applications by studying the phenomenon essence of friction and wear [1, 2]. The friction and wear phenomenon is much more complex and friction and wear tests should be conducted under certain conditions according to various test methods, so different types of testing machines are needed. Measurement and control system is a key part of testing machines, which can achieve data collection, transmission and processing [3].

Most measurement and control systems of testing machines have similar functions and basically include three function modules. The first one is control function module, which is used to control test conditions (such as test load, speed, temperature and etc.) of friction and wear test within setting ranges. The second one is data collection module which is used to collect test parameters (including friction force or torque, speed, temperature and so on) in real-time. The last module is data processing module, used to calculate performance of friction & wear with data collected according to formulas corresponding to different testing methods.

The measurement and control system design includes hardware design and software design. The functions of hardware include: (1) analyzing and processing sensor signals to convert it to measurement values; (2) outputting control signals to control heater, load,

G. Shen and X. Huang (Eds.): ECWAC 2011, Part I, CCIS 143, pp. 291–297, 2011.

rotate speed and other servo systems. The functions of software are showing measurement values in real-time and dealing with data collected to generate a test report.

Aiming to reduce design cost and enhance versatility of measurement and control system, this paper designed an Ethernet-based measurement and control system suitable for conventional friction & wear testing machines. On hardware design, the presented system used DSP as processor and successfully integrated touch screen into system as user interface. On software, a reconfigurable software system was designed according to ideas of virtual instruments theory. Functions and implementation processes of each module were introduced in detail.

The reminder of this paper is organized as follows. Section 2 introduces the configuration of the presented measurement and control system for conventional friction & wear testing machines. Section 3 presents the details of hardware circuit design. Section 4 gives the communication interface design of touch screen system. Section 5 introduces the principles and methods of software design, and the last section gives the conclusions of this paper.

2   Software and Hardware Configuration of System

A measurement and control system for friction & wear testing machines can be divided into two parts namely hardware and software. Basic function modules are shown in Fig. 1. The hardware system, using TMS320LF2407 DSP as processor, includes analog signal input-output channels, pulse signal input-output channels and communication interfaces (such as serial communication interface and Ethernet communication interface). Data collecting software collects measurement values from hardware in

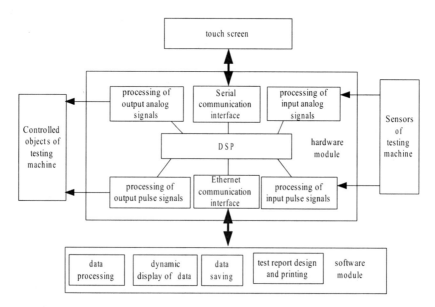

Fig. 1. Basic modules of testing machine

real-time via Ethernet interface, and displays data collected in designed virtual instruments. By automatically analyzing all data collected, a test report can be designed and generated automatically. Touch screen and hardware circuit can communicated with each other through RS232 serial communication interface by Modbus protocol, so the operator can control and watch the running states of testing machine on touch screen.

3 Hardware Circuit Design

The circuit includes input channels, output channels and communication interfaces. The input channels can read and process signals from sensors and convert them to measurement values, and output channels can output different types of signals which are used to control motor, heater or other servo systems. With communication interfaces, the measurement and control system can send or receive information to or from other devices.

3.1 Analog Signals Input and Output

Analog signals from the sensors should be converted into digital signals, which can be input into DSP. As the voltage of analog signals from sensors is every weak, it must be proceed by sequential amplifying, filtering and A/D conversion. To improve the versatility of the presented measurement and control system, this design used two-stage gain-controllable amplifier to amplify the sensor signals. The first amplifier used PGA202, which gain can be switched to 1,2,4,8 by programming. The second amplifier used PGA203, which gain can be switched to 1,10,100,1000 by programming. So the combination gain of the two- stage amplifier can be changed to 16 classes among 1-8000, which can meet the need of sensors with different output voltage.

In most cases, the signals measured (such as temperature, load, speed and so on) in friction & wear testing machines are low frequency signal, so classic low-pass filters were adopted in this design. The 24-bit precision A/D converter ADS1256 was used to convert 4 channel analog signals into digital signals in time-sharing manner. The connection diagram between DSP and ADS1256 is shown in Fig. 2(a), Input reference voltage of ADS1256 (VREFN and VREFP in Fig. 2 (a)) are connected to +2.5V and -2.5V respectively. Through serial peripheral interface protocol, the digital values can be transmitted to DSP for displaying and processing.

Output analog signals are to be used to control friction & wear testing conditions such as speed of servo motor, heater and loader. Analog signal output circuit includes a D/A converters and amplifiers. This design used 12-bit DAC7625 chip as the D/A converter. The connection diagram between DSP and DAC7625 is shown in Fig. 2(b), As reference voltage of DAC7625 are connected to +2.5 V and -2.5V respectively, the voltage of the output analog signals is be restricted within 2.5V and -2.5V. In order to meet the voltage requirements of different control system, this design used 4052-type analog multiplexer and AD623 amplifier to form a gain-programmable amplifier, With which, the output analog signals from DAC7625 can be amplified by 1,2,4 and 8 times.

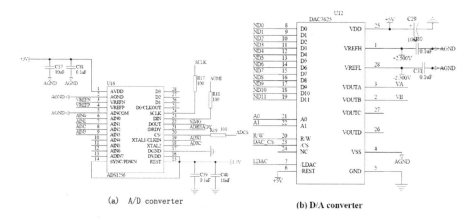

(a)   A/D converter

(b) D/A converter

Fig. 2. A /D and D/A converter interface

3.2   Ethernet Control Interface Design

With the development and popularity of network technologies, Ethernet interface becomes a popular communication interface for measurement and control systems [4]. This paper used highly-integrated Ethernet chip named RTL8019AS as Ethernet controller to design an embedded Ethernet-based measurement and control system. With the embedded Ethernet interface, data collected from sensor can be sent to the host computer by TCP/IP protocol for virtual instrument displaying. The connection diagram between DSP and RTL8019AS is shown in Fig. 3. In which, 20F001N is the twisted-pair driver/receiver, which was used for improving anti-jamming capability of Ethernet communication. On the right of 20F001N is a standard RJ45 Ethernet interface, which will be connected with RJ45 plug.

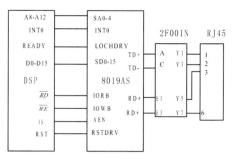

Fig. 3. DSP and 8019AS connection diagram

4   Touch Screen Interface Design

Touch Screen is a new man-machine interface, which not only can intuitively display a variety of parameters and states but also enable operators to modify parameters directly and conveniently. So it has been widely used in industry area [5]. This paper designed a touch screen system for testing machine, in which the touch screen was used as host, and hardware circuit was used as slave. Then a Modbus protocol-based asynchronous serial communication method between DSP and touch screen was realized.

Modbus protocol is a serial master-slave communication protocol which is widely used in industry measure and control area. It has two information transmission modes, namely ASCII mode and RTU mode. With the same baud rate, RTU mode can transmit more information than ASCII mode. So in application of this design, we hope to transmit more information within the same time interval, so the RTU mode was adopted. The basic communication unit of Modbus protocol is known as packets. Each packet includes three parts, namely packet header (such as address, command code and the number of bytes), data and Cyclic Redundancy Check (CRC). Table 1 shows the format of RTU packets.

Table 1. RTU packets format

Device address	Function code	Data	CRC
1 byte	1 byte	N bytes	2 bytes

Device address: Each slave machine has a unique device address code, which is used to receive information from host machine or send information to host machine. When a slave machine receives information, only information with its address code is validated. At the same time, information sent from slave machine to host must begin with its address code, so the host machine can recognize the source of information.

Function code: The function number of Modbus protocol can be defined with the code from 1 to 127. With function code, host machine can inform slave machine what to do, and slave machine can inform host machine what has been done according to the request of host machine.

Data area: Data area represents contents of command from host machine or contents of response from slave.

CRC: CRC can distinguish error messages transmitted between host and slave from right messages. So the data safety and effectiveness of communication can be enhanced.

Both DSP and touch screen used in this design do not provide Modbus protocol for communicating with each other. So in order to realize serial communication between touch screen and DSP, the Modbus protocol must be implemented in both touch screen and DSP. On touch screen, The Macro commands are used to implement Modbus protocol. On DSP, the Modbus protocol program is carefully coded using C language according to the workflow shown in Fig. 4.

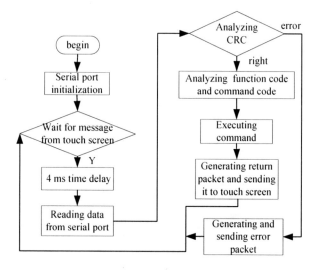

Fig. 4. Flowchart of Modbus protocol implementation on DSP

5   Software Design

In accordance with the theory of virtual instrument, this paper developed a measurement and control software using VC + + platform. A virtual oscillogram widget and some virtual instrument widgets were developed to display data collected in real-time. Meanwhile an application programming interface (API) for secondary development of EXCEL system was used to make the data can be saved in "excel"

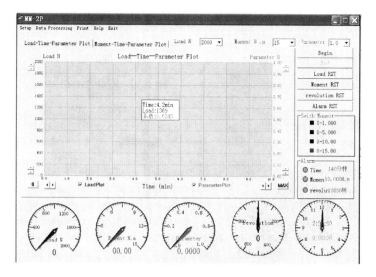

Fig. 5. Main graphic interface of the software

formats, so the operator can edit or analyze the data conveniently. One thing to be pointed out is that the data collected can also be saved in text and bitmap formats in the designed software. This design provides operators with a user interface to edit the template of test report in Excel at their pleasure. The main graphic interface of the software designed in this paper is shown in Fig. 5. The graphical interfaces of touch screen can be designed in special software named Screen Editor.

6 Conclusions

To reduce design cost and enhance the versatility of measurement and control system, this paper designed an Ethernet-based measurement and control system for friction & wear testing machines. The DSP processor and touch screen system were successfully integrated into the presented system. And a reconfigurable software system was designed according to ideas of virtual instrument theory. The hardware and software designed in this paper have been used in a number of friction & wear testing machines.

References

1. Ludema Kenneth, C.: Seventy years of research on wear. Achievements in Tribology (1), 111–127 (1990)
2. Wen, S.: Centurial Review and Prospect-The Development tendency of Tribology. Chinese Journal of Mechanical Engineering 36(6), 1–6 (2000)
3. Fan, J., Dai, Z., Jiang, C.: Development and Application of Multifunctional Wear Testing Machine. Journal of Nanjing University of Aeronautics & Astronautics 32(4), 405–409 (2000)
4. Fang, H., Fang, K.: The design of remote embedded monitoring system based on internet. In: 2010 International Conference on Measuring Technology and Mechatronics Automation, vol. 3, pp. 852–854 (2010)
5. Zhang, Z.-Q., Zhang, Y.-L.: Realization of communication between DSP and PC based on modbus protocol. In: 1st International Conference on Multimedia Information Networking and Security, vol. 2, pp. 258–261 (2009)

Research on a Photovoltaic Control System Scheme

Jiuhua Zhang

Department of Physics and Electrical Engineering,
Leshan Teachers College,
Leshan, China
LSTCWD@163.com

Abstract. This paper explains a small power photovoltaic control system based on PLD. And a new way is applied to trace the maximum power point based on the improved accelerating simplex method. The system perfects the management and protection for the charge and discharge of storage battery also for the load and solar power supply. It's very important part that the techniques of maximum power point tracking and islanding protecting, but also the technique for inverter to connected with grid are discussed at emphasis. This system scheme can be made use of in several photovoltaic products and obtain the satisfied result.

Keywords: photovoltaic, PLD, solar power, SPWM.

1 Introduction

In resent years, solar energy is especially concerned because of its high efficiency and free pollution. Many countries attach great importance to developing solar photovoltaic (PV) system. Solar PV system has more reliable ensure in stabilities and low running costs, and can work continuously compared with power grid. With the development of technology, solar power generation technology into people's daily life has become a reality. With the solar cell efficiency and reduction in the prices of PV systems, PV power generation increasingly wide range of applications and its market is getting bigger and bigger. So the PV power generation increasingly is showing the bright prospect. The core of photovoltaic system is logical link control that not only responsible for the entire system of state control but also ensure the safe operation of the system, at the same time it provides the necessary interface Human-Computer Interaction. Rational design of logical link control can ensure not the perfect process of electrification but the system life cycle. With the popularization of PLD in the field of electronics that high performance/price ration gradually exhibits its superiority. This paper mainly introduces the design of a small power photovoltaic control system based on PLD.

1.1 Checking the PDF File

Kindly assure that the Contact Volume Editor is given the name and email address of the contact author for your paper. The Contact Volume Editor uses these details to compile a list for our

G. Shen and X. Huang (Eds.): ECWAC 2011, Part I, CCIS 143, pp. 298–302, 2011.

production department at SPS in India. Once the files have been worked upon, SPS sends a copy of the final pdf of each paper to its contact author. The contact author is asked to check through the final pdf to make sure that no errors have crept in during the transfer or preparation of the files. This should not be seen as an opportunity to update or copyedit the papers, which is not possible due to time constraints. Only errors introduced during the preparation of the files will be corrected.

This round of checking takes place about two weeks after the files have been sent to the Editorial by the Contact Volume Editor, i.e., roughly seven weeks before the start of the conference for conference proceedings, or seven weeks before the volume leaves the printer's, for post-proceedings. If SPS does not receive a reply from a particular contact author, within the timeframe given, then it is presumed that the author has found no errors in the paper. The tight publication schedule of LNCS does not allow SPS to send reminders or search for alternative email addresses on the Internet.

In some cases, it is the Contact Volume Editor that checks all the pdfs. In such cases, the authors are not involved in the checking phase.

2   PV System Summary

The Grid-connected PV system is divided into two categories according to function: one is non-scheduling type without battery; another is schedulable type with battery. In this paper, the main research object is the latter. The schedulable Grid-connected PV system has significant expansion and improvement than the non-scheduling system in the way of function and performance. First, the core controller generally consists of two main parts - Grid inverter and battery charger. Its function is not only to be able to inverter DC after the transmission to the grid, but also to charge the battery. Second, the system is equipped with the main switch and an important load switches. When the AC power grid power is interrupted the core controller disconnect the grid main switch, but the important load switch remains closed so as to the DC power provided by solar arrays and batteries still supply important AC loads.

Generally, in PV system the control core is made up of DSP or SCM which disadvantage is that the whole system has more separate components and bad stability. In this paper, an alternative system architecture based on PLD is provided to replace the above-mentioned. PLD has many advantages such as large-capacity, high speed, low power consumption and so on, and the SCM or DSP controller core can be embedded in PLD. So PLD can greatly improve system integration, enhance system reliability, and reduce system cost.

3   PV System General Scheme Based PLD

As shown in Figure 1, the grad PV system is schedulable type, and its control core is PLD which complete all control and operation work. PLD unit consist of several modules: MCU, SPWM and data process, etc. In which MCU module is responsible for coordination throughout the system control, such as Human-Computer Interaction Information Processing, to control battery charging and discharging, to control SPWM and to process other emergencies; SPWM module's function is under the control of the MCU to generate SPWM signal, which is delivered to convertor to convert the DC from storage battery to AC, which can directly drive AC loads or be added to the power network after phase synchronization; Data process module is used to compute the parameter's value, which contains direct voltage, direct current, direct current power, storage battery charging and discharging state, power network phase, MPPT(maximum power point tracking), island monitoring, the system's total generated energy, etc.

This paper adopts the current control method based on SPWM, which can be gained through processing the sampling signal and can be used to drive the former MOSFET and the latter IGBT. The System's overall work process is relatively simple. The first is system initialization, which contains PWM initialization, capture initialization and A/D is initialized. And then the timer is started to enter the loop waiting for interrupts.

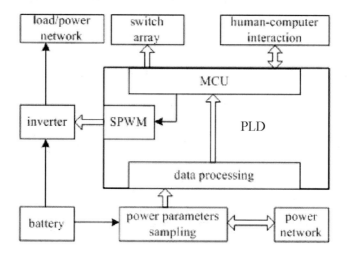

Fig. 1. System hardware architecture

3.1 Inverter Function Strategy

There are many ways to achieve inverter function in PV system, in which full-bridge method based on SPWM is usually adopted. The important link in this scheme is pulser and genlock, so the control system is relatively complex. There is also a relatively new control strategy that the power network voltage signal is used the given signal to trace current, and the sinusoidal output current in phase with the power network voltage can be gained.

3.2 AC Parameters Sample Strategy

The way of sampling AC parameters generally contains synchronous sampling, quasi-synchronous sampling, non-synchronous sampling, non-integer-period sampling, etc. Among them, synchronous sampling is also called interval the whole cycle of sampling, which contains hardware synchronous sampling and software synchronous and is a more common method to measure AC parameters. In this system software synchronous sample scheme is implemented through the MCU module which is the part of PLD. MCU measures the power network cycle through capturing level changing and Calculates the sampling time interval, and then gives the synchronous pulse to start sampling.

3.3 Grid-Connected Current Control Strategy

Controller's output current and the power grid must be in phase with the same frequency in order to achieve generation system's power is added to the power network safely. So this system adopts a control strategy which combines dual-loop phase-locked and synchronization. Inner loop phase control system is used to real-time track current. Outer loop phase control system is used to eliminate the error generated by inner control. Synchronous phase-locked loop is used to generate synchronized with the grid voltage reference current signal.

4 Conclusion

This paper presents a PV grid-connected control system scheme based on PLD, which expanded the scheme to build solar power generation system and can effectively control the battery charging and discharging and the power to be added to network. In addition, due to the PLD as the core building control system makes the system has more compact and simple structure, which improves the stability, while reducing power consumption.

Acknowledgments. This work is supported by important foundation of Leshan Teachers College(No. Z0909) and the Science and Technology of Leshan Town(No. 10GXP037).

References

1. Smith, T.F., Waterman, M.S.: Identification of Common Molecular Subsequences. J. Mol. Biol. 147, 195–197 (1981)
2. Koutroulis, E., Kalaitzakis, K.: Development of a Microcont roller-Based Photovoltaic Maximum Power Point Tracking Control System. IEEE Trans. Power Electronics 16(1), 46–54 (2001)
3. Ikegami, T., et al.: Estimation of equivalent circuit parameters module and its application to optimal of PV system. Solar Energy Materials&Solar Cells 67, 389–395 (2001)
4. Tse, K.K., et al.: A Comparative Study of Maximum Power Point Tracker for Photovoltaic Panel Using Switching Frequency Modulation Scheme. IEEE Trans. and Electron 51(2), 410–418 (2004)
5. Veeraehary, M., et al.: Feed forward maximum Power Point tracking of PV systems using fuzzy controller. IEEE Trans. Aerosp. Electron System 38(3), 969–981 (2002)
6. Buso, S., Fasolo, S., Malesani, L.: A dead-beat adaptive hysteresis current control. IEEE Transactions on Industry Applications 36, 1174–1180 (2000)

7. Sharaf, A.M.: A Low Cost Stand Alone PV Scheme for Motorized Hybrid Loads System Theory. In: Proceedings of the Thirty-Sixth Southeastern Symposium, pp.175–179 (2004)
8. Guo, K., Chang, C.: Automatic Phase-Shift Method for Islanding Detection of Grid-connected Photovoltaic Inverters. IEEE Transactions on Energy Conversion 18, 169–173 (2003)
9. Kuo, Y.C., Liang, T.J., Chen, J.F.: Novel Maximum Power Point Tracking Controller for Photovoltaic Energy Conversion System. IEEE Trans Industrial Electronics 48, 594–601 (2001)

A New Approach to the Provision
of Non-simple Node-Protecting p-Cycles
in WDM Mesh Networks

Honghui Li[1,2], Brigitte Jaumard[2], and Xueliang Fu[1]

[1] CCIE, Inner Mongolia Agricultural University,
Hohhot, Inner Mongolia, 010018, P.R. China
[2] CSE, Concordia University, Montreal, Qc, H3G 1M8, Canada

Abstract. This paper proposed a new approach to the provision of nonsimple node-protecting p-cycles in survivable WDM mesh networks. The traditional designs of non-simple p-cycles model the problem as an Integer Linear Program (ILP), and require the pre-enumeration of all possible p-cycles. The resulting ILP becomes less tractable for a large network because there may exist a huge number of p-cycles. We proposed a new solution method using large scale optimization tools, i.e., Column Generation (CG). With CG, p-cycles are generated dynamically when needed. Numerical results show clearly that our new proposed method has a big advantage over the existing one in the capacity efficiency.

Keywords: Non-simple p-cycles, node protection.

1 Introduction

Survivability is a paramount requirement for WDM mesh networks. To ensure the survivability, all kinds of protection approaches have been proposed. Among them, p-cycles [1] are most attractive thanks to its exclusive properties, i.e., ring-like recovery speed and mesh-like capacity efficiency. A large number of studies have been done on the design of p-cycles. However, most of studies deal with a single link failure; only a few studies investigate node protection. Node-encircling p-cycles are proposed in [2] for node protection. An enhanced APS protocol is present in [3] to provide methods of node protection with p-cycles. The authors in [4] proposed a two-hop-segment strategy for node protection using p-cycleswhile retaining the simplicity of the operation. All of these studies are all based on simple p-cycles for node protection.

Non-simple p-cycles are proposed in [5] which can visit an on-cycle node or link more than one time. Here we only consider non-simple p-cycles which can only go through an on-cycle node multiple times because we consider an undirected network. Non-simple p-cycles can be of a great interest for node protection based on the two-hop-segment strategy for efficiently use spare capacity.

The conventional way to design non-simple node-protecting p-cycles is to model the problem as Integer Linear Program (ILP). The associated solution methods require the pre-enumeration of all possible p-cycle candidates. Then, the resulting ILP becomes less tractable for a large network instance where a large number of p-cycles may exist. On the other hand, the solution quality may not be guaranteed if only a

G. Shen and X. Huang (Eds.): ECWAC 2011, Part I, CCIS 143, pp. 303–308, 2011.

subset of candidates is considered. A scalable approach is proposed in [6] where candidates are generation dynamically when needed. However, the design in [6] is restricted which only allows a non-simple p-cycle to protect one affected working path from a single node failure.

In this paper, we propose a new design approach to the provision of nonsimple p-cycles for node protection. The objective is to minimize the spare capacity cost in such a way that a WDM mesh network can survive from a single failure of a link or a node. Note that for a node failure, only the working paths passing through the node are considered for recovery. In contrast with the design in [6], our new proposed design approach enable a p-cycle to recover multiple simultaneously disrupted working paths against a single node failure as long as the associated protection paths are disjoint (see Section 2). We also develop a new design method using large scale optimization tools, namely, Column Generation (CG). With CG, our approach generates p-cycle candidates on-line when needed in the course of the optimization process.

The rest of the paper is organized as follows. Section 2 illustrates the new proposed design of non-simple p-cycles for node protection. In Section 3, a CG model is developed for the provision of non-simple node-protecting p-cycles. Simulation results are present in Section 4. Conclusions are drawn in Section 5.

2 Non-simple Node-Protecting p-Cycles

The authors in [4] proposed a two-hop-segment strategy for node protection with p-cycles. A 2-hop segment of a path consists in the two links which are on the path and are adjacent to the relay node of the path. If the two end nodes of a 2-hop segment sit on the same p-cycle as each other, then this p-cycle can protect the related path against the failure of the relay node. If the relay node sit on the same p-cycle as its end nodes of the 2-hop segment, the p-cycle provides one protection path; otherwise, the p-cycle provides two protection paths. In the same way, non-simple p-cycles can also be used for node protection.

Fig. 1 illustrates non-simple p-cycles for node protection. Fig. 1(a) shows an example network with three demands routed on paths w_1, w_2 and w_3, respectively. Fig. 1(b) shows an optimal solution of the design [6]. Upon the failure of node A, end nodes B and D of the path w_1 switch the traffic to the protection path D-E-C-B on the p-cycle c_1. The design in [6] only allows a non-simple p-cycle to protect ONE affected working path from a node failure. Thus, two pcycles c_1 and c_2 are required to protect paths w_2 and w_3 from the failure of node E. The spare capacity usage is nine units, and the redundancy is $9 \div 6 = 150\%$.

2.1 A New Design Approach

The new proposed design enables a non-simple p-cycle protect multiple affected working paths against the single node failure only if the associated protection paths are link disjoint. An optimal solution of the new design is present in Fig. 1(c). Only one p-cycle c_1 is employed to protect all traffic against a single failure. Upon the failure of node E, protection paths A-D and B-C on c_1 are available to reroute the affected paths w_2 and w_3 respectively. The spare capacity usage is six units, and the redundancy is $6 \div 6 = 100\%$. Obviously, the new design can achieve a big improvement in capacity efficiency over the existing one.

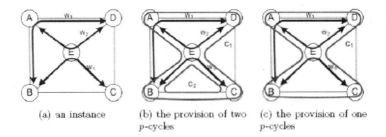

(a) an instance (b) the provision of two *p*-cycles (c) the provision of one *p*-cycles

Fig. 1. Link and node protection of *p*-cycles

3 A Column Generation Model

A WDM mesh network considered is represented by a graph $G = (V, L)$, where V and L denotes the set of all nodes and all links, indexed by v and ℓ, respectively. Let ω_ℓ be the traffic load on link $\ell \in L$. For a given demand carried on a working path $p \in P$, let w_p be the number of connection requests in the bundle, and V_p be the relay-node set of the path.

In the design of non-simple node-protecting *p*-cycles [6], a *p*-cycle is only used to recover one affected working path upon a node failure. In contrast with this design, our design enable a *p*-cycle to protect multiple simultaneously affected working paths through the failed node as long as the associated working paths are link disjoint. We propose an optimization method based on a large scale optimization tool, i.e., column generation (CG) for the provision of non-simple *p*-cycles. The objective is to minimize the spare capacity utilization such that 100% survivability can be guaranteed against a single failure of a node or a link. With CG, our proposed optimization method generates non-simple nodeprotecting *p*-cycles when needed in the course of the optimization process. Then, the design problem is decomposed into two subproblems: the master problem and the pricing problem. The master problem calculates an optimal solution using the *p*-cycles, each of which is generated dynamically by the pricing problem at each iteration of the CG algorithm.

3.1 The Master Problem

The master problem takes care of selecting candidates for protecting against a single failure. The objective is to minimize the total spare capacity usage.

Candidates are associated with the configuration set C. A configuration c consists in a non-simple *p*-cycle that protects a set of links and a set of the relay nodes of working paths. A configuration c is associated with a vector $(a_\ell^c)_{\ell \in L}$ and a matrix $(a_{pv}^c)_{p \in P, v \in V_p}$. The element $a_\ell^c \in \{2, 1, 0\}$ denotes the number of protection paths for link ℓ provided by the configuration c. a_ℓ^c is 2 if the link ℓ is the straddling link of the current non-simple *p*-cycle c; 1 if the link ℓ is the on-cycle link; 0 otherwise. The element $a_{pv}^c \in \{2, 1, 0\}$ represents the number of protection paths provided by non-simple *p*-cycle c for the relay-node v of working path p. Let COST^c be the spare capacity cost of the configuration c, which relies on the cost of on-cycle links.

Variables z^c denotes the number of copies of configuration c that are selected in the current solution. The mathematical model can then be written as follows.

$$\min \quad \sum_{c \in C} \text{COST}^c \, z^c$$

$$\text{subject to:} \quad \sum_{c \in C} a_\ell^c \, z^c \geq w_\ell \qquad \ell \in L \tag{1}$$

$$\sum_{c \in C} a_{pv}^c \, z^c \geq w_p \qquad p \in P, \; v \in V_p \tag{2}$$

$$z^c \in \mathbb{Z}^+ \qquad c \in C \tag{3}$$

Constraints (1) ensure that all traffic units are protected against a single link failure. Constraints (2) ensure that all demands are protected against a single node failure. (Note that only the associated relay-node failure is considered here.) Constraints (3) are variable domain constraints.

3.2 The Pricing Problem

The pricing problem corresponds to the optimization problem with the objective of minimizing the so-called reduced cost of the master problem. The reduced cost can be written as follows.

$$\overline{\text{COST}^c} = \text{COST}^c - \sum_{\ell \in L} u_\ell^1 \, a_\ell^c - \sum_{p \in P} \sum_{v \in V_p} u_{pv} \, a_{pv}^c$$

where u_ℓ and u_{pv} are dual variables associated with constraints (1) and (2) respectively.

The pricing problem includes the two parts of constraints. The first part defines a non-simple p-cycle, and identifies the protected on-cycle links and straddling links. The second part of the constraints is used for determining a set of working paths protected against the associated relay-node failure by the cycle satisfying the first part of the constraints. Due to the space limitation, the detailed constraints of the pricing problem are omitted.

4 Experimental results

Extensive experiments have been carried out on four network instances for evaluation and comparison. We compared our proposed design approach (NPC-MUL) with the one (NPC-UNI) in [6]. There, non-simple p-cycles are also exploited for full node protection. The designs NPC-MUL and NPC-UNI were all implemented in C++ and were solved by CPLEX 11.0.1 MIP solver.

4.1 Data Instances

The network instances are presented in Table 1. For each instance, the table presents network name for reference, the number of nodes, the number of links, average nodal degree for approximately representing connectivity. Moreover, the table presents the number of demand relations and working capacity usage (the number of wavelength channels) for each instance. Each demand relation is routed a priori on the shortest path.

Table 1. Network Instances

Networks	Nodes	Edges	Node Degree	Num. Demands	Working Cost
GERMANY [4]	17	26	3.1	136	4050
BELLCORE [4]	15	28	3.7	105	2610
NJ LATA [7]	11	23	4.2	55	943
COST239 [4]	11	26	4.7	55	792

4.2 Numerical Comparisons

In Fig. 2(a), we present the comparisons of the capacity redundancy of NPCUNI with NPC-MUL over four network instances. The capacity redundancy is defined as the ratio of the spare capacity cost over the working capacity cost. We can observe clearly that NPC-MUL is much more capacity efficient (less capacity redundant) than NPC-UNI. The differences of the capacity redundancy range from ~8% to ~29%. The differences of the redundancy between NPC-UNI and NPC-MUL become larger with the increase of the network density.

Fig. 2(b) shows the average size of the solutions of NPC-UNI versus NPCMUL, which are measured as the average number of on-cycle links. For each network, in general, the average length of the p-cycles calculated by NPC-MUL is longer than NPC-UNI. The larger the p-cycle is, the more likely it is to enable working paths share the protection path against a single node failure. Thus, the resulting solutions are more capacity efficient.

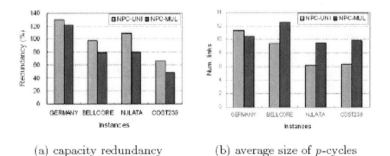

(a) capacity redundancy   (b) average size of p-cycles

Fig. 2. Solution performances: NPC-UNI vs. NPC-MUL

5 Conclusion

This paper investigates the provision of non-simple p-cycles for node protection in WDM mesh networks. The new proposed design method enable a non-simple p-cycle to protect multiple simultaneously failed working paths from a node failure as long as the associated protection paths are disjoint. We cope with the scalability issue using large scale optimization tools, i.e., Column Generation (CG). In contrast with the traditional non-simple p-cycle designs, our new proposed CG-based method calculates the promising set of p-cycle candidates on-line when needed. Extensive experiments have been conducted on four network instances. Numerical results show clearly that our proposed design method outperforms the existing one in terms of capacity efficiency.

References

1. Grover, W., Stamatelakis, D.: Cycle-oriented distributed preconfiguration: ringlike speed with mesh-like capacity for self-planning network restoration. In: IEEE International Conference on Communications - ICC, vol. 1, pp. 537–543 (June 1998)
2. Stamatelakis, D., Grover, W.D.: IP layer restoration and network planning based on virtual protection cycles. IEEE Journal on Selected Areas in Communications 18, 1938–1949 (2000)
3. Schupke, D.A.: Automatic protection switching for p-cycless in WDM networks. Optical Switching and Networking 2(1), 35–48 (2005)
4. Grover, W., Onguetou, D.: A new approach to node-failure protection with span protecting p-cycles. In: 11th International Conference on Transparent Optical Networks, pp. 1–5 (July 2009)
5. Gruber, C.: Resilient networks with non-simple p-cycles. In: Proceedings of International Conference on Telecommunication (ICT 2003), vol. 2, pp. 1027–1032 (2003)
6. Li, H., Jaumard, B., Fu., X.: Addressing node protection using non-simple p-cycles in survivable wdm mesh networks. In: The 9th International Conference on Optical Communications and Networks (ICOCN 2010), pp. 1–5 (October 2010)
7. Yoo, Y., Ahn, S., Kim, C.S.: Adaptive routing considering the number of available wavelengths inWDM networks. IEEE Journal on Selected Areas in Communications 21(8), 1263–1273 (2003)

Research about Memory Detection Based on the Embedded Platform

Hao Sun[1] and Jian Chu[2]

[1] School of Automation and Electrical Engineering
[2] Tianjin University of Technology and Education
Tianjin, China
sunhao.27@163.com

Abstract. As is known to us all, the resources of memory detection of the embedded systems are very limited. Taking the Linux-based embedded arm as platform, this article puts forward two efficient memory detection technologies according to the characteristics of the embedded software. Especially for the programs which need specific libraries, the article puts forwards portable memory detection methods to help program designers to reduce human errors, improve programming quality and therefore make better use of the valuable embedded memory resource.

Keywords: memory detection, embedded, arm, Linux.

1 Summary

With the development of software and hardware technologies, the embedded systems have been widely used in our daily life. More and more people go in for the development of the embedded products. As one of the core techniques in the embedded systems, embedded software has more requirements about reliability and stability, which are very important to the embedded memory in the designing process.

As a result of the wide use of Linux operating system, this article provides some memory test methods in connection with the embedded arm platform and some practical examples.

2 Introduction of Memory Problems

The incorrect use of the memory is one common problem in program developments. The mistakes may bring us many unpredictable problems when we are going on code debugging, and we may also waste much of our time to deal with the mistakes. Among the mistakes, heap corruption and memory leak are the two main ones.

2.1 MemoryLeak

Memory leak means that we don't us some memories because the programs fail to be released due to our negligence and mistakes. It doesn't mean the physical disappearance

G. Shen and X. Huang (Eds.): ECWAC 2011, Part I, CCIS 143, pp. 309–314, 2011.

of memory. It refers to the waste of memory because of the lack of some memory control resulting from our design mistakes.

Memory leak may impair the computer quality because it can reduce the available memory. In the worst case, the excessive loss of the available memory may lead the whole equipment or part of the equipment to stop work or lead to the application breakage.

2.2 Heap Corruption

Heap Corruption means when the memory input exceeds the pre-allocated space, it will cover the latter period of storage area, which may cause the system to be abnormal. There are many unusual phenomena, for example, codes suddenly perform in irrelevant area, access exceptionally or provide wrong data in normal operation, and so on.

2.3 Memory Detection Methods

With regard to memory leak and heap corruption, there are many memory detection tools that can help program designers to find out more memory problems. Therefore we can improve our efficiency of product development with time saved. However, the embedded memory detection tools are still few at the moment. In connection with the codes to be performed on the embedded arm platform, this article provides two relative methods, as follows:

(1) To test the codes independent of a specific library or platform, it's required to compile the codes into the executable file in the PC. First, use the PC memory detection tools to detect the codes, and then cross-compile the debugged modes into the executable file of the arm platform;

(2) During the software development, the written programs often rely on manufactures to provide the compiled library files based on a specific platform. In this case, we can only use the memory detection technologies which are not related to the platform instead of the first method.

3 Memory Detection Tools based on Linux

In terms of the first case 2.3, one memory detection tool based on Linux in the PC is just enough. The open source software-Valgrind is adopted in this article.

3.1 Introduction of Valgrind

Valgrind is a highly modular suite of Linux-based program debugger and parser software. It runs on the following platforms: X86/Linux, AMD64/Linux, PPC32/Linux, PPC64/Linux, and X86/Darwin (Mac OS X). Valgrind contains a core that provides a virtual CPU running the program and a series of tools, which you can use to run your program to monitor the memory use of the compiled binaries in its environment, thus completing the testing, analysis and other similar tasks.

Valgrind has a great function. It can detect most of the relative memory leaks and heap corruptions, especially the followings:

(1) Use of uninitialized memory;
(2) Reading/writing memory after it has been freed;
(3) Reading/writing off the end of malloc'd blocks;
(4) Reading/writing inappropriate areas on the stack;
(5) Memory leaks -- where pointers to malloc'd blocks are lost forever;
(6) Mismatched use of malloc/new/new [] vs free/delete/delete [];
(7) Overlapping src and dst pointers in memcpy () and related functions.

3.2 Memory Detecting Process of Valgrind

(1) For more information about Valgrind installation process, see Reference [3].
(2) To edit files in the computer, as shown in Fig. 1:
(3) Execute the following command; executable file-valtest can be generated now

```
[root@localhost valgrind]# gcc memtest.c -g -o valtest
```

(4) Using Valgrind tools for code testing

```
[root@localhost valgrind]# ./valgrind \
> --tool=memcheck --leak-check=yes ./valtest
```

Then the test results will appear on the screen. You can also add ---log-file parameter, and output the test results into the specified file.

```
root@localhost:/memcheck/mmutest
File  Edit  View  Terminal  Tabs  Help
[root@localhost mmutest]# ls
memtest.c   memwatch.c   memwatch.h
[root@localhost mmutest]# cat memtest.c
#include <stdio.h>
#include <stdlib.h>
#include "memwatch.h"

void main(void)
{
        char *p;
        p = malloc(210);
        free(p);
        p = malloc(20);
        p = malloc(200);        /* causes unfreed error */
        p[-1] = 0;              /* causes underflow error */
        free(p);
}
[root@localhost mmutest]#
```

Fig. 1.

3.3 Cautions for Valgrind

(1) Valgrind supports a number of tools: memcheck, addrcheck, cachegrind, massif, helgrind and callgrind, etc. When running Valgrind, you must specify which tools to use. For example, use the following parameters:

> ---tool=memcheck: use memcheck to analyze the programs

Regardless of which tool t use, valgrind will always obtain your control of the programs before starting them and read the debugged information from the executable library association .And then run the programs in a virtual CPU provided by valgrind. Valgrind will deal with the codes according to the chosen tools which can add test codes into the codes and return the codes to Valgrind core as the final codes. At last, Valgrind core runs these codes.

(2) Some compiler optimization options (eg-O2 or higher optimization options) may make the wrong uninitialized memcheck reports submitted. Therefore, in order to make Valgrind reports more precise, it's better not to use the optimization options.

(3) If the program is started by the script, modify the code in the boot, or use parameter option -trace-children=yes to run the script.

3.4 Description of Valgrind's Porting to Arm Platform

Valgrind is a powerful tool for memory testing. Unfortunately, Valgrind does not currently support arm structure, but there is a brief porting description of the documents from the source files such as ../docs/internals/porting-to-ARM.txt, which we can use for reference.

The following is a Valgrind-based memory detection method that introduces porting to arm platform. It can be used to detect memory leaks and help improve program development efficiency, although it's not as powerful as Valgrind.

4   Portable Memory Detection

Memcheck is an open source memory error detection tool. It provides results, logs and records and can detect double-free, erroneous free, unfreed memory, overflow and underflow and so on. Memwatch is free from platform restrictions, and can be ported on different platforms. It is just a set of C codes, without requirement of installation, so when compiling the program, just links it.

4.1 Porting Method of Memcheck

(1) Download the source file memwatch-2.71.tar.gz

(2) Use the following command to extract

```
[root@localhost memcheck]# \
> tar -zxvf memwatch-2.71.tar.gz

[root@localhost memcheck]# ls
memwatch-2.71  memwatch-2.71.tar.gz
```

(3) Edit the source file memtest.c which is to be tested in the PC, and copy memwatch.c and memwatch.h files from memwatch-2.71 .As shown in Fig 1.

(4) Run the following command

```
[root@localhost mmutest]# arm-linux-gcc -o memtest \
> -DMEMWATCH -DMW_STDIO memtest.c memwatch.c
```

Then the executable file -memtest is generated on the arm platform.

```
[root@localhost mmutest]# ls
memtest memtest.c memwatch.c memwatch.h
[root@localhost mmutest]# file memtest
memtest: ELF 32-bit LSB executable, ARM, version 1 (ARM),
dynamically linked (uses shared libs), not stripped
```

(5) Copy the executable file memtest into the arm development board, and run
     ./memtest.

       Then memwatch.log document is generated which can record memory prob-
     lems in this process, as shown in Fig. 2:

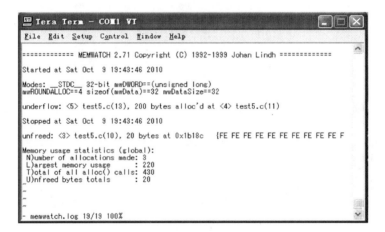

Fig. 2.

4.2 Analyze Log Files

Memwatch.log contains the following parts:

(1) Test date;
(2) Information of status collector;
(3) Use the output function of MemWatch or macro (such as TRACE, etc.);
(4) The wrong information captured by MemWatch ;
(5) The whole information about memory use includes four parts: ①The number of
     memory allocation; ②Maximum memory usage; ③The amount of memory
     allocated; ④The amount of Memory for the release.

4.3 The Operation Instructions of Memcheck

As memwatch requires no special configuration and installation, it will be able to show clearly the location of memory leaks and memory size by the generated logs. So memwatch can provide the memory test for all the codes ported to arm platform, but it also has some disadvantages:

(1) It will slow down the speed of the program, especially when it releases the memory for a large number of checks;
(2) It mainly detects the memory leak, but can not detect the heap corruption.

5 Summary

Embedded systems resources are relatively limited. The importance of memory resources is out of question. How to use the limited memory to the fullest becomes programmers' key problem. The memory leak and the heap corruption which tend to be different to be detected are the two common problems during memory processing.

This article discusses the two arm-based embedded memory testing methods, which greatly simplify the testing process and identify memory problems, therefore improving software development efficiency. And because the second method has portable quality, it makes the memory test of the codes that are to be ported on the arm platform possible.

References

1. Wang, X., Wang, Z., Sun, Y., Liu, Y., Zhang, B., Luo, Y.: Detecting Memory Leak Via VMM. Chinese Journal of Computers 33(3) (2010)
2. Wang, Y., Zeng, Q.: Dynamic Approach to Detecting Memory Errors. Application Research of Computers (May 2008)
3. Pan, Z., Tong, W., Zhou, Z.: Debug Technology of Embedded Program based on Valgrind. Microcomputer Information (May 2009)
4. Qin, F., Lu, S., Zhou, Y.: SafeMem: Exploiting ECC memory for detecting memory leaks and memory corruption during production runs. In: Proceedings of the HPCA 2005, San Franciso, USA, pp. 391–302 (2005)

An Algorithm of Semi-structured Data Scheme Extraction Based on OEM Model

An Gong and Xue-wei Yang

College of Computer and Communication Engineering,
China University of Petroleum (East China),
Dongying, 257061
gongan0328@sina.com, yangxuewei.com@126.com

Abstract. In order to get the target model of semi-structured data rapidly, effectively and accurately, by combining the related nature of label path in the paper, this paper proposes an algorithm that can extract target model from the OEM model of semi-structured data directly. The basic idea of the Algorithm is: Using a Depth_First Search to get all of the label path expressions, with the help of the nature2 in this paper can reducing the number of path matching, we can generate all frequent label path expressions by layer. Finally, with the strategy of deletion we can get all of the longest frequent label path expressions effectively. Theoretical analysis and Experimental result shows that this algorithm can improve the accuracy of target model and reduce the size of candidate sets in pattern extraction.

Keywords: Semi-structured data, frequent patterns mining, OEM, the longest frequent label path.

1 Introduction

With the development of the network technology and its maturity, rapid growth of the Web data, E-commerce and the application of heterogeneous data integration, there generated a lot of semi-structured data. Semi-structured data is a type of self-descriptive data between structure-less natural raw data (such as voice, image files) and traditional database with strictly structured data [1]. The structure of Semi-structured data is hidden, irregular, lack of strict type constraints, and dynamic variable. Therefore, lack of a predictable, clear and fixed external schema that is separated from data store, which leads to inefficiency in querying, optimizing and integration of Web data. Therefore, it was hoped that Web data can be operated effectively by data structures just as conventional database, and we can found the data structure and the relationship between data objects of Semi-structured data. So it needs a technique to extract the structural pattern from semi-structured data, which is named as scheme extraction. In order to extract scheme from semi-structured data, the foremost problem is to describe semi-structured data. OEM (Object Exchange Model) model which is based on graph is a classic way of describing semi-structured data, and it provides a tool and carrier for semi-structured data.

G. Shen and X. Huang (Eds.): ECWAC 2011, Part I, CCIS 143, pp. 315–319, 2011.

2 The Basic Concepts, Definitions and Nature of OEM Model

The OEM model (which can contain ring) was proposed by professor Papakonstanti-nou of Stanford University, it has nests and tags, and a main feature of OEM is that it is self-describing object exchange model, we need not define in advance the structure of an object, and there is no notion of a fixed schema or object class [2], it was de-signed for the expression of semi-structured data, and it is very useful in integration of heterogeneous data sources. The model which consists of object vertices and directed edge labels can be viewed as a directed graph. Each vertex represents a data object, and the label represents the level of reference between the two vertices. In this paper, we adopt OEM example model form literature [3] to illustrate related concepts and algorithms.

2.1 The Relevant Natures of OEM Model

Nature 1. lp is a frequent label path expression, but if there is a frequent label path expression lp1 which contains lp, then the lp is not a maximal frequent label path expression [5].

In order to reduce the number of matching label path expression and improve the efficiency of the algorithm, in this paper we propose nature 2.

Nature 2. In the OEM graph, there is a label path $lp= l_1,l_2,...,l_n$, if $sup(l_n)<$ min_sup(the support of l_n which is the n-layer label of lp),then also the support of lp $sup(lp) <$ min_sup.

2.2 Scheme Extraction

The aim of Scheme extraction is to get the target model of semi-structured data and find the relationship among data objects, so we are more interested in label which links object and its child objects than the object itself. Simple path expression is cho-sen over data path dp. This is because the former better reflects the general structure of semi-structured data, while the latter node is associated with object node and can only reflect the local characteristics of data. A label path expression can describe the relationship among data objects, so in order to find communal and complete internal structure, Scheme extraction needs to find out the entire longest frequent label path expressions (lflp) form semi-structured, the set of all of the longest frequent label path expressions in OEM is defined as target model.

3 Analysis of Related Work

Literature [4] [5] exist two serious problems: produced a large number of candidate sets and needed to scan the database repeatedly.

Literature [6] used MFRO (Minimal Full Representative Objects) to succinctly ex-press semi-structured hierarchical data schema. But the schema is too large and ex-tremely time-consuming.

All of the literatures used the pruning strategy which based on Apriori nature- Nature 1.Used Apriori nature to prune in two ways: method 1 saw OEM model diagram as a transaction database, it used Apriori nature top-down to prune strategy. Method 2 generated the longest frequent label path expression from the OEM model directly, if the support of label path (lp) is less than min_sup, then it deleted all of the supersets of lp. But used the nature of Apriori to prune did not apply to the OEM which its branch paths contain the same label. If used method 1 to prune, it leads to count repeatedly. If used method 2 to prune, it can not extract the target mode accurately. Therefore, this paper presents an algorithm of semi-structured scheme extraction; it can address the following issues effectively:

① How to resolve problem of the impact by branching path effectively?
② How to select an efficient prune strategy to improve the accuracy of scheme extraction?
③ How to reduce the number of scanning database and the size of candidate sets?

4   Algorithm for Scheme Extraction

4.1   The Storage Structure of OEM Model

In order to find out all of the longest frequent label path expressions (lflp) directly by using a Depth-first traversal strategy, this paper uses variant adjacency list to store OEM model, the structure of head node and arc of adjacency list shown in Figure 1:

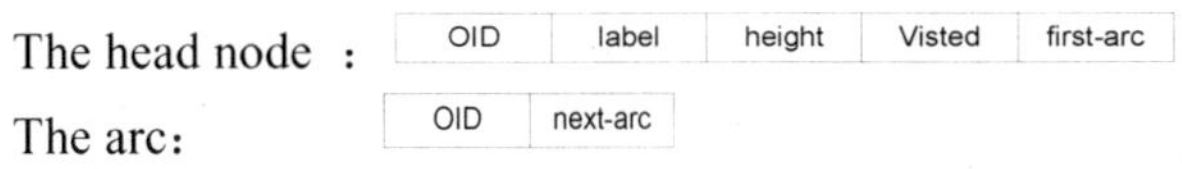

The head node : | OID | label | height | Visted | first-arc |

The arc: | OID | next-arc |

Fig. 1. The structure of head node and arc

The head node, OID is the object identity (object-id); label is a label which points to OID; height is the height-storey of OID; Visited is a mark of visit; first-arc is a pointer which points to the first arc form vertex OID.The arc, OID is the object-id of vertex which leads from this arc; next-arc is a pointer which points to the next arc.

4.2   The Thread of Scheme Extraction Algorithm

Because the hierarchy of OEM model, so we use a Depth-first traversal strategy since the root node from short to long to get all the label path expressions serially, then according to the min_sup which was set by the user and using the Nature 2 to reduce the number of path matching, then deleting all non-frequent label path expressions. Finally, using the Nature1 to judge whether label path lp is a subset of other label paths and get all the longest frequent label path expressions. The specific thread of Scheme extraction algorithm as follows:

① Using a Depth-first traversal strategy to traversal OEM model and deal with loop path, marking the height of each node from top to down by the layer, the root node as the first layer, Obtaining all the label path expressions from the root node to each layer. lp_{hi} is a label path expression of layer (h) ($1<h\leq n$, $i\geq1$), n is the height of OEM model which through loop handle. The approach to deal with loop is: in the process of traversal OEM model, if an object node V points to the next object node V_i which has been traversed, so the object node V_i is not necessary to traverse again, continue to traverse the next object node V_j which leads from object node V.

② Firstly, using Nature 2 to match label path expressions, if the support of the last label path $label_{hi}$ of lphi is less than min_sup (sup ($label_{hi}$) <min_sup), then delete the label path expression lp_{hi}, else continue to match until completion of all of the label path expressions. Then count the number (count) of the label path expression lp_{hi} appears in the same layer, according to the min_sup, if count $\geq$ min_sup, so the support of lphi sup (lp_{hi}) $\geq$ min_sup, then save the label path expression lp_{hi}, else delete it, at last get all of the frequent label path expressions.

③ According to the Nature1, if the label path expression lp is a subset of another label path expression lp_i, then delete the label path expression lp, finally, we get all of the longest frequent label path expressions.

This algorithm can use a Depth-first traversal to get all of the unique label path expressions by layer, so each label path expression was counted only once, it can avoid to repeat the count of the public path of label path expression effectively, after that it only needs to operate on the label path expression, so it can solve the problem of the branch path on the impact of support effectively; Because the algorithm did not use Apriori nature to prune, it also avoids when OEM's branch paths contain the same label on the impact of accuracy of target model, so that it can improve the accuracy of target model; At the same time used Nature 2 can reduce the number of the label path expression matching, it can improve the efficiency of the algorithm.

5 Experimental Results and Analysis

The algorithm was used in the OEM model [3]; it could get the corresponding model by setting different min_sup. The algorithm in this paper can compensate for the shortage; it can improve the accuracy of the target model.

In order to evaluate the performance of the algorithm, the experiment environment used in this paper is: Intel (R) Core (TM) 2 CPU, memory 1.00GB, Windows XP, the algorithm used C# to implement. Experimental data sets were taken from the Chinese Movie Database (www.dianying.com). Under the same experiment environment, each method was implemented 10 times independently, taken the average time of 10 experiments to compare as shown in Table 1:

Table 1. Execution time comparison between algorithms

min_sup time	Literature[5]	SHDP-mine Algorithm	Algorithm in this paper
1	4317s	3551s	2476s
500	2325s	1877s	839s
1000	1472s	993s	174s

6 Conclusions

In this paper, the algorithm used a Depth-first traversal strategy to get all frequent label path expressions; finally, it used Nature 1 to obtain all of the longest frequent label path expressions. It solves the branch path on the impact of support effectively; it avoids using the Apriori nature to prune on the impact of target pattern; thus it improves the accuracy of the target model, meanwhile reducing the size of candidates and improving the efficiency of the algorithm.

References

1. Buneman, P.: Semi- structured data. In: The 16th ACM Symposium on Principles of Database Systems, Tucson, Arizona, USA, pp. 117–121 (May 1997)
2. Papakonstantinou, Y., Garcia- Molina, H., Widom, J.: Object exchange across heterogeneous information sources. In: The 11th International Conference on Data Engineering, Taipei, Taiwan, pp. 251–260 (1995)
3. Li, J.Z., Shi, Y.: Minimized schema discovery for semi-structured. Computer Applications and Software 26(4), 51–54 (2009)
4. Lu, M.Y., Lu, Y.C.: OEM-based schema extraction of semi-structured data. Tsinghua University (Sci. & Tech.) 44(9), 29–36 (2004)
5. Liu, F., Hu, H.P., Lu, S.F.: Schema discovery for semi-structured hierarchical data. Mini-Micro Computer System 22(1), 84–88 (2001)
6. Nestorov, S., Ullman, J., Wiener, J.: Representative objects: concise representations of semi-structured, hierarchical data. In: The Thirteenth International Conference on Data Engineering, Birmingham, England, pp. 79–90 (April 1997)

Improved KNN Classification Algorithm by Dynamic Obtaining K

An Gong and Yanan Liu

College of Computer and Communication Engineering
China University of Petroleum (East China), Dongying, China
gongan0328@sina.com, jsjliuyanan@163.com

Abstract. KNN algorithm which is one of the best methods of text classifying in the vector space model (VSM) is a simple, example based and none-parameter method. But in the KNN algorithm, the fixed K value ignores the influence of the category and the document number of training text. So, selecting the correct K value can achieve better classification results. This paper proposes a kind of dynamic obtain k-valued for KNN classification algorithm, experimental results show that the dynamic obtain k-valued KNN classification algorithm with high performance.

Keywords: KNN classification algorithm, k-valued, dynamic obtain.

1 Instruction

KNN classification algorithm is widely used in the field of machine learning and data mining, and has been proved to be one of the best text classification methods under vector space model (VSM) [1]. However, KNN algorithm has inherent disadvantages [2]: (1) When the training sample set is too large or too many feature items, the algorithm's complexity of time and space is high, its time complexity is O (n*m) (n is the characteristic dimension, m is the sample set size), leading to the efficiency of KNN algorithm will be decreased; (2) There is not a strong basis for the selection of the value of K, when the value of K is small, the neighbors' interference is small, but following low accuracy; when the K value is large, the method has good accuracy, but the interference of neighbor is very large.

For the lacking of KNN classification algorithm, domestic and foreign scholars put forwards some improves, which can be divided into three categories: (1)Sample cutting;(2)Reducing the dimension of high-dimensional vectors, such as the method based on Latent Semantic Analysis (LSA) [3], the method based on feature vector polymerization [4]; (3)Improving the feature selection method.

In the KNN classification algorithm, many experimenters use a fixed K value. This value is an empirical value, which is the result of a large number of experiments and has no reliable theoretical basis. If the K value is too large, the text tends to belong to the class which contains more texts, classification performance is poor; If K value is too small, text has too few neighbors, this will reduce the classification accuracy. Almost all of the calculations have taken place in the classification stage, and the classification results depend on the K value. Therefore, how to select appropriate K values is critical

G. Shen and X. Huang (Eds.): ECWAC 2011, Part I, CCIS 143, pp. 320–324, 2011.
© Springer-Verlag Berlin Heidelberg 2011

to improve the performance of KNN classification algorithm and it will be a research focus in the field of data mining. Then this paper proposes a kind of dynamic obtain k-valued for KNN classification algorithm.

2   Classical KNN Classification Algorithm

KNN classification algorithm is based on the examples and the parameters of text classification method, which is a relatively mature theory of simple machines for learning algorithm [5]. The method has simple idea: According to the traditional vector space model, the content of the text is formalized as the weighted feature vector in feature space, as $D=D(T_0, W_0; T_1, W_1; ...; T_n, W_n)$,the various dimensions of the various features used to corresponding to characterize properties of the document. Calculate the similarity that between the test text vector and the training set vector, then by sorting the similarity to select the K most similar to the test text. Accumulate the same type of text similarity; the test text belongs to that obtaining the maximum similarity. The algorithm steps are:

(1).   Using the collection of features items to descript the training text vectors.
(2).   Upon the test text's arrival, using the word segmentation to process the test text, determining its vector representation.
(3).   Calculate the similarity between the test text vector and the training set vector, the formula as follows:

$$sim\left(d_i, d_j\right) = \frac{\sum_{k=1}^{n} a_{ik} \times a_{jk}}{\sqrt{\left(\sum_{k=1}^{n} a^2_{ik}\right)\left(\sum_{k=1}^{n} a^2_{jk}\right)}}$$

Where, d_i is the text feature vector under test, d_j is the text feature vector for the j type, a_{ik}, a_{jk} for the K-dimensional vector corresponding to the first.

(4).   According to the similarity of text, select the K most similar to the test text. Calculate the weight of each class according to the following formula:

$$P\left(i,C_x\right) = \sum sim\left(d_i, d_j\right) y\left(d_j, C_x\right)$$

Where, $y\left(d_j, C_x\right)$ is class attribute function, if d_j belongs to class C_x, the function value is 1, otherwise the function values is 0.

(5).   Comparison of the various weights, the test text was assigned to the class that has the maximum weight.

3   The Selection of K Value

The selection of K value has relationship with the class of texts and the number of texts in every class. Taking different categories with the different number of texts into account, this paper proposes a dynamic obtain K value.

Suppose the class of training text is N, the total number of the text is M. Each class contains different number of text. We use this training set to classify the test text X and still use the Euclidean distance between the two calculation methods to calculate the similarity between X and other training texts.

$$sim(d_x, d_i) = \frac{\sum_{k=1}^{s} a_{xk} \times a_{ik}}{\sqrt{\left(\sum_{k=1}^{s} a_{xk}^2\right) \times \left(\sum_{k=1}^{s} a_{ik}^2\right)}} \tag{1}$$

Where, d_x is the text feature vector for X, d_i is the text feature vector for the i type, a_{xk}, a_{ik} for the K-dimensional vector corresponding to the first. S is the number of dimension.

Taking different categories with the different number of texts into account, the paper proposes using the number of various types of training set and the average similarity to fix the selection of K value. Can avoid large different numbers of training texts leads to the results of classification for test text tend to the class which has the larger number of training texts.

We use formula (1) to calculate the similarity between X and other training texts. After the similarity calculation with one class, we use the number of the training texts to fix the total value of similarity. The formula as follows:

$$\text{Sim}(j) = \left(1 - \frac{n}{M}\right) \sum_{i=1}^{n} sim(d_x, d_i) \tag{2}$$

Where, j is the type of training set, n is number of training texts for j types, M is the total number of the text. In formula (2), the class containing a larger number of training text, the value of n / M is larger, and the value of is smaller. Using (1-n/M) to fix the j type's similarity values, can eliminate the classification results are not accurate because of the number of training text is too large or too small.

From the formula (2), we can get the amendment similarity of the various types of training text. Then cumulate the amendment similarity, we can get an average of SIM (avg), as shown in formula (3), where N is the class of training text.

$$\text{SIM}(\text{avg}) = \frac{1}{N} \sum_{j=1}^{N} \text{Sim}(j) \tag{3}$$

To SIM(avg) as a standard, we can divided the similarity which between X and other training texts   into two parts. One sim is greater than SIM(avg), the other part's sim is less than SIM(avg). We reserve part which has larger values. We calculate the number of texts in this part, and then assigned the value of this number to K. Therefore, we obtain the dynamic K value.

4   Experimental Results and Analysis

4.1   Experimental Data

This experimental data is provided by Tan Songbo who is the doctor form CAS Institute of Computing. This corpus is divided into two layers, the first layer of 12 categories, and the second layer of 60 categories which collects 14,150 documents. We select 8 categories of document data which from the first player to test. There are 1647 documents, including finance, geography, computers, property, education, automobile, health, entertainment. The training set has 896 documents and the test set has 751 documents (Table 1).

Table 1. Experimental data

Category	The training set	The test set
Finance	120	95
Geography	80	70
Computers	130	110
Property	95	80
Education	125	90
Automobile	100	93
Health	156	138
Entertainment	90	75

4.2 Experimental Results

This paper uses two kind of KNN classification algorithm to classify the selected documents, one is the fixed K value KNN classification algorithm, the other is the dynamic obtain K value KNN classification algorithm. For the first method, we assign 8, 20 to K, because the large number of experiments show that assign 8 or 20 to K, the classification can get better accuracy.

Internationally accepted the basis of the evaluation for the classification results are the recall (R), precision (P) and the value of F1 [6].

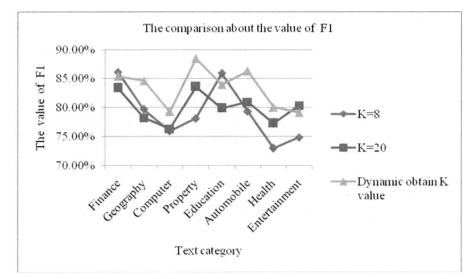

Fig. 2.

Fig.2 shows the comparison of F1, which from two kinds of KNN classification algorithm, and one of the K value is 8 or 20, and the other's k value is obtained by a dynamic method. From the line chart, in the KNN classification algorithm, the F1 value of the dynamic K value is higher than that of the fixed K value. From table1, we know that, the geography's number of training set and test set is about twice more than that of health category .As shown in chart4.3, when K=8 or k=20, the F1 values of the two categories are varied. For geography category, when k=8 there is better classification results, but for health category, it will get better classification results when k=20.However, the dynamic obtain k value algorithm can get the best classification results. For property category and education category, there is little difference in their numbers of training set and test set. Using the fixed K value algorithm, the F1 values of the two categories are varied, too and the dynamic obtain k value algorithm can get the better classification results. Therefore, we conclude that the dynamic K value for the classification algorithm can effectively avoid the impact of the size of the training text set and the test text set and has high classification efficiency.

5   Conclusion

Based on the analysis and studying classical KNN classification algorithm, this paper proposes a kind of dynamic obtain k value for KNN classification algorithm. In this new method, after the similarity calculation with one class, we use the number of the training texts to fix the total value of similarity, then cumulative the amendment similarity of each class; we can get an average of SIM (avg). We assign the number of the text whose value of similarity is larger than the SIM (avg) to K. Experimental results show that the dynamic obtain k-valued KNN classification algorithm can effectively avoid the impact of the size of the training text set and the test text set and can get high classification efficiency.

References

[1] Pang, J., Bu, D., Bai, S.: Based on vector space model the automatic Text Classification System and implementation. Computer Applications 18(9), 23–26 (2001)
[2] Han, E.H., George, K., Vipin, K.: Text categorization using weight adjusted k-nearest neighbor classification: Technical Report. University of Minnesota (2000)
[3] Deerwester, S., Dumas, S., Furnas, G., Landauer, T., Harsrtian, R.: Indexing by Laent Semantic Analysis. Journal of the American Society for Information Science 41(6), 391–417 (1994)
[4] Zhang, X., Li, Y., Wang, H.: Using Characteristics of polymerization to improve the KNN algorithm for Chinese Text Classification. Northeastern University (Natural Science) (3), 229–232 (2003)
[5] Liu, B., Yang, L., Yuan, F.: Improved KNN method and its application in Chinese text categorization. West China University of Technology (Natural Science) 27(2), 33 (2008)
[6] Song, F., Gao, L.: The evaluation about text classification performance. Computer Engineering 30(13), 107–109 (2004)

Safety Psychology Applicating on Coal Mine Safety Management Based on Information System

Baoyue Hou and Fei Chen

College of Safety Science and Engineering,
Liaoning Technical University, Fuxin 123000, China
Houbaoyue2010@163.com

Abstract. In recent years, with the increase of intensity of coal mining, a great number of major accidents happen frequently, the reason mostly due to human factors, but human's unsafely behavior are affected by insecurity mental control. In order to reduce accidents, and to improve safety management, with the help of application security psychology, we analyse the cause of insecurity psychological factors from human perception, from personality development, from motivation incentive, from reward and punishment mechanism, and from security aspects of mental training , and put forward countermeasures to promote coal mine safety production,and to provide information for coal mining to improve the level of safety management.

Keywords: Safety Psychology, safety management, perception, personality development, motivation incentives, incentive mechanism, Security psychological training.

1 Introduction

Modern coal mine safety management is an important part of enterprise management that reflects the level of overall quality of coal mine. Mine safety not only depend on human's behavior but also depends on physical security the security environment, and human's security behavior relates to psychology closely.Safety management is mainly to people, to equipment and to mine protection management of the natural environment , and people management is the most important.

Safety Psychology is a subject that research on handling the relationships between "man - machine - environment" correctly in security organization.with the application of management in coal mine safety system,it directly reflects the main features of project management: advanced prevention. In accordance with the laws of human psychology and objective laws of development of safety precautions, the introduction and application of psychology means to provide better services for the mine safety management, on this basis, to establish a new security management system. Coal mine production safety in coal mine refers to legitimate security configuration between "man, machine and environment" in the cycle of operation, in order to achieve human security act, ultimately achieve the production of safe state. Because people are the core of the operation of safety factors. Security Management focus on research

G. Shen and X. Huang (Eds.): ECWAC 2011, Part I, CCIS 143, pp. 325–329, 2011.
© Springer-Verlag Berlin Heidelberg 2011

and control the people with great degrees of freedom during production activities, which is the basic premise of safety production. Coal mine accidents, in addition to environmental and underground equipment and other factors, mainly man-made accidents and duty accidents, to avoid man-made accidents, we must use the principles of safety engineering psychology, to develop and to improve mine workers self-control standard operation quality to reduce errors gradually, thereby reducing the unsafety acts of people to avoid accidents.

2 Perception Used in Safety Production

Percertion plays an important role on the aspect of safe protection.Because the awareness level of the attributes on objective things has a direct impact and restrict. on w human behavior.Miners work underground, how to work efficiently and safety, of course is a special cognitive processes, primarily through a series of perception on complex objects and special environment underground, and to reach adaptation and coordination on human and character, production and and security. Only clear and objective perception on the environment underground lays foundation on eliminating hidden dangers. Meanwhile, only the miners perceived the hidden dangers can ensure safe production. Accordance the miners should follow the laws of perception to understand and observe underground environment, specifically as follows.

2.1 Useing the Strength to Increase Irritation

Things to be perceived can achieve a clear perception must have a certain strength. In general, a strong stimulus can be perceived easily, while the weak stimulation are easily overlooked. During mine safety management, we should adapt to the use of sensitive features on the strength of perception, building more safety signs, and engaging in some relative strength, such as static and dynamic, white and black, etc., and to suggest the miners to pay attention to enhance the perceived effect.We should take full advantage of reflecting the perception of the strength of law, to improve and perfect the mine safety signs, in order to improve the safety vigilance of miners furtherly in the process of management.

2.2 Useing Contrast to Enhance a Sense Impression

In order to enhance attention of staff on the safety, it is important to usecontrast on different things consciously to enhance people's perception impression in the management Such as comparison of different colors, different shapes, different voices, different environments, etc., these can enhance the security perceived impression of the staff ,and to enhance the ability to observe the security risks. ntribution, with numbers enclosed in parentheses and set on the right margin.

2.3 Useing Synergies to Enhance the Effective sense

In the course of safety education, we should apply principles of synergy, mobilizating of the senses, to participate in awareness campaign, and to a more effective level on people's perception. Psychological research shows that thing that you listened can only be remembered 15%, and you saw can be remember 25%. Therefore, safety education should be engaged in various forms, not only the ears listening,the eyes seeing,but also the hands reaching. Particularly, the operation of new equipment and new technologies should be jioned in conduct test operations and pre-job training.

3 Safe Behavior in Personality Development

(1). According to the different character of the miners to allocate work.Personality can be divided into inward and outward, lazy stagnation and aggressive type,calm and impatient type from different angles Weak strong sense of responsibility and accountability, etc. Useing scientific management to establish a management mechanism through analysis of the character of each miner, according different personalities of operators, to transfer a favorable safety positions. For example, a man who have a strong sense of responsibility can be underground gas inspectors,and blasters need a man who is calm.

(2). We should choose different management methods in the coal mine safety management according to different character of the miners.From the technical point of view of science, it is not the same in dealing with the relationship between security and miners,as the character of miners are different.After careful analysising according to different objects, use different management methods with their different personalities.So the positive role of personality can be played effectively, and to ensure workplace safety. For example, underground coal mine should establish safety mental effective configuration management system, researching and analysising on psychological law and changes on esch miners,timely adjusting the work position in order to reduce the probability of the potential emergence.

(3). Setting a reasonable team members according to the miners personalities. for the coal mining enterprises, each team is the most basic safety production units underground, the stability of their work is directly related to the whole security situation. In our security management process, setting a reasonable team members is a very important part.Miners with the same character, interests and hobbies should be dived into one team.So that the team work strong complementarity,and there is more mutual aid, and also fully team spirit,so they are easily to reduce operational errors and to achieve the purpose of safety production.

4 Safety Incentive Motivation Behavior

Security motive is an internal motivation to promote the safety of miners produced.It promote staff to focus on security, security energy concentration achieveing a high degree, and making a directional force. Whether the employee safety motivation suits for safety production requirements or not, can they really put safety first as the production needs,can they correctly handle the contradiction between safety and production, all depend on their employees insisting on the implementation safety system make in the production of every aspect of operation. By predicting the motivation to improve miners miners safety motivated behavior, mainly in the following two ways, from the perspective of coal mine safety management.

(1). Strengthen the goals of the appeal. We can carry out the "Hundred Days safety rectification", "no accident Season," "Safety Month" activities in practice. Different types of work proposed by different objectives and requirements, such as types of machinery carring out "1,000 days of safe operation" ,while individuals carring out"security model", "Top Ten security experts" and "safe Hongqi Shou" and so on. The objectives to be implemened must be strengthened, so the staff can be actived, so that they can produce positive, strong reactions and feelings.

(2). External pressure increased security motivation. Carring out the "Safe Home", "security assistance and education" activities, and the family of the miners should "knocked the safety bell, the wind blowing security", "provide hope of security," and so on, the safety of miners have some form of motivation effect.

5   Incentive Mechanism and the Relationship between Coal Mine Safety Management

American psychologist Skinner believes that people will influence future behavior. though learning the results of past actions and behavior.When the behavior results in his favor, they will tend to repeat it.while,if the behavior results against him, that act would tend to be weaken or disappear. This situation is called " reinforcement " in psychology.And " positive reinforcement " is to further strengthen there actions by giving grant reward for individual behavior. Positive reinforcement methods include bonuses, recognition of achievement, recognition, improved working conditions, promotion, arrangements challenging work, given the opportunities to learn and grow. Negative reinforcement is to punish the behavior that who do not meet the organizational goals,in order to weaken until the disappearance of these acts. Negative reinforcement methods include criticism, discipline, demotion, and sometimes no reward or lessen reward is also a negative reinforcement.

Negative reinforcement is a basic means of coal mine safety management, it can promptly correct the unsafety behavior of miners and ensure an effectiveand safety organizations operation.But,if it is taken inappropriately, not only can not mobilize the enthusiasm and creativity of the miners, but also will seriously dampen the enthusiasm of employees,and will affect the communication between security managers and employees, or even appearing some extreme behavior. Therefore, the application of negative reinforcement should be scientific, and insisting on the principle of combing positive reinforcement with negative reinforcement.

(1). Security wages.That is, and to quantitative evaluation indexes safe behavior, and its positive,and to carry on positive and negative reinforce on the material through evaluating personal accident, significant rectification of non-physical risks, safety inspection and other indicators monthly.

(2). Security risk mortgage payment. Namely it is to take a certain proportion monthly mortgage from each independent system units and relevant leaders respectively. That is,who conform to the examination conditions will reach the guaranty amount as monthly mortgage for reward, while,fail to meet the appropriate assessment criteria required deposit should be deducted.

(3). Security fine.Mainly the responsible person should be fined related to the ratio of the basis of "three violations" level and "three violations"

(4). Safety bonus points. That is to arouse area teams and management cadres the initiative on catching security production,by integral evaluation and point plan prize in order to give positive incentives area teams and management cadres,which will enable them to directly calculate the amount of money received.

In the implementation of strengthen theory measures we also should adhere to the principle of fairness, adhere to the combination of punishment and human concern.

6 Conclusion

In the process of coal production, people's mental affect by human perception, personality development, motivation, incentive, reward and punishment mechanism, it plays a vital role impact on coal mine safety management. Psychology is an important theoretical basis for safety production.For a person's mental activity is based on its external behavior and the driving force within,behavior is manifested in his internal mental activity, dominated by the internal psychological. so people's behave must have psychological causes. If abnormal psychology, behavior will go wrong, can lead to accidents. Therefore, researching on the rule of mental activity and external factors ompacting on workers psychological, strengthen the security psychological guidance of employees, and to identify positive and effective response measures, is important to ensure safety production in coal mines.

References

1. Rasmussen, J.: Skill, rules, and knowledge, Signals, signs, and symbols, and other distinctions in human performance models. IEEE Transactions on Systems, Man, and Cybernetics 13(3), 257–268 (1983)
2. Reason, J.: Human Error. Cambridge University Press, Cambridge (1990)
3. Neal, A., Griffin, M.A., Hart, P.M.: The impact of organizational climate on safety climate and individual behavior. Safety Science 34, 99–109 (2000)
4. Glendon, A.I., Litherland, D.K.: Safety climate factors, group differences and safety behavior in road construction. Safety Science 39, 157–188 (2001)
5. Wagenaar, W.A.: A model—based analysis of automation problems. In: Wilpert, B., Qvale, T. (eds.) Reliability and Safety in Hazardous Work Systems, pp. 71–85. Lawrence Erlbaum, Hove (1993)
6. Entin, E.E., Serfaty, D.: Adaptive team coordination. Human Factors 41(2), 312–325 (1999)

Applications of the Soave-Redlich-Kwong Equations of State Using Mathematic

Lanyi Sun, Cheng Zhai, and Hui Zhang

State Key Laboratory of Heavy Oil Processing,
China University of Petroleum, Qingdao,
Shandong Province, 266555, China
sunlanyi@upc.edu.cn

Abstract. The application of the Peng-Robinson equations of state (PR EOS) using Matlab and Mathematic has already been demonstrated. In this paper, using Mathematic to solve Soave-Redlich-Kwong (SRK) EOS, as well as the estimation of pure component properties, plotting of vapor-liquid equilibrium (VLE) diagram and calculation of chemical equilibrium, is presented. First the SRK EOS is used to predict several pure-component properties, such as liquid and gas molar volumes for isobutane. The vapor-liquid isobaric diagram is then plotted for a binary mixture composed of n-pentane and n-hexane under the pressures of $2*10^5$ and $8*10^5$ Pa respectively.

Keywords: Applied Thermodynamics, Soave-Redlich-Kwong Equations of State, Mathematic.

1 Introduction

The Soave-Redlich-Kwong EOS has become the most popular equation of state for natural gas systems in the petroleum industry. SRK EOS conserves the temperature dependency of the attractive term and the acentric factor of SRK EOS. SRK EOS has a better performance near critical point than SRK EOS, thus is suitable for calculating temperature, pressure, compressibility factor and density of liquid. Parameters of the EOS are defined in terms of the critical properties and the acentric factor. Coefficients "a" and "b" of the equation are functions of the critical properties by imposing the criticality conditions.

Mathematic is one of the industry-standard mathematics-based technical calculation tools for professionals, educators and college students worldwide. Mathematic helps engineers design and document engineering calculations simultaneously with comprehensive applied math functionality and dynamic, unit-aware calculations. And it provides excellent coverage of numerical methods while simultaneously demonstrating the general applicability of Mathematic to problem solving.

G. Shen and X. Huang (Eds.): ECWAC 2011, Part I, CCIS 143, pp. 330–334, 2011.

2 Estimation of Pure Component Properties

The Soave-Redlich-Kwong equation of state [1-3] is

$$p = \frac{R \cdot T}{V - b} - \frac{a(T)}{V \cdot (V + b) + b \cdot (V - b)} . \tag{1}$$

where

$$a(T) = a_c \cdot \alpha(T) = \frac{0.45724 R^2 T_c^{\,2}}{p_c} \cdot \alpha(T) \tag{2}$$

$$b = \frac{0.077880 \cdot R \cdot T_c}{p_c} . \tag{3}$$

$$\alpha(T) = (1 + k(1 - T_r^{\,0.5}))^2 . \tag{4}$$

$$k = 0.3746 + 1.54226\omega - 0.26992\omega^2 . \tag{5}$$

$$T_r = \frac{T}{T_c} . \tag{6}$$

Fig.1. shows isotherms (of the P/V relationship) for isobutane at temperatures ranging from 273.15K to 313.15K. Isobutane's critical temperature and pressure and acentric factor [3] are shown as follows:
Pc=3.468*10^6, Tc=408.1, ω=0.176

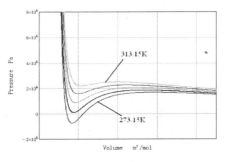

Fig. 1. Isotherms for isobutane with spacing of 10 K

In Fig.2, we can read the vapor pressure as well as the liquid and gas molar volumes at different temperatures using the tracking options from context menu of Mathematic.

To get the properties of isobutene, we assumed that the two shaded areas in the picture are equal.

The reason for the equality is that the area in the P-V diagram corresponds to mechanical work, and the change of free energy, $\Delta A(T,V)$, is equal to that work. As a state function, the change of free energy $A(T,V)$ is independent of the paths [1]. Thus, the work from point A to point B on the horizontal line drawn by Maxwell and work by the isotherm obtained from SRK EOS are equal. The flat line portion of the isotherm now corresponds to liquid-vapor equilibrium. The point A (0.000129577, 1.654e+006) represents liquid phase state parameters, while the point B (0.001264, 1.6611e+006) represents vapor phase state parameters.

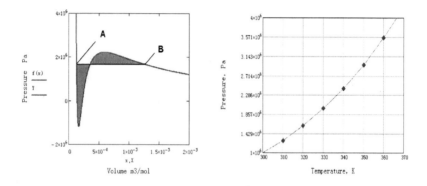

Fig.2. Isotherm at 363.15K (two areas are equal)

Fig. 3. Vapor pressure versus temperature for propane

Fig.3. shows the relation between the vapor's pressure and temperature. The curve agree with the results calculated by the modified Antoine equation from HYSYS 3.2, a major process simulator by Aspen Technology, which is

$$P^{sat} = \exp(53.3785 - \frac{3.4905510^3}{T} - 6.10875\ln(T) + 1.11869*10^{-5}T^2)*1000 \cdot \tag{7}$$

3   Vapor-Liquid Equilibrium Diagram for Binary Mixtures

In this part, the vapor-liquid isobaric equilibrium diagram for the binary mixture composed of n-pentane and n-hexane is plotted using the SRK EOS. In this case, K-values are functions of pressure, temperature, and composition. Therefore, the programming function in Mathematic is employed to solve the problem. The program scheme for calculating vapor-liquid equilibrium of binary mixture [3, 4] involves two loops, with the inner loop for y and the outer for T. The mole fraction of vapor is determined by the following equilibrium relation:

$$y_i = K_i \cdot x_i \ where \ i = 1 \ or \ 2 \tag{8}$$

Where K_i is the equilibrium constant.

The SRK EOS can be written in cubic equation form by using the mixing and combining rules. The compressibility factor, Z, is a solution of the following cubic equation for a multi-component mixture.

$$Z^3 + (1-B)Z^2 + (A - 3B^2 - 2B)Z + (-AB + B^2 + B^3) = 0 \tag{9}$$

Where

$$A = \sum_{i=1}^{c}\sum_{j=1}^{c} y_i y_j A_{ij} \ or \ A = \sum_{i=1}^{c}\sum_{j=1}^{c} x_i x_j A_{ij} \tag{10}$$

$$A_{ij} = (A_i A_j)^{0.5}(1-k_{ij}) \tag{11}$$

$$B = \sum_{i=1}^{c} y_i B_i \ or \ B = \sum_{i=1}^{c} x_i B_i \tag{12}$$

$$A_i = 0.45724 a_i \frac{P_{r,i}}{T_{r,i}^2} \ and \ B_i = 0.07780 \frac{P_{r,i}}{T_{r,i}} \tag{13}$$

For each component, the reduced pressure and temperature are defined by $P_{r,i} = P / P_{c,i}$ and $T_{r,i} = T / T_{c,i}$, and a_i is given by an equation similar to Eq.(2) for the pure component case. The binary interaction parameter, k_{ij}, is assumed to be zero. The equilibrium constants are obtained using the φ-φ method as follows,

$$K_i = \frac{\phi_{l,i}}{\phi_{v,i}}, i \ from \ 1 \ to \ c \tag{14}$$

Where

$$\phi_{v,i} = \exp[(Z_v - 1)\frac{B_i}{B} - \ln(Z_v - B) - \frac{A}{2\sqrt{2}B}(\frac{2\sum_j y_j A_{ij}}{A} - \frac{B_i}{B})\ln(\frac{Z_v + (1+\sqrt{2})B}{Z_v + (1-\sqrt{2})B})] \tag{15}$$

A similar expression is obtained for the liquid phase fugacity coefficient, $\phi_{l,i}$, by replacing the gas phase compressibility factor, Z_v with its liquid phase counterpart, Z_l. These two compressibility factors are the largest and smallest roots of Eq. (9), respectively.

Fig. 4 and 5 are obtained at pressures of 2*10^5 and 8*10^5 Pa. These results agree with those given by ASPEN. These two figures show that the binary mixture is ideal at low pressure since both n-hexane and n-pentane are non-polar molecules.

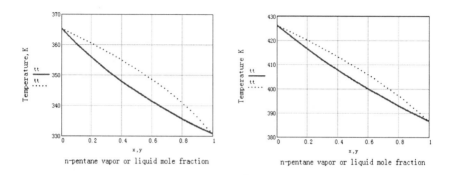

Fig. 4. Isobaric VLE diagram for n-pentane /nhexane mixture at 2*10^5pa

Fig. 5. Isobaric VLE diagram for n-pentane/n-hexane mixture at 8*10^5pa

4 Conclusion

The advantages of the numerical and graphical capabilities of Mathematic have been shown in this paper. "Given-find" function and programming in Mathematic are applied to solve problems. When the initial data, such as critical pressure and temperature and acentric factor is given, the results agree with the experimental data. Like Matlab and Mathmatic, Mathematic can also be successfully used in applications of SRK EOS. It can simplify the procedure and solve it in a clean, expressive, readable way.

References

1. Zakia, N., Housam, B.: Application of the Peng-Robinson Equation of State using Matlab. J. C E E 43, 115–124 (2009)
2. Zakia, N., Housam, B.: Application of the Peng-Robinson Equation of State using Mathmatic. J. Che. Eng. Jpn. 40, 534–538 (2007)
3. Chen, Z., Gu, F., Hu, W.: Chemical Engineering Thermodynamics. Chemical Industry Press, Beijing (2006)
4. Henley, E.J., Seader, J.D.: Equilibrium-Stage Separation Operations in Chemical Engineering. Wiley, New York (1982)
5. Sandler, S.I.: Chemical and Engineering Thermodynamics. Wiley, New York (1999)

Research on Configurations of Thermally Integrated Distillation Column(TIDC)

Lanyi Sun, Jun Li, Xuenuan Liu, and Qingsong Li

State Key Laboratory of Heavy Oil Processing, China University of Petroleum,
Qingdao, Shandong Province, 266555, China
sunlanyi@upc.edu.cn

Abstract. Taking a C3 distillation column as the base case, possible configurations for Thermally Integrated Distillation Columns (TIDC) are proposed and compared to a conventional column and a column with a vapor recompression system (VRC). Thermal efficiency of the TIDC appears to be strongly sensitive to column configuration and a highly efficient asymmetrical configuration with stripping section stages thermally interconnected with the same number of stages in the upper part of the rectifying section emerges as the most promising option. The relationships among pressure ratio of rectifying section to stripping section and energy consumption were also discussed.

Keywords: Thermal Efficiency, Configuration, Thermally Integrated Distillation Column.

1 Introduction

Distillation column, the workhorse of process industries is notorious for the inefficiency with respect to energy consumption. A possibility for a breakthrough in this direction is the adoption of the internally heat integrated distillation column concept known as TIDC[1-2], a well-known but due to complexity never implemented column configuration.

Fig. 1 illustrates schematically the operating principles of a conventional column (CC), a column with the direct vapor recompression system (VRC) and a TIDC. In case of a TIDC, the rectifying section operated at elevated pressure/temperature fulfils the role of a reboiler. Namely, the heat released during continuous condensation along the rectifying section is used to effect a roughly the same amount of progressive evaporation of liquid to maintain continuously increasing vapor traffic along the stripping section.

A potential problem with practical implementation of TIDC is the fact that an ideal TIDC inherently requires symmetrical distribution of stages, i.e. equal number of stages in both sections. Namely, this is conflicting with optimum feed position. So the main conceptual design question is how to arrange a TIDC with different number of stages in rectifying and stripping sections. Possible configurations, compared in this study are shown in Fig. 2.

G. Shen and X. Huang (Eds.): ECWAC 2011, Part I, CCIS 143, pp. 335–339, 2011.

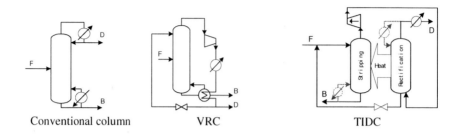

Fig. 1. Schematic illustration of the operating principle of a conventional column, a column with the direct vapor recompression (VRC) and a TIDC

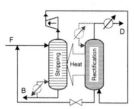

(TIDC_all)

(TIDC_optimum middle)

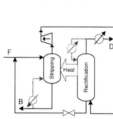

(TIDC_upper)

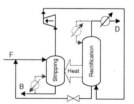

(TIDC_lower)

Fig. 2. Other possible configurations of the TIDC, in addition to that (TIDC_middle) shown in Figure 1

TIDC_middle, shown in Fig. 1 is the fully symmetrical configuration configuration as known from the literature[1-2]. TIDC_optimum middle is the modification of TIDC_middle where the feed is introduced on the stage. TIDC_upper and TIDC_lower represent two extreme asymmetric configurations, with the stripping section stages connected with the same number of stages in the rectifying section in the respectively upper and lower part of the rectifying section. Finally, TIDC_all can be arranged to have equal length of the sections, simply by adapting the stripping section tray spacing accordingly.

The objective of the current work is to present the results of a thermal analysis study indicating a strikingly strong effect of TIDC configuration on the exergy consumption of a hypothetical PP-splitter.

2 Base Case Configurations

Table 1. summarizes operating conditions of seven PP-splitter configurations compared in this study. The thermal analysis of the PP-splitter configurations evaluated in this study was carried out using ASPEN Plus facilities.

The conventional distillation column uses the heat added into the reboiler as the separating agent. In case of both the VRC and TIDC, the only energy supplied from outside is the electrical energy used to drive the compressor. To account properly for the difference in the qualities of thermal and electric energies the exergy analysis was adopted employing the following relation:

$$Ex_R = Q_R \left(1 - \frac{T_0}{T_B + \Delta T} \right). \tag{1}$$

where Ex_R is the exergy of reboiler [kW], Q_R is the reboiler duty [kW], T_0 is ambient temperature [K], T_B is bottoms temperature [K], and ΔT is the temperature difference in the reboiler [K].

Table 1. Operating conditions of the TIDC

Configurations		CC	VRC	TIDC_middle	TIDC_opt. middle	TIDC_upper TIDC_lower TIDC_all
No. of stages	Rectifying section	138	140	91	91	138
	Stripping section	44	42	91	91	44
Feed stage		139	141	92	125	139
Top rectifying pressure, $P_R/10^{-1}$MPa		18.34	9.15	18.34	18.34	1.834
Top stripping pressure, $P_S/10^{-1}$MPa				13, 15	13, 15	1.3, 1.5
Pressure drop per stage/ 10^{-3}MPa		8	8	8	8	0.008
Feed flow rate/(kmol/s)		100	100	100	100	100
Feed mole fraction	(Propylene)	0.5	0.5	0.5	0.5	0.5
	(Propane)	0.5	0.5	0.5	0.5	0.5
Feed thermal condition, q		1	1	1	1	1
Top propylene mole fraction		0.995	0.995	0.995	0.995	0.995
Bottom propylene mole fraction		0.04	0.04	0.04	0.04	0.04

3   Results and Discussion

Fig. 3 shows the energy and exergy consumptions of the VRC (column with vapor recompression system) and the TIDC relative to that of the conventional column. As expected a VCR enables a huge energy saving with respect to conventional column and the asymmetric TIDC with upper part of rectification section coupled thermally to the striping section seems to be the best configuration in this respect. As expected, each of TIDC configurations with lower compression ratio (TIDC(15), PR/PS = 1.2) consumes less energy/exergy than its counterpart operating at the higher compression ratio (TIDC(13), PR/PS = 1.4). Striking is the extent of bad performance of the TIDC with the bottom part of the rectification section coupled to the stripping section (TIDC_lower). The relative exergy consumption plot shown in Fig. 3 indicates that the exergy efficiency of this configuration is more than factor two worse than that of the conventional column. An explanation for the difference in the performance of five TIDC configurations, particularly the extreme one, is suggested in Fig. 4 which shows vapor flow rate profiles for each configuration, with stage number increasing from the top to the bottom of the column. Namely, in addition to the compression ratio, which is equal for all TIDC configurations, the compressor duty depends also on the mass flow rate of the vapor. As indicated in Fig. 4 the latter one varies considerably, in one case extremely, depending on the configuration. It should be noted that the vapor flow rate in a TIDC increases from say zero at the bottom of stripping section to the maximum at the top of the stripping section. The vapor flow that enters the rectification section starts to decrease continuously while ascending through the rectification section reaching the minimum rate at the top, which is equivalent to that of the distillate product.

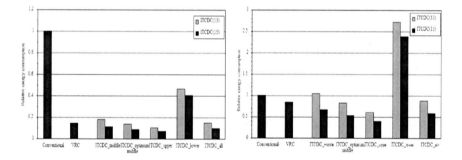

Fig. 3. Relative energy (left) and exergy (right) consumption compared to the conventional column (TIDC with bottom section pressure of respectively $13*10^{-1}$MPa and $15*10^{-1}$MPa)

The peaks of vapor rate curves shown in Fig. 4 indicate the compressor load associated with TIDC configurations considered here. It can be seen that the vapor flows through compressors of TIDC(13)_upper, TIDC(13)_optimum middle, TIDC(13)_all, TIDC(13)_middle and TIDC(13)_lower are 1.7, 2.4, 2.4, 3.1 and 7.5 times of that of the VRC, respectively. Therefore it is not surprising that in some cases a TIDC consumes more energy/exergy than the VRC.

An inspection of the propylene composition profile along the column for two asymmetric TIDC's and the conventional column shown in Fig. 5 indicates that in case of TIDC(13)_lower the separation effort is concentrated in the thermally coupled part of the column. In fact, this part of the column operates with a rather low number of theoretical stages, which must be compensated by correspondingly increased internal reflux ratio (roughly 75!). This is needed to compensate effectively for highly inefficient performance of the upper. As shown in Fig. 4, the vapor flow in the normally operating lower part of the rectification section is somewhat larger indicating correspondingly larger internal reflux (around 24.5). As indicated in Fig. 5, this leads to somewhat enhanced separation performance in this part of the column, which compensates certain loss in the thermally coupled part of the column.

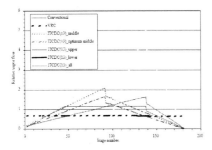
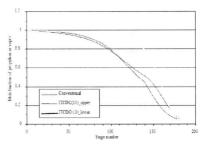

Fig. 4. Comparison of vapor flow profiles for the high compression ratio TIDC in vapor along the column

Fig. 5. Comparison of propylene fraction

4   Conclusions

The performance of a TIDC with different number of stages in rectifying and stripping section depends strongly on the configuration chosen. For the PP-splitter, the best option appeared to be a configuration with stripping section stages thermally interconnected with a corresponding number of stages in the upper part of the rectifying section, with the lower part of rectification section operating as a normal column. With this configuration it appears possible to reduce the energy consumption associated with a heat-pump distillation column by nearly 25~40%.

References

1. Nakaiwa, M., Huang, K., Endo, A.: Internally Heat Integrated Distillation Columns: A Review. Trans IchemE, Part A, Chem. Eng. Res. Des. 81, 162–177 (2003)
2. Olujic, Z., Fakhri, F., de Rijke, A.: Internal heat integration – the key to energy-conserving distillation column. J. Chem. Technol. Biotechnol. 78, 241–248 (2003)

Study on Vibratory Stress Relief Technology for the Structural Parts of Hydraulic Support

Lianmin Cao[1], Shunqiang Hou[2], Qingliang Zeng[1], and Jintao Liu[3]

[1] Shandong University of Science and Technology, Qingdao, 266510, China
[2] Qingdao Binhai University, Qingdao, 266555, China
[3] Qingdao Hotel Management College, Qingdao, 266100, China
skdclm@163.com, hellospring111@163.com, qlzeng@sdust.edu.cn,
qdliujintao@tom.com

Abstract. This paper mainly compares two methods thermal aging and VSR for structural parts of the hydraulic support. VSR using the spectrum harmonic vibration aging technology has the same effect in the elimination of stress with thermal aging, and is superior to thermal aging in stabling dimensional accuracy and increasing payload capacity of the works.

Keywords: support, structural parts, Vibratory Stress Relief, thermal aging.

1 Introduction

With the increasing amount of mine output, hydraulic support requires a higher quality of working resistance and reliability on the coalface. It is imperative that the structural parts of hydraulic support needs high strength steel products with 550Mpa, 690 MPa and 890 MPa tensile strength. On the assumption of strength proof, we can reduce the weight of hydraulic support, and save the cost. However, high strength steel plates are weak in notch sensitivity, and weldment always causes rupture, snap and low fatigue strength in use. Aging treatment after high strength steel plates welding makes the key point in increasing using reliability and working life of hydraulic support[1]. So it is much more important to choose suitable high strength steel plate and welding technology in support design to ensure the support strength. Welding is the key technology in hydraulic support production in fully-mechanized coal face. The character of material weldability decides the special welding technology for each steel, and aging treatment after high strength steel plates welding makes the key point in increasing using reliability and working life of hydraulic support. At present, there are two methods-thermal aging and VSR-of aging treatments after high strength steel plates welding [2].

2 Vibratory Stress Relief

VSR is short for Vibratory Stress Relief. It makes use of controlled vibrational energy to treat metal work-piece, in order to eliminate remaining stress of the work-piece. VSR has good effect in stabling dimensional accuracy of the work. In the working

G. Shen and X. Huang (Eds.): ECWAC 2011, Part I, CCIS 143, pp. 340–345, 2011.

practice, VSR can not only eliminate remaining stress of the work-piece, but also increase strength indicators of work-piece[3].VSR technology has the obvious advantages of high efficiency, energy conservation and environmental protection. However, the traditional technology calls for strict requirements of supporting point, excitation vibration point, vibration picking point and direction, etc., constantly sweeping frequency and adjusting position. In addition to unstable stress relief and high pitch of noise, VSR can not be widely applied in industrial production[4].

3   Comparison between the Spectrum Harmonic Vibration Aging Application and Thermal Aging Application

With spectrum analysis, the spectrum harmonic aging technology can automatically make a vibration treatment, analyze and collect harmonic frequency of work-pieces, select 7 optimum vibration frequencies, automatically treat 5 frequencies and eliminate remaining stress in many vibrations and dimensions. It solves high rigidity and high natural frequency problems of work-piece in traditonal subresonance method, and the handle frequency is under 6000 r/min. In some cases, it reduces the noise, saves sources and protect environment[5].In this test, VSR treats two work-pieces: upper beam and caving shield, and thermal aging treats chassis and caving shield.The whole working process of vibration aging strictly follows mechanical industry standards of The People's Republic of China-Vibrations Age Effect Evaluation Method. It uses spectrum harmonic method to treat 5 harmonic frequencies and ensures the two frequency accelerations between 30m/s2� 70 m/s2. The work-pieces are steadily supported by rubber matting before aging. In vibration aging destressing, we take two-point excitation vibration on upper beam and one-point excitation vibration on caving shield[6].The following charts are three-dimensional distribution of each check point stress before and after work-piece vibration. X-axis is path length of work-piece(mm); Y-axis is the number of channels. Z-axis is gradient change of magnetic field dH/dX, the unit is (A/m)/mm, and the right number is gradient of each point.

The following charts are three-dimensional distribution of each check point stress before and after work-piece VSR.Fig. 1 and Fig. 2 show the three-dimensional distribution of upper beam check point before and after VSR.

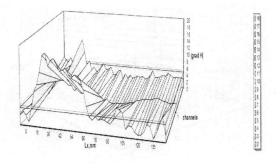

Fig. 1. Distribution of upper beam check point before VSR

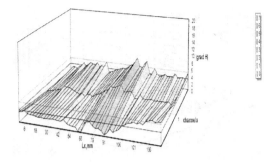

Fig. 2. Distribution of upper beam check point after VSR

Fig. 3 and Fig. 4 show the three-dimensional distribution of caving shield check point before and after VSR.

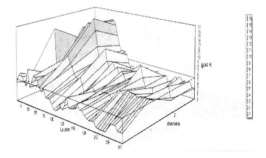

Fig. 3. Distribution of caving shield check point before VSR

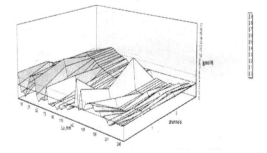

Fig. 4. Distribution caving shield check point after VSR

The following charts are three-dimensional distribution of each check point stress before and after work-piece thermal aging.Fig. 5 and Fig. 6 show the three-dimensional distribution of chassis check point before and after thermal aging.

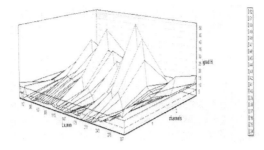

Fig. 5. Distribution of chassis check point before thermal aging

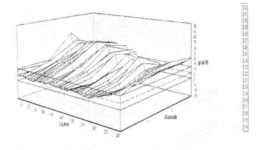

Fig. 6. Distribution of chassis check point after thermal aging

Fig. 7 and Fig. 8 show the three-dimensional distribution of caving shield check point before and after thermal aging.

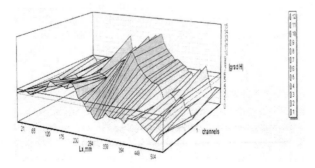

Fig. 7. Distribution of caving shield check point before thermal aging

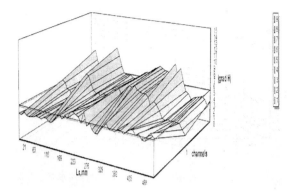

Fig. 8. Distribution of caving shield check point after thermal aging

4 Data Statistics

Before and after VSR on upper beam, the average decreasing ratio of | gradeH | is 43.8%; while on caving shield, the average decreasing ratio of | gradeH | is 43.53%; before and after thermal aging on chassis, the average decreasing ratio of | gradeH | is 40.32%; while on caving shield, the average decreasing ratio of | gradeH | is 40.00%.

5 Conclusion

By checking the magnetic stress before and after vibration elimination stress test, it is found that before vibration elimination stress, magnetic field gradient is unevenly distributed and the gradient magnitude is much higher, which indicate that the remaining stress is unevenly distributed in the inner part and there still exists stress concentration in some parts; after vibration elimination stress, leakage magnetic field is evenly distributed and the amplitude is relatively decreased, which indicate that the remaining stress is gradually distributed, and remaining stress concentration is eliminated. From the gradient magnitude chart, it is seen that both the max gradient magnitudes are decreasing inordinately before and after vibration, and the stress is obviously decreased. What's more, from the decreasing rate of gradient magnitude, both thermal aging and VSR have the approaching magnetic field decreasing rate, and the same effect in vibration elimination. However, spectrum harmonic aging is superior to thermal aging in stabling dimensional accuracy and increasing payload capacity of the works. Consequently, the new spectrum harmonic technology (VSR) can take place of thermal aging aiming at the elimination of stress, especially applied in high strength steel plate after welding of hydraulic support.

Acknowledgment. This paper is founded by the National Natural Science Foundation of China (No. 50875158), Shandong soft science research project of China (No. 2009RKB163), and Scientific fund of shandong university of science and technology.

References

1. He, W., Ren, Y., Chen, C., Ma, F.: Analysis on technology of high-frequency vibratory stress relief. In: Proceedings of the ASME Power Conference, vol. PART A, pp. 119–122 (2005)
2. Jiang, G., He, W., Zheng, J.-Y.: Mechanism and experimental research on high frequency vibratory stress relief. Zhejiang Daxue Xuebao (Gongxue Ban)/Journal of Zhejiang University (Engineering Science) 43(7), 1269–1272 (2009)
3. Bilal Khan, M., Iqbal, T.: Vibratory stress relief in D-406 aerospace alloy. In: TMS Annual Meeting, pp. 807–814 (2009)
4. Dryga, A.I.: Vibratory stress-relief units for stabilizing cast and fabricated parts. Soviet Engineering Research 10(6), 111–113 (1990)
5. Sun, M.C., Sun, Y.H., Wang, R.K.: The vibratory stress relief of a marine shafting of 35# bar steel. Materials Letters 58(3-4), 299–303 (2004)
6. Jurcius, A., Valiulis, A.V., Cernašejus, O.: Effects of vibration energy input on stress concentration in weld and heat-affected zone of S355J2 steel. Diffusion and Defect Data Pt.B: Solid State Phenomena 165, 73–78 (2010)

Application Research of QRCode Barcode in Validation of Express Delivery

Zhihai Liu[1], Qingliang Zeng[1], Chenglong Wang[1], and Qing Lu[2]

[1] College of Mechanical and Electrical Engineering, Shandong University of Science and Technology, Qingdao 266510, China
[2] The Logistic Service General Establishment, Shandong University of Science and Technology, Qingdao 266510, China
zhihliu@126.com, qlzeng@sdust.edu.cn, wcllym@hotmail.com, sdqingl@163.com

Abstract. The barcode technology has become an important way in the field of information input and identify automatically. With the outstanding features of big storage capacity, secure, rich encoding character set and fast decoding, the two-dimensional(2D) QRcode(Quick Response Barcode) has become an important choice of commerce barcode. The development of wireless communications technology and the popularization and application of mobile device has set the foundation of 2D barcode used in business. In this paper, the characteristics and the compositions of 2D QRcode are described, the secure validation workflows and contents of QRcode in goods express delivery are discussed, the encoding process of QRcode is showed, and the system framework is analyzed and established. At last, the system compositions and functions of each part are discussed.

Keywords: QRcode, mobile commerce, barcode validation.

1 Introduction

The barcode is a emerging technology on the basis of computer and information technology, has become an import means in the process of information automatically input and validation. The barcode has the following characteristics: (1) fast input speed and high efficiency; (2) high reliability; (3) low cost in production and use; (4) practical and flexible.

In recent years, with the development and application of wireless technology and with the improving of people's living standards and with the needs of social intercourse, mobile phones and other mobile devices has become an important communication and entertainment. The promotion of mobile phones equipped with camera and the function of MMS (Multimedia Messaging Service), and the rapid growth of mobile communication services, make it possible that 2D barcode can be used in mobile phones. The 2D barcodes used in mobile phone means that encoding the useful information into a barcode image file, transmit and store it in the way of multimedia message. The 2D barcodes saved in the mobile phone can be recognized by using the external scanning device, or can be decoded by the embedded or downloaded decoding software, so

G. Shen and X. Huang (Eds.): ECWAC 2011, Part I, CCIS 143, pp. 346–351, 2011.

people can get the information encoded in the barcode image. According to [1], 2D barcodes can be used to support pre-sale, buy-and-sell, and post-sale activities for mobile commerce transactions.

On the basis of studying the encoding and decoding, the 2D QRcode is used in security validation process of cargo express delivery to ensure the delivery safety of goods, and improved the information reading and processing efficiency.

2 Brief Introduction to QRcode

The research of 2D barcode technology on the world began from late of 1980s, and has developed a variety of 2D barcode types. According to [2], different approaches can be classified into composite codes, stacked codes, dot codes and matrix codes. QR codes are a variation of matrix codes.

QRCode is a 2D matrix code symbol, developed by Denso corporation of Japan in September 1994. QRcode not only has the merits of one-dimensional barcode, but also has the advantages of the other 2D barcodes, such as large capacity, high reliability, can encode Chinese words and images effectively, strong confidentiality and anti-counterfeiting, etc.. The most outstanding characteristics are super-fast decoding (it can decode 30 QRcode image symbols which has the capacity of 100 codewords) and omni-directional to read(rotates 360 degree within a plane). QRcode has the maximum storage of 7089 digital data, or 4296 characters, or 2953 bytes data, or 1817 Chinese words. The error correction of QRcode can be divided into 4 levels. The lowest correction level is L level, which can correct about 7% of codewords mistakes, and the lower correction level is M level, which can correct about 15% of codewords mistakes, and the higher correction level is Q level, which can correct about 25% of codewords mistakes, and the highest correction level is H level, which can correct about 30% of codewords mistakes. The QRcode is standardized in several international bodies, i.e. AIM International, JIS and JAMA, ISO, Chinese and Korea National Standard, Vietnam National Standard and further utilized in several application standards, i.e. ISO and IEC[2].

Fig.1 is the structure of QRcode.

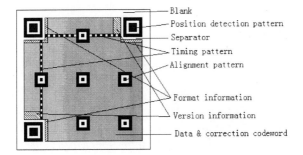

Fig. 1. The structure of QRcode

3   Related Works

In recent years, the one-dimensional barcodes have been widely used all over the world in the field of supermarket, logistics, warehousing, books, etc.. By using database and scanning device or software, the merchandise will be automatically and quickly recognized. The 2D barcode can store large amount of data, and the information safety has been greatly improved, thus all the information of goods can be decoded and obtained directly from the 2D barcode, so made it to use more widely. In all 2D barcodes, QRcode is thought as the fastest conversational 2D barcode.

As we all known, QRcode technology has been adopted in China's railway ticking system, when people buy the railway ticket, the system will encode the buyer's information, such as identification card number, ticket booth, starting railway station, destination railway station, distance, etc., and print the encrypted QRcode on the ticket. When passengers enter the waiting room or leave from the railway station, the QRcode will be read by using special equipment, and the passenger's information will be compared by railway station staff.

Besides encoding the goods name and manufacturer's name, it can also encode the date, price, telephone number, email address and graphics into a QRcode image file, and the hypertext links can also be encoded with the support of network environment. For example, in Japan, QRcodes are attached to fruits or vegetables, providing information on cultivation, used pesticides, crop and packing date[3].

In Japan and South Korea, many businesses encode the information of discounted goods or new goods with hypertext links into QRcode, and post it on the shop doorway, so people can take photo via embedded camera of mobile phone and login the related website to query or browse the goods information after decode the QRcode by using the built-in or downloaded decoding software.

In mobile ticketing the QRcode is used to transfer authorization information in a secure way and offers a paperless alternative to print-out tickets[4].

2D Barcode Medical Prescription System. The Taiwan government developed a 2D barcode prescription system (2DBPS) for its National Health Insurance (NHI) [5]. With this system, doctors' medical prescriptions are encoded as 2D barcodes and given to patients. When patients arrive at a pharmacy, the pharmacist only needs to scan the barcode to validate the prescription with the back-end server.

4   Verification System

At present, one-dimensional barcode system has been applied in the express delivery, and the barcode text is send to the company's server and registered in system database. But the storage capacity of one-dimensional barcode is limited, so the application of one-dimensional barcode is mainly to resolve the real-time tracking of the goods by the shipper or consignee. Several shortcomings are listed as follows.

(1)   The sorting or recognition of goods still mainly depend on manual labor, so the labor intensity is not reduced.
(2)   As a result of limited capacity, it can not encode the consignee's name, the shipper's name, the address and other contact information.
(3)   The papery receipt is not convenient to carry, and is easy to damage or lost.

(4)   There is only one check codeword, so if one-dimensional barcode is defaced, it will not be able to be read.
(5)   Each goods will be pasted several papers, so there will be some waste of papers.
(6)   The information validation process is fulfilled by people, so there will be some mistakes.

When we use QRcode in express delivery, the sequential number of this delivery express process will be encoded into the QRcode image, and the shipper's contact information, the consignee's contact information, the shipment information, date time and the delivery company's web site will be encoded into the QRcode image also. If you think there are some other important information should be encoded into the QRcode image, so you can input these important information by sequence into the user interface of the encoding software. During the process of goods delivery, there might be some damage to the QRcode image, such as covered with dust or scrapped by other things, etc. So the correction level should be set to the highest level in order to recover all the damaged codewords. After encoding the QRcode image, it will be sent to the shipper's mobile phone by the means of multimedia message as a receipt, or be sent to and the consignee's mobile phone as evidence of receiving goods. If the mobile phone has setup QRcode decode software or equipped with built-in decode hardware, people can decode the QRcode in the multimedia message, get the useful information, and then login the delivery company's website to query the transportation status of goods. For the sake of security and avoid to falsely claim the goods, the shipper can set a password to the QRcode image file.

The process of giving goods to consignee as follows.

(1)   The goods is transported to the destination.
(2)   The consignee go to the site carrying the mobile phone which stored the QRcode image file, and the courier receive the password input by the consignee through handheld devices, scanning QRcode graphics on the mobile phone, if the encoded information is decoded correctly and the information on system server shows that the delivery process is not completed, so the goods will be delivered to the consignee, and set a mark to the system database automatically at the same time which means the completion of this delivery process.

5 System Design and Architecture

The 2D QRcode validation system consists of three parts, the system server, the client and the terminal user. Each part is composed by different devices and communication protocols. The communication channel can divided into wireless and internet network. The system framework is shown in Figure 2.

The system server is composed by database server, print server, web server and application server, aims to receive the submitted delivery information and fulfill the query process by courier, and provide the online tracking of goods for the terminal

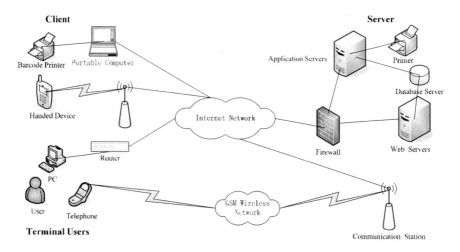

Fig. 2. The system framework

user based on internet or GSM wireless network. The system administrator can maintain and view the system data.

The client is mainly composed by portable computer, mobile handheld encoder and decoder, portable printer, etc.. The client device is used to encode the shipper's contact information, consignee's contact information, goods description, expected time of arrival, and the other useful information into a QRcode graphics, so send the encoded graphics into the shipper's or consignee's mobile phone by MMS, and print the barcode as a receipt of delivering goods.

The terminal user mainly means the shipper and the consignee and the potential users, they can login the delivery company's application server to view the delivery position or status of the goods by using the website in internet explorer browser on the computer or on the mobile phone.

6 Encoding Example

In the test, we fill out the encoding information by the following sequence. Shipper's name/ postcode/ address/ phone number/ Consignee's name/ postcode/ address/ phone number/ Goods name and description/ fees / password mark (zero means there is no password), each part is separated by return key symbol. For example, Zhang san want to send an import letter from Shanghai to Beijing, and ask Li Si to pick the letter, the input information as follows. Zhang San/ 201100/ commercial street 1, Minhang district of Shanghai/ 18918835998/ Li Si/ 100000/ Zhongguancun street 123, Beijing/ 19812345436/ important letter (commercial contract)/ 25.0Yuan/0. The QRcode encoded in Chinese words is shown in Fig.3(a), and the encoded QRcode in English words is shown in Fig.3(b).

(a) Correction level: H   Version: 8   (b) Correction level: H   Version: 10

Fig. 3. Two versions of QRcode

7 Conclusion

The development of wireless network and the popularization of mobile device such as mobile phone brought brilliant prospects for the commercial use of 2D barcode. At present, the commercial application of QRcode is in the preliminary stage. The business process and system framework of QRcode used in the validation of goods express delivery is put forward in this paper, the security and operability are ensured, and the efficiency of validation process are also improved. This research also provides technical reference for commercial application of the other 2D barcodes.

Acknowledgement. The paper is supported by the National Natural Science Foundation of China (No.50875158) and Shandong Natural Science Foundation for Distinguished Young scholars of China (No. JQ200816).

References

1. Gao, J., Prakash, L., Jagatesan, R.: Understanding 2D-BarCodes Technology and Applications in M-Commerce – Design and Implementation of A 2D Barcode Processing Solution. In: The Proceedings of COMPSAC 2007, vol. 2, pp. 49–56 (2007)
2. Canadi, M., Hoepken, W., Fuchs, M.: Information and Communication Technologies in Tourism 2010: Application of QR Codes in Online Travel Distribution. In: Gretzel, U., Law, R., Fuchs, M. (eds.), vol. 4, pp. 137–148. Springer, New York (2010)
3. QR Code Enables Easy Access to Food Production Data via Cell Phone I Japan for Sustainability, http://www.japanfs.org/en/pages/025772.html
4. Ivancsits, R.G.: Mobile Couponing und Mobile Ticketing – Instrument des Customer Relationship Management in Mobile Marketing. Müller, Saarbrücken, pp.7–109 (2006)
5. Wang, W.L., Lin, C.H.: A Study of Two-dimensional Barcode Prescription System for Pharmacists Activities of NHI Contracted Pharmacy. Yakugaku Zasshi 128, 123–127 (2008)
6. Kuo, D., Wong, D., Gao, J., Chang, L.: A 2D Barcode Validation System for Mobile Commerce. In: Chang, R.-S., Bellavista, P., Chao, H.-C., Lin, S.-F., Sloot, P.M.A. (eds.) GPC 2010. LNCS, vol. 6104, pp. 150–161. Springer, Heidelberg (2010)

Digital Library Billing Management System Design and Implementation

Ying Nie

Library, Henan University of Science and Technology, Luoyang, China
luodenglin@sohu.com

Abstract. Based on the database of SQL Server, a new automated billing and management system was designed using a range of forms, menus and control room provided by VB. In this new design, WINDOWS registry and API functions ware used, as well DAO and ADO data access and other advanced means. A good interactive interface was available and users could obtain a fresh and different feeling. Demonstrated by the application, the system provided accurate and reliable function and satisfied the needs of modern managements. The system is suitable for automatic billing of colleges and internet cafes management.

Keywords: digital library management, automatic billing, SQL Server database.

1 Introduction

With the rapid development of the digital library, numbers of users are growing, more and more users realize the rich network resources and the convenience exchange of information. However, due to purchasing figure resources and the computer network equipment spoilage and promotion cost, the use of the digital library must be compensable, the consumer need to pay appropriate cost. Therefore, the billing management is the important function that the computer network manages[1-2]. At present, the billing software is essentially standalone running under network environment. In case of this machine breakdown or interruption, the cost data would lose and cause the losses. Therefore, a good and mature billing management system can make the network healthy and steady development.

2 System Design

The accounting management system for internet bar used C/S model and included client and server end. Here we main analysis the function of client end.

2.1 Digital Library Billing Management System Structure

The accounting management system for internet bar used C/S model and the database was placed on the server side. The system was connects the database through client[3]. The structure of accounting management system for internet bar was showed in Figure 1.

G. Shen and X. Huang (Eds.): ECWAC 2011, Part I, CCIS 143, pp. 352–358, 2011.

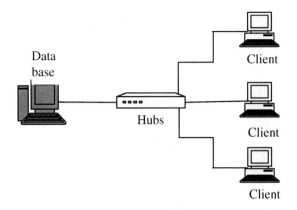

Fig. 1. System structure of billing management

2.2 Digital Library Billing Management Systems Design Process

2.2.1 The Customer Online Registration Module Design

First of all, it needs to get the information how many idle machines for customers to choose in Internet cafe now. Through database query get free machine, and the information added to the drop-down list box. Then, the system must receive the users' card number and password before carry out the automatic settlement business .The system make user's card number and password checked in the data base. If correct, the database preserved the machine number which user choose and card number (only identifiers) and start time of Internet. If the user card number and password does not match, then prompt card name or password is not correct, and keep the page is changeless, make the user re-enter the card number and password.

2.2.2 Referral Automatic Settlement Module Design

First, the system gets information from database about which machines are using at present (including some off-line), add the information of card number into the drop-down list box of "machine number". Transmit the user's machine number and the current time from system (user can modify) to the database, settlement the time of online in this machine.

In the database to start time and end time subtraction, get the time which machine use each time. The checking of the machine and the Internet card number were depended on the online registration data. Use time depending on the machine, machine number (for each machine number, system can be designed for different charging method), calculate the amount payable, and automatically from this card to send in amount. The system make the machine number, card number, and use of the time, modem remaining sum returns to the front desk page that allows users to check card number and overage.

2.2.3 Modem Design on the Card Overage Inquiry

First, the system make user to input the card number and password of inquiry. Then system sent this card number and password to the database for checking. If card number and password match, then from the database query card overage and displayed it on the front desk page. If card number and password does not match, indicate the card number or password is not correct, and then keep the page is changeless, let the user input again.

2.2.4 Internet Records Inquiry Module Design

First, the system make user to input the card number and password of inquiry and sent this card number and password to the database for checking. If the card number and password match, system for details about Internet records from the database and return it to the client, client use the List Control show the records. If card number and password does not match, indicate the card number or password is not correct, and then keep the page is changeless, let the user input again.

3 The Establishment of Database of E-R Model

According to the system design requirements, the information on the card, the machine information and the Internet business should be the main consideration, the designed system ER diagram, as shown in Figure 2.

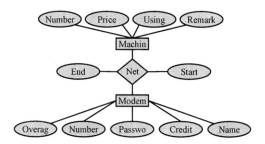

Fig. 2. ER diagram system

4 Set Up the Database of Billing Management System in Internet Cafe

4.1 The Table Design of Database

According to the design of the ER diagram in the previous section, there are two entities, as well as a contact, so in the digital library billing management system should be designed including three tables, which are on the card information table, the machine information table, and online contact form, and all property from the ER diagram to extract. The forms required for the system design are as follows: save modem information of table design as shown in figure 3; then save computer design of the machine information table shown in figure 4; finally, save the form for more information for Internet access event design shown in Figure 5.

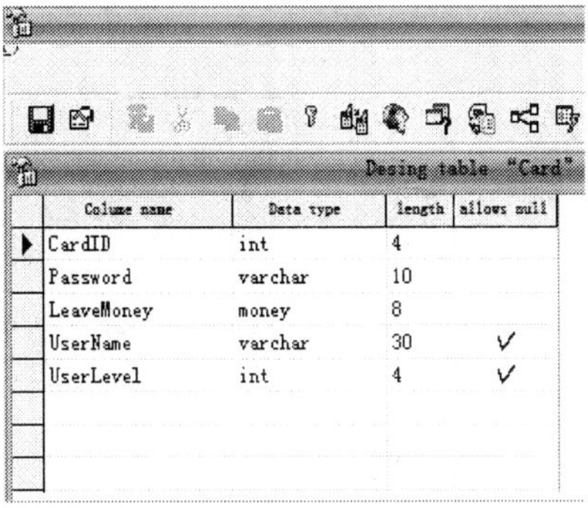

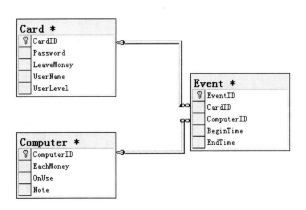

Fig. 3. Card table design interface

4.2 Database of Relationship Chart and View Design

In SQL server, to establish contacts for the three tables shown in Figure 6 [4]. To read the machine state (from the Event table), the establishment view card of surfing internet, as shown in Figure 7. To get the user's online time and the price of the machine

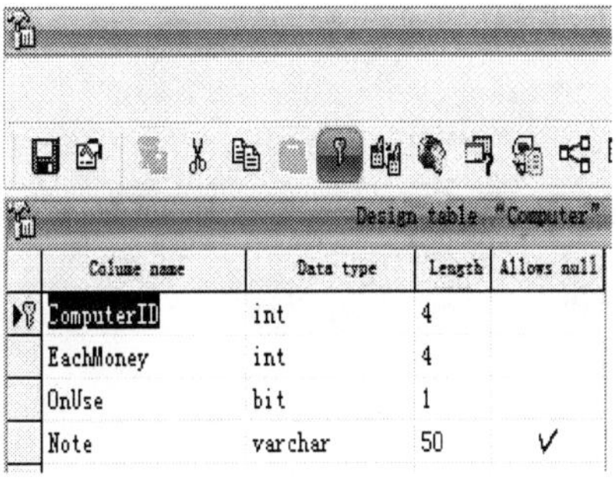

Fig. 4. Computer table design interface 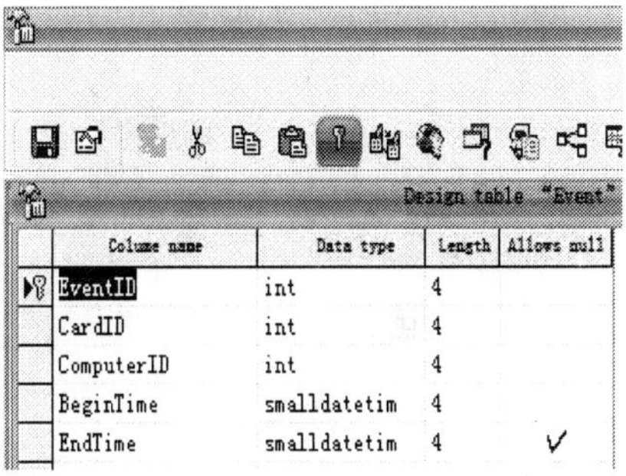   **Fig. 5.** Event table design interface

Fig. 6. The connection between the table

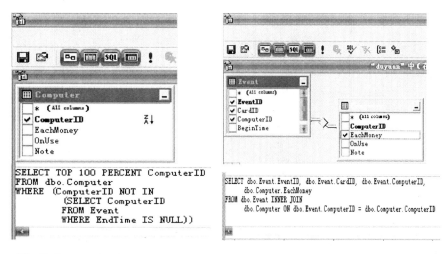

Fig. 7. ComputerIDView design interface   **Fig. 8.** TimeMoneyView design interface

on the machine, the system established view TimeMoneyView, shown in Figure 8. Here, the system settings database connection user name is sa, password is blank. Since not much data, So there is no optimization of the database.

5   System Graphic Interface Implementation

In the process, the main function of the system is on the card balance inquiries, online records information, online registration and automatic billing, etc. under the machines. These features are the digital library billing management system functionality.

5.1   Online Registration and Settlement Functions under the Automatic

"On machine" menu item, when users register online, click "Use" the system can switch to the interface shown in Figure 9.

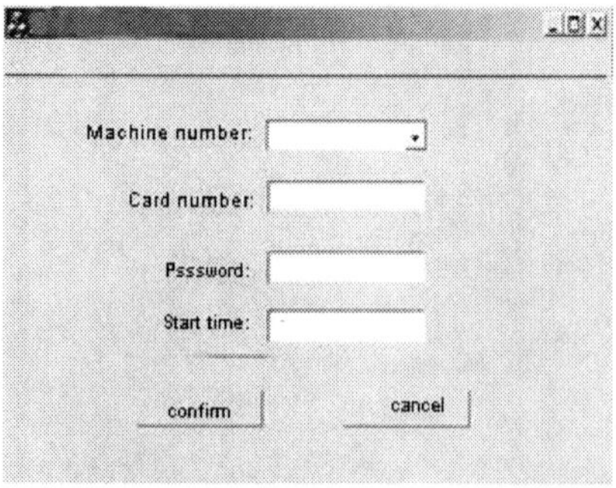

Fig. 9. Online registration interface 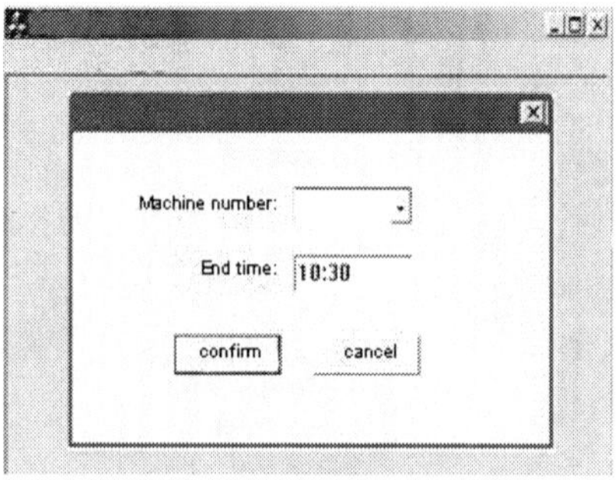   **Fig. 10.** Offline automatic billing interface

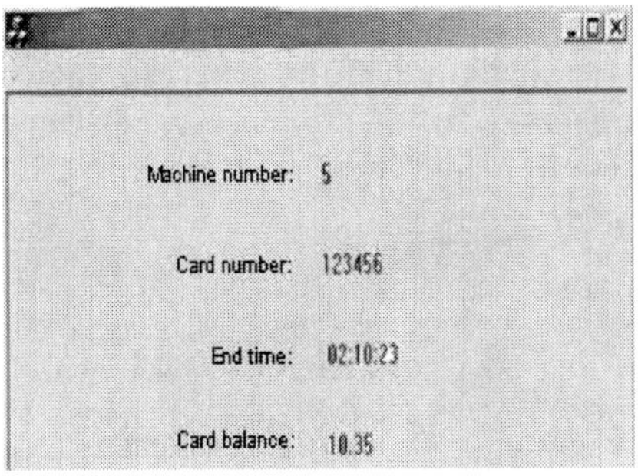

Fig. 11. Use the display interface 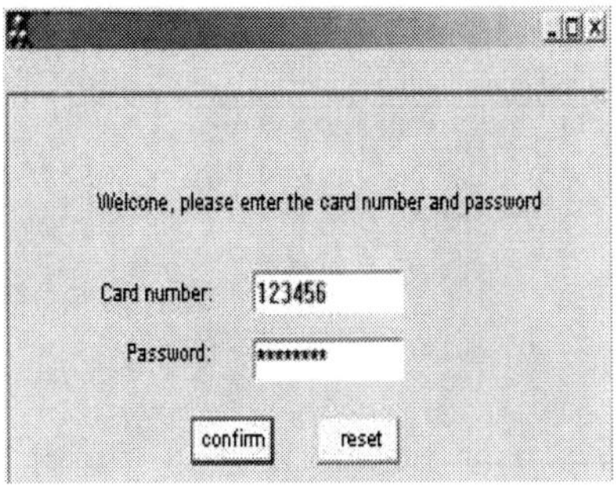   **Fig. 12.** Inquiry interface

Select a s ispare machine (Caution: "Machine number" drop-down list box displays the machines are idle, if a machine already in use, it is no longer displayed), then enter the card number, password; "Start Time" text box shows the system time, you can manually modified. Click "OK" button to complete the registration.

"The plane" when the client under the machine, click the "Use" menu item, the system will pop up the interface shown in Figure 10.

Under the settlement interface will automatically display the current system time (which can be manually modified.) Click "OK" button, you can get the case of Internet users, the interface shown in Figure 11.

5.2 Recorded on the Card Check and Internet Search Functions

"Records Search" menu→" balance inquiry" menu item or "query" Click "Search" item can pop the card number, password input screen shown in Figure 12.

Click "OK" button to find the balance of this card, the interface shown in Figure 13.

To view a detailed record of the Internet, click the "Search" "Records Search" menu item, the system will pop up the interface shown in Figure 12, enter the card number and password, you can get a detailed record of the card access system interface shown in Figure 14.

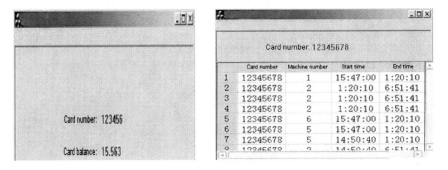

Fig. 13. Inquire the login screen   **Fig. 14.** User access records detailed query interface

Design code to use as much as possible on the class designed to reduce the amount of code, database design also emphasizes data integrity and for the speed, after the actual operation, the system can be better applied to the count room fee management. However, the system is only designed a relatively simple client billing system can not fully meet the needs of practical applications.

6 Conclusions

Based on the database of SQL Server, a new automated billing and management system was designed using a range of forms, menus and control room provided by VB. Demonstrated by the application, the system provided accurate and reliable function and satisfied the needs of modern managements. The system is suitable for automatic billing of colleges and internet cafes management.

References

1. Guo, Y.Y., Shou, J.X.: Campus network accounting system based on SNMP. Journal of Zhengjiang University of Technology 32, 78–81 (2004)
2. Qing, L.P.: The accounting system of the online reading-room on the wide area networks. New Technology of Library and Information Service 81, 53–55 (2000)
3. Brustoloni, J., Garay, J.: MicroISPs: providing convenient and low-cost high-bandwidth Internet access. Computer Networks 33, 789–802 (2000)
4. Shi, M.H., Shen, X.M., Mark, J.W., Zhao, D.M., Jiang, Y.X.: User authentication and undeniable billing support for agent-based roaming service in WLAN/cellular integrated mobile networks. Computer Networks 52, 1693–1702 (2008)

The Impact of Individual Differences on E-Learning System Behavioral Intention

PeiWen Liao[1,2,*], Chien Yu[1], and ChinCheh Yi[1]

[1] Department of Applied Technology and Human Resource Development,
National Taiwan Normal University, R.O.C.
[2] 162, Sec.1, ho-Ping E. Rd, Taipei, Taiwan
pearl908m015@hotmail.com

Abstract. This study investigated the impact of contingent variables on the relationship between four predictors and employees' behavioral intention with e-learning. Seven hundred and twenty-two employees in online training and education were asked to answer questionnaires about their learning styles, perceptions of the quality of the proposed predictors and behavioral intention with e-learning systems. The results of analysis showed that three contingent variables, gender, job title and industry, significantly influenced the perceptions of predictors and employees' behavioral intention with the e-learning system. This study also found a statistically significant moderating effect of two contingent variables, gender, job title and industry, on the relationship between predictors and e-learning system behavioral intention. The results suggest that a serious consideration of contingent variables is crucial for improving e-learning system behavioral intention. The implications of these results for the management of e-learning systems are discussed.

Keywords: e-learning system, behavioral intention, quality perceptions.

1 Introduction and Research Hypotheses

There are many benefits to using e-learning systems; they can be used at any time and place, allowing learners to proceed at their own pace and facilitators to track the trajectory of each learner's progress more easily and objectively [1]. As the use of e-learning has increased, so has research into the factors affecting learners' behavioral intention with e-learning systems. One reason for gaining a better understanding of learners' satisfaction with e-learning system is to help managers improve e-learning system quality and enhance learners' behavioral intention. In other words, managers can improve these predictors' quality so that e-learners' behavioral intention can be enhanced. This model proposed three major determinants of IS satisfaction: system quality, information quality and service quality [2] [3]. Among them, Wang's [4], Lu's and Chiou's model was selected because it provides a better mapping with the IS satisfaction model. This study combines the research from a designer's viewpoint: interface friendliness (IF), content richness (CR), perceived flexibility (PF) and perceived community (PC). Instead, management style and organizational structure are influenced by environmental aspects: the contingency factors [1]. In keeping with the

---

* Corresponding author.

G. Shen and X. Huang (Eds.): ECWAC 2011, Part I, CCIS 143, pp. 359–364, 2011.

basic concepts of contingency theory, the premise of this study is that there cannot be 'one best way' for attaining e-learning behavioral intention. This research identifies and investigates the impact of three contingency factors on e-learning system satisfaction: gender, job title, and industry [5][6][7].

On the basis of the research literature, four predictors of e-learning system satisfaction and three contingent variables were selected for investigation. Figure 1 depicts the research model that examines the effect of perceptions of quality on e-learning satisfaction; to investigate the impact of three contingent variables—gender, job title and industry—on IF, PC, CR, PF and behavioral intention (BI); and to explore the moderating effects of contingent variables on the relationships among the four predictors and e-learning system behavioral intention. Four groups of hypotheses are to be evaluated: the e-learners' perceptions of quality mean IF, PC, CR and PF (see Fig. 1):

H1: e-Learners' perceptions of qualities are positively related to the BI.
H2: e-Learners' perceptions of qualities are correlated with the contingent variables of gender, job title and industry.
H3: e-Learners' BI is correlated with these three contingent variables.
H4: These three contingent variables have moderating effects on the relationship between various perceptions of qualities and BI.

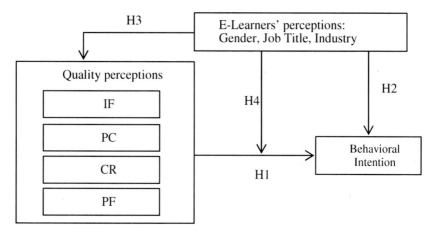

Fig. 1. Research model

2   Research Method

2.1   Sample

The 722 usable responses were received. These respondents were female (369), and male (353). Their job title was manager (119), and employee (603). These respondents were service industry (244), technology industry (245), and finance industry (233).

2.2   Model Estimation and Hypotheses Testing

Initial scale reliability and validity were verified. Finally, this study was assessed on a 5-point Likert-type scale. In this study, interface friendliness is the degree to which employees perceived the interface of the e-learning system as friendly, easy to use and stable in operation. Perceived community is the degree to which employees perceived that the e-learning system provided an easy communication platform to share learning content and collaborate with their classmates. Content richness is the degree to which employees perceived that the learning content provided by the e-learning system was rich, sufficient, relevant and updated. Perceived flexibility is the degree to which employees perceived that the e-learning system enabled them to control the pace and sequence of course progress, and to choose the learning content they preferred.

3   Data Analysis and Results

3.1   Analysis of Measurement Validity

In verifying the scale for measuring these constructs, the coefficient alpha values for IF, PC, CR, PF and BI were 0.73, 0.79, 0.88, 0.86 and 0.90 respectively. Because the Cronbach's alpha values were above the conventional level of 0.7, the scales for these constructs were deemed to exhibit adequate reliability. An SEM approach allows researchers to find the five latent variables. Composite reliability for IF, PC, CR, PF and BI were 0.73, 0.79, 0.89, 0.86, 0.90. Loading were between the 0.61-0.90. All goodness-of-fit indices (GFI = 0.92, CFI = 0.98, NFI = 0.98, RMSEA = 0.085, RMSR = 0.026) were within the acceptable range recommended by the previous researchers [8][9], suggesting that the research model provided a good fit to the data. Therefore, the research model fit was adequate to assess the results for the structural model.

3.2   Hypotheses Testing

The significance of each path from predictors to e-learning behavioral intention in the structural model was tested with data from the entire sample. The paths of all three—interface friendliness-satisfaction (IF- BI), content richness-satisfaction (CR- BI) and perceived flexibility-satisfaction (PF- BI)—exhibited significant path coefficients of 0.35, 0.37 and 0.27 respectively, while the path from perceived community to e-learning satisfaction (PC- BI) was significant at a p-value of 0.05.

The effects of gender, job title and industry on IF, PC, CR, PF and BI were examined using analyses of variance (ANOVAs). Table 1 shows the mean scores, standard deviations, together with significant F ratios. No significant differences were found in the gender, job title contingent variables. Finally, there were differences in perception among the industry, perceptions of all four predictors—IF, PC, CR and PF—and of BI. The path model was tested with the data from the entire data sample (i.e., all employees) and each of the contingent subsamples (for example, male and female). The comparison of path coefficients between predictors and e-learning system behavioral intention is shown in Table 2 for each contingent subsample. Significant differences were found in two groups of contingent subsamples. For manager versus employee, significant differences appeared in the path coefficients: IF-BI. Different industries also showed significant differences. In the CR-BI dimension, two path coefficients were significantly different, whereas in the PF-BI dimension, two path coefficients were significantly different. The testing result is shown in Table 3. Each group of hypotheses (H1, H2, H3 and H4) is partially supported.

Table 1. Descriptive statistics and ANOVAs testing results

			IF	PC	CR	PF	BI
Gender	Male(n=353)	Mean	3.588	3.554	3.732	3.665	3.749
		SD	.661	.698	.696	.765	.780
	Female(n=369)	Mean	3.592	3.539	3.656	3.734	3.757
		SD	.648	.676	.684	.726	.772
	Significance of difference (F ratios)		ns	ns	ns	ns	ns
Job title	Manager(n=119)	Mean	3.669	3.627	3.725	3.703	3.878
		SD	.640	.614	.668	.694	.698
	Employee(n=603)	Mean	3.574	3.531	3.687	3.700	3.729
		SD	.656	.699	.695	.755	.788
	Significance of difference (F ratios)		ns	ns	ns	ns	ns
Industry	Service(n=244)	Mean	3.515	3.441	3.570	3.551	3.648
		SD	.649	.643	.648	.704	.790
	Technology(n=245)	Mean	3.731	3.739	3.841	3.884	3.908
		SD	.572	.642	.659	.628	.700
	Finance(n=233)	Mean	3.521	3.455	3.667	3.664	3.702
		SD	.716	.734	.739	.855	.812
	Significance of difference (F ratios)		8.756***	15.128***	9.912***	13.104***	7.814***

$*p \leq 0.05$; $***p < 0.001$.

Table 2. Comparison of path coefficients among predictors and satisfaction

			BI	IF-BI	PC-BI	CR-BI	PF-BI
Entire sample		R^2	.520				
		γ		.349***	.186***	.142**	.133***
Gender differences	Male	R_1^2	.525				
		γ_1		.445***	.099	.115	.138*
	Female	R_2^2	.524				
		γ_2		.270***	.264***	.160**	.128**
	Significant difference			*	ns	ns	ns
Job title differences	Manager	R_1^2	.450				
		γ_1		.184	.128	.333**	.152
	Employee	R_2^2	.536				
		γ_2		.392***	.189***	.102*	.127**
	Significant difference			*	ns	ns	ns
Industry differences	Service	R_1^2	.488				
		γ_1		.357***	.185*	.162*	.089
	Technology	R_1^2	.486				
		γ_1		.269***	.255**	.006	.271***
	Finance	R_1^2	.576				
		γ_1		.401***	.136	.250**	.038
	Significant difference	D1	ns	ns	ns	ns	*
		D2	ns	ns	ns	*	**

$**p < 0.01$; $***p \leq 0.001$. BI, behavioral intention; IF, interface friendliness; PC, perceived community; CR, content richness; PF, perceived flexibility; AC, abstract concept; CE, concrete experience; AE, active experiment; RO, reflective observation; D1 Service-other(technology and finance), D2 Finance-other(service and technology) ; ns, not significant.

Table 3. The significant differences among contingent groups

Perception	Contingent variable	Result	Relationship	Contingent variable	Result
IF	Gender	ns	IF-BI	Gender	male>female
IF	Job title	ns	IF-BI	Job title	employee>manager
IF	Industry	technology>service, finance	IF-BI	industry	ns
PC	Gender	ns	PC-BI	Gender	ns
PC	Job title	ns	PC-BI	Job title	ns
PC	Industry	technology>service, finance	PC-BI	industry	ns
CR	Gender	ns	CR-BI	Gender	ns
CR	Job title	ns	CR-BI	Job title	ns
CR	Industry	technology>service, finance	CR-BI	industry	service >technology
PF	Gender	ns	PF-BI	Gender	ns
PF	Job title	ns	PF-BI	Job title	ns
PF	Industry	technology>service, finance	PF-BI	industry	technology>service> finance
BI	Gender	ns			
BI	Job title	ns			
BI	Industry	technology>service, finance			

4 Discussion

The findings of this study offer the following insights and suggestions. First, this study provides strong support for the industry difference in perceptions of all predictors and e-learning system behavioral intentions. Technology industry's ratings of all predictors and e-learning behavioral intention were higher than those of the service and finance industries. Second, this study provides strong evidence that males perceived greater IF experienced more behavioral intention than females did, and job title provides strong evidence that employees who perceived greater IF experienced more behavioral intention than managers did.

Acknowledgment

This research was substantially supported by the National Science Council (NSC) of Taiwan under grant number NSC 99-2511-S-003-001.

References

1. Lu, H.P., Chiou, M.J.: The impact of individual differences on e-learning system satisfaction: A contingency approach. British Journal of Educational Technology 41(2), 307–323 (2010)
2. DeLone, W.D., McLean, E.R.: Information systems success: the quest for the dependent variable. Information Systems Research 3, 60–95 (1992)
3. DeLone, W.D., McLean, E.R.: The DeLone and McLean model of information systems success: a ten-year update. Journal of Management Information Systems 19, 9–30 (2003)
4. Wang, Y.S.: Assessment of learner satisfaction with asynchronous electronic learning systems. Information & Management 41, 75–86 (2003)

5. Garland, D., Martin, B.N.: Do gender and learning style play a role in how online courses should be designed? Journal of Interactive Online Learning 4, 67–81 (2005)
6. Ong, C.S., Lai, J.Y.: Gender differences in perceptions and relationships among dominants of e-learning acceptance. Computers in Human Behavior 22, 816–829 (2006)
7. Lee, Y.K.: Understanding e-learning consumers: the moderating effects of gender and learner diversity. The Journal of American Academy of Business 11, 223–230 (2007)
8. Bagozzi, R.P., Yi, Y.: On the evaluation of structural equation models. Journal of the Academy of Marking Science 16, 74–94 (1988)
9. McDonald, R.P., Ho, M.R.: Principles and practice in reporting structural equation analysis. Psychological Methods 7, 64–82 (2002)

A Research on Performance Measurement Based on Economic Valued-Added Comprehensive Scorecard

Qin Chen and XiaoMei Zhang

Northeast Agricultural University Economic Management School
150030, Harbin, China

Abstract. With the development of economic, the traditional performance mainly rely on financial indicators could not satisfy the need of work. In order to make the performance measurement taking the best services for business goals, this paper proposed Economic Valued-Added Comprehensive Scorecard based on research of shortages and advantages of EVA and BSC .We used Analytic Hierarchy Process to build matrix to solve the weighting of EVA Comprehensive Scorecard. At last we could find the most influence factors for enterprise value forming the weighting.

Keywords: economic value-added, the balanced scorecard, economic valued-added comprehensive scorecard, performance measurement.

1 Introduction

Business performance evaluation refers to use specific indicators and benchmarks, and uses the scientific evaluation methods to make value judgments about enterprise's performance, the aim of it is to achieve enterprise strategic objectives and promote the sustainable development of enterprise.

Traditional performance evaluation are single and passive, and largely focused on measurements of performance on financial aspects . In order to adapt to enterprises' development, performance appraisal should evaluate the type of financial indicators and non-financial indicators reasonable to evaluate the enterprise' performance . The another shortages is that the capital cost factors are ignored and may lead to business focuses on short-term goals., the traditional performance appraisals can not satisfy the modern enterprise to maintain the long term competition.

This article proposed a new kind of performance evaluation method-Valued-Added Comprehensive Scorecard based on the research of EVA and BSC.

2 EVA Performance Measurement System

2.1 The Basic Principles of EVA

Economic Value-Added is the profits that corporate income deducts total capital costs(include capital cost and debt cost).

G. Shen and X. Huang (Eds.): ECWAC 2011, Part I, CCIS 143, pp. 365–370, 2011.

$$EVA=NOPAT-NA_0 \times WACC$$

NOPAT is the net business profit after adjusted ;NA_0 is the initial investment capital which include capital cost and debt cost; WACC is the rate of weighted average capital cost.

2.2 The Advantages and Shortages of EVA Performance Measurement System

EVA have the following advantages:(1) EVA makes up for the shortages of accounting profit that not considers total capital costs. EVA considers capital cost so that businesses should ignore to overestimate profit and can reflect the real wealth of owners.(2)EVA can not be easily operated.. All the expenditures associated with profit look as investment not cost ,in the same time ,the all capitals look as the costs of capital whatever where is its source.(3)EVA can establish stimulant system effectively. Eva may set up a set of stimulant system which can have influence the owners, managers and staff and can integrate their interests.

EVA has the following shortages:(1) EVA force only on the financial indicators. EVA is calculated according to historical data so indicators for the next performance are difficult to predict.(2) EVA lead to easily short-term action. EVA is consequential indicator and easy to make the operators concerns only for final results and ignores the effects of course, therefore, may make owners pursuit one-sided profits lead to short-term action.(3)EVA do not consider the interests of another related people. The objective of EVA is to maximize shareholders' wealth and do not consider the other stakeholders, such as customers, suppliers, etc.

3 BSC Performance Measurement System

3.1 The Basic Concents of BSC

Balanced Scorecard includes four aspects of contents: customer, internal process, study and development and financial ability.(1)Customer. In the first time, how to meet the needs of the clients is the key to get to the sustainable development for enterprises. (2)Internal Process. It concerns the internal process that is important to achieve the organization's financial objectives.(3)Study and Development. Enterprises must keep up learning and innovating.(4)Financial Ability. Enterprise's final goal is to pursue profit.

3.2 The Advantages and Shortages of BSC Performance Measurement System

BSC has the following advantages:(1)The balance between financial and-non-financial .It makes up for the shortages of the traditional performance appraisals by carring out strategic management form the four aspects of BSC.(2) The balance between result and reason. BSC associate result with reason so that organizations can determine reasons of things and work out the plan of action.(3)The balance between long-term and short-term. BSC discloses short-term objectives form business strategies.(4)The balance between external and internal. In BSC, the shareholders and customers are external groups ,staff and internal process are internal groups.

BSC has the following advantages:(1)Parts of the indicators to measure. Such as customer satisfaction and clients retention.(2)The complex problems of the distribution of weighting. BSC need to have a comprehensive consideration form four dimensions, this will increase complexity of BSC.

4 Economic Valued-Added Comprehensive Scorecard

4.1 The Overview of Economic Valued-Added Comprehensive Scorecard

We can put EVA and BSC into together to constitute a new kind of index system-EVA comprehensive scorecard. EVA is placed in the top of the system and the final link of cause-and-effect relationship in BSC. Enterprise development strategy and business advantage is to achieve the growth of EVA ,under the goal , the departmental plans are not carried out alone but for the promotion of EVA .

The structure steps of EVA comprehensive scorecard:

(1)   EVA is placeg the top of the comprehensive scorecard.
(2)   Making indicators form the four aspects of BSC and every indicators are associated with the goals to achieve the growth of EVA.
(3)   Using the performance evaluation tables to estimate performance in the whole business.

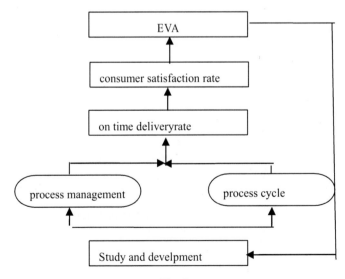

Fig. 1.

4.2 Using AHP (Analytic Hierarchy Process)to Build the Model EVA Comprehensive Scorecard

AHP is the method which discloses elements associated with decision-making into the level of goals, principles and proposals.

Build pairwise comparison matrix. The top of AHP is objective level, the bottom is normal level, the middle is index level. From the second floor of hierarchical model ,for all factors of the level belong to the last level, Using the method of 1-9scale ratio ,we compare every two indicators of each level by consulting experts and receive pairwise comparison matrix $X=[X_1, X_2, ..., X_n]^T$, indicators belong to X_1 is $[W_{i1}, W_{i2}, ..., W_{in}]$ $(i=1, 2......n)$, W_{ij} show the relative importance of indicators i for indicators j. The following matrix is pairwise comparison matrix:

$$X = \begin{bmatrix} W_{11}W_{12}...W_{1n} \\ W_{21}W_{22}...W_{2n} \\ ... \\ W_{n1}W_{n2}...W_{nn} \end{bmatrix}$$

Calculate weighting. According to pairwise comparison matrix ,we calculate feature vector of each matrix so that we can obtain the weighting of each indicator.

Table 1. The figure of 1-9 ratio scale

Scale	Meaning
1	i and j is equally important
3	i is a little important than j
5	i is important than j
7	i is more important than j
9	i is extremely important than j
2,4,6,8	the median value

5 Taking Analysis from a Example

H company has a large scale of production and strength, according to the actual conditions of business to establish the hierarchical model of EVA comprehensive scorecard. The hierarchical model: the objective level A; the normal level(financial ability b_1,customer b_2,internal process b_3,study and development b_4); the index level sales growth ratec_1,rate of return on investmentc_2,asset turnover ratec$_3$,customer retention rate c$_4$,consumer satisfaction rate c$_5$,on time delivery rate c$_6$, quality products ratec$_7$,products refund rate c$_8$,new product development time c$_9$,research costs of the total income c$_{10}$,the number of staff training c$_{11}$,employee turnover rate c$_{12}$,research cost growth rate c$_{13}$.

The following figure is the structure of EVA comprehensive scorecard of H company.

Forming this figure we can see fairly the structure of EVA comprehensive scorecard. Each indicator is to implement the growth of EVA.

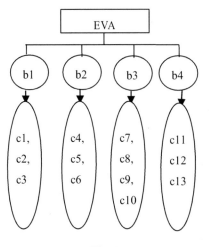

Fig. 2.

According to actual situation and AHP principle, we can get the pairwise comparison matrix by consulting experts.

The pairwise comparison matrix between the objective level and the normal level.

$$\begin{bmatrix} 1 & 2 & 1/3 & 1/2 \\ 1/2 & 1 & 1/5 & 1/2 \\ 3 & 5 & 1 & 2 \\ 2 & 2 & 1/2 & 1 \end{bmatrix}$$

The feature vector of it is H=[0.18,0.12,0.45,0.25].

The pairwise comparison matrix between the normal level and the normal level. In the financial ability b1,the matrix among c$_1$,c$_2$,and c$_3$ is k$_1$.In the customer b$_2$,the matrix among c$_4$,c$_5$and c$_6$ is k$_2$.In the internal process b$_3$,the matrix among c$_7$,c$_8$,c$_9$and c$_{10}$ is k$_3$.In the study and development b$_4$,the matrix among c$_{11}$,c$_{12}$and c$_{13}$ is k$_4$.

$$k_1=\begin{bmatrix} 1 & 2 & 5 \\ 1/2 & 1 & 4 \\ 1/5 & 1/4 & 1 \end{bmatrix} \quad k2=\begin{bmatrix} 1 & 1/2 & 3 \\ 2 & 1 & 4 \\ 1/3 & 1/4 & 1 \end{bmatrix} \quad k3=\begin{bmatrix} 1 & 1/2 & 3 & 5 \\ 2 & 1 & 5 & 7 \\ 1/3 & 1/5 & 1 & 1/2 \\ 1/5 & 1/7 & 2 & 1 \end{bmatrix} \quad k_4=\begin{bmatrix} 1 & 1/4 & 1/4 \\ 4 & 1 & 4 \\ 4 & 3 & 1 \end{bmatrix}$$

The following is feature vector of k1,k2,k3,k4 :
H_1=[0.544,0.347,0.109],H_2=[0.342,0.526,0.132],H_3=[0.336,0.087,0.159,0.518],H_4= [0.096,0.281,0.623].According to feature vectors of matrixs, we can calculate the weighting of each indicator. the following table is the weighting of indicator in EVA comprehensive scorecard.

Table 2.

The objective level	Weighting	The normal level	Weighting	Weighting
financial ability	0.18	sales growth rate	0.544	0.098
		rate of return on investment	0.347	0.062
		asset turnover rate	0.109	0.019
customer	0.12	customer retention rate	0.342	0.041
		consumer satisfactional rate	0.526	0.063
		on time delivery rate	0.132	0.016
internal process	0.45	rate of quality products	0.336	0.151
		products refund rate	0.087	0,039
		new product development time	0.159	0.072
		research costs of total income	0.518	0.207
study and development	0.25	the number of staff training	0.096	0.024
		employee turnover rate	0.281	0.070
		research cost growth rate	0.623	0.156

Forming the figure we can find that the indicator of internal process is best important for the growth of EVA, secondly is the indicator of study and development.

References

1. Liu, X.: A Research on Performance Measurement Based on EVA comprehensive scorecard. J. Statistics and policy-making (2009)
2. Wan, L., Li, Z.: A Research on BSC Based on AHP and Fuzzy. J. Technology and Management Research (2010)
3. Lin, Z.: Performance Measurement, pp. 242–251. Northeast University of Finance and Economic Press (2008)

A Method to Reduce Error When Synthesizing Signal with Adjustable Frequency by Using DDS

Jian Guo, Jie Zhu, Li Zhou, and Pingping Dong

Information School, Beijing Wuzi University, Beijing, 101149, China
{guojian,zhujie,zhouli}@bwu.edu.cn

Abstract. Because of its own advantages, direct digital synthesis technology (DDS) is applied widely in traditional fields which need signal source. Based on the working principle of DDS, in the applying process, it is very important to calculate the frequency control word. To address the shortcoming of large computation, low efficiency of frequency setting, more storage space occupied or significant cumulative errors of frequency setting when calculating frequency control word with traditional methods, a novel calculation way for frequency control word is researched in this paper. This new method does not need large computation and more space and simultaneously it can decrease the error greatly, which plays an important role in improving the frequency setting speed and precision in signal generator.

Keywords: Direct Digital Synthesis, Frequency Control Word, Adjustable Frequency, Signal Source.

1 Introduction

Direct digital frequency synthesis (DDS or DDFS) is a novel technology following direct synthesis, coherent phase-locked-type synthesis and digital phase-locked synthesis technologies [1]. DDS is far beyond the traditional frequency synthesis in a series of performance indicators such as the frequency resolution, frequency hopping speed, frequency stability and so on. At the same time, because almost all elements in DDS are belong to digital circuit, it has advantages of easy integration, low power consumption, small size, light weight, high reliability, easily programmed, flexible usage, et al. Therefore, it is applied in many fields such as portable communications, radar systems, and frequency hopping communication [2].

2 DDS Working Principle

DDS chip consists of clock, phase increment register, phase accumulator, waveform memory, D/A converter and low-pass filter. The diagram of working principle of DDS is shown as Fig.1. Under the reference clock with certain frequency, the output frequency can be changed by changing the phase interval represented by each reference

G. Shen and X. Huang (Eds.): ECWAC 2011, Part I, CCIS 143, pp. 371–376, 2011.

clock pulse (that is, M, shown in Fig.1). The working principle of DDS is described in Fig.1. The waveform memory usually is a read-only memory which is used to store the coded quantization value of waveform amplitude. The working process is as following. When the clock pulse arrives, the frequency control word will be added to the data stored in phase accumulator. And the output of phase accumulator is used as an addressing address of waveform memory after it is latched and the contents of this address unit is the amplitude of a waveform synthesis point. The amplitude value is converted by D/A converter and filtered by low-pass filter, and then the analog signal meet requirement is obtained [3-6].

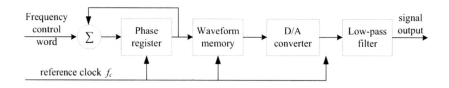

Fig. 1. The diagram of working principle of DDS

If the reference clock frequency is f_c and the bit of phase accumulator is N, the output

frequency of DDS is $f_{out} = \dfrac{M * f_c}{2^N}$ .Here, M is the frequency control word and it value

is preset by the external control circuit. When the frequency of reference clock f_c and the number of phase accumulator bit is certain, the output frequency f_{out} is decided by

M. So, the frequency control word M is obtained as $M = \dfrac{2^N * f_{out}}{f_c}$. When M is equal to

1, the lowest frequency of signal synthesized is $f_{out}=f_c/2^N$, which is the frequency resolution of DDS. The highest output frequency is determined by Nyquist sampling theorem and it is $f_c/2$.

3   The Usual Method of Calculating Frequency Control Word M

When the reference clock frequency f_c is equal to $2f$Hz, the bit of phase accumulator is N, and the range of frequency output is aHz$\sim f$Hz and frequency resolution is tHz, the calculation of frequency control word M is analyzed. Under the above condition, there are $(f-a)/t+1$ optional frequency output which are aHz, $(a+t)$Hz,$(a+2t)$Hz,......,$(f-t)$Hz, fHz. Here the least frequency also should be the integral times of frequency resolution t.

3.1   One of the Usual Methods to Compute the Frequency Control Word

At first, the value of frequency control word M written to frequency register corresponding to $(f-a)/t+1$ frequency is calculated by hand calculation. And $(f-a)/t+1$ numbers which are represented with N bits are stored into system memory. After the frequency setting value is accepted by the signal generator, the value chased down from $(f-a)/t+1$ numbers is written to frequency register.

The advantage of this method is high setting frequency accuracy which can be up to frequency resolution of DDS chip,$f_c/2^N$. However, when the system is designed, the amount of data needed to compute is large, speed frequency setting is low and storage space required is more.

3.2   Another Usual Method to Compute the Frequency Control Word

Another method is that the frequency control words are calculated by programming based on above formula. At first, the frequency control word M_1 corresponding to $f_{out} = t\mathrm{Hz}$ is computed, and then M_1 is truncated and $M_1^{'}$.is gotten. Then under a certain frequency, the value M is written into the frequency register is $M = B * M_1^{'}$, where $B(=1,2,3,...)$ is the quotient when a certain frequency is divided by $t\mathrm{Hz}$ since t is the frequency resolution. Taking $t=0.1\mathrm{Hz}$ as an example, when the frequency is 35.4Hz, the value needed to be written to the frequency register is $M = 354 * M_1^{'}$.

This algorithm has the advantages such as simple programming, small hand calculation working and little storage space. But there are accumulating error of setting frequency. With the frequency increasing, the absolute error of frequency Δ is increasing too and its value is $\Delta = \dfrac{(M_1 - M_1^{'}) B}{M_1} \mathrm{Hz}$. For example, if $f_c = 2MHz$, N=28, $t=0.1\mathrm{Hz}$ and the output frequency is 1KHz, the absolute error is about 31Hz. And such a large error in the instrument calibration applications is not allowed

4   A New Method to Compute the Frequency Control Word

To solve the problem of methods used in 3.1 and 3.2, a new algorithm to compute the frequency control word is put forward. The new method under the circumstance of no reducing the setting speed of frequency, a lot of storage space is saved and the absolute error of setting frequency is decreased clearly.

At first, we will calculate the values of frequency control word M truncated corresponding to the output frequency M1$\{t,2t, ...,9t\mathrm{Hz}\}$,M2$\{10t, 20t, ...,90t\mathrm{Hz}\}$, M3$\{100t, 200t, ..., 900t\mathrm{Hz}\}$,......,M$i\{10^{i-1}\times t, 10^{i-1}\times 2t, ...,10^{i-1}\times 9t\ \mathrm{Hz}\}$,......,

$\mathrm{M}q\{\,10^{q-1}\times t\,,\;10^{q-1}\times 2t\,,\;...,\;10^{q-1}\times 9t\,\}$ and write them into the frequency register. Here, $q=\lceil\log_{10}^{f/t}\rceil$. And then all the values will be saved into q arrays such as M1, M2,..., Mi, ..., Mq. Then the rounding part of M1~Mq data are going to be stored with q arrays. We can get the value of frequency control word M corresponding to mHz frequency from the following four steps.

Step 1: calculate the multiple of m to t: $B=m/t$. Then the maximum of B is f/t(f is the largest output frequency)

Setp 2: display B with an expression as

$$B=n_1+n_2\times 10+n_3\times 10^2+......+n_i\times 10^{i-1}+......n_p\times 10^{p-1},\;0\le n_i\le 9,\;1\le i\le p,n_p\ne 0.$$

Step 3: When the setting frequency is mHz, we can extract the value M1$[n_1]$ from M1, M2$[n_2]$ from M2,..., M$i[n_i]$ from Mi, ..., and M$p[n_p]$ from Mp and then add all these value, which means that M= M1$[n_1]$+ M2$[n_2]$+M3$[n_3]$+...M$i[n_i]$+...M$p[n_p]$. Here, when ni=0, there is no data extracted from Mi.

Step 4: We can extract the value $\triangle 1[n_1]$ from $\triangle 1$, $\triangle 2[n_2]$ from $\triangle 2$,..., $\triangle i[n_i]$from $\triangle i$, ..., and $\triangle p[n_p]$ from $\triangle p$ and then add all these value, which means that $\triangle$= $\triangle 1[n_1]$+ $\triangle 2[n_2]$+$\triangle 3[n_3]$+...$\triangle i[n_i]$+...$\triangle p[n_p]$. Then the result is rounded and is added to the result of step3, which is the data needed to write to the frequency register.

Taking a=0.1Hz,f=1MHz, t=0.1Hz as an example, when the setting output frequency m equals to 7893.4Hz, we can get the value of frequency control word M according to the next four steps.

Step 1: calculate the multiple of m to t: $B=m/t$=7893.4/0.1=78934.

Setp 2: display B with an expression as $B=4+3\times 10+9\times 10^2+8\times 10^3+7\times 10^4$.

Step 3: extract the value M1[4] from M1, M2[3] from M2, M3[9] from M3, M4[8] from M4 and M5[7] from M7 and then add all these value. We can get that M= M1[4] +M2[3] +M3[9]+M4[8] + M5[7].

Step 4: We can extract the value $\triangle 5[7]$from $\triangle 5$, $\triangle 4[8]$ from $\triangle 4$, $\triangle 3[9]$ from $\triangle 3$, $\triangle 2[3]$from $\triangle 2$ and$\triangle 1[4]$from $\triangle 1$, and then add all these value, which means that $\triangle$=$\triangle 1[4]$ +$\triangle 2[3]$ +$\triangle 3[9]$ +$\triangle 4[8]$ + $\triangle 5[7]$. Then the result is rounded and is added to the result of step3, which is the data needed to write to the frequency register, that is, the frequency control word.

Summing up the above, we can get the advantages of this new method as following. (1) The data stored into memory is small. There are only $2 \times q$ groups, which mean $2 \times 9 \times q$ n-bit binary numbers. (2) Comparing to the method in 2.1, the speed of frequency setting is much faster since the value is retrieved from only q groups instead of from $(f-a)/t+1$ numbers. (3) The new method significantly reduces the error accumulating effect since each array is calculated by hands. So the maximum error is 0.5 when getting each array values of frequency control word M truncated corresponding to setting frequency. The absolute error of output frequency is less than $\dfrac{0.5 \times f_c}{2^N}$ Hz, which is the half of frequency resolution. When $f_c=2\text{MHz}$ and $N=28$, the absolute error of frequency is less than $\dfrac{0.5 \times f_c}{2^N} = \dfrac{0.5 \times 2 \times 10^6}{2^{28}} = 0.003725\text{Hz}$.

5 Conclusions

DDS is an important means to synthesize frequency. Because it has superiority in a series of performance such as bandwidth, frequency conversion time, frequency resolution, phase continuity and integration, DDS is used widely in a variety of instruments. To address the disadvantages of large computation, low efficiency of frequency setting, more storage space occupied or significant cumulative errors of frequency setting when calculating frequency control word with usual methods, a new calculation algorithm of frequency control word is developed in this paper. This new method does not need large computation and more space and simultaneously it can decrease the error greatly and improve the frequency setting speed and precision. The method can be employed in synthesizing adjustable frequency signal generators when adopting DDS technology.

Acknowledgment

The paper is supported by the Funding Project for Academic Human Resources Development in Institutions of Higher Learning Under the Jurisdiction of Beijing Municipality(PHR201007145, PHR201108311), Funding Project for Base Construction of Scientific Research of Beijing Municipal Commission of Education(WYJD200902) and Funding project for Beijing excellent talents (2010D005009000002).

References

1. Zhang, H.-d., Liu, J.: Analysis of the Spurious Caused by Phase Truncation in DDS and the Ways to Restrain It. Automation & Instrumentation 3, 26–29 (2007)
2. Chen, Y.-y., Hu, Q.-q., Zhang, J., Ge, L.-f.: Design of Low Frequency Program-controlled Signal Source Based on DDS Technology. Automation & Instrumentation 2, 26–29 (2007)
3. Chen, J., Pan, Z., Wang, T.: A High Accurate Signal Generator Based on DDS Chip AD9959. Process Automation Instrumentation 28, 50–53 (2007)
4. Cheng, M., Chen, Y., Zhao, H.: A kind of signal source based on DDS chip AD9959. Automation and Instruments 6, 25–28 (2005)
5. Salmer, I.M., Mencattia, B., et al.: High spectral purity digital direct synthesizer implementation by means of a fuzzy approximator. Applied Soft Computing 4, 241–257 (2004)
6. Chen, J.: Design of High Frequency Signal Generator Based on AT89S51 and AD9850. Industrial Control Computer 9, 118–120 (2003)

Task-Based Teaching of English-Chinese Translation under "Caliber-Oriented Education to Success" Based on Web

Zhongyan Duan

Zhongnan Language Research Institute,
Wuhan University of Science and Technology Zhongnan Branch,
Wuhan 430223

Abstract. This paper, under 3–using principle in the philosophy of caliber-oriented education to success (CETS), makes a tentative qualitative study on the application of task-based approach in the teaching of English-Chinese translation based on the web. Translation teaching is characterized by its practicality. Therefore, the task-based approach can be employed to guide the web-based content collection and the process of English translation teaching. In this way, the prospect for enhancing student's translation ability is quite encouraging, which has been verified by one year's teaching.

Keywords: task-based teaching of translation, teaching content, teaching process.

1 Introduction

Translation teaching reform is urgently needed, for translation course is one of the core curriculum for English majors, and translation teaching plays a quite important role in the enhancement of students' language competence as well as their translation ability, or caliber. As early as in 1996, delegates of the first National Translation Teaching Conference proposed that the teaching of translation must be based on some theory because the simple skill teaching is obviously difficult to meet the present teaching needs, and they also pointed out that equal emphasis should be placed on translation theory and practice in appropriate combination.

However, the present translation textbooks, with no more than two types of given exercises of a long or short history, fail to meet such requirement and have lost their attraction in students who are curious and fashionable. Undoubtedly, new contents should be offered. But what are they? where are they from? How could they be arranged to satisfy the practicality of translation teaching? The answer is the web where you can find almost any information you want and the 3-using principle which can guide you collect appropriate information and arrange it logically.

1.1 The 3-Using Principle

It is hold in the CETS philosophy that caliber is basically innate and that its improvement is determined by education. In addition to the innate ones, caliber cannot be

G. Shen and X. Huang (Eds.): ECWAC 2011, Part I, CCIS 143, pp. 377–382, 2011.
© Springer-Verlag Berlin Heidelberg 2011

transferred directly; internalization is the fundamental law of its formation and development. Therefore, college education should be innovative in education models, mechanisms, content and methods, through the organization of autonomous learning, nurture, training, experience, practice sublimation, contributing to the internalization and enhancement of students' success caliber. (Zuobin Zhao, 2009: 104)

In the CETS philosophy, the most important principle in teaching is 3-using principle, namely, being applicable, being enough, and being capable of using. Being applicable means that the course content should be applicable and conducive to the cultivation of students' specialized caliber. Being enough means that the specialized education should be systematized and the teaching content should be enough to achieve the training objective. Being capable of using means the course content should be ensured to be mastered by students. The 3-using principle is a new requirement of caliber-oriented education for teachers in independent institutes, and it is also a kind of concrete CETS embodiment in teaching. The three items of this principle are not simply paralleled but intrinsically linked. The first one is the basic principle of the CETS teaching philosophy; the second one is the requirement for the amount of teaching material and it says the specialized education should be systematic.

1.2 Task-Based Approach

Task-based approach could be well employed in the teaching of translation. This approach, based on the education theory pragmatism by the American educator John Dewey, is student–centered, claiming learning by doing. Mr. John Dewey advocated that the center of teaching should be turned to students from the teacher and the textbooks and students should be guided to learn in various activities. Classroom teaching should be always started around the given tasks, which enables each lesson clear in purpose, practical in content, and best in effect(Jia Zhigao, 2005).

Under this principle, the teacher has to substitute the traditional cramming teaching mode with a heuristic, interactive, and practical teaching mode, give full play to the autonomy of the students, and help them acquire applicable knowledge, enough skills and practical capability for the future in the teacher-student interaction. The paper below is mainly about the application of task-based approach to the English-Chinese translation teaching based on the web in terms of teaching content and process.

2 Web-Based Collection of Teaching Content and Development of Teaching Program

The beginning step is to summarize, according to the characteristics of translation teaching, translation methods and techniques accompanied by enough typical examples and exercises which include sentences, short passages and the materials for regular translation practice in teaching. As Table 1 indicates, most teaching contents are from the web because the information of the textbooks are out of date. Here the author has tried her best to make full use of the textbooks and network resources to get an extensive collection of the translation teaching materials, such as syllabus and courseware, of the domestic colleges and universities. Then, under the guidance of the principle being applicable and enough in the CETS philosophy, the most widely used translation

Table 1. Percentages of teaching content from the textbooks and from the web

Teaching content	From the textbooks	From the web
theory (skills)	70	30
examples	20	80
sentence practices	40	60
paragraph practices	0	100
passage practices	0	100

methods and skills are drawn from them based on her personal experience. These summarized methods and techniques are what students should master in the translation course, hence they could be regarded as tasks for the course.

The second step is to stratify tasks according to the requirements of the task-based approach. The translation course, which is itself one task among the language teaching, is divided into several main tasks, such as translation methods and skills; the main tasks as translation methods are then subdivided into sub-tasks as liberal and literal translation or domestication and alienation. It should be clear that translation methods belong to the sub-task, literal and liberal translation to the sub-sub-tasks. The task chain should be consistent in logic and in difficulty with the principle of continuity according to Krashen's "i+1" theory.

With logic stratification of the summarized translation methods and techniques, the following step is to develop the teaching programs in accordance with the principle of "First practice, first exercises" and the practical features of translation (Bocheng Zhang, 2008). The specific approach in the preparation of lesson plans for each task is to supply exercises which embody the relevant theory and technique in the beginning, then the theory summarized from the previous exercises, and finally curricular and extracurricular training materials for further consolidation and sublimation of the relevant technique. The teaching system should take sentence as the basic translation unit and take as the main line the translation in comparison between English and Chinese.

3   Web-Based Teaching Process

In the specific process of teaching, task-based approach is employed to deal with the content about methods such as translation methods and techniques except for the intellectual content in the first part, the brief history of the Chinese translation, which is given by traditional lectures.

3.1   The Basic Premise of the Task Implementation

According to the practicality of translation course and requirements of the task-based approach, the class grouping is completed before the second lesson, which the monitor and the commissary in charge of studies are responsible for. The principle of free combination is adopted in the grouping. And after that, group members sit together in class, which facilitates the completion of group tasks. Usually the course subtasks are completed in groups.

The amount of exercises in each task depends on the acceptance of most students rather than the knowledge points included in the textbooks or in the subject. Therefore, proper adjustments should be made in the design of the task chain for each class according to the completion of the previous and, or the immediate classroom tasks. In the following section, the author will take the task the technique negation in E-C translation as an example to illustrate the specific steps to implement the task.

3.2   The Specific Steps to Implement the Task Based on the Web

(1) Lead-in of the main task:
At the beginning of each chapter, three to five sentences of "i" level are provided for students to translate rapidly, which is followed by a guided syntactic comparison between the original and the translated version, or a piece of bilingual news with pictures from the well-known website is displayed which is succeeded by a similar job to summarize the specific technique. For instance, the technique negation is introduced by "Most Unwanted Tattoos" from the Global Times. Seeing the picture, the students are quite excited. Reading the English text, they would take the initiative to think about the Chinese version and derive the technique after the bilingual comparison under the guidance of the teacher.

(2) Presentation of the focal points of the main task in the form of questions for students to consider
In the main task negation, there are the following five questions.

1)   What is negation in translation?
2)   What is the role of the technique negation in translation?
3)   How many categories can negation be divided into?
4)   What kind of positive English expressions should be rendered into negative Chinese expressions?
5)   What kind of negative English expressions should be converted into positive Chinese expressions?

(3) Conduction of the subtask
The subtask here is translation and discussion of the carefully selected sentences from the web in groups. During this process, the teacher should make random visit and give necessary guidance. Discussions between members are followed by between groups. One group report their final work and other groups make a comment, which part of the version is good if it is well translated and which part should be improved if it is a poor job. Group contests can also be adopted. For example, in the task negation, students are encouraged to offer the most positive expressions with negative meaning (verbs, nouns, adjectives, prepositions, etc.) which should be translated into negative forms in Chinese. Sometimes, for the sake of efficiency, the teacher can comment directly, guide students to analyze the characteristics of language rendering and summarize the employed technique, and give detailed explanation of the cause and full illustration of its application.

(4) Consolidation and sublimation of the technique in practice
After the completion of the third task, students are required to translate a number of similar but slightly more difficult sentences ("i+1" level). And they are encouraged to

make conscious use of the skill summarized immediately just before. Finishing all relevant subtasks, a conclusion will be made to help students get the answers to the questions of the main task and conduct comprehensive exercises, most of which are from the language column of well-known newspapers online, in order to ensure the authenticity of the task. Sometimes, a quiz is given. The psychology of getting good grades can stimulate students to work hard.

(5) Homework for consolidation of the technique through the web
Homework is assigned by the online class group to consolidate the techniques generalized in class. Upon completion of the after-school exercises, a passage of moderate difficulty should be provided monthly for students to do translation practice. At the same time the teacher should try to understand the students' feedback. By marking this kind of exercises and practice, the teacher can find the student's progress and problems. And with communication with their caliber mentor and other teachers as well as with students themselves, he learns about the reasons for such problems, figures out possible solutions, and makes proper adjustments to the next task.

4   Teaching Effectiveness

After the implementation of web task-based approach in the translation course, students become more interested in learning, which can be easily drawn from their increasing lecture rate. Often some students have the initiative to require practice. Chief Inspector also expressed his recognition and encouragement for the approach. In this method, teachers encourage students' free translation, and then guide them to analyze and summarize the common features of these sentences to obtain the corresponding translation theory and techniques, and after that give a detailed explanation of the technique sources and application and then offer enough exercises to students to practice until they can instinctively understand and use related skills. This teaching mode, warm-up practice - analysis and induction - understanding and comprehension - consolidation practice, is consistent with the student's cognitive process, and can therefore stimulate their thinking. This kind of teaching content highlights the translation practicality and follows the acquisition law of internalization by practice in the CETS philosophy. With enough practice, knowledge can be internalized and become part of a person, namely his caliber. Here in the translation course, knowledge mainly refers to the theory such as the translation methods and techniques, and practice refers to all kinds of exercises. Both are arranged and conducted in the form of tasks. It is safely to say such teaching content is quite applicable.

5   Conclusion

The application of web task-based approach to translation course, a specialized practice-based course guided by theory, can make an effective improvement of the learners' translation ability. All lectures are organized in the form of tasks. During the performance of a series of tasks, the learners often adopt the ways of participation, experience, interaction, communication, and cooperation, which give full play to their own cognitive ability and enable them to perceive, understand, and apply the target language in practice by mobilizing the target language resources they already have. This is a kind of studying by doing and by applying. And this is a teaching model consistent with the 3-using principle in the CETS philosophy which advocates caliber internalization by practice. When a teacher guides his students to induce the technique from their exercises during his teaching process and adjusts his teaching plan according to his students' feedback, his role in teaching has been completely changed, a shift from the traditional centre to a real guide and mentor; meanwhile, the learners own a dominant position in the learning activities in that they get to explore actively the knowledge rather than accept passively what the teacher or the textbook says. A famous educator Rogers believed that all the knowledge taught by others are relatively useless, and what influence the individual behavior is the internalized knowledge discovered by himself. In the task-based teaching of translation, the techniques which the students take the initiative to explore and induce from the exercises under the guidance of their teacher belong to what they discover and can become part of their own language schemata with appropriated amount of practice and internalization. This kind of teaching, can of course achieve the purpose enabling the learners to make use of what they get from the class.

Of course, the model should be further improved systematically, the arrangement of specific practice under each task should be further adjusted according to the level of difficulty, in order to effectively meet the "i +1" principle; the examples as well as the exercises should be enhanced in their embedded value and the typical level to offer maximum benefit for students, arousing their learning interests, and facilitating their understanding, memory, and imitation. At the same time, empirical studies can be conducted to the feasibility of the model.

References

1. Zhao, Z.: Practice and Theory of Caliber-oriented Education to Success, p. 104. Wuhan University Press, Wuhan (2009)
2. Fang, W.: On Task-based Language Approach. J. Foreign Language and Foreign Language Teaching 9, 17–20 (2003)
3. Jia, Z.: Discussion of Several Core Issues on Task-based Approach. J. Curriculum · Coursebook · teaching 1 (2005)
4. Zhang, M.: On Textbooks of English-Chinese Translation in China (1949-1998). Shanghai Foreign Language Press, Shanghai (2001)
5. Zhang, B.: Practicality of Translation and Translation Teaching, http://www.zhushenhai.anyp.cn

Comparison and Research on New Rural Community Management Patterns of Shan Dong Province

Lei Fang and XiaoMei Zhang

Northeast Agricultural university, Economic Management School
150030 , Harbin, China

Abstract. Rural community is an important institutional innovation,which has important effect and edification to future new rural management.There are three new rural community management patterns in shandong province:divisions of the village community,many villages community and village merge community. This article not only introduce three models,but also compare them in four aspects: community scale, community management,infrastructure,resource utilization.Pointing out the strength and weakness of three models.Drawing a conclusion that village merge community is the active reaction for rural urbanization. And could be the important recommended breed.

Keywords: rural community, divisions of the village community, many villages community, village merge community.

1 Introduction

Rural community is a gather life community based on style of rural life,which has many shortcomings.For example,small,simple construction,weak infrastructure, imperfect service.For the moment,Shandong province has discovered many effective community management.divisions of the village community,many villages community and village merge community are the very representative ones.This article not only introduce three modes,but also compare them in four aspects:community scale,community management,infrastructure,resource utilization.

2 Introduction of New Rural Community Management Patterns

2.1 The Divisions of the Village Community

Based on divisions of the village,Divisions Of The Village Community set up build a rural community and a comprehensive service center.,relying mainly on the old committee of the villagers and party committee.

G. Shen and X. Huang (Eds.): ECWAC 2011, Part I, CCIS 143, pp. 383–388, 2011.
© Springer-Verlag Berlin Heidelberg 2011

Divisions Of The Village Community gaine prominence of nationwide rural community.Because it has high position accuracy distinguish the concept between urban community and rural community;without additions administrative level and cost;can realize community self-governing;it combines the committee of the villagers and Party Committee into one, which is beneficial to build closer relations between cadres and the masses;convenient services to meet the needs of everyday life.The flaw is that too small village in resources to waste but several villages are assembled together divided carefully.

2.2 The Many Village Community

Counted by villages and towns,Many Villages Community does not combine old villages.Based on economic powerful village or center village and focus on countryside community garden,bring about around five villages, community rely on the Community Development Commission for managing.

Many Villages Community only establish community service centers at the center village,so that could concentrate the authority and budget.And this is the best approach to rural-urban basicpublic service equally.It is beneficial to led the villagers gathered to center village,and the Community Development Commission and Party Committee are favorable to cadre serve inhabitant face each other. The drawback is position imprecisely,and associate with community self-governing weekly.The pattern attaches great importance to community services but neglect.others of the community construction.Moreover,extra staff increase the financial expenditure.

2.3 The Village Merge Community

Radius of the Village Merge Community isn't more than 3 kilometers,and scale covers three to six villages or 3000~6000 inhabits. Establishing community service centers and reorganizing functional districts by 5 types:centre project,resources complementary,historical origins, town promoting, strong-weak co-operation.

The Village Merge Community rethought on in China Lin Yi and Wei Fang,which have the superior of the Divisions Of The Village Community and The Many Village Community.So it is helpful to resources integration and utilization.However, the integration of assets and debts involve in collective assets and debts and the villagers' vital interests.The demolition bring up many questions,such as the villagers unwilling to leave their homelands,the financial input on new houses,make it's difficult to pressing ahead.

3 Comparison of Three Models

This article compareabove-mentioned three models in four aspects:community scale,community management,infrastructure and resource utilization.Take 3-5 villages for instance(see Table 1).

Table 1. The situation of three community patterns

	Community Scale	Community Management	Infrastructure	Resource Utilization
Divisions of the village	small	Construction Coordinating Committee anAd Party Committee	3-5 groups	low
The Many Villages Community	large	Party Organizations and Community Development Commission	1 group	heigh
The Village Merge Community	large	community general Party branch and neighborhood committee	1group	heigh

3.1 In the Community Scale (See Figure 1)

Every divisions of the village has its rural community,whose scale is different because of the difference between and the economic factors.But many villages community and village merge community establish community ineconomic powerful village or center village,so that they have relatively great scale.

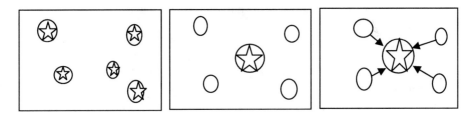

Divisions of the village The Many Villages Community The Village Merge Community
◯ mean the village,☆mean the community service center, ⟶mean movement

Fig. 1. Three kinds of rural communities and service center

3.2 In the Community Management

The Construction Coordinating Committee of Divisions Of The Village Community is formed by representatives of Party branch work as director,director of villagers committees work as deputy director and personnel of various kinds ,such as the People's Congress at different levels and the CPPCC Members, representatives of the unit, villager representatives,whiz at wealth,old cadres,old teachers,older Party members.And using "University Student Village Officer";carrying out decision system of "4 authority",working system is Party make a decision ⟶ the villagers meeting and the villager congress vote it ⟶ villagers committees execute it ⟶ the masses and organizations above them supervise it.

Party Organizations in the Many Villages Community is formed by Party branch of representatives of the Community Service Center,village Party organizations in the community and other unit in the community Party organizations.Party Organization isn't a leading body but a services agency.It mainly surround community service and construction.Party Organization integrate community resources by means of communication,coordination, guarantee,education and training.The relationship between Community Development Commission and villages in community isn't led and be led.Commissiones work surrounding community service under the direct leadership of township Party committee,government.

Divisions Of The Village Community repeal old Party branch and villagers committees,and reorganize community general Party branch and neighborhood committee,and explore on switch fromfour spheres: establish Residential Areas;set up party organizations at profession,group or industry chain,to form new organization system with the community general Party branch as the mainstay,Party branch of industrial associationas backbones, professional Party groups as the base;add peasant to Cooperation and particular way is cancelling the conventional villager groupadding Community Residents to trade, industrialization and group in kinds of cooperation;strengthen democratic management,and particular way is carrying out"together put up and vote"in terms of group election,carrying out consultation service of decision and democratic decision and open invite bidding and bid in terms of affair administer,change "what be published by the village,what be known by the villagers" to "what be desired by the neighbourhood,what be published by the community".

3.3 In the Infrastructure

Divisions Of The Village Community establish service center in every community,take "neighborhood center" as the breakthrough point-which bring together Community Party building,civilization construction,villagers' autonomy,double support work,convenience service,cultural education, exercise and amusement-keep promoting the construction of public service of rural community in mind.So that villagers demands could be resolved at their own door.

The service center of Many Villages Community usually set up 8 service station,such as medical and health,community policing, community sanitation, culture and sport,family planning,and a office hall.Because of "all the townships are connected by roads" ,it is convenient for villagers to go to the service center in the center village.

The Village Merge Community located in being supported by "one net and two platform" of supply and sales system,and establish service center in the large village community.By using reform of township mechanism,community decentralize power of 7 station and 8 agency.Therefore 13 service are decentralized to service center,such as family planning,residence migration.All together,the Joyous Farmer's House supermarket, the Rural Credit Cooperatives, professional cooperatives and postal savings are extended to the community could abundant the connotations of the service.

3.4 In the Resource Utilization

Although villages in divisions of the village model lie in developed region of Shandong Bandao,there are varying degrees of villages.The small villages(less than four thousand inhabitants)are small,so it is always comes forth the three appearance:villages scattered and crowd in dimple type;the peasant household are scattered and weak,Scale and Industrialization are low;party organizations are not as one of a group.The utilization of resources is low.Land and other resources and debts are not change because the community is built on the spot.

Collective debts are not change because the Many Villages Community requiring no demolition.Leading the villagers gathered to center village.Thus will gradually form large a village even a jerkwatertown.And the utilization of resources will raise naturally.But center villages have difficulty in designing,demolition and collecting land.

The Village Merge Community is beneficial to integration and utilization,for example Jvnan integrate assets,both real and personal property are put under the community.Community is beneficial to integrate the land and land contract isn't change,for example Xianggou Xiang give within 5 percent house sites, flexible sites,allowance sites for construction and 4 kings of wasteland to the community to govern. Community is also beneficial to integrate claims and debts,such as debts inside the community could be resolve each other,or else other original collective claims and debts could be undertaken by the community.

4 Conclusion

Overall,we shouldn't discuss 3 patterns in themselves,but should put them in the macroscopic broadview of entire modernizations:the reasonability and validity of any local system lie in the coupling,and whether construction logic of the modern state.Divisions Of The Village Community   suit larger villages ,otherwise it will cause the waste of resources.The Many Villages Community pay more attention to economy development,but because of leading the villagers gathered to center village. After a long development will inevitably form large villages,which resemble Divisions Of The Village Community and need a relatively long time.Represent active reaction for urbanization and surpassing System of Villagers' Autonomy make The Village Merge Community real modern meaning.So it is a ideal pattern of rural community that we could predict and adapts the economic development level of nation should be recommended majorly.The question is debts and demolition in the development should be active reaction by all levels.

References

1. Research team of the Construction Party Team of the Central Party School: Rural development and The basis of consolidating the party's ruling:Innovative rural development approach to building a new life for farmers Practice of ZhuCheng of ShanDong province. People's Publishing House (2009)
2. Li, Y.: MC rural communities: Villagers fill a vacancy on the Elimination of defects. J. Learning and Exploration, 79–80 (2009)

3. Xu, Y.: The construction of socialist new countryside construction of rural communities. JingHan Form (2007)
4. Xin, C.: Some Reflections of community building a new socialist countryside. J. NanJing Agricultural University, 15–21 (2008)
5. Zhang, X., You, Y., Tan, J.: Construction and Management of Rural Community. South China University of Technology Press (2007)
6. Uphoff, N., Esman, M.J., Krishna, A.: Reasons for Success: Learning fromm Instructive Experiences in Rural Development. Guangdong People's Publishing House (2006)

An Incremental Updating Method for Computing Approximations by Matrix While the Universe Evolves over Time

Lei Wang [1,2], Tianrui Li [1], and Jun Ye [2]

[1] School of Information Science and Technology,
Southwest Jiaotong University, Chengdu, China
[2] Information Engineering School, Nanchang Institute of Technology,
Nanchang, China
ezhoulei@163.com, trli@home.swjtu.edu.cn

Abstract. Most of the methods for calculation of the upper and lower approximations of a concept are presently based on static information systems. In fact, the information system usually evolves over time, including the change of its universe, attribute set and values of attributes. In this paper, from the point of view of matrix, an incremental updating method is proposed for updating β-approximations under variable precision rough sets while the universe of information system evolves with time. Furthermore, the theorems on updating the approximations of a concept by the tool of matrix are given. The process of calculation on this updating method is presented. Finally, a numeric example is given to illustrate the correctness of the proposed incremental updating method based on the matrix point of view.

Keywords: Matrix, approximations, incremental updating, variable precision rough set.

1 Introduction

The rough set theory [1] was proposed by Z. Pawlak in 1982. It is an effective method and tool to deal with inconsistent problems. Owing to no need of the priori knowledge in certain field, it has obtained successful applications in pattern recognition, machine learning[2]. The lower approximation and the upper approximation are two important concepts in rough set theory. At present, most of the methods for calculation of the upper approximation and the lower approximation are based on static information systems. In fact, the information system usually varies over time, including the change of its universe, attribute set and values of attributes. How to quickly compute the approximations of concept under a changing circumstance is a crucial task in dynamic knowledge discovery. When a new object insert into or delete from the universe of information systems, there are many results on how to update approximations incrementally while the universe varies over time under the classic rough set model[3-5]. However, there are few reports on the research on the incremental updating approximations by the tool of matrix [11]. Ziarko introduced a probability value β and

G. Shen and X. Huang (Eds.): ECWAC 2011, Part I, CCIS 143, pp. 389–395, 2011.
© Springer-Verlag Berlin Heidelberg 2011

proposed the variable precision rough sets (VPRS) model [6]. It has many applications in real-life world. In this paper, we use the matrix method to incrementally update approximations in VPRS.

The remainder of the paper is organized as follows. Section 2 provides the basic concepts of information system and the matrix representation of the subset, the lower approximation and the upper approximation. In Section 3, the incremental updating approach to calculate the approximations of a concept by the matrix method is presented. In Section 4, examples are employed to validate the proposed approach. The paper ends with conclusions and further research topics in Section 5.

2   Preliminaries

Basic concepts, notations and results of VPRS as well as the matrix representation of the subset of the universe are briefly reviewed in this section [7-10].

Definition 1. [7] A quadruple $S =<U,A,V,f>$ is an information system, where U is a nonempty finite set of object; A is a nonempty finite set of attributes; $A=C \cup D$, $C \cap D = \emptyset$, where C and D denote the set of condition attributes and the set of decision attributes respectively. $V = \bigcup_{a \in A} V_a$, V_a is a domain of attribute a, $f : U \times A \to V$ is an information function, which gives value to every object on each attribute.

Definition 2. [8] Let $U=\{u_1, u_2, \ldots\ldots, u_n\}$ be a finite universe set, and X a subset of U. Thus X can be represented by a n-row matrix $X_{n \times 1} = (x_1, x_2, \ldots, x_n)^T$ (T denotes the transpose operation), and $x_i = \begin{cases} 1, & u_i \in X \\ 0, & u_i \notin X \end{cases}$

Here, we do not distinguish the subset X of U and its corresponding n-column boolean vector.

For instance, if $U = \{u_1, u_2, u_3, u_4, u_5\}$, $X = \{u_1, u_3, u_4\}$, then we write $X = \{1,0,1,1,0\}^T$.

Definition 3. [9] The matrix A is partitioned into many little matrices with some vertical and horizontal lines and each little matrix is called the sub-block of matrix A. The nominal matrix whose elements is sub-block is called partitioned matrices.

For example, $A = \begin{bmatrix} a_{11} & a_{12} & a_{13} & a_{14} \\ a_{21} & a_{22} & a_{23} & a_{24} \\ a_{31} & a_{32} & a_{33} & a_{34} \end{bmatrix}$. The method for partition is denoted as

$A = \begin{bmatrix} A_{11} & A_{12} \\ A_{21} & A_{22} \end{bmatrix}$, where, $A_{11} = \begin{bmatrix} a_{11} & a_{12} \\ a_{21} & a_{22} \end{bmatrix}$, $A_{12} = \begin{bmatrix} a_{13} & a_{14} \\ a_{23} & a_{24} \end{bmatrix}$, $A_{21} = \begin{bmatrix} a_{31} & a_{32} \end{bmatrix}$, $A_{22} = \begin{bmatrix} a_{33} & a_{34} \end{bmatrix}$

The operation law of partitioned matrices is similar to that of the ordinary matrix.

In[10], we have proposed a new method for calculation of the approximations of rough sets based on the matrix method, namely, the column matrix of upper and lower approximations of a subset can be derived from the operation among the column matrix of the subset, the induced matrix and the equivalence relation matrix. The method is shown as follows.

Theorem 1. [10] Let $U=\{u_1, u_2, \ldots\ldots, u_n\}$ be a finite universe set, R an equivalence relation on U, $(m_{ij})_{n\times n}$ a matrix representation of R, and X an arbitrary subset of U,

$$\Lambda_{n\times n} \overset{\Delta}{=} diag(1/\sum_{k=1}^{n} m_{1k}, 1/\sum_{k=1}^{n} m_{2k}, \ldots, 1/\sum_{k=1}^{n} m_{nk})$$ be the induced diagonal matrix of M_R. Then the method for calculation of approximations based on the matrix is as follows.

(1) The n-column boolean vector of β-lower approximation of X:
$$\underline{R}_\beta(X) = (\Lambda \bullet (M_R \bullet X))_{1-\beta} = (\Lambda \bullet C_{n\times 1})_{1-\beta}$$

(2) The n-column boolean vector of β-upper approximation of X:
$$\overline{R}_\beta(X) = (\Lambda \bullet (M_R \bullet X))_\beta = (\Lambda \bullet C_{n\times 1})_\beta$$

where $\bullet$ is the dot product of matrices, $(\Lambda \bullet C_{n\times 1})_{1-\beta}$ is the $(1-\beta)$-cut of matrix $(\Lambda \bullet C_{n\times 1})$ and. $(\Lambda \bullet C_{n\times 1})_\beta$ is the β-cut of matrix $(\Lambda \bullet C_{n\times 1})$.

3   An Incremental Method for Updating Approximations of VPRS While the Universe Evolves over Time

In this paper, the case that only one object insert into or delete from the universe is considered, namely, the incremental updating method for computing approximations by the matrix is studied only under this case and then only the incremental updating matrix $M_R \bullet X$ will be taken into account.

3.1   One Object Is Deleted from the Universe

Theorem 2. Let $U=\{u_1, u_2, \ldots\ldots, u_n\}$ be a finite universe set. The element deleted from the universe is ui ($1\leq i\leq n$). M_R and M'_R are two $n\times n$ matries representing the equivalent relation R before and after the element u_i deleting from the universe respectively; X and X' are two subsets of U before and after the element ui deleting from the universe respectively. Then the matrix $M'_R \bullet X'$ can derived form $M_R \bullet X$ according to following methods.

(1) Matrix M'_R can be derived after all the ith row's elements and all the jth column's elements of matrix M_R are removed;

(2) If $u_i \notin X$, then matrix $M'_R \bullet X'$ can be obtained by deleting the ith row's elements of matrix $M_R \bullet X$;

(3) If $u_i \in X$, then $M'_R \bullet X'$ can derived from $M_R \bullet X$ by two steps: a) If $(M_R)_{ri} = 1(1 \leq r \leq |U|)$, then the element $(M_R \bullet X)_{r1}$ minus one, else remained unchanged; b) Delete all the elements of the ith row of matrix $M_R \bullet X$.

Proof

(1) M'_R can be derived after all the ith row's elements and all the ith column's elements of M_R are removed , this property can derived from the definitions of equivalent relation matrix M_R and M'_R easily.

Denote $c_{j1} = (M_R \bullet X)_{j1}(1 \leq j \leq n)$, $c'_{j1} = (M'_R \bullet X')_{j1}(1 \leq j \leq n-1)$.

(2) Since $u_i \notin X$, namely, $x_i = 0$. Then

If $j < i : c_{j1} = \sum_{k=1}^{n} m_{jk} x_k = \sum_{k=1}^{i-1} m_{jk} x_k + m_{ji} x_i + \sum_{k=i+1}^{n} m_{jk} x_k = \sum_{k=1}^{n-1} m'_{jk} x'_k = c'_{j1}$ Otherwise, $j > i$:

$c_{j1} = \sum_{k=1}^{n} m_{jk} x_k = \sum_{k=1}^{i-1} m_{jk} x_k + m_{ji} x_i + \sum_{k=i+1}^{n} m_{jk} x_k = \sum_{k=1}^{i-1} m'_{(j-1)k} x'_k + \sum_{k=i}^{n-1} m'_{(j-1)k} x'_k = \sum_{k=1}^{n-1} m'_{(j-1)k} x'_k = c'_{(j-1)1}$

Therefore, $M'_R \bullet X'$ can derived from $M_R \bullet X$ by deleting all the ith row's elements of $M_R \bullet X$.

(3) Since $u_i \in X$, namely, $x_i = 1$. Then

case 1 $j < i$: If $(M_R)_{ji} = 1$, this indicates that $u_i \in [u_j]$:

then $c_{j1} = \sum_{k=1}^{n} m_{jk} x_k = \sum_{k=1}^{i-1} m_{jk} x_k + m_{ji} x_i + \sum_{k=i+1}^{n} m_{jk} x_k = \sum_{k=1}^{n-1} m'_{jk} x'_k + 1 = c'_{j1} + 1$ else $(M_R)_{ji} = 0 : c_{j1} = c'_{j1}$

case 2 $j > i$: If $(M_R)_{ji} = 1$ then

$c_{j1} = \sum_{k=1}^{n} m_{jk} x_k = \sum_{k=1}^{i-1} m_{jk} x_k + m_{ji} x_i + \sum_{k=i+1}^{n} m_{jk} x_k = \sum_{k=1}^{i-1} m'_{(j-1)k} x'_k + 1 + \sum_{k=i}^{n-1} m'_{(j-1)k} x'_k = \sum_{k=1}^{n-1} m'_{(j-1)k} x'_k + 1 = c'_{(j-1)1} + 1$

else $(M_R)_{ji} = 0 : c_{j1} = c'_{(j-1)1}$. overall, proposition (3) can be demonstrated .

The algorithm is shown as follows to update the β-approximations incrementally based on the matrix while an object deleted from the universe :

Input: The universe set U; The equivalence relation R on U; The subset X of U; Threshold value: β; The object u_i which will be removed.

Output: The β-lower approximation and the β-upper approximation of X' after the removal of the object u_i.

Method

Step 1. Delete the ith row and the jth column of matrix M_R and the matrix M'_R can be obtained.

Step 2. The matrix $M'_R \bullet X'$ can derived from the matrix $M_R \bullet X$

Step 3. According to the definition of induced matrix the matrix $\Lambda'_{(n-1)\times(n-1)}$ can be obtained

Step 4. Calculate the matrix representation of β-upper approximation and β-lower approximation of subset X' after the deletion of object u_i respectively

Step 5. Get the β-upper and the β-lower approximation of subset X' after the deletion of object u_i according to the meaning of matrix representation of X'.

3.2   One Object Inserts into the Universe

When a object inserts into the universe U, the matrix $M'_R \bullet X'$ can be updated by the matrix's block-divided method. For sake of convenience, let the inserted object be u_{n+1}. U={$u_1, u_2, \ldots\ldots, u_n$} be the original finite universe. X is the arbitrary subset of U. After the insertion of the u_{n+1}, the universe turns into U'={$u_1, u_2, \ldots, u_i, \ldots, u_n, u_{n+1}$}.

Theorem 3: Let U={$u_1, u_2, \ldots\ldots, u_n$} be a finite universe, X an arbitrary subset of U, the element which will be inserted into the universe U is u_{n+1}. M_R and M'_R are two $n \times n$ matrix representing equivalent relation R before and after the element u_{n+1} is inserted into the universe, respectively; X and X' are two subsets of U before and after the element u_{n+1} is inserted into the universe, respectively. R and Q are denoted as follows:

$$(R)_{1\times 1} = [1], \quad Q = (q_{1j})_{1\times n} = \begin{cases} 1, & u_{n+1}Ru_j \quad j=1,2,3,\cdots,n \\ 0, & u_{n+1}\cancel{R}u_j \quad j=1,2,3,\cdots,n \end{cases}$$

Thus: 1) $M_R' = \left[\begin{array}{c|c} M_R & Q^T \\ \hline Q & R \end{array}\right]$, T denotes the transpose operation; 2) $M_R' \bullet X' = \left[\begin{array}{c} M_R \bullet X \\ \hline Q \bullet X \end{array}\right]$.

Proof: Firstly, construct matrices Q and Q^T by using the relations between the inserted object u_{n+1} and the original object $u_i (1 \le i \le n)$. Their orders are 1×n and n×1, respectively.

Then, get the partitioned representation of M_R' and the column matrix X' after updating as follows by using M_R and subset X.

$$M_R' = \left[\begin{array}{c|c} M_R & Q^T \\ \hline Q & R \end{array}\right], \quad X' = \left[\begin{array}{c} X \\ \hline O \end{array}\right], \text{ and } O = [0] \text{ Then, } M_R' \bullet X' = \left[\begin{array}{c|c} M_R & Q^T \\ \hline Q & R \end{array}\right] \bullet \left[\begin{array}{c} X \\ \hline O \end{array}\right]$$

$$= \left[\begin{array}{c} M_R \bullet X + Q^T \bullet O \\ \hline Q \bullet X + R \bullet O \end{array}\right] = \left[\begin{array}{c} M_R \bullet X \\ \hline Q \bullet X \end{array}\right], \text{ The order of } M_R' \bullet X' \text{ is (n+1)×1.}$$

The algorithm is shown as follows to update the β-approximations incrementally based on the matrix while an object insert into the universe U:

Input: U; The equivalence relation R on U; The subset X of U; Threshold value: β; The object u_i which will be inserted into the universe.

Output: The β-lower and the β-upper approximations of X' after the insertion of u_{n+1}.

Method:

After the insertion u_{n+1}, the partitioned representation of M_R' can be obtained

Step 1. Matrix $M_R' \bullet X'$ can be obtained in accordance with Theorem 3.

Step 2. The updated induced matrix $\Lambda'_{(n+1)\times(n+1)}$ can be derived from M_R' according to the definition.

Step 3. Calculate the matrix representation of β-upper approximation and β-lower approximation of subset X' after the insertion of object u_i respectively.

Step 4. Get the β-upper approximation and the β-lower approximation of X' after the insertion of u_{n+1} according to the meaning of matrix representation of X'.

4   An Illustration

Let $U = \{u_1,u_2,u_3,u_4,u_5,u_6,u_7\}$, the partitions of equivalent R on U is: $U/R = \{\{u_1,u_6\},\{u_2,u_3,u_4,u_5\},\{u_7\}\}$ and subset of U is: $X = \{1,1,1,0,0,0,1\}^T$, $\beta=0.4$. and $\Lambda_{7\times 7} = diag(1/2,1/4,1/4,1/4,1/4,1/2,1)$. So, $M_R \bullet X = \{1,2,2,2,2,1,1\}^T$.

Calculate the column matrix representation of β-approximations of X

$$\underline{R}_{0.4}(X) = (\Lambda_{7\times7} \bullet (M_R \bullet X))_{0.6} = (\Lambda_{7\times7} \bullet \{1,2,2,2,2,1,1\}^T)_{0.6} = \{0,0,0,0,0,0,1\}^T$$

$$\overline{R}_{0.4}(X) = (\Lambda_{7\times7} \bullet (M_R \bullet X))_{0.4} = (\Lambda_{7\times7} \bullet \{1,2,2,2,2,1,1\}^T)_{0.4} = \{1,1,1,1,1,1,1\}^T$$

$$(M_R)_{7\times7} = \begin{bmatrix} 1 & 0 & 0 & 0 & 0 & 1 & 0 \\ 0 & 1 & 1 & 1 & 1 & 0 & 0 \\ 0 & 1 & 1 & 1 & 1 & 0 & 0 \\ 0 & 1 & 1 & 1 & 1 & 0 & 0 \\ 0 & 1 & 1 & 1 & 1 & 0 & 0 \\ 1 & 0 & 0 & 0 & 0 & 1 & 0 \\ 0 & 0 & 0 & 0 & 0 & 0 & 1 \end{bmatrix} \qquad (M'_R)_{6\times6} = \begin{bmatrix} 1 & 0 & 0 & 0 & 1 & 0 \\ 0 & 1 & 1 & 1 & 0 & 0 \\ 0 & 1 & 1 & 1 & 0 & 0 \\ 0 & 1 & 1 & 1 & 0 & 0 \\ 1 & 0 & 0 & 0 & 1 & 0 \\ 0 & 0 & 0 & 0 & 0 & 1 \end{bmatrix}$$

Get the β-upper approximations of subset X according to the meaning of matrix representation of subset X'. $\underline{R}_{0.4}(X) = \{u_7\}$, $\overline{R}_{0.4}(X) = \{u_1,u_2,u_3,u_4,u_5,u_6,u_7\}$.

The incremental updatoffing of β-approximations will be discussed respectively when an object deleted from or inserted into the universe U.

Suppose object u_3 will be deleted from U, namely, $U' = U - \{u_3\}$, $X' = \{u_1,u_2,u_7\}$.

Firstly, $(M'_R)_{6\times6}$ after update can derived from $(M_R)_{7\times7}$.

Secondly, updated $M'_R \bullet X' = \{1,1,1,1,1,1\}^T$ can derived from $M_R \bullet X$.

Thirdly, $\Lambda'_{6\times6} = diag(1/2,1/3,1/3,1/3,1/2,1)$.

So the matrix representations of the β-approximations of X' can be calculated:

$$\underline{R}_{0.4}(X') = (\Lambda'_{6\times6} \bullet (M'_R \bullet X'))_{0.6} = (\Lambda'_{6\times6} \bullet \{1,1,1,1,1,1\}^T)_{0.6} = \{1/2,1/3,1/3,1/3,1/2,1\}^T_{0.6} = \{0,0,0,0,0,1\}^T$$

$$\overline{R}_{0.4}(X') = (\Lambda'_{6\times6} \bullet (M'_R \bullet X'))_{0.4} = (\Lambda'_{6\times6} \bullet \{1,1,1,1,1,1\}^T)_{0.4} = \{1/2,1/3,1/3,1/3,1/2,1\}^T_{0.4} = \{1,0,0,0,1,1\}^T$$

At last, the β-upper approximation and the β-lower approximation of subset X' are obtained respectively according to the meaning of matrix representation of subset X'. $\underline{R}_{0.4}(X') = \{u_7\}$, $\overline{R}_{0.4}(X') = \{u_1,u_6,u_7\}$.

Suppose u_8 will be inserted into U, namely, $U' = U + \{u_8\}$, $X' = \{u_1,u_2,u_3,u_7,u_8,\}$. Let β=0.4. And suppose the partition of equivalent R on U after the insertion of u_8 is: $U/R = \{\{u_1,u_6\},\{u_2,u_3,u_4,u_5\},\{u_7,u_8\}\}$ In accordance with the relations between u_8 and the original object, Q is constructed and Thus: $Q_{1\times n} = \begin{bmatrix} 0 & 0 & 0 & 0 & 0 & 0 & 1 \end{bmatrix}$ $(Q^T)_{n\times1} = \begin{bmatrix} 0 & 0 & 0 & 0 & 0 & 0 & 1 \end{bmatrix}^T$ and $R_{1\times1} = [1]$ .So,

$$M'_R = \begin{bmatrix} M_R & Q^T \\ \hline Q & R \end{bmatrix} = \left[\begin{array}{ccccccc|c} 1 & 0 & 0 & 0 & 0 & 1 & 0 & 0 \\ 0 & 1 & 1 & 1 & 1 & 0 & 0 & 0 \\ 0 & 1 & 1 & 1 & 1 & 0 & 0 & 0 \\ 0 & 1 & 1 & 1 & 1 & 0 & 0 & 0 \\ 0 & 1 & 1 & 1 & 1 & 0 & 0 & 0 \\ 1 & 0 & 0 & 0 & 0 & 1 & 0 & 0 \\ 0 & 0 & 0 & 0 & 0 & 0 & 1 & 1 \\ \hline 0 & 0 & 0 & 0 & 0 & 0 & 1 & 1 \end{array}\right] \qquad X' = \begin{bmatrix} X \\ O \end{bmatrix} = \begin{bmatrix} 1 & 1 & 1 & 0 & 0 & 0 & 1 \,|\, 0 \end{bmatrix}^T$$

after updating: $M'_R \cdot X' = \begin{bmatrix} M_R \cdot X \\ \hline Q \cdot X \end{bmatrix} = [1,2,2,2,2,1,1,1]^T$

$\Lambda'_{8\times8} = diag(1/2,1/4,1/4,1/4,1/4,1/2,1/2,1/2)$

The column matrix representation of theβ-upper approximation and theβ-lower approximation of subset X' can be calculated respectively.

$$\overline{R}_{0.4}(X') = (\Lambda'_{8\times8} \bullet (M'_R \bullet X'))_{0.4} = (\Lambda'_{8\times8} \bullet \{1,2,2,2,2,1,1,1\}^T)_{0.4} = \{1,1,1,1,1,1,1,1\}^T$$

At last, theβ-approximations of subset X' are obtained according to the meaning of matrix representation of subset X' : $\underline{R}_{0.4}(X') = \phi$, $\overline{R}_{0.4}(X') = \{u_1, u_2, u_3, u_4, u_5, u_6, u_7, u_8\}$.

5 Summary

The incremental updating method for computing approximations of VPRS by the matrix while the universe varies over time was proposed in this paper. It may help to improve the efficiency of knowledge discovery by rough set theory. Our future work will focus on the development of algorithms to validate the proposed methods.

Acknowledgement

The paper is funded by National Science Foundation of China (60873108) and Jiangxi science and technology project (2009ZDG08000).

References

1. Pawlak, Z.: Rough sets. J. International Journal of Computer and Information Science 11, 341–356 (1982)
2. Skowron, A., Swiniarski, R., Synak, P.: Approximation spaces and information granulation. In: Peters, J.F., Skowron, A., Van, A.D. (eds.) Transactions on Rough Sets III. LNCS, vol. 3400, pp. 175–189. Springer, Heidelberg (2005)
3. Wang, L., Wu, Y., Wang, G.-Y.: An incremental rule acquisition algorithm based on variable precision rough set model. J. Journal of Chongqing University of Posts and Telecommunications (Natural Science) 17(6), 709–713 (2005)
4. Chen, H., Li, T., Hu, C., Ji, X.: An Incremental Updating Principle for Computing Approximations in Information Systems While the Object Set Varies with Time. In: 2009 IEEE International Conference on Granular Computing, pp. 49–52. IEEE Press, New York (2009)
5. Zheng, Z., Wang, G.Y., Wu, Y.: A Rough Set and Rule Tree Based Incremental Knowledge Acquisition Algorithm. In: Wang, G., Liu, Q., Yao, Y., Skowron, A. (eds.) RSFDGrC 2003. LNCS (LNAI), vol. 2639, pp. 122–129. Springer, Heidelberg (2003)
6. Ziarko, W.: Variable Precision Rough Set Model. J. Journal of Computer and system Siences 46(1), 39–59 (1993)
7. Liu, Q.: Rough Set and Rough Reasoning. Science Press, Beijing (2001) (in Chinese)
8. Liu, G.-L.: The Axiomatization of the Rough Set Upper Approximation Operations. J. Fundamenta Informaticae. 69, 331–342 (2006)
9. Applied Mathematics of Tongji University, Linear Algebra, 4th edn., pp. 29–38. Higher Education Press, Beijing (2003) (in Chinese)
10. Wang, L., Li, T.: Research on the Method of Calculation of Upper and Lower Approximations Based on Matrix. In: Proceedings of CRSSC-CWI-CGrC 2010 (2010) (in Chinese)
11. Liu, D., Li, T., Ruan, D., Zou, W.: An Incremental Approach for Inducing Knowledge from Dynamic Information Systems. Fundamenta Informaticae 94(2), 245–260 (2009)

Movement Simulation for Wheeled Mobile Robot Based on Stereo Vision

Hongwei Gao*, Fuguo Chen, Dong Li, and Yang Yu

School of Information Science & Engineering,
Shenyang Ligong University, Shenyang, 110159 China
ghw1978@sohu.com

Abstract. According to the application of the planet detection, the kinematics model of six wheels rock-bogie robot was studied in this paper. A corresponding robot movement simulation system based on stereo vision and virtual reality was developed. The system provided motion parameters of virtual robot to real robot by means of out-line teaching, which ensured the robot's safety. The visual orientation theory and the simulation system realization based on OpenGL were introduced in detail. The simulation was finished based on synthesis terrain and real terrain, and the results show that the system possesses preferable interactive characteristic, and will provide some key techniques for virtual navigation, teleoperation of planetary exploration robot.

Keywords: Wheeled mobile robot (WMR), Kinematics model, Stereo vision, Off-line teaching.

1 Introduction

The motion of wheeled mobile robot (WMR) with appropriate suspension system is rapid and steady which will get a strong ability to adapt terrain, and it plays an important role in planetary exploration and dangerous operation environment. In general, the working process of robot's teleoperation system is as follows: The camera carried by robot will take the photos of its position, these photos and the status of robot itself will be sent back to control center. All of those will be passed to teleoperation system as well, then the system could generate environment model by using 3D reconstruction techniques. After that, a virtual robot which has the same geometrical model and kinematics model deduced from the real robot will be put into the 3D environment model, so as to the operator could act、 trajectory planning and test off-line according to science mission. Then, the planned information of action and trajectory will be sent to control center, and the distal robot will execute the operation when it receives the information from control center[1,2]. The paper builds a visual and humanly teleoperation environment by use of stereo vision and virtual reality technique on the basis

---

* Associate professor, his research interest includes computer vision, image processing and intelligent computation and control.

G. Shen and X. Huang (Eds.): ECWAC 2011, Part I, CCIS 143, pp. 396–401, 2011.

of WMR kinematics model. The simulation results show that the scheme is effective and practical based on the synthesis terrain and the real terrain.

2 The Simulation Platform for the Motion of WMR

2.1 3D Terrain Modelling Based on Stereo Vision

The raw data of terrain is composed of a series of 3D points; the initial data points are triangulated to represent the surface of terrain.

2.1.1 Binocular Camera Calibration
The calibration is processed on a high-precision calibration platform by using Tsai two-step method which is realized based on 3D re-projection error[3], it has stronger anti-interference ability for the noise of image coordinate.

2.1.2 Image Dense Matching
The paper adopted dense matching algorithm based on the max flow mini cut theory in graph theory[4].Image matching is equivalent to search for the minimum cut of net, and the curve surface which run through all edges of minimum cut is called minimum cut curve. The capacity (cost) of all edges on the curve is minimum[5], it is similar to variable curve of disparity d in two images overlapping region following image coordinate (x, y). The global optimization function can be defined as:

$$E(f) = E_{data}(f) + E_{occ}(f) + E_{smooth}(f) \tag{1}$$

Where, E_{data} is data item which represents the degree of consistency of pixel matching; E_{occ} is penalty item which make sure each pixel could find its corresponding relationship; E_{smooth} is smooth item which restrain corresponding disparity between adjacent pixels.

2.1.3 Generation of 3D Cloud Points on Object Surface
3D cloud points could reflect object's appearance, they could be obtained by triangulation after dense matching, the paper adopts least square method to calculate 3D cloud points of terrain surface[6]. Then, triangulation and texture paste could generate a vivid terrain scene on computer screen.

2.2 WMR Kinematics Modeling

2.2.1 Mechanical Configuration of WMR
Take series planetary exploration robot as example to modeling and simulation, which is six-wheel- rocker-bogie Rocky that developed by JPL of USA. Its basic structure is shown in figure 1. It consists of eudipleural rocker-bogie, two terminals of rocker connect to front wheel and bogie, and the two terminals of bogie connect middle wheel and rear wheel.

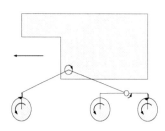

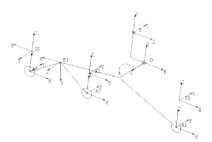

Fig. 1. Mechanical configuration   **Fig. 2.** Coordinate frames for right side of WMR

2.2.2 The Definition of Coordinate and Joint Angle

The right side coordinate of six-wheel WMR is defined as figure 2: Left side coordinate is similar to right side coordinate, the number of wheels from font to rear in the right side coordinate in order are 1、 2、 3; The left side are 4、 5、 6 that corresponds with the right side. The meaning of coordinate is as follows: R: the coordinate of car body; D: the coordinate of differential ream center; $\bar{B}_1,\bar{B}_2$:the coordinate of right and left vice rocker; rf, lf: the steering coordinate of right and left front wheel; rr, lr: the steering coordinate of right and left rear wheel; x_i : the transitional coordinate of right and left rear wheel; A_i :the wheel center coordinate of each wheels.

2.2.3 Kinematics Model

Kinematics model formula of WMR can be obtained by analyzing Jacobin matrix of wheel and combining with velocity projection method. Take the 3rd wheel as example:

$$\begin{bmatrix} \dot{X} \\ \dot{Y} \\ \dot{Z} \end{bmatrix} + \begin{bmatrix} 0 & -K_1 & d_2 \\ K_1 & 0 & K_2 \\ -d_2 & -K_2 & 0 \end{bmatrix} \cdot \begin{bmatrix} \dot{\phi}_x \\ \dot{\phi}_y \\ \dot{\phi}_z \end{bmatrix} + \begin{bmatrix} K_1 \\ 0 \\ K_2 \end{bmatrix} \dot{\beta} + \begin{bmatrix} d_4 \cdot c(\beta+\rho_1)+a_4 \cdot s(\beta+\rho_1) \\ 0 \\ d_4 \cdot s(\beta+\rho_1)-a_4 \cdot c(\beta+\rho_1) \end{bmatrix} \dot{\rho}_1 = \begin{bmatrix} J_{18} \\ J_{28} \\ J_{38} \end{bmatrix} \cdot R \cdot \dot{\theta}_3 \quad (2)$$

According to Jacobin matrix of 1st and 2nd wheel, we can get formula (3), (4):

$$\begin{bmatrix} \dot{X} \\ \dot{Y} \\ \dot{Z} \end{bmatrix} + \begin{bmatrix} 0 & -K_1 & d_2 \\ K_1 & 0 & K_2 \\ -d_2 & -K_2 & 0 \end{bmatrix} \cdot \begin{bmatrix} \dot{\phi}_x \\ \dot{\phi}_y \\ \dot{\phi}_z \end{bmatrix} + \begin{bmatrix} K_1 \\ 0 \\ K_2 \end{bmatrix} \dot{\beta} + \begin{bmatrix} 0 \\ 0 \\ 0 \end{bmatrix} \dot{\rho}_1 = \begin{bmatrix} J_{17} \\ J_{27} \\ J_{37} \end{bmatrix} \cdot R \cdot \dot{\theta}_1 \quad (3)$$

$$\begin{bmatrix} \dot{X} \\ \dot{Y} \\ \dot{Z} \end{bmatrix} + \begin{bmatrix} 0 & -K_1 & d_2 \\ K_1 & 0 & K_2 \\ -d_2 & -K_2 & 0 \end{bmatrix} \begin{bmatrix} \dot{\phi}_x \\ \dot{\phi}_y \\ \dot{\phi}_z \end{bmatrix} + \begin{bmatrix} K_1 \\ 0 \\ K_2 \end{bmatrix} \dot{\beta} + \begin{bmatrix} d_4 c(\beta+\rho_1)-a_4 s(\beta+\rho_1) \\ 0 \\ d_4 c(\beta+\rho_1)+a_4 s(\beta+\rho_1) \end{bmatrix} \cdot \dot{\rho}_1 = \begin{bmatrix} J_{17} \\ 0 \\ J_{37} \end{bmatrix} \cdot R \cdot \dot{\theta}_2 \quad (4)$$

According to formula (2)、 (3)、 (4), the new form of kinematics model can be obtained:

$$\dot{V} + D_{1i}\dot{\Phi} + D_{1i}\dot{\beta} + D_{2i}\dot{\rho} = M_i R \dot{\theta}_i \tag{5}$$

2.2.4 Model of Car Body

We utilize Solidworks to generate accurate geometrical model of WMR, then import the model into code and generate accurate model by using OpenGL. The 3-D model of WMR is presented accurately in such a virtual environment.

2.3 Simulation Mechanism

The simulation process can be divided into four steps:

(1) Initialize the position and orientation of car body, and rotation angle of rocker-bogie to ensure that the wheel of WMR cling to ground in initialization status.
(2) The inverse solution and integral for kinematics.
(3) Matrix transformation:

      According to the relation between car body coordinate R and wheel joint point coordinate C_i, we get the new position and orientation of joint point coordinate. The transformation matrix from wheel joint point coordinates C_i to world coordinate W: $T_{W,Ci}(U,q,\delta_i) = T_{W,R}(U)T_{R,Ai}(q)T_{Ai,Ci}(\delta_i)$

(4) The terrain angle needs to be changed to get inverse solution from new kinematics if there is mutation, so that solve new structure status parameter of WMR to adapt to mutational terrain.

3 Results and Analysis of Motion Simulation

3.1 Virtual Terrain Generated by Program

According to above relevant theory, we realized virtual roam system of WMR by using VC++ OpenGL, and achieve the motion experiment on sine curve. Figure 3 shows the simulation result of linear motion ($\dot{\phi}_z = 0$) on the sine curve surface. The curve line equation for the trace of left and right wheels: $20 * \sin(3.14 * x / 200)$; and $20 * \sin(3.14 * x / 180)$. Figure 4 shows the changes for each joint angle of WMR, as well it includes rotation angle (β) of cradle, rotation angle (ρ_1, ρ_2) of bogie. The mutation of β, ρ_1 appeared when left front wheel begin to go uphill, and ρ_2 changed later. Because the length of cradle is longer than the length of bogie, so the amplitude of β is smaller than the amplitude of (ρ_1, ρ_2). Figure 5 represents changing law between pitch angle ϕ_y of car body and roll angle ϕ_x. ϕ_y ranges from 0 to negative value which increase firstly and then decrease; ϕ_y become 0 when the center of car body reaches peak; And then, increase firstly and decrease later; Finally, its value approach to 0. The changing lay of curve line ϕ_y verified that the change of ϕ_y reflected the change of curve's tangent line. The change of roll angle ϕ_x is caused by the different touched terrain of left and right wheels. At last, ϕ_x, ϕ_y approach to 0 because the car body return to the initial state and its movement is on plane.

Fig. 3. WMR roving on sine surface

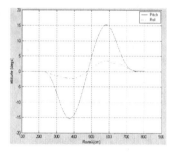

Fig. 4. Rocker and bogie joint angle

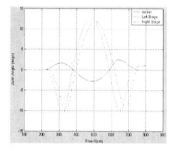

Fig. 5. WMR pitch and roll

a   b

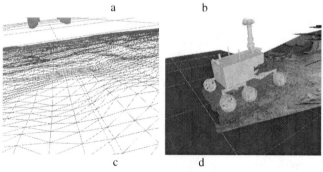

c   d

Fig. 6. Rocker and bogie joint angle

3.2 The Real Terrain Obtained by Stereo Vision

The Experiment environment is on the flat ground covered by sand in 15×20 meters room. In the environment, a 6×3 meters slope road was set up by human. The experiment environmental images were sampled firstly by using stereo camera on mast, as shown in figure 6(a). Subsequently, 3D point cloud data are calculated which is shown in figure 6(b). Figure 6(c) shows the triangulation partition result. Then, the operator chose one planning path in the virtual environment (terrain), and verified the path in the environment by the above algorithms, as shown in figure 6(d).The process is examined time and again to verify that if there is any dangerous during the movement until the planning path is verified exactly.

4 Conclusion

This paper utilized stereo vision and virtual environment technique to generate a visual, humanly teleoperation environment on the basis of kinematics model for WMR. The operator can interact with WMR system conveniently, thus realize the location and navigation for WMR. The research will be significant in virtual navigation, real time collision prevention and teleoperation for planetary exploration robot.

Acknowledgments. This work is supported by China Liaoning Provice Educational Office fund (No.20080611).

References

1. Castano, R., Judd, M., Estlin, T., et al.: Onborad Autonomous Rover Science. In: Proc. IEEE Aerospace Conference, pp. 1–13. Big Sky, Pasadena (2007)
2. Pedersen, L.: Science target assessment for Mars rover instrument deployment. In: Proc. IEEE/RSJ International Conference on Intelligent Robots and System, vol. 1, pp. 817–822 (2002)
3. Gao, H.W., Wu, C.D., Gao, L.F., Li, B.: An Improved Two-Stage Camera Calibration Method. In: Proc. The 6th World Congress on Control and Automation, Dalian, China, June 21-23, pp. 9514–9518 (2006)
4. Kolmogorov, V., Zabih, R.: Computing visual correspondence with occlusions using graph cuts. In: Proc.The Eighth International Conference on Computer Vision, pp. 508–515 (2001)
5. Cook, W.J., Cunningham, W.H., Pulleyblank, W.R.: Combinatorial Optimization. John Wiley & Sons, Chichester (1998)
6. Ma, S.D., Zhang, Z.Z.: Computer Vision-calculation theory and algorithm. Science Press, Beijing (2003)
7. Liu, W.J., Zhu, F., Dong, Z.L.: Virtual reality aided robot teleoperation techniques. Robot 23, 385–390 (2001)

Disparity Vector Based Depth Information Calculation

Hongwei Gao[1,*], Fuguo Chen[1], Ben Niu[2], and Yang Yu[1]

[1] School of Information Science & Engineering, Shenyang Ligong University,
Shenyang, 110159 China
[2] College of Management, Shenzhen University, Shenzhen, 518060 China
ghw1978@sohu.com

Abstract. The depth information contained in the image sequence which produced by the movement of the camera along the each axis is analyzed in this paper, especially for the depth information along the optical axis. Then, the corresponding relationship of the translational vector and the disparity vector under the translational movement of the camera is deduced. Finally, the algorithm for extracting the depth information based on the resolution of disparity vector is given, and the validity of the algorithm is proved by experiment.

Keywords: Image sequence, Translational vector, Disparity vector, Depth information.

1 Introduction

Stereo vision getting the depth information of scene form plane image is one of hot topics in computer vision. Its basic principle is that sample the images from different (two or more)views firstly and calculate positional deviation(i.e. disparity) between pixels in different images to get 3D information through triangulation principle[1]. According to different numbers used in stereo vision, the vision system is divided into monocular vision, binocular vision and multi-vision, etc. Binocular vision system is undoubtedly one of the most basic models in stereo vision, but monocular can also realize 3D reconstruction through the movement of single camera to get more than two views. Binocular vision system is used in navigation for mobile robot working in the complex environment and it has widely application perspective[2]. In general model for binocular vision system, the solution of matching points on the corresponding radial will realize 3D reconstruction for space point. The parallel binocular vision is degraded model of general binocular vision system, its geometrical relationship is simple and it can easily realize the image matching through epipolar line collineation constraint, thus the model is applied widely. However, the constraint condition of parallel binocular vision is not easy to realize, the situation of epipolar line non-collinear for matching point is usually to appear in practical application. The recover of epipolar line geometry[3-4] is proposed just for the reason of epipolar constraint, the method will increase the accuracy of parallel binocular vision. This

---

* Associate professor, his research interest includes computer vision, image processing and intelligent computation and control.

G. Shen and X. Huang (Eds.): ECWAC 2011, Part I, CCIS 143, pp. 402–407, 2011.
© Springer-Verlag Berlin Heidelberg 2011

paper discussed the binocular model with the relationship of translation position, and researched the method of extracting depth information by use of translation sequence in the model. The simulation results shows the validity of the proposed algorithm.

2   The Decomposition Analysis of Translational Movement

A series of translational sequence images could be obtained by the translational movement of camera. If two images are obtained from camera with a translational vector $T=(\Delta x,\Delta y,\Delta z)$, scenery point W and a pair of points $P_1(u_1,v_1)$ and $P_2(u_2,v_2)$ could be always found in two images, where P_1 is imaging point before moving and P_2 is imaging point after moving, and we assume that the camera coordinate of scenery point W is (x,y,z) before moving. We first consider that the situation of the camera movement along X axis, i.e. $T=(\Delta x,0,0)$, the translation vector of camera. The below equation is obtained easily according to parallel binocular vision principle[5]:

$$z = \frac{f\Delta x}{u_1 - u_2} \tag{1}$$

Where, u_1-u_2 is horizontal disparity, Δx is the length of baseline.

After that, we consider that the situation of the camera movement along Y axis, i.e. $T=(0, \Delta y, 0)$, the translation vector of camera. We can also get the following equation according to parallel binocular vision principle:

$$z = \frac{f\Delta y}{v_1 - v_2} \tag{2}$$

Where, v_1-v_2 is vertical disparity, Δx is the length of baseline.

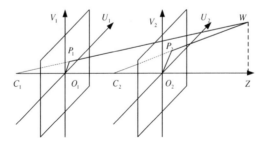

Fig. 1. Schematic diagram of imaging when the camera moves along the optical axis

Finally we analyses the situation of the camera movement along Z axis, i.e. $T=(0, 0, \Delta z$, the translation vector of camera. We can see in figure 1, it shows that W, P_1, P_2 all located on the plane which pass through optical axis, and $C_1O_1=C_2O_2=f, O_1O_2=\Delta z$. Let $r_1=O_1P_1, r_1=O_2P_2, R=WZ$, and we can get the following equation from geometry relationship in the figure:

$$\frac{f}{z} = \frac{r_1}{R} \tag{3}$$

$$\frac{f}{z - \Delta z} = \frac{r_2}{R} \tag{4}$$

The ratio of above two equations can be ordered as:

$$z = \frac{r_2 \Delta z}{r_2 - r_1} = \frac{r_2 \Delta z}{\sqrt{u_{21}^2 + v_{21}^2}} \tag{5}$$

3 The Corresponding Relationship between Translational Vector and Disparity Vector

As shown in figure 2, we assume that the camera execute translational movement among four positions in 3D space, and suppose that the camera move from point W_1 to point W_2 firstly along X axis, and then move from point W_2 to point W_3 along Y axis, finally move from point W_3 to point W_4 along Z axis, and the points have been projected to images in each position as well. If the matching points of the scene point W in space are P_1, P_2, P_3, P_4 respectively in the four images, so P_1, P_2 is in the same horizontal direction and P_2, P_3 is in the same vertical direction according to the analysis of above section, therefore they are in the same radial direction. We can confirm the relationship between each disparity by ignoring the real length of distance between matching points just according to the direction relationship for the matching points, as it is shown in figure 3. Obviously, disparity P_1P_4 represents the disparity obtained by the movement of camera from W_1 to W_4. In vector analysis, if the translational vector of camera in 3D space is $T=(\Delta x, \Delta y, \Delta z)$, we can obtain a disparity vector $D=\Delta u + \Delta v + \Delta r$, and Δu, Δv, Δr are the disparity vectors produced by the components Δx, Δy, Δz of translational vector.

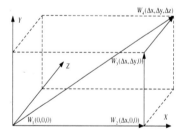

Fig. 2. Camera movement in 3D space

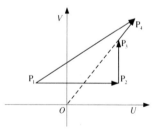

Fig. 3. Disparity at four positions

4   Solve Depth Information in the View of Decomposing Disparity Vector

Without loss of generality, we assume that two images are obtained by the camera movement with translational vector $T=(\Delta x, \Delta y, \Delta z)$, we can always find a pair of matching points $P_1(u_1,v_1)$和$P_2(u_2,v_2)$ in two images that the points correspond to the scene point W in space, where P_1 is image point before moving, P_2 is image point after moving, the coordinate of scene point W is (x,y,z) in camera coordinate before moving. Now, we mark the pair points in the same coordinate, and their relationship is shown in figure 4.

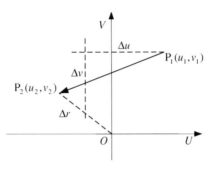

Fig. 4. Resolution of disparity vector

The disparity could be decomposed into 3 sections according to previous analysis: horizontal disparity Δu, vertical disparity Δv and a radial disparity Δr. Then, we can get four equation according to the corresponding relationship between their translational vector:

$$\Delta u = -\frac{f\Delta x}{z} \tag{6}$$

$$\Delta v = -\frac{f\Delta y}{z} \tag{7}$$

$$\Delta r = \frac{r_2 \Delta z}{z} \tag{8}$$

$$\Delta r = \sqrt{(u_2 - u_1 - \Delta u)^2 + (v_2 - v_1 - \Delta v)^2} \tag{9}$$

Where, $r_2 = \sqrt{(u_2 - u_0)^2 + (v_2 - v_0)^2}$.

Take equation (6), (7), (8) into equation (9), we will obtain a quadratic equation with one unknown about z:

$$(u_2 - u_1 + \frac{f\Delta x}{z})^2 + (v_2 - v_1 + \frac{f\Delta y}{z})^2 = \frac{r_2^2 \Delta z^2}{z^2} \qquad (10)$$

Let $u_{21} = u_2 - u_1$, $v_{21} = v_2 - v_1$, and solve the equation:

$$z = [\pm \sqrt{r_2^2 (u_{21}^2 + v_{21}^2) \Delta z^2 - f^2 (v_{21} \Delta x - u_{21} \Delta y)^2}$$
$$- f(u_{21} \Delta x + v_{21} \Delta y)] / (u_{21}^2 + v_{21}^2) \qquad (11)$$

We can get two real roots by solving equation (10) and it is obvious that the two real roots could not be decided which should be kept or rejected in their mathematical sense. We have known that the relationship between depth and translational movement when the camera moved in the direction of axis, and the relationship between depth and general translation movement in equation (10), so we can decide which should be kept or rejected in equation (11) according to principle of the general situation containing the special situation, and at the same time we can also verify the validity of the equation.

5   Experimental Result and Analysis

Experiment condition: binocular vision system: Bumblebee2 stereo camera of PointGrey company, resolution 1024×768; Homemade simple calibration board: The printing black-and-white checkerboard paste into foam board, the number of square are 7×9, the size of single square is 28×28 mm; The software for calibration is MATLAB calibration toolbox.

Fig. 5. Stereo vision camera Bumblebee2   **Fig. 6.** Image pair obtained by two cameras

In the experiment, the simple calibration board need to be placed in front of stereo camera and parallel to it as much as possible, the distance is mainly about 1m. Then, sample a pair of stereo images, as it is shown in figure 6. We can get 80 matching points from two images, and all these points are marked from left to right and later from top to bottom. Finally, we estimate the depth for calibration board through two algorithms by use of 80 pairs of matching points, the experimental results are shown in figure 7. Curve 1 is the results based on the algorithm of the paper whose mean value is 1(939.7651 mm); Curve 2 is the results based on parallel binocular vision algorithm whose mean value is 2 (925.4962 mm). The experimental results show that the accuracy of the algorithm proposed in the paper is higher under the same condition. There is still deviation between the estimated value and the real value for two algorithms which is limited to experimental condition.

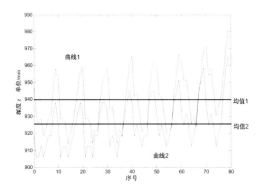

Fig. 7. Comparison of estimation for depths

6 Conclusion

In conclusion, there is obvious relationship between the translational movement and disparity for camera from decomposition of disparity vector perspective, i.e., horizontal movement correspond to horizontal disparity as well as vertical movement correspond to vertical disparity, and the movement in the direction of optical axis correspond to radial disparity; we can get the depth information of plane image through the corresponding relationship .Because the movement between camera and scene is relative, so we can also estimate the translational movement of scene from decomposition of disparity vector perspective, even achieve self calibration from decomposition of disparity vector perspective. These problems will be solved in the future research and the practical application of robot system.

Acknowledgments. This work is supported by China Liaoning Provice Educational Office fund (No. 20080611). National Natural Science Foundation (No. 71001072).

References

1. Pan, H., Guo, G.: Review of stereo vision. Computer measure and control 12(12), 1121–1124 (2004)
2. Liu, J.G., Wang, Y.C., Li, B., et al.: Current Research, Key Performance, and Future Development of Search and Rescue Robot. Frontiers of Mechanical Engineering 2(4), 404–416 (2007)
3. Gao, H.G., Wu, C.D., Li, B.: Study of a high-accuracy eppolar geometry restoration method. Hightechniqueletter 16(1), 51–54 (2006)
4. Zhang, Z.Z., Deriche, R., Faugeras, O.: A robust technique for matching two uncalibrated images through the recovery of the unknown epipolar geometry. Artificial Intelligence, 87–119 (1995)
5. Ma, S.D., Zhang, Z.Z.: Computer Vision-calculation theory and algorithm. Science Press, Beijing (2003)

Single Pile Side Friction Prediction for Super-Long and Large-Diameter Steel Pipe Piles of a Bridge under Vertical Load

Huazhu Song, Cong Cheng, and Bo Liu

School of Computer Science and Technology, Wuhan University of Technology,
Wuhan, Hubei, China
mingjs@vip.163.com

Abstract. A novel prediction algorithm LearnPre-Q was proposed by inversing the *Soil-feature SVM* created. After studying the domain knowledge, soil layer compressibility coefficient and void ratio variation were abstracted to describe the soil characters, and the pile data were transformed and divided into the active data and the passive data. Through learning from the data of one pile, the first independent component *firstIC* was got by fastICA algorithm which reflected the same or similar features of the soil; and then made the passive data as input and *firstIC* as ouput to create *Soil-feature SVM* model. When predicting, the transformed data of other pile was input to the *Soil-feature SVM* model, whose output was the soil feature of other pile. This feature and the corresponding active data were input to predict the pile side friction through SVM-Q algorithm. The result of experiment show the LearnPre-Q algorithm could predict very precisely.

Keywords: super-long and large-diameter steel pile piles, pile side friction, support vector machine (SVM), independent component analysis (ICA).

1 Introduction

As we all known, the number of super-long and large-diameter steel pipe piles in general projects is less, and the static load test data are lacking as well. So the data set used to research super-long and large-diameter steel pipe piles belong to small data set, and it is very difficult to get complete data about one project due to many factors such as construction, survey and so on. The existed research on the bearing capability of super-long and large-diameter steel pipe piles is rare. A new problem was proposed that was whether there is a model to predict pile side friction and bearing capability of other piles after learning the data from one pile in the same bridge with multiple piles.

For the single pile bearing capacity confirmation, there are two kinds of traditional methods. One is a direct method, namely to practical test pile static or dynamic test, direct determination of single pile bearing capacity; the other is the indirect method, which combined with other methods to estimate the parameters of pile and soil resistance and pile resistance, then determined on the basis of single pile bearing capacity [1]. Among them, the static load test pile is the most reliable method, but its cost is

G. Shen and X. Huang (Eds.): ECWAC 2011, Part I, CCIS 143, pp. 408–414, 2011.

very expensive, tested time is very long, and the number of piles tested is very small, especially for the bridge across the sea. In addition, there are some intelligent methods to predict the single pile bearing capability for the foundation or composite foundation [2]. Support vector machine (SVM) based on statistics learning theory is the focus of researchers because it can be good at solving finite sample learning issue [3]. Independent component analysis (ICA) is a good method to abstract the feature [4,5], our experiences show that ICA combined with SVM made a good prediction model [6]. These intelligent methods can reduce the cost for measuring and be very useful.

According to the super-long and large-diameter steel pipe piles data and our previous experiments, we found that the mutual effect among soil layers and pile soil is very important. It is well known that there exist the same or similar geologic characters in the environment of the bridge, and we found the commonness and discovered and applied it to prediction. Therefore, we built the model through study one pile to predict the pile side friction and bearing capability of other piles in the same geological conditions. The data used were introduced in Section 2. Section 3 gave the LearnPre-Q algorithm. Experiments were done and explained in Section 4.

2 Data Analysis

2.1 Pile Data

The study used the static load test data of the third test pile and the first test pile of a bridge shown in Table 1 and Table 2.

Table 1. Test data of the third test pile   **Table 2.** Test data of the first test pile

level	pile-length (m)	layer thickness (m)	void ratio	modulus of compressibility (Mpa)	standard penetration test	pile side friction (kPa)	level	pile-length (m)	layer thickness (m)	void ratio	modulus of compressibility (Mpa)	standard penetration test	pile side friction (kPa)
2	18.75	5	0.696	11.1	5	9	2.	19.716	5.9	0.663	14.5	8.5	13.
4	23.25	4.5	0.78	10.07	6	7	4.	23.516	3.8	0.814	6.07	8.5	14.
1	26.25	3	1.021	2.74	5	6	1.	28.616	5.1	1.056	2.93	6.5	11.
2	28.85	2.6	1.323	2.18	4	6	2.	36.416	7.8	1.265	2.59	8.	9.
5	30.75	1.9	0.562	12.1	23	41	3.	41.616	4.2	0.643	9.65	21.	46.
1	37.775	7	0.789	5.33	19.5	33	1.	47.016	5.4	0.663	7.76	28.	39.
3	41.25	3.5	0.647	8.52	25	41	4.	58.616	11.6	1.073	5.305	10.5	31.
1	43.25	2	0.865	4.81	20	33	5.	63.416	4.8	0.863	5.87	26.	31.
2	47.65	4.4	0.96	3.885	18	31	1.	64.916	1.5	0.651	10.	23.	42.
3	57.85	10.2	0.696	9.19	28	46	4.	73.316	8.4	0.758	6.55	19.	37.
4	64.75	6.9	0.871	5.5	21	31	1.	84.016	10.7	0.653	12.22	24.5	54.
5	69.15	4.4	0.751	5.21	21.5	51	1.	85.7	1.684	0.717	7.94	31.	64.
2	71.75	2.6	0.557	12.6	40	73	2.	19.716	5.9	0.663	14.5	8.5	13.
5	76.7	4.95	0.56	13	44.3	73	4.	23.516	3.8	0.814	6.07	8.5	14.

Geological situation of each soil layer is displayed in Table 3.

Table 3. Geological situation of each soil layer

No.	level	lithological character description	No.	level	lithological character description
1	2	Sandy Loam:	8	1	Loam
2	4	Sandy loam	9	2	Loam
3	1	Silty loam	10	3	Fine sand with loam sandwiched
4	2	Silty clay	11	4	Loam
5	5	Medium sand	12	5	Loam
6	1	Mild clay	13	2	Fine sand
7	3	Clayey silt	14	5	Medium sand with gravels

2.2 Analysis of Pile Data

Since geologic parameters in a same location have some similarity, we need to find these similarities and build the model through learning data of one pile, then use the model to predict the lateral friction resistance and bearing capability of other piles.

In the previous sections, we used level, pile-length, layer thickness, void ratio, modulus of compressibility and standard penetration test as learning data, and pile side friction as output data. Among these data, layer thickness, void ratio, modulus of compressibility and standard penetration test are related with geologic information more closely, the effect of geologic parameters to piles have similarity in spite of different pile-length.

1) Coefficient of Compressibility

As an important factor in evaluating the compression of the soil, the coefficient of compressibility is the slope of a random point in e-p curve, suppose a as coefficient of compressibility,

$$a = -\frac{de}{dp}$$

(1)

While the pressure variation scope is small, the soil compressibility curve can be expressed as following:

$$a = -\frac{\Delta e}{\Delta p} = \frac{e_1 - e_2}{p_2 - p_1}$$

(2)

in which:

e_1 and e_2 are void ratios under the effect of P_1 and P_2 while compression stabilizes before and after voltage increase;

P_1 is the intensity of pressure before voltage increase which can keep model compression stability, in general refers to the vertical weight stress in deep soil of foundation, and its unit is kPa;

P_2 is the intensity of pressure after voltage increase, in general refers to the sum of weight stress and subsidiary stress in deep soil of foundation, and its unit is kPa; So

$$\Delta e = e_1 - e_2 = a\Delta p$$

(3)

It is clear that Δe is very important, for it reflects a variation, and should be considered as a parameter.

2) Modulus of compressibility

Modulus of compressibility Es is another expression of reflecting soil compression parameter; it is the ratio of vertical subsidiary stress and corresponding strain increment under completely lateral confinement condition shown in Fig.1.

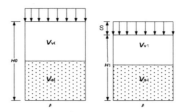

Fig. 1. Relation between the variation of layer thickness with void ratio

$$E_s = \frac{\sigma_z}{\varepsilon_z} \qquad (4)$$

Since $\sigma_z = \Delta P$, $\Delta H = H_1 - H_2 = \frac{e_1 - e_2}{1 + e_1} H_1$, and $\varepsilon_s = -\frac{\Delta P}{\dfrac{\Delta H}{H_1}}$, we get

$$\varepsilon_s = -\frac{\Delta P}{\dfrac{\Delta H}{H_1}} = -\frac{\Delta P}{\dfrac{-\Delta e}{1 + e_1}} = \frac{1 + e_1}{a} \ ,$$

Layer thickness is one of the important parameters.
So we can get the *soil layer compressibility coefficient*

$$a = \frac{1 + e_1}{\varepsilon_s} \qquad (5)$$

We can conclude from the derivation process, the *compressibility coefficient 'a'* is very important too, so it can be considered as a parameter.

So we converted the learning data (*layer thickness, void ratio, modulus of compressibility, standard penetration test*) to transformed data (*layer thickness, void ratio variation – detae, soil layer compressibility coefficient – a* and *standard penetration test*), the output data is pile side friction.

According to the different measures, transformed data (*layer thickness, void ratio variation, soil layer compressibility coefficient, standard penetration test*) was separated into active factor (*standard penetration test*) and passive factors (*layer thickness, void ratio variation, soil layer compressibility coefficient*) in which shows the commonness or similarity soil features among the different piles in a same location.

3   Learnpre-Q Predict Algorithm

3.1   SVM-Q Model

The study used the static load test data of the third test pile and the first test pile of a bridge shown in Table 1 and Table 2.

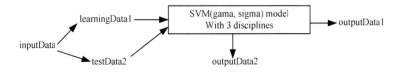

Fig. 2. SVM-Q algorithm block diagram

SVM-Q algorithm was to predict pile side friction of super-long, and large-diameter steel pipe pile. Its block diagram was illustrated in Fig.2: divide input data into learning data (learningData1) and test data (testData2), and divide corresponding solving target into practical output data (outputData1) for learning data and model output data (outputData2) for test data; then using learning data with (gama, sigma) to build SVM model and adjustment (gama, sigma) to make SVM model meet convergent condition and three disciplines, from this to obtain SVM model of solving target;

At last, predict solving target based on the SVM model with testData2 as input to get the output data outputData2 from the SVM model.

In which, the three disciplines were got from the domain knowledge and requirements, and they were show as following:

- The training data error is more than 10%, or around 10%;
- The solved data model error is more than 10% or around 10%;
- Sum of training data error as least as possible and sum of the solved model error as small as possible.

They could ensure the accuracy to the rain and prediction, avoid the overfitting, made the SVM-Q model fit for predicting more test data and show the good generating capability and prediction accuracy.

outputData SVM-Q(inputData)
//inputData: {*pile length, layer thickness, void ratio, modulus of compressibility, standard penetration test* };
//outputData: {*pile side friction*};

3.2 LearnPre-Q Prediction Algorithm

LearnPre-Q predicts algorithm block diagram was shown in Fig.3. There were two procedures – learning procedure and predicting procedure. Both learning data and predicting data were transformed according to (3) and (5). In learning procedure, one pile data was processed and *Soil-feature SVM* model was setup according to the abstracted the first independent component through fastICA model. In fact, more than one independent component was obtained, but the first independent component was abstracted as the feature of the environment after analyzing the components and more experiments. Therefore, Soil-feature SVM could be setup with abstracted passive *ldata* as input and abstracted *firstIC* as output. Meantime, abstracted active *ldata* combined with abstracted *firstIC* was regarded as input for building *learningSVM* model to show its accurate prediction ability. In predicting procedure, the other pile data was processed. After transformation, abstracted passive data was as input to *Soil-feature SVM* model, and outputSoil feature *pdata* was obtained which show the soil features about this pile. And then, ouputSoil feature *pdata* combined with abstracted active *pdata* were input to setup *Predicting SVM* model with *poutputGoal* – pile side friction. LearnPre-Q predict algorithm was shown in Fig. 4.

4 Examples

According to the LearnPre-Q algorithm, the experiment was done as following.

The data of third test pile was chosen as learning data, and transformed the learning data.

We chose the first independent component from which we obtained as a component for the following predict. Get $firstIC$ = (0.4210, 0.3689, 0.3129, 0.2931, 1.9145, 1.5621, 1.9541, 1.5700, 1.4604, 2.1938, 1.5200, 2.2430, 3.3896, 3.4745)^{T} with (100,0.005);

According to SVM-Q algorithm, *Soil-feature SVM* model(1000,0.25) was created with abstracted passive *ldata* as input and abstracted *firstIC* as output, whose relative model error was (-0.0604, -0.0014, -0.0045, -0.0048, 0.0001, -0.0000, -0.0002, -0.0001, -0.0002, 0.0002, -0.0001, 0.0006, 0.0005, 0.0075).

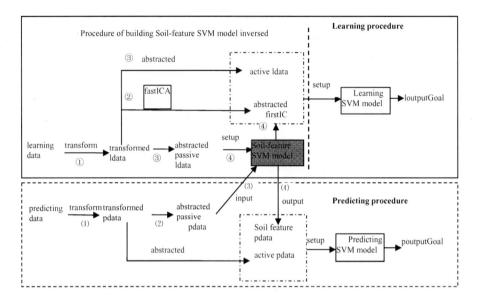

Fig. 3. LearnPre-Q predict algorithm block diagram

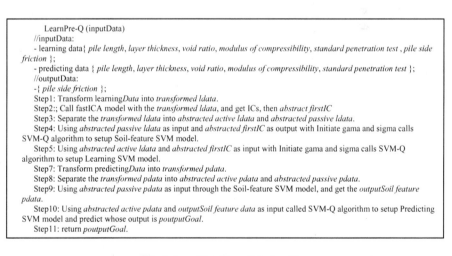

Fig. 4. LearnPre-Q predict algorithm

Input abstracted passive *pdata* to *Soil-feature SVM* model and got the outputSoil-feature *pdata* = (1.977, 2.1463, 1.7136, 1.7133, 1.7133, -2.8905, 1.7169, 1.3731, 1.7052, 1.7203, 1.7136, 1.895).

Using abstracted active *pdata* and outputSoil-feature *pdata* to predict pile side friction, the predicted result and relative error with (1000, 0.05) displayed in Table 4.

Table 4. LearnPre-Q algorithm predict pile side friction

Practical pile side friction (kPa)	Predict pile side friction (kPa)	Relative error
13.0000	12.9976	0.0002
14.0000	14.0204	-0.0015
11.0000	11.0142	-0.0013
9.0000	9.0168	-0.0019
46.0000	45.9838	0.0004
39.0000	38.9964	0.0001
31.0000	31.0000	0.0000
31.0000	31.0083	-0.0003
42.0000	42.0146	-0.0003
37.0000	37.0041	-0.0001
54.0000	53.9725	0.0005
64.0000	63.9714	0.0004

So we accurately predicted the first pile side friction with LearnPre-Q after learning the third pile.

5   Conclusion

The large bridge across the sea has more super-long and large-diameter steel pipe piles which are in the same or similar geologic environment. Based on SVM-Q and ICASVM-Q, LearnPre-Q was proposed to predict other pile side friction after learning one pile. The experiment results indicated that LearnPre-Q is feasible, effective and predicts result very accurately. In addition, the parameters of '*a*' and *detae* are useful, and they combined with layer thickness could reflect some relation with the pile side friction. The idea of LearnPre-Q was novel.

References

1. Huang, F., Liu, C., Li, G., Lu, H.: Study of the method for the determination of load bearing capacity of piles. Journal of Tsinghua University (Science And Technology) 38(1), 28–32 (1998)
2. Peng, W.: Study on Testing Analysis and Prediction Methods for Bearing Properties of Super-long and Large-diameter Steel Pipe Piles under Vertical Load. Wuhan University of Technology, Wuhan (2010)
3. Vapnik, V.: The Nature of Statistical Learning Theory. Springer, Heidelberg (1995)
4. Lee, T.W.: Independent Component Analysis: Theory and Application. Kluwer Academic Publishers, Dordrecht (1998)
5. Roberts, S.J., Everson, R.: Independent component analysis: principles and practice. Cambridge University Press, Cambridge (2001)
6. Song, H., Zhong, L., Han, B.: Structural damage detection by integrating independent component analysis and support vector machine. Int. J. Systems Science 37(13), 961–967 (2006)

Simulation Analysis of Stability for Fuzzy Systems Based on Efficient Maximal Overlapped-Rules Group

Song-tao Zhang

School of Management, Harbin University of Commerce,
Harbin, PR China
zst0626@163.com

Abstract. For relaxing the conservatism of stability analysis methods of fuzzy systems, this paper defines a concept of the efficient maximal overlapped-rules group (EMORG), then a theorem is proposed to reduce the difficulty of stability analysis for T-S fuzzy systems, which can guarantee the quadratic stability of the open-loop T-S fuzzy systems globally. This theorem only requires finding a local common positive definite matrix in each EMORG. Finally, simulation studies for two illustrative examples are conducted to show the effectiveness of the proposed method.

Keywords: stability condition, simulation analysis, EMORG.

1 Introduction

Recently, the stability analysis of T-S fuzzy systems has been difficult and hot issue. Since Tanaka and Sugeno[1] proposed the stability condition which is to find a common positive definite matrix $\mathbf{P}$ for all subsystems, many scholars[2-6] have been applying themselves to reducing its conservatism that finding a common matrix $\mathbf{P}$ is difficult if the number of fuzzy rules is large. Among of them, Reference [6] proposed a new stability condition, which utilizes a set of local common matrices $\mathbf{P}_1, \mathbf{P}_2, \cdots, \mathbf{P}_G$ to satisfy the Lyapunov inequalities of rules included in the maximal overlapped-rules groups (MORGs) respectively, where G denotes the number of MORGs. But if the number of the MORGs can be reduced, both the number of Lyapunov inequalities and the number of the local common matrices to be found can be reduced greatly. Therefore, the conservatism of two approaches mentioned above will be overcome.

In this paper, the concept of the efficient maximal overlapped-rules group (EMORG) is defined. Subsequently an improved stability condition of T-S fuzzy systems is proposed. The improved condition only requires finding a local common positive definite matrix in each EMORG. The feasibility and the validity of the proposed approach are illustrated by the simulation results of two examples.

2 Preliminary

Consider T-S fuzzy model as follows:

G. Shen and X. Huang (Eds.): ECWAC 2011, Part I, CCIS 143, pp. 415–420, 2011.

$$R_i : \text{IF } x_1(t) \text{ is } M_1^i \text{ and} \cdots \text{and } x_n(t) \text{ is } M_n^i \text{ THEN } \dot{x}(t) = A_i x(t), \, i=1,2,\cdots,r, \quad (1)$$

where r and n are the numbers of rules (sub-models) and input variables (state variables) respectively, $x(t) = [x_1(t), x_2(t), \cdots, x_n(t)]^\mathrm{T}$ is the state vector, M_j^i ($j=1,\cdots,n$) is the fuzzy set, A_i is system matrix with appropriate dimension. By the singleton fuzzifier, the product inference engine and center average defuzzification, the final output of (1) is inferred as:

$$\dot{x}(t) = \sum_{i=1}^{r} h_i \left(x(t) \right) A_i x(t), \quad (2)$$

where $h_i \left(x(t) \right) = \prod_{j=1}^{n} M_j^i \left(x_j(t) \right) \Big/ \sum_{i=1}^{r} \prod_{j=1}^{n} M_j^i \left(x_j(t) \right)$, and $\sum_{i=1}^{r} h_i \left(x(t) \right) = 1$.

Lemma 1[1]. The equilibrium point of (2) is asymptotically stable in the large if there exists a common positive definite matrix P satisfying

$$A_i^\mathrm{T} P + P A_i < 0, \quad i=1,2,\cdots,r. \quad (3)$$

Lemma 1 shows that a common positive definite matrix P must satisfy r inequalities (3) in order to guarantee the stability of T-S fuzzy systems. It might be difficult to find the common positive definite matrix P, if the number of rules is large.

To reduce the difficulty, Reference [6] proposed a relaxed stability condition given in Lemma 2 based on the definition of the maximal overlapped-rules group (MORG).

Definition 1[6]. For a given fuzzy system, an overlapped-rules group with the largest amount of rules is said to be a maximal overlapped-rules group (MORG).

Lemma 2[6]. For a T-S fuzzy system described by (2), if input variables adopt SFPs, then the equilibrium point of the fuzzy system is asymptotically stable in the large if there exists a local common positive definite matrix P_l in lth MORG such that

$$A_i^\mathrm{T} P_l + P_l A_i < 0, \quad l=1,2,\cdots,G, \quad (4)$$

for $i \in$ {the sequence numbers of rules included in the lth MORG}, G denotes the number of MORGs, $G = \prod_{j=1}^{n} (q_j - 1)$, and q_j denotes the number of the fuzzy partitions of the jth input variable.

3   Stability Analysis

Definition 2. A set of maximal overlapped-rules groups (MORGs) is said to be an efficient maximal overlapped-rules group set (EMORGS) if the set is composed of the least number of MORGs which include all rules of a T-S fuzzy system. And each MORG included in an EMORGS is said to be an efficient maximal overlapped-rules group (EMORG).

Theorem 1. For a T-S fuzzy system described by (2), if input variables adopt SFPs, then the equilibrium point of the fuzzy system is asymptotically stable in the large if there exists a local common positive definite matrix P_l in lth EMORG such that

$$\mathbf{A}_i^{\mathrm{T}}\mathbf{P}_l + \mathbf{P}_l\mathbf{A}_i < 0, \quad l=1,2,\cdots, g, \tag{5}$$

where $i \in$ {the sequence numbers of rules included in the lth EMORG}, g denotes the number of EMORGs,

$$
g = \begin{cases}
\displaystyle\prod_{j=1}^{n}\left(\frac{q_j+1}{2}\right) & q_j \in \text{odd set} \\[3mm]
\displaystyle\prod_{j=1}^{n}\left(\frac{q_j}{2}\right) & q_j \in \text{even set} \\[3mm]
\displaystyle\prod_{q_{j'}\in even}\left(\frac{q_{j'}}{2}\right)\prod_{q_{j''}\in odd}\left(\frac{q_{j''}+1}{2}\right), j', j'' \in \{1,2,\cdots,n\} & q_j \in \text{other}
\end{cases}
$$

and q_j denotes the number of the fuzzy partitions of the jth input variable.

4 Numerical Examples

In this section, two numerical examples are given to illustrate the stability examination for an open-loop T-S fuzzy system in detail. An open-loop T-S fuzzy system is considered as follows:

$$R_i : \text{IF } x_1(t) \text{ is } \mathbf{M}_1^i \text{ and } x_2(t) \text{ is } \mathbf{M}_2^i \text{ THEN } \dot{x}(t)=\mathbf{A}_i x(t). \tag{6}$$

4.1 $q_j \in$ Even Set

For (6), we select $i = 1,2,\cdots,16$, and the fuzzy partitions of $x_1(t)$ and $x_2(t)$ are $F_1^m(x_1(t))$ $(m=1,2,\cdots,4)$ and $F_2^s(x_2(t))$ $(s=1,2,\cdots,4)$ respectively as shown in Fig. 1. From Fig. 1 we can see that the input variables of the fuzzy system employ SFPs.

The fuzzy sets and the system parameters are shown as follows:

$\mathbf{M}_1^1=\mathbf{M}_1^2=\mathbf{M}_1^3=\mathbf{M}_1^4=\mathbf{F}_1^1$, $\mathbf{M}_1^5=\mathbf{M}_1^6=\mathbf{M}_1^7=\mathbf{M}_1^8=\mathbf{F}_1^2$, $\mathbf{M}_1^9=\mathbf{M}_1^{10}=\mathbf{M}_1^{11}=\mathbf{M}_1^{12}=\mathbf{F}_1^3$,

$\mathbf{M}_1^{13}=\mathbf{M}_1^{14}=\mathbf{M}_1^{15}=\mathbf{M}_1^{16}=\mathbf{F}_1^4$, $\mathbf{M}_2^1=\mathbf{M}_2^5=\mathbf{M}_2^9=\mathbf{M}_2^{13}=\mathbf{F}_2^1$, $\mathbf{M}_2^2=\mathbf{M}_2^6=\mathbf{M}_2^{10}=\mathbf{M}_2^{14}=\mathbf{F}_2^2$,

$\mathbf{M}_2^3=\mathbf{M}_2^7=\mathbf{M}_2^{11}=\mathbf{M}_2^{15}=\mathbf{F}_2^3$, $\mathbf{M}_2^4=\mathbf{M}_2^8=\mathbf{M}_2^{12}=\mathbf{M}_2^{16}=\mathbf{F}_2^4$.

$$\mathbf{A}_1 = \begin{bmatrix} -0.01 & 0.3 \\ 0 & -3.26 \end{bmatrix}, \mathbf{A}_2 = \begin{bmatrix} -2 & 3 \\ 1 & -4 \end{bmatrix}, \mathbf{A}_3 = \begin{bmatrix} -2 & 2 \\ 0 & -4 \end{bmatrix}, \mathbf{A}_4 = \begin{bmatrix} -0.01 & 3 \\ 0 & -3 \end{bmatrix},$$

$$\mathbf{A}_5 = \begin{bmatrix} -1 & 1.99 \\ 1 & -2 \end{bmatrix}, \mathbf{A}_6 = \begin{bmatrix} -2 & 1.99 \\ 1 & -2 \end{bmatrix}, \mathbf{A}_7 = \begin{bmatrix} -0.01 & 3 \\ 0 & -3.26 \end{bmatrix}, \mathbf{A}_8 = \begin{bmatrix} -1 & 3 \\ 1 & -4 \end{bmatrix},$$

$$\mathbf{A}_9 = \begin{bmatrix} -20 & 3 \\ 1 & -4 \end{bmatrix}, \mathbf{A}_{10} = \begin{bmatrix} -0.01 & 0.3 \\ 0 & -3 \end{bmatrix}, \mathbf{A}_{11} = \begin{bmatrix} -1.2 & 1.99 \\ 1 & -2 \end{bmatrix}, \mathbf{A}_{12} = \begin{bmatrix} -1 & 1.99 \\ 0 & -2 \end{bmatrix},$$

$$\mathbf{A}_{13} = \begin{bmatrix} -0.01 & 2 \\ 0 & -3.26 \end{bmatrix}, \mathbf{A}_{14} = \begin{bmatrix} -1 & 2 \\ 1 & -4 \end{bmatrix}, \mathbf{A}_{15} = \begin{bmatrix} -2 & 3 \\ -1 & -4 \end{bmatrix}, \mathbf{A}_{16} = \begin{bmatrix} -10.01 & 3 \\ 0 & -30 \end{bmatrix}.$$

There are 16 rules in this fuzzy system. For Lemma 1, a common positive definite matrix **P** must satisfy 16 Lyapunov inequalities (3). On the other hand, for Lemma 2, local common positive definite matrices $P_1 - P_9$ must satisfy the inequalities formed by the rules included in 9 MORGs ($G_1 - G_9$) respectively. By using LMI method, the common matrix **P** and the set of matrices $P_1 - P_9$ to satisfy (3) and (4) respectively can not be found. Therefore, neither Lemma 1 nor Lemma 2 can guarantee the stability of the system.

Four local common positive definite matrices are found to satisfy inequalities (5) in Theorem 1.

$$\mathbf{P}_1 = \begin{bmatrix} 0.9815 & 0.1378 \\ 0.1378 & 1.7612 \end{bmatrix} \quad , \quad \mathbf{P}_3 = \begin{bmatrix} 2.2942 & 2.1614 \\ 2.1614 & 3.2057 \end{bmatrix} \quad , \quad \mathbf{P}_7 = \begin{bmatrix} 0.4567 & 0.4060 \\ 0.4060 & 1.1983 \end{bmatrix} \quad ,$$

$$\mathbf{P}_9 = \begin{bmatrix} 0.3184 & 0.1340 \\ 0.1340 & 0.5222 \end{bmatrix} .$$

The approach only requires solving 16 Lyapunov inequalities. By Theorem 1, the equilibrium of this system should be asymptotically stable. The results of this simulation are shown in Fig. 2.

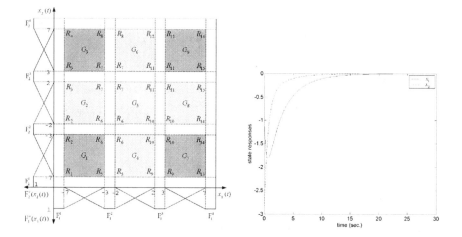

Fig. 1. The fuzzy partitions with $q_1 = q_2 = 4$ **Fig. 2.** State responses with $x(0) = \begin{bmatrix} -1 & -3 \end{bmatrix}^{\mathrm{T}}$

4.2 $q_j \in$ **Odd Set**

For (6), we select $i = 1, 2, \cdots, 25$, and the fuzzy partitions of $x_1(t)$ and $x_2(t)$ are $F_1^m(x_1(t))$ $(m = 1, 2, \cdots, 5)$ and $F_2^s(x_2(t))$ $(s = 1, 2, \cdots, 5)$ respectively as shown in Fig. 3. From Fig. 3 we can see that the input variables of the fuzzy system employ SFPs. The fuzzy sets and the system parameters are shown as follows:

$M_1^1 = M_1^2 = M_1^3 = M_1^4 = M_1^5 = F_1^1$, $M_1^6 = M_1^7 = M_1^8 = M_1^9 = M_1^{10} = F_1^2$,

$M_1^{11} = M_1^{12} = M_1^{13} = M_1^{14} = M_1^{15} = F_1^3$, $M_1^{16} = M_1^{17} = M_1^{18} = M_1^{19} = M_1^{20} = F_1^4$,

$M_1^{21} = M_1^{22} = M_1^{23} = M_1^{24} = M_1^{25} = F_1^5$, $M_2^1 = M_2^6 = M_2^{11} = M_2^{16} = M_2^{21} = F_2^1$,

$M_2^2 = M_2^7 = M_2^{12} = M_2^{17} = M_2^{22} = F_2^2$, $M_2^3 = M_2^8 = M_2^{13} = M_2^{18} = M_2^{23} = F_2^3$,

$M_2^4 = M_2^9 = M_2^{14} = M_2^{19} = M_2^{24} = F_2^4$, $M_2^5 = M_2^{10} = M_2^{15} = M_2^{20} = M_2^{25} = F_2^5$.

$$\mathbf{A}_1 = \mathbf{A}_6 = \mathbf{A}_{11} = \begin{bmatrix} -1 & 3 \\ 0.01 & -2.99 \end{bmatrix}, \quad \mathbf{A}_2 = \mathbf{A}_7 = \mathbf{A}_{12} = \mathbf{A}_{17} = \mathbf{A}_{22} = \begin{bmatrix} -1 & 3 \\ 1 & -4 \end{bmatrix},$$

$$\mathbf{A}_3 = \mathbf{A}_8 = \mathbf{A}_{13} = \mathbf{A}_{18} = \mathbf{A}_{23} = \begin{bmatrix} -2 & 3 \\ 1 & -4 \end{bmatrix}, \quad \mathbf{A}_5 = \begin{bmatrix} -1 & 1 \\ 1 & -1 \end{bmatrix}, \quad \mathbf{A}_{25} = \begin{bmatrix} -1 & 4.8 \\ 1 & -5 \end{bmatrix},$$

$$\mathbf{A}_4 = \mathbf{A}_9 = \mathbf{A}_{14} = \mathbf{A}_{19} = \mathbf{A}_{24} = \begin{bmatrix} -1 & 3 \\ 0 & -3 \end{bmatrix}, \quad \mathbf{A}_{10} = \mathbf{A}_{15} = \mathbf{A}_{20} = \begin{bmatrix} -1 & 2 \\ 1 & -5 \end{bmatrix},$$

$$\mathbf{A}_{16} = \mathbf{A}_{21} = \begin{bmatrix} -1 & 3 \\ 0 & -2.99 \end{bmatrix}.$$

For the fuzzy system (6), by using Lemma 1 and Lemma 2, there do not exist the common positive definite matrix and the set of 16 local common positive definite matrices to satisfy (3) and (4) respectively. But using Theorem 1, we can respectively find different three sets of local common positive definite matrices for 3 different EMORGSs chosen at random.

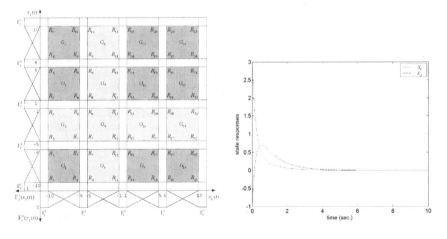

Fig. 3. The fuzzy partitions with $q_1 = q_2 = 5$ **Fig. 4.** State responses with $x(0) = \begin{bmatrix} -1 & 3 \end{bmatrix}^T$

For the EMORGS $\{G_1, G_3, G_4, G_9, G_{11}, G_{12}, G_{13}, G_{15}, G_{16}\}$, 9 local common positive definite matrices are found as follows:

$$\mathbf{P}_1 = \begin{bmatrix} 448.8383 & 304.9255 \\ 304.9255 & 386.5180 \end{bmatrix}, \quad \mathbf{P}_3 = \mathbf{P}_{11} = \mathbf{P}_{15} = \begin{bmatrix} 297.0426 & 197.4118 \\ 197.4118 & 288.4769 \end{bmatrix},$$

$$\mathbf{P}_4 = \begin{bmatrix} 283.1442 & 147.1164 \\ 147.1164 & 283.1442 \end{bmatrix}, \quad \mathbf{P}_9 = \begin{bmatrix} 448.2100 & 304.2547 \\ 304.2547 & 385.8544 \end{bmatrix}, \quad \mathbf{P}_{12} = \begin{bmatrix} 277.5240 & 135.5835 \\ 135.5835 & 225.1697 \end{bmatrix},$$

$$\mathbf{P}_{13} = \begin{bmatrix} 447.5875 & 303.5889 \\ 303.5889 & 385.1953 \end{bmatrix}, \quad \mathbf{P}_{16} = \begin{bmatrix} 215.4814 & 162.2243 \\ 162.2243 & 289.2484 \end{bmatrix}.$$

The approach only needs solving 36 Lyapunov inequalities. By Theorem 1, the equilibrium of this system should be asymptotically stable. The results of this simulation are shown in Fig. 4.

5 Conclusions

This paper has developed a relaxed stability condition for T-S fuzzy systems in terms of the definition of the efficient maximal overlapped-rules group. This stability condition only requires finding a local common positive definite matrix in each efficient maximal overlapped-rules group. To demonstrate the effectiveness of the proposed stability condition, an open-loop T-S fuzzy system with different numbers of fuzzy partition q_j has been considered as a platform or a test bed for illustration. Simulation results have verified the effectiveness of the relaxed conditions.

Acknowledgment

The author would like to acknowledge the financial support of Heilongjiang Province Education Bureau Foundation (No. 11541075).

References

1. Tanaka, K., Sugeno, M.: Stability analysis and design of fuzzy control systems. Fuzzy Sets and Systems 45(2), 135–156 (1992)
2. Zhang, S., Bai, S.-z.: Controller design of uncertain nonlinear systems based on T-S fuzzy model. Journal of Control Theory and Applications 7(2), 139–143 (2009)
3. Sala, A., Ariño, C.: Relaxed stability and performance LMI conditions for Takagi-Sugeno fuzzy systems with Polynomial constraints on membership function shapes. IEEE Transactions on Fuzzy Systems 16(5), 1328–1336 (2008)
4. Tanaka, K., Hori, T., Wang, H.O.: A multiple Lyapunov function approach to stabilization of fuzzy control systems. IEEE Transactions on Fuzzy Systems 11(4), 582–589 (2003)
5. Sala, A., Ariño, C.: Relaxed stability and performance LMI conditions for Takagi-Sugeno fuzzy systems with Polynomial constraints on membership function shapes. IEEE Transactions on Fuzzy Systems 16(5), 1328–1336 (2008)
6. Xiu, Z.H., Ren, G.: Stability analysis and systematic design of Takagi-Sugeno fuzzy control systems. Fuzzy Sets and Systems 151(1), 119–138 (2005)

The Animation Design of Fusible Material Based on Graphics

Yun Yang and Hongli Yang

School of Electrical and Information Engineering of
Shaanxi University of Science and Technology of
Xi'an, China
yangyun11@163.com

Abstract. In the animation production process, often of different elements to describe the fusion state, this paper takes the single phase reaction–feldspar fusion in the process of ceramic body as example, adopts graphics in its graphics technology to generate fusion style animation design, and makes use of the software Visual C + + language to realize the formation process showing the ceramics microstructure with animation procedure.

Keywords: ceramic body, fusion process, graphics technology, fusion style animation.

1 Introduction

In ceramic technology, ceramic materials microstructure and the relationship between raw material burn system and product performance is critical. Because the ceramic microstructure formation process involves a wide range and can not be directly observed, it is difficult to understand. From the point of view of traditional ceramic and start with ceramic green theoretical model, the use of computer animation methods to quartz-feldspar-clay firing process in the physic-chemical reaction and phase formation process of the display more depth, so that people can effectively understand the ceramic microstructure and its development. This text takes the single phase reaction--feldspar fusion in the process of ceramic body as example, Introduction of a based graphics generation of graphics technology [1] for animation design method.

2 Animation Production Basal Principle and Method

The animation production [2] is as illustrated step by step as follows:

- Generate the first dissolution frame in the motion process. It is real-time generated by computer graphics system, or was pre-organize to form images stored in computer.
- Erase the frame which is showing.

G. Shen and X. Huang (Eds.): ECWAC 2011, Part I, CCIS 143, pp. 421–426, 2011.

- Generate the next frame or fetch next frame from the computer graphics buffer area.
- Repeat these step, can form the people's animation visual effects.

Four methods of traditional animation production:

- Draw the dissolution frame of the motion by hand, then the information of these frames is recorded enter a computer, them is stored after appropriate deal with. This method is suitable to the motion in not certain law comparatively;
- Make use of display to transform: the motions are generated by comparison transform, translation transform, rotation transform, and composite transform form animation effects;
- Make use of the relativity moving to generated an animation, for example, when making the animation which is a running train in the computer, you can let the train do not move but the roadside trees do move, then to form the visual effect of the running train.
- Use of equations of motion generated the animation; this method is suitable for regular motion.

While we are talking about the ceramic body after change temperature and calcinations, the ceramic microstructure and the formation of the majority of reactions are no regular motion, and its animation effects is similar to volcanic eruptions and the flow of water ripples.

In this paper, the graphics principle and random technology are used to the design of fusion-style animation [3].

3   Design and Implementation of the Ceramic Body - Feldspar Fusion Style Animation

Feldspar shape round or oval-shaped can be used to express, and its reaction to generate the melt point. If designed as a circular shape, is used for animation arc fitting design; if designed to be oval, elliptical arc is used for animation to be legitimate. This article feldspar into a circular shape of the design, first of all express feldspar in the circle N random check points, then these N random points based fitting of the use of arc-by-point comparison arc interpolation algorithm to achieve melting of feldspar animation [4].

3.1   Fusions-Style Design of the Basic Principles of Animation

We use graphics-by-point comparison arc interpolation, so that more detailed mapping of the arc, making a very realistic animation effects.

The basic principle [4,5] is: in the output arc process, each after the end of a unit length on the arc and should draw a comparison, according to the results of this comparison, and then decide on the next direction; This will be step by step approximation of the draw the arc. Arc interpolation process should be based on circular interpolation discriminated locus to determine the location of the point, are located outside the circle or circle, and then be able to track points by quadrants in different sports at the time to decide to go walking along the x direction or Walking along the y direction, where sport and clockwise or counterclockwise to draw the relationship between arc has.

3.2 Algorithm implementation

Procedures defined in the array of five variables, of which (x [N], y [N]) is used to store the coordinates of N points, d [N] express feldspar melting when the direction of -1 to express the internal melting feldspar , +1 to express external feldspar melting (because at melting feldspar volume change), r [N] express draw circle radius, if the internal melt-down, then r [N] gradually decreased, on the contrary, if the external melting , then r [N] is gradually increasing, n [N] that the melting rate of the control parameter [6,7].

First of all, in feldspar edge set N random check points.

```
for(i=0;i<N;i++)
{
x[i]=random(2*r0+1)+x0-r0;
for(j=0;j<=r0;j++)
if(r0*r0-(x[i]-x0)*(x[i]-x0)<=j*j)
{
y[i]=(random(2)= =1?1:-1)*j+y0;
break;
}
d[i]=random(4)>0?-1:1;
r[i]=r0+1; n[i]=0;
}
```

In which,(x0, y0) to the center of a circle drawn feldspar, r0 to draw a radius of feldspar.

Then, this N-point arc drawn as the starting point, according to the different quadrants decided the direction of trajectory points.

```
for (i=0;i<N;i++)
Trajectories in the circle
if((x[i]-x0)*(x[i]-x0)+(y[i]-y0)*(y[i]-y0)<r[i]*r[i])
if(right>x[i]&&x[i]>x0&&y0>y[i]&&y[i]>=top) y[i]--;
else if (y0>y[i]&&y[i]>=top)
x[i]--;
else if (x0>x[i]&&x[i]>=left)
y[i]++;
```

```
else if (bottom>=y[i]&&y[i]>y0)
x[i]++;
else
if(bottom>=y[i]&&y[i]>y0 &&x0>=x[i]&&x[i]>=left)  x[i]++;
else if (x0>x[i]&&x[i]>=left)
y[i]++;
else if (y0>y[i]&&y[i]>=top)
x[i]--;
else if (right>=x[i]&& x[i]>x0)
    y[i]--;
```

Drawing with circular arc fitting, when the melting rate of the control parameters n [N] must meet the conditions, then the radius becomes: r [N] + d [N], since then draw a radius of the arc after the Change.

```
if (r[i]<53)
{
n [i]++;
if (n[i]>20)
{
n[i]=0; r[i]+=d[i];
}
}
```

Since drawing with painting point arc, the resulting leakage points more, especially in the circle of the place. So the introduction of xn, yn two variables, they are stored in the (x [N], y [N]) and (x0, y0), composed of a straight line up, and to (x0, y0) for the center of a circle, r0 is the radius of the circle on the coordinates of a point. Will be painted point arc painted expanded to draw line method painted a round cake, so we can have a melt-down process of feldspar animation procedures, and minimal leakage point, because the procedure used random numbers are the way to generate graphics at the basic laws on the use of stochastic techniques, so that when the graphics in the demo more realistic, and when each call to the animation effects are not identical. One of (xn, yn) Determination:

```
for (m=1;m<=((x0-x[i])*(x0-x[i])+(y0-y[i])*(y0-y[i]))/2;m++)
if (x0-x[i])*(x0-x[i])+(y0-y[i])*(y0-y[i])<=m*m)
{
xn=x0+r0*(x[i]-x0)/m;
yn=y0+r0*(y[i]-y0)/m;  }
break;
}
```

Finally from (x[i],y[i]) to (xn,yn) draw a straight line.
  Draw a straight line function as follows:

```
line (x[i],y[i],xn,yn);
```

The flow chart of this program is following as figure1:

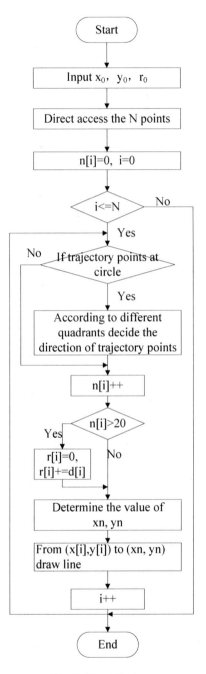

Fig. 1. Flow Chart

4 Conclusion

More than introduce the use of Visual C + + to achieve fusion-style animation applications, this paper, random function of technology and graphics principles of the graphics generation technology, arc fitting of point-by-point comparison method. Master the technical side can take full advantage of graphics in the other principle, not only the form of the rules of the sport graphics irregular melting-style animation procedures can also be prepared to meet the user needs into a graphics irregularly irregular sports-style animation of the melting process, Ways to use the design of its effect is very realistic animation. The design idea can draw on to other areas of animation, design, facilitate the promotion and use.

Acknowledgments. This research is financially supported by the Doctor Scientific Research Start Fund (BJ10-01) and the Graduate Innovation Fund of Shaanxi University of Science and Technology.

References

1. Sun, J.: Computer Graphics. Tsinghua University Press, Beijing (1995)
2. Ye, Y.: Computer animated film in the teaching of design and application. J. China's cable TV (January 2007)
3. Feng, G., Feng, G., Zhang, H.: "Organic Chemistry" CAI courseware production and application. J. China's modern educational equipment (September 2006)
4. Guo, L., Liu, X., Lei, J.: Organic-based integrated design of computer simulation experiments. J. Computer and Applied Chemistry (February 2006)
5. Chu, Y.P.: A mathematical model to evaluate a CAI courseware. J. Mathematical and Computer Modeling 22(2), 39–49 (1995)
6. de v Steyn, M.M., Alexander, P.M., Röhm, D.: CAL for first year analytical chemistry by distance education. J.Computers & Education 27(2), 95–101 (1996)
7. Song, K.-S., Hu, X., Olney, A., Graesser, A.C.: A framework of synthesizing tutoring conversation capability with web-based distance education courseware. J.Computers & Education 42(4), 375–388 (2004)

Least Square Support Vector Machine
for the Simultaneous Learning of a Function
and Its Derivative

Rui Zhang[1] and Guozhen Liu[2]

[1] School of Science, Shandong University of Technology
Zibo, P.R. China
zrlgz@sdut.edu.cn
[2] Zibo Fifth Senior High School, Zibo, P.R. China

Abstract. In this paper, the problem of simultaneously approximating a function and its derivatives is formulated. First, the problem is solved for a one-dimensional input space by using the least square support vector machines and introducing additional constraints in the approximation of the derivative. To optimize the regression estimation problem, we have derived an algorithm that works fast and more accuracy for moderate-size problems. The proposed method shows that using the information about derivatives significantly improves the reconstruction of the function.

Keywords: SVM, SVR, LS-SVR, regression.

1 Introduction

Regression approximation of a given data set is a very common problem in a number of applications. In some of these applications, like economy, device modeling, telemetry, etc., it is necessary to fit not only the underlying characteristic function but also its derivatives, which are often available. The problem of learning a function and its derivatives has been addressed, for instance, in the neural networks literature, to analyze the capability of several kinds of networks [1, 2], or in some applications [3, 4]. Some other methods have been employed to simultaneously approximate a set of samples of a function and its derivative: splines, or filter bank based methods are some examples [5]. On the other hand, support vector machines (SVMs) are state-of-the-art tools for linear and nonlinear input output knowledge discovery [6,7]. The SVMs, given a labeled data set (x_i, y_i) where $x_i \in R^d$ for $i = 1, \cdots, N$ and a function $\phi(\cdot)$ that nonlinearly transforms the input vector x_i to a higher-dimensional space, solve either classification ($y_i \in \{\pm 1\}$) or regression $y_i \in R$ problems.

In this paper, we will deal with the regression approximation problem using the least square support vector regression (LS--SVR) method and we will extend this framework when prior knowledge about the derivative of the functional relation between x and y is known. We will solve this problem for one dimensional problem

G. Shen and X. Huang (Eds.): ECWAC 2011, Part I, CCIS 143, pp. 427–433, 2011.

(d= 1), but it can be readily extended to multidimensional input and the gradient information, as we will show herein. We would like to find the functional relation between x and y giving a labeled data set (x_i, y_i, y_i'), where $y_i \in R$ and $y_i' \in R$, which is the derivative of the function to be approximated at x_i.

The rest of the paper is outlined as follows. In section 2, we briefly introduce the SVM for regression approximation to include the derivative information. In Section 3, we apply LS--SVR to solve the simultaneous learning of a function and its derivative. Experimental results and conclusions are presented in Section 4.

2 One-dimensional SVM-Based Approach

In this section, we briefly introduce the SVM for regression approximation to include the derivative information (see [8] for details).

The one-dimensional problem can be stated as follows: to find the functional relation between x and y giving a labeled data set (x_i, y_i, y_i') , where $y_i \in R$ and $y_i' \in R$ is the derivative of the function to be approximated at x_i. The proposed method is an extension of the SVM for regression (SVR) employing Vapnik's ε-insensitive loss function . The SVR obtains a linear regressor in the transformed space (feature space)

$$f(x) = w^T \phi(x) + b$$

where w and b define the linear regression, which is nonlinear in the input space (unless $\phi(x)$ is linear). Roughly speaking, the SVR minimizes the squared norm of the weight vector w, while it linearly penalizes deviations greater than ε.

With respect to the conventional SVR cost function, the proposed method adds a new penalty term: the errors in the derivative that are out of its associated insensitive region. In the general case, a different parameter is employed to define the insensitive region size for the function (ε) and for the derivative (ε'). Taking this extension into account, the proposed approach minimizes

$$\min \quad \frac{1}{2} w^T w + C_1 \sum_{i=1}^{N} (\xi_i + \xi_i^*) + C_2 \sum_{i=1}^{N} (\tau_i + \tau_i^*)$$

$$\begin{aligned} s.t. \quad & w^T \phi(x_i) + b - y_i \le \varepsilon + \xi_i \\ & y_i - w^T \phi(x_i) - b \le \varepsilon + \xi_i^* \\ & w^T \phi'(x_i) - y_i' \le \varepsilon' + \tau_i' \\ & y_i' - w^T \phi'(x_i) \le \varepsilon' + \tau_i' \\ & \xi_i, \xi_i', \tau_i, \tau_i^* \ge 0 \end{aligned} \tag{1}$$

for $i = 1, \cdots, N$. The positive slack variables ξ_i, ξ_i^*, τ_i and τ_i^* are responsible for penalizing errors greater than ε and ε', respectively, in the function and derivative, and $\phi'(x)$ denotes the derivative of $\phi(x)$. To solve this problem, a Lagrangian functional is used to introduce the previous linear constraints, as usual in the classical SVM framework.

The Lagrangian has to be minimized with respect to w, b, ξ, ξ^*, τ and τ^*, and maximized with respect to the Lagrange multipliers. The solution to this problem can be obtained considering the Karush-Kuhn-Tucker (KKT) complementary conditions, which lead to a weight vector w taking the form

$$w = \sum_{i=1}^{N}(\alpha_i^* - \alpha_i)\phi(x_i) + \sum_{i=1}^{N}(\lambda_i^* - \lambda_i)\phi'(x_i) \tag{2}$$

where $\alpha_i, \alpha_i^*, \lambda_i$ and λ_i^* are, respectively, the Lagrange multipliers. Therefore, the regression estimation for a new sample x can be computed as follows:

$$f(x) = \sum_{i=1}^{N}(\alpha_i^* - \alpha_i)\phi^T(x_i)\phi(x) + \sum_{i=1}^{N}(\lambda_i^* - \lambda_i)\phi'^T(x)\phi(x) + b \tag{3}$$

In the SVM framework, the nonlinear transformation $\phi(x)$ is not needed to be explicitly known and it can be replaced by the kernel of the nonlinear transformation. In this case, $\phi^T(x_i)\phi(x_j)$ is substituted by $K(x_i, x_j)$, a kernel satisfying the Mercer theorem [13]. From this definition for the kernel, it is easy to demonstrate that

$$\begin{cases} \phi'^T(x_i)\phi(x_j) = \dfrac{\partial k(x_i, x_j)}{\partial x_i} \overset{\Delta}{=} K'(x_i, x_j) \\[3mm] \phi^T(x_i)\phi'(x_j) = \dfrac{\partial k(x_i, x_j)}{\partial x_j} \overset{\Delta}{=} G(x_i, x_j) \\[3mm] \phi'^T(x_i)\phi'(x_j) = \dfrac{\partial^2 k(x_i, x_j)}{\partial x_i \partial x_j} \overset{\Delta}{=} J(x_i, x_j) \end{cases} \tag{4}$$

Although $K(\cdot, \cdot)$ must be a Mercer Kernel, its derivatives do not necessarily have to be so. Therefore, using a valid kernel $K(\cdot, \cdot)$, once the Lagrange multipliers have been obtained, the regression estimate takes the form

$$f(x) = \sum_{i=1}^{N}(\alpha_i^* - \alpha_i)K(x_i, x) + \sum_{i=1}^{N}(\lambda_i^* - \lambda_i)K'(x_i, x) + b \tag{5}$$

where we have only used the kernel of the transformation without explicitly computing the nonlinear transformation. We will show, in the following subsection, that the resolution of the minimization problem can also be done using kernels, so one does not need to know the nonlinear transformation, as in the regular SVM framework.

3 Least Square Support Vector Machines for the Simultaneous Learning of a Function and Its Derivative

The problem (1) can be solved following the classical SVM method [6]: to arrive at Wolfe's dual problem, which gives a quadratic functional depending only on the Lagrange multipliers that can be solved by Quadratic Programming (QP) techniques. However, the QP solution of the system can be computationally expensive, especially when a large number of samples are employed, which can make the problem unaffordable. In order to reduce the computational burden, we apply least square support vector machines (LS--SVM) to solve this problem. We will first state it as an unconstrained optimization problem

$$
\begin{aligned}
\min \quad & J(w,\xi,\tau) = \frac{1}{2}w^T w + \frac{1}{2}C_1 \sum_{i=1}^{N}\xi_i^2 + \frac{1}{2}C_2 \sum_{i=1}^{N}\tau_i^2 \\
s.t. \quad & y_i = w^T \phi(x_i) + b + \xi_i, (1 \le i \le N) \\
& y_i' = w^T \phi'(x_i) + \tau_i, (1 \le i \le N)
\end{aligned} \tag{6}
$$

To solve this optimization problem (12) , we construct the Lagrangian

$$
\begin{aligned}
L(w,b,\xi,\alpha) = \; & J(w,\xi,\tau) - \sum_{i=1}^{N}\alpha_k \{w^T \phi(x_k) + b + \xi_k - y_k\} \\
& - \sum_{i=1}^{N}\beta_k \{w^T \phi'(x_k) + \tau_k - y_k'\}
\end{aligned} \tag{7}
$$

with Lagrange multipliers $\alpha_k \in R, \beta_k \in R$. The conditions for optimality are given by

$$
\begin{cases}
\dfrac{\partial L}{\partial w} = 0 & \to \quad w = \sum_{k=1}^{N}\alpha_k \phi(x_k) + \sum_{k=1}^{N}\beta_k \phi'(x_k) \\[2mm]
\dfrac{\partial L}{\partial b} = 0 & \to \quad \sum_{k=1}^{N}\alpha_k = 0 \\[2mm]
\dfrac{\partial L}{\partial \xi_k} = 0 & \to \quad \alpha_k = C_1 \xi_k \\[2mm]
\dfrac{\partial L}{\partial \tau_k} = 0 & \to \quad \beta_k = C_2 \xi_k \\[2mm]
\dfrac{\partial L}{\partial \alpha_k} = 0 & \to \quad w^T \phi(x_k) + b + \xi_k - y_k = 0 \\[2mm]
\dfrac{\partial L}{\partial \beta_k} = 0 & \to \quad w^T \phi'(x_k) + \tau_k - y_k' = 0
\end{cases} \tag{8}
$$

These conditions (8) for optimality can be written immediately as the solution to the following set of linear equations

$$
\begin{bmatrix}
0 & 1_v^T & 0 \\
1_v & \Omega + \dfrac{1}{C_1} I & K' \\
0 & G & J + \dfrac{1}{C_2} I
\end{bmatrix}
\begin{bmatrix} b \\ \alpha \\ \beta \end{bmatrix}
=
\begin{bmatrix} 0 \\ y \\ y' \end{bmatrix}
\tag{9}
$$

with $\quad y = [y_1, \cdots, y_N]^T, \qquad y' = [y_1', \cdots, y_N']^T, \qquad 1_v = [1, \cdots 1]^T,$

$\alpha = [\alpha_1, \cdots, \alpha_N]^T, \quad \beta = [\beta_1, \cdots, \beta_N]^T \quad$ and $\quad \Omega_{kl} = \phi(x_k)^T \phi(x_l) \quad$ for

$k, l = 1, \cdots, N$.

Once the Lagrange multipliers have been obtained, the regression estimate takes the form

$$
f(x) = \sum_{k=1}^{N} \alpha_k K(x, x_k) + \sum_{k=1}^{N} \beta_k K'(x, x_k) + b
\tag{10}
$$

where we have only used the kernel of the transformation without explicitly computing the nonlinear transformation.

4   Experiment Results and Conclusion

The classical ε-SVR method and LS-SFD were all implemented in MATLAB running on a PC with an Intel P4 processor(1.8MHz), 512 MB RAM, with Windows XP operating system. To help in making a comparison, the value of C_1 has been chosen to be ten numbers (listed in the following tables), and $C_2 = \dfrac{1}{C_1}, \varepsilon = 0.1$.

In this paper, sinc function is considered and defined as

$$
y = \frac{\sin(x)}{x} \text{ with } x \in [-10, 10]
$$

In this example, 50 equally spaced sampling points in the range -10-10 have been employed by the ε-SVR (50 samples o the function) and by the proposed method , labeled LS-SFD (in this case 100 total samples: 50 samples of the function +50 samples of the derivative). Moreover, we have tested the proposed method using the same number of total samples, which means to subsample (we will label this option by LS-SFD^s). This method uses 25 sampling points (25 samples of the function +25 samples of the derivative). In this way, the number of total available data is the same. The root mean square error (RMSE) of the testing data is used to measure the performance of the learned network (generalization capability). The kernel function adopts the radial basic function

$$K(x, x_i) = \exp(-\frac{\|x - x_i\|^2}{\sigma^2}) \text{ with } \sigma = 2$$

From table 1, it can be seen that the proposed method, using twice the data(LS-FSD), but more interestingly, even using the same amount of data(LS-FSD^s), provides better results than the ε-SVR.

Table 2 shows a comparison between a traditional ε-SVR and the LS-FSD in terms of computation time. The mean computation times of ε-SVR and the LS-FSD are 1.47742, 0.05395 respectively, the LS-FSD is about 27 times faster than the ε-SVR.

Table 1. Testing RMSRs of ε-SVR and of LS-FSD with $\varepsilon = 0.1$ for the sinc function

RMSE	$C_1 = 10^{-4}$	$C_1 = 10^{-3}$	$C_1 = 10^{-2}$	$C_1 = 10^{-1}$
y(LS-FSD)	0.0465	0.0384	0.0608	0.2041
y(LS-FSD^s)	0.0401	0.0361	0.0350	0.1401
y(ε-SVR)	0.4257	0.3484	0.3898	0.0842
y'(LS-FSD)	2.6370×10^{-4}	0.0025	0.0199	0.0828
y'(LS-FSD^s)	1.3103×10^{-4}	0.0013	0.0109	0.0502
RMSE	$C_1 = 10$	$C_1 = 10^2$	$C_1 = 10^3$	$C_1 = 10^4$
y(LS-FSD)	0.0764	0.0098	0.0010	1.1257×10^{-4}
y(LS-FSD^s)	0.0380	0.0045	5.0555×10^{-4}	6.9187×10^5
y(ε-SVR)	0.0675	0.0675	0.0675	0.0675
y'(LS-FSD)	0.0462	0.0070	0.0016	5.2523×10^{-4}
y' (LS-FSD^s)	0.0227	0.0064	0.0029	0.0017

Table 2. Training times for ε-SVR and LS-FSD with $\varepsilon = 0.1$ for the sinc function

Time	$C_1 = 10^{-4}$	$C_1 = 10^{-3}$	$C_1 = 10^{-2}$	$C_1 = 10^{-1}$
y(LS-FSD)	0.0499	0.0556	0.0538	0.0563
y(ε-SVR)	1.4195	1.3761	1.6266	1.4766
Time	$C_1 = 10$	$C_1 = 10^2$	$C_1 = 10^3$	$C_1 = 10^4$
y(LS-FSD)	0.0532	0.0521	0.0557	0.0537
y(ε-SVR)	1.3355	1.4106	1.3293	1.6403

The experimental results demonstrate that the LS-FSD method provides improved generalization ability and shortens computation time in comparison with traditional ε-SVR.

Acknowledgements

This work is financially supported by the National Natural Science Foundation of China (No. 10926194) and Doctor Foundation of Shandong University of Technology (No.4041-410002).

References

1. Gallant, A.R., White, H.: On learning the derivatives of an unknown mapping with multi-layer feedforward networks. Neural Networks 5, 129–138 (1992)
2. Hornik, K., Stinchcombe, M., White, H.: Universal approximation of an unknown mapping and its derivatives using multilayer feedforward networks. Neural Networks 3, 551–560 (1990)
3. Li, X.: Simultaneous approximations of multivariate functions and their derivatives by neural networks with one hidden layer. Neurocomputing 12, 327–343 (1996)
4. Nguyen-Thien, T., Tran-Cong, T.: Approximation of functions and their derivatives: a neural network implementation with applications. Neurocomputing 23, 687–704 (1999)
5. Lázaro, M., Santamaría, I., Pantaleón, C., Ibáñez, J., Vielva, L.: A regularized technique for the simultaneous reconstruction of a function and its derivatives with application to nonlinear transistor modeling. Signal Processing 83, 1859–1870 (2003)
6. Schölkopf, B., Smola, A.: Learning with Kernels. MIT Press, Cambridge (2002)
7. Vapnik, V.N.: Statistical Learning Theory. Wiley, New York (1998)
8. Lázaro, M., Santamaría, I., et al.: Support Vector Regression for the simultaneous learning of a multivariate function and its derivatives. Neurocomputing 67, 42–61 (2005)

Study on the Web Information Search Prediction Algorithm

Zhong-Sheng Wang and Mei Cao

Xi'an Technological University
Xi'an, 710032, China
wzhsh1681@163.com,
Caomei1225@126.com

Abstract. This paper introduces the methods of tailing after user's browsing action and forecasting users' download action. In order to foresee user's download action, when user is applying for a web page at browser, the query string based on hierarchical information directory, which is presented to database server, is recorded. When these query strings have been processed with certain algorithm, user's interested strength level to certain product can be obtained.

Keywords: Electronic Information, Interested Strength Level, Two Smoothing Index.

1 Introduction

With the growing popularity of Internet applications, electronic information and intelligence is increasingly in the important position in the future economic development. At present, most e-book reading system simply display these books, with customer-oriented Integrated information service system research and development. Contrary to the behavior that network customers can click on the information and intelligence, it can provide not only real-time analysis, the estimate,and take some measures to improve the information that provided, but also more proper personalized information and products to achieve a satisfactory trade-line information services.

In this paper, we use hierarchical directory of network information management technology and Double Exponential Smoothing based on the time series, proposed algorithm that can calculate the strength of users' interest according to the users' browsing records in order to provide a solution for predicting users' tapping target.

2 The Tracking Information of User Browsing Process

When users are interested in certain types of information and intelligence, they will often browse through the information related catalog, view the information details which he cares about, and he could eventually download or online payment. Therefore,

G. Shen and X. Huang (Eds.): ECWAC 2011, Part I, CCIS 143, pp. 434–438, 2011.

as long as tracking the browsing process of a user, you can discover what products they are interested in recently and make sure the user's shopping goals, so as to provide network electronic information which meet their needs and achieve personal service. Currently, most of the e-commerce solutions and application systems at the market are based on the B/W/D tertiary structure of the client browser, Web server, data server, and from this it appends multi-level structure that information used by hierarchical management according catalog, each page is dynamically generated from the query. Therefore, we can use hierarchical directory technology and record a query condition according to a chronological which a user submits to the database service when browsing the information; you can abstract the user's browsing activities into forms of orderly array, and achieve the purpose of tracking browsing process of users.

UNSPSC (United Nations Standard Product and Services Classification) is first applied to classification system of e-commerce products and services. With the popularity of electronic reading and downloading, the electronic information transactions which completed through the network are broad promising developments. Using UNSPSC to encode information make a more accurate and efficient communication between information providers, information services and users. Use this coding system, information services institution needs provide a specific code for every pieces of electronic information products. Only do this can the information service institution will be able to track each of the activities sectors of the information using process ,but traditional commodity classification method can not meet the demand of detailed data on product during the transaction .

UNSPSC classification method consists of four levels of classification, there are Segment, Family, Class, and Commodity, each level consists of two numbers, so a UNSPSC code would have eight numbers, two are in a group which represent attribute of the product at different levels.

3   The Model of the Mathematical

3.1   The Weight of the Link

For understanding conveniently, after using the ordered sequence expresses the users browsing process, we give the following definition:

The weight of the link: we called the two adjacent node as pre-node and post-node; The weight of the link between the two adjacent nodes d_i ,d_j, in a user browsing period is the time of link emerging. Namely:

$$w_{ij} = \sum_{n=0}^{m} g_k \tag{1}$$

$k = 0,1,...,m$, m is the process number of the users in browsing period; If the some process includes l_{ij}, then $g_k = 1$, otherwise $g_k = 0$.

It can be seen that the weight between two adjacent nodes in ordered sequence reflects the user access frequency that the users visit the post-node.

3.2 Double Exponential Smoothing

The weight formula reflected the user access frequency that the users visit the post-node is just based on the statistic characteristics of notes; it does not reflect the effect the user's concern about the notes by time.

The mathematical model of single exponential smoothing:

$$\hat{X}_{t+1}^{(1)} = S_t^{(1)} = \alpha^{(1)} X_t + (1 - \alpha^{(1)} \hat{X}_t^{(1)}) \tag{2}$$

$S_t^{(1)}$ is the value of single exponential smoothing for the t term; X_t is the observed value for the t term; $\hat{X}_t^{(1)}$ is the predictive value of single exponential smoothing for the t term; $\alpha^{(1)}$ is the smoothing factor of single exponential smoothing $(0 \leq \alpha^{(1)} \leq 1)$; $X_{t+1}^{(1)}$ is the predictive value of single exponential smoothing for the t+1 term.

We predict using the formula of single exponential smoothing, when the trend of actual data rising, the predictive values is lower than the actual value; when the actual data is on the decline, the predictive value is higher than the actual value. To compensate for this defect, and make the predictive value is closer than the actual value, we correct it using double exponential smoothing.

The calculation formula of double exponential smoothing:

$$S_t^{(2)} = \alpha^{(2)} S_t^{(1)} + (1 - \alpha^{(2)}) S_{t-1}^{(2)} \tag{3}$$

$S_t^{(2)}, S_{t-1}^{(2)}$ is the value of double exponential smoothing for the t term and t+1 term; $\alpha^{(2)}$ is the smoothing factor of double exponential smoothing ; $S_t^{(1)}$ is the value of single exponential smoothing for the t term.

When we make sure the time-series is on the linear trend, you can set up linear predictive equation as follows:

$$\hat{X}_{t+T}^{(2)} = \hat{a}_t + \hat{b}_t \cdot T \tag{4}$$

$\hat{X}_{t+T}^{(2)}$ is the predictive value of double exponential smoothing for the first t + T term; T is the predictive pre-term; $\hat{a}_t, \hat{b}_t$ is the estimate value of parameter, the calculate method is:

$$\hat{a}_t = 2S_t^{(1)} - S^{(2)}t \tag{5}$$

$$\hat{b}_t = \frac{a^{(2)}}{1 - a^{(2)}} (S_t^{(1)} - S_t^{(2)}) \tag{6}$$

Exponential smoothing is the method of time series analysis, which based on past actual figures and projections, it can be short-term behavior forecast by the method of moving weighted average. When using this method to predict, it is no need for large amounts of historical data, the calculated amount is relatively small, and it can eliminate the effect of random factors, and is well in reflecting the change of forecast object by time. Therefore, we can make the sum of the weights as the observations, and get the weight of each node using exponential smoothing.

4 Experiments

In a network of bookstores, tracking the browsing process of all our online websites for a month, and comparing the weight of each node for the user with the subsequent purchase behavior, we found that the weight of the node is often much greater than purchase rate, that is to say the big weight of node does not lead to high purchase rate. Through the research, we found mainly reasons as follows:

① The purchasing habits of users is different, some users turn the matter over for a long time before buying, while other users only have a short time from planning to actual purchasing behavior ;

② The books on test site are similar to the books on many other sites, some users take into account some problems as price, transport costs after scanning the books, and turn to other web site or nearby bookstore to buy ;

③Many users just randomly visit the website or read the book online; they are no intention to buy.

In response to these problems, the following improved methods are proposed:

① Change the experimental site to the website of web e-book feed reader, make a expedition according to the downloads of information, and choose different types of content of different information site to achieve bright characteristics of content, minimize the similar repeated site;

②The sampling period extended to 2 months due to the less visits numbers of characteristically websites;

③The weight is large for a single node, but we did not return a visit for the users who did not purchase books from this site's, so we should understand the actual purchase intent. If they have purchased the same electronic information from other similar information websites, the purchase rate should be included;

④ Make the node weights that reached to a certain critical quantity as the sample, and count the purchase rate.

Through modifying, the experimental results shown in Table 1(in case of a subscription to download e-reader) :

Table 1. The contradistinction between note weights and purchasing behavior

Node level	Weight	Purchase rate
0	>50	17241
	>80	23366
1	>20	15133
	>40	21236
2	>10	13721
	>20	19828
3	>2	12913
	>5	21680

Node-level reflects the location of information on the level directory structure, the node-level belonging to 3 is leaf nodes. According to the proposed algorithm, even if the user visit electronic information not according to the directory order, it can increase the weight to the all the upper nodes of current note automatically. So for the upper node, it represents a certain type of the level directory structure, and its value is always greater than the lower nodes. The experimental value according to this prediction algorithm compared with different prediction methods which emphasizing on coming from different information (including time series models, regression prediction, gray model, etc.) is closer to the actual situation, the forecasting method is simple and the results have higher credibility.

5   Conclusion

In this paper, we use the method of information directory classification management technology tracking users' browsing method, effectively avoided the problem of work-load, slow operational speed of the traditional Web Usage Mine. In addition, we adopt the method that based on time series of double exponential smoothing to calculate the strength of links' interest, not only can it honestly reflect the frequency of user access node, but also have a good simulation of the situation of user's interest by time, so that the predicting results can be more accurate.

References

1. Ou, Y.-f.: E-commerce Solutions, July 13-15. Tsinghua university Press, Beijing (2008)
2. Cai, Y.-p., Zang, G.-x.: Research on Classification of Commodity Data in the Electronics Commerce Marketplace. Journal of Hangzhou Medical College 23(4) (2003) (12-15)
3. Li, Y.-c., Liu, W.-q.: Study on the Feature Extraction in the Course of Personal Information on Internet. Journal of Intelligence (December 2006)
4. Yu, Q., Zhang, H.-s.: Study of personalized web information service technology. Application Research of Computers (February 2006)
5. Luo, Q., Yu, Y., Zhao, C.-l.: Research on personalized service system in E-supermaket by using adaptive recommendation algorithm. Journal of Communications (November 2006)
6. Liu, R., Chen, P., Zhang X.-y.: Research on nenral network based adaptive user model in automatic Web personalization. Electronic Measurement Technology (April 2007)

Two-Level Verification of Data Integrity for Data Storage in Cloud Computing

Guangwei Xu[1], Chunlin Chen[1], Hongya Wang[1], Zhuping Zang[1], Mugen Pang[1], and Ping Jiang[2]

[1] School of Computer Science and Technology, Donghua University, Shanghai
[2] The Faculty of Finance and Accounting, Shanghai Business School, Shanghai
gwxu@dhu.edu.cn

Abstract. Data storage in cloud computing can save capital expenditure and relive burden of storage management for users. As the lose or corruption of files stored may happen, many researchers focus on the verification of data integrity. However, massive users often bring large numbers of verifying tasks for the auditor. Moreover, users also need to pay extra fee for these verifying tasks beyond storage fee. Therefore, we propose a two-level verification of data integrity to alleviate these problems. The key idea is to routinely verify the data integrity by users and arbitrate the challenge between the user and cloud provider by the auditor according to the MACs and φ values. The extensive performance simulations show that the proposed scheme obviously decreases auditor's verifying tasks and the ratio of wrong arbitration.

Keywords: Data storage, integrity, verification, challenge arbitration.

1 Introduction

Cloud computing is a computing model that enables users to conveniently and on-demand access a shared pool of configurable computing resources, e.g., networks, servers, storage, applications, and services, that can be rapidly provided and released with minimal management effort or service provider interaction. This cloud model promotes availability and is composed of five essential characteristics: on-demand self-service, broad network access, resource pooling, rapid elasticity, and measured service. A great number of large scale storage service systems, e.g., Amazon, Google, Yahoo!, can profit via storing and maintaining lots of user data. However, no storage service can be completely reliable, and all services may potentially loss or corrupt customer data.

The motivation which users centralize and store their data files into the cloud is to save their capital expenditure and relive their burden of storage management [1]. However, the corruption of data files stored into the cloud may go contrary to users' wish. Because some storage service providers may neglect those data files stored or intentionally delete few rarely accessed data files of users for their own benefits, users will suffer huge loss, especially while local copies of those files deleted.

G. Shen and X. Huang (Eds.): ECWAC 2011, Part I, CCIS 143, pp. 439–445, 2011.

In order to avoid the lose or corruption of files stored, the cloud provider should periodically verify the integrity of these files. Unfortunately, some cloud providers often hide data loss and corruption to deceive users for their profit and reputation. Moreover, capability of users restricts them to independently verify the integrity of files. Many schemes resort to a third party to verify the integrity of files stored into the cloud [2] [3]. At the same time, MAC-based approach is widely applied in the verification of file integrity [2]. Therefore, these schemes need users to provide many prior value of MACs for the third party to compare them with new MACs computed by the cloud provider. However, the reliability of MACs is difficult to be ensured when some provided MACs are tampered by a malicious user. Moreover, even if the third party can provide a fair result of file verification, it needs the user or the cloud provider to pay extra cost for the storage service. We consider verifying the integrity of files using two-level scheme to decrease the cost of the user and cloud provider. At the first level, the user and the cloud provider respectively computes and verifies the MAC and φ values of files, and then judge the integrity of files. At the second level, when there exits a challenge on the result of verification between the user and cloud provider, the third party will arbitrate the challenge via extracting the mixed and re-aggregated file and recomputing the φ value.

2   Related Work

There are many recent solutions to verify the outsourced data and audit the storage service responsibility. One method is to extract the outsourced data and verify them with local stored copy of data periodically, e.g., OceanStore. However, there are some disadvantages in this method, e.g. the expensive I/O and bandwidth cost, the insufficiently accessing and detecting the data, the challenge of user data and privacy leaked. Another alternative method is proposed to decrease the overhead of computation and network and protect privacy via MACs computed and encryption technique. Ateniese et al. [2] defined the "provable data possession" (PDP) model for ensuring possession of file, and described techniques based on homomorphic tags for auditing the file. Ateniese et al. [4] described a PDP scheme that uses symmetric-key encryption and MACs to verify integrity of stored data. This MAC-based approach is quite efficient on file-expansion and bandwidth overhead, and computational costs, however it does not permit the prover to return a digest via hashing or XOR these responses together. Juels et al. [3] mentioned another possible way in which a Merkle tree was constructed to verify the correctness of file blocks. Wang et al. [5] proposed a cloud data auditing system to utilize and combine the public key based homomorphic authenticator with random masking to achieve privacy-preserving without the local copy of data and new vulnerabilities towards user data privacy.

3   Problem Statement and System Model

Because cloud services may resort for a third party to arbitrate the challenge of commitments between cloud provider and users, each cloud data storage service involves three different entities [5] in Fig. 1: the cloud user, the cloud provider, and the third party auditor. The key ideal of the existing integrity auditing schemes is designed to pre-compute MACs of each block of a data file F via a function $hash$, and then compare these remote MACs to the local MACs to verify the integrity of the data file by the auditor.

However, some malicious users may release the false local MACs to the auditor, and thus the results of MACs compared between the local MAC and remote MAC are unequal. There are several problems requiring to be resolved in proposed scheme of data integrity verification: 1) Data privacy can not be invaded; 2) Corruption of user's outsourced data should be found in time, and it can not introduce overfull burden of communication and storage; 3) Malicious users maligning the cloud providers for corruption of their outsourced data should be distinguished.

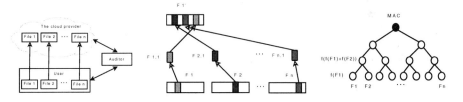

Fig. 1. System model   **Fig. 2.** The files sliced and mixed   **Fig. 3.** The Merkle tree

4   Verifying Auditing Scheme of Data Integrity

In our scheme, the user stores his data files into the cloud. In general, the use verifies the integrity of stored data files by himself. When he has a challenge with the cloud provider on the integrity of these files, he requests the auditor to arbitrate it. Some terminologies and notations are defined as follows. The $storeddatanfile$ which are decrypted using the secure key and delivered into the cloud by the user are denoted as F_i, $i \in \{1, ..., n\}$. The MAC value is computed according to $MAC(F_i, k_j) = hash(F_i, k_j), i \in \{1, ..., n\}$, $j \in \{1, ..., m\}$, where the function $hash$ is a one-way hash function such as MD5 or SHA, and the k_j is the secure key which size is commonly used by 128 bits. There are two $verifiers$ in our scheme: one is the user, and another is the auditor. They commonly verify the integrity of files. The $arbitrator$ is the auditor who arbitrates the challenges between the cloud provider and user. The user is denoted as U, the cloud provider is denoted as P, and the auditor is denoted as T. Our scheme proposes that the user periodically verifies the integrity of data files, and the auditor arbitrates the challenge between the user and cloud provider while MAC values are different using uniform hash function and key. The scheme is divided into five phases, i.e. file slicing and mixing, file uploading and MAC computing, MACs storage, self-verifying, and challenge arbitrating.

4.1 File Slicing and Mixing

If a user wants to store n files, denoted as $\{F_i\}_{i=1}^n$, into the cloud, he needs to use a slicing technique to ensure privacy preserving. The slicing technique adopts the similar idea as PriSense [6]. The key idea of the slicing technique is as follows. Firstly, each file F_i of n files is sliced into s random slices, denoted by $\{F_{i,j}\}_{j=1}^s$. Secondly, the file F_i keeps 1 random slice of s slices to itself while sending residual slices to the other different $n-1$ files. Finally, every slice from different files is mixed and aggregated into a new file F_i'. The process is shown in Fig. 2. The user stores the mapping between the original files and the mixing files at local place.

4.2 File Uploading and MAC Computing

When the user wants to store the mixed data files into the cloud, he contracts with the cloud provider to ensure the integrity of all data files after they are uploaded. We construct a binary Merkle tree as CBS [7] to check the integrity of all files as following rule in Fig. 3: each leaf node of the tree L_i is deployed a data file F_i, and each tree node is assigned a value φ which is a hash value. The φ value at the leaf node is the hash value of its data file, and these φ values at the leaf node are defined as the equation $\varphi(L_i) = f(F_i)$, $i \in \{1, ..., n\}$, where the function f is a one-way hash function such as MD5 or SHA. Each φ value at other nodes N_i except leaf nodes is the hash value of the concatenation of φ values of its two children, and is defined as the equation $\varphi(N_i) = f(\varphi(n_i) + \varphi(n_i + 1))$, $i \in \{1, ..., n\}$, where $+$ denotes concatenation. From the leaf nodes to root node, all φ values are computed. The φ value at the tree root is computed as the message authentication code (MAC).

Before files are uploaded, the user constructs a Merkle tree of all files and computes an initial MAC value of the tree root node, MAC_0, via using a hash function f and an initial key K_0. In the tree, all leaves are deployed with files which are ordered by file names. Whereafter, the user samples t files from all files every times to compute a set of the MAC values, i.e., φ_i ($i \in \{1, ..., t+1\}$), where the values from φ_1 to φ_t are corresponding to the leaf nodes (each sampled files) and the φ_{t+1} is corresponding to the MAC of the tree via using a uniform hash function f and one of a set of keys, i.e., K_i ($i \in \{1, ..., m\}$).

When he uploads all files into the cloud, he also releases the construction of the Merkle tree, the hush function f and the initial key K_0 to the cloud provider. After the cloud provider receives these files, theoretically, he can construct the similar Merkle tree, and compute a set of remote MAC values, i.e., a new set of φ values, φ_i' ($i \in \{1, ..., n\}$), for each tree node.

4.3 MACs Storage

The verification of metadata between the auditor and the user includes many MACs and φ values computed by the user and cloud provider. The count of auditing tasks will be promised in the lifetime of the contract and denoted as T.

As some malicious users may send false MACs or φ values to the auditor, the MACs and φ corresponding to the different keys are sampled by the auditor. The process of the hash function and keys chosen and sent is as following.

Firstly, the user sends the hash function f, the initial key K_0, MAC_0, and $\varphi(L_i)$ ($i \in \{1, ..., n\}$) to the auditor. Secondly, after the cloud provider computes the remote $\varphi(L_i')$ ($i \in \{1, ..., n\}$) and MAC_0', he sends these data to the auditor. Thirdly, the auditor compares these local metadata to the remote metadata. If these metadata are equal respectively, all files is intact; otherwise, some files may be corrupted or metadata provided are wrong. Those files corresponding to the unequal φ value at the tree need to be re-uploaded. Finally, after the initial check is finished, the auditor accepts user's request of verification and stores the MAC_0 and $\varphi(L_i')$ ($i \in \{1, ..., n\}$) corresponding to K_0. At the same time, the user can delete his local copies of files.

4.4 Self-verifying

To evaluate the integrity of files in the cloud, there are two primary self-verifying phases: one is the process of files uploading, another is the MAC value compared periodically. For the former, the integrity of files can be verified whether to be intact or not after they have been uploaded according to the Section 4.2. For the latter, user generally stores their data files into the cloud for a long time, e.g., one year. It is convenient for user to find whether any file is deleted or not when he needs download a file to view, because the original file comes from every files mixed in the cloud. Moreover, the user periodically requests the cloud provider to computer the remote MAC_i' via randomly sampling t files and choosing any K_i. If the remote MAC_i' is equal to the local MAC_i, files is intact. Otherwise, files may be corrupted.

4.5 Challenge Arbitrating

The user finds that a file is not intact, after he compares the local MAC and φ values of each file to the remote ones. However, if the cloud provider disagrees this result which is informed by the user, they can request the auditor to arbitrate the challenge. The loser will pay the money for auditing. Because it dose not need the auditor to frequently verify the MACs and φ values, the user will save his money and would like to store his data in the cloud.

In the process of auditing, if the local and remote MACs is unequal, the auditor will extract the corresponding files from the cloud. The auditor computes the new φ values of these files using the stored hash function f and K_0. If a new φ value is unequal to the stored φ value of the file, the file is not intact; otherwise it is intact. If the cloud provider is of the loser, he will pay money to the auditor and user; otherwise the user pays money to the auditor.

5 Discussion

We assume that the size of an original file F is L. After the file is sliced into n slices and mixed into a new file F', the new file size is also L. Thus, there is $\frac{1}{n}$ of the F existing in the F'. Assume the probability of the challenge for each file is P_f. Therefore, there is $\frac{1}{n}$ of the F accessed by the auditor in each challenge. For all n files, the probability of any original file recovered is $n \times P_f \times \frac{L}{n} \times \frac{1}{L} = P_f$. As the P_f is generally few, the probability of the original file recovered will be close to 0. Therefore, the original file can not be recovered.

In the process of file slicing, the size of each original file is denoted as z_i ($i \in \{1, ..., n\}$) and sliced into s pieces. Let the size of any aggregated file be z. We have $z = \frac{1}{s} \sum_{i=1}^{n} z_i$. When the s is big enough, the z will be small. Therefore, if a challenged file is extracted and φ recomputed by the auditor, the overhead of network transmission will decrease.

6   Performance Evaluation

We design an experiment using $c++$ to evaluate the performance of the proposed scheme. In this experiment, each file will be checked only one times during the storage service. Let the amount of files be $12,000$, the size of key be 128 $bits$, the size of MAC and φ be 128 $bits$, and the average size of each file be $1M$ $bytes$. The proposed scheme is denoted as TLA, and the scheme in [5] is denoted as TPA.

Auditing tasks need the user to pay extra money for the auditor. We assume the user pays extra money M for each auditing task. Thus, the cost of file verification will be determined by the number of auditing tasks. The number of auditing tasks are shown in the Fig. 4 and Fig. 5. We can see the number of auditing tasks executed by the auditor in the TPA scheme is nearly 100 times than the number in our scheme when $\alpha \leq 0.01$. Therefore, the user in the TPA needs to pay money more 100 times than that in our scheme. The reason is that all auditing tasks are assigned to the auditor in the TPA scheme, whereas many auditing tasks are executed by user himself in our scheme.

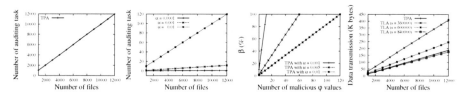

Fig. 4. Number of auditing tasks for TPA **Fig. 5.** Number of auditing tasks for TLA **Fig. 6.** Ratio of wrong arbitration for TPA **Fig. 7.** Overhead of network transmission

When a tampered MAC is applied to arbitrate the challenge by the auditor, a wrong result of arbitration will be returned. Fig. 6 reveals the ratio of wrong arbitration at the different ratio of the challenge by the TPA scheme. However, our proposed scheme can achieve ratio of wrong arbitration to 0, as it extracts the challenged file and recomputes the MAC using the hash function and initial key k_0.

The overhead of network transmission affects the performance of the proposed scheme. As the overhead associates with the number of file slicing s and ratio of the challenge α. The overhead of network transmission when $\alpha = 0.001$ is shown in Fig. 7. While the s is more and more big, the overhead in the TLA is less than that in the TPA.

7 Conclusion

In this paper, we propose a two-level verification of file integrity, i.e., the user verifying and third party verifying. The user verifying deals with the daily integrity of data. When there is a challenge on the result of the verification, the third party auditor will be requested to arbitrate the challenge. The auditor extracts the aggregated file responding to the challenge and recomputes the φ using the uniform hash function and initial key. Our scheme protects the privacy of files and ensures the correct result of the verification of file integrity.

References

1. Armbrust, M., Fox, A., Griffith, R., Joseph, A.D., Katz, R., Konwinski, A., Lee, G., Patterson, D., Rabkin, A., Stoica, I., Zaharia, M.: Above the clouds: A berkeley view of cloud computing. University of California, Berkeley, Tech. Rep. UCB-EECS-2009-28 (February 2009)
2. Ateniese, G., Burns, R., Curtmola, R., Herring, J., Kissner, L., Peterson, Z., Song, D.: Provable data possession at untrusted stores. In: Proceedings of the 14th ACM Conference on Computer and Communications Security, pp. 598–609 (2007)
3. Juels, A., Kaliski, B.S.: Pors: proofs of retrievability for large files. In: Proceedings of the 14th ACM Conference on Computer and Communications Security, pp. 584–597 (2007)
4. Ateniese, G., Di Pietro, R., Mancini, L.V., Tsudikd, G.: Scalable and efficient provable data possession. Technical Report 2008/114, Cryptology ePrint Archive (March 2007)
5. Wang, C., Wang, Q., Ren, K., Lou, W.: Privacy-Preserving Public Auditing for Data Storage Security in Cloud Computing. In: Proceedings of IEEE INFOCOM (March 2010)
6. Shi, J., Zhang, R., Liu, Y., Zhang, Y.: PriSense: Privacy- Preserving Data Aggregation in People-Centric Urban Sensing Systems. In: Proceedings of IEEE INFOCOM (March 2010)
7. Du, W., Jia, J., Mangal, M., Murugesan, M.: Uncheatable Grid Computing. In: Proceedings of the 24th IEEE International Conference on Distributed Computing Systems, pp. 4–11 (March 2004)

Vessel Traffic Flow Forecasting Model Study Based on Support Vector Machine

Hongxiang Feng, Fancun Kong, and Yingjie Xiao

Engineering Research Center of Shipping Simulation,
Ministry of Education, Shanghai Maritime University,
Shanghai, P.O. Box 1290, 1550 Pu Dong Da Dao,
Shanghai, Post Code: 200135,
Tel.: +86 21 58850828
yiyouyishi@163.com

Abstract. Based on vessel traffic flow data and Support Vector Machine theory, SVM regression model for short-term vessel traffic flow forecasting was presented. The forecasted vessel traffic flow and abserved ones, which by SVM regression model, coincide properly, and the forecasting results show that mean absolute percentage error of forecasting are smaller than that by SPSS regress model, which validates the feasibility of SVM regression model in the vessel traffic flow forecasting.

Keywords: support vector machine (SVM), regress analysis, vessel traffic flow, forecasting, matlab, SPSS regress.

1 Introduction

With the rapid development of China economy and international trade, vessel traffic over China's navigational waters increased quickly. At the mean time, due to the increase of vessel traffic flow, maritime accident occurred frequently; and maritime safety situation came to be grim, which called higher request for the planning, design and marine supervision of harbor and lane engineering. Study on the vessel traffic flow forecasting is to provide a fundation to the planning, design and marine supervision of harbor and lane engineering. Therefore, it's important to retionally forecast the vessel traffic flow and find out its ragularity for the purpose of maritime safety improvemnt. The popular methods for vessel traffic flow forecasting include regression analysis[1], neural network[2], combination forecast model[3] and so on. The paper tried to introduce support vector machine (SVM) into the study of vessel traffic flow forecasting. By utilization of abservation data at Sutong Bridge and based on SVM theory, the paper attempted the prectical applicability for SVM in the vessel traffic flow forecasting and forecasted the short-term vessel traffic.

G. Shen and X. Huang (Eds.): ECWAC 2011, Part I, CCIS 143, pp. 446–451, 2011.

2 Principle for SVM Classification[4]

2.1 Regression Algorithm for SVM

Supposed that the training data is $\{(xi, yi)\}_{i=1}^{N}$, here x_i is the i sample of input vectors $(x \in R^d)$, and y_i is corresponding expectation response to xi $(y \in R)$, the linear regression function can be defined as $f(x)=w^T x+b$; and the optimization regression problem becomes:

$$\min \varphi(w,\xi,\xi^*) = \frac{1}{2} \| w \|^2 + C(\sum_{i=1}^{N} \xi_i + \sum_{i=1}^{N} \xi_i^*)$$

$$s.t.\begin{cases} f(x_i) - y_i \le \xi_i^* + \varepsilon, i = 1, \cdots, N \\ y_i - f(x_i) \le \xi_i + \varepsilon, i = 1, \cdots, N \\ \xi, \xi^* \ge 0, i = 1, \cdots, N \end{cases} \quad (1)$$

By introduction of Lagrangian function, get the dual problem:

$$\max w(a,a^*) = \sum_{i=1}^{N}(a_i - a_i^*)y_i + \sum_{j=1}^{N}(a_j - a_j^*)\varepsilon y_j - \frac{1}{2}\sum_{i,j=1}^{t}(a_i - a_i^*)(a_j - a_j^*)(x_i^T \cdot x_j)$$

$$s.t.\begin{cases} \sum_{i=1}^{N}(a_i - a_i^*) = 0 \\ 0 \le a_i, a_i^* \le C, i = 1, \cdots, N \end{cases} \quad (2)$$

Parameters' solution for linear regression are as same as ones for classification.

$$f(x) = \sum_{i=1}^{N}(a_i - a_i^*)k(x_i, x) + b \quad (3)$$

For nonlinear regression problems, firstly map the original sample space to high dimensional space with a nonlinear mapping function, then analyse it with the linear regression method. In the circumstance, key problem is to find out the nonlinear mapping function. Now, nonlinear regression problem converts into abtaining the maximum of $w(a,a^*)$ in constrained conditions. Here $w = \sum_{i=1}^{N}(a_i - a_i^*)\varphi(x_i)$. The parameters' solution is as same as ones for nonlinear classification and the nonlinear regression function can be expressed as:

$$f(x) = \sum_{i=1}^{l}(a_i - a_i^*)k(x, x_i) + b \qquad (4)$$

2.2 Kernel Functions

(1) RBF kernel function (Gaussian Radial Basis Function): $K(x_i \bullet x_j) = exp(x,x_i) + b$

(2) polynomial kernel function: $K(x_i \bullet x_j) = (x_i \bullet x_j + r)^d$

Because based on small sample learning thoery, and with no need for the gradation requirement of sample tending to infinity, SVM can abtain satisfactory effect in the condition of small sample[5]. In the paper, Matlab Libsvm 3.0[6] is adopted as tool in programming and data handling.

3 Forecasting Model for Vessel Traffic Based on SVM

3.1 Establishment of SVM Forecasting Model

Supposed that data sequences varying with time is $\{x_t, t=1,2,...,N\}$, map the original sample data into the high dimentional space by a nonlinear function, then forecasting can be proceeded to the data sequences through the mapping convertion. Now creat a mapping relationship $f:R^m \rightarrow R$, , here m is slide number; construct samlpe (X_t,Y_t), and train $n-m$the first N sample data, here $X_t=\{x_{t-m},x_{t-m+1},...,x_{t-1}\}$, $Y_t=x_t$, $Y_t = \sum_{i=1}^{l}(a_i - a_i^*)k(X_i, X) + b$, $t=m+1,...,N$, then obtain SVM forecasting model:

$$x_{N+1} = \begin{cases} \{x_{N-m+1}, \hat{x}_{N+1}, \cdots, \hat{x}_{N+l-1}\} & l = 1 \\ \{x_{N-m+1}, \hat{x}_{N+1}, \cdots, \hat{x}_{N+l-1}\} & l = 2,3,\cdots \end{cases}$$

$$Y_{N+1} = \sum_{i=1}^{n-m}(a_i - a_i^*)k(X_i, X_{N+1}) + b \qquad (5)$$

3.2 Parameter Determination of SVM Forecasting Model

SVM parameters mainly include kernel function form, insensitive loss function, model regularization parameter, embedding dimension of data sequence and kernel parameter. Kernel parameter requires choosing maximum in the range of forecasting accuracy; loss function and model regularization parameter are chosen by cross validation method; and embedding dimension is determinated by minimum forecasting error.

3.3 Evaluation Criterion of SVM Forecasting Model

Effect of SVM forecasting can be evaluated by Mean Absolute Percentage Error and Mean Absolute Error[7].

$$MAPE = \frac{1}{n}\sum_{i=1}^{n}\frac{|Y_t - \hat{Y}|_i}{Y_i}\times100\% \quad MAE = \frac{1}{n}\sum_{i=1}^{n}|Y_t - \hat{Y}|\times100\% \quad (6)$$

4   An Example of Vessel Traffic Forecasting Based on SVM

4.1   Training Sample and Test Sample

Table 1. Abservation result of vessel traffic flow at Sutong Bridge (unit: ship/hour)

clock	1	2	3	4	5	6	7	8	9	10	11	12
$7^{th}/8^{th}$	33	27	20	30	22	14	14	15	25	13	8	4
$10^{th}/11^{th}$	16	19	50	29	27	21	23	13	11	13	17	13
$16^{th}/17^{th}$	28	13	18	28	23	10	17	21	20	27	17	23
clock	13	14	15	16	17	18	19	20	21	22	23	24
$7^{th}/8^{th}$	25	34	11	11	7	8	10	11	10	11	9	10
$10^{th}/11^{th}$	5	7	21	30	17	12	23	16	27	13	14	17
$16^{th}/17^{th}$	20	21	30	12	9	6	11	9	19	18	21	16

The paper adopts absevation data of Yangtze River (Sutong Bridge section) on Oct 7th $\sim8^{th}$, $10^{th}\sim11^{th}$, $16^{th}\sim17^{th}$ 2010 (table 1) as data sample. Here, datas of $7^{th}\sim8^{th}$ and $10^{th}\sim11^{th}$ are input variables, and those of $16^{th}\sim17^{th}$ are output results; datas of $1\sim20$ clock on $7^{th}\sim8^{th}$ and $10^{th}\sim11^{th}$ are training samples and those on $16^{th}\sim17^{th}$ are test samples. Based on SVM, establish forecasting model for vessel traffic flow, and forecast the traffic flow value of $21\sim24$ clock on $16^{th}\sim17^{th}$.

4.2   Determination of Model Parameters

Loss function ε, penalty factor C and kernel parameter δ^2 are key factors which determinate forecasting precision. ε controls fitting error; if ε bigger, number of support vector becomes less and model trending to be simpler, but fitting precision decreases; conversely, if ε smaller, model precision increases, but sloving time would add up, and at the mean time with the increase of model complexity, extending capacity would be impacted because of over-fitting. Value range of ε is generally $0.0001\sim0.1$. Function of C is to punish datas of which fitting function error are greater than ε. bigger C means bigger punishment. In addition, C also controls model complexity and moderateness of function approximate error. If C bigger, fitting degree of data would be higher, but extending capacity would be worse. For the virtue of excellent learning ability of RBF, we adopt it as kernel function, and determinate δ^2 to be 90, ε to be 0.001, and C to be 5.

4.3 Analysis of Forecasting Results

Use the established forecasting model and forecast the vessel traffic flow of Yangtze River (Sutong Bridge section) on Oct $16^{th} \sim 17^{th}$, 2010. Results are listed in table 2 and figure 1,2 and shown that: 1) The relative forecasting error is larger only in few points, most are relatively ideal, and the average relative error is only 1.4% compared with 33.1% of SPSS; 2)The shorter the forecasting period, the forecasting accuracy is higher; Above results validate the feasibility of SVM theory in short-term vessel traffic flow forecasting.

Table 2. Forecasting result (unit for traffic flow: ship/hour; for error: %)

clock	1	2	3	4	5	6	7	8	9	10	11	12
observation	28.0	13.0	18.0	28.0	23.0	10.0	17.0	21.0	20.0	27.0	17.0	23.0
SSPS	23.5	21.5	18.9	22.4	19.8	17.1	17.1	17.5	20.9	16.8	15.1	13.8
SVM	28.0	13.0	18.0	28.0	23.0	10.0	17.0	21.0	20.0	27.0	17.0	23.0
SSPS error	15.9	65.4	5.1	19.8	14.1	70.9	0.5	16.8	4.4	37.8	11.2	40.2
SVM error	0.1	0.1	0.2	0.1	0.1	0.2	0.1	0.2	0.1	0.1	0.1	0.1
clock	13	14	15	16	17	18	19	20	21	22	23	24
observation	20.0	21.0	30.0	12.0	9.0	6.0	11.0	9.0	19.0	18.0	21.0	16.0
SSPS	20.9	23.9	16.1	16.0	14.8	15.1	15.7	16.1	15.7	16.1	15.4	15.8
SVM	20.0	21.0	30.0	12.0	9.0	6.0	11.0	9.0	18.5	19.0	19.2	18.0
SSPS error	4.6	14.0	46.4	33.5	63.9	152.0	43.0	79.0	17.4	10.4	26.4	1.5
SVM error	0.1	0.1	0.1	0.1	0.4	0.5	0.2	0.4	2.7	5.4	8.5	12.3

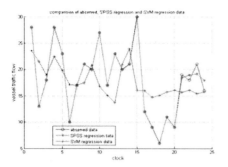

Fig. 1 Comparision of baserved, SPSS regression and SVM regression data

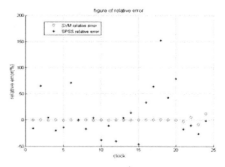
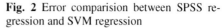

Fig. 2 Error comparision between SPSS regression and SVM regression

References

1. Zhang, X.: The Application of Regressive Analyais in VTS Forecast Research. Navigation of China 39(2), 032–035 (1996)
2. Xu, X., Shi, X.: BP neural network based container throughput predicting model for Shenzhen Port. Journal of Hohai University 30(4), 041–044 (2002)
3. Lv, J., Fang, X.: Composite systematic forecasting model and method for vessel traffic flow forecasting. Journal of Dalian Maritime University 22(2), 033–035 (1996)
4. Deng, N., Tian, Y.: New Method of Data Mining-Support Vector Machine, pp. 120–122. Science press, Beijing
5. Chen, Y., Liu, Y., Zhao, G., Wang, W., Li, F.: Chinese Traditional Medicine Recognition by Support Vector Machine (SVM)Terahertz Spectrum. Spectroscopy and Spectral Analysis 29(9), 2346–2350 (2009)
6. http://www.csie.ntu.edutw/-cjlin
7. Qu, W., Fan, G., Yang, B.: Research on complicated time series prediction based on support vector machines. Computer Engineering 23(12), 1 (2005)

Local Analytic Solutions of a Functional Differential Equation

LingXia Liu

Department of Mathematics, Weifang University,
Weifang, Shandong 261061, P.R. China
llxmath@126.com

Abstract. This paper is concerned with the existence of analytic solutions of an iterative functional differential equation. Employing the method of majorant series, we need to discuss the constant α given in *Schröder* transformation. we study analytic solutions of the equation in the case of α at resonance and the case of α near resonance under the Brjuno condition.

Keywords: Iterative functional differential equation, analytic solution, resonance, Diophantine condition, Brjuno condition.

1 Introduction

In the last few years there has been a growing interest in studying functional differential equations with state dependent delay [1-4]. In [5], analytic solutions of the following iterative functional differential equations

$$x'(z) = x^{[m]}(z)$$

were found, where $x^{[m]}(z) = x(x^{[m-1]}(z))$. More general form

$$x'(z) = c_1 x(z) + c_2 x^{[2]}(z) + \cdots + c_m x^{[m]}(z), \ \sum_{i=1}^{m} c_i \neq 0 \tag{1}$$

was discussed in [6], where $c_1, c_2, \cdots c_m$ are complex numbers, and $x^{[k]}(z)$ denotes the k-th iterative of the function $x(z)$.

   In this paper existence of local analytic solutions of an iterative functional differential equation (1) is studied. As well as in previous work [4, 5], we reduce this problem with the *Schröder* transformation

$$x(z) = y(\alpha y^{-1}(z)) \tag{2}$$

to the auxiliary equation

$$\alpha y'(\alpha z) = y'(z) \sum_{i=1}^{m} c_i y(\alpha^i z), \ z \in C, \tag{3}$$

where iteration of the unknown function is not involved but an indeterminate complex α needs to be discussed. We need to find invertible analytic solutions of the equation (3) for possible choices of α. When the complex α in (2) is not the unit circle in $\mathbf{C}$ (i.e. $0 < |\alpha| < 1$) or α is lies on the unit circle in $\mathbf{C}$ but satisfies the Diophantine condition:

G. Shen and X. Huang (Eds.): ECWAC 2011, Part I, CCIS 143, pp. 452–457, 2011.
© Springer-Verlag Berlin Heidelberg 2011

$|\mu|=1$, μ *is not a root of unity, and* $\log\dfrac{1}{|\mu^n-1|}\leq T\log n$, $n=2,3,\cdots$ *for some positive*

constant T. The existence of analytic solutions of (3) was given in [6]. Since then, we have been striving to give a result of analytic solutions for those α near a root of the unity, i.e., neither being roots of the unity nor satisfying the Diophantine condition. The Brjuno condition provides such a chance for us. In this paper we assume that α in [5] satisfies the following hypotheses:

(H1) $\mu=e^{2\pi i\theta}$, where $\theta\in$ **R\Q** is a Brjuno number ([7, 8]), i.e., $B(\theta)=$
$\displaystyle\sum_{k=0}^{\infty}\frac{\log q_{k+1}}{q_k}<\infty$, where $\{p_k/q_k\}$ denotes the sequence of partial fraction of the continued fraction expansion of θ, and is said to satisfy the Brjuno condition.

(H2) $\alpha=e^{2\pi iq/p}$ for some integers $p\in$ **N** with $p\geq 2$ and $q\in$ **Z** \{0\}, and $\alpha\neq e^{2\pi il/k}$ for all $1\leq k\leq p-1$ and $l\in$ **Z** \{0\}.

We observe that α is on the unit circle s^1 in (H1) and (H2). More difficult are encountered for α on s^1, since the small divisor α^n-1 is involved in (H1) and (H2). In this paper, we discuss the existence analytic solution of (3) in the case of (H1) and (H2). α is a p-th unit root (or called p-order resonance) in (H2)., while the case (H1) contains a part of α near resonance.

2 Analytic Solution of Auxiliary Equation

We now discuss the existence of an analytic solution of (3) in the initial condition

$$y(0)=\alpha\left/\sum_{i=1}^{m}c_i\right. . \tag{4}$$

First, we devote attention to the existence of analytic solutions of (3) under the Brjuno condition. To do this, we first recall briefly the definition of Brjuno number and some basic facts. As state in [9], for a for a real number θ we let θ denote its integer part and let $\{\theta\}=\theta-[\theta]$. Then every national number θ has a unique expression of the Gauss' continued fraction $\theta=a_0+\theta_0=a_0+\dfrac{1}{a_1+\theta_1}=...$, denoted simply by $\theta=[a_0,a_1,...,a_n,...]$, where a_j 's and θ_j 's are calculated by the algorithm: **(a)** $a_0=[\theta]$, $\theta_0=\{\theta\}$ and **(b)** $a_n=\left[\dfrac{1}{\theta_{n-1}}\right],\theta_n=\left\{\dfrac{1}{\theta_{n-1}}\right\}$ for all $n\geq 1$. Define the sequences $(p_n)_{n\in\text{N}}$ and $(q_n)_{n\in\text{N}}$ as follows $q_{-2}=1,q_{-1}=0,q_n=a_nq_{n-1}+q_{n-2}$; $p_{-2}=0,p_{-1}=1$, $p_n=a_np_{n-1}+p_{n-2}$. It is easy to show that $p_n/q_n=[a_0,a_1,...,a_n]$. Thus, for every $\theta\in$ **R\Q** we associate, using its convergence, an arithmetical function $B(\theta)=\displaystyle\sum_{n\geq 0}\frac{\log q_{n+1}}{q_n}$.

We say that θ is a Brjuno number or that it satisfies Brjuno condition if $B(\theta)<+\infty$. The Brjuno condition is weaker than the Diophantine condition. For example, if $a_{n+1}\leq ce^{a_n}$ for all $n\geq 0$, where $c>0$ is a constant, then $\theta=[a_0,a_1,...,a_n,...]$ is a Brjuno number but is not a Diophantine number. So, the case (H1) contains both Diophantine condition and a part of μ ``near" resonance.

In order to discuss analytic solutions of the auxiliary equation (3) under (H1), we need to introduce Davie's Lemma. First, we recall some facts in [10] briefly. Let $\theta \in \mathbf{R}\backslash\mathbf{Q}$ and $(q_n)_{n\in\mathbb{N}}$ be the sequence of partial denominators of the Gauss's continued fraction for θ as in the Introduction. As in [9], let $A_k = \{n \geq 0 \mid \|n\theta\| \leq \frac{1}{8q_k}\}$, $E_k = \max(q_k, \frac{q_{k+1}}{4})$, $\eta_k = \frac{q_k}{E_k}$. Let A_k^* be the set of integers $j \geq 0$ such that either $j \in A_k$ or for some j_1 and j_2 in A_k, with $j_2 - j_1 < E_k$, one has $j_1 < j < j_2$ and q_k divide $j - j_1$. For any integer $n \geq 0$, define $l_k(n) = \max\left((1+\eta_k)\frac{n}{q_k}-2, \ (m_n\eta_k+n)\frac{1}{q_k}-1\right)$, where $m_n = \max\{j \mid 0 \leq j \leq n, j \in A_k^*\}$. We then define function $h_k : \mathbf{N} \to \mathbf{R}_+$ as follows:

$$
\begin{cases}
\dfrac{m_n + \eta_k n}{q_k} - 1, & \text{if } m_n + q_k \in A_k^*, \\[2mm]
l_k(n), & \text{if } m_n + q_k \notin A_k^*.
\end{cases}
$$

Let $g_k(n) := \max\left(h_k(n), \left[\dfrac{n}{q_k}\right]\right)$, and define $k(n)$ by the condition $q_{k(n)} \leq n \leq q_{k(n)+1}$. Clearly, $k(n)$ is non-decreasing. Then we are able to state the following result:

Lemma 1. (Davie's Lemma [10]) Let $K(n) = n\log 2 + \sum_{k=0}^{k(n)} g_k(n)\log(2q_{k+1})$. Then

(a) There is a universal constant $\gamma > 0$ (independent of n and θ) such that
$$
K(n) \leq n\left(\sum_{k=0}^{k(n)} \frac{\log q_{k+1}}{q_k} + \gamma\right),
$$

(b) $K(n_1) + K(n_2) \leq K(n_1 + n_2)$ for all n_1 and n_2, and

(c) $-\log|\alpha^n - 1| \leq K(n) - K(n-1)$.

Now we state and prove the following theorem under Brjuno condition. The idea of our proof is acquired from [10].

Theorem 1. Suppose (H1) holds, then for any complex number $\eta \neq 0$, the equation (3) has an analytic solution of the form

$$
y(z) = \alpha\Big/ \sum_{i=1}^{m} c_i + \eta z + \sum_{n=2}^{\infty} b_n z^n \tag{5}
$$

on a neighborhood of the origin.

Proof. We seek a solution of (3) in a power series of the form (3). Substituting (5) into (3), we see that the sequence $\{b_n\}_{n=0}^{\infty}$ is successively determined by the condition $b_0 = \alpha\Big/\sum_{i=1}^{m} c_i$, $b_1 = \eta$ and

$$
\alpha(\alpha^n - 1)(n+1)b_{n+1} = \sum_{k=0}^{n-1}(k+1)\sum_{i=1}^{m} c_i \alpha^{i(n-k)} b_{k+1} b_{n-k}, \ n = 1, 2, \cdots \tag{6}
$$

in a unique manner. Since

$$\left| \frac{(k+1)\sum_{i=1}^{m} c_i \alpha^{i(n-k)}}{(n+1)\alpha} \right| \le \sum_{i=1}^{m} |c_i|, \, 0 \le k \le n-1,$$

let $M = \sum_{i=1}^{m} |c_i|$, then we have

$$|b_{n+1}| \le \frac{M}{|\alpha^n - 1|} \sum_{k=0}^{n-1} |b_{k+1}||b_{n-k}|, \, n = 1, 2, \cdots. \quad (7)$$

Thus, if we define a sequence $\{B_n\}_{n=1}^{\infty}$ by $B_1 = |\eta|$ and

$$B_{n+1} = M \sum_{k=0}^{n-1} B_{k+1} B_{n-k}, \, n = 1, 2, \cdots, \quad (8)$$

and

$$G(z) =: G(z, \eta, M) = \sum_{n=1}^{\infty} B_n z^n, \quad (9)$$

then

$$G^2(z) = \sum_{n=2}^{\infty} (B_1 B_{n-1} + B_2 B_{n-2} + \cdots + B_{n-1} B_1) z^n = \sum_{n=1}^{\infty} (B_1 B_n + B_2 B_{n-1} + \cdots + B_n B_1) z^{n+1}$$

$$= \frac{1}{M} \sum_{n=1}^{\infty} B_{n+1} z^{n+1} = \frac{1}{M} G(z) - \frac{1}{M} |\eta| z,$$

that is, $G^2(z) - \frac{1}{M} G(z) + \frac{1}{M} |\eta| z = 0.$ Let

$$R(z, w) =: R(z, w, \eta, M) = w^2 - \frac{1}{M} w + \frac{1}{M} |\eta| z, \quad (10)$$

for (z, w) from a neighborhood of the origin. Since $R(0,0) = 0$ and $R'_w(0,0) = -\frac{1}{M} \ne 0$, there exists a unique function $w(z)$, analytic in a neighborhood of zero, such that $w(0) = 0$, $w'(0) = |\eta|$ and $R(z, w(z)) = 0.$ By (8) (9) and (10) we have $G(z) = w(z).$ It follows that the power series (9) converges in a neighborhood of the origin. Hence, this is a constant $T > 0$ such that

$$B_n < T^n, \, n = 1, 2, \cdots. \quad (11)$$

Now, we can deduce, by induction, that $|b_n| \le B_n e^{K(n-1)}, n = 1, 2, \cdots$, where $K : N \to R$ is defined in Lemma 1. In fact, $b_1 = |\eta| = B_1.$ For inductive proof, we assume that $|b_j| \le B_j e^{K(j-1)}, j \le m.$ From (7) and Lemma 1

$$|b_{m+1}| \le \frac{M}{|\alpha^m - 1|} |b_{k+1}||b_{m-k}| \le \frac{M}{|\alpha^m - 1|} \sum_{k=0}^{m-1} B_{k+1} B_{m-k} e^{K(k) + K(m-k-1)}.$$

Note that $K(k) + K(m-k-1) \le K(m-1) \le \log|\alpha^m - 1| + K(m)$, then

$$|b_{m+1}| \le \frac{e^{K(m-1)}}{|\alpha^m - 1|} M \sum_{k=0}^{m-1} B_{k+1} B_{m-k} = B_{m+1} e^{K(m)}$$

as desired. Moreover, from Lemma 1, we have $K(n) \le n(B(\theta) + \gamma)$ for some universal constant $\gamma > 0.$ Then $|b_n| \le T^n e^{(n-1)(B(\theta) + \gamma)}$, that is,

$$\limsup_{n\to\infty}\left(|b_n|^{\frac{1}{n}}\right)\le\limsup_{n\to\infty}\left(T^n e^{(n-1)(B(\theta)+\gamma)}\right)^{\frac{1}{n}}=Te^{B(\theta)+\gamma}.$$

This implies that the convergence radius of (5) is at least $\left(Te^{B(\theta)+\gamma}\right)^{-1}$. This completes the proof.

In case (H2), the constant α is not only on the unit circle in $\mathbf{C}$, but also a root of unity. In the resonant case, both the Diophantine condition and the Brjuno condition are not satisfied. Let $\{C_n\}_{n=1}^{\infty}$ be a sequence define by $C_1=|\eta|$ and

$$C_{n+1}=\Gamma M\sum_{k=0}^{n-1}C_{k+1}C_{n-k},\quad n=1,2,\cdots,\tag{12}$$

where $\Gamma=\max\left\{1,|\alpha^i-1|^{-1},i=1,2,\cdots,p-1\right\}$, and M is defined in Theorem 1.

Theorem 2. Suppose (H2) holds and P is given as above. Suppose that for $b_0=\alpha\Big/\sum_{i=1}^{m}c_i$ and $\eta\ne0$ the system

$$\begin{cases}b_1=\eta\\ \alpha(\alpha^n-1)(n+1)b_{n+1}=\sum_{k=0}^{n-1}(k+1)\sum_{i=1}^{m}c_i\alpha^{i(n-k)}b_{k+1}b_{n-k}\end{cases}\tag{13}$$

has a solution $\{b_n\}_{n=1}^{\infty}$ such that $b_{lp+1}=0$ and $\sum_{k=0}^{lp-1}(k+1)\sum_{i=1}^{m}c_i\alpha^{i(lp-k)}b_{k+1}b_{lp-k}=0,l=1,2,\cdots$. Then the initial value problem (3) and (4) has an analytic solution of the form

$$y(z)=\alpha\Big/\sum_{i=1}^{m}c_i+\eta z+\sum_{\substack{n\ne vp+1\\v=1,2,\cdots}}b_n z^n\tag{14}$$

on a neighborhood of the origin.

Proof. If $\{b_n\}_{n=1}^{\infty}$ is a solution of system (13) such that $b_{lp+1}=0$, then

$$y(z)=\sum_{n=1}^{\infty}b_n z^n\tag{15}$$

is the form solution of the auxiliary equation (3). Now we prove that the power series (15) is convergent. From (7) we have $|b_{n+1}|\le M\Gamma\sum_{k=0}^{n-1}|b_{k+1}||b_{n-k}|,n\ne lp,l=1,2,\cdots$. Let

$$\psi(z,\eta,\Gamma M)=\sum_{n=1}^{\infty}C_n z^n,\ C_1=|\eta|,\tag{16}$$

where $\{C_n\}_{n=1}^{\infty}$ is defined in (12). It is easy to check that (16) satisfies the implicit functional equation

$$R(z,\psi,\eta,M)=0,\tag{17}$$

where R is defined in (10). Similarly to the proof of Theorem 1, we can prove that (17) has a unique analytic solution $\psi(z,\eta,M)$ in a neighborhood of the origin such that $\psi(0,\eta,M)=0$ and $\psi_z'(0,\eta,M)=|\eta|$. Thus (16) converges on a neighborhood of the origin. Moreover, it is easy to show that, by induction, $|b_n|\le C_n,n=1,2,\cdots$. Therefore, the series (5) converges in a neighborhood of the origin. This completes the proof.

3   Analytic Solution of Equation (1)

Theorem 3. Suppose the condition of Theorem 1 or Theorem 2 are satisfied, then equation (1) has an analytic solution $y(z)$ of the form

$$x(z) = y(\alpha y^{-1}(z)) \tag{18}$$

on a neighborhood of the number $\alpha \big/ \sum_{i=0}^{m} c_i$, $x(\alpha \big/ \sum_{i=0}^{m} c_i) = \alpha \big/ \sum_{i=0}^{m} c_i$, $x'(\alpha \big/ \sum_{i=0}^{m} c_i) = \alpha$, where $y(z)$ is an analytic solution of (3).

Proof. In view of Theorem 1 and Theorem 2, we may find a sequence $\{b_n\}_{n=0}^{\infty}$ such that the function $y(z)$ of the form (5) is an analytic solution of (3) on a neighborhood of the origin. Since $y'(0) = \eta \neq 0$, the function $y^{-1}(z)$ is analytic in a neighborhood of $y(0) = \alpha \big/ \sum_{i=0}^{m} c_i$. If we now define $x(z) = y(\alpha y^{-1}(z))$, then

$$x^{[k]}(z) = y(\alpha^k y^{-1}(z)), \quad x'(z) = \frac{\alpha y'(\alpha y^{-1}(z))}{y'(y^{-1}(z))}.$$

So from (3) we have

$$x'(z) = \frac{\alpha y'(\alpha y^{-1}(z))}{y'(y^{-1}(z))} = \sum_{i=1}^{m} c_i y(\alpha^i y^{-1}(z)) = \sum_{i=1}^{m} c_i x^{[i]}(z),$$

that is, the function $x(z)$ in (18), defined on a neighborhood of the origin, satisfies Eq. (1) and $x\left(\alpha \big/ \sum_{i=0}^{m} c_i\right) = y(\alpha y^{-1}\left(\alpha \big/ \sum_{i=0}^{m} c_i\right)) = y(0) = \alpha \big/ \sum_{i=0}^{m} c_i$, $x'\left(\alpha \big/ \sum_{i=0}^{m} c_i\right) = \frac{\alpha y'(0)}{y'(y^{-1}(0))} = \alpha$. This completes the proof.

References

1. Eder, E.: The functional differential equation x´(t)=x(x(t)). J. Differential Equations 54, 390–400 (1984)
2. Wang, K.: On the equation x´(t)=f(x(x(t))). Funkcial. Ekvac. 33, 405–425 (1990)
3. Feckan, E.: On certain type of functional differential equations. Math. Slovaca 43, 39–43 (1993)
4. Stanek, S.: On global properties of solutions of functional differential equations x´(t)=x(x(t))+x(t). Dynam. Systems Appl. 4, 263–278 (1995)
5. Si, J.G., Li, W.R., Cheng, S.S.: Analytic solutions of an iterative functional differential equations. Comput. Math. Appl. 33(6), 47–51 (1997)
6. Si, J.G., Cheng, S.S.: Note on an iterative functional-differential equations. Demonstratio Math. 31(3), 609–614 (1998)
7. Bjuno, A.D.: Analytic form of differential equations. Trans. Moscow Math. Soc. 25, 131–288 (1971)
8. Marmi, S., Moussa, P., Yoccoz, J.C.: The Brjuno functions and their regularity properties. Comm. Math. Phys. 186(2), 265–293 (1997)
9. Carletti, T., Marmi, S.: Linearization of Analytic and Non-Analytic Germs of Diffeomorphisms of (C, 0). Bull. Soc. Math. 128, 69–85 (2000)
10. Davie, A.M.: The critical function for the semistandard map. Nonlinearity 7, 219–229 (1994)

Swarm Intelligence Optimization and Its Applications

Caichang Ding, Lu Lu, Yuanchao Liu, and Wenxiu Peng

School of Computer Science, Yangtze University,
Jingzhou, Hubei Province, China
hamigua_ping@hotmail.com

Abstract. Swarm Intelligence is a computational and behavioral metaphor for solving distributed problems inspired from biological examples provided by social insects such as ants, termites, bees, and wasps and by swarm, herd, flock, and shoal phenomena in vertebrates such as fish shoals and bird flocks. An example of successful research direction in Swarm Intelligence is ant colony optimization (ACO), which focuses on combinatorial optimization problems. Ant algorithms can be viewed as multi-agent systems (ant colony), where agents (individual ants) solve required tasks through cooperation in the same way that ants create complex social behavior from the combined efforts of individuals.

Keywords: Swarm Intelligence, ant colony optimization, combinatorial optimization, multi-agent.

1 Introduction

Swarm Intelligence (SI) is based on the principles underlying the behavior of natural systems consisting of many agents, and exploiting local communication forms and highly distributed control. Thus, the SI approach constitutes a very practical and powerful model that greatly simplifies the design of distributed solutions to different kind of problems. In the last few years, SI principles have been successfully applied to a series of applications including optimization algorithms, communications networks, and robotics.

SI systems are typically made up of a population of simple agents or boids interacting locally with one another and with their environment. The agents follow very simple rules, and although there is no centralized control structure dictating how individual agents should behave, local, and to a certain degree random, interactions between such agents lead to the emergence of "intelligent" global behavior, unknown to the individual agents. Natural examples of SI include ant colonies, bird flocking, animal herding, bacterial growth, and fish schooling.

2 Swarm Intelligence Overview

Swarm Intelligence is, intrinsically, a bottom-up approach. Bottom-up approaches are carried out by programming large numbers of independent entities with relatively simple sets of rules. Brought together, constructive behavior emerges, as it does in

G. Shen and X. Huang (Eds.): ECWAC 2011, Part I, CCIS 143, pp. 458–464, 2011.

insects that create complex social behavior and structures from the combined efforts of individuals with extremely limited intelligence. In contrast, the top-down approach is based on the classic centralized method (e.g., the Client/Server approach), where in central coordination should take place. SI can be applied to fully distributed systems that consist of several autonomous agents working together with local communication and minimal perception capabilities to complete one or more tasks.

Collective behavior demonstrated by social insects (ants, bees, termites, etc.) often emerges from a small set of simple low-level interactions between individuals, and between individuals and the environment.

The following example illustrates the concept of emergence. To solve a given task, for example, to sort elements scattered on the ground, one can write an algorithm wherein a centralized part distributes the task to achieve between a set of distributed agents. The centralized program, based on the global goal and plans, the current input, and the current state, collects agent results, analyzes them, and decides the actions to be executed next.

Swarm Intelligence is a new way to control multiple agent systems. The swarm-type approach to emergent strategy deals with large numbers of homogeneous agents, each of which has fairly limited capabilities on its own. However, when many such simple agents are brought together, globally interesting behavior can emerge as a result of the local interactions of the agents and the interactions between the agents and the environment. A key research issue in such a scenario is determining the proper design of the local control laws that will allow the collection of agents to solve a given problem.

3 Organizing Principles

A study of the SI approach reveals a useful set of organizing principles that can guide the design of efficient distributed applications for different kinds of problems. SI has the following notable features:

Autonomy: The system does not require outside management or maintenance. Individuals are autonomous, controlling their own behavior both at the detector and effector levels in a self-organized way.

Adaptability: Interactions between individuals can arise through direct or indirect communication via the local environment; two individuals interact indirectly when one of them modifies the environment and the other responds to the new environment at a later time. By exploiting such local communication forms, individuals have the ability to detect changes in the environment dynamically. They can then autonomously adapt their own behavior to these new changes. Thus, swarm systems emphasize auto-configuration capabilities.

Scalability: SI abilities can be performed using groups consisting of a few, up to thousands of individuals with the same control architecture.

Flexibility: No single individual of the swarm is essential, that is, any individual can be dynamically added, removed, or replaced.

Robustness: SI provides a good example of a highly distributed architecture that greatly enhances robustness; no central coordination takes place,which means that there is no single point of failure. Moreover, like most biological and social systems, and by combining scalability and flexibility capabilities, the swarm system enables redundancy, which is essential for robustness.

Massively parallel: The swarm system is massively parallel and its functioning is truly distributed. Tasks performed by each individual within its group are the same. If we view each individual as a processing unit, SI architecture can be thought of as single instruction stream–multiple data stream (SIMD) architecture or systolic networks.

Self-organization: Swarmsystems emphasize self-organization capabilities. The intelligence exhibited is not present in the individuals, but rather emerges somehowout of the entire swarm. In otherwords, if we view every individual as a processing unit, solutions to problems obtained are not predefined or preprogrammed but are determined collectively as a result of the running program.

Cost effectiveness: The swarm-type system consists of a finite collection of homogeneous agents, each of which has fairly limited capabilities on its own. Also, each agent has the same capabilities and control algorithm. It is clear that the autonomy and the highly distributed control afforded by the swarm model greatly simplify the task of designing the implementation of parallel algorithms and hardware. For example, for swarm-type multi-robotic systems, robots are relatively simple and their design process effort can be kept minimal in terms of sensors, actuators, and resources for computation and communication.

4 Swarm Intelligence Communication Forms

SI exploits local communication forms. Interactions between individuals can arise through direct or indirect communication.

4.1 Indirect Communication

Indirect communication is implicit communication that takes place between individuals via the environment. This is known as Stigmergy communication. The Stigmergy concept describes a class of mechanisms mediating animal–animal interactions through stimuli. When an animal does not explicitly distinguish between its own activity and the activities of others, its actions include modification of its local environment. By sensing its environment, an animal will perform an appropriate action as a response to the new environment at a later time. Thus, interaction takes place in stages through changes in the local environment. Note that the behavior of each insect can then be described as a series of stimulus–response sequences.

There are two forms of Stigmergy. In the Stigmergy Sematectonic communication form, information is communicated through physical modification of the environment. For example, opening a hole in the body of a termitary causes a disruption of the termitary's carefully maintained internal atmosphere (intense gradients in temperature, humidity, carbon dioxide, and oxygen). Sensing some problem in the body of the termitary, termites perform the rebuilding function and attack intruders while repairing the breach in order to restore the termitary's equilibrium.

In the second form of Stigmergy, some signal substance is deposited in the environment that makes no direct contribution to the task being undertaken but is used to influence the subsequent behavior that is task related [1]. For example, for building their nests, termites use highly volatile chemicals called pheromones. Termites place tiny balls of mud near other balls of mud that have high pheromone concentrations and, as a consequence, mounds develop. As the mounds grow, pheromones at the bases evaporate and the termites bring the mud to the top, driving the height of some mounds upward of 30 ft and causing adjacent mounds to meet in arches.

Pheromone-based Stigmergy is well developed in ants. Ants are capable of finding the shortest path from a food source to the nest. Also, they are capable of adapting to changes in the environment, and find a new shortest path once the old one is no longer feasible due to an obstacle [2]. Ants deposit a certain amount of pheromone while walking, and each ant probabilistically prefers to follow a direction rich in pheromone rather than a poorer one. Hence, the shorter path will receive a higher amount of pheromone and this will in turn cause a higher number of ants to choose the shorter path. This elementary behavior of real ants explains how they can find the shortest path. The collective behavior that emerges is a form of autocatalytic behavior (or positive feedback), whereby the more the ants follow the trail the more likely they are to do so.

4.2 Direct Communication

Direct communication is explicit communication that can also take place between individuals. Examples of such interactions are the waggle dance of the honeybee, using antennas, trophallaxis (food or liquid exchange, e.g., mouth-to-mouth food exchange in honeybees), mandibular contact, visual contact, chemical contact (the odor of nearby nest mates), etc.

Direct communication can be implemented by mobile wireless ad hoc networks. Individuals have a very limited memory with the added feature that they are mobile; therefore, they can be considered mobile agents. Indirect interactions through the environment can be thought of as distributed shortterm memory. Indeed, agents communicate through pheromone trails.When walking toward the colony or food sources, ants will simply walk toward a high concentration of pheromone. The accumulated pheromone then serves as a distributed shared memory. Note also that we need an analog for indirect interaction through the local environment to implement the autoadaptive mechanism. Such a system can adapt to changes in user behavior and system software through the pheromones. In other words, pheromones will monitor the state of the machines and the network.

5 The Main Applications of Swarm Intelligence

Swarm Intelligence principles have been successfully applied in a variety of problem domains and applications. An example of successful research direction in SI is ant colony optimization (ACO)[3], which focuses on combinatorial optimization problems[5].

Ant-Colony Optimization (ACO) is a metaheuristics approach proposed by Dorigo et al.[3]. The inspiration for ACO is the foraging behavior of real ants. This behavior allows the ants to find the shortest paths between food sources and their nest. Ants deploy a chemical trail (or pheromone trail) as they walk; this trail attracts other ants to take the path that has the most pheromone. This reinforcement process results in the selection of the shortest path[4]: the first ants coming back to the nest are those that took the shortest path twice (from the nest to the source and back to the nest), so that more pheromone is present on the shortest path than on the longer paths immediately after these ants have returned, stimulating nest mates to choose the shortest path.

Ant-colony optimization algorithms(see Fig. 1) are based on a parameterized probabilistic model (pheromone model) that is used to model the chemical pheromone trails[6]. Artificial ants incrementally construct solutions by adding opportunely defined solution components to a partial solution under consideration. In order to do this, artificial ants perform randomized walks on a completely connected graph $G(C,L)$, called a construction graph, whose vertices are the solution components C, and the set L composed of the connections. When a constrained combinatorial optimization problem is considered, the problem constraints are built into the ants' constructive procedure in such a way that in every step of the construction process only feasible solution components can be added to the current partial solution.

While termination condition not satisfied **Do**
   ScheduleActivicies
     Ant_activity( )
     Pheromone_evaporation( )
     Deamon_actions( )
   EndscheduleActivities
EndWhile

Fig. 1. Ant-colony optimization algorithm

Ant_activity( ): In the construction phase an ant incrementally builds a solution by adding solution components to the partial solution constructed so far. The probabilistic choice of the next solution component to be added is done by means of transition probabilities. More specifically, ant n in step t moves from vertex $i \in C$ to vertex $j \in C$ with a probability given by:

$$p_{ij,n}(t) = \begin{cases} \dfrac{\tau_{ij}^{a} \eta_{ij}^{b}}{\sum_{m \in N_{i,n}} \tau_{im}^{a} \eta_{im}^{b}} \\ 0 \end{cases} \quad (1)$$

where η_{ij} is a priori available heuristic information, a and b are two parameters that determine the relative influence of the pheromone trail $\tau_{ij}(t)$ and heuristic information, respectively, and $N_{i,n}$ is the feasible neighborhood of vertex i. If $a = 0$, then only heuristic information is considered. Similarly, if $b = 0$, then only pheromone information is at work. Once an ant builds a solution, or while a solution is being built, the pheromone is being deposited (on nodes or connections) according to the evaluation of a (partial) solution. This pheromone information will direct the search of the ants in the following iterations. The solution construction ends when an ant comes to the ending vertex (where the food is located).

Pheromone_evaporation( ): Pheromone-trail evaporation is a procedure that simulates the reduction of pheromone intensity. It is needed in order to avoid a too quick convergence of the algorithm to a suboptimal solution.

Daemon_actions( ): Daemon actions can be used to implement centralized actions that cannot be performed by single ants. Examples are the use of a local search procedure applied to the solutions built by the ants, or the collection of global information that can be used to decide whether it is useful or not to deposit additional pheromone to bias the search process from a nonlocal perspective. As we can see from the pseudo code, the ScheduleActivities construct does not specify how the three included activities should be scheduled or synchronized. This means it is up to the programmer to specify how these procedures will interact (parallel or independent).

Within the ACO metaheuristic framework the currently best-performing versions in practice are Ant Colony System [6][7] and MAX–MIN Ant System [8]. Recently, researchers have been dealing with finding similarities between ACO algorithms and Estimation of Distribution Algorithms. Furthermore, connections between ACO algorithms and Stochastic Gradient–Descent algorithms are shown in [9].

6 Conclusion

Swarm Intelligence is a rich source of inspiration for our computer systems. Specifically, SI has many features that are desirable for distributed computing. These include auto-configuration, auto-organization, autonomy, scalability, flexibility, robustness, emergent behavior, and adaptability. These capabilities suggest a wide variety of applications that can be solved by SI principles. We believe that the emergence paradigm and the highly distributed control paradigm will be fruitful to new technologies, such as nanotechnology, massively parallel supercomputers, embedded systems, and scalable systems for deep space applications.

References

1. White, T.: Swarm intelligence and problem solving in telecommunications. Canadian Artificial Intelligence Magazine (Spring 1997)
2. Beckers, R., Deneubourg, J.L., Goss, S.: Trails and U-turns in the selection of the shortest path by the ant Lasius niger. Journal of Theoretical Biology 159, 397–415 (1992)
3. Dorigo, M., Gambardella, L.M.: Ant colony system: A cooperative learning approach to the traveling salesman problem. IEEE Transactions on Evolutionary Computation 1, 53–66 (1997)
4. Michel, R., Middendorf, M.: An ACO algorithm for the shortest common supersequence problem. In: Corne, D., Dorigo, M., Glover, F. (eds.) New Ideas in Optimization, pp. 51–62. McGraw-Hill, New York (1999)

5. Branke, J., Guntsch, M.: Solving the probabilistic tsp with ant colony optimization. Journal of Mathematical Modelling and Algorithms 3, 403–425 (2004)
6. Leguizamón, G., Michalewicz, Z.: A new version of ant system for subset problems. In: Angeline, P.J., Michalewicz, Z., Schoenauer, M., Yao, X., Zalzala, A. (eds.) Congress of Evolutionary Computation, vol. 2, pp. 1459–1464. IEEE Press, Washington (1999)
7. Stützle, T., Dorigo, M.: ACO algorithms for the traveling salesman problem. In: Miettinen, K., Makela, M., Neittaanmaki, P., Periaux, J. (eds.) Evolutionary Algorithms in Engineering and Computer Science, pp. 163–183. Wiley, New Jersey (1999)
8. Fenet, S., Solnon, C.: Searching for maximum cliques with ant colony optimization. In: Raidl, G.R., Cagnoni, S., Cardalda, J.J.R., Corne, D.W., Gottlieb, J., Guillot, A., Hart, E., Johnson, C.G., Marchiori, E., Meyer, J.-A., Middendorf, M. (eds.) EvoWorkshops 2003. LNCS, vol. 2611, pp. 236–245. Springer, Heidelberg (2003)
9. Branke, J., Guntsch, M.: New ideas for applying ant colony optimization to the probabilistic TSP. In: Raidl, G.R., Cagnoni, S., Cardalda, J.J.R., Corne, D.W., Gottlieb, J., Guillot, A., Hart, E., Johnson, C.G., Marchiori, E., Meyer, J.-A., Middendorf, M. (eds.) EvoWorkshops 2003. LNCS, vol. 2611, pp. 165–175. Springer, Heidelberg (2003)

Author Index